THE THIRD REICH FROM ORIGINAL SOURCES

MEIN KAMPF

The Official 1939 Edition

BY ADOLF HITLER

With a new introduction
by Bob Carruthers

Translated into English
by James Murphy

C✛DA
BOOKS LTD

This hardback edition is published in Great Britain in 2011 by

Coda Books Ltd, Unit 1, Cutlers Farm Business Centre, Edstone, Wootton Wawen,
Henley in Arden, Warwickshire, B95 6DJ
www.codahistory.com

A CIP catalogue record for this book is available from the British Library
ISBN 978 1 908538 69 7

Contents

MEIN KAMPF - The 1939 edition translated by James Murphy

This is the book which every historian and student of 20th century history should read. You hold in your hands the 1939 translation of *Mein Kampf* by James Murphy as published in the UK by Hutchison and Co Ltd during World War II. This version of the text is important as it was the only version officially sanctioned by the Nazi Foreign Office. It made its appearance during the Nazi era and it was this version which was read by the mass of British readers at the time in question.

Mein Kampf clearly sets out in the writer's own words the pan-German nationalist agenda which formed the basis of Hitler's political outlook. For many years I have been of the opinion that the influence of German nationalism, his willingness to take risks and an innate love of violence for the sake of violence were the key factors which shaped Hitler's *weltanschauung* (or world view). The anti-Semitic element of his agenda, although fully formed by 1924, was always subordinate to his pan-German nationalist aspirations. The proof of that theory can be found in Hitler's own version of events as published by him in the pages of *Mein Kampf*.

The officially sanctioned English language version of *Mein Kampf* was translated and introduced by James Murphy who travelled to Germany in 1938 to prepare Hitler's work for translation. Murphy quickly grew to despise the National Socialist regime and was asked to leave Germany. However, he managed to salvage most of his work and his translation was first published in the UK in 1939. It also appeared in magazine form as a collection of 22 weekly parts prepared and published by Hutchison and Co Ltd. This authentic hardback edition brings together both of the original volumes complete with Murphy's 1939 introduction.

As Murphy's was the only translation which was officially endorsed by the Nazi party during Hitler's lifetime, this edition represents an opportunity to approach the work as it was presented to contemporary readers. This was the version of *Mein Kampf* which the Nazi party hoped would spread the gospel of National Socialism throughout the UK, but by the time publication was underway World War II had commenced. Somewhat surprisingly, publication of the weekly illustrated edition was allowed to continue into 1940 although all proceeds from the sale were diverted to the British Red Cross.

This new publication of the entire primary source provides the reader with access to the complete historical document and provides a unique insight into the past by reproducing Mein Kampf as it was presented to British readers in the thirties.

Mein Kampf is routinely dismissed as unreadable and this was certainly the case in contemporary circles where many Nazi functionaries, including Göring, privately joked that they had never read the thing. Italian Fascist dictator and Nazi ally, Benito Mussolini, was famously critical, stating that the book was "…a boring tome that I have never been able to read." He also remarked that Hitler's beliefs, as expressed in the book, were "… little more than commonplace clichés." For students of history, politics and general readers with an interest in the period that is certainly not the case. While it is true those large sections of political exposition are rambling and turgid, they do nonetheless repay the reader with an insight into the workings of the mind of Adolf Hitler. The book also contains highly accessible elements of autobiography which are intriguing as they afford

4

us the ultimate primary source glimpse into the private world of Adolf Hitler. On balance I'm sure most readers would side with Winston Churchill who stated, shortly after Hitler's ascension to power, that no other book deserved more intensive scrutiny. I still believe that Churchill was right - *Mein Kampf* should not be dismissed as readily as is so often the case. Some effort is required on the part of the reader during the long-winded political expositions, but Hitler's hopes, aspirations, fears and prejudices are plainly set out for us in these pages. The kind of world which he hoped to create, and did create, is clearly depicted in the pages of *Mein Kampf* which represented a strong and unambiguous warning which Chamberlain was fool-hardy enough to ignore.

We should never lose sight of the fact that Hitler was a masterful politician writing for political purposes. We should obviously approach his words with extreme caution, but they should nonetheless be studied and carefully considered, and where there is no reason to do otherwise, we should be prepared to give them weight. This is especially the case where Hitler's autobiographical account can be cross referenced with other accounts by the likes of Kubizek and Hanisch.

It is interesting to note that at the time this book was written Hitler was simply just "one more fanatic" spouting rhetoric on the fringes of the *völkisch* movement. However, the experience of actually hearing Hitler promulgate the ideas contained in these pages awed and inspired his audiences, and many, such as Kurt Ludecke, underwent a conversion to Nazism of almost religious proportions. Ludecke, in common with so many others was ecstatic in response to Hitler's amazing powers of rhetoric which in the pages of his book "I knew Hitler" he describes in glowing terms: "His appeal to German manhood was like a call to arms, the gospel he preached a sacred truth."

The published opinion of Ludecke is representative of the views millions of ordinary Germans who fell under Hitler's spell and although anti-Semitism was rife, it was not something which was on the personal agenda of all conservatives in Germany while the desire to re-build national prestige undoubtedly was a common rallying point.

Hitler began work on his book while imprisoned Landsberg. We know that Hitler received many visitors in the early part of his incarceration, but soon afterwards he became engrossed in his work and devoted himself entirely to writing *Mein Kampf*, the bulk of which seems to have been written in 1924 with work continuing into 1925. The prison governor of Landsberg noted at the time that "he [Hitler] hopes the book will run into many editions, thus enabling him to fulfil his financial obligations and to defray the expenses incurred at the time of his trial."

Hitler's crimes against humanity are now synonymous with the fate of the Jewish people in Germany and throughout occupied Europe. Accordingly *Mein Kampf* has today assumed a key place in identifying the roots of Hitler's anti-Semitism which is often depicted as his life's work. My own view is that nationalism came first with anti-Semitism following behind. *Mein Kampf* if taken at face value, certainly seems to back up that point of view and as such now forms a key part of the functionalist versus intentionalist debate. The Intentionalists insist with considerable force that the infamous passage stating that if 12,000–15,000 Jews were gassed, then "the sacrifice of millions of soldiers would not have been in vain," proves quite clearly that Hitler had a master plan for the genocide of the Jewish people all along. Functionalist historians reject this assertion, noting that the passage does not call for the destruction of the entire Jewish people and also stress that although Mein Kampf is suffused with an extreme anti-Semitism, it is the only time in the entire book that Hitler ever explicitly refers to the murder of Jews. Given that *Mein Kampf* is 720 pages long, Functionalist historians caution that it may be making too much out of one sentence. Regardless of which school of thought we fall into, what certainly comes over loud and clear is Hitler's willingness to advocate violent and inhumane solutions to political issues.

My own view accords with the Functionalist historians who broadly argue that by 1935 Hitler had triumphed in his war against the Jews and with the introduction of the Nuremberg laws he felt his goal had been achieved. From that point onwards Hitler's expansionist agenda was his main focus and the dealings with the rump of the Jewish problem were no longer his concern. Many Functionalists have supported the view that the memorandum written by Heinrich Himmler to Hitler on May 25, 1940, regarding the "Final Solution to the Jewish Question," which proposals Hitler accepted, proves that there was no master plan for genocide stemming back to the 1920s. In the memorandum, Himmler famously rejects a programme of state sanctioned murder on the grounds that one must reject "...the Bolshevik method of physical extermination of a people out of inner conviction as un-German and impossible." Himmler goes on to state that something similar to the "Madagascar Plan" should be the preferred "territorial solution" to the "Jewish Question."

Additionally, Functionalist historians have noted that in *Mein Kampf* the only anti-Semitic policies are the 25 Point Platform of the Nazi Party (adopted in February 1920), which demands that only "Aryan" Germans be allowed to publish newspapers and own department stores, places a ban on Jewish immigration, expels all Ostjuden (Eastern Jews; i.e. Jews from Eastern Europe who had arrived in Germany since 1914) and strips all German Jews of their German citizenship. Although these demands do reflect a hateful anti-Semitism, they do not amount to a programme for genocide. In addition , some historians have claimed although Hitler was clearly imbued with anti-Semitism, his degree of anti-Semitic hatred contained in *Mein Kampf* is no greater or less than that contained in the writings and speeches of earlier völkisch leaders such as Wilhelm Marr, Georg Ritter von Schönerer, Houston Stewart Chamberlain and Karl Lueger, all of whom routinely called Jews a "disease" and "vermin.

I trust that you will find this book compelling as a historical document and that you will come to form your own views on the debate. However, the discussions stemming from the events of the last century continue to unfold to-day and it is important to keep an open mind. There really is no final answer and the judgement of each individual reader is as valid as the next. What really matters is the sum of the knowledge we accumulate and a reading of *Mein Kampf* helps us to better explore the past.

Thank you for buying this edition, I sincerely hope it repays your investment in time and money.

Bob Carruthers

INTRODUCTION: Author's Preface

On April 1st, 1924, I began to serve my sentence of detention in the Fortress of Landsberg am Lech, following the verdict of the Munich People's Court of that time. After years of uninterrupted labour it was now possible for the first time to begin a work which many had asked for and which I myself felt would be profitable for the Movement. So I decided to devote two volumes to a description not only of the aims of our Movement but also of its development. There is more to be learned from this than from any purely doctrinaire treatise.

This has also given me the opportunity of describing my own development in so far as such a description is necessary to the understanding of the first as well as the second volume and to destroy the legendary fabrications which the Jewish Press have circulated about me.

In this work I turn not to strangers but to those followers of the Movement whose hearts belong to it and who wish to study it more profoundly. I know that fewer people are won over by the written word than by the spoken word and that every great movement on this earth owes its growth to great speakers and not to great writers.

Nevertheless, in order to produce more equality and uniformity in the defence of any doctrine, its fundamental principles must be committed to writing. May these two volumes therefore serve as the building stones which I contribute to the joint work.

The Fortress, Landsberg AM Lech

At half-past twelve in the afternoon of November 9th, 1923, those whose names are given below fell in front of the FELDHERRNHALLE and in the forecourt of the former War Ministry in Munich for their loyal faith in the resurrection of their people:

Alfarth, Felix, Merchant, born July 5th, 1901
Bauriedl, Andreas, Hatmaker, born May 4th, 1879
Casella, Theodor, Bank Official, born August 8th, 1900
Ehrlich, Wilhelm, Bank Official, born August 19th, 1894
Faust, Martin, Bank Official, born January 27th, 1901
Hechenberger, Anton, Locksmith, born September 28th, 1902
Koerner, Oskar, Merchant, born January 4th, 1875
Kuhn, Karl, Head Waiter, born July 25th, 1897
Laforce, Karl, Student of Engineering, born October 28th, 1904
Neubauer, Kurt, Waiter, born March 27th, 1899
Pape, Claus von, Merchant, born August 16th, 1904
Pfordten, Theodor von der, Councillor to the Superior Provincial Court,
born May 14th, 1873
Rickmers, Johann, retired Cavalry Captain, born May 7th, 1881
Scheubner-Richter, Max Erwin von, Dr. of Engineering, born January 9th, 1884
Stransky, Lorenz Ritter von, Engineer, born March 14th, 1899
Wolf, Wilhelm, Merchant, born October 19th, 1898

So-called national officials refused to allow the dead heroes a common burial. So I dedicate the first volume of this work to them as a common memorial, that the memory of those martyrs may be a permanent source of light for the followers of our Movement.

The Fortress, Landsberg a/L.,
October 16th, 1924

Translator's Introduction

In placing before the reader this unabridged translation of Adolf Hitler's book, MEIN KAMPF, I feel it my duty to call attention to certain historical facts which must be borne in mind if the reader would form a fair judgment of what is written in this extraordinary work. The first volume of MEIN KAMPF was written while the author was imprisoned in a Bavarian fortress. How did he get there and why? The answer to that question is important, because the book deals with the events which brought the author into this plight and because he wrote under the emotional stress caused by the historical happenings of the time. It was the hour of Germany's deepest humiliation, somewhat parallel to that of a little over a century before, when Napoleon had dismembered the old German Empire and French soldiers occupied almost the whole of Germany.

In the beginning of 1923 the French invaded Germany, occupied the Ruhr district and seized several German towns in the Rhincland. This was a flagrant breach of international law and was protested against by every section of British political opinion at that time. The Germans could not effectively defend themselves, as they had been already disarmed under the provisions of the Versailles Treaty. To make the situation more fraught with disaster for Germany, and therefore more appalling in its prospect, the French carried on an intensive propaganda for the separation of the Rhineland from the German Republic and the establishment of an independent Rhenania. Money was poured out lavishly to bribe agitators to carry on this work, and some of the most insidious elements of the German population became active in the pay of the invader. At the same time a vigorous movement was being carried on in

Bavaria for the secession of that country and the establishment of an independent Catholic monarchy there, under vassalage to France, as Napoleon had done when he made Maximilian the first King of Bavaria in 1805.

The separatist movement in the Rhineland went so far that some leading German politicians came out in favour of it, suggesting that if the Rhineland were thus ceded it might be possible for the German Republic to strike a bargain with the French in regard to Reparations. But in Bavaria the movement went even farther. And it was more far-reaching in its implications; for, if an independent Catholic monarchy could be set up in Bavaria, the next move would have been a union with Catholic German-Austria. possibly under a Habsburg King. Thus a Catholic BLOC would have been created which would extend from the Rhineland through Bavaria and Austria into the Danube Valley and would have been at least under the moral and military, if not the full political, hegemony of France. The dream seems fantastic now, but it was considered quite a practical thing in those fantastic times. The effect of putting such a plan into action would have meant the complete dismemberment of Germany; and that is what French diplomacy aimed at. Of course such an aim no longer exists. And I should not recall what must now seem "old, unhappy, far-off things" to the modern generation, were it not that they were very near and actual at the time MEIN KAMPF was written and were more unhappy then than we can even imagine now.

By the autumn of 1923 the separatist movement in Bavaria was on the point of becoming an accomplished fact. General von Lossow, the Bavarian chief of the

REICHSWEHR no longer took orders from Berlin. The flag of the German Republic was rarely to be seen, Finally, the Bavarian Prime Minister decided to proclaim an independent Bavaria and its secession from the German Republic. This was to have taken place on the eve of the Fifth Anniversary of the establishment of the German Republic (November 9th, 1918.)

Hitler staged a counter-stroke. For several days he had been mobilizing his storm battalions in the neighbourhood of Munich, intending to make a national demonstration and hoping that the REICHSWEHR would stand by him to prevent secession. Ludendorff was with him. And he thought that the prestige of the great German Commander in the World War would be sufficient to win the allegiance of the professional army.

A meeting had been announced to take place in the Bürgerbräu Keller on the night of November 8th. The Bavarian patriotic societies were gathered there, and the Prime Minister, Dr. von Kahr, started to read his official PRONUNCIAMENTO, which practically amounted to a proclamation of Bavarian independence and secession from the Republic. While von Kahr was speaking Hitler entered the hall, followed by Ludendorff. And the meeting was broken up.

Next day the Nazi battalions took the street for the purpose of making a mass demonstration in favour of national union. They marched in massed formation, led by Hitler and Ludendorff. As they reached one of the central squares of the city the army opened fire on them. Sixteen of the marchers were instantly killed, and two died of their wounds in the local barracks of the REICHSWEHR. Several others were wounded also. Hitler fell on the pavement and broke a collar-bone. Ludendorff marched straight up to the soldiers who were firing from the barricade, but not a man dared draw a trigger on his old Commander.

Hitler was arrested with several of his comrades and imprisoned in the fortress of Landsberg on the River Lech. On February 26th, 1924, he was brought to trial before the VOLKSGERICHT, or People's Court in Munich. He was sentenced to detention in a fortress for five years. With several companions, who had been also sentenced to various periods of imprisonment, he returned to Landsberg am Lech and remained there until the 20th of the following December, when he was released. In all he spent about thirteen months in prison. It was during this period that he wrote the first volume of MEIN KAMPF.

If we bear all this in mind we can account for the emotional stress under which MEIN KAMPF was written. Hitler was naturally incensed against the Bavarian government authorities, against the footling patriotic societies who were pawns in the French game, though often unconsciously so, and of course against the French. That he should write harshly of the French was only natural in the circumstances. At that time there was no exaggeration whatsoever in calling France the implacable and mortal enemy of Germany. Such language was being used by even the pacifists themselves, not only in Germany but abroad. And even though the second volume of MEIN KAMPF was written after Hitler's release from prison and was published after the French had left the Ruhr, the tramp of the invading armies still echoed in German ears, and the terrible ravages that had been wrought in the industrial and financial life of Germany, as a consequence of the French invasion, had plunged the country into a state of social and economic chaos. In France itself the franc fell to fifty per cent of its previous value. Indeed, the whole of Europe had been brought to the brink of ruin, following the French invasion of the Ruhr and Rhineland.

But, as those things belong to the limbo of a dead past that nobody wishes to have remembered now, it is often asked: Why doesn't Hitler revise MEIN KAMPF? The answer, as I think, which would immediately come into the mind of an impartial critic is that MEIN KAMPF is an historical document which bears the imprint of its own time. To revise it would involve taking it out of its historical context. Moreover Hitler has declared that his acts and public statements constitute a partial revision of his book and are to be taken as such. This refers especially to the statements in MEIN KAMPF regarding France and those German kinsfolk that have not yet been incorporated in the REICH. On behalf of Germany he has definitely acknowledged the German portion of South Tyrol as permanently belonging to Italy and, in regard to France, he has again and again declared that no grounds now exist for a conflict of political interests between Germany and France and that Germany has no territorial claims against France. Finally, I may note here that Hitler has also declared that, as he was only a political leader and not yet a statesman in a position of official responsibility, when he wrote this book, what he stated in MEIN KAMPF does not implicate him as Chancellor of the REICH.

I now come to some references in the text which are frequently recurring and which may not always be clear to every reader. For instance, Hitler speaks indiscriminately of the German REICH. Sometimes he means to refer to the first REICH, or Empire, and sometimes to the German Empire as founded under William I in 1871. Incidentally the regime which he inaugurated in 1933 is generally known as the THIRD REICH, though this expression is not used in MEIN KAMPF. Hitler also speaks of the Austrian REICH and the East Mark, without always explicitly distinguishing between the Habsburg Empire and Austria proper. If the reader will bear the following historical outline in mind, he will understand the references as they occur.

The word REICH, which is a German form of the Latin word REGNUM, does not mean Kingdom or Empire or Republic. It is a sort of basic word that may apply to any form of Constitution. Perhaps our word, Realm, would be the best translation, though the word Empire can be used when the REICH was actually an Empire. The forerunner of the first German Empire was the Holy Roman Empire which Charlemagne founded in A.D. 800. Charlemagne was King of the Franks, a group of Germanic tribes that subsequently became Romanized. In the tenth century Charlemagne's Empire passed into German hands when Otto I (936-973) became Emperor. As the Holy Roman Empire of the German Nation, its formal appellation, it continued to exist under German Emperors until Napoleon overran and dismembered Germany during the first decade of the last century. On August 6th, 1806, the last Emperor, Francis II, formally resigned the German crown. In the following October Napoleon entered Berlin in triumph, after the Battle of Jena.

After the fall of Napoleon a movement set in for the reunion of the German states in one Empire. But the first decisive step towards that end was the foundation of the Second German Empire in 1871, after the Franco-Prussian War. This Empire, however, did not include the German lands which remained under the Habsburg Crown. These were known as German Austria. It was Bismarck's dream to unite German Austria with the German Empire; but it remained only a dream until Hitler turned it into a reality in 1938'. It is well to bear that point in mind, because this dream of reuniting all the German states in one REICH has been a dominant feature of German patriotism and statesmanship for over a century and has been one of Hitler's ideals since his childhood.

In MEIN KAMPF Hitler often speaks of the East Mark. This East Mark—i.e. eastern frontier land—was founded by Charlemagne as the eastern bulwark of the Empire. It was inhabited principally by Germano-Celtic tribes called Bajuvari and stood for centuries as the firm bulwark of Western Christendom against invasion from the East, especially against the Turks. Geographically it was almost identical with German Austria.

There are a few points more that I wish to mention in this introductory note. For instance, I have let the word WELTANSCHAUUNG stand in its original form very often. We have no one English word to convey the same meaning as the German word, and it would have burdened the text too much if I were to use a circumlocution each time the word occurs. WELTANSCHAUUNG literally means "Outlook-on-the World". But as generally used in German this outlook on the world means a whole system of ideas associated together in an organic unity—ideas of human life, human values, cultural and religious ideas, politics, economics, etc., in fact a totalitarian view of human existence. Thus Christianity could be called a WELTANSCHAUUNG, and Mohammedanism could be called a WELTANSCHAUUNG, and Socialism could be called a WELTANSCHAUUNG, especially as preached in Russia. National Socialism claims definitely to be a WELTANSCHAUUNG.

Another word I have often left standing in the original is VÖLKISCH. The basic word here is VOLK, which is sometimes translated as PEOPLE; but the German word, VOLK, means the whole body of the PEOPLE without any distinction of class or caste. It is a primary word also that suggests what might be called the basic national stock. Now, after the defeat in 1918, the downfall of the Monarchy and the destruction of the aristocracy and the upper classes, the concept of DAS VOLK came into prominence as the unifying co-efficient which would embrace the whole German people. Hence the large number of VÖLKISCH societies that arose after the war and hence also the National Socialist concept of unification which is expressed by the word VOLKSGEMEINSCHAFT, or folk community. This is used in contradistinction to the Socialist concept of the nation as being divided into classes. Hitler's ideal is the VÖLKISCHER STAAT, which I have translated as the People's State.

Finally, I would point out that the term Social Democracy may be misleading in English, as it has not a democratic connotation in our sense. It was the name given to the Socialist Party in Germany. And that Party was purely Marxist; but it adopted the name Social Democrat in order to appeal to the democratic sections of the German people.

JAMES MURPHY.
Abbots Langley, February, 1939

VOLUME I: A RETROSPECT

CHAPTER I: In the Home of My Parents

It has turned out fortunate for me to-day that destiny appointed Braunau-on-the-Inn to be my birthplace. For that little town is situated just on the frontier between those two States the reunion of which seems, at least to us of the younger generation, a task to which we should devote our lives and in the pursuit of which every possible means should be employed.

German-Austria must be restored to the great German Motherland. And not indeed on any grounds of economic calculation whatsoever. No, no. Even if the union were a matter of economic indifference, and even if it were to be disadvantageous from the economic standpoint, still it ought to take place. People of the same blood should be in the same REICH. The German people will have no right to engage in a colonial policy until they shall have brought all their children together in the one State. When the territory of the REICH embraces all the Germans and finds itself unable to assure them a livelihood, only then can the moral right arise, from the need of the people to acquire foreign territory. The plough is then the sword; and the tears of war will produce the daily bread for the generations to come.

And so this little frontier town appeared to me as the symbol of a great task. But in another regard also it points to a lesson that is applicable to our day. Over a hundred years ago this sequestered spot was the scene of a tragic calamity which affected the whole German nation and will be remembered for ever, at least in the annals of German history. At the time of our Fatherland's deepest humiliation a bookseller, Johannes Palm, uncompromising nationalist and enemy of the French, was put to death here because he had the misfortune to have loved Germany well. He obstinately refused to disclose the names of his associates, or rather the principals who were chiefly responsible for the affair. Just as it happened with Leo Schlageter. The former, like the latter, was denounced to the French by a Government agent. It was a director of police from Augsburg who won an ignoble renown on that occasion and set the example which was to be copied at a later date by the neo-German officials of the REICH under Herr Severing's regime [1].

In this little town on the Inn, haloed by the memory of a German martyr, a town that was Bavarian by blood but under the rule of the Austrian State, my parents were domiciled towards the end of the last century. My father was a civil servant who fulfilled his duties very conscientiously. My mother looked after the household and lovingly devoted herself to the care of her children. From that period I have not retained very much in my memory; because after a few years my father had to leave that frontier town which I had come to love so much and take up a new post farther down the Inn valley, at Passau, therefore actually in Germany itself.

In those days it was the usual lot of an Austrian civil servant to be transferred periodically from one post to another. Not long after coming to Passau my father was transferred to Linz, and while there he retired finally to live on his pension. But this did not mean that the old gentleman would now rest from his labours.

He was the son of a poor cottager, and while still a boy he grew restless and left home. When he was barely thirteen years old he buckled on his satchel and set forth from his native woodland parish. Despite the dissuasion of villagers who could speak from 'experience,' he went to Vienna to learn a trade there. This was in the fiftieth year of the last century. It was a sore trial, that of deciding to leave home and face the unknown, with three gulden in his pocket. By when the boy of thirteen was a lad of seventeen and had passed his apprenticeship examination as a craftsman he was not content. Quite the contrary. The persistent economic depression of that period and the constant want and misery strengthened his resolution to give up working at a trade and strive for 'something higher.' As a boy it had seemed to him that the position of the parish priest in his native village was the highest in the scale of human attainment; but now that the big city had enlarged his outlook the young man looked up to the dignity of a State official as the highest of all. With the tenacity of one whom misery and trouble had already made old when only half-way through his youth the young man of seventeen obstinately set out on his new project and stuck to it until he won through. He became a civil servant. He was about twenty-three years old, I think, when he succeeded in making himself what he had resolved to become. Thus he was able to fulfil the promise he had made as a poor boy not to return to his native village until he was 'somebody.'

He had gained his end. But in the village there was nobody who had remembered him as a little boy, and the village itself had become strange to him.

Now at last, when he was fifty-six years old, he gave up his active career; but he could not bear to be idle for a single day. On the outskirts of the small market town of Lambach in Upper Austria he bought a farm and tilled it himself. Thus, at the end of a long and hard-working career, he came back to the life which his father had led.

It was at this period that I first began to have ideals of my own. I spent a good deal of time scampering about in the open, on the long road from school, and mixing up with some of the roughest of the boys, which caused my mother many anxious moments. All this tended to make me something quite the reverse of a stay-at-home. I gave scarcely any serious thought to the question of choosing a vocation in life; but I was certainly quite out of sympathy with the kind of career which my father had followed. I think that an inborn talent for speaking now began to develop and take shape during the more or less strenuous arguments which I used to have with my comrades. I had become a juvenile ringleader who learned well and easily at school but was rather difficult to manage. In my freetime I practised singing in the choir of the monastery church at Lambach, and thus it happened that I was placed in a very favourable position to be emotionally impressed again and again by the magnificent splendour of ecclesiastical ceremonial. What could be more natural for me than to look upon the Abbot as representing the highest human ideal worth striving for, just as the position of the humble village priest had appeared to my father in his own boyhood days? At least, that was my idea for a while. But the juvenile disputes I had with my father did not lead him to appreciate his son's oratorical gifts in such a way as to see in them a favourable promise for such a career, and so he naturally could not understand the boyish ideas I had in my head at that time. This contradiction in my character made him feel somewhat anxious.

As a matter of fact, that transitory yearning after such a vocation soon gave way to hopes that were better suited to my temperament. Browsing through my father's books, I chanced to come across some publications that dealt with military subjects. One of these publications was a popular history of the Franco-German War of 1870-71. It consisted of two volumes of an illustrated periodical dating from those years. These became my favourite reading. In a little while that great and heroic conflict began to take first place in my mind. And from that time onwards I became more and more enthusiastic about everything that was in any way connected with war or military affairs.

But this story of the Franco-German War had a special significance for me on other grounds also. For the first time, and as yet only in quite a vague way, the question began to present itself: Is there a difference — and if there be, what is it — between the Germans who fought that war and the other Germans? Why did not Austria also take part in it? Why did not my father and all the others fight in that struggle? Are we not the same as the other Germans? Do we not all belong together?

That was the first time that this problem began to agitate my small brain. And from the replies that were given to the questions which I asked very tentatively, I was forced to accept the fact, though with a secret envy, that not all Germans had the good luck to belong to Bismarck's Empire. This was something that I could not understand.

It was decided that I should study. Considering my character as a whole, and especially my temperament, my father decided that the classical subjects studied at the Lyceum were not suited to my natural talents. He thought that the REALSCHULE [2] would suit me better. My obvious talent for drawing confirmed him in that view; for in his opinion drawing was a subject too much neglected in the Austrian GYMNASIUM. Probably also the memory of the hard road which he himself had travelled contributed to make him look upon classical studies as unpractical and accordingly to set little value on them. At the back of his mind he had the idea that his son also should become an official of the Government. Indeed he had decided on that career for me. The difficulties through which he had to struggle in making his own career led him to overestimate what he had achieved, because this was exclusively the result of his own indefatigable industry and energy. The characteristic pride of the self-made man urged him towards the idea that his son should follow the same calling and if possible rise to a higher position in it. Moreover, this idea was strengthened by the consideration that the results of his own life's industry had placed him in a position to facilitate his son's advancement in the same career.

He was simply incapable of imagining that I might reject what had meant everything in life to him. My father's decision was simple, definite, clear and, in his eyes, it was something to be taken for granted. A man of such a nature who had become an autocrat by reason of his own hard struggle for existence, could not think of allowing 'inexperienced' and irresponsible young fellows to choose their own careers. To act in such a way, where the future of his own son was concerned, would have been a grave and reprehensible weakness in the exercise of parental authority and responsibility, something utterly incompatible with his characteristic sense of duty.

And yet it had to be otherwise.

For the first time in my life — I was then eleven years old — I felt myself forced into open opposition. No matter how hard and determined my father might be about putting his own plans and opinions into action, his son was no less obstinate in refusing to accept ideas on which he set little or no value.

I would not become a civil servant.

No amount of persuasion and no amount of 'grave' warnings could break down that opposition. I would not become a State official, not on any account. All the attempts which my father made to arouse in me a love or liking for that profession, by picturing his own career for me, had only the opposite effect. It nauseated me to think that one day I might be fettered to an office stool, that I could not dispose of my own time but would be forced to spend the whole of my life filling out forms.

One can imagine what kind of thoughts such a prospect awakened in the mind of a young fellow who was by no means what is called a 'good boy' in the current sense of that term. The ridiculously easy school tasks which we were given made it possible for me to spend far more time in the open air than at home. To-day, when my political opponents pry into my life with diligent scrutiny, as far back as the days of my boyhood, so as finally to be able to prove what disreputable tricks this Hitler was accustomed to in his young days, I thank heaven that I can look back to those happy days and find the memory of them helpful. The fields and the woods were then the terrain on which all disputes were fought out.

Even attendance at the REALSCHULE could not alter my way of spending my time. But I had now another battle to fight.

So long as the paternal plan to make a State functionary contradicted my own inclinations only in the abstract, the conflict was easy to bear. I could be discreet about expressing my personal views and thus avoid constantly recurrent disputes. My own resolution not to become a Government official was sufficient for the time being to put my mind completely at rest. I held on to that resolution inexorably. But the situation became more difficult once I had a positive plan of my own which I might present to my father as a counter-suggestion. This happened when I was twelve years old. How it came about I cannot exactly say now; but one day it became clear to me that I would be a painter—I mean an artist. That I had an aptitude for drawing was an admitted fact. It was even one of the reasons why my father had sent me to the REALSCHULE; but he had never thought of having that talent developed in such a way that I could take up painting as a professional career. Quite the contrary. When, as a result of my renewed refusal to adopt his favourite plan, my father asked me for the first time what I myself really wished to be, the resolution that I had already formed expressed itself almost automatically. For a while my father was speechless. "A painter? An artist-painter?" he exclaimed.

He wondered whether I was in a sound state of mind. He thought that he might not have caught my words rightly, or that he had misunderstood what I meant. But when I had explained my ideas to him and he saw how seriously I took them, he opposed them with that full determination which was characteristic of him. His decision was exceedingly simple and could not be deflected from its course by any consideration of what my own natural qualifications really were.

"Artist! Not as long as I live, never." As the son had inherited some of the father's obstinacy, besides having other qualities of his own, my reply was equally energetic. But it stated something quite the contrary.

At that our struggle became stalemate. The father would not abandon his 'Never', and I became all the more consolidated in my 'Nevertheless'.

Naturally the resulting situation was not pleasant. The old gentleman was bitterly annoyed; and indeed so was I, although I really loved him. My father forbade me to entertain any hopes of taking up the art of painting as a profession. I went a step further and declared that I would not study anything else. With such declarations the situation became still more strained, so that the old gentleman irrevocably decided to assert his parental authority at all costs. That led me to adopt an attitude of circumspect silence, but I put my threat into execution. I thought that, once it became clear to my father that

I was making no progress at the REALSCHULE, for weal or for woe, he would be forced to allow me to follow the happy career I had dreamed of.

I do not know whether I calculated rightly or not. Certainly my failure to make progress became quite visible in the school. I studied just the subjects that appealed to me, especially those which I thought might be of advantage to me later on as a painter. What did not appear to have any importance from this point of view, or what did not otherwise appeal to me favourably, I completely sabotaged. My school reports of that time were always in the extremes of good or bad, according to the subject and the interest it had for me. In one column my qualification read 'very good' or 'excellent'. In another it read 'average' or even 'below average'. By far my best subjects were geography and, even more so, general history. These were my two favourite subjects, and I led the class in them.

When I look back over so many years and try to judge the results of that experience I find two very significant facts standing out clearly before my mind.

First, I became a nationalist.

Second, I learned to understand and grasp the true meaning of history.

The old Austria was a multi-national State. In those days at least the citizens of the German Empire, taken through and through, could not understand what that fact meant in the everyday life of the individuals within such a State. After the magnificent triumphant march of the victorious armies in the Franco-German War the Germans in the REICH became steadily more and more estranged from the Germans beyond their frontiers, partly because they did not deign to appreciate those other Germans at their true value or simply because they were incapable of doing so.

The Germans of the REICH did not realize that if the Germans in Austria had not been of the best racial stock they could never have given the stamp of their own character to an Empire of 52 millions, so definitely that in Germany itself the idea arose — though quite an erroneous one — that Austria was a German State. That was an error which led to dire consequences; but all the same it was a magnificent testimony to the character of the ten million Germans in that East Mark.[3] Only very few of the Germans in the REICH itself had an idea of the bitter struggle which those Eastern Germans had to carry on daily for the preservation of their German language, their German schools and their German character. Only to-day, when a tragic fate has torn several millions of our kinsfolk away from the REICH and has forced them to live under the rule of the stranger, dreaming of that common fatherland towards which all their yearnings are directed and struggling to uphold at least the sacred right of using their mother tongue — only now have the wider circles of the German population come to realize what it means to have to fight for the traditions of one's race. And so at last perhaps there are people here and there who can assess the greatness of that German spirit which animated the old East Mark and enabled those people, left entirely dependent on their own resources, to defend the Empire against the Orient for several centuries and subsequently to hold fast the frontiers of the German language through a guerilla warfare of attrition, at a time when the German Empire was sedulously cultivating an interest for colonies but not for its own flesh and blood before the threshold of its own door.

What has happened always and everywhere, in every kind of struggle, happened also in the language fight which was carried on in the old Austria. There were three groups — the fighters, the hedgers and the traitors. Even in the schools this sifting already began to take place. And it is worth noting that the struggle for the language was waged perhaps in its bitterest form around the school; because this was the nursery where the seeds had to be watered which were to spring up and form the future generation. The tactical objective of the fight was the winning over of the child, and it was to the child that the first rallying cry was addressed:

"German youth, do not forget that you are a German," and "Remember, little girl, that one day you must be a German mother."

Those who know something of the juvenile spirit can understand how youth will always lend a glad ear to such a rallying cry. Under many forms the young people led the struggle, fighting in their own way and with their own weapons. They refused to sing non-German songs. The greater the efforts made to win them away from their German allegiance, the more they exalted the glory of their German heroes. They stinted themselves in buying things to eat, so that they might spare their pennies to help the war chest of their elders. They were incredibly alert in the significance of what the non-German teachers said and they contradicted in unison. They wore the forbidden emblems of their own kinsfolk and were happy when penalised for doing so, or even physically punished. In miniature they were mirrors of loyalty from which the older people might learn a lesson.

And thus it was that at a comparatively early age I took part in the struggle which the nationalities were waging against one another in the old Austria. When meetings were held for the South Mark German League and the School League we wore cornflowers and black-red-gold colours to express our loyalty. We greeted one another with HEIL! and instead of the Austrian anthem we sang our own DEUTSCHLAND ÜBER ALLES, despite warnings and penalties. Thus the youth were educated politically at a time when the citizens of a so-called national State for the most part knew little of their own nationality except the language. Of course, I did not belong to the hedgers. Within a little while I had become an ardent 'German National', which has a different meaning from the party significance attached to that phrase to-day.

I developed very rapidly in the nationalist direction, and by the time I was 15 years old I had come to understand the distinction between dynastic patriotism and nationalism based on the concept of folk, or people, my inclination being entirely in favour of the latter.

Such a preference may not perhaps be clearly intelligible to those who have never taken the trouble to study the internal conditions that prevailed under the Habsburg Monarchy.

Among historical studies universal history was the subject almost exclusively taught in the Austrian schools, for of specific Austrian history there was only very little. The fate of this State was closely bound up with the existence and development of Germany as a whole; so a division of history into German history and Austrian history would be practically inconceivable. And indeed it was only when the German people came to be divided between two States that this division of German history began to take place.

The insignia of a former imperial sovereignty[4] which were still preserved in Vienna appeared to act as magical relics rather than as the visible guarantee of an everlasting bond of union.

When the Habsburg State crumbled to pieces in 1918 the Austrian Germans instinctively raised an outcry for union with their German fatherland. That was the voice of a unanimous yearning in the hearts of the whole people for a return to the unforgotten home of their fathers. But such a general yearning could not be explained except by attributing the cause of it to the historical training through which the individual Austrian Germans had passed. Therein lay a spring that never dried up. Especially in times of distraction and forgetfulness its quiet voice was a reminder of the past, bidding the people to look out beyond the mere welfare of the moment to a new future.

The teaching of universal history in what are called the middle schools is still very unsatisfactory. Few teachers realize that the purpose of teaching history is not the memorizing of some dates and facts, that the student is not interested in knowing the exact date of a battle or the birthday of some marshal or other, and not at all — or at least only very insignificantly — interested in knowing when the crown of his fathers was placed on the brow of some monarch. These are certainly not looked upon as important matters.

To study history means to search for and discover the forces that are the causes of those results which appear before our eyes as historical events. The art of reading and studying consists in remembering the essentials and forgetting what is not essential.

Probably my whole future life was determined by the fact that I had a professor of history who understood, as few others understand, how to make this viewpoint prevail in teaching and in examining. This teacher was Dr. Leopold Poetsch, of the REALSCHULE at Linz. He was the ideal personification of the qualities necessary to a teacher of history in the sense I have mentioned above. An elderly gentleman with a decisive manner but a kindly heart, he was a very attractive speaker and was able to inspire us with his own enthusiasm. Even to-day I cannot recall without emotion that venerable personality whose enthusiastic exposition of history so often made us entirely forget the present and allow ourselves to be transported as if by magic into the past. He penetrated through the dim mist of thousands of years and transformed the historical memory of the dead past into a living reality. When we listened to him we became afire with enthusiasm and we were sometimes moved even to tears.

It was still more fortunate that this professor was able not only to illustrate the past by examples from the present but from the past he was also able to draw a lesson for the present. He understood better than any other the everyday problems that were then agitating our minds. The national fervour which we felt in our own small way was utilized by him as an instrument of our education, inasmuch as he often appealed to our national sense of honour; for in that way he maintained order and held our attention much more easily than he could have done by any other means. It was because I had such a professor that history became my favourite subject. As a natural consequence, but without the conscious connivance of my professor, I then and there became a young rebel. But who could have studied German history under such a teacher and not become an enemy of that State whose rulers exercised such a disastrous influence on the destinies of the German nation? Finally, how could one remain the faithful subject of the House of Habsburg, whose past history and present conduct proved it to be ready ever and always to betray the interests of the German people for the sake of paltry personal interests? Did not we as youngsters fully realize that the House of Habsburg did not, and could not, have any love for us Germans?

What history taught us about the policy followed by the House of Habsburg was corroborated by our own everyday experiences. In the north and in the south the poison of foreign races was eating into the body of our people, and even Vienna was steadily becoming more and more a non-German city. The 'Imperial House' favoured the Czechs on every possible occasion. Indeed it was the hand of the goddess of eternal justice and inexorable retribution that caused the most deadly enemy of Germanism in Austria, the Archduke Franz Ferdinand, to fall by the very bullets which he himself had helped to cast. Working from above downwards, he was the chief patron of the movement to make Austria a Slav State.

The burdens laid on the shoulders of the German people were enormous and the sacrifices of money and blood which they had to make were incredibly heavy.

Yet anybody who was not quite blind must have seen that it was all in vain. What affected us most bitterly was the consciousness of the fact that this whole system was morally shielded by the alliance with Germany, whereby the slow extirpation of Germanism in the old Austrian Monarchy seemed in some way to be more or less sanctioned by Germany herself. Habsburg hypocrisy, which endeavoured outwardly to make the people believe that Austria still remained a German State, increased the feeling of hatred against the Imperial House and at the same time aroused a spirit of rebellion and contempt.

But in the German Empire itself those who were then its rulers saw nothing of what all this meant. As if struck blind, they stood beside a corpse and in the very symptoms of decomposition they believed that they recognized the signs of a renewed vitality. In that unhappy alliance between the young German Empire and the illusory Austrian State lay the germ of the World War and also of the final collapse.

In the subsequent pages of this book I shall go to the root of the problem. Suffice it to say here that in the very early years of my youth I came to certain conclusions which I have never abandoned. Indeed I became more profoundly convinced of them as the years passed. They were: That the dissolution of the Austrian Empire is a preliminary condition for the defence of Germany; further, that national feeling is by no means identical with dynastic patriotism; finally, and above all, that the House of Habsburg was destined to bring misfortune to the German nation.

As a logical consequence of these convictions, there arose in me a feeling of intense love for my German-Austrian home and a profound hatred for the Austrian State.

That kind of historical thinking which was developed in me through my study of history at school never left me afterwards. World history became more and more an inexhaustible source for the understanding of contemporary historical events, which means politics. Therefore I will not "learn" politics but let politics teach me.

A precocious revolutionary in politics I was no less a precocious revolutionary in art. At that time the provincial capital of Upper Austria had a theatre which, relatively speaking, was not bad. Almost everything was played there. When I was twelve years old I saw William Tell performed. That was my first experience of the theatre. Some months later I attended a performance of LOHENGRIN, the first opera I had ever heard. I was fascinated at once. My youthful enthusiasm for the Bayreuth Master knew no limits. Again and again I was drawn to hear his operas; and to-day I consider it a great piece of luck that these modest productions in the little provincial city prepared the way and made it possible for me to appreciate the better productions later on.

But all this helped to intensify my profound aversion for the career that my father had chosen for me; and this dislike became especially strong as the rough corners of youthful boorishness became worn off, a process which in my case caused a good deal of pain. I became more and more convinced that I should never be happy as a State official. And now that the REALSCHULE had recognized and acknowledged my aptitude for drawing, my own resolution became all the stronger. Imprecations and threats had no longer any chance of changing it. I wanted to become a painter and no power in the world could force me to become a civil servant. The only peculiar feature of the situation now was that as I grew bigger I became more and more interested in architecture. I considered this fact as a natural development of my flair for painting and I rejoiced inwardly that the sphere of my artistic interests was thus enlarged. I had no notion that one day it would have to be otherwise. The question of my career was decided much sooner than I could have expected.

When I was in my thirteenth year my father was suddenly taken from us. He was still in robust health when a stroke of apoplexy painlessly ended his earthly wanderings and left us all deeply bereaved. His most ardent longing was to be able to help his son to advance in a career and thus save me from the harsh ordeal that he himself had to go through. But it appeared to him then as if that longing were all in vain. And yet, though he himself was not conscious of it, he had sown the seeds of a future which neither of us foresaw at that time.

At first nothing changed outwardly.

My mother felt it her duty to continue my education in accordance with my father's wishes, which meant that she would have me study for the civil service. For my own part I was even more firmly determined than ever before that under no circumstances would I become an official of the State. The curriculum and teaching methods followed in the middle school were so far removed from my ideals that I became profoundly indifferent. Illness suddenly came to my assistance. Within a few weeks it decided my future and put an end to the long-standing family conflict. My lungs became so seriously affected that the doctor advised my mother very strongly not under any circumstances to allow me to take up a career which would necessitate working in an office. He ordered that I should give up attendance at the REALSCHULE for a year at least. What I had secretly desired for such a long time, and had persistently fought for, now became a reality almost at one stroke.

Influenced by my illness, my mother agreed that I should leave the REALSCHULE and attend the Academy.

Those were happy days, which appeared to me almost as a dream; but they were bound to remain only a dream. Two years later my mother's death put a brutal end to all my fine projects. She succumbed to a long and painful illness which from the very beginning permitted little hope of recovery. Though expected, her death came as a terrible blow to me. I respected my father, but I loved my mother.

Poverty and stern reality forced me to decide promptly.

The meagre resources of the family had been almost entirely used up through my mother's severe illness. The allowance which came to me as an orphan was not enough for the bare necessities of life. Somehow or other I would have to earn my own bread.

With my clothes and linen packed in a valise and with an indomitable resolution in my heart, I left for Vienna. I hoped to forestall fate, as my father had done fifty years before. I was determined to become 'something' — but certainly not a civil servant.

CHAPTER II:
Years of Study and Suffering in Vienna

When my mother died my fate had already been decided in one respect. During the last months of her illness I went to Vienna to take the entrance examination for the Academy of Fine Arts. Armed with a bulky packet of sketches, I felt convinced that I should pass the examination quite easily. At the REALSCHULE I was by far the best student in the drawing class, and since that time I had made more than ordinary progress in the practice of drawing. Therefore I was pleased with myself and was proud and happy at the prospect of what I considered an assured success.

But there was one misgiving: It seemed to me that I was better qualified for drawing than for painting, especially in the various branches of architectural drawing. At the same time my interest in architecture was constantly increasing. And I advanced in this direction at a still more rapid pace after my first visit to Vienna, which lasted two weeks. I was not yet sixteen years old. I went to the Hof Museum to study the paintings in the art gallery there; but the building itself captured almost all my interest, from early morning until late at night I spent all my time visiting the various public buildings. And it was the buildings themselves that were always the principal attraction for me. For hours and hours I could stand in wonderment before the Opera and the Parliament. The whole Ring Strasse had a magic effect upon me, as if it were a scene from the Thousand-and-one-Nights.

And now I was here for the second time in this beautiful city, impatiently waiting to hear the result of the entrance examination but proudly confident that I had got through. I was so convinced of my success that when the news that I had failed to pass was brought to me it struck me like a bolt from the skies. Yet the fact was that I had failed. I went to see the Rector and asked him to explain the reasons why they refused to accept me as a student in the general School of Painting, which was part of the Academy. He said that the sketches which I had brought with me unquestionably showed that painting was not what I was suited for but that the same sketches gave clear indications of my aptitude for architectural designing. Therefore the School of Painting did not come into question for me but rather the School of Architecture, which also formed part of the Academy. At first it was impossible to understand how this could be so, seeing that I had never been to a school for architecture and had never received any instruction in architectural designing.

When I left the Hansen Palace, on the SCHILLER PLATZ, I was quite crestfallen. I felt out of sorts with myself for the first time in my young life. For what I had heard about my capabilities now appeared to me as a lightning flash which clearly revealed a dualism under which I had been suffering for a long time, but hitherto I could give no clear account whatsoever of the why and wherefore.

Within a few days I myself also knew that I ought to become an architect. But of course the way was very difficult. I was now forced bitterly to rue my former conduct in neglecting and despising certain subjects at the REALSCHULE. Before taking up the courses at the School of Architecture in the Academy it was necessary to attend the Technical Building School; but a necessary qualification for entrance into this school was a Leaving Certificate from the Middle School. And this I simply did not have. According to the human measure of things my dream of following an artistic calling seemed beyond the limits of possibility.

After the death of my mother I came to Vienna for the third time. This visit was destined to last several years. Since I had been there before I had recovered my old calm and resoluteness. The former self-assurance had come back, and I had my eyes steadily fixed on the goal. I would be an architect. Obstacles are placed across our path in life, not to be boggled at but to be surmounted. And I was fully determined to surmount these obstacles, having the picture of my father constantly before my mind, who had raised himself by his own efforts to the position of a civil servant though he was the poor son of a village shoemaker. I had a better start, and the possibilities of struggling through were better. At that time my lot in life seemed to me a harsh one; but to-day I see in it the wise workings of Providence. The Goddess of Fate clutched me in her hands and often threatened to smash me; but the will grew stronger as the obstacles increased, and finally the will triumphed.

I am thankful for that period of my life, because it hardened me and enabled me to be as tough as I now am. And I am even more thankful because I appreciate the fact that I was thus saved from the emptiness of a life of ease and that a mother's darling was taken from tender arms and handed over to Adversity as to a new mother. Though I then rebelled against it as too hard a fate, I am grateful that I was thrown into a world of misery and poverty and thus came to know the people for whom I was afterwards to fight.

It was during this period that my eyes were opened to two perils, the names of which I scarcely knew hitherto and had no notion whatsoever of their terrible significance for the existence of the German people. These two perils were Marxism and Judaism.

For many people the name of Vienna signifies innocent jollity, a festive place for happy mortals. For me, alas, it is a living memory of the saddest period in my life. Even to-day the mention of that city arouses only gloomy thoughts in my mind. Five years of poverty in that Phaecian[5] town. Five years in which, first as a casual labourer and then as a painter of little trifles, I had to earn my daily bread. And a meagre morsel indeed it was, not even sufficient to still the hunger which I constantly felt. That hunger was the faithful guardian which never left me but took part in everything I did. Every book that I bought meant renewed hunger, and every visit I paid to the opera meant the intrusion of that inalienabl companion during the following days. I was always struggling with my unsympathic friend. And yet during that time I learned more than I had ever learned before. Outside my architectural studies and rare visits to the opera, for which I had to deny myself food, I had no other pleasure in life except my books.

I read a great deal then, and I pondered deeply over what I read. All the free time after work was devoted exclusively to study. Thus within a few years I was able to acquire a stock of knowledge which I find useful even to-day.

But more than that. During those years a view of life and a definite outlook on the world took shape in my mind. These became the granite basis of my conduct at that time. Since then I have extended that foundation only very little, and I have changed nothing in it.

On the contrary: I am firmly convinced to-day that, generally speaking, it is in youth that men lay the essential groundwork of their creative thought, wherever that creative thought exists. I make a distinction between the wisdom of age—which can only arise from the greater profundity and foresight that are based on the experiences of a long life—and the creative genius of youth, which blossoms out in thought and ideas with inexhaustible fertility, without being able to put these into practice immediately, because of their very superabundance. These furnish the building materials and plans for the future; and it is from them that age takes the stones and builds the edifice, unless the so-called wisdom of the years may have smothered the creative genius of youth.

The life which I had hitherto led at home with my parents differed in little or nothing from that of all the others. I looked forward without apprehension to the morrow, and there was no such thing as a social problem to be faced. Those among whom I passed my young days belonged to the small bourgeois class. Therefore it was a world that had very little contact with the world of genuine manual labourers. For, though at first this may appear astonishing, the ditch which separates that class, which is by no means economically well-off; from the manual labouring class is often deeper than people think. The reason for this division, which we may almost call enmity, lies in the fear that dominates a social group which has only just risen above the level of the manual labourer—a fear lest it may fall back into its old condition or at least be classed with the labourers. Moreover, there is something repulsive in remembering the cultural indigence of that lower class and their rough manners with one another; so that people who are only on the first rung of the social ladder find it unbearable to be forced to have any contact with the cultural level and standard of living out of which they have passed.

And so it happens that very often those who belong to what can really be called the upper classes find it much easier than do the upstarts to descend to and intermingle with their fellow beings on the lowest social level. For by the word upstart I mean everyone who has raised himself through his own efforts to a social level higher than that to which he formerly belonged. In the case of such a person the hard struggle through which he passes often destroys his normal human sympathy. His own fight for existence kills his sensibility for the misery of those who have been left behind.

From this point of view fate had been kind to me. Circumstances forced me to return to that world of poverty and economic insecurity above which my father had raised himself in his early days; and thus the blinkers of a narrow PETIT BOURGEOIS education were torn from my eyes. Now for the first time I learned to know men and I learned to distinguish between empty appearances or brutal manners and the real inner nature of the people who outwardly appeared thus.

At the beginning of the century Vienna had already taken rank among those cities where social conditions are iniquitous. Dazzling riches and loathsome destitution were intermingled in violent contrast. In the centre and in the Inner City one felt the pulse-beat of an Empire which had a population of fifty-two millions, with all the perilous charm of a State made up of multiple nationalities. The dazzling splendour of the Court acted like a magnet on the wealth and intelligence of the whole Empire. And this attraction was further strengthened by the dynastic policy of the Habsburg Monarchy in centralizing everything in itself and for itself.

This centralizing policy was necessary in order to hold together that hotchpotch of heterogeneous nationalities. But the result of it was an extraordinary concentration of higher officials in the city, which was at one and the same time the metropolis and imperial residence. But Vienna was not merely the political and intellectual centre of the Danubian Monarchy; it was also the commercial centre. Besides the horde of military officers of high rank, State officials, artists and scientists, there was the still vaster horde of workers. Abject poverty confronted the wealth of the aristocracy and the merchant class face to face. Thousands of unemployed loitered in front of the palaces on the Ring Strasse; and below that VIA TRIUMPHALIS of the old Austria the homeless huddled together in the murk and filth of the canals.

There was hardly any other German city in which the social problem could be studied better than in Vienna. But here I must utter a warning against the illusion that this problem can be 'studied' from above downwards. The man who has never been in the clutches of that crushing viper can never know what its poison is. An attempt to study it in any other way will result only in superficial talk and sentimental delusions. Both are harmful. The first because it can never go to the root of the question, the second because it evades the question entirely. I do not know which is the more nefarious: to ignore social distress, as do the majority of those who have been favoured by fortune and those who have risen in the social scale through their own routine labour, or the equally supercilious and often tactless but always genteel condescension displayed by people who make a fad of being charitable and who plume themselves on 'sympathising with the people.' Of course such persons sin more than they can imagine from lack of instinctive understanding. And thus they are astonished to find that the 'social conscience' on which they pride themselves never produces any results, but often causes their good intentions to be resented; and then they talk of the ingratitude of the people.

Such persons are slow to learn that here there is no place for merely social activities and that there can be no expectation of gratitude; for in this connection there is no question at all of distributing favours but essentially a matter of retributive justice. I was protected against the temptation to study the social question in the way just mentioned, for the simple reason that I was forced to live in the midst of poverty-stricken people. Therefore it was not a question of studying the problem objectively, but rather one of testing its effects on myself. Though the rabbit came through the ordeal of the experiment, this must not be taken as evidence of its harmlessness.

When I try to-day to recall the succession of impressions received during that time I find that I can do so only with approximate completeness. Here I shall describe only the more essential impressions and those which personally affected me and often staggered me. And I shall mention the few lessons I then learned from this experience.

At that time it was for the most part not very difficult to find work, because I had to seek work not as a skilled tradesman but as a so-called extra-hand ready to take any job that turned up by chance, just for the sake of earning my daily bread.

Thus I found myself in the same situation as all those emigrants who shake the dust of Europe from their feet, with the cast-iron determination to lay the foundations of a new existence in the New World and acquire for themselves a new home. Liberated from all the paralysing prejudices of class and calling, environment and tradition, they enter any service that opens its doors to them, accepting any work that comes their way, filled more and more with the idea that honest work never disgraced anybody, no matter what kind it may be. And so I was resolved to set both feet in what was for me a new world and push forward on my own road.

I soon found out that there was some kind of work always to be got, but I also learned that it could just as quickly and easily be lost. The uncertainty of being able to earn a regular daily livelihood soon appeared to me as the gloomiest feature in this new life that I had entered.

Although the skilled worker was not so frequently thrown idle on the streets as the unskilled worker, yet the former was by no means protected against the same fate; because though he may not have to face hunger as a result of unemployment due to the lack of demand in the labour market, the lock-out and the strike deprived the skilled worker of the chance to earn his bread. Here the element of uncertainty in steadily earning one's daily bread was the bitterest feature of the whole social-economic system itself.

The country lad who migrates to the big city feels attracted by what has been described as easy work—which it may be in reality—and few working hours. He is especially entranced by the magic glimmer spread over the big cities. Accustomed in the country to earn a steady wage, he has been taught not to quit his former post until a new one is at least in sight. As there is a great scarcity of agricultural labour, the probability of long unemployment in the country has been very small. It is a mistake to presume that the lad who leaves the countryside for the town is not made of such sound material as those who remain at home to work on the land. On the contrary, experience shows that it is the more healthy and more vigorous that emigrate, and not the reverse. Among these emigrants I include not merely those who emigrate to America, but also the servant boy in the country who decides to leave his native village and migrate to the big city where he will be a stranger. He is ready to take the risk of an uncertain fate. In most cases he comes to town with a little money in his pocket and for the first few days he is not discouraged if he should not have the good fortune to find work. But if he finds a job and then loses it in a little while, the case is much worse. To find work anew, especially in winter, is often difficult and indeed sometimes impossible. For the first few weeks life is still bearable He receives his out-of-work money from his trade union and is thus enabled to carry on. But when the last of his own money is gone and his trade union ceases to pay out because of the prolonged unemployment, then comes the real distress. He now loiters about and is hungry. Often he pawns or sells the last of his belongings. His clothes begin to get shabby and with the increasing poverty of his outward appearance he descends to a lower social level and mixes up with a class of human beings through whom his mind is now poisoned, in addition to his physical misery. Then he has nowhere to sleep and if that happens in winter, which is very often the case, he is in dire distress. Finally he gets work. But the old story repeats itself. A second time the same thing happens. Then a third time; and now it is probably much worse. Little by little he becomes indifferent to this everlasting insecurity. Finally he grows used to the repetition. Thus even a man who is normally of industrious habits grows careless in his whole attitude towards life and gradually becomes an instrument in the hands of unscrupulous people who exploit him for the sake of their own ignoble aims. He has been so often thrown out of employment through no fault of his own that he is now more or less indifferent whether the strike in which he takes part be for the purpose of securing his economic rights or be aimed at the destruction of the State, the whole social order and even civilization itself. Though the idea of going on strike may not be to his natural liking, yet he joins in it out of sheer indifference.

I saw this process exemplified before my eyes in thousands of cases. And the longer I observed it the greater became my dislike for that mammoth city which greedily attracts men to its bosom, in order to break them mercilessly in the end. When they came they still felt themselves in communion with their own people at home; if they remained that tie was broken.

I was thrown about so much in the life of the metropolis that I experienced the workings of this fate in my own person and felt the effects of it in my own soul. One thing stood out clearly before my eyes: It was the sudden changes from work to idleness and vice versa; so that the constant fluctuations thus caused by earnings and expenditure finally destroyed the 'sense of thrift for many people and also the habit of regulating expenditure in an intelligent way. The body appeared to grow accustomed to the vicissitudes of food and hunger, eating heartily in good times and going hungry in bad. Indeed hunger shatters all plans for rationing expenditure on a regular scale in better times when employment is again found. The reason for this is that the deprivations which the unemployed worker has to endure must be compensated for psychologically by a persistent mental mirage in which he imagines himself eating heartily once again. And this dream develops into such a longing that it turns into a morbid impulse to cast off all self-restraint when work and wages turn up again. Therefore the moment work is found anew he forgets to regulate the expenditure of his earnings but spends them to the full without thinking of to-morrow. This leads to confusion in the little weekly housekeeping budget, because the expenditure is not rationally planned. When the phenomenon which I have mentioned first happens, the earnings will last perhaps for five days instead of seven; on subsequent occasions they will last only for three days; as the habit recurs, the earnings will last scarcely for a day; and finally they will disappear in one night of feasting.

Often there are wife and children at home. And in many cases it happens that these become infected by such a way of living, especially if the husband is good to them and wants to do the best he can for them and loves them in his own way and according to his own lights. Then the week's earnings are spent in common at home within two or three days. The family eat and drink together as long as the money lasts and at the end of the week they hunger together. Then the wife wanders about furtively in the neighbourhood, borrows a little, and runs up small debts with the shopkeepers in an effort to pull through the lean days towards the end of the week. They sit down together to the midday meal with only meagre fare on the table, and often even nothing to eat. They wait for the coming payday, talking of it and making plans; and while they are thus hungry they dream of the plenty that is to come. And so the little children become acquainted with misery in their early years.

But the evil culminates when the husband goes his own way from the beginning of the week and the wife protests, simply out of love for the children. Then there are quarrels and bad feeling and the husband takes to drink according as he becomes estranged from his wife. He now becomes drunk every Saturday. Fighting for her own existence and that of the children, the wife has to hound him along the road from the factory to the tavern in order to get a few shillings from him on payday. Then when he finally comes home, maybe on the Sunday or the Monday, having parted with his last shillings and pence, pitiable scenes follow, scenes that cry out for God's mercy.

I have had actual experience of all this in hundreds of cases. At first I was disgusted and indignant; but later on I came to recognize the whole tragedy of their misfortune and to understand the profound causes of it. They were the unhappy victims of evil circumstances.

Housing conditions were very bad at that time. The Vienna manual labourers lived in surroundings of appalling misery. I shudder even to-day when I think of the woeful dens in which people dwelt, the night shelters and the slums, and all the tenebrous spectacles of ordure, loathsome filth and wickedness.

What will happen one day when hordes of emancipated slaves come forth from these dens of misery to swoop down on their unsuspecting fellow men? For this other world does not think about such a possibility. They have allowed these things to go on without caring and even without suspecting—in their total lack of instinctive understanding—that sooner or later destiny will take its vengeance unless it will have been appeased in time.

To-day I fervidly thank Providence for having sent me to such a school. There I could not refuse to take an interest in matters that did not please me. This school soon taught me a profound lesson.

In order not to despair completely of the people among whom I then lived I had to set on one side the outward appearances of their lives and on the other the reasons why they had developed in that way. Then I could hear everything without discouragement; for those who emerged from all this misfortune and misery, from this filth and outward degradation, were not human beings as such but rather lamentable results of lamentable laws. In my own life similar hardships prevented me from giving way to a pitying sentimentality at the sight of these degraded products which had finally resulted from the pressure of circumstances. No, the sentimental attitude would be the wrong one to adopt.

Even in those days I already saw that there was a two-fold method by which alone it would be possible to bring about an amelioration of these conditions. This method is: first, to create better fundamental conditions of social development by establishing a profound feeling for social responsibilities among the public; second, to combine this feeling for social responsibilities with a ruthless determination to prune away all excrescences which are incapable of being improved.

Just as Nature concentrates its greatest attention, not to the maintenance of what already exists but on the selective breeding of offspring in order to carry on the species, so in human life also it is less a matter of artificially improving the existing generation—which, owing to human characteristics, is impossible in ninety-nine cases out of a hundred—and more a matter of securing from the very start a better road for future development.

During my struggle for existence in Vienna I perceived very clearly that the aim of all social activity must never be merely charitable relief, which is ridiculous and useless, but it must rather be a means to find a way of eliminating the fundamental deficiencies in our economic and cultural life—deficiencies which necessarily bring about the degradation of the individual or at least lead him towards such degradation. The difficulty of employing every means, even the most drastic, to eradicate the hostility prevailing among the working classes towards the State is largely due to an attitude of uncertainty in deciding upon the inner motives and causes of this contemporary phenomenon. The grounds of this uncertainty are to be found exclusively in the sense of guilt which each individual feels for having permitted this tragedy of degradation. For that feeling paralyses every effort at making a serious and firm decision to act. And thus because the people whom it concerns are vacillating they are timid and half-hearted in putting into effect even the measures which are indispensable for self-preservation. When the individual is no longer burdened with his own consciousness of blame in this regard, then and only then will he have that inner tranquillity and outer force to cut off drastically and ruthlessly all the parasite growth and root out the weeds.

But because the Austrian State had almost no sense of social rights or social legislation its inability to abolish those evil excrescences was manifest.

I do not know what it was that appalled me most at that time: the economic misery of those who were then my companions, their crude customs and morals, or the low level of their intellectual culture.

How often our bourgeoisie rises up in moral indignation on hearing from the mouth of some pitiable tramp that it is all the same to him whether he be a German or not and that he will find himself at home wherever he can get enough to keep body and soul together. They protest sternly against such a lack of 'national pride' and strongly express their horror at such sentiments.

But how many people really ask themselves why it is that their own sentiments are better? How many of them understand that their natural pride in being members of so favoured a nation arises from the innumerable succession of instances they have encountered which remind them of the greatness of the Fatherland and the Nation in all spheres of artistic and cultural life? How many of them realize that pride in the Fatherland is largely dependent on knowledge of its greatness in all those spheres? Do our bourgeois circles ever think what a ridiculously meagre share the people have in that knowledge which is a necessary prerequisite for the feeling of pride in one's fatherland?

It cannot be objected here that in other countries similar conditions exist and that nevertheless the working classes in those countries have remained patriotic. Even if that were so, it would be no excuse for our negligent attitude. But it is not so. What we call chauvinistic education—in the case of the French people, for example—is only the excessive exaltation of the greatness of France in all spheres of culture or, as the French say, civilization. The French boy is not educated on purely objective principles. Wherever the importance of the political and cultural greatness of his country is concerned he is taught in the most subjective way that one can imagine.

This education will always have to be confined to general ideas in a large perspective and these ought to be deeply engraven, by constant repetition if necessary, on the memories and feelings of the people. In our case, however, we are not merely guilty of negative sins of omission but also of positively perverting the little which some individuals had the luck to learn at school. The rats that poison our body-politic gnaw from the hearts and memories of the broad masses even that little which distress and misery have left.

Let the reader try to picture the following:

There is a lodging in a cellar and this lodging consists of two damp rooms. In these rooms a workman and his family live—seven people in all. Let us assume that one of the children is a boy of three years. That is the age at which children first become conscious of the impressions which they receive. In the case of highly gifted people traces of the impressions received in those early years last in the memory up to an advanced age. Now the narrowness and congestion of those living quarters do not conduce to pleasant inter-relations. Thus quarrels and fits of mutual anger arise. These people can hardly be said to live with one another, but rather down on top of one another. The small misunderstandings which disappear of themselves in a home where there is enough space for people to go apart from one another for a while, here become the source of chronic disputes. As far as the children are concerned the situation is tolerable from this point of view. In such conditions they are constantly quarrelling with one another, but the quarrels are quickly and entirely forgotten. But when the parents fall out with one another these daily bickerings often descend to rudeness such as cannot be adequately imagined. The results of such experiences must become apparent later on in the children. One must have practical experience of such a MILIEU so as to be able to picture the state of affairs that arises from these mutual recriminations when the father physically assaults the mother and maltreats her in a fit of drunken rage. At the age of six the child can no longer ignore those sordid details which even an adult would find revolting. Infected with moral poison, bodily undernourished, and the poor little head filled with vermin, the young 'citizen' goes to the primary school. With difficulty he barely learns to read and write. There is no possibility of learning any lessons at home. Quite the contrary. The father and mother themselves talk before the children in the most disparaging way about the teacher and the school and they are much more inclined to insult the teachers than to put their offspring across the knee and knock sound reason into him. What the little fellow hears at home does not tend to increase respect for his human surroundings. Here nothing good is said of human nature as a whole and every institution, from the school to the government, is reviled. Whether religion and morals are concerned or the State and the social order, it is all the same; they are all scoffed at. When the young lad leaves school, at the age of fourteen, it would be difficult to say what are the most striking features of his character, incredible ignorance in so far as real knowledge is concerned or cynical impudence combined with an attitude towards morality which is really startling at so young an age.

What station in life can such a person fill, to whom nothing is sacred, who has never experienced anything noble but, on the contrary, has been intimately acquainted with the lowest kind of human existence? This child of three has got into the habit of reviling all authority by the time he is fifteen. He has been acquainted only with moral filth and vileness, everything being excluded that might stimulate his thought towards higher things. And now this young specimen of humanity enters the school of life.

He leads the same kind of life which was exemplified for him by his father during his childhood. He loiters about and comes home at all hours. He now even black-guards that broken-hearted being who gave him birth. He curses God and the world and finally ends up in a House of Correction for young people. There he gets the final polish.

And his bourgeois contemporaries are astonished at the lack of 'patriotic enthusiasm' which this young 'citizen' manifests.

Day after day the bourgeois world are witnesses to the phenomenon of spreading poison among the people through the instrumentality of the theatre and the cinema, gutter journalism and obscene books; and yet they are astonished at the deplorable 'moral standards' and 'national indifference' of the masses. As if the cinema bilge and the gutter press and suchlike could inculcate knowledge of the greatness of one's country, apart entirely from the earlier education of the individual.

I then came to understand, quickly and thoroughly, what I had never been aware of before. It was the following:

The question of 'nationalizing' a people is first and foremost one of establishing healthy social conditions which will furnish the grounds that are necessary for the education of the individual. For only when family upbringing and school education have inculcated in the individual a knowledge of the cultural and economic and, above all, the political greatness of his own country—then, and then only, will it be possible for him to feel proud of being a citizen of such a country. I can fight only for something that I love. I can love only what I respect. And in order to respect a thing I must at least have some knowledge of it.

As soon as my interest in social questions was once awakened I began to study them in a fundamental way. A new and hitherto unknown world was thus revealed to me.

In the years 1909-10 I had so far improved my, position that I no longer had to earn my daily bread as a manual labourer. I was now working independently as draughtsman, and painter in water colours. This MÉTIER was a poor one indeed as far as earnings were concerned; for these were only sufficient to meet the bare exigencies of life. Yet it had an interest for me in view of the profession to which I aspired. Moreover, when I came home in the evenings I was now no longer dead-tired as formerly, when I used to be unable to look into a book without falling asleep almost immediately. My present occupation therefore was in line with the profession I aimed at for the future. Moreover, I was master of my own time and could distribute my working-hours now better than formerly. I painted in order to earn my bread, and I studied because I liked it.

Thus I was able to acquire that theoretical knowledge of the social problem which was a necessary complement to what I was learning through actual experience. I studied all the books which I could find that dealt with this question and I thought deeply on what I read. I think that the MILIEU in which I then lived considered me an eccentric person.

Besides my interest in the social question I naturally devoted myself with enthusiasm to the study of architecture. Side by side with music, I considered it queen of the arts. To study it was for me not work but pleasure. I could read or draw until the small hours of the morning without ever getting tired. And I became more and more confident that my dream of a brilliant future would become true, even though I should have to wait long years for its fulfilment. I was firmly convinced that one day I should make a name for myself as an architect.

The fact that, side by side with my professional studies, I took the greatest interest in everything that had to do with politics did not seem to me to signify anything of great importance. On the contrary: I looked upon this practical interest in politics merely as part of an elementary obligation that devolves on every thinking man. Those who have no understanding of the political world around them have no right to criticize or complain. On political questions therefore I still continued to read and study a great deal. But reading had probably a different significance for me from that which it has for the average run of our so-called 'intellectuals'.

I know people who read interminably, book after book, from page to page, and yet I should not call them 'well-read people'. Of course they 'know' an immense amount; but their brain seems incapable of assorting and classifying the material which they have gathered from books. They have not the faculty of distinguishing between what is useful and useless in a book; so that they may retain the former in their minds and if possible skip over the latter while reading it, if that be not possible, then—when once read— throw it overboard as useless ballast. Reading is not an end in itself, but a means to an end. Its chief purpose is to help towards filling in the framework which is made up of the talents and capabilities that each individual possesses. Thus each one procures for himself the implements and materials necessary for the fulfilment of his calling in life, no matter whether this be the elementary task of earning one's daily bread or a calling that responds to higher human aspirations. Such is the first purpose of reading. And the second purpose is to give a general knowledge of the world in which we live. In both cases, however, the material which one has acquired through reading must not be stored up in the memory on a plan that corresponds to the successive chapters of the book; but each little piece of knowledge thus gained must be treated as if it were a little stone to be inserted into a mosaic, so that it finds its proper place among all the other pieces and particles that help to form a general world-picture in the brain of the reader. Otherwise only a confused jumble of chaotic notions will result from all this reading. That jumble is not merely useless, but it also tends to make the unfortunate possessor of it conceited. For he seriously considers himself a well-educated person and thinks that he understands something of life. He believes that he has acquired knowledge, whereas the truth is that every increase in such 'knowledge' draws him more and more away from real life, until he finally ends up in some sanatorium or takes to politics and becomes a parliamentary deputy.

Such a person never succeeds in turning his knowledge to practical account when the opportune moment arrives; for his mental equipment is not ordered with a view to meeting the demands of everyday life. His knowledge is stored in his brain as a literal transcript of the books he has read and the order of succession in which he has read them. And if Fate should one day call upon him to use some of his book-knowledge for certain practical ends in life that very call will have to name the book and give the number of the page; for the poor noodle himself would never be able to find the spot where he gathered the information now called for. But if the page is not mentioned at the critical moment the widely-read intellectual will find himself in a state of hopeless embarrassment. In a high state of agitation he searches for analogous cases and it is almost a dead certainty that he will finally deliver the wrong prescription.

If that is not a correct description, then how can we explain the political achievements of our Parliamentary heroes who hold the highest positions in the government of the country? Otherwise we should have to attribute the doings of such political leaders, not to pathological conditions but simply to malice and chicanery.

On the other hand, one who has cultivated the art of reading will instantly discern, in a book or journal or pamphlet, what ought to be remembered because it meets one's personal needs or is of value as general knowledge. What he thus learns is incorporated in his mental analogue of this or that problem or thing, further correcting the mental picture or enlarging it so that it becomes more exact and precise. Should some practical problem suddenly demand examination or solution, memory will immediately select the opportune information from the mass that has been acquired through years of reading and will place this information at the service of one's powers of judgment so as to get a new and clearer view of the problem in question or produce a definitive solution.

Only thus can reading have any meaning or be worth while.

The speaker, for example, who has not the sources of information ready to hand which are necessary to a proper treatment of his subject is unable to defend his opinions against an opponent, even though those opinions be perfectly sound and true. In every discussion his memory will leave him shamefully in the lurch. He cannot summon up arguments to support his statements or to refute his opponent. So long as the speaker has only to defend himself on his own personal account, the situation is not serious; but the evil comes when Chance places at the head of public affairs such a soi-disant know-it-all, who in reality knows nothing.

From early youth I endeavoured to read books in the right way and I was fortunate in having a good memory and intelligence to assist me. From that point of view my sojourn in Vienna was particularly useful and profitable. My experiences of everyday life there were a constant stimulus to study the most diverse problems from new angles. Inasmuch as I was in a position to put theory to the test of reality and reality to the test of theory, I was safe from the danger of pedantic theorizing on the one hand and, on the other, from being too impressed by the superficial aspects of reality.

The experience of everyday life at that time determined me to make a fundamental theoretical study of two most important questions outside of the social question.

It is impossible to say when I might have started to make a thorough study of the doctrine and characteristics of Marxism were it not for the fact that I then literally ran head foremost into the problem.

What I knew of Social Democracy in my youth was precious little and that little was for the most part wrong. The fact that it led the struggle for universal suffrage and the secret ballot gave me an inner satisfaction; for my reason then told me that this would weaken the Habsburg regime, which I so thoroughly detested. I was convinced that even if it should sacrifice the German element the Danubian State could not continue to exist. Even at the price of a long and slow Slaviz-ation of the Austrian Germans the State would secure no guarantee of a really durable Empire; because it was very questionable if and how far the Slavs possessed the necessary capacity for constructive politics. Therefore I welcomed every movement that might lead towards the final disruption of that impossible State which had decreed that it would stamp out the German character in ten millions of people. The more this babel of tongues wrought discord and disruption, even in the Parliament, the nearer the hour approached for the dissolution of this Babylonian Empire. That would mean the liberation of my German Austrian people, and only then would it become possible for them to be re-united to the Motherland.

Accordingly I had no feelings of antipathy towards the actual policy of the Social Democrats. That its avowed purpose was to raise the level of the working classes — which in my ignorance I then foolishly believed — was a further reason why I should speak in favour of Social Democracy rather than against it. But the features that contributed most to estrange me from the Social Democratic movement was its hostile attitude towards the struggle for the conservation of Germanism in Austria, its lamentable cocotting with the Slav 'comrades', who received these approaches favourably as long as any practical advantages were forthcoming but otherwise maintained a haughty reserve, thus giving the importunate mendicants the sort of answer their behaviour deserved.

And so at the age of seventeen the word 'Marxism' was very little known to me, while I looked on 'Social Democracy' and 'Socialism' as synonymous expressions. It was only as the result of a sudden blow from the rough hand of Fate that my eyes were opened to the nature of this unparalleled system for duping the public.

Hitherto my acquaintance with the Social Democratic Party was only that of a mere spectator at some of their mass meetings. I had not the slightest idea of the social-democratic teaching or the mentality of its partisans. All of a sudden I was brought face to face with the products of their teaching and what they called their WELTANSCHAUUNG. In this way a few months sufficed for me to learn something which under other circumstances might have necessitated decades of study — namely, that under the cloak of social virtue and love of one's neighbour a veritable pestilence was spreading abroad and that if this pestilence be not stamped out of the world without delay it may eventually succeed in exterminating the human race.

I first came into contact with the Social Democrats while working in the building trade.

From the very time that I started work the situation was not very pleasant for me. My clothes were still rather decent. I was careful of my speech and I was reserved in manner. I was so occupied with thinking of my own present lot and future possibilities that I did not take much of an interest in my immediate surroundings. I had sought work so that I shouldn't starve and at the same time so as to be able to make further headway with my studies, though this headway might be slow. Possibly I should not have bothered to be interested in my companions were it not that on the third or fourth day an event occurred which forced me to take a definite stand. I was ordered to join the trade union.

At that time I knew nothing about the trades unions. I had had no opportunity of forming an opinion on their utility or inutility, as the case might be. But when I was told that I must join the union I refused. The grounds which I gave for my refusal were simply that I knew nothing about the matter and that anyhow I would not allow myself to be forced into anything. Probably the former reason saved me from being thrown out right away. They probably thought that within a few days I might be converted' and become more docile. But if they thought that they were profoundly mistaken. After two weeks I found it utterly impossible for me to take such a step, even if I had been willing to take it at first. During those fourteen days I came to know my fellow workmen better, and no power in the world could have moved me to join an organization whose representatives had meanwhile shown themselves in a light which I found so unfavourable.

During the first days my resentment was aroused.

At midday some of my fellow workers used to adjourn to the nearest tavern, while the others remained on the building premises and there ate their midday meal, which in most cases was a very scanty one. These were married men. Their wives brought them the midday soup in dilapidated vessels. Towards the end of the week there was a gradual increase in the number of those who remained to eat their midday meal on the building premises. I understood the reason for this afterwards. They now talked politics.

I drank my bottle of milk and ate my morsel of bread somewhere on the outskirts, while I circumspectly studied my environment or else fell to meditating on my own harsh lot. Yet I heard more than enough. And I often thought that some of what they said was meant for my ears, in the hope of bringing me to a decision. But all that I heard had the effect of arousing the strongest antagonism in me. Everything was disparaged—the nation, because it was held to be an invention of the 'capitalist' class (how often I had to listen to that phrase!); the Fatherland, because it was held to be an instrument in the hands of the bourgeoisie for the exploitation of' the working masses; the authority of the law, because that was a means of holding down the proletariat; religion, as a means of doping the people, so as to exploit them afterwards; morality, as a badge of stupid and sheepish docility. There was nothing that they did not drag in the mud.

At first I remained silent; but that could not last very long. Then I began to take part in the discussion and to reply to their statements. I had to recognize, however, that this was bound to be entirely fruitless, as long as I did not have at least a certain amount of definite information about the questions that were discussed. So I decided to consult the source from which my interlocutors claimed to have drawn their so-called wisdom. I devoured book after book, pamphlet after pamphlet.

Meanwhile, we argued with one another on the building premises. From day to day I was becoming better informed than my companions in the subjects on which they claimed to be experts. Then a day came when the more redoubtable of my adversaries resorted to the most effective weapon they had to replace the force of reason. This was intimidation and physical force. Some of the leaders among my adversaries ordered me to leave the building or else get flung down from the scaffolding. As I was quite alone I could not put up any physical resistance; so I chose the first alternative and departed, richer however by an experience.

I went away full of disgust; but at the same time so deeply moved that it was quite impossible for me to turn my back on the whole situation and think no more about it. When my anger began to calm down the spirit of obstinacy got the upper hand and I decided that at all costs I would get back to work again in the building trade. This decision became all the stronger a few weeks later, when my little savings had entirely run out and hunger clutched me once again in its merciless arms. No alternative was left to me. I got work again and had to leave it for the same reasons as before.

Then I asked myself: Are these men worthy of belonging to a great people? The question was profoundly disturbing; for if the answer were 'Yes', then the struggle to defend one's nationality is no longer worth all the trouble and sacrifice we demand of our best elements if it be in the interests of such a rabble. On the other hand, if the answer had to be 'No—these men are not worthy of the nation', then our nation is poor indeed in men. During those days of mental anguish and deep meditation I saw before my mind the ever-increasing and menacing army of people who could no longer be reckoned as belonging to their own nation.

It was with quite a different feeling, some days later, that I gazed on the interminable ranks, four abreast, of Viennese workmen parading at a mass demonstration. I stood dumbfounded for almost two hours, watching that enormous human dragon which slowly uncoiled itself there before me. When I finally left the square and wandered in the direction of my lodgings I felt dismayed and depressed. On my way I noticed the ARBEITERZEITUNG (The Workman's Journal) in a tobacco shop. This was the chief press-organ of the old Austrian Social Democracy. In a cheap café, where the common people used to foregather and where I often went to read the papers, the ARBEITERZEITUNG was also displayed. But hitherto I could not bring myself to do more than glance at the wretched thing for a couple of minutes: for its whole tone was a sort of mental vitriol to me. Under the depressing influence of the demonstration I had witnessed, some interior voice urged me to buy the paper in that tobacco shop and read it through. So I brought it home with me and spent the whole evening reading it, despite the steadily mounting rage provoked by this ceaseless outpouring of falsehoods.

I now found that in the social democratic daily papers I could study the inner character of this politico-philosophic system much better than in all their theoretical literature.

For there was a striking discrepancy between the two. In the literary effusions which dealt with the theory of Social Democracy there was a display of high-sounding phraseology about liberty and human dignity and beauty, all promulgated with an air of profound wisdom and serene prophetic assurance; a meticulously-woven glitter of words to dazzle and mislead the reader. On the other hand, the daily Press inculcated this new doctrine of human redemption in the most brutal fashion. No means were too base, provided they could be exploited in the campaign of slander. These journalists were real virtuosos in the art of twisting facts and presenting them in a deceptive form. The theoretical literature was intended for the simpletons of the soi-disant intellectuals belonging to the middle and, naturally, the upper classes. The newspaper propaganda was intended for the masses.

This probing into books and newspapers and studying the teachings of Social Democracy reawakened my love for my own people. And thus what at first seemed an impassable chasm became the occasion of a closer affection.

Having once understood the working of the colossal system for poisoning the popular mind, only a fool could blame the victims of it. During the years that followed I became more independent and, as I did so, I became better able to understand the inner cause of the success achieved by this Social Democratic gospel. I now realized the meaning and purpose of those brutal orders which prohibited the reading of all books and newspapers that were not 'red' and at the same time demanded that only the 'red' meetings should be attended. In the clear light of brutal reality I was able to see what must have been the inevitable consequences of that intolerant teaching.

The PSYCHE of the broad masses is accessible only to what is strong and uncompromising. Like a woman whose inner sensibilities are not so much under the sway of abstract reasoning but are always subject to the influence of a vague emotional longing for the strength that completes her being, and who would rather bow to the strong man than dominate the weakling—in like manner the masses of the people prefer the ruler to the suppliant and are filled with a stronger sense of mental security by a teaching that brooks no rival than by a teaching which offers them a liberal choice. They have very little idea of how to make such a choice and thus they are prone to feel that they have been abandoned. They feel very little shame at being terrorized intellectually and they are scarcely conscious of the fact that their freedom as human beings is impudently abused; and thus they have not the slightest suspicion of the intrinsic fallacy of the whole doctrine. They see only the ruthless force and brutality of its determined utterances, to which they always submit.

IF SOCIAL DEMOCRACY SHOULD BE OPPOSED BY A MORE TRUTHFUL TEACHING, THEN EVEN, THOUGH THE STRUGGLE BE OF THE BITTEREST KIND, THIS TRUTHFUL TEACHING WILL FINALLY PREVAIL PROVIDED IT BE ENFORCED WITH EQUAL RUTHLESSNESS.

Within less than two years I had gained a clear understanding of Social Democracy, in its teaching and the technique of its operations.

I recognized the infamy of that technique whereby the movement carried on a campaign of mental terrorism against the bourgeoisie, who are neither morally nor spiritually equipped to withstand such attacks. The tactics of Social Democracy consisted in opening, at a given signal, a veritable drum-fire of lies and calumnies against the man whom they believed to be the most redoubtable of their adversaries, until the nerves of the latter gave way and they sacrificed the man who was attacked, simply in the hope of being allowed to live in peace. But the hope proved always to be a foolish one, for they were never left in peace.

The same tactics are repeated again and again, until fear of these mad dogs exercises, through suggestion, a paralysing effect on their Victims. Through its own experience Social Democracy learned the value of strength, and for that reason it attacks mostly those in whom it scents stuff of the more stalwart kind, which is indeed a very rare possession. On the other hand it praises every weakling among its adversaries, more or less cautiously, according to the measure of his mental qualities known or presumed. They have less fear of a man of genius who lacks will-power than of a vigorous character with mediocre intelligence and at the same time they highly commend those who are devoid of intelligence and will-power.

The Social Democrats know how to create the impression that they alone are the protectors of peace. In this way, acting very circumspectly but never losing sight of their ultimate goal, they conquer one position after another, at one time by methods of quiet intimidation and at another time by sheer daylight robbery, employing these latter tactics at those moments when public attention is turned towards other matters from which it does not wish to be diverted, or when the public considers an incident too trivial to create a scandal about it and thus provoke the anger of a malignant opponent.

These tactics are based on an accurate estimation of human frailties and must lead to success, with almost mathematical certainty, unless the other side also learns how to fight poison gas with poison gas. The weaker natures must be told that here it is a case of to be or not to be.

I also came to understand that physical intimidation has its significance for the mass as well as for the individual. Here again the Socialists had calculated accurately on the psychological effect.

Intimidation in workshops and in factories, in assembly halls and at mass demonstrations, will always meet with success as long as it does not have to encounter the same kind of terror in a stronger form.

Then of course the Party will raise a horrified outcry, yelling blue murder and appealing to the authority of the State, which they have just repudiated. In doing this their aim generally is to add to the general confusion, so that they may have a better opportunity of reaching their own goal unobserved. Their idea is to find among the higher government officials some bovine creature who, in the stupid hope that he may win the good graces of these awe-inspiring opponents so that they may remember him in case of future eventualities, will help them now to break all those who may oppose this world pest.

The impression which such successful tactics make on the minds of the broad masses, whether they be adherents or opponents, can be estimated only by one who knows the popular mind, not from books but from practical life. For the successes which are thus obtained are taken by the adherents of Social Democracy as a triumphant symbol of the righteousness of their own cause; on the other hand the beaten opponent very often loses faith in the effectiveness of any further resistance.

The more I understood the methods of physical intimidation that were employed, the more sympathy I had for the multitude that had succumbed to it.

I am thankful now for the ordeal which I had to go through at that time; for it was the means of bringing me to think kindly again of my own people, inasmuch as the experience enabled me to distinguish between the false leaders and the victims who have been led astray.

We must look upon the latter simply as victims. I have just now tried to depict a few traits which express the mentality of those on the lowest rung of the social ladder; but my picture would be disproportionate if I do not add that amid the social depths I still found light; for I experienced a rare spirit of self-sacrifice and loyal comradeship among those men, who demanded little from life and were content amid their modest surroundings. This was true especially of the older generation of workmen. And although these qualities were disappearing more and more in the younger generation, owing to the all-pervading influence of the big city, yet among the younger generation also there were many who were sound at the core and who were able to maintain themselves uncontaminated amid the sordid surroundings of their everyday existence. If these men, who in many cases meant well and were upright in themselves, gave the support to the political activities carried on by the common enemies of our people, that was because those decent workpeople did not and could not grasp the downright infamy of the doctrine taught by the socialist agitators. Furthermore, it was because no other section of the community bothered itself about the lot of the working classes. Finally, the social conditions became such that men who otherwise would have acted differently were forced to submit to them, even though unwillingly at first. A day came when poverty gained the upper hand and drove those workmen into the Social Democratic ranks.

On innumerable occasions the bourgeoisie took a definite stand against even the most legitimate human demands of the working classes. That conduct was ill-judged and indeed immoral and could bring no gain whatsoever to the bourgeois class. The result was that the honest workman abandoned the original concept of the trades union organization and was dragged into politics.

There were millions and millions of workmen who began by being hostile to the Social Democratic Party; but their defences were repeatedly stormed and finally they had to surrender. Yet this defeat was due to the stupidity of the bourgeois parties, who had opposed every social demand put forward by the working class. The short-sighted refusal to make an effort towards improving labour conditions, the refusal to adopt measures which would insure the workman in case of accidents in the factories, the refusal to forbid child labour, the refusal to consider protective measures for female workers, especially expectant mothers—all this was of assistance to the Social Democratic leaders, who were thankful for every opportunity which they could exploit for forcing the masses into their net. Our bourgeois parties can never repair the damage that resulted from the mistake they then made. For they sowed the seeds of hatred when they opposed all efforts at social reform. And thus they gave, at least, apparent grounds to justify the claim put forward by the Social Democrats—namely, that they alone stand up for the interests of the working class.

And this became the principal ground for the moral justification of the actual existence of the Trades Unions, so that the labour organization became from that time onwards the chief political recruiting ground to swell the ranks of the Social Democratic Party.

While thus studying the social conditions around me I was forced, whether I liked it or not, to decide on the attitude I should take towards the Trades Unions. Because I looked upon them as inseparable from the Social Democratic Party, my decision was hasty—and mistaken. I repudiated them as a matter of course. But on this essential question also Fate intervened and gave me a lesson, with the result that I changed the opinion which I had first formed.

When I was twenty years old I had learned to distinguish between the Trades Union as a means of defending the social rights of the employees and fighting for better living conditions for them and, on the other hand, the Trades Union as a political instrument used by the Party in the class struggle.

The Social Democrats understood the enormous importance of the Trades Union movement. They appropriated it as an instrument and used it with success, while the bourgeois parties failed to understand it and thus lost their political prestige. They thought that their own arrogant VETO would arrest the logical development of the movement and force it into an illogical position. But it is absurd and also untrue to say that the Trades Union movement is in itself hostile to the nation. The opposite is the more correct view. If the activities of the Trades Union are directed towards improving the condition of a class, and succeed in doing so, such activities are not against the Fatherland or the State but are, in the truest sense of the word, national. In that way the trades union organization helps to create the social conditions which are indispensable in a general system of national education. It deserves high recognition when it destroys the psychological and physical germs of social disease and thus fosters the general welfare of the nation.

It is superfluous to ask whether the Trades Union is indispensable.

So long as there are employers who attack social understanding and have wrong ideas of justice and fair play it is not only the right but also the duty of their employees—who are, after all, an integral part of our people—to protect the general interests against the greed and unreason of the individual. For to safeguard the loyalty and confidence of the people is as much in the interests of the nation as to safeguard public health.

Both are seriously menaced by dishonourable employers who are not conscious of their duty as members of the national community. Their personal avidity or irresponsibility sows the seeds of future trouble. To eliminate the causes of such a development is an action that surely deserves well of the country.

It must not be answered here that the individual workman is free at any time to escape from the consequences of an injustice which he has actually suffered at the hands of an employer, or which he thinks he has suffered—in other words, he can leave. No. That argument is only a ruse to detract attention from the question at issue. Is it, or is it not, in the interests of the nation to remove the causes of social unrest? If it is, then the fight must be carried on with the only weapons that promise success. But the individual workman is never in a position to stand up against the might of the big employer; for the question here is not one that concerns the triumph of right. If in such a relation right had been recognized as the guiding principle, then the conflict could not have arisen at all. But here it is a question of who is the stronger. If the case were otherwise, the sentiment of justice alone would solve the dispute in an honourable way; or, to put the case more correctly, matters would not have come to such a dispute at all.

No. If unsocial and dishonourable treatment of men provokes resistance, then the stronger party can impose its decision in the conflict until the constitutional legislative authorities do away with the evil through legislation. Therefore it is evident that if the individual workman is to have any chance at all of winning through in the struggle he must be grouped with his fellow workmen and present a united front before the individual employer, who incorporates in his own person the massed strength of the vested interests in the industrial or commercial undertaking which he conducts.

Thus the trades unions can hope to inculcate and strengthen a sense of social responsibility in workaday life and open the road to practical results. In doing this they tend to remove those causes of friction which are a continual source of discontent and complaint.

Blame for the fact that the trades unions do not fulfil this much-desired function must be laid at the doors of those who barred the road to legislative social reform, or rendered such a reform ineffective by sabotaging it through their political influence.

The political bourgeoisie failed to understand—or, rather, they did not wish to understand the importance of the trades union movement. The Social Democrats accordingly seized the advantage offered them by this mistaken policy and took the labour movement under their exclusive protection, without any protest from the other side. In this way they established for themselves a solid bulwark behind which they could safely retire whenever the struggle assumed a critical aspect. Thus the genuine purpose of the movement gradually fell into oblivion, and was replaced by new objectives. For the Social Democrats never troubled themselves to respect and uphold the original purpose for which the trade unionist movement was founded. They simply took over the Movement, lock, stock and barrel, to serve their own political ends.

Within a few decades the Trades Union Movement was transformed, by the expert hand of Social Democracy, from an instrument which had been originally fashioned for the defence of human rights into an instrument for the destruction of the national economic structure. The interests of the working class were not allowed for a moment to cross the path of this purpose; for in politics the application of economic pressure is always possible if the one side be sufficiently unscrupulous and the other sufficiently inert and docile. In this case both conditions were fulfilled.

By the beginning of the present century the Trades Unionist Movement had already ceased to recognize the purpose for which it had been founded. From year to year it fell more and more under the political control of the Social Democrats, until it finally came to be used as a battering-ram in the class struggle. The plan was to shatter, by means of constantly repeated blows, the economic edifice in the building of which so much time and care had been expended. Once this objective had been reached, the destruction of the State would become a matter of course, because the State would already have been deprived of its economic foundations. Attention to the real interests of the working-classes, on the part of the Social Democrats, steadily decreased until the cunning leaders saw that it would be in their immediate political interests if the social and cultural demands of the broad masses remained unheeded; for there was a danger that if these masses once felt content they could no longer be employed as mere passive material in the political struggle.

The gloomy prospect which presented itself to the eyes of the CONDOTTIERI of the class warfare, if the discontent of the masses were no longer available as a war weapon, created so much anxiety among them that they suppressed and opposed even the most elementary measures of social reform. And conditions were such that those leaders did not have to trouble about attempting to justify such an illogical policy.

As the masses were taught to increase and heighten their demands the possibility of satisfying them dwindled and whatever ameliorative measures were taken became less and less significant; so that it was at that time possible to persuade the masses that this ridiculous measure in which the most sacred claims of the working-classes were being granted represented a diabolical plan to weaken their fighting power in this easy way and, if possible, to paralyse it. One will not be astonished at the success of these allegations if one remembers what a small measure of thinking power the broad masses possess.

In the bourgeois camp there was high indignation over the bad faith of the Social Democratic tactics; but nothing was done to draw a practical conclusion and organize a counter attack from the bourgeois side. The fear of the Social Democrats, to improve the miserable conditions of the working-classes ought to have induced the bourgeois parties to make the most energetic efforts in this direction and thus snatch from the hands of the class-warfare leaders their most important weapon; but nothing of this kind happened.

Instead of attacking the position of their adversaries the bourgeoisie allowed itself to be pressed and harried. Finally it adopted means that were so tardy and so insignificant that they were ineffective and were repudiated. So the whole situation remained just as it had been before the bourgeois intervention; but the discontent had thereby become more serious.

Like a threatening storm, the 'Free Trades Union' hovered above the political horizon and above the life of each individual. It was one of the most frightful instruments of terror that threatened the security and independence of the national economic structure, the foundations of the State and the liberty of the individual. Above all, it was the 'Free Trades Union' that turned democracy into a ridiculous and scorned phrase, insulted the ideal of liberty and stigmatized that of fraternity with the slogan 'If you will not become our comrade we shall crack your skull'.

It was thus that I then came to know this friend of humanity. During the years that followed my knowledge of it became wider and deeper; but I have never changed anything in that regard.

The more I became acquainted with the external forms of Social Democracy, the greater became my desire to understand the inner nature of its doctrines.

For this purpose the official literature of the Party could not help very much. In discussing economic questions its statements were false and its proofs unsound. In treating of political aims its attitude was insincere. Furthermore, its modern methods of chicanery in the presentation of its arguments were profoundly repugnant to me. Its flamboyant sentences, its obscure and incomprehensible phrases, pretended to contain great thoughts, but they were devoid of thought, and meaningless. One would have to be a decadent Bohemian in one of our modern cities in order to feel at home in that labyrinth of mental aberration, so that he might discover 'intimate experiences' amid the stinking fumes of this literary Dadism. These writers were obviously counting on the proverbial humility of a certain section of our people, who believe that a person who is incomprehensible must be profoundly wise.

In confronting the theoretical falsity and absurdity of that doctrine with the reality of its external manifestations, I gradually came to have a clear idea of the ends at which it aimed.

During such moments I had dark presentiments and feared something evil. I had before me a teaching inspired by egoism and hatred, mathematically calculated to win its victory, but the triumph of which would be a mortal blow to humanity.

Meanwhile I had discovered the relations existing between this destructive teaching and the specific character of a people, who up to that time had been to me almost unknown.

Knowledge of the Jews is the only key whereby one may understand the inner nature and therefore the real aims of Social Democracy.

The man who has come to know this race has succeeded in removing from his eyes the veil through which he had seen the aims and meaning of his Party in a false light; and then, out of the murk and fog of social phrases rises the grimacing figure of Marxism.

To-day it is hard and almost impossible for me to say when the word 'Jew' first began to raise any particular thought in my mind. I do not remember even having heard the word at home during my father's lifetime. If this name were mentioned in a derogatory sense I think the old gentleman would just have considered those who used it in this way as being uneducated reactionaries. In the course of his career he had come to be more or less a cosmopolitan, with strong views on nationalism, which had its effect on me as well. In school, too, I found no reason to alter the picture of things I had formed at home.

At the REALSCHULE I knew one Jewish boy. We were all on our guard in our relations with him, but only because his reticence and certain actions of his warned us to be discreet. Beyond that my companions and myself formed no particular opinions in regard to him.

It was not until I was fourteen or fifteen years old that I frequently ran up against the word 'Jew', partly in connection with political controversies. These references aroused a slight aversion in me, and I could not avoid an uncomfortable feeling which always came over me when I had to listen to religious disputes. But at that time I had no other feelings about the Jewish question.

There were very few Jews in Linz. In the course of centuries the Jews who lived there had become Europeanized in external appearance and were so much like other human beings that I even looked upon them as Germans. The reason why I did not then perceive the absurdity of such an illusion was that the only external mark which I recognized as distinguishing them from us was the practice of their strange religion. As I thought that they were persecuted on account of their Faith my aversion to hearing remarks against them grew almost into a feeling of abhorrence. I did not in the least suspect that there could be such a thing as a systematic anti-Semitism.

Then I came to Vienna.

Confused by the mass of impressions I received from the architectural surroundings and depressed by my own troubles, I did not at first distinguish between the different social strata of which the population of that mammoth city was composed. Although Vienna then had about two hundred thousand Jews among its population of two millions, I did not notice them. During the first weeks of my sojourn my eyes and my mind were unable to cope with the onrush of new ideas and values. Not until I gradually settled down to my surroundings, and the confused picture began to grow clearer, did I acquire a more discriminating view of my new world. And with that I came up against the Jewish problem.

I will not say that the manner in which I first became acquainted with it was particularly unpleasant for me. In the Jew I still saw only a man who was of a different religion, and therefore, on grounds of human tolerance, I was against the idea that he should be attacked because he had a different faith. And so I considered that the tone adopted by the anti-Semitic Press in Vienna was unworthy of the cultural traditions of a great people. The memory of certain events which happened in the middle ages came into my mind, and I felt that I should not like to see them repeated. Generally speaking, these anti-Semitic newspapers did not belong to the first rank—but I did not then understand the reason of this—and so I regarded them more as the products of jealousy and envy rather than the expression of a sincere, though wrong-headed, feeling.

My own opinions were confirmed by what I considered to be the infinitely more dignified manner in which the really great Press replied to those attacks or simply ignored them, which latter seemed to me the most respectable way.

I diligently read what was generally called the World Press—NEUE FREIE PRESSE, WIENER TAGEBLATT, etc.—and I was astonished by the abundance of information they gave their readers and the impartial way in which they presented particular problems. I appreciated their dignified tone; but sometimes the flamboyancy of the style was unconvincing, and I did not like it. But I attributed all this to the overpowering influence of the world metropolis.

Since I considered Vienna at that time as such a world metropolis, I thought this constituted sufficient grounds to excuse these shortcomings of the Press. But I was frequently disgusted by the grovelling way in which the Vienna Press played lackey to the Court. Scarcely a move took place at the Hofburg which was not presented in glorified colours to the readers. It was a foolish practice, which, especially when it had to do with 'The Wisest Monarch of all Times', reminded one almost of the dance which the mountain cock performs at pairing time to woo his mate. It was all empty nonsense. And I thought that such a policy was a stain on the ideal of liberal democracy. I thought that this way of currying favour at the Court was unworthy of the people. And that was the first blot that fell on my appreciation of the great Vienna Press.

While in Vienna I continued to follow with a vivid interest all the events that were taking place in Germany, whether connected with political or cultural question. I had a feeling of pride and admiration when I compared the rise of the young German Empire with the decline of the Austrian State. But, although the foreign policy of that Empire was a source of real pleasure on the whole, the internal political happenings were not always so satisfactory. I did not approve of the campaign which at that time was being carried on against William II. I looked upon him not only as the German Emperor but, above all, as the creator of the German Navy. The fact that the Emperor was prohibited from speaking in the Reichstag made me very angry, because the prohibition came from a side which in my eyes had no authority to make it. For at a single sitting those same parliamentary ganders did more cackling together than the whole dynasty of Emperors, comprising even the weakest, had done in the course of centuries.

It annoyed me to have to acknowledge that in a nation where any half-witted fellow could claim for himself the right to criticize and might even be let loose on the people as a 'Legislator' in the Reichstag, the bearer of the Imperial Crown could be the subject of a 'reprimand' on the part of the most miserable assembly of drivellers that had ever existed.

I was even more disgusted at the way in which this same Vienna Press salaamed obsequiously before the meanest steed belonging to the Habsburg royal equipage and went off into wild ecstacies of delight if the nag wagged its tail in response. And at the same time these newspapers took up an attitude of anxiety in matters that concerned the German Emperor, trying to cloak their enmity by the serious air they gave themselves. But in my eyes that enmity appeared to be only poorly cloaked. Naturally they protested that they had no intention of mixing in Germany's internal affairs—God forbid! They pretended that by touching a delicate spot in such a friendly way they were fulfilling a duty that devolved upon them by reason of the mutual alliance between the two countries and at the same time discharging their obligations of journalistic truthfulness. Having thus excused themselves about tenderly touching a sore spot, they bored with the finger ruthlessly into the wound.

That sort of thing made my blood boil. And now I began to be more and more on my guard when reading the great Vienna Press.

I had to acknowledge, however, that on such subjects one of the anti-Semitic papers—the DEUTSCHE VOLKSBLATT—acted more decently.

What got still more on my nerves was the repugnant manner in which the big newspapers cultivated admiration for France. One really had to feel ashamed of being a German when confronted by those mellifluous hymns of praise for 'the great culture-nation'. This wretched Gallomania more often than once made me throw away one of those 'world newspapers'. I now often turned to the VOLKSBLATT, which was much smaller in size but which treated such subjects more decently. I was not in accord with its sharp anti-Semitic tone; but again and again I found that its arguments gave me grounds for serious thought.

Anyhow, it was as a result of such reading that I came to know the man and the movement which then determined the fate of Vienna. These were Dr. Karl Lueger and the Christian Socialist Movement. At the time I came to Vienna I felt opposed to both. I looked on the man and the movement as 'reactionary'.

But even an elementary sense of justice enforced me to change my opinion when I had the opportunity of knowing the man and his work, and slowly that opinion grew into outspoken admiration when I had better grounds for forming a judgment. To-day, as well as then, I hold Dr. Karl Lueger as the most eminent type of German Burgermeister. How many prejudices were thrown over through such a change in my attitude towards the Christian-Socialist Movement!

My ideas about anti-Semitism changed also in the course of time, but that was the change which I found most difficult. It cost me a greater internal conflict with myself, and it was only after a struggle between reason and sentiment that victory began to be decided in favour of the former. Two years later sentiment rallied to the side of reasons and became a faithful guardian and counsellor.

At the time of this bitter struggle, between calm reason and the sentiments in which I had been brought up, the lessons that I learned on the streets of Vienna rendered me invaluable assistance. A time came when I no longer passed blindly along the street of the mighty city, as I had done in the early days, but now with my eyes open not only to study the buildings but also the human beings.

Once, when passing through the inner City, I suddenly encountered a phenomenon in a long caftan and wearing black side-locks. My first thought was: Is this a Jew? They certainly did not have this appearance in Linz. I watched the man stealthily and cautiously; but the longer I gazed at the strange countenance and examined it feature by feature, the more the question shaped itself in my brain: Is this a German?

As was always my habit with such experiences, I turned to books for help in removing my doubts. For the first time in my life I bought myself some anti-Semitic pamphlets for a few pence. But unfortunately they all began with the assumption that in principle the reader had at least a certain degree of information on the Jewish question or was even familiar with it. Moreover, the tone of most of these pamphlets was such that I became doubtful again, because the statements made were partly superficial and the proofs extraordinarily unscientific. For weeks, and indeed for months, I returned to my old way of thinking. The subject appeared so enormous and the accusations were so far-reaching that I was afraid of dealing with it unjustly and so I became again anxious and uncertain.

Naturally I could no longer doubt that here there was not a question of Germans who happened to be of a different religion but rather that there was question of an entirely different people. For as soon as I began to investigate the matter and observe the Jews, then Vienna appeared to me in a different light. Wherever I now went I saw Jews, and the more I saw of them the more strikingly and clearly they stood out as a different people from the other citizens. Especially the Inner City and the district northwards from the Danube Canal swarmed with a people who, even in outer appearance, bore no similarity to the Germans.

But any indecision which I may still have felt about that point was finally removed by the activities of a certain section of the Jews themselves. A great movement, called Zionism, arose among them. Its aim was to assert the national character of Judaism, and the movement was strongly represented in Vienna.

To outward appearances it seemed as if only one group of Jews championed this movement, while the great majority disapproved of it, or even repudiated it. But an investigation of the situation showed that those outward appearances were purposely misleading. These outward appearances emerged from a mist of theories which had been produced for reasons of expediency, if not for purposes of downright deception. For that part of Jewry which was styled Liberal did not disown the Zionists as if they were not members of their race but rather as brother Jews who publicly professed their faith in an unpractical way, so as to create a danger for Jewry itself.

Thus there was no real rift in their internal solidarity.

This fictitious conflict between the Zionists and the Liberal Jews soon disgusted me; for it was false through and through and in direct contradiction to the moral dignity and immaculate character on which that race had always prided itself.

Cleanliness, whether moral or of another kind, had its own peculiar meaning for these people. That they were water-shy was obvious on looking at them and, unfortunately, very often also when not looking at them at all. The odour of those people in caftans often used to make me feel ill. Beyond that there were the unkempt clothes and the ignoble exterior.

All these details were certainly not attractive; but the revolting feature was that beneath their unclean exterior one suddenly perceived the moral mildew of the chosen race.

What soon gave me cause for very serious consideration were the activities of the Jews in certain branches of life, into the mystery of which I penetrated little by little. Was there any shady undertaking, any form of foulness, especially in cultural life, in which at least one Jew did not participate? On putting the probing knife carefully to that kind of abscess one immediately discovered, like a maggot in a putrescent body, a little Jew who was often blinded by the sudden light.

In my eyes the charge against Judaism became a grave one the moment I discovered the Jewish activities in the Press, in art, in literature and the theatre. All unctuous protests were now more or less futile. One needed only to look at the posters announcing the hideous productions of the cinema and theatre, and study the names of the authors who were highly lauded there in order to become permanently adamant on Jewish questions. Here was a pestilence, a moral pestilence, with which the public was being infected. It was worse than the Black Plague of long ago. And in what mighty doses this poison was manufactured and distributed. Naturally, the lower the moral and intellectual level of such an author of artistic products the more inexhaustible his fecundity. Sometimes it went so far that one of these fellows, acting like a sewage pump, would shoot his filth directly in the face of other members of the human race. In this connection we must remember there is no limit to the number of such people. One ought to realize that for one, Goethe, Nature may bring into existence ten thousand such despoilers who act as the worst kind of germ-carriers in poisoning human souls. It was a terrible thought, and yet it could not be avoided, that the greater number of the Jews seemed specially destined by Nature to play this shameful part.

And is it for this reason that they can be called the chosen people?

I began then to investigate carefully the names of all the fabricators of these unclean products in public cultural life. The result of that inquiry was still more disfavourable to the attitude which I had hitherto held in regard to the Jews. Though my feelings might rebel a thousand time, reason now had to draw its own conclusions.

The fact that nine-tenths of all the smutty literature, artistic tripe and theatrical banalities, had to be charged to the account of people who formed scarcely one per cent. of the nation—that fact could not be gainsaid. It was there, and had to be admitted. Then I began to examine my favourite 'World Press', with that fact before my mind.

The deeper my soundings went the lesser grew my respect for that Press which I formerly admired. Its style became still more repellent and I was forced to reject its ideas as entirely shallow and superficial. To claim that in the presentation of facts and views its attitude was impartial seemed to me to contain more falsehood than truth. The writers were—Jews.

Thousands of details that I had scarcely noticed before seemed to me now to deserve attention. I began to grasp and understand things which I had formerly looked at in a different light.

I saw the Liberal policy of that Press in another light. Its dignified tone in replying to the attacks of its adversaries and its dead silence in other cases now became clear to me as part of a cunning and despicable way of deceiving the readers. Its brilliant theatrical criticisms always praised the Jewish authors and its adverse, criticism was reserved exclusively for the Germans.

The light pin-pricks against William II showed the persistency of its policy, just as did its systematic commendation of French culture and civilization. The subject matter of the feuilletons was trivial and often pornographic. The language of this Press as a whole had the accent of a foreign people. The general tone was openly derogatory to the Germans and this must have been definitely intentional.

What were the interests that urged the Vienna Press to adopt such a policy? Or did they do so merely by chance? In attempting to find an answer to those questions I gradually became more and more dubious.

Then something happened which helped me to come to an early decision. I began to see through the meaning of a whole series of events that were taking place in other branches of Viennese life. All these were inspired by a general concept of manners and morals which was openly put into practice by a large section of the Jews and could be established as attributable to them. Here, again, the life which I observed on the streets taught me what evil really is.

The part which the Jews played in the social phenomenon of prostitution, and more especially in the white slave traffic, could be studied here better than in any other West-European city, with the possible exception of certain ports in Southern France. Walking by night along the streets of the Leopoldstadt, almost at every turn whether one wished it or not, one witnessed certain happenings of whose existence the Germans knew nothing until the War made it possible and indeed inevitable for the soldiers to see such things on the Eastern front.

A cold shiver ran down my spine when I first ascertained that it was the same kind of cold-blooded, thick-skinned and shameless Jew who showed his consummate skill in conducting that revolting exploitation of the dregs of the big city. Then I became fired with wrath.

I had now no more hesitation about bringing the Jewish problem to light in all its details. No. Henceforth I was determined to do so. But as I learned to track down the Jew in all the different spheres of cultural and artistic life, and in the various manifestations of this life everywhere, I suddenly came upon him in a position where I had least expected to find him. I now realized that the Jews were the leaders of Social Democracy. In face of that revelation the scales fell from my eyes. My long inner struggle was at an end.

In my relations with my fellow workmen I was often astonished to find how easily and often they changed their opinions on the same questions, sometimes within a few days and sometimes even within the course of a few hours. I found it difficult to understand how men who always had reasonable ideas when they spoke as individuals with one another suddenly lost this reasonableness the moment they acted in the mass. That phenomenon often tempted one almost to despair. I used to dispute with them for hours and when I succeeded in bringing them to what I considered a reasonable way of thinking I rejoiced at my success. But next day I would find that it had been all in vain. It was saddening to think I had to begin it all over again. Like a pendulum in its eternal sway, they would fall back into their absurd opinions.

I was able to understand their position fully. They were dissatisfied with their lot and cursed the fate which had hit them so hard. They hated their employers, whom they looked upon as the heartless administrators of their cruel destiny. Often they used abusive language against the public officials, whom they accused of having no sympathy with the situation of the working people. They made public protests against the cost of living and paraded through the streets in defence of their claims. At least all this could be explained on reasonable grounds. But what was impossible to understand was the boundless hatred they expressed against their own fellow citizens, how they disparaged their own nation, mocked at its greatness, reviled its history and dragged the names of its most illustrious men in the gutter.

This hostility towards their own kith and kin, their own native land and home was as irrational as it was incomprehensible. It was against Nature.

One could cure that malady temporarily, but only for some days or at least some weeks. But on meeting those whom one believed to have been converted one found that they had become as they were before. That malady against Nature held them once again in its clutches.

I gradually discovered that the Social Democratic Press was predominantly controlled by Jews. But I did not attach special importance to this circumstance, for the same state of affairs existed also in other newspapers. But there was one striking fact in this connection. It was that there was not a single newspaper with which Jews were connected that could be spoken of as National, in the meaning that my education and convictions attached to that word.

Making an effort to overcome my natural reluctance, I tried to read articles of this nature published in the Marxist Press; but in doing so my aversion increased all the more. And then I set about learning something of the people who wrote and published this mischievous stuff. From the publisher downwards, all of them were Jews. I recalled to mind the names of the public leaders of Marxism, and then I realized that most of them belonged to the Chosen Race — the Social Democratic representatives in the Imperial Cabinet as well as the secretaries of the Trades Unions and the street agitators. Everywhere the same sinister picture presented itself. I shall never forget the row of names — Austerlitz, David, Adler, Ellenbogen, and others. One fact became quite evident to me. It was that this alien race held in its hands the leadership of that Social Democratic Party with whose minor representatives I had been disputing for months past. I was happy at last to know for certain that the Jew is not a German.

Thus I finally discovered who were the evil spirits leading our people astray. The sojourn in Vienna for one year had proved long enough to convince me that no worker is so rooted in his preconceived notions that he will not surrender them in face of better and clearer arguments and explanations. Gradually I became an expert in the doctrine of the Marxists and used this knowledge as an instrument to drive home my own firm convictions. I was successful in nearly every case. The great masses can be rescued, but a lot of time and a large share of human patience must be devoted to such work.

But a Jew can never be rescued from his fixed notions.

It was then simple enough to attempt to show them the absurdity of their teaching.

Within my small circle I talked to them until my throat ached and my voice grew hoarse. I believed that I could finally convince them of the danger inherent in the Marxist follies. But I only achieved the contrary result. It seemed to me that immediately the disastrous effects of the Marxist Theory and its application in practice became evident, the stronger became their obstinacy.

The more I debated with them the more familiar I became with their argumentative tactics. At the outset they counted upon the stupidity of their opponents, but when they got so entangled that they could not find a way out they played the trick of acting as innocent simpletons. Should they fail, in spite of their tricks of logic, they acted as if they could not understand the counter arguments and bolted away to another field of discussion. They would lay down truisms and platitudes; and, if you accepted these, then they were applied to other problems and matters of an essentially different nature from the original theme. If you faced them with this point they would escape again, and you could not bring them to make any precise statement. Whenever one tried to get a firm grip on any of these apostles one's hand grasped only jelly and slime which slipped through the fingers and combined again into a solid mass a moment afterwards. If your adversary felt forced to give in to your argument, on account of the observers present, and if you then thought that at last you had gained ground, a surprise was in store for you on the following day. The Jew would be utterly oblivious to what had happened the day before, and he would start once again by repeating his former absurdities, as if nothing had happened. Should you become indignant and remind him of yesterday's defeat, he pretended astonishment and could not remember anything, except that on the previous day he had proved that his statements were correct. Sometimes I was dumbfounded. I do not know what amazed me the more—the abundance of their verbiage or the artful way in which they dressed up their falsehoods. I gradually came to hate them.

Yet all this had its good side; because the more I came to know the individual leaders, or at least the propagandists, of Social Democracy, my love for my own people increased correspondingly. Considering the Satanic skill which these evil counsellors displayed, how could their unfortunate victims be blamed? Indeed, I found it extremely difficult myself to be a match for the dialectical perfidy of that race. How futile it was to try to win over such people with argument, seeing that their very mouths distorted the truth, disowning the very words they had just used and adopting them again a few moments afterwards to serve their own ends in the argument! No. The more I came to know the Jew, the easier it was to excuse the workers.

In my opinion the most culpable were not to be found among the workers but rather among those who did not think it worth while to take the trouble to sympathize with their own kinsfolk and give to the hard-working son of the national family what was his by the iron logic of justice, while at the same time placing his seducer and corrupter against the wall.

Urged by my own daily experiences, I now began to investigate more thoroughly the sources of the Marxist teaching itself. Its effects were well known to me in detail. As a result of careful observation, its daily progress had become obvious to me. And one needed only a little imagination in order to be able to forecast the consequences which must result from it. The only question now was: Did the founders foresee the effects of their work in the form which those effects have shown themselves to-day, or were the founders themselves the victims of an error? To my mind both alternatives were possible.

If the second question must be answered in the affirmative, then it was the duty of

48

every thinking person to oppose this sinister movement with a view to preventing it from producing its worst results. But if the first question must be answered in the affirmative, then it must be admitted that the original authors of this evil which has infected the nations were devils incarnate. For only in the brain of a monster, and not that of a man, could the plan of this organization take shape whose workings must finally bring about the collapse of human civilization and turn this world into a desert waste.

Such being the case the only alternative left was to fight, and in that fight to employ all the weapons which the human spirit and intellect and will could furnish leaving it to Fate to decide in whose favour the balance should fall.

And so I began to gather information about the authors of this teaching, with a view to studying the principles of the movement. The fact that I attained my object sooner than I could have anticipated was due to the deeper insight into the Jewish question which I then gained, my knowledge of this question being hitherto rather superficial. This newly acquired knowledge alone enabled me to make a practical comparison between the real content and the theoretical pretentiousness of the teaching laid down by the apostolic founders of Social Democracy; because I now understood the language of the Jew. I realized that the Jew uses language for the purpose of dissimulating his thought or at least veiling it, so that his real aim cannot be discovered by what he says but rather by reading between the lines. This knowledge was the occasion of the greatest inner revolution that I had yet experienced. From being a soft-hearted cosmopolitan I became an out-and-out anti-Semite.

Only on one further occasion, and that for the last time, did I give way to oppressing thoughts which caused me some moments of profound anxiety.

As I critically reviewed the activities of the Jewish people throughout long periods of history I became anxious and asked myself whether for some inscrutable reasons beyond the comprehension of poor mortals such as ourselves, Destiny may not have irrevocably decreed that the final victory must go to this small nation? May it not be that this people which has lived only for the earth has been promised the earth as a recompense? is our right to struggle for our own self-preservation based on reality, or is it a merely subjective thing? Fate answered the question for me inasmuch as it led me to make a detached and exhaustive inquiry into the Marxist teaching and the activities of the Jewish people in connection with it.

The Jewish doctrine of Marxism repudiates the aristocratic principle of Nature and substitutes for it the eternal privilege of force and energy, numerical mass and its dead weight. Thus it denies the individual worth of the human personality, impugns the teaching that nationhood and race have a primary significance, and by doing this it takes away the very foundations of human existence and human civilization. If the Marxist teaching were to be accepted as the foundation of the life of the universe, it would lead to the disappearance of all order that is conceivable to the human mind. And thus the adoption of such a law would provoke chaos in the structure of the greatest organism that we know, with the result that the inhabitants of this earthly planet would finally disappear.

Should the Jew, with the aid of his Marxist creed, triumph over the people of this world, his Crown will be the funeral wreath of mankind, and this planet will once again follow its orbit through ether, without any human life on its surface, as it did millions of years ago.

And so I believe to-day that my conduct is in accordance with the will of the Almighty Creator. In standing guard against the Jew I am defending the handiwork of the Lord.

CHAPTER III: Political reflections arising out of My Sojourn in Vienna

Generally speaking a man should not publicly take part in politics before he has reached the age of thirty, though, of course, exceptions must be made in the case of those who are naturally gifted with extraordinary political abilities. That at least is my opinion to-day. And the reason for it is that until he reaches his thirtieth year or thereabouts a man's mental development will mostly consist in acquiring and sifting such knowledge as is necessary for the groundwork of a general platform from which he can examine the different political problems that arise from day to day and be able to adopt a definite attitude towards each. A man must first acquire a fund of general ideas and fit them together so as to form an organic structure of personal thought or outlook on life — a WELTANSCHAUUNG. Then he will have that mental equipment without which he cannot form his own judgments on particular questions of the day, and he will have acquired those qualities that are necessary for consistency and steadfastness in the formation of political opinions. Such a man is now qualified, at least subjectively, to take his part in the political conduct of public affairs.

If these pre-requisite conditions are not fulfilled, and if a man should enter political life without this equipment, he will run a twofold risk. In the first place, he may find during the course of events that the stand which he originally took in regard to some essential question was wrong. He will now have to abandon his former position or else stick to it against his better knowledge and riper wisdom and after his reason and convictions have already proved it untenable. If he adopt the former line of action he will find himself in a difficult personal situation; because in giving up a position hitherto maintained he will appear inconsistent and will have no right to expect his followers to remain as loyal to his leadership as they were before. And, as regards the followers themselves, they may easily look upon their leader's change of policy as showing a lack of judgment inherent in his character. Moreover, the change must cause in them a certain feeling of discomfiture VIS-À-VIS those whom the leader formerly opposed.

If he adopts the second alternative — which so very frequently happens to-day — then public pronouncements of the leader have no longer his personal persuasion to support them. And the more that is the case the defence of his cause will be all the more hollow and superficial. He now descends to the adoption of vulgar means in his defence. While he himself no longer dreams seriously of standing by his political protestations to the last — for no man will die in defence of something in which he does not believe-he makes increasing demands on his followers. Indeed, the greater be the measure of his own insincerity, the more unfortunate and inconsiderate become his claims on his party adherents. Finally, he throws aside the last vestiges of true leadership and begins to play politics. This means that he becomes one of those whose only consistency is their inconsistency, associated with overbearing insolence and oftentimes an artful mendacity developed to a shamelessly high degree.

Should such a person, to the misfortune of all decent people, succeed in becoming a parliamentary deputy it will be clear from the outset that for him the essence of political activity consists in a heroic struggle to keep permanent hold on this milk-bottle as a source of livelihood for himself and his family. The more his wife and children are dependent on him, the more stubbornly will he fight to maintain for himself the representation of his parliamentary constituency. For that reason any other person who gives evidence of political capacity is his personal enemy. In every new movement he will apprehend the possible beginning of his own downfall. And everyone who is a better man than himself will appear to him in the light of a menace.

I shall subsequently deal more fully with the problem to which this kind of parliamentary vermin give rise.

When a man has reached his thirtieth year he has still a great deal to learn. That is obvious. But henceforward what he learns will principally be an amplification of his basic ideas; it will be fitted in with them organically so as to fill up the framework of the fundamental WELTANSCHAUUNG which he already possesses. What he learns anew will not imply the abandonment of principles already held, but rather a deeper knowledge of those principles. And thus his colleagues will never have the discomforting feeling that they have been hitherto falsely led by him. On the contrary, their confidence is increased when they perceive that their leader's qualities are steadily developing along the lines of an organic growth which results from the constant assimilation of new ideas; so that the followers look upon this process as signifying an enrichment of the doctrines in which they themselves believe, in their eyes every such development is a new witness to the correctness of that whole body of opinion which has hitherto been held.

A leader who has to abandon the platform founded on his general principles, because he recognizes the foundation as false, can act with honour only when he declares his readiness to accept the final consequences of his erroneous views. In such a case he ought to refrain from taking public part in any further political activity. Having once gone astray on essential things he may possibly go astray a second time. But, anyhow, he has no right whatsoever to expect or demand that his fellow citizens should continue to give him their support.

How little such a line of conduct commends itself to our public leaders nowadays is proved by the general corruption prevalent among the cabal which at the present moment feels itself called to political leadership. In the whole cabal there is scarcely one who is properly equipped for this task.

Although in those days I used to give more time than most others to the consideration of political question, yet I carefully refrained from taking an open part in politics. Only to a small circle did I speak of those things which agitated my mind or were the cause of constant preoccupation for me. The habit of discussing matters within such a restricted group had many advantages in itself. Rather than talk at them, I learned to feel my way into the modes of thought and views of those men around me. Oftentimes such ways of thinking and such views were quite primitive. Thus I took every possible occasion to increase my knowledge of men.

Nowhere among the German people was the opportunity for making such a study so favourable as in Vienna.

In the old Danubian Monarchy political thought was wider in its range and had a richer variety of interests than in the Germany of that epoch—excepting certain parts of Prussia, Hamburg and the districts bordering on the North Sea. When I speak of Austria here I mean that part of the great Habsburg Empire which, by reason of its German population, furnished not only the historic basis for the formation of this State but whose population was for several centuries also the exclusive source of cultural life in that political system whose structure was so artificial. As time went on the stability of the Austrian State and the guarantee of its continued existence depended more and more on the maintenance of this germ-cell of that Habsburg Empire.

The hereditary imperial provinces constituted the heart of the Empire. And it was this heart that constantly sent the blood of life pulsating through the whole political and cultural system. Corresponding to the heart of the Empire, Vienna signified the brain and the will. At that time Vienna presented an appearance which made one think of her as an enthroned queen whose authoritative sway united the conglomeration of heterogenous nationalities that lived under the Habsburg sceptre. The radiant beauty of the capital city made one forget the sad symptoms of senile decay which the State manifested as a whole.

Though the Empire was internally rickety because of the terrific conflict going on between the various nationalities, the outside world—and Germany in particular—saw only that lovely picture of the city. The illusion was all the greater because at that time Vienna seemed to have risen to its highest pitch of splendour. Under a Mayor, who had the true stamp of administrative genius, the venerable residential City of the Emperors of the old Empire seemed to have the glory of its youth renewed. The last great German who sprang from the ranks of the people that had colonized the East Mark was not a 'statesman', in the official sense. This Dr. Luegar, however, in his rôle as Mayor of 'the Imperial Capital and Residential City', had achieved so much in almost all spheres of municipal activity, whether economic or cultural, that the heart of the whole Empire throbbed with renewed vigour. He thus proved himself a much greater statesman than the so-called 'diplomats' of that period.

The fact that this political system of heterogeneous races called AUSTRIA, finally broke down is no evidence whatsoever of political incapacity on the part of the German element in the old East Mark. The collapse was the inevitable result of an impossible situation. Ten million people cannot permanently hold together a State of fifty millions, composed of different and convicting nationalities, unless certain definite pre-requisite conditions are at hand while there is still time to avail of them.

The German-Austrian had very big ways of thinking. Accustomed to live in a great Empire, he had a keen sense of the obligations incumbent on him in such a situation. He was the only member of the Austrian State who looked beyond the borders of the narrow lands belonging to the Crown and took in all the frontiers of the Empire in the sweep of his mind. Indeed when destiny severed him from the common Fatherland he tried to master the tremendous task which was set before him as a consequence. This task was to maintain for the German-Austrians that patrimony which, through innumerable struggles, their ancestors had originally wrested from the East. It must be remembered that the German-Austrians could not put their undivided strength into this effort, because the hearts and minds of the best among them were constantly turning back towards their kinsfolk in the Motherland, so that only a fraction of their energy remained to be employed at home.

The mental horizon of the German-Austrian was comparatively broad. His commercial interests comprised almost every section of the heterogeneous Empire. The conduct of almost all important undertakings was in his hands. He provided the State, for the most part, with its leading technical experts and civil servants. He was responsible for carrying on the foreign trade of the country, as far as that sphere of activity was not under Jewish control, The German-Austrian exclusively represented the political cement that held the State together. His military duties carried him far beyond the narrow frontiers of his homeland. Though the recruit might join a regiment made up of the German element, the regiment itself might be stationed in Herzegovina as well as in Vienna or Galicia. The officers in the Habsburg armies were still Germans and so was the predominating element in the higher branches of the civil service. Art and science were in German hands. Apart from the new artistic trash, which might easily have been produced by a negro tribe, all genuine artistic inspiration came from the German section of the population. In music, architecture, sculpture and painting, Vienna abundantly supplied the entire Dual Monarchy. And the source never seemed to show signs of a possible exhaustion. Finally, it was the German element that determined the conduct of foreign policy, though a small number of Hungarians were also active in that field.

All efforts, however, to save the unity of the State were doomed to end in failure, because the essential pre-requisites were missing.

There was only one possible way to control and hold in check the centrifugal forces of the different and differing nationalities. This way was: to govern the Austrian State and organize it internally on the principle of centralization. In no other way imaginable could the existence of that State be assured.

Now and again there were lucid intervals in the higher ruling quarters when this truth was recognized. But it was soon forgotten again, or else deliberately ignored, because of the difficulties to be overcome in putting it into practice. Every project which aimed at giving the Empire a more federal shape was bound to be ineffective because there was no strong central authority which could exercise sufficient power within the State to hold the federal elements together. It must be remembered in this connection that conditions in Austria were quite different from those which characterized the German State as founded by Bismarck. Germany was faced with only one difficulty, which was that of transforming the purely political traditions, because throughout the whole of Bismarck's Germany there was a common cultural basis. The German Empire contained only members of one and the same racial or national stock, with the exception of a few minor foreign fragments.

Demographic conditions in Austria were quite the reverse. With the exception of Hungary there was no political tradition, coming down from a great past, in any of the various affiliated countries. If there had been, time had either wiped out all traces of it, or at least, rendered them obscure. Moreover, this was the epoch when the principle of nationality began to be in ascendant; and that phenomenon awakened the national instincts in the various countries affiliated under the Habsburg sceptre. It was difficult to control the action of these newly awakened national forces; because, adjacent to the frontiers of the Dual Monarchy, new national States were springing up whose people were of the same or kindred racial stock as the respective nationalities that constituted the Habsburg Empire. These new States were able to exercise a greater influence than the German element. Even Vienna could not hold out for a lengthy period in this conflict. When Budapest had developed into a metropolis a rival had grown up whose mission was, not to help in holding together the various divergent parts of the Empire, but rather to strengthen one part. Within a short time Prague followed the example of Budapest; and later on came Lemberg, Laibach and others. By raising these places which had formerly been provincial towns to the rank of national cities, rallying centres were provided for an independent cultural life. Through this the local national instincts acquired a spiritual foundation and therewith gained a more profound hold on the people. The time was bound to come when the particularist interests of those various countries would become stronger than their common imperial interests. Once that stage had been reached, Austria's doom was sealed.

The course of this development was clearly perceptible since the death of Joseph II. Its rapidity depended on a number of factors, some of which had their source in the Monarchy itself; while others resulted from the position which the Empire had taken in foreign politics.

It was impossible to make anything like a successful effort for the permanent consolidation of the Austrian State unless a firm and persistent policy of centralization were put into force. Before everything else the principle should have been adopted that only one common language could be used as the official language of the State. Thus it would be possible to emphasize the formal unity of that imperial commonwealth. And thus the administration would have in its hands a technical instrument without which the State could not endure as a political unity. In the same way the school and other forms of education should have been used to inculcate a feeling of common citizenship. Such an objective could not be reached within ten or twenty years. The effort would have to be envisaged in terms of centuries; just as in all problems of colonization, steady perseverance is a far more important element than the output of energetic effort at the moment.

It goes without saying that in such circumstances the country must be governed and administered by strictly adhering to the principle of uniformity.

For me it was quite instructive to discover why this did not take place, or rather why it was not done. Those who were guilty of the omission must be held responsible for the break-up of the Habsburg Empire.

More than any other State, the existence of the old Austria depended on a strong and capable Government. The Habsburg Empire lacked ethnical uniformity, which constitutes the fundamental basis of a national State and will preserve the existence of such a State even though the ruling power should be grossly inefficient. When a State is composed of a homogeneous population, the natural inertia of such a population will hold the Stage together and maintain its existence through astonishingly long periods of misgovernment and maladministration. It may often seem as if the principle of life had died out in such a body-politic; but a time comes when the apparent corpse rises up and displays before the world an astonishing manifestation of its indestructible vitality.

But the situation is utterly different in a country where the population is not homogeneous, where there is no bond of common blood but only that of one ruling hand. Should the ruling hand show signs of weakness in such a State the result will not be to cause a kind of hibernation of the State but rather to awaken the individualist instincts which are slumbering in the ethnological groups. These instincts do not make themselves felt as long as these groups are dominated by a strong central will-to-govern. The danger which exists in these slumbering separatist instincts can be rendered more or less innocuous only through centuries of common education, common traditions and common interests. The younger such States are, the more their existence will depend on the ability and strength of the central government. If their foundation was due only to the work of a strong personality or a leader who is a man of genius, in many cases they will break up as soon as the founder disappears; because, though great, he stood alone. But even after centuries of a common education and experiences these separatist instincts I have spoken of are not always completely overcome. They may be only dormant and may suddenly awaken when the central government shows weakness and the force of a common education as well as the prestige of a common tradition prove unable to withstand the vital energies of separatist nationalities forging ahead towards the shaping of their own individual existence.

The failure to see the truth of all this constituted what may be called the tragic crime of the Habsburg rulers.

Only before the eyes of one Habsburg ruler, and that for the last time, did the hand of Destiny hold aloft the torch that threw light on the future of his country. But the torch was then extinguished for ever.

Joseph II, Roman Emperor of the German nation, was filled with a growing anxiety when he realized the fact that his House was removed to an outlying frontier of his Empire and that the time would soon be at hand when it would be overturned and engulfed in the whirlpool caused by that

Babylon of nationalities, unless something was done at the eleventh hour to overcome the dire consequences resulting from the negligence of his ancestors. With superhuman energy this 'Friend of Mankind' made every possible effort to counteract the effects of the carelessness and thoughtlessness of his predecessors. Within one decade he strove to repair the damage that had been done through centuries. If Destiny had only granted him forty years for his labours, and if only two generations had carried on the work which he had started, the miracle might have been performed. But when he died, broken in body and spirit after ten years of rulership, his work sank with him into the grave and rests with him there in the Capucin Crypt, sleeping its eternal sleep, having never again showed signs of awakening.

His successors had neither the ability nor the will-power necessary for the task they had to face.

When the first signs of a new revolutionary epoch appeared in Europe they gradually scattered the fire throughout Austria. And when the fire began to glow steadily it was fed and fanned not by the social or political conditions but by forces that had their origin in the nationalist yearnings of the various ethnic groups.

The European revolutionary movement of 1848 primarily took the form of a class conflict in almost every other country, but in Austria it took the form of a new racial struggle. In so far as the German-Austrians there forgot the origins of the movement, or perhaps had failed to recognize them at the start and consequently took part in the revolutionary uprising, they sealed their own fate. For they thus helped to awaken the spirit of Western Democracy which, within a short while, shattered the foundations of their own existence.

The setting up of a representative parliamentary body, without insisting on the preliminary that only one language should be used in all public intercourse under the State, was the first great blow to the predominance of the German element in the Dual Monarchy. From that moment the State was also doomed to collapse sooner or later. All that followed was nothing but the historical liquidation of an Empire.

To watch that process of progressive disintegration was a tragic and at the same time an instructive experience. The execution of history's decree was carried out in thousands of details. The fact that great numbers of people went about blindfolded amid the manifest signs of dissolution only proves that the gods had decreed the destruction of Austria.

I do not wish to dwell on details because that would lie outside the scope of this book. I want to treat in detail only those events which are typical among the causes that lead to the decline of nations and States and which are therefore of importance to our present age. Moreover, the study of these events helped to furnish the basis of my own political outlook.

Among the institutions which most clearly manifested unmistakable signs of decay, even to the weak-sighted Philistine, was that which, of all the institutions of State, ought to have been the most firmly founded—I mean the Parliament, or the Reichsrat (Imperial Council) as it was called in Austria.

The pattern for this corporate body was obviously that which existed in England, the land of classic democracy. The whole of that excellent organization was bodily transferred to Austria with as little alteration as possible.

As the Austrian counterpart to the British two-chamber system a Chamber of Deputies and a House of Lords (HERRENHAUS) were established in Vienna. The Houses themselves, considered as buildings were somewhat different. When Barry built his palaces, or, as we say the Houses of Parliament, on the shore of the Thames, he could look to the history of the British Empire for the inspiration of his work. In that history he found sufficient material to fill and decorate the 1,200 niches, brackets, and pillars of his magnificent edifice. His statues and paintings made the House of Lords and the House of Commons temples dedicated to the glory of the nation.

There it was that Vienna encountered the first difficulty. When Hansen, the Danish architect, had completed the last gable of the marble palace in which the new body of popular representatives was to be housed he had to turn to the ancient classical world for subjects to fill out his decorative plan. This theatrical shrine of 'Western Democracy' was adorned with the statues and portraits of Greek and Roman statesmen and philosophers. As if it were meant for a symbol of irony, the horses of the quadriga that surmounts the two Houses are pulling apart from one another towards all four quarters of the globe. There could be no better symbol for the kind of activity going on within the walls of that same building.

The 'nationalities' were opposed to any kind of glorification of Austrian history in the decoration of this building, insisting that such would constitute an offence to them and a provocation. Much the same happened in Germany, where the Reich-stag, built by Wallot, was not dedicated to the German people until the cannons were thundering in the World War. And then it was dedicated by an inscription.

I was not yet twenty years of age when I first entered the Palace on the Franzens-ring to watch and listen in the Chamber of Deputies. That first experience aroused in me a profound feeling of repugnance.

I had always hated the Parliament, but not as an institution in itself. Quite the contrary. As one who cherished ideals of political freedom I could not even imagine any other form of government. In the light of my attitude towards the House of Habsburg I should then have considered it a crime against liberty and reason to think of any kind of dictatorship as a possible form of government.

A certain admiration which I had for the British Parliament contributed towards the formation of this opinion. I became imbued with that feeling of admiration almost without my being conscious of the effect of it through so much reading of newspapers while I was yet quite young. I could not discard that admiration all in a moment. The dignified way in which the British House of Commons fulfilled its function impressed me greatly, thanks largely to the glowing terms in which the Austrian Press reported these events. I used to ask myself whether there could be any nobler form of government than self-government by the people.

But these considerations furnished the very motives of my hostility to the Austrian Parliament. The form in which parliamentary government was here represented seemed unworthy of its great prototype. The following considerations also influenced my attitude:

The fate of the German element in the Austrian State depended on its position in Parliament. Up to the time that universal suffrage by secret ballot was introduced the German representatives had a majority in the Parliament, though that majority was not a very substantial one. This situation gave cause for anxiety because the Social-Democratic fraction of the German element could not be relied upon when national questions were at stake. In matters that were of critical concern for the German element, the Social-Democrats always took up an anti-German stand because they were afraid of losing their followers among the other national groups. Already at that time—before the introduction of universal suffrage—the Social-Democratic Party could no longer be considered as a German Party. The introduction of universal suffrage put an end even to the purely numerical predominance of the German element. The way was now clear for the further 'de-Germanization' of the Austrian State.

The national instinct of self-preservation made it impossible for me to welcome a representative system in which the German element was not really represented as such, but always betrayed by the Social-Democratic fraction. Yet all these, and many others, were defects which could not be attributed to the parliamentary system as such, but rather to the Austrian State in particular. I still believed that if the German majority could be restored in the representative body there would be no occasion to oppose such a system as long as the old Austrian State continued to exist.

Such was my general attitude at the time when I first entered those sacred and contentious halls. For me they were sacred only because of the radiant beauty of that majestic edifice. A Greek wonder on German soil.

But I soon became enraged by the hideous spectacle that met my eyes. Several hundred representatives were there to discuss a problem of great economical importance and each representative had the right to have his say.

That experience of a day was enough to supply me with food for thought during several weeks afterwards.

The intellectual level of the debate was quite low. Some times the debaters did not make themselves intelligible at all. Several of those present did not speak German but only their Slav vernaculars or dialects. Thus I had the opportunity of hearing with my own ears what I had been hitherto acquainted with only through reading the newspapers. A turbulent mass of people, all gesticulating and bawling against one another, with a pathetic old man shaking his bell and making frantic efforts to call the House to a sense of its dignity by friendly appeals, exhortations, and grave warnings.

I could not refrain from laughing.

Several weeks later I paid a second visit. This time the House presented an entirely different picture, so much so that one could hardly recognize it as the same place. The hall was practically empty. They were sleeping in the other rooms below. Only a few deputies were in their places, yawning in each other's faces. One was speechifying. A deputy speaker was in the chair. When he looked round it was quite plain that he felt bored.

Then I began to reflect seriously on the whole thing. I went to the Parliament whenever I had any time to spare and watched the spectacle silently but attentively. I listened to the debates, as far as they could be understood, and I studied the more or less intelligent features of those 'elect' representatives of the various nationalities which composed that motley State. Gradually I formed my own ideas about what I saw.

A year of such quiet observation was sufficient to transform or completely destroy my former convictions as to the character of this parliamentary institution. I no longer opposed merely the perverted form which the principle of parliamentary representation had assumed in Austria. No. It had become impossible for me to accept the system in itself. Up to that time I had believed that the disastrous deficiencies of the Austrian Parliament were due to the lack of a German majority, but now I recognized that the institution itself was wrong in its very essence and form.

A number of problems presented themselves before my mind. I studied more closely the democratic principle of 'decision by the majority vote', and I scrutinized no less carefully the intellectual and moral worth of the gentlemen who, as the chosen representatives of the nation, were entrusted with the task of making this institution function.

Thus it happened that at one and the same time I came to know the institution itself and those of whom it was composed. And it was thus that, within the course of a few years, I came to form a clear and vivid picture of the average type of that most lightly worshipped phenomenon of our time—the parliamentary deputy. The picture of him which I then formed became deeply engraved on my mind and I have never altered it since, at least as far as essentials go.

Once again these object-lessons taken from real life saved me from getting firmly entangled by a theory which at first sight seems so alluring to many people, though that theory itself is a symptom of human decadence.

Democracy, as practised in Western Europe to-day, is the fore-runner of Marxism. In fact, the latter would not be conceivable without the former. Democracy is the breeding-ground in which the bacilli of the Marxist world pest can grow and spread. By the introduction of parliamentarianism, democracy produced an abortion of filth and fire[6], the creative fire of which, however, seems to have died out.

I am more than grateful to Fate that this problem came to my notice when I was still in Vienna; for if I had been in Germany at that time I might easily have found only a superficial solution. If I had been in Berlin when I first discovered what an illogical thing this institution is which we call Parliament, I might easily have gone to the other extreme and believed—as many people believed, and apparently not without good reason—that the salvation of the people and the Empire could be secured only by restrengthening the principle of imperial authority. Those who had this belief did not discern the tendencies of their time and were blind to the aspirations of the people.

In Austria one could not be so easily misled. There it was impossible to fall from one error into another. If the Parliament were worthless, the Habsburgs were worse; or at least not in the slightest degree better. The problem was not solved by rejecting the parliamentary system. Immediately the question arose: What then? To repudiate and abolish the Vienna Parliament would have resulted in leaving all power in the hands of the Habsburgs. For me, especially, that idea was impossible.

Since this problem was specially difficult in regard to Austria, I was forced while still quite young to go into the essentials of the whole question more thoroughly than I otherwise should have done.

The aspect of the situation that first made the most striking impression on me and gave me grounds for serious reflection was the manifest lack of any individual responsibility in the representative body.

The parliament passes some acts or decree which may have the most devastating consequences, yet nobody bears the responsibility for it. Nobody can be called to account. For surely one cannot say that a Cabinet discharges its responsibility when it retires after having brought about a catastrophe. Or can we say that the responsibility is fully discharged when a new coalition is formed or parliament dissolved? Can the principle of responsibility mean anything else than the responsibility of a definite person?

Is it at all possible actually to call to account the leaders of a parliamentary government for any kind of action which originated in the wishes of the whole multitude of deputies and was carried out under their orders or sanction? Instead of developing constructive ideas and plans, does the business of a statesman consist in the art of making a whole pack of blockheads understand his projects? Is it his business to entreat and coach them so that they will grant him their generous consent?

Is it an indispensable quality in a statesman that he should possess a gift of persuasion commensurate with the statesman's ability to conceive great political measures and carry them through into practice?

Does it really prove that a statesman is incompetent if he should fail to win over a majority of votes to support his policy in an assembly which has been called together as the chance result of an electoral system that is not always honestly administered.

Has there ever been a case where such an assembly has worthily appraised a great political concept before that concept was put into practice and its greatness openly demonstrated through its success?

In this world is not the creative act of the genius always a protest against the inertia of the mass?

What shall the statesman do if he does not succeed in coaxing the parliamentary multitude to give its consent to his policy? Shall he purchase that consent for some sort of consideration?

Or, when confronted with the obstinate stupidity of his fellow citizens, should he then refrain from pushing forward the measures which he deems to be of vital necessity to the life of the nation? Should he retire or remain in power?

In such circumstances does not a man of character find himself face to face with an insoluble contradiction between his own political insight on the one hand and, on the other, his moral integrity, or, better still, his sense of honesty?

Where can we draw the line between public duty and personal honour?

Must not every genuine leader renounce the idea of degrading himself to the level of a political jobber?

And, on the other hand, does not every jobber feel the itch to 'play politics', seeing that the final responsibility will never rest with him personally but with an anonymous mass which can never be called to account for their deeds?

Must not our parliamentary principle of government by numerical majority necessarily lead to the destruction of the principle of leadership?

Does anybody honestly believe that human progress originates in the composite brain of the majority and not in the brain of the individual personality?

Or may it be presumed that for the future human civilization will be able to dispense with this as a condition of its existence?

But may it not be that, to-day, more than ever before, the creative brain of the individual is indispensable?

The parliamentary principle of vesting legislative power in the decision of the majority rejects the authority of the individual and puts a numerical quota of anonymous heads in its place. In doing so it contradicts the aristrocratic principle, which is a fundamental law of nature; but, of course, we must remember that in this decadent era of ours the aristrocratic principle need not be thought of as incorporated in the upper ten thousand.

The devastating influence of this parliamentary institution might not easily be recognized by those who read the Jewish Press, unless the reader has learned how to think independently and examine the facts for himself. This institution is primarily responsible for the crowded inrush of mediocre people into the field of politics. Confronted with such a phenomenon, a man who is endowed with real qualities of leadership will be tempted to refrain from taking part in political life; because under these circumstances the situation does not call for a man who has a capacity for constructive statesmanship but rather for a man who is capable of bargaining for the favour of the majority. Thus the situation will appeal to small minds and will attract them accordingly.

The narrower the mental outlook and the more meagre the amount of knowledge in a political jobber, the more accurate is his estimate of his own political stock, and thus he will be all the more inclined to appreciate a system which does not demand creative genius or even high-class talent; but rather that crafty kind of sagacity which makes an efficient town clerk. Indeed, he values this kind of small craftiness more than the political genius of a Pericles. Such a mediocrity does not even have to worry about responsibility for what he does. From the beginning he knows that whatever be the results of his 'statesmanship' his end is already prescribed by the stars; he will one day have to clear out and make room for another who is of similar mental calibre. For it is another sign of our decadent times that the number of eminent statesmen grows according as the calibre of individual personality dwindles. That calibre will become smaller and smaller the more the individual politician has to depend upon parliamentary majorities. A man of real political ability will refuse to be the beadle for a bevy of footling cacklers; and they in their turn, being the representatives of the majority—which means the dunder-headed multitude—hate nothing so much as a superior brain.

For footling deputies it is always quite a consolation to be led by a person whose intellectual stature is on a level with their own. Thus each one may have the opportunity to shine in debate among such compeers and, above all, each one feels that he may one day rise to the top. If Peter be boss to-day, then why not Paul tomorrow?

This new invention of democracy is very closely connected with a peculiar phenomenon which has recently spread to a pernicious extent, namely the cowardice of a large section of our so-called political leaders. Whenever important decisions have to be made they always find themselves fortunate in being able to hide behind the backs of what they call the majority.

In observing one of these political manipulators one notices how he wheedles the majority in order to get their sanction for whatever action he takes. He has to have accomplices in order to be able to shift responsibility to other shoulders whenever it is opportune to do so. That is the main reason why this kind of political activity is abhorrent to men of character and courage, while at the same time it attracts inferior types; for a person who is not willing to accept responsibility for his own actions, but is always seeking to be covered by something, must be classed among the knaves and the rascals. If a national leader should come from that lower class of politicians the evil consequences will soon manifest themselves. Nobody will then have the courage to take a decisive step. They will submit to abuse and defamation rather than pluck up courage to take a definite stand. And thus nobody is left who is willing to risk his position and his career, if needs be, in support of a determined line of policy.

One truth which must always be borne in mind is that the majority can never replace the man. The majority represents not only ignorance but also cowardice. And just as a hundred blockheads do not equal one man of wisdom, so a hundred poltroons are incapable of any political line of action that requires moral strength and fortitude.

The lighter the burden of responsibility on each individual leader, the greater will be the number of those who, in spite of their sorry mediocrity, will feel the call to place their immortal energies at the disposal of the nation. They are so much on the tip-toe of expectation that they find it hard to wait their turn. They stand in a long queue, painfully and sadly counting the number of those ahead of them and calculating the hours until they may eventually come forward. They watch every change that takes place in the personnel of the office towards which their hopes are directed, and they are grateful for every scandal which removes one of the aspirants waiting ahead of them in the queue. If somebody sticks too long to his office stool they consider this as almost a breach of a sacred understanding based on their mutual solidarity. They grow furious and give no peace until that inconsiderate person is finally driven out and forced to hand over his cosy berth for public disposal. After that he will have little chance of getting another opportunity. Usually those placemen who have been forced to give up their posts push themselves again into the waiting queue unless they are hounded away by the protestations of the other aspirants.

The result of all this is that, in such a State, the succession of sudden changes in public positions and public offices has a very disquieting effect in general, which may easily lead to disaster when an adverse crisis arises. It is not only the ignorant and the incompetent person who may fall victim to those parliamentary conditions, for the genuine leader may be affected just as much as the others, if not more so, whenever Fate has chanced to place a capable man in the position of leader. Let the superior quality of such a leader be once recognized and the result will be that a joint front will be organized against him, particularly if that leader, though not coming from their ranks, should fall into the habit of intermingling with these illustrious nincompoops on their own level. They want to have only their own company and will quickly take a hostile attitude towards any man who might show himself obviously above and beyond them when he mingles in their ranks. Their instinct, which is so blind in other directions, is very sharp in this particular.

The inevitable result is that the intellectual level of the ruling class sinks steadily. One can easily forecast how much the nation and State are bound to suffer from such a condition of affairs, provided one does not belong to that same class of 'leaders'.

The parliamentary régime in the old Austria was the very archetype of the institution as I have described it.

Though the Austrian Prime Minister was appointed by the King-Emperor, this act of appointment merely gave practical effect to the will of the parliament. The huckstering and bargaining that went on in regard to every ministerial position showed all the typical marks of Western Democracy. The results that followed were in keeping with the principles applied. The intervals between the replacement of one person by another gradually became shorter, finally ending up in a wild relay chase. With each change the quality of the 'statesman' in question deteriorated, until finally only the petty type of political huckster remained. In such people the qualities of statesmanship were measured and valued according to the adroitness with which they pieced together one coalition after another; in other words, their craftiness in manipulating the pettiest political transactions, which is the only kind of practical activity suited to the aptitudes of these representatives.

In this sphere Vienna was the school which offered the most impressive examples.

Another feature that engaged my attention quite as much as the features I have already spoken of was the contrast between the talents and knowledge of these representatives of the people on the one hand and, on the other, the nature of the tasks they had to face. Willingly or unwillingly, one could not help thinking seriously of the narrow intellectual outlook of these chosen representatives of the various constituent nationalities, and one could not avoid pondering on the methods through which these noble figures in our public life were first discovered.

It was worth while to make a thorough study and examination of the way in which the real talents of these gentlemen were devoted to the service of their country; in other words, to analyse thoroughly the technical procedure of their activities.

The whole spectacle of parliamentary life became more and more desolate the more one penetrated into its intimate structure and studied the persons and principles of the system in a spirit of ruthless objectivity. Indeed, it is very necessary to be strictly objective in the study of the institution whose sponsors talk of 'objectivity' in every other sentence as the only fair basis of examination and judgment. If one studied these gentlemen and the laws of their strenuous existence the results were surprising.

There is no other principle which turns out to be quite so ill-conceived as the parliamentary principle, if we examine it objectively.

In our examination of it we may pass over the methods according to which the election of the representatives takes place, as well as the ways which bring them into office and bestow new titles on them. It is quite evident that only to a tiny degree are public wishes or public necessities satisfied by the manner in which an election takes place; for everybody who properly estimates the political intelligence of the masses can easily see that this is not sufficiently developed to enable them to form general political judgments on their own account, or to select the men who might be competent to carry out their ideas in practice.

Whatever definition we may give of the term 'public opinion', only a very small part of it originates from personal experience or individual insight. The greater portion of it results from the manner in which public matters have been presented to the people through an overwhelmingly impressive and persistent system of 'information'. In the religious sphere the profession of a denominational belief is largely the result of education, while the religious yearning itself slumbers in the soul; so too the political opinions of the masses are the final result of influences systematically operating on human sentiment and intelligence in virtue of a method which is applied sometimes with almost-incredible thoroughness and perseverance.

By far the most effective branch of political education, which in this connection is best expressed by the word 'propaganda', is carried on by the Press. The Press is the chief means employed in the process of political 'enlightenment'. It represents a kind of school for adults. This educational activity, however, is not in the hands of the State but in the clutches of powers which are partly of a very inferior character. While still a young man in Vienna I had excellent opportunities for coming to know the men who owned this machine for mass instruction, as well as those who supplied it with the ideas it distributed. At first I was quite surprised when I realized how little time was necessary for this dangerous Great Power within the State to produce a certain belief among the public; and in doing so the genuine will and convictions of the public were often completely misconstrued. It took the Press only a few days to transform some ridiculously trivial matter into an issue of national importance, while vital problems were completely ignored or filched and hidden away from public attention.

The Press succeeded in the magical art of producing names from nowhere within the course of a few weeks. They made it appear that the great hopes of the masses were bound up with those names. And so they made those names more popular than any man of real ability could ever hope to be in a long lifetime. All this was done, despite the fact that such names were utterly unknown and indeed had never been heard of even up to a month before the Press publicly emblazoned them. At the same time old and tried figures in the political and other spheres of life quickly faded from the public memory and were forgotten as if they were dead, though still healthy and in the enjoyment of their full viguour. Or sometimes such men were so vilely abused that it looked as if their names would soon stand as permanent symbols of the worst kind of baseness. In order to estimate properly the really pernicious influence which the Press can exercise one had to study this infamous Jewish method whereby honourable and decent people were besmirched with mud and filth, in the form of low abuse and slander, from hundreds and hundreds of quarters simultaneously, as if commanded by some magic formula.

These highway robbers would grab at anything which might serve their evil ends.

They would poke their noses into the most intimate family affairs and would not rest until they had sniffed out some petty item which could be used to destroy the reputation of their victim. But if the result of all this sniffing should be that nothing derogatory was discovered in the private or public life of the victim, they continued to hurl abuse at him, in the belief that some of their animadversions would stick even though refuted a thousand times. In most cases it finally turned out impossible for the victim to continue his defence, because the accuser worked together with so many accomplices that his slanders were re-echoed interminably. But these slanderers would never own that they were acting from motives which influence the common run of humanity or are understood by them. Oh, no. The scoundrel who defamed his contemporaries in this villainous way would crown himself with a halo of heroic probity fashioned of unctuous phraseology and twaddle about his 'duties as a journalist' and other mouldy nonsense of that kind. When these cuttle-fishes gathered together in large shoals at meetings and congresses they would give out a lot of slimy talk about a special kind of honour which they called the professional honour of the journalist. Then the assembled species would bow their respects to one another.

These are the kind of beings that fabricate more than two-thirds of what is called public opinion, from the foam of which the parliamentary Aphrodite eventually arises.

Several volumes would be needed if one were to give an adequate account of the whole procedure and fully describe all its hollow fallacies. But if we pass over the details and look at the product itself while it is in operation I think this alone will be sufficient to open the eyes of even the most innocent and credulous person, so that he may recognize the absurdity of this institution by looking at it objectively.

In order to realize how this human aberration is as harmful as it is absurd, the test and easiest method is to compare democratic parliamentarianism with a genuine German democracy.

The remarkable characteristic of the parliamentary form of democracy is the fact that a number of persons, let us say five hundred—including, in recent time, women also— are elected to parliament and invested with authority to give final judgment on anything and everything. In practice they alone are the governing body; for although they may appoint a Cabinet, which seems outwardly to direct the affairs of state, this Cabinet has not a real existence of its own. In reality the so-called Government cannot do anything against the will of the assembly. It can never be called to account for anything, since the right of decision is not vested in the Cabinet but in the parliamentary majority. The Cabinet always functions only as the executor of the will of the majority. Its political ability can be judged only according to how far it succeeds in adjusting itself to the will of the majority or in persuading the majority to agree to its proposals. But this means that it must descend from the level of a real governing power to that of a mendicant who has to beg the approval of a majority that may be got together for the time being. Indeed, the chief preoccupation of the Cabinet must be to secure for itself, in the case of' each individual measure, the favour of the majority then in power or, failing that, to form a new majority that will be more favourably disposed. If it should succeed in either of these efforts it may go on 'governing' for a little while. If it should fail to win or form a majority it must retire. The question whether its policy as such has been right or wrong does not matter at all.

Thereby all responsibility is abolished in practice. To what consequences such a state of affairs can lead may easily be understood from the following simple considerations:

Those five hundred deputies who have been elected by the people come from various dissimilar callings in life and show very varying degrees of political capacity, with the result that the whole combination is disjointed and sometimes presents quite a sorry picture. Surely nobody believes that these chosen representatives of the nation are the choice spirits or first-class intellects. Nobody, I hope, is foolish enough to pretend that hundreds of statesmen can emerge from papers placed in the ballot box by electors who are anything else but averagely intelligent. The absurd notion that men of genius are born out of universal suffrage cannot be too strongly repudiated. In the first place, those times may be really called blessed when one genuine statesman makes his appearance among a people. Such statesmen do not appear all at once in hundreds or more. Secondly, among the broad masses there is instinctively a definite antipathy towards every outstanding genius. There is a better chance of seeing a camel pass through the eye of a needle than of seeing a really great man 'discovered' through an election.

Whatever has happened in history above the level of the average of the broad public has mostly been due to the driving force of an individual personality.

But here five hundred persons of less than modest intellectual qualities pass judgment on the most important problems affecting the nation. They form governments which in turn learn to win the approval of the illustrious assembly for every legislative step that may be taken, which means that the policy to be carried out is actually the policy of the five hundred.

And indeed, generally speaking, the policy bears the stamp of its origin.

But let us pass over the intellectual qualities of these representatives and ask what is the nature of the task set before them. If we consider the fact that the problems which have to be discussed and solved belong to the most varied and diverse fields we can very well realize how inefficient a governing system must be which entrusts the right of decision to a mass assembly in which only very few possess the knowledge and experience such as would qualify them to deal with the matters that have to be settled. The most important economic measures are submitted to a tribunal in which not more than one-tenth of the members have studied the elements of economics. This means that final authority is vested in men who are utterly devoid of any preparatory training which might make them competent to decide on the questions at issue.

The same holds true of every other problem. It is always a majority of ignorant and incompetent people who decide on each measure; for the composition of the institution does not vary, while the problems to be dealt with come from the most varied spheres of public life. An intelligent judgment would be possible only if different deputies had the authority to deal with different issues. It is out of the question to think that the same people are fitted to decide on transport questions as well as, let us say, on questions of foreign policy, unless each of them be a universal genius. But scarcely more than one genius appears in a century. Here we are scarcely ever dealing with real brains, but only with dilettanti who are as narrow-minded as they are conceited and arrogant, intellectual DEMI-MONDES of the worst kind. This is why these honourable gentlemen show such astonishing levity in discussing and deciding on matters that would demand the most painstaking consideration even from great minds. Measures of momentous importance for the future existence of the State are framed and discussed in an atmosphere more suited to the card-table. Indeed the latter suggests a much more fitting occupation for these gentlemen than that of deciding the destinies of a people.

Of course it would be unfair to assume that each member in such a parliament was endowed by nature with such a small sense of responsibility. That is out of the question.

But this system, by forcing the individual to pass judgment on questions for which he is not competent gradually debases his moral character. Nobody will have the courage to say: "Gentlemen, I am afraid we know nothing about what we are talking about. I for one have no competency in the matter at all." Anyhow if such a declaration were made it would not change matters very much; for such outspoken honesty would not be understood. The person who made the declaration would be deemed an honourable ass who ought not to be allowed to spoil the game. Those who have a knowledge of human nature know that nobody likes to be considered a fool among his associates; and in certain circles honesty is taken as an index of stupidity.

Thus it happens that a naturally upright man, once he finds himself elected to parliament, may eventually be induced by the force of circumstances to acquiesce in a general line of conduct which is base in itself and amounts to a betrayal of the public trust. That feeling that if the individual refrained from taking part in a certain decision his attitude would not alter the situation in the least, destroys every real sense of honour which might occasionally arouse the conscience of one person or another. Finally, the otherwise upright deputy will succeed in persuading himself that he is by no means the worst of the lot and that by taking part in a certain line of action he may prevent something worse from happening.

A counter argument may be put forward here. It may be said that of course the individual member may not have the knowledge which is requisite for the treatment of this or that question, yet his attitude towards it is taken on the advice of his Party as the guiding authority in each political matter; and it may further be said that the Party sets up special committees of experts who have even more than the requisite knowledge for dealing with the questions placed before them. At first sight, that argument seems sound. But then another question arises—namely, why are five hundred persons elected if only a few have the wisdom which is required to deal with the more important problems?

It is not the aim of our modern democratic parliamentary system to bring together an assembly of intelligent and well-informed deputies. Not at all. The aim rather is to bring together a group of nonentities who are dependent on others for their views and who can be all the more easily led, the narrower the mental outlook of each individual is. That is the only way in which a party policy, according to the evil meaning it has to-day, can be put into effect. And by this method alone it is possible for the wirepuller, who exercises the real control, to remain in the dark, so that personally he can never be brought to account for his actions. For under such circumstances none of the decisions taken, no matter how disastrous they may turn out for the nation as a whole, can be laid at the door of the individual whom everybody knows to be the evil genius responsible for the whole affair. All responsibility is shifted to the shoulders of the Party as a whole.

In practice no actual responsibility remains. For responsibility arises only from personal duty and not from the obligations that rest with a parliamentary assembly of empty talkers.

The parliamentary institution attracts people of the badger type, who do not like the open light. No upright man, who is ready to accept personal responsibility for his acts, will be attracted to such an institution.

That is the reason why this brand of democracy has become a tool in the hand of that race which, because of the inner purposes it wishes to attain, must shun the open light, as it has always done and always will do. Only a Jew can praise an institution which is as corrupt and false as himself.

As a contrast to this kind of democracy we have the German democracy, which is a true democracy; for here the leader is freely chosen and is obliged to accept full responsibility for all his actions and omissions. The problems to be dealt with are not put to the vote of the majority; but they are decided upon by the individual, and as a guarantee of responsibility for those decisions he pledges all he has in the world and even his life.

The objection may be raised here that under such conditions it would be very difficult to find a man who would be ready to devote himself to so fateful a task. The answer to that objection is as follows:

We thank God that the inner spirit of our German democracy will of itself prevent the chance careerist, who may be intellectually worthless and a moral twister, from coming by devious ways to a position in which he may govern his fellow-citizens. The fear of undertaking such far-reaching responsibilities, under German democracy, will scare off the ignorant and the feckless.

But should it happen that such a person might creep in surreptitiously it will be easy enough to identify him and apostrophize him ruthlessly. somewhat thus: "Be off, you scoundrel. Don't soil these steps with your feet; because these are the steps that lead to the portals of the Pantheon of History, and they are not meant for place-hunters but for men of noble character."

Such were the views I formed after two years of attendance at the sessions of the Viennese Parliament. Then I went there no more.

The parliamentary regime became one of the causes why the strength of the Habsburg State steadily declined during the last years of its existence. The more the predominance of the German element was whittled away through parliamentary procedure, the more prominent became the system of playing off one of the various constituent nationalities against the other. In the Imperial Parliament it was always the German element that suffered through the system, which meant that the results were detrimental to the Empire as a whole; for at the close of the century even the most simple-minded people could recognize that the cohesive forces within the Dual Monarchy no longer sufficed to counterbalance the separatist tendencies of the provincial nationalities. On the contrary!

The measures which the State adopted for its own maintenance became more and more mean spirited and in a like degree the general disrespect for the State increased. Not only Hungary but also the various Slav provinces gradually ceased to identify themselves with the monarchy which embraced them all, and accordingly they did not feel its weakness as in any way detrimental to themselves. They rather welcomed those manifestations of senile decay. They looked forward to the final dissolution of the State, and not to its recovery.

The complete collapse was still forestalled in Parliament by the humiliating concessions that were made to every kind of importunate demands, at the cost of the German element. Throughout the country the defence of the State rested on playing off the various nationalities against one another. But the general trend of this development was directed against the Germans. Especially since the right of succession to the throne conferred certain influence on the Archduke Franz Ferdinand, the policy of increasing the power of the Czechs was carried out systematically from the upper grades of the administration down to the lower. With all the means at his command the heir to the Dual Monarchy personally furthered the policy that aimed at eliminating the influence of the German element, or at least he acted as protector of that policy. By the use of State officials as tools, purely German districts were gradually but decisively brought within the danger zone of the mixed languages. Even in Lower Austria this process began to make headway with a constantly increasing tempo and Vienna was looked upon by the Czechs as their biggest city.

In the family circle of this new Habsburger the Czech language was favoured. The wife of the Archduke had formerly been a Czech Countess and was wedded to the Prince by a morganatic marriage. She came from an environment where hostility to the Germans had been traditional. The leading idea in the mind of the Archduke was to establish a Slav State in Central Europe, which was to be constructed on a purely Catholic basis, so as to serve as a bulwark against Orthodox Russia.

As had happened often in Habsburg history, religion was thus exploited to serve a purely political policy, and in this case a fatal policy, at least as far as German interests were concerned. The result was lamentable in many respects.

Neither the House of Habsburg nor the Catholic Church received the reward which they expected. Habsburg lost the throne and the Church lost a great State. By employing religious motives in the service of politics, a spirit was aroused which the instigators of that policy had never thought possible.

From the attempt to exterminate Germanism in the old monarchy by every available means arose the Pan-German Movement in Austria, as a response.

In the 'eighties of the last century Manchester Liberalism, which was Jewish in its fundamental ideas, had reached the zenith of its influence in the Dual Monarchy, or had already passed that point. The reaction which set in did not arise from social but from nationalistic tendencies, as was always the case in the old Austria. The instinct of self-preservation drove the German element to defend itself energetically. Economic considerations only slowly began to gain an important influence; but they were of secondary concern. But of the general political chaos two party organizations emerged. The one was more of a national, and the other more of a social, character; but both were highly interesting and instructive for the future.

After the war of 1866, which had resulted in the humiliation of Austria, the House of Habsburg contemplated a REVANCHE on the battlefield. Only the tragic end of the Emperor Maximilian of Mexico prevented a still closer collaboration with France. The chief blame for Maximilian's disastrous expedition was attributed to Napoleon III and the fact that the Frenchman left him in the lurch aroused a general feeling of indignation. Yet the Habsburgs were still lying in wait for their opportunity. If the war of 1870-71 had not been such a singular triumph, the Viennese Court might have chanced the game of blood in order to get its revenge for Sadowa. But when the first reports arrived from the Franco-German battlefield, which, though true, seemed miraculous and almost incredible, the 'most wise' of all monarchs recognized that the moment was inopportune and tried to accept the unfavourable situation with as good a grace as possible.

The heroic conflict of those two years (1870-71) produced a still greater miracle; for with the Habsburgs the change of attitude never came from an inner heartfelt urge but only from the pressure of circumstances. The German people of the East Mark, however, were entranced by the triumphant glory of the newly established German Empire and were profoundly moved when they saw the dream of their fathers resurgent in a magnificent reality.

For—let us make no mistake about it—the true German-Austrian realized from this time onward, that Königgrätz was the tragic, though necessary, pre-condition for the re-establishment of an Empire which should no longer be burdened with the palsy of the old alliance and which indeed had no share in that morbid decay. Above all, the German-Austrian had come to feel in the very depths of his own being that the historical mission of the House of Habsburg had come to an end and that the new Empire could choose only an Emperor who was of heroic mould and was therefore worthy to wear the 'Crown of the Rhine'. It was right and just that Destiny should be praised for having chosen a scion of that House of which Frederick the Great had in past times given the nation an elevated and resplendent symbol for all time to come.

After the great war of 1870-71 the House of Habsburg set to work with all its determination to exterminate the dangerous German element—about whose inner feelings and attitude there could be no doubt—slowly but deliberately. I use the word exterminate, because that alone expresses what must have been the final result of the Slavophile policy. Then it was that the fire of rebellion blazed up among the people whose extermination had been decreed. That fire was such as had never been witnessed in modern German history.

For the first time nationalists and patriots were transformed into rebels.

Not rebels against the nation or the State as such but rebels against that form of government which they were convinced, would inevitably bring about the ruin of their own people. For the first time in modern history the traditional dynastic patriotism and national love of fatherland and people were in open conflict.

It was to the merit of the Pan-German movement in Austria during the closing decade of the last century that it pointed out clearly and unequivocally that a State is entitled to demand respect and protection for its authority only when such authority is administered in accordance with the interests of the nation, or at least not in a manner detrimental to those interests.

The authority of the State can never be an end in itself; for, if that were so, any kind of tyranny would be inviolable and sacred.

If a government uses the instruments of power in its hands for the purpose of leading a people to ruin, then rebellion is not only the right but also the duty of every individual citizen. The question of whether and when such a situation exists cannot be answered by theoretical dissertations but only by the exercise of force, and it is success that decides the issue.

Every government, even though it may be the worst possible and even though it may have betrayed the nation's trust in thousands of ways, will claim that its duty is to uphold the authority of the State. Its adversaries, who are fighting for national self-preservation, must use the same weapons which the government uses if they are to prevail against such a rule and secure their own freedom and independence. Therefore the conflict will be fought out with 'legal' means as long as the power which is to be overthrown uses them; but the insurgents will not hesitate to apply illegal means if the oppressor himself employs them.

Generally speaking, we must not forget that the highest aim of human existence is not the maintenance of a State of Government but rather the conservation of the race.

If the race is in danger of being oppressed or even exterminated the question of legality is only of secondary importance. The established power may in such a case employ only those means which are recognized as 'legal'. yet the instinct of self-preservation on the part of the oppressed will always justify, to the highest degree, the employment of all possible resources.

Only on the recognition of this principle was it possible for those struggles to be carried through, of which history furnishes magnificent examples in abundance, against foreign bondage or oppression at home.

Human rights are above the rights of the State. But if a people be defeated in the struggle for its human rights this means that its weight has proved too light in the scale of Destiny to have the luck of being able to endure in this terrestrial world.

The world is not there to be possessed by the faint-hearted races.

Austria affords a very clear and striking example of how easy it is for tyranny to hide its head under the cloak of what is called 'legality'.

The legal exercise of power in the Habsburg State was then based on the anti-German attitude of the parliament, with its non-German majorities, and on the dynastic House, which was also hostile to the German element. The whole authority of the State was incorporated in these two factors. To attempt to alter the lot of the German element through these two factors would have been senseless. Those who advised the 'legal' way as the only possible way, and also obedience to the State authority, could offer no resistance; because a policy of resistance could not have been put into effect through legal measures. To follow the advice of the legalist counsellors would have meant the inevitable ruin of the German element within the Monarchy, and this disaster would not have taken long to come. The German element has actually been saved only because the State as such collapsed.

The spectacled theorist would have given his life for his doctrine rather than for his people.

Because man has made laws he subsequently comes to think that he exists for the sake of the laws.

A great service rendered by the pan-German movement then was that it abolished all such nonsense, though the doctrinaire theorists and other fetish worshippers were shocked.

When the Habsburgs attempted to come to close quarters with the German element, by the employment of all the means of attack which they had at their command, the Pan-German Party hit out ruthlessly against the 'illustrious' dynasty. This Party was the first to probe into and expose the corrupt condition of the State; and in doing so they opened the eyes of hundreds of thousands. To have liberated the high ideal of love for one's country from the embrace of this deplorable dynasty was one of the great services rendered by the Pan-German movement.

When that Party first made its appearance it secured a large following—indeed, the movement threatened to become almost an avalanche. But the first successes were not maintained. At the time I came to Vienna the pan-German Party had been eclipsed by the Christian-Socialist Party, which had come into power in the meantime. Indeed, the Pan-German Party had sunk to a level of almost complete insignificance.

The rise and decline of the Pan-German movement on the one hand and the marvellous progress of the Christian-Socialist Party on the other, became a classic object of study for me, and as such they played an important part in the development of my own views.

When I came to Vienna all my sympathies were exclusively with the Pan-German Movement.

I was just as much impressed by the fact that they had the courage to shout HEIL HOHENZOLLERN as I rejoiced at their determination to consider themselves an integral part of the German Empire, from which they were separated only provisionally. They never missed an opportunity to explain their attitude in public, which raised my enthusiasm and confidence. To avow one's principles publicly on every problem that concerned Germanism, and never to make any compromises, seemed to me the only way of saving our people. What I could not understand was how this movement broke down so soon after such a magnificent start; and it was no less incomprehensible that the Christian-Socialists should gain such tremendous power within such a short time. They had just reached the pinnacle of their popularity.

When I began to compare those two movements Fate placed before me the best means of understanding the causes of this puzzling problem. The action of Fate in this case was hastened by my own straitened circumstances.

I shall begin my analysis with an account of the two men who must be regarded as the founders and leaders of the two movements. These were George von Schönerer and Dr. Karl Lueger.

As far as personality goes, both were far above the level and stature of the so-called parliamentary figures. They lived lives of immaculate and irreproachable probity amidst the miasma of all-round political corruption. Personally I first liked the Pan-German representative, Schönerer, and it was only afterwards and gradually that I felt an equal liking for the Christian-Socialist leader.

When I compared their respective abilities Schönerer seemed to me a better and more profound thinker on fundamental problems. He foresaw the inevitable downfall of the Austrian State more clearly and accurately than anyone else. If this warning in regard to the Habsburg Empire had been heeded in Germany the disastrous world war, which involved Germany against the whole of Europe, would never have taken place.

But though Schönerer succeeded in penetrating to the essentials of a problem he was very often much mistaken in his judgment of men.

And herein lay Dr. Lueger's special talent. He had a rare gift of insight into human nature and he was very careful not to take men as something better than they were in reality. He based his plans on the practical possibilities which human life offered him, whereas Schönerer had only little discrimination in that respect. All ideas that this Pan-German had were right in the abstract, but he did not have the forcefulness or understanding necessary to put his ideas across to the broad masses. He was not able to formulate them so that they could be easily grasped by the masses, whose powers of comprehension are limited and will always remain so. Therefore all Schönerer's knowledge was only the wisdom of a prophet and he never could succeed in having it put into practice.

This lack of insight into human nature led him to form a wrong estimate of the forces behind certain movements and the inherent strength of old institutions.

Schönerer indeed realized that the problems he had to deal with were in the nature of a WELTANSCHAUUNG; but he did not understand that only the broad masses of a nation can make such convictions prevail, which are almost of a religious nature.

Unfortunately he understood only very imperfectly how feeble is the fighting spirit of the so-called bourgeoisie. That weakness is due to their business interests, which individuals are too much afraid of risking and which therefore deter them from taking action. And, generally speaking, a WELTANSCHAUUNG can have no prospect of success unless the broad masses declare themselves ready to act as its standard-bearers and to fight on its behalf wherever and to whatever extent that may be necessary.

This failure to understand the importance of the lower strata of the population resulted in a very inadequate concept of the social problem.

In all this Dr. Lueger was the opposite of Schönerer. His profound knowledge of human nature enabled him to form a correct estimate of the various social forces and it saved him from under-rating the power of existing institutions. And it was perhaps this very quality which enabled him to utilize those institutions as a means to serve the purposes of his policy.

He saw only too clearly that, in our epoch, the political fighting power of the upper classes is quite insignificant and not at all capable of fighting for a great new movement until the triumph of that movement be secured. Thus he devoted the greatest part of his political activity to the task of winning over those sections of the population whose existence was in danger and fostering the militant spirit in them rather than attempting to paralyse it. He was also quick to adopt all available means for winning the support of long-established institutions, so as to be able to derive the greatest possible advantage for his movement from those old sources of power.

Thus it was that, first of all, he chose as the social basis of his new Party that middle class which was threatened with extinction. In this way he secured a solid following which was willing to make great sacrifices and had good fighting stamina. His extremely wise attitude towards the Catholic Church rapidly won over the younger clergy in such large numbers that the old Clerical Party was forced to retire from the field of action or else, which was the wiser course, join the new Party, in the hope of gradually winning back one position after another.

But it would be a serious injustice to the man if we were to regard this as his essential characteristic. For he possessed the qualities of an able tactician, and had the true genius of a great reformer; but all these were limited by his exact perception of the possibilities at hand and also of his own capabilities.

The aims which this really eminent man decided to pursue were intensely practical. He wished to conquer Vienna, the heart of the Monarchy. It was from Vienna that the last pulses of life beat through the diseased and worn-out body of the decrepit Empire. If the heart could be made healthier the others parts of the body were bound to revive. That idea was correct in principle; but the time within which it could be applied in practice was strictly limited. And that was the man's weak point.

His achievements as Burgomaster of the City of Vienna are immortal, in the best sense of the word. But all that could not save the Monarchy. It came too late.

His rival, Schönerer, saw this more clearly. What Dr. Lueger undertook to put into practice turned out marvellously successful. But the results which he expected to follow these achievements did not come. Schönerer did not attain the ends he had proposed to himself; but his fears were realized, alas, in a terrible fashion. Thus both these men failed to attain their further objectives. Lueger could not save Austria and Schönerer could not prevent the downfall of the German people in Austria.

To study the causes of failure in the case of these two parties is to learn a lesson that is highly instructive for our own epoch. This is specially useful for my friends, because in many points the circumstances of our own day are similar to those of that time. Therefore such a lesson may help us to guard against the mistakes which brought one of those movements to an end and rendered the other barren of results.

In my opinion, the wreck of the Pan-German Movement in Austria must be attributed to three causes.

The first of these consisted in the fact that the leaders did not have a clear concept of the importance of the social problem, particularly for a new movement which had an essentially revolutionary character. Schönerer and his followers directed their attention principally to the bourgeois classes. For that reason their movement was bound to turn out mediocre and tame. The German bourgeoisie, especially in its upper circles, is pacifist even to the point of complete self-abnegation—though the individual may not be aware of this—wherever the internal affairs of the nation or State are concerned. In good times, which in this case means times of good government, such a psychological attitude makes this social layer extraordinarily valuable to the State. But when there is a bad government, such a quality has a destructive effect. In order to assure the possibility of carrying through a really strenuous struggle, the Pan-German Movement should have devoted its efforts to winning over the masses. The failure to do this left the movement from the very beginning without the elementary impulse which such a wave needs if it is not to ebb within a short while.

In failing to see the truth of this principle clearly at the very outset of the movement and in neglecting to put it into practice the new Party made an initial mistake which could not possibly be rectified afterwards. For the numerous moderate bourgeois elements admitted into the movements increasingly determined its internal orientation and thus forestalled all further prospects of gaining any appreciable support among the masses of the people. Under such conditions such a movement could not get beyond mere discussion and criticism. Quasi-religious faith and the spirit of sacrifice were not to be found in the movement any more. Their place was taken by the effort towards 'positive' collaboration, which in this case meant the acknowledgment of the existing state of affairs, gradually whittling away the rough corners of the questions in dispute, and ending up with the making of a dishonourable peace.

Such was the fate of the Pan-German Movement, because at the start the leaders did not realize that the most important condition of success was that they should recruit their following from the broad masses of the people. The Movement thus became bourgeois and respectable and radical only in moderation.

From this failure resulted the second cause of its rapid decline.

The position of the Germans in Austria was already desperate when Pan-Germanism arose. Year after year Parliament was being used more and more as an instrument for the gradual extinction of the German-Austrian population. The only hope for any eleventh-hour effort to save it lay in the overthrow of the parliamentary system; but there was very little prospect of this happening.

Therewith the Pan-German Movement was confronted with a question of primary importance.

To overthrow the Parliament, should the Pan-Germanists have entered it 'to undermine it from within', as the current phrase was? Or should they have assailed the institution as such from the outside?

They entered the Parliament and came out defeated. But they had found themselves obliged to enter.

For in order to wage an effective war against such a power from the outside, indomitable courage and a ready spirit of sacrifice were necessary weapons. In such cases the bull must be seized by the horns. Furious drives may bring the assailant to the ground again and again; but if he has a stout heart he will stand up, even though some bones may be broken, and only after a long and tough struggle will he achieve his triumph. New champions are attracted to a cause by the appeal of great sacrifices made for its sake, until that indomitable spirit is finally crowned with success.

For such a result, however, the children of the people from the great masses are necessary. They alone have the requisite determination and tenacity to fight a sanguinary issue through to the end. But the Pan-German Movement did not have these broad masses as its champions, and so no other means of solution could be tried out except that of entering Parliament.

It would be a mistake to think that this decision resulted from a long series of internal hesitations of a moral kind, or that it was the outcome of careful calculation. No. They did not even think of another solution. Those who participated in this blunder were actuated by general considerations and vague notions as to what would be the significance and effect of taking part in such a special way in that institution which they had condemned on principle. In general they hoped that they would thus have the means of expounding their cause to the great masses of the people, because they would be able to speak before 'the forum of the whole nation'. Also, it seemed reasonable to believe that by attacking the evil in the root they would be more effective than if the attack came from outside. They believed that, if protected by the immunity of Parliament, the position of the individual protagonists would be strengthened and that thus the force of their attacks would be enhanced.

In reality everything turned out quite otherwise.

The Forum before which the Pan-German representatives spoke had not grown greater, but had actually become smaller; for each spoke only to the circle that was ready to listen to him or could read the report of his speech in the newspapers.

But the greater forum of immediate listeners is not the parliamentary auditorium: it is the large public meeting. For here alone will there be thousands of men who have come simply to hear what a speaker has to say, whereas in the parliamentary sittings only a few hundred are present; and for the most part these are there only to earn their daily allowance for attendance and not to be enlightened by the wisdom of one or other of the 'representatives of the people'.

The most important consideration is that the same public is always present and that this public does not wish to learn anything new; because, setting aside the question of its intelligence, it lacks even that modest quantum of will-power which is necessary for the effort of learning.

Not one of the representatives of the people will pay homage to a superior truth and devote himself to its service. No. Not one of these gentry will act thus, except he has grounds for hoping that by such a conversion he may be able to retain the representation of his constituency in the coming legislature. Therefore, only when it becomes quite clear that the old party is likely to have a bad time of it at the forthcoming elections—only then will those models of manly virtue set out in search of a new party or a new policy which may have better electoral prospects; but of course this change of position will be accompanied by a veritable deluge of high moral motives to justify it. And thus it always happens that when an existing Party has incurred such general disfavour among the public that it is threatened with the probability of a crushing defeat, then a great migration commences. The parliamentary rats leave the Party ship.

All this happens not because the individuals in the case have become better informed on the questions at issue and have resolved to act accordingly. These changes of front are evidence only of that gift of clairvoyance which warns the parliamentary flea at the right moment and enables him to hop into another warm Party bed.

To speak before such a forum signifies casting pearls before certain animals.

Verily it does not repay the pains taken; for the result must always be negative.

And that is actually what happened. The Pan-German representatives might have talked themselves hoarse, but to no effect whatsoever.

The Press either ignored them totally or so mutilated their speeches that the logical consistency was destroyed or the meaning twisted round in such a way that the public got only a very wrong impression regarding the aims of the new movement. What the individual members said was not of importance. The important matter was what people read as coming from them. This consisted of mere extracts which had been torn out of the context of the speeches and gave an impression of incoherent nonsense, which indeed was purposely meant. Thus the only public before which they really spoke consisted merely of five hundred parliamentarians; and that says enough.

The worst was the following:

The Pan-German Movement could hope for success only if the leaders realized from the very first moment that here there was no question so much of a new Party as of a new WELTANSCHAUUNG. This alone could arouse the inner moral forces that were necessary for such a gigantic struggle. And for this struggle the leaders must be men of first-class brains and indomitable courage. If the struggle on behalf of a WELTANSCHAUUNG is not conducted by men of heroic spirit who are ready to sacrifice, everything, within a short while it will become impossible to find real fighting followers who are ready to lay down their lives for the cause. A man who fights only for his own existence has not much left over for the service of the community.

In order to secure the conditions that are necessary for success, everybody concerned must be made to understand that the new movement looks to posterity for its honour and glory but that it has no recompense to offer to the present-day members. If a movement should offer a large number of positions and offices that are easily accessible the number of unworthy candidates admitted to membership will be constantly on the increase and eventually a day will come when there will be such a preponderance of political profiteers among the membership of a successful Party that the combatants who bore the brunt of the battle in the earlier stages of the movement can now scarcely recognize their own Party and may be ejected by the later arrivals as unwanted ballast. Therewith the movement will no longer have a mission to fulfil.

Once the Pan-Germanists decided to collaborate with Parliament they were no longer leaders and combatants in a popular movement, but merely parliamentarians. Thus the Movement sank to the common political party level of the day and no longer had the strength to face a hostile fate and defy the risk of martyrdom. Instead of fighting, the Pan-German leaders fell into the habit of talking and negotiating. The new parliamentarians soon found that it was a more satisfactory, because less risky, way of fulfilling their task if they would defend the new WELTANSCHAUUNG with the spiritual weapon of parliamentary rhetoric rather than take up a fight in which they placed their lives in danger, the outcome of which also was uncertain and even at the best could offer no prospect of personal gain for themselves.

When they had taken their seats in Parliament their adherents outside hoped and waited for miracles to happen. Naturally no such miracles happened or could happen. Whereupon the adherents of the movement soon grew impatient, because reports they read about their own deputies did not in the least come up to what had been expected when they voted for these deputies at the elections. The reason for this was not far to seek. It was due to the fact that an unfriendly Press refrained from giving a true account of what the Pan-German representatives of the people were actually doing.

According as the new deputies got to like this mild form of 'revolutionary' struggle in Parliament and in the provincial diets they gradually became reluctant to resume the more hazardous work of expounding the principles of the movement before the broad masses of the people.

Mass meetings in public became more and more rare, though these are the only means of exercising a really effective influence on the people; because here the influence comes from direct personal contact and in this way the support of large sections of the people can be obtained.

When the tables on which the speakers used to stand in the great beer-halls, addressing an assembly of thousands, were deserted for the parliamentary tribune and the speeches were no longer addressed to the people directly but to the so-called 'chosen' representatives, the Pan-German Movement lost its popular character and in a little while degenerated to the level of a more or less serious club where problems of the day are discussed academically.

The wrong impression created by the Press was no longer corrected by personal contact with the people through public meetings, whereby the individual representatives might have given a true account of their activities. The final result of this neglect was that the word 'Pan-German' came to have an unpleasant sound in the ears of the masses.

The knights of the pen and the literary snobs of to-day should be made to realize that the great transformations which have taken place in this world were never conducted by a goosequill. No. The task of the pen must always be that of presenting the theoretical concepts which motivate such changes. The force which has ever and always set in motion great historical avalanches of religious and political movements is the magic power of the spoken word.

The broad masses of a population are more amenable to the appeal of rhetoric than to any other force. All great movements are popular movements. They are the volcanic eruptions of human passions and emotions, stirred into activity by the ruthless Goddess of Distress or by the torch of the spoken word cast into the midst of the people. In no case have great movements been set afoot by the syrupy effusions of aesthetic littérateurs and drawing-room heroes.

The doom of a nation can be averted only by a storm of glowing passion; but only those who are passionate themselves can arouse passion in others. It is only through the capacity for passionate feeling that chosen leaders can wield the power of the word which, like hammer blows, will open the door to the hearts of the people.

He who is not capable of passionate feeling and speech was never chosen by Providence to be the herald of its will. Therefore a writer should stick to his ink-bottle and busy himself with theoretical questions if he has the requisite ability and knowledge. He has not been born or chosen to be a leader.

A movement which has great ends to achieve must carefully guard against the danger of losing contact with the masses of the people. Every problem encountered must be examined from this viewpoint first of all and the decision to be made must always be in harmony with this principle.

The movement must avoid everything which might lessen or weaken its power of influencing the masses; not from demagogical motives but because of the simple fact that no great idea, no matter how sublime and exalted it may appear, can be realized in practice without the effective power which resides in the popular masses. Stern reality alone must mark the way to the goal. To be unwilling to walk the road of hardship means, only too often in this world, the total renunciation of our aims and purposes, whether that renunciation be consciously willed or not.

The moment the Pan-German leaders, in virtue of their acceptance of the parliamentary principle, moved the centre of their activities away from the people and into Parliament, in that moment they sacrificed the future for the sake of a cheap momentary success. They chose the easier way in the struggle and in doing so rendered themselves unworthy of the final victory.

While in Vienna I used to ponder seriously over these two questions, and I saw that the main reason for the collapse of the Pan-German Movement lay in the fact that these very questions were not rightly appreciated. To my mind at that time the Movement seemed chosen to take in its hands the leadership of the German element in Austria.

These first two blunders which led to the downfall of the Pan-German Movement were very closely connected with one another. Faulty recognition of the inner driving forces that urge great movements forward led to an inadequate appreciation of the part which the broad masses play in bringing about such changes. The result was that too little attention was given to the social problem and that the attempts made by the movement to capture the minds of the lower classes were too few and too weak. Another result was the acceptance of the parliamentary policy, which had a similar effect in regard to the importance of the masses.

If there had been a proper appreciation of the tremendous powers of endurance always shown by the masses in revolutionary movements a different attitude towards the social problem would have been taken, and also a different policy in the matter of propaganda. Then the centre of gravity of the movement would not have been transferred to the Parliament but would have remained in the workshops and in the streets.

There was a third mistake, which also had its roots in the failure to understand the worth of the masses. The masses are first set in motion, along a definite direction, by men of superior talents; but then these masses once in motion are like a flywheel inasmuch as they sustain the momentum and steady balance of the offensive.

The policy of the Pan-German leaders in deciding to carry through a difficult fight against the Catholic Church can be explained only by attributing it to an inadequate understanding of the spiritual character of the people.

The reasons why the new Party engaged in a violent campaign against Rome were as follows:

As soon as the House of Habsburg had definitely decided to transform Austria into a Slav State all sorts of means were adopted which seemed in any way serviceable for that purpose. The Habsburg rulers had no scruples of conscience about exploiting even religious institutions in the service of this new 'State Idea'. One of the many methods thus employed was the use of Czech parishes and their clergy as instruments for spreading Slav hegemony throughout Austria. This proceeding was carried out as follows:

Parish priests of Czech nationality were appointed in purely German districts. Gradually but steadily pushing forward the interests of the Czech people before those of the Church, the parishes and their priests became generative cells in the process of de-Germanization.

Unfortunately the German-Austrian clergy completely failed to counter this procedure. Not only were they incapable of taking a similar initiative on the German side, but they showed themselves unable to meet the Czech offensive with adequate resistance. The German element was accordingly pushed backwards, slowly but steadily, through the perversion of religious belief for political ends on the one side, and the Jack of proper resistance on the other side. Such were the tactics used in dealing with the smaller problems; but those used in dealing with the larger problems were not very different.

The anti-German aims pursued by the Habsburgs, especially through the instrumentality of the higher clergy, did not meet with any vigorous resistance, while the clerical representatives of the German interests withdrew completely to the rear. The general impression created could not be other than that the Catholic clergy as such were grossly neglecting the rights of the German population.

Therefore it looked as if the Catholic Church was not in sympathy with the German people but that it unjustly supported their adversaries. The root of the whole evil, especially according to Schönerer's opinion, lay in the fact that the leadership of the Catholic Church was not in Germany, and that this fact alone was sufficient reason for the hostile attitude of the Church towards the demands of our people.

The so-called cultural problem receded almost completely into the background, as was generally the case everywhere throughout Austria at that time. In assuming a hostile attitude towards the Catholic Church, the Pan-German leaders were influenced not so much by the Church's position in questions of science but principally by the fact that the Church did not defend German rights, as it should have done, but always supported those who encroached on these rights, especially then Slavs.

George Schönerer was not a man who did things by halves. He went into battle against the Church because he was convinced that this was the only way in which the German people could be saved. The LOS-VON-ROM (Away from Rome) Movement seemed the most formidable, but at the same time most difficult, method of attacking and destroying the adversary's citadel. Schönerer believed that if this movement could be carried through successfully the unfortunate division between the two great religious denominations in Germany would be wiped out and that the inner forces of the German Empire and Nation would be enormously enhanced by such a victory.

But the premises as well as the conclusions in this case were both erroneous.

It was undoubtedly true that the national powers of resistance, in everything concerning Germanism as such, were much weaker among the German Catholic clergy than among their non-German confrères, especially the Czechs. And only an ignorant person could be unaware of the fact that it scarcely ever entered the mind of the German clergy to take the offensive on behalf of German interests.

But at the same time everybody who is not blind to facts must admit that all this should be attributed to a characteristic under which we Germans have all been doomed to suffer. This characteristic shows itself in our objective way of regarding our own nationality, as if it were something that lay outside of us.

While the Czech priest adopted a subjective attitude towards his own people and only an objective attitude towards the Church, the German parish priest showed a subjective devotion to his Church and remained objective in regard to his nation. It is a phenomenon which, unfortunately for us, can be observed occurring in exactly the same way in thousands of other cases.

It is by no means a peculiar inheritance from Catholicism; but it is something in us which does not take long to gnaw the vitals of almost every institution, especially institutions of State and those which have ideal aims. Take, for example, the attitude of our State officials in regard to the efforts made for bringing about a national resurgence and compare that attitude with the stand which the public officials of any other nation would have taken in such a case. Or is it to be believed that the military officers of any other country in the world would refuse to come forward on behalf of the national aspirations, but would rather hide behind the phrase 'Authority of the State', as has been the case in our country during the last five years and has even been deemed a meritorious attitude? Or let us take another example. In regard to the Jewish problem, do not the two Christian denominations take up a standpoint to-day which does not respond to the national exigencies or even the interests of religion? Consider the attitude of a Jewish Rabbi towards any question, even one of quite insignificant importance, concerning the Jews as a race, and compare his attitude with that of the majority of our clergy, whether Catholic or Protestant.

We observe the same phenomenon wherever it is a matter of standing up for some abstract idea.

'Authority of the State', 'Democracy', 'Pacifism', 'International Solidarity', etc., all such notions become rigid, dogmatic concepts with us; and the more vital the general necessities of the nation, the more will they be judged exclusively in the light of those concepts.

This unfortunate habit of looking at all national demands from the viewpoint of a pre-conceived notion makes it impossible for us to see the subjective side of a thing which objectively contradicts one's own doctrine. It finally leads to a complete reversion in the relation of means to an end. Any attempt at a national revival will be opposed if the preliminary condition of such a revival be that a bad and pernicious regime must first of all be overthrown; because such an action will be considered as a violation of the 'Authority of the State'. In the eyes of those who take that standpoint, the 'Authority of the State' is not a means which is there to serve an end but rather, to the mind of the dogmatic believer in objectivity, it is an end in itself; and he looks upon that as sufficient apology for his own miserable existence. Such people would raise an outcry, if, for instance, anyone should attempt to set up a dictatorship, even though the man responsible for it were Frederick the Great and even though the politicians for the time being, who constituted the parliamentary majority, were small and incompetent men or maybe even on a lower grade of inferiority; because to such sticklers for abstract principles the law of democracy is more sacred than the welfare of the nation. In accordance with his principles, one of these gentry will defend the worst kind of tyranny, though it may be leading a people to ruin, because it is the fleeting embodiment of the 'Authority of the State', and another will reject even a highly beneficent government if it should happen not to be in accord with his notion of 'democracy'.

In the same way our German pacifist will remain silent while the nation is groaning under an oppression which is being exercised by a sanguinary military power, when this state of affairs gives rise to active resistance; because such resistance means the employment of physical force, which is against the spirit of the pacifist associations. The German International Socialist may be rooked and plundered by his comrades in all the other countries of the world in the name of 'solidarity', but he responds with fraternal kindness and never thinks of trying to get his own back, or even of defending himself. And why? Because he is a—German.

It may be unpleasant to dwell on such truths, but if something is to be changed we must start by diagnosing the disease.

The phenomenon which I have just described also accounts for the feeble manner in which German interests are promoted and defended by a section of the clergy.

Such conduct is not the manifestation of a malicious intent, nor is it the outcome of orders given from 'above', as we say; but such a lack of national grit and determination is due to defects in our educational system. For, instead of inculcating in the youth a lively sense of their German nationality, the aim of the educational system is to make the youth prostrate themselves in homage to the idea, as if the idea were an idol.

The education which makes them the devotees of such abstract notions as 'Democracy', 'International Socialism', 'Pacifism', etc., is so hard-and-fast and exclusive and, operating as it does from within outwards, is so purely subjective that in forming their general picture of outside life as a whole they are fundamentally influenced by these A PRIORI notions. But, on the other hand, the attitude towards their own German nationality has been very objective from youth upwards. The Pacifist—in so far as he is a German—who surrenders himself subjectively, body and soul, to the dictates of his dogmatic principles, will always first consider the objective right or wrong of a situation when danger threatens his own people, even though that danger be grave and unjustly wrought from outside. But he will never take his stand in the ranks of his own people and fight for and with them from the sheer instinct of self-preservation.

Another example may further illustrate how far this applies to the different religious denominations. In so far as its origin and tradition are based on German ideals, Protestantism of itself defends those ideals better. But it fails the moment it is called upon to defend national interests which do not belong to the sphere of its ideals and traditional development, or which, for some reason or other, may be rejected by that sphere.

Therefore Protestantism will always take its part in promoting German ideals as far as concerns moral integrity or national education, when the German spiritual being or language or spiritual freedom are to be defended: because these represent the principles on which Protestantism itself is grounded. But this same Protestantism violently opposes every attempt to rescue the nation from the clutches of its mortal enemy; because the Protestant attitude towards the Jews is more or less rigidly and dogmatically fixed. And yet this is the first problem which has to be solved, unless all attempts to bring about a German resurgence or to raise the level of the nation's standing are doomed to turn out nonsensical and impossible.

During my sojourn in Vienna I had ample leisure and opportunity to study this problem without allowing any prejudices to intervene; and in my daily intercourse with people I was able to establish the correctness of the opinion I formed by the test of thousands of instances.

In this focus where the greatest varieties of nationality had converged it was quite clear and open to everybody to see that the German pacifist was always and exclusively the one who tried to consider the interests of his own nation objectively; but you could never find a Jew who took a similar attitude towards his own race. Furthermore, I found that only the German Socialist is 'international' in the sense that he feels himself obliged not to demand justice for his own people in any other manner than by whining and wailing to his international comrades. Nobody could ever reproach Czechs or Poles or other nations with such conduct.

In short, even at that time, already I recognized that this evil is only partly a result of the doctrines taught by Socialism, Pacifism, etc., but mainly the result of our totally inadequate system of education, the defects of which are responsible for the lack of devotion to our own national ideals.

Therefore the first theoretical argument advanced by the Pan-German leaders as the basis of their offensive against Catholicism was quite entenable.

The only way to remedy the evil I have been speaking of is to train the Germans from youth upwards to an absolute recognition of the rights of their own people, instead of poisoning their minds, while they are still only children, with the virus of this curbed 'objectivity', even in matters concerning the very maintenance of our own existence. The result of this would be that the Catholic in Germany, just as in Ireland, Poland or France, will be a German first and foremost. But all this presupposes a radical change in the national government.

The strongest proof in support of my contention is furnished by what took place at that historical juncture when our people were called for the last time before the tribunal of History to defend their own existence, in a life-or-death struggle.

As long as there was no lack of leadership in the higher circles, the people fulfilled their duty and obligations to an overwhelming extent. Whether Protestant pastor or Catholic priest, each did his very utmost in helping our powers of resistance to hold out, not only in the trenches but also, and even more so, at home. During those years, and especially during the first outburst of enthusiasm, in both religious camps there was one undivided and sacred German Empire for whose preservation and future existence they all prayed to Heaven.

The Pan-German Movement in Austria ought to have asked itself this one question: Is the maintenance of the German element in Austria possible or not, as long as that element remains within the fold of the Catholic Faith? If that question should have been answered in the affirmative, then the political Party should not have meddled in religious and denominational questions. But if the question had to be answered in the negative, then a religious reformation should have been started and not a political party movement.

Anyone who believes that a religious reformation can be achieved through the agency of a political organization shows that he has no idea of the development of religious conceptions and doctrines of faith and how these are given practical effect by the Church. No man can serve two masters. And I hold that the foundation or overthrow of a religion has far greater consequences than the foundation or overthrow of a State, to say nothing of a Party.

It is no argument to the contrary to say that the attacks were only defensive measures against attacks from the other side. Undoubtedly there have always been unscrupulous rogues who did not hesitate to degrade religion to the base uses of politics. Nearly always such a people had nothing else in their minds except to make a business of religions and politics. But on the other hand it would be wrong to hold religion itself, or a religious denomination, responsible for a number of rascals who exploit the Church for their own base interests just as they would exploit anything else in which they had a part.

Nothing could be more to the taste of one of these parliamentary loungers and tricksters than to be able to find a scapegoat for his political sharp-practice—after the event, of course. The moment religion or a religious denomination is attacked and made responsible for his personal misdeeds this shrewd fellow will raise a row at once and call the world to witness how justified he was in acting as he did, proclaiming that he and his eloquence alone have saved religion and the Church. The public, which is mostly stupid and has a very short memory, is not capable of recognizing the real instigator of the quarrel in the midst of the turmoil that has been raised. Frequently it does not remember the beginning of the fight and so the rogue gets by with his stunt.

A cunning fellow of that sort is quite well aware that his misdeeds have nothing to do with religion. And so he will laugh up his sleeve all the more heartily when his honest but artless adversary loses the game and, one day losing all faith in humanity, retires from the activities of public life.

But from another viewpoint also it would be wrong to make religion, or the Church as such, responsible for the misdeeds of individuals. If one compares the magnitude of the organization, as it stands visible to every eye, with the average weakness of human nature we shall have to admit that the proportion of good to bad is more favourable here than anywhere else. Among the priests there may, of course, be some who use their sacred calling to further their political ambitions. There are clergy who unfortunately forget that in the political mêlée they ought to be the paladins of the more sublime truths and not the abettors of falsehood and slander. But for each one of these unworthy specimens we can find a thousand or more who fulfil their mission nobly as the trustworthy guardians of souls and who tower above the level of our corrupt epoch, as little islands above the seaswamp.

I cannot condemn the Church as such, and I should feel quite as little justified in doing so if some depraved person in the robe of a priest commits some offence against the moral law. Nor should I for a moment think of blaming the Church if one of its innumerable members betrays and besmirches his compatriots, especially not in epochs when such conduct is quite common. We must not forget, particularly in our day, that for one such Ephialtes[7] there are a thousand whose hearts bleed in sympathy with their people during these years of misfortune and who, together with the best of our nation, yearn for the hour when fortune will smile on us again.

If it be objected that here we are concerned not with the petty problems of everyday life but principally with fundamental truths and questions of dogma, the only way of answering that objection is to ask a question:

Do you feel that Providence has called you to proclaim the Truth to the world? If so, then go and do it. But you ought to have the courage to do it directly and not use some political party as your mouthpiece; for in this way you shirk your vocation. In the place of something that now exists and is bad put something else that is better and will last into the future.

If you lack the requisite courage or if you yourself do not know clearly what your better substitute ought to be, leave the whole thing alone. But, whatever happens, do not try to reach the goal by the roundabout way of a political party if you are not brave enough to fight with your visor lifted.

Political parties have no right to meddle in religious questions except when these relate to something that is alien to the national well-being and thus calculated to undermine racial customs and morals. If some ecclesiastical dignitaries should misuse religious ceremonies or religious teaching to injure their own nation their opponents ought never to take the same road and fight them with the same weapons.

To a political leader the religious teachings and practices of his people should be sacred and inviolable. Otherwise he should not be a statesman but a reformer, if he has the necessary qualities for such a mission.

Any other line of conduct will lead to disaster, especially in Germany. In studying the Pan-German Movement and its conflict with Rome I was then firmly persuaded, and especially in the course of later years, that by their failure to understand the importance of the social problem the Pan-Germanists lost the support of the broad masses, who are the indispensable combatants in such a movement. By entering Parliament the Pan-German leaders deprived themselves of the great driving force which resides in the masses and at the same time they laid on their own shoulders all the defects of the parliamentary institution. Their struggle against the Church made their position impossible in numerous circles of the lower and middle class, while at the same time it robbed them of innumerable high-class elements — some of the best indeed that the nation possessed. The practical outcome of the Austrian Kulturkampf was negative.

Although they succeeded in winning 100,000 members away from the Church, that did not do much harm to the latter. The Church did not really need to shed any tears over these lost sheep, for it lost only those who had for a long time ceased to belong to it in their inner hearts. The difference between this new reformation and the great Reformation was that in the historic epoch of the great Reformation some of the best members left the Church because of religious convictions, whereas in this new reformation only those left who had been indifferent before and who were now influenced by political considerations. From the political point of view alone the result was as ridiculous as it was deplorable.

Once again a political movement which had promised so much for the German nation collapsed, because it was not conducted in a spirit of unflinching adherence to naked reality, but lost itself in fields where it was bound to get broken up.

The Pan-German Movement would never have made this mistake if it had properly understood the PSYCHE of the broad masses. If the leaders had known that, for psychological reasons alone, it is not expedient to place two or more sets of adversaries before the masses—since that leads to a complete splitting up of their fighting strength—they would have concentrated the full and undivided force of their attack against a single adversary. Nothing in the policy of a political party is so fraught with danger as to allow its decisions to be directed by people who want to have their fingers in every pie though they do not know how to cook the simplest dish.

But even though there is much that can really be said against the various religious denominations, political leaders must not forget that the experience of history teaches us that no purely political party in similar circumstances ever succeeded in bringing about a religious reformation. One does not study history for the purpose of forgetting or mistrusting its lessons afterwards, when the time comes to apply these lessons in practice. It would be a mistake to believe that in this particular case things were different, so that the eternal truths of history were no longer applicable. One learns history in order to be able to apply its lessons to the present time and whoever fails to do this cannot pretend to be a political leader. In reality he is quite a superficial person or, as is mostly the case, a conceited simpleton whose good intentions cannot make up for his incompetence in practical affairs.

The art of leadership, as displayed by really great popular leaders in all ages, consists in consolidating the attention of the people against a single adversary and taking care that nothing will split up that attention into sections. The more the militant energies of the people are directed towards one objective the more will new recruits join the movement, attracted by the magnetism of its unified action, and thus the striking power will be all the more enhanced. The leader of genius must have the ability to make different opponents appear as if they belonged to the one category; for weak and wavering natures among a leader's following may easily begin to be dubious about the justice of their own cause if they have to face different enemies.

As soon as the vacillating masses find themselves facing an opposition that is made up of different groups of enemies their sense of objectivity will be aroused and they will ask how is it that all the others can be in the wrong and they themselves, and their movement, alone in the right.

Such a feeling would be the first step towards a paralysis of their fighting vigour. Where there are various enemies who are split up into divergent groups it will be necessary to block them all together as forming one solid front, so that the mass of followers in a popular movement may see only one common enemy against whom they have to fight.

Such uniformity intensifies their belief in the justice of their own cause and strengthens their feeling of hostility towards the opponent.

The Pan-German Movement was unsuccessful because the leaders did not grasp the significance of that truth. They saw the goal clearly and their intentions were right; but they took the wrong road. Their action may be compared to that of an Alpine climber who never loses sight of the peak he wants to reach, who has set out with the greatest determination and energy, but pays no attention to the road beneath his feet. With his eye always fixed firmly on the goal he does not think over or notice the nature of the ascent and finally he fails.

The manner in which the great rival of the Pan-German Party set out to attain its goal was quite different. The way it took was well and shrewdly chosen; but it did not have a clear vision of the goal. In almost all the questions where the Pan-German Movement failed, the policy of the Christian-Socialist Party was correct and systematic.

They assessed the importance of the masses correctly, and thus they gained the support of large numbers of the popular masses by emphasizing the social character of the Movement from the very start. By directing their appeal especially to the lower middle class and the artisans, they gained adherents who were faithful, persevering and self-sacrificing.

The Christian-Socialist leaders took care to avoid all controversy with the institutions of religion and thus they secured the support of that mighty organization, the Catholic Church. Those leaders recognized the value of propaganda on a large scale and they were veritable virtuosos in working up the spiritual instincts of the broad masses of their adherents.

The failure of this Party to carry into effect the dream of saving Austria from dissolution must be attributed to two main defects in the means they employed and also the lack of a clear perception of the ends they wished to reach.

The anti-Semitism of the Christian-Socialists was based on religious instead of racial principles. The reason for this mistake gave rise to the second error also.

The founders of the Christian-Socialist Party were of the opinion that they could not base their position on the racial principle if they wished to save Austria, because they felt that a general disintegration of the State might quickly result from the adoption of such a policy. In the opinion of the Party chiefs the situation in Vienna demanded that all factors which tended to estrange the nationalities from one another should be carefully avoided and that all factors making for unity should be encouraged.

At that time Vienna was so honeycombed with foreign elements, especially the Czechs, that the greatest amount of tolerance was necessary if these elements were to be enlisted in the ranks of any party that was not anti-German on principle. If Austria was to be saved those elements were indispensable. And so attempts were made to win the support of the small traders, a great number of whom were Czechs, by combating the liberalism of the Manchester School; and they believed that by adopting this attitude they had found a slogan against Jewry which, because of its religious implications, would unite all the different nationalities which made up the population of the old Austria.

It was obvious, however, that this kind of anti-Semitism did not upset the Jews very much, simply because it had a purely religious foundation. If the worst came to the worst a few drops of baptismal water would settle the matter, hereupon the Jew could still carry on his business safely and at the same time retain his Jewish nationality.

On such superficial grounds it was impossible to deal with the whole problem in an earnest and rational way. The consequence was that many people could not understand this kind of anti-Semitism and therefore refused to take part in it.

The attractive force of the idea was thus restricted exclusively to narrow-minded circles, because the leaders failed to go beyond the mere emotional appeal and did not ground their position on a truly rational basis. The intellectuals were opposed to such a policy on principle. It looked more and more as if the whole movement was a new attempt to proselytize the Jews, or, on the other hand, as if it were merely organized from the wish to compete with other contemporary movements.

Thus the struggle lost all traces of having been organized for a spiritual and sublime mission. Indeed, it seemed to some people—and these were by no means worthless elements—to be immoral and reprehensible. The movement failed to awaken a belief that here there was a problem of vital importance for the whole of humanity and on the solution of which the destiny of the whole Gentile world depended.

Through this shilly-shally way of dealing with the problem the anti-Semitism of the Christian-Socialists turned out to be quite ineffective.

It was anti-Semitic only in outward appearance. And this was worse than if it had made no pretences at all to anti-Semitism; for the pretence gave rise to a false sense of security among people who believed that the enemy had been taken by the ears; but, as a matter of fact, the people themselves were being led by the nose.

The Jew readily adjusted himself to this form of anti-Semitism and found its continuance more profitable to him than its abolition would be.

This whole movement led to great sacrifices being made for the sake of that State which was composed of many heterogeneous nationalities; but much greater sacrifices had to be made by the trustees of the German element.

One did not dare to be 'nationalist', even in Vienna, lest the ground should fall away from under one's feet. It was hoped that the Habsburg State might be saved by a silent evasion of the nationalist question; but this policy led that State to ruin. The same policy also led to the collapse of Christian Socialism, for thus the Movement was deprived of the only source of energy from which a political party can draw the necessary driving force.

During those years I carefully followed the two movements and observed how they developed, one because my heart was with it and the other because of my admiration for that remarkable man who then appeared to me as a bitter symbol of the whole German population in Austria.

When the imposing funeral CORTÈGE of the dead Burgomaster wound its way from the City Hall towards the Ring Strasse I stood among the hundreds of thousands who watched the solemn procession pass by. As I stood there I felt deeply moved, and my instinct clearly told me that the work of this man was all in vain, because a sinister Fate was inexorably leading this State to its downfall. If Dr. Karl Lueger had lived in Germany he would have been ranked among the great leaders of our people. It was a misfortune for his work and for himseif that he had to live in this impossible State.

When he died the fire had already been enkindled in the Balkans and was spreading month by month. Fate had been merciful in sparing him the sight of what, even to the last, he had hoped to prevent.

I endeavoured to analyse the cause which rendered one of those movements futile and wrecked the progress of the other. The result of this investigation was the profound conviction that, apart from the inherent impossibility of consolidating the position of the State in the old Austria, the two parties made the following fatal mistake: The Pan-German Party was perfectly right in its fundamental ideas regarding the aim of the Movement, which was to bring about a German restoration, but it was unfortunate in its choice of means. It was nationalist, but unfortunately it paid too little heed to the social problem, and thus it failed to gain the support of the masses. Its anti-Jewish policy, however, was grounded on a correct perception of the significance of the racial problem and not on religious principles. But it was mistaken in its assessment of facts and adopted the wrong tactics when it made war against one of the religious denominations.

The Christian-Socialist Movement had only a vague concept of a German revival as part of its object, but it was intelligent and fortunate in the choice of means to carry out its policy as a Party. The Christian-Socialists grasped the significance of the social question; but they adopted the wrong principles in their struggle against Jewry, and they utterly failed to appreciate the value of the national idea as a source of political energy.

If the Christian-Socialist Party, together with its shrewd judgment in regard to the worth of the popular masses, had only judged rightly also on the importance of the racial problem—which was properly grasped by the Pan-German Movement—and if this party had been really nationalist; or if the Pan-German leaders, on the other hand, in addition to their correct judgment of the Jewish problem and of the national idea, had adopted the practical wisdom of the Christian-Socialist Party, and particularly their attitude towards Socialism—then a movement would have developed which, in my opinion, might at that time have successfully altered the course of German destiny. If things did not turn out thus, the fault lay for the most part in the inherent nature of the Austrian State.

I did not find my own convictions upheld by any party then in existence, and so I could not bring myself to enlist as a member in any of the existing organizations or even lend a hand in their struggle. Even at that time all those organizations seemed to me to be already jaded in their energies and were therefore incapable of bringing about a national revival of the German people in a really profound way, not merely outwardly.

My inner aversion to the Habsburg State was increasing daily. The more I paid special attention to questions of foreign policy, the more the conviction grew upon me that this phantom State would surely bring misfortune on the Germans. I realized more and more that the destiny of the German nation could not be decisively influenced from here but only in the German Empire itself. And this was true not only in regard to general political questions but also—and in no less a degree—in regard to the whole sphere of cultural life.

Here, also, in all matters affecting the national culture and art, the Austrian State showed all the signs of senile decrepitude, or at least it was ceasing to be of any consequence to the German nation, as far as these matters were concerned. This was especially true of its architecture. Modern architecture could not produce any great results in Austria because, since the building of the Ring Strasse—at least in Vienna—architectural activities had become insignificant when compared with the progressive plans which were being thought out in Germany.

And so I came more and more to lead what may be called a twofold existence. Reason and reality forced me to continue my harsh apprenticeship in Austria, though I must now say that this apprenticeship turned out fortunate in the end. But my heart was elsewhere.

A feeling of discontent grew upon me and made me depressed the more I came to realize the inside hollowness of this State and the impossibility of saving it from collapse. At the same time I felt perfectly certain that it would bring all kinds of misfortune to the German people.

I was convinced that the Habsburg State would balk and hinder every German who might show signs of real greatness, while at the same time it would aid and abet every non-German activity.

This conglomerate spectacle of heterogeneous races which the capital of the Dual Monarchy presented, this motley of Czechs, Poles, Hungarians, Ruthenians, Serbs and Croats, etc., and always that bacillus which is the solvent of human society, the Jew, here and there and everywhere—the whole spectacle was repugnant to me. The gigantic city seemed to be the incarnation of mongrel depravity.

The German language, which I had spoken from the time of my boyhood, was the vernacular idiom of Lower Bavaria. I never forgot that particular style of speech, and I could never learn the Viennese dialect. The longer I lived in that city the stronger became my hatred for the promiscuous swarm of foreign peoples which had begun to batten on that old nursery ground of German culture. The idea that this State could maintain its further existence for any considerable time was quite absurd.

Austria was then like a piece of ancient mosaic in which the cohesive cement had dried up and become old and friable. As long as such a work of art remains untouched it may hold together and continue to exist; but the moment some blow is struck on it then it breaks up into thousands of fragments. Therefore it was now only a question of when the blow would come.

Because my heart was always with the German Empire and not with the Austrian Monarchy, the hour of Austria's dissolution as a State appeared to me only as the first step towards the emancipation of the German nation.

All these considerations intensified my yearning to depart for that country for which my heart had been secretly longing since the days of my youth.

I hoped that one day I might be able to make my mark as an architect and that I could devote my talents to the service of my country on a large or small scale, according to the will of Fate.

A final reason was that I longed to be among those who lived and worked in that land from which the movement should be launched, the object of which would be the fulfilment of what my heart had always longed for, namely, the union of the country in which I was born with our common fatherland, the German Empire.

There are many who may not understand how such a yearning can be so strong; but I appeal especially to two groups of people. The first includes all those who are still denied the happiness I have spoken of, and the second embraces those who once enjoyed that happiness but had it torn from them by a harsh fate. I turn to all those who have been torn from their motherland and who have to struggle for the preservation of their most sacred patrimony, their native language, persecuted and harried because of their loyalty and love for the homeland, yearning sadly for the hour when they will be allowed to return to the bosom of their father's household. To these I address my words, and I know that they will understand.

Only he who has experienced in his own inner life what it means to be German and yet to be denied the right of belonging to his fatherland can appreciate the profound nostalgia which that enforced exile causes. It is a perpetual heartache, and there is no place for joy and contentment until the doors of paternal home are thrown open and all those through whose veins kindred blood is flowing will find peace and rest in their common REICH.

Vienna was a hard school for me; but it taught me the most profound lessons of my life. I was scarcely more than a boy when I came to live there, and when I left it I had grown to be a man of a grave and pensive nature. In Vienna I acquired the foundations of a WELTANSCHAUUNG in general and developed a faculty for analysing political questions in particular. That WELTANSCHAUUNG and the political ideas then formed have never been abandoned, though they were expanded later on in some directions. It is only now that I can fully appreciate how valuable those years of apprenticeship were for me.

That is why I have given a detailed account of this period. There, in Vienna, stark reality taught me the truths that now form the fundamental principles of the Party which within the course of five years has grown from modest beginnings to a great mass movement. I do not know what my attitude towards Jewry, Social-Democracy, or rather Marxism in general, to the social problem, etc., would be to-day if I had not acquired a stock of personal beliefs at such an early age, by dint of hard study and under the duress of Fate.

For, although the misfortunes of the Fatherland may have stimulated thousands and thousands to ponder over the inner causes of the collapse, that could not lead to such a thorough knowledge and deep insight as a man may develop who has fought a hard struggle for many years so that he might be master of his own fate.

CHAPTER IV: Munich

At last I came to Munich, in the spring of 1912. The city itself was as familiar to me as if I had lived for years within its walls. This was because my studies in architecture had been constantly turning my attention to the metropolis of German art. One must know Munich if one would know Germany, and it is impossible to acquire a knowledge of German art without seeing Munich.

All things considered, this pre-war sojourn was by far the happiest and most contented time of my life. My earnings were very slender; but after all I did not live for the sake of painting. I painted in order to get the bare necessities of existence while I continued my studies. I was firmly convinced that I should finally succeed in reaching the goal I had marked out for myself. And this conviction alone was strong enough to enable me to bear the petty hardships of everyday life without worrying very much about them.

Moreover, almost from the very first moment of my sojourn there I came to love that city more than any other place known to me. A German city! I said to myself. How different to Vienna. It was with a feeling of disgust that my imagination reverted to that Babylon of races. Another pleasant feature here was the way the people spoke German, which was much nearer my own way of speaking than the Viennese idiom. The Munich idiom recalled the days of my youth, especially when I spoke with those who had come to Munich from Lower Bavaria. There were a thousand or more things which I inwardly loved or which I came to love during the course of my stay. But what attracted me most was the marvellous wedlock of native folk-energy with the fine artistic spirit of the city, that unique harmony from the Hofbräuhaus to the Odeon, from the October Festival to the PINAKOTHEK, etc. The reason why my heart's strings are entwined around this city as around no other spot in this world is probably because Munich is and will remain inseparably connected with the development of my own career; and the fact that from the beginning of my visit I felt inwardly happy and contented is to be attributed to the charm of the marvellous Wittelsbach Capital, which has attracted probably everybody who is blessed with a feeling for beauty instead of commercial instincts.

Apart from my professional work, I was most interested in the study of current political events, particularly those which were connected with foreign relations. I approached these by way of the German policy of alliances which, ever since my Austrian days, I had considered to be an utterly mistaken one. But in Vienna I had not yet seen quite clearly how far the German Empire had gone in the process of' self-delusion. In Vienna I was inclined to assume, or probably I persuaded myself to do so in order to excuse the

German mistake, that possibly the authorities in Berlin knew how weak and unreliable their ally would prove to be when brought face to face with realities, but that, for more or less mysterious reasons, they refrained from allowing their opinions on this point to be known in public. Their idea was that they should support the policy of alliances which Bismarck had initiated and the sudden discontinuance of which might be undesirable, if for no other reason than that it might arouse those foreign countries which were lying in wait for their chance or might alarm the Philistines at home.

But my contact with the people soon taught me, to my horror, that my assumptions were wrong. I was amazed to find everywhere, even in circles otherwise well informed, that nobody had the slightest intimation of the real character of the Habsburg Monarchy. Among the common people in particular there was a prevalent illusion that the Austrian ally was a Power which would have to be seriously reckoned with and would rally its man-power in the hour of need. The mass of the people continued to look upon the Dual Monarchy as a 'German State' and believed that it could be relied upon. They assumed that its strength could be measured by the millions of its subjects, as was the case in Germany. First of all, they did not realize that Austria had ceased to be a German State and, secondly, that the conditions prevailing within the Austrian Empire were steadily pushing it headlong to the brink of disaster.

At that time I knew the condition of affairs in the Austrian State better than the professional diplomats. Blindfolded, as nearly always, these diplomats stumbled along on their way to disaster. The opinions prevailing among the bulk of the people reflected only what had been drummed into them from official quarters above. And these higher authorities grovelled before the 'Ally', as the people of old bowed down before the Golden Calf. They probably thought that by being polite and amiable they might balance the lack of honesty on the other side. Thus they took every declaration at its full face value.

Even while in Vienna I used to be annoyed again and again by the discrepancy between the speeches of the official statesmen and the contents of the Viennese Press. And yet Vienna was still a German city, at least as far as appearances went. But one encountered an utterly different state of things on leaving Vienna, or rather German-Austria, and coming into the Slav provinces. It needed only a glance at the Prague newspapers in order to see how the whole exalted hocus-pocus of the Triple Alliance was judged from there. In Prague there was nothing but gibes and sneers for that masterpiece of statesmanship. Even in the piping times of peace, when the two emperors kissed each other on the brow in token of friendship, those papers did not cloak their belief that the alliance would be liquidated the moment a first attempt was made to bring it down from the shimmering glory of a Nibelungen ideal to the plane of practical affairs.

Great indignation was aroused a few years later, when the alliances were put to the first practical test. Italy not only withdrew from the Triple Alliance, leaving the other two members to march by themselves. but she even joined their enemies. That anybody should believe even for a moment in the possibility of such a miracle as that of Italy fighting on the same side as Austria would be simply incredible to anyone who did not suffer from the blindness of official diplomacy. And that was just how people felt in Austria also.

In Austria only the Habsburgs and the German-Austrians supported the alliance. The Habsburgs did so from shrewd calculation of their own interests and from necessity. The Germans did it out of good faith and political ignorance. They acted in good faith inasmuch as they believed that by establishing the Triple Alliance they were doing a great service to the German Empire and were thus helping to strengthen it and consolidate its defence. They showed their political ignorance, however, in holding such ideas, because, instead of helping the German Empire they really chained it to a moribund State which might bring its associate into the grave with itself; and, above all, by championing this alliance they fell more and more a prey to the Habsburg policy of de-Germanization. For the alliance gave the Habsburgs good grounds for believing that the German Empire would not interfere in their domestic affairs and thus they were in a position to carry into effect, with more ease and less risk, their domestic policy of gradually eliminating the German element. Not only could the 'objectiveness' of the German Government be counted upon, and thus there need be no fear of protest from that quarter, but one could always remind the German-Austrians of the alliance and thus silence them in case they should ever object to the reprehensible means that were being employed to establish a Slav hegemony in the Dual Monarchy.

What could the German-Austrians do, when the people of the German Empire itself had openly proclaimed their trust and confidence in the Habsburg régime? Should they resist, and thus be branded openly before their kinsfolk in the REICH as traitors to their own national interests? They, who for so many decades had sacrificed so much for the sake of their German tradition!

Once the influence of the Germans in Austria had been wiped out, what then would be the value of the alliance? If the Triple Alliance were to be advantageous to Germany, was it not a necessary condition that the predominance of the German element in Austria should be maintained? Or did anyone really believe that Germany could continue to be the ally of a Habsburg Empire under the hegemony of the Slavs?

The official attitude of German diplomacy, as well as that of the general public towards internal problems affecting the Austrian nationalities was not merely stupid, it was insane. On the alliance, as on a solid foundation, they grounded the security and future existence of a nation of seventy millions, while at the same time they allowed their partner to continue his policy of undermining the sole foundation of that alliance methodically and resolutely, from year to year. A day must come when nothing but a formal contract with Viennese diplomats would be left. The alliance itself, as an effective support, would be lost to Germany.

As far as concerned Italy, such had been the case from the outset. If people in Germany had studied history and the psychology of nations a little more carefully not one of them could have believed for a single hour that the Quirinal and the Viennese Hofburg could ever stand shoulder to shoulder on a common battle front. Italy would have exploded like a volcano if any Italian government had dared to send a single Italian soldier to fight for the Habsburg State. So fanatically hated was this State that the Italians could stand in no other relation to it on a battle front except as enemies. More than once in Vienna I have witnessed explosions of the contempt and profound hatred which 'allied' the Italian to the Austrian State. The crimes which the House of Habsburg committed against Italian freedom and independence during several centuries were too grave to be forgiven, even with the best of goodwill. But this goodwill did not exist, either among the rank and file of the population or in the government. Therefore for Italy there were only two ways of co-existing with Austria—alliance or war. By choosing the first it was possible to prepare leisurely for the second. Especially since relations between Russia and Austria tended more and more towards the arbitrament of war, the German policy of alliances was as senseless as it was dangerous. Here was a classical instance which demonstrated the lack of any broad or logical lines of thought.

But what was the reason for forming the alliance at all? It could not have been other than the wish to secure the future of the REICH better than if it were to depend exclusively on its own resources. But the future of the REICH could not have meant anything else than the problem of securing the means of existence for the German people.

The only questions therefore were the following: What form shall the life of the nation assume in the near future—that is to say within such a period as we can forecast? And by what means can the necessary foundation and security be guaranteed for this development within the framework of the general distribution of power among the European nations? A clear analysis of the principles on which the foreign policy of German statecraft were to be based should have led to the following conclusions:

The annual increase of population in Germany amounts to almost 900,000 souls. The difficulties of providing for this army of new citizens must grow from year to year and must finally lead to a catastrophe, unless ways and means are found which will forestall the danger of misery and hunger. There were four ways of providing against this terrible calamity:

(1) It was possible to adopt the French example and artificially restrict the number of births, thus avoiding an excess of population. Under certain circumstances, in periods of distress or under bad climatic condition, or if the soil yields too poor a return, Nature herself tends to check the increase of population in some countries and among some races, but by a method which is quite as ruthless as it is wise. It does not impede the procreative faculty as such; but it does impede the further existence of the offspring by submitting it to such tests and privations that everything which is less strong or less healthy is forced to retreat into the bosom of tile unknown. Whatever survives these hardships of existence has been tested and tried a thousandfold, hardened and renders fit to continue the process of procreation; so that the same thorough selection will begin all over again. By thus dealing brutally with the individual and recalling him the very moment he shows that he is not fitted for the trials of life, Nature preserves the strength of the race and the species and raises it to the highest degree of efficiency.

The decrease in numbers therefore implies an increase of strength, as far as the individual is concerned, and this finally means the invigoration of the species.

But the case is different when man himself starts the process of numerical restriction. Man is not carved from Nature's wood. He is made of 'human' material. He knows more than the ruthless Queen of Wisdom. He does not impede the preservation of the individual but prevents procreation itself. To the individual, who always sees only himself and not the race, this line of action seems more humane and just than the opposite way. But, unfortunately, the consequences are also the opposite.

By leaving the process of procreation unchecked and by submitting the individual to the hardest preparatory tests in life, Nature selects the best from an abundance of single elements and stamps them as fit to live and carry on the conservation of the species. But man restricts the procreative faculty and strives obstinately to keep alive at any cost whatever has once been born. This correction of the Divine Will seems to him to be wise and humane, and he rejoices at having trumped Nature's card in one game at least and thus proved that she is not entirely reliable. The dear little ape of an all-mighty father is delighted to see and hear that he has succeeded in effecting a numerical restriction; but he would be very displeased if told that this, his system, brings about a degeneration in personal quality.

For as soon as the procreative faculty is thwarted and the number of births diminished, the natural struggle for existence which allows only healthy and strong individuals to survive is replaced by a sheer craze to 'save' feeble and even diseased creatures at any cost. And thus the seeds are sown for a human progeny which will become more and more miserable from one generation to another, as long as Nature's will is scorned.

But if that policy be carried out the final results must be that such a nation will eventually terminate its own existence on this earth; for though man may defy the eternal laws of procreation during a certain period, vengeance will follow sooner or later. A stronger race will oust that which has grown weak; for the vital urge, in its ultimate form, will burst asunder all the absurd chains of this so-called humane consideration for the individual and will replace it with the humanity of Nature, which wipes out what is weak in order to give place to the strong.

Any policy which aims at securing the existence of a nation by restricting the birth-rate robs that nation of its future.

(2) A second solution is that of internal colonization. This is a proposal which is frequently made in our own time and one hears it lauded a good deal. It is a suggestion that is well-meant but it is misunderstood by most people, so that it is the source of more mischief than can be imagined.

It is certainly true that the productivity of the soil can be increased within certain limits; but only within defined limits and not indefinitely. By increasing the productive powers of the soil it will be possible to balance the effect of a surplus birth-rate in Germany for a certain period of time, without running any danger of hunger. But we have to face the fact that the general standard of living is rising more quickly than even the birth rate. The requirements of food and clothing are becoming greater from year to year and are out of proportion to those of our ancestors of, let us say, a hundred years ago. It would, therefore, be a mistaken view that every increase in the productive powers of the soil will supply the requisite conditions for an increase in the population. No. That is true up to a certain point only, for at least a portion of the increased produce of the soil will be consumed by the margin of increased demands caused by the steady rise in the standard of living. But even if these demands were to be curtailed to the narrowest limits possible and if at the same time we were to use all our available energies in the intenser cultivation, we should here reach a definite limit which is conditioned by the inherent nature of the soil itself. No matter how industriously we may labour we cannot increase agricultural production beyond this limit. Therefore, though we may postpone the evil hour of distress for a certain time, it will arrive at last. The first phenomenon will be the recurrence of famine periods from time to time, after bad harvests, etc. The intervals between these famines will become shorter and shorter the more the population increases; and, finally, the famine times will disappear only in those rare years of plenty when the granaries are full. And a time will ultimately come when even in those years of plenty there will not be enough to go round; so that hunger will dog the footsteps of the nation.

Nature must now step in once more and select those who are to survive, or else man will help himself by artificially preventing his own increase, with all the fatal consequences for the race and the species which have been already mentioned.

It may be objected here that, in one form or another, this future is in store for all mankind and that the individual nation or race cannot escape the general fate.

At first glance, that objection seems logical enough; but we have to take the following into account:

The day will certainly come when the whole of mankind will be forced to check the augmentation of the human species, because there will be no further possibility of adjusting the productivity of the soil to the perpetual increase in the population. Nature must then be allowed to use her own methods or man may possibly take the task of regulation into his own hands and establish the necessary equilibrium by the application of better means than we have at our disposal to-day. But then it will be a problem for mankind as a whole, whereas now only those races have to suffer from want which no longer have the strength and daring to acquire sufficient soil to fulfil their needs. For, as things stand to-day, vast spaces still lie uncultivated all over the surface of the globe. Those spaces are only waiting for the ploughshare. And it is quite certain that Nature did not set those territories apart as the exclusive pastures of any one nation or race to be held unutilized in reserve for the future. Such land awaits the people who have the strength to acquire it and the diligence to cultivate it.

Nature knows no political frontiers. She begins by establishing life on this globe and then watches the free play of forces. Those who show the greatest courage and industry are the children nearest to her heart and they will be granted the sovereign right of existence.

If a nation confines itself to 'internal colonization' while other races are perpetually increasing their territorial annexations all over the globe, that nation will be forced to restrict the numerical growth of its population at a time when the other nations are increasing theirs.

This situation must eventually arrive. It will arrive soon if the territory which the nation has at its disposal be small. Now it is unfortunately true that only too often the best nations—or, to speak more exactly, the only really cultured nations, who at the same time are the chief bearers of human progress—have decided, in their blind pacifism, to refrain from the acquisition of new territory and to be content with 'internal colonization.' But at the same time nations of inferior quality succeed in getting hold of large spaces for colonization all over the globe. The state of affairs which must result from this contrast is the following:

Races which are culturally superior but less ruthless would be forced to restrict their increase, because of insufficient territory to support the population, while less civilized races could increase indefinitely, owing to the vast territories at their disposal. In other words: should that state of affairs continue, then the world will one day be possessed by that portion of mankind which is culturally inferior but more active and energetic.

A time will come, even though in the distant future, when there can be only two alternatives: Either the world will be ruled according to our modern concept of democracy, and then every decision will be in favour of the numerically stronger races; or the world will be governed by the law of natural distribution of power, and then those nations will be victorious who are of more brutal will and are not the nations who have practised self-denial.

Nobody can doubt that this world will one day be the scene of dreadful struggles for existence on the part of mankind. In the end the instinct of self-preservation alone will triumph. Before its consuming fire this so-called humanitarianism, which connotes only a mixture of fatuous timidity and self-conceit, will melt away as under the March sunshine.

Man has become great through perpetual struggle. In perpetual peace his greatness must decline.

For us Germans, the slogan of 'internal colonization' is fatal, because it encourages the belief that we have discovered a means which is in accordance with our innate pacifism and which will enable us to work for our livelihood in a half slumbering existence. Such a teaching, once it were taken seriously by our people, would mean the end of all effort to acquire for ourselves that place in the world which we deserve. If. the average German were once convinced that by this measure he has the chance of ensuring his livelihood and guaranteeing his future, any attempt to take an active and profitable part in sustaining the vital demands of his country would be out of the question. Should the nation agree to such an attitude then any really useful foreign policy might be looked upon as dead and buried, together with all hope for the future of the German people.

Once we know what the consequences of this 'internal colonization' theory would be we can no longer consider as a mere accident the fact that among those who inculcate this quite pernicious mentality among our people the Jew is always in the first line. He knows his softies only too well not to know that they are ready to be the grateful victims of every swindle which promises them a gold-block in the shape of a discovery that will enable them to outwit Nature and thus render superfluous the hard and inexorable struggle for existence; so that finally they may become lords of the planet partly by sheer DOLCE FAR NIENTE and partly by working when a pleasing opportunity arises.

It cannot be too strongly emphasised that any German 'internal colonization' must first of all be considered as suited only for the relief of social grievances. To carry out a system of internal colonization, the most important preliminary measure would be to free the soil from the grip of the speculator and assure that freedom. But such a system could never suffice to assure the future of the nation without the acquisition of new territory.

If we adopt a different plan we shall soon reach a point beyond which the resources of our soil can no longer be exploited, and at the same time we shall reach a point beyond which our man-power cannot develop. In conclusion, the following must be said: The fact that only up to a limited extent can internal colonization be practised in a national territory which is of definitely small area and the restriction of the procreative faculty which follows as a result of such conditions—these two factors have a very unfavourable effect on the military and political standing of a nation.

The extent of the national territory is a determining factor in the external security of the nation. The larger the territory which a people has at its disposal the stronger are the national defences of that people. Military decisions are more quickly, more easily, more completely and more effectively gained against a people occupying a national territory which is restricted in area, than against States which have extensive territories. Moreover, the magnitude of a national territory is in itself a certain assurance that an outside Power will not hastily risk the adventure of an invasion; for in that case the struggle would have to be long and exhausting before victory could be hoped for. The risk being so great. there would have to be extraordinary reasons for such an aggressive adventure. Hence it is that the territorial magnitude of a State furnishes a basis whereon national liberty and independence can be maintained with relative ease; while, on the contrary, a State whose territory is small offers a natural temptation to the invader.

As a matter of fact, so-called national circles in the German REICH rejected those first two possibilities of establishing a balance between the constant numerical increase in the population and a national territory which could not expand proportionately. But the reasons given for that rejection were different from those which I have just expounded.

94

It was mainly on the basis of certain moral sentiments that restriction of the birth-rate was objected to. Proposals for internal colonization were rejected indignantly because it was suspected that such a policy might mean an attack on the big landowners, and that this attack might be the forerunner of a general assault against the principle of private property as a whole. The form in which the latter solution — internal colonization — was recommended justified the misgivings of the big landowners.

But the form in which the colonization proposal was rejected was not very clever, as regards the impression which such rejection might be calculated to make on the mass of the people, and anyhow it did not go to the root of the problem at all.

Only two further ways were left open in which work and bread could be secured for the increasing population.

(3) It was possible to think of acquiring new territory on which a certain portion of' the increasing population could be settled each year; or else

(4) Our industry and commerce had to be organized in such a manner as to secure an increase in the exports and thus be able to support our people by the increased purchasing power accruing from the profits made on foreign markets.

Therefore the problem was: A policy of territorial expansion or a colonial and commercial policy. Both policies were taken into consideration, examined, recommended and rejected, from various standpoints, with the result that the second alternative was finally adopted. The sounder alternative, however, was undoubtedly the first.

The principle of acquiring new territory, on which the surplus population could be settled, has many advantages to recommend it, especially if we take the future as well as the present into account. In the first place, too much importance cannot be placed on the necessity for adopting a policy which will make it possible to maintain a healthy peasant class as the basis of the national community. Many of our present evils have their origin exclusively in the disproportion between the urban and rural portions of the population. A solid stock of small and medium farmers has at all times been the best protection which a nation could have against the social diseases that are prevalent to-day. Moreover, that is the only solution which guarantees the daily bread of a nation within the framework of its domestic national economy.

With this condition once guaranteed, industry and commerce would retire from the unhealthy position of foremost importance which they hold to-day and would take their due place within the general scheme of national economy, adjusting the balance between demand and supply. Thus industry and commerce would no longer constitute the basis of the national subsistence, but would be auxiliary institutions. By fulfilling their proper function, which is to adjust the balance between national production and national consumption, they render the national subsistence more or less independent of foreign countries and thus assure the freedom and independence of the nation, especially at critical junctures in its history. Such a territorial policy, however, cannot find its fulfilment in the

Cameroons but almost exclusively here in Europe. One must calmly and squarely face the truth that it certainly cannot be part of the dispensation of Divine Providence to give a fifty times larger share of the soil of this world to one nation than to another. In considering this state of affairs to-day, one must not allow existing political frontiers to distract attention from what ought to exist on principles of strict justice. If this earth has sufficient room for all, then we ought to have that share of the soil which is absolutely necessary for our existence.

Of course people will not voluntarily make that accommodation. At this point the right of self-preservation comes into effect. And when attempts to settle the difficulty in an amicable way are rejected the clenched hand must take by force that which was refused to the open hand of friendship. If in the past our ancestors had based their political decisions on similar pacifist nonsense as our present generation does, we should not possess more than one-third of the national territory that we possess to-day and probably there would be no German nation to worry about its future in Europe. No. We owe the two Eastern Marks[8] of the Empire to the natural determination of our forefathers in their struggle for existence, and thus it is to the same determined policy that we owe the inner strength which is based on the extent of our political and racial territories and which alone has made it possible for us to exist up to now.

And there is still another reason why that solution would have been the correct one: Many contemporary European States are like pyramids standing on their apexes. The European territory which these States possess is ridiculously small when compared with the enormous overhead weight of their colonies, foreign trade, etc. It may be said that they have the apex in Europe and the base of the pyramid all over the world; quite different from the United States of America, which has its base on the American Continent and is in contact with the rest of the world only through its apex. Out of that situation arises the incomparable inner strength of the U.S.A. and the contrary situation is responsible for the weakness of most of the colonial European Powers.

England cannot be suggested as an argument against this assertion, though in glancing casually over the map of the British Empire one is inclined easily to overlook the existence of a whole Anglo-Saxon world. England's position cannot be compared with that of any other State in Europe, since it forms a vast community of language and culture together with the U.S.A.

Therefore the only possibility which Germany had of carrying a sound territorial policy into effect was that of acquiring new territory in Europe itself. Colonies cannot serve this purpose as long as they are not suited for settlement by Europeans on a large scale. In the nineteenth century it was no longer possible to acquire such colonies by peaceful means. Therefore any attempt at such a colonial expansion would have meant an enormous military struggle. Consequently it would have been more practical to undertake that military struggle for new territory in Europe rather than to wage war for the acquisition of possessions abroad.

Such a decision naturally demanded that the nation's undivided energies should be devoted to it. A policy of that kind which requires for its fulfilment every ounce of available energy on the part of everybody concerned, cannot be carried into effect by half-measures or in a hesitating manner. The political leadership of the German Empire should then have been directed exclusively to this goal. No political step should have been taken in response to other considerations than this task and the means of accomplishing it. Germany should have been alive to the fact that such a goal could have been reached only by war, and the prospect of war should have been faced with calm and collected determination.

The whole system of alliances should have been envisaged and valued from that standpoint. If new territory were to be acquired in Europe it must have been mainly at Russia's cost, and once again the new German Empire should have set out on its march along the same road as was formerly trodden by the Teutonic Knights, this time to acquire soil for the German plough by means of the German sword and thus provide the nation with its daily bread.

For such a policy, however, there was only one possible ally in Europe. That was England.

Only by alliance with England was it possible to safeguard the rear of the new German crusade. The justification for undertaking such an expedition was stronger than the justification which our forefathers had for setting out on theirs. Not one of our pacifists refuses to eat the bread made from the grain grown in the East; and yet the first plough here was that called the 'Sword'.

No sacrifice should have been considered too great if it was a necessary means of gaining England's friendship. Colonial and naval ambitions should have been abandoned and attempts should not have been made to compete against British industries.

Only a clear and definite policy could lead to such an achievement. Such a policy would have demanded a renunciation of the endeavour to conquer the world's markets, also a renunciation of colonial intentions and naval power. All the means of power at the disposal of the State should have been concentrated in the military forces on land. This policy would have involved a period of temporary self-denial, for the sake of a great and powerful future.

There was a time when England might have entered into negotiations with us, on the grounds of that proposal. For England would have well understood that the problems arising from the steady increase in population were forcing Germany to look for a solution either in Europe with the help of England or, without England, in some other part of the world.

This outlook was probably the chief reason why London tried to draw nearer to Germany about the turn of the century. For the first time in Germany an attitude was then manifested which afterwards displayed itself in a most tragic way. People then gave expression to an unpleasant feeling that we might thus find ourselves obliged to pull England's chestnuts out of the fire. As if an alliance could be based on anything else than mutual give-and-take! And England would have become a party to such a mutual bargain. British diplomats were still wise enough to know that an equivalent must be forthcoming as a consideration for any services rendered.

Let us suppose that in 1904 our German foreign policy was managed astutely enough to enable us to take the part which Japan played. It is not easy to measure the greatness of the results that might have accrued to Germany from such a policy.

There would have been no world war. The blood which would have been shed in 1904 would not have been a tenth of that shed from 1914 to 1918. And what a position Germany would hold in the world to-day? In any case the alliance with Austria was then an absurdity. For this mummy of a State did not attach itself to Germany for the purpose of carrying through a war, but rather to maintain a perpetual state of peace which was meant to be exploited for the purpose of slowly but persistently exterminating the German element in the Dual Monarchy.

Another reason for the impossible character of this alliance was that nobody could expect such a State to take an active part in defending German national interests, seeing that it did not have sufficient strength and determination to put an end to the policy of de-Germanization within its own frontiers. If Germany herself was not moved by a sufficiently powerful national sentiment and was not sufficiently ruthless to take away from that absurd Habsburg State the right to decide the destinies of ten million inhabitants who were of the same nationality as the Germans themselves, surely it was out of the question to expect the Habsburg State to be a collaborating party in any great and courageous German undertaking. The attitude of the old REICH towards the Austrian question might have been taken as a test of its stamina for the struggle where the destinies of the whole nation were at stake.

In any case, the policy of oppression against the German population in Austria should not have been allowed to be carried on and to grow stronger from year to year; for the value of Austria as an ally could be assured only by upholding the German element there. But that course was not followed.

Nothing was dreaded so much as the possibility of an armed conflict; but finally, and at a most unfavourable moment, the conflict had to be faced and accepted. They thought to cut loose from the cords of destiny, but destiny held them fast.

They dreamt of maintaining a world peace and woke up to find themselves in a world war. And that dream of peace was a most significant reason why the above-mentioned third alternative for the future development of Germany was not even taken into consideration. The fact was recognized that new territory could be gained only in the East; but this meant that there would be fighting ahead, whereas they wanted peace at any cost. The slogan of German foreign policy at one time used to be: The use of all possible means for the maintenance of the German nation. Now it was changed to: Maintenance of world peace by all possible means. We know what the result was. I shall resume the discussion of this point in detail later on.

There remained still another alternative, which we may call the fourth. This was: Industry and world trade, naval power and colonies. Such a development might certainly have been attained more easily and more rapidly. To colonize a territory is a slow process, often extending over centuries. Yet this fact is the source of its inner strength, for it is not through a sudden burst of enthusiasm that it can be put into effect, but rather through a gradual and enduring process of growth quite different from industrial progress, which can be urged on by advertisement within a few years. The result thus achieved, however, is not of lasting quality but something frail, like a soap-bubble. It is much easier to build quickly than to carry through the tough task of settling a territory with farmers and establishing farmsteads. But the former is more quickly destroyed than the latter. In adopting such a course Germany must have known that to follow it out would necessarily mean war sooner or later. Only children could believe that sweet and unctuous expressions of goodness and persistent avowals of peaceful intentions could get them their bananas through this 'friendly competition between the nations', with the prospect of never having to fight for them.

No. Once we had taken this road, England was bound to be our enemy at some time or other to come. Of course it fitted in nicely with our innocent assumptions, but still it was absurd to grow indignant at the fact that a day came when the English took the liberty of opposing our peaceful penetration with the brutality of violent egoists.

Naturally, we on our side would never have done such a thing. If a European territorial policy against Russia could have been put into practice only in case we had England as our ally, on the other hand a colonial and world-trade policy could have been carried into effect only against English interests and with the support of Russia. But then this policy should have been adopted in full consciousness of all the consequences it involved and, above all things, Austria should have been discarded as quickly as possible.

At the turn of the century the alliance with Austria had become a veritable absurdity from all points of view. But nobody thought of forming an alliance with Russia against

England, just as nobody thought of making England an ally against Russia; for in either case the final result would inevitably have meant war. And to avoid war was the very reason why a commercial and industrial policy was decided upon. It was believed that the peaceful conquest of the world by commercial means provided a method which would permanently supplant the policy of force. Occasionally, however, there were doubts about the efficiency of this principle, especially when some quite incomprehensible warnings came from England now and again. That was the reason why the fleet was built. It was not for the purpose of attacking or annihilating England but merely to defend the concept of world-peace, mentioned above, and also to protect the principle of conquering the world by 'peaceful' means. Therefore this fleet was kept within modest limits, not only as regards the number and tonnage of the vessels but also in regard to their armament, the idea being to furnish new proofs of peaceful intentions.

The chatter about the peaceful conquest of the world by commercial means was probably the most completely nonsensical stuff ever raised to the dignity of a guiding principle in the policy of a State, This nonsense became even more foolish when England was pointed out as a typical example to prove how the thing could be put into practice. Our doctrinal way of regarding history and our professorial ideas in that domain have done irreparable harm and offer a striking 'proof' of how people 'learn' history without understanding anything of it. As a matter of fact, England ought to have been looked upon as a convincing argument against the theory of the pacific conquest of the world by commercial means. No nation prepared the way for its commercial conquests more brutally than England did by means of the sword, and no other nation has defended such conquests more ruthlessly. Is it not a characteristic quality of British statecraft that it knows how to use political power in order to gain economic advantages and, inversely, to turn economic conquests into political power? What an astounding error it was to believe that England would not have the courage to give its own blood for the purposes of its own economic expansion! The fact that England did not possess a national army proved nothing; for it is not the actual military structure of the moment that matters but rather the will and determination to use whatever military strength is available. England has always had the armament which she needed. She always fought with those weapons which were necessary for success. She sent mercenary troops, to fight as long as mercenaries sufficed; but she never hesitated to draw heavily and deeply from the best blood of the whole nation when victory could be obtained only by such a sacrifice. And in every case the fighting spirit, dogged determination, and use of brutal means in conducting military operations have always remained the same.

But in Germany, through the medium of the schools, the Press and the comic papers, an idea of the Englishman was gradually formed which was bound eventually to lead to the worst kind of self-deception. This absurdity slowly but persistently spread into every quarter of German life. The result was an undervaluation for which we have had to pay a heavy penalty. The delusion was so profound that the Englishman was looked upon as a shrewd business man, but personally a coward even to an incredible degree. Unfortunately our lofty teachers of professorial history did not bring home to the minds of their pupils the truth that it is not possible to build up such a mighty organization as the British Empire by mere swindle and fraud. The few who called attention to that truth were either ignored or silenced. I can vividly recall to mind the astonished looks of my comrades when they found themselves personally face to face for the first time with the Tommies in Flanders. After a few days of fighting the consciousness slowly dawned on our soldiers that those Scotsmen were not like the ones we had seen described and caricatured in the comic papers and mentioned in the communiqués. It was then that I formed my first ideas of the efficiency of various forms of propaganda.

Such a falsification, however, served the purpose of those who had fabricated it. This caricature of the Englishman, though false, could be used to prove the possibility of conquering the world peacefully by commercial means. Where the Englishman succeeded we should also succeed. Our far greater honesty and our freedom from that specifically English 'perfidy' would be assets on our side. Thereby it was hoped that the sympathy of the smaller nations and the confidence of the greater nations could be gained more easily.

We did not realize that our honesty was an object of profound aversion for other people because we ourselves believed in it. The rest of the world looked on our behaviour as the manifestation of a shrewd deceitfulness; but when the revolution came, then they were amazed at the deeper insight it gave them into our mentality, sincere even beyond the limits of stupidity.

Once we understand the part played by that absurd notion of conquering the world by peaceful commercial means we can clearly understand how that other absurdity, the Triple Alliance, came to exist. With what State then could an alliance have been made? In alliance with Austria we could not acquire new territory by military means, even in Europe. And this very fact was the real reason for the inner weakness of the Triple Alliance. A Bismarck could permit himself such a makeshift for the necessities of the moment, but certainly not any of his bungling successors, and least of all when the foundations no longer existed on which Bismarck had formed the Triple Alliance. In Bismarck's time Austria could still be looked upon as a German State; but the gradual introduction of universal suffrage turned the country into a parliamentary Babel, in which the German voice was scarcely audible. From the viewpoint of racial policy, this alliance with Austria was simply disastrous. A new Slavic Great Power was allowed to grow up close to the frontiers of the German Empire. Later on this Power was bound to adopt towards Germany an attitude different from that of Russia, for example. The Alliance was thus bound to become more empty and more feeble, because the only supporters of it were losing their influence and were being systematically pushed out of the more important public offices.

About the year 1900 the Alliance with Austria had already entered the same phase as the Alliance between Austria and Italy. Here also only one alternative was possible: Either to take the side of the Habsburg Monarchy or to raise a protest against the oppression of the German element in Austria. But, generally speaking, when one takes such a course it is bound eventually to lead to open conflict.

From the psychological point of view also, the Triple decreases according as such an alliance limits its object to the defence of the STATUS QUO. But, on the other hand, an alliance will increase its cohesive strength the more the parties concerned in it may hope to use it as a means of reaching some practical goal of expansion. Here, as everywhere else, strength does not lie in defence but in attack.

This truth was recognized in various quarters but, unfortunately, not by the so-called elected representatives of the people. As early as 1912 Ludendorff, who was then Colonel and an Officer of the General Staff, pointed out these weak features of the Alliance in a memorandum which he then drew up. But of course the 'statesmen' did not attach any importance or value to that document. In general it would seem as if reason were a faculty that is active only in the case of ordinary mortals but that it is entirely absent when we come to deal with that branch of the species known as 'diplomats'.

It was lucky for Germany that the war of 1914 broke out with Austria as its direct cause, for thus the Habsburgs were compelled to participate. Had the origin of the War been otherwise, Germany would have been left to her own resources. The Habsburg State would never have been ready or willing to take part in a war for the origin of which Germany was responsible. What was the object of so much obloquy later in the case of Italy's decision would have taken place, only earlier, in the case of Austria. In other words, if Germany had been forced to go to war for some reason of its own, Austria would have remained 'neutral' in order to safeguard the State against a revolution which might begin immediately after the war had started. The Slav element would have preferred to smash up the Dual Monarchy in 1914 rather than permit it to come to the assistance of Germany. But at that time there were only a few who understood all the dangers and aggravations which resulted from the alliance with the Danubian Monarchy.

In the first place, Austria had too many enemies who were eagerly looking forward to obtain the heritage of that decrepit State, so that these people gradually developed a certain animosity against Germany, because Germany was an obstacle to their desires inasmuch as it kept the Dual Monarchy from falling to pieces, a consummation that was hoped for and yearned for on all sides. The conviction developed that Vienna could be reached only by passing through Berlin. In the second place, by adopting this policy Germany lost its best and most promising chances of other alliances. In place of these possibilities one now observed a growing tension in the relations with Russia and even with Italy. And this in spite of the fact that the general attitude in Rome was just as favourable to Germany as it was hostile to Austria, a hostility which lay dormant in the individual Italian and broke out violently on occasion.

Since a commercial and industrial policy had been adopted, no motive was left for waging war against Russia. Only the enemies of the two countries, Germany and Russia, could have an active interest in such a war under these circumstances. As a matter of fact, it was only the Jews and the Marxists who tried to stir up bad blood between the two States. In the third place, the Alliance constituted a permanent danger to German security; for any great Power that was hostile to Bismarck's Empire could mobilize a whole lot of other States in a war against Germany by promising them tempting spoils at the expense of the Austrian ally.

It was possible to arouse the whole of Eastern Europe against Austria, especially Russia, and Italy also. The world coalition which had developed under the leadership of King Edward could never have become a reality if Germany's ally, Austria, had not offered such an alluring prospect of booty. It was this fact alone which made it possible to combine so many heterogeneous States with divergent interests into one common phalanx of attack. Every member could hope to enrich himself at the expense of Austria if he joined in the general attack against Germany. The fact that Turkey was also a tacit party to the unfortunate alliance with Austria augmented Germany's peril to an extraordinary degree.

Jewish international finance needed this bait of the Austrian heritage in order to carry out its plans of ruining Germany; for Germany had not yet surrendered to the general control which the international captains of finance and trade exercised over the other States. Thus it was possible to consolidate that coalition and make it strong enough and brave enough, through the sheer weight of numbers, to join in bodily conflict with the 'horned' Siegfried. [9]

The alliance with the Habsburg Monarchy, which I loathed while still in Austria, was the subject of grave concern on my part and caused me to meditate on it so persistently that finally I came to the conclusions which I have mentioned above.

In the small circles which I frequented at that time I did not conceal my conviction that this sinister agreement with a State doomed to collapse would also bring catastrophe to Germany if she did not free herself from it in time. I never for a moment wavered in that firm conviction, even when the tempest of the World War seemed to have made shipwreck of the reasoning faculty itself and had put blind enthusiasm in its place, even among those circles where the coolest and hardest objective thinking ought to have held sway. In the trenches I voiced and upheld my own opinion whenever these problems came under discussion. I held that to abandon the Habsburg Monarchy would involve no sacrifice if Germany could thereby reduce the number of her own enemies; for the millions of Germans who had donned the steel helmet had done so not to fight for the maintenance of a corrupt dynasty but rather for the salvation of the German people.

Before the War there were occasions on which it seemed that at least one section of the German public had some slight misgivings about the political wisdom of the alliance with Austria. From time to time German conservative circles issued warnings against being over-confident about the worth of that alliance; but, like every other reasonable suggestion made at that time, it was thrown to the winds. The general conviction was that the right measures had been adopted to 'conquer' the world, that the success of these measures would be enormous and the sacrifices negligible.

Once again the 'uninitiated' layman could do nothing but observe how the 'elect' were marching straight ahead towards disaster and enticing their beloved people to follow them, as the rats followed the Pied Piper of Hamelin.

If we would look for the deeper grounds which made it possible to foist on the people this absurd notion of peacefully conquering the world through commercial penetration, and how it was possible to put forward the maintenance of world-peace as a national aim, we shall find that these grounds lay in a general morbid condition that had pervaded the whole body of German political thought.

The triumphant progress of technical science in Germany and the marvellous development of German industries and commerce led us to forget that a powerful State had been the necessary pre-requisite of that success. On the contrary, certain circles went even so far as to give vent to the theory that the State owed its very existence to these phenomena; that it was, above all, an economic institution and should be constituted in accordance with economic interests. Therefore, it was held, the State was dependent on the economic structure. This condition of things was looked upon and glorified as the soundest and most normal arrangement.

Now, the truth is that the State in itself has nothing whatsoever to do with any definite economic concept or a definite economic development. It does not arise from a compact made between contracting parties, within a certain delimited territory, for the purpose of serving economic ends. The State is a community of living beings who have kindred physical and spiritual natures, organized for the purpose of assuring the conservation of their own kind and to help towards fulfilling those ends which Providence has assigned to that particular race or racial branch. Therein, and therein alone, lie the purpose and meaning of a State. Economic activity is one of the many auxiliary means which are necessary for the attainment of those aims. But economic activity is never the origin or purpose of a State, except where a State has been originally founded on a false and unnatural basis. And this alone explains why a State as such does not necessarily need a certain delimited territory as a condition of its establishment. This condition becomes a necessary pre-requisite only among those people who would provide and assure subsistence for their kinsfolk through their own industry, which means that they are ready to carry on the struggle for existence by means of their own work. People who can sneak their way, like parasites, into the human body politic and make others work for them under various pretences can form a State without possessing any definite delimited territory. This is chiefly applicable to that parasitic nation which, particularly at the present time preys upon the honest portion of mankind; I mean the Jews.

The Jewish State has never been delimited in space. It has been spread all over the world, without any frontiers whatsoever, and has always been constituted from the membership of one race exclusively. That is why the Jews have always formed a State within the State. One of the most ingenious tricks ever devised has been that of sailing the Jewish ship-of-state under the flag of Religion and thus securing that tolerance which Aryans are always ready to grant to different religious faiths. But the Mosaic Law is really nothing else than the doctrine of the preservation of the Jewish race. Therefore this Law takes in all spheres of sociological, political and economic science which have a bearing on the main end in view.

The instinct for the preservation of one's own species is the primary cause that leads to the formation of human communities. Hence the State is a racial organism, and not an economic organization. The difference between the two is so great as to be incomprehensible to our contemporary so-called 'statesmen'. That is why they like to believe that the State may be constituted as an economic structure, whereas the truth is that it has always resulted from the exercise of those qualities which are part of the will to preserve the species and the race. But these qualities always exist and operate through the heroic virtues and have nothing to do with commercial egoism; for the conservation of the species always presupposes that the individual is ready to sacrifice himself. Such is the meaning of the poet's lines: UND SETZET IHR NICHT DAS LEBEN EIN, NIE WIRD EUCH DAS LEBEN GEWONNEN SEIN. (AND IF YOU DO NOT STAKE YOUR LIFE, YOU WILL NEVER WIN LIFE FOR YOURSELF.)[10]

The sacrifice of the individual existence is necessary in order to assure the conservation of the race. Hence it is that the most essential condition for the establishment and maintenance of a State is a certain feeling of solidarity, wounded in an identity of character and race and in a resolute readiness to defend these at all costs. With people who live on their own territory this will result in a development of the heroic virtues; with a parasitic people it will develop the arts of subterfuge and gross perfidy unless we admit that these characteristics are innate and that the varying political forms through which the parasitic race expresses itself are only the outward manifestations of innate characteristics. At least in the beginning, the formation of a State can result only from a manifestation of the heroic qualities I have spoken of. And the people who fail in the struggle for existence, that is to say those, who become vassals and are thereby condemned to disappear entirely sooner or later, are those who do not display the heroic virtues in the struggle, or those who fall victims to the perfidy of the parasites. And even in this latter case the failure is not so much due to lack of intellectual powers, but rather to a lack of courage and determination. An attempt is made to conceal the real nature of this failing by saying that it is the humane feeling.

The qualities which are employed for the foundation and preservation of a State have accordingly little or nothing to do with the economic situation. And this is conspicuously demonstrated by the fact that the inner strength of a State only very rarely coincides with what is called its economic expansion. On the contrary, there are numerous examples to show that a period of economic prosperity indicates the approaching decline of a State. If it were correct to attribute the foundation of human communities to economic forces, then the power of the State as such would be at its highest pitch during periods of economic prosperity, and not vice versa.

It is specially difficult to understand how the belief that the State is brought into being and preserved by economic forces could gain currency in a country which has given proof of the opposite in every phase of its history. The history of Prussia shows in a manner particularly clear and distinct, that it is out of the moral virtues of the people and not from their economic circumstances that a State is formed. It is only under the protection of those virtues that economic activities can be developed and the latter will continue to flourish until a time comes when the creative political capacity declines. Therewith the economic structure will also break down, a phenomenon which is now happening in an alarming manner before our eyes. The material interest of mankind can prosper only in the shade of the heroic virtues. The moment they become the primary considerations of life they wreck the basis of their own existence.

Whenever the political power of Germany was specially strong the economic situation also improved. But whenever economic interests alone occupied the foremost place in the life of the people, and thrust transcendent ideals into the back.-ground, the State collapsed and economic ruin followed readily.

If we consider the question of what those forces actually are which are necessary to the creation and preservation of a State, we shall find that they are: The capacity and readiness to sacrifice the individual to the common welfare. That these qualities have nothing at all to do with economics can be proved by referring to the simple fact that man does not sacrifice himself for material interests. In other words, he will die for an ideal but not for a business. The marvellous gift for public psychology which the English have was never shown better than the way in which they presented their case in the World War. We were fighting for our bread; but the English declared that they were fighting for 'freedom', and not at all for their own freedom. Oh, no, but for the freedom of the small nations. German people laughed at that effrontery and were angered by it; but in doing so they showed how political thought had declined among our so-called diplomats in Germany even before the War. These diplomatists did not have the slightest notion of what that force was which brought men to face death of their own free will and determination.

As long as the German people, in the War of 1914, continued to believe that they were fighting for ideals they stood firm. As soon as they were told that they were fighting only for their daily bread they began to give up the struggle.

Our clever 'statesmen' were greatly amazed at this change of feeling. They never understood that as soon as man is called upon to struggle for purely material causes he will avoid death as best he can; for death and the enjoyment of the material fruits of a victory are quite incompatible concepts. The frailest woman will become a heroine when the life of her own child is at stake. And only the will to save the race and native land or the State, which offers protection to the race, has in all ages been the urge which has forced men to face the weapons of their enemies.

The following may be proclaimed as a truth that always holds good: A State has never arisen from commercial causes for the purpose of peacefully serving commercial ends; but States have always arisen from the instinct to maintain the racial group, whether this instinct manifest itself in the heroic sphere or in the sphere of cunning and chicanery. In the first case we have the Aryan States, based on the principles of work and cultural development. In the second case we have the Jewish parasitic colonies. But as soon as economic interests begin to predominate over the racial and cultural instincts in a people or a State, these economic interests unloose the causes that lead to subjugation and oppression.

The belief, which prevailed in Germany before the War, that the world could be opened up and even conquered for Germany through a system of peaceful commercial penetration and a colonial policy was a typical symptom which indicated the decline of those real qualities whereby States are created and preserved, and indicated also the decline of that insight, will-power and practical determination which belong to those qualities. The World War with its consequences, was the natural liquidation of that decline.

To anyone who had not thought over the matter deeply, this attitude of the German people—which was quite general—must have seemed an insoluble enigma. After all, Germany herself was a magnificent example of an empire that had been built up purely by a policy of power. Prussia, which was the generative cell of the German Empire, had been created by brilliant heroic deeds and not by a financial or commercial compact. And the Empire itself was but the magnificent recompense for a leadership that had been conducted on a policy of power and military valour.

How then did it happen that the political instincts of this very same German people became so degenerate? For it was not merely one isolated phenomenon which pointed to this decadence, but morbid symptoms which appeared in alarming numbers, now all over the body politic, or eating into the body of the nation like a gangrenous ulcer. It seemed as if some all-pervading poisonous fluid had been injected by some mysterious hand into the bloodstream of this once heroic body, bringing about a creeping paralysis that affected the reason and the elementary instinct of self-preservation.

During the years 1912-1914 I used to ponder perpetually on those problems which related to the policy of the Triple Alliance and the economic policy then being pursued by the German Empire. Once again I came to the conclusion that the only explanation of this enigma lay in the operation of that force which I had already become acquainted with in Vienna, though from a different angle of vision. The force to which I refer was the Marxist teaching and WELTANSCHAUUNG and its organized action throughout the nation.

For the second time in my life I plunged deep into the study of that destructive teaching. This time, however, I was not urged by the study of the question by the impressions and influences of my daily environment, but directed rather by the observation of general phenomena in the political life of Germany. In delving again into the theoretical literature of this new world and endeavouring to get a clear view of the possible consequences of its teaching, I compared the theoretical principles of Marxism with the phenomena and happenings brought about by its activities in the political, cultural, and economic spheres.

For the first time in my life I now turned my attention to the efforts that were being made to subdue this universal pest. I studied Bismarck's exceptional legislation in its original concept, its operation and its results. Gradually I formed a basis for my own opinions, which has proved as solid as a rock, so that never since have I had to change my attitude towards the general problem. I also made a further and more thorough analysis of the relations between Marxism and Jewry.

During my sojourn in Vienna I used to look upon Germany as an imperturbable colossus; but even then serious doubts and misgivings would often disturb me. In my own mind and in my conversation with my small circle of acquaintances I used to criticize Germany's foreign policy and the incredibly superficial way, according to my thinking, in which Marxism was dealt with, though it was then the most important problem in Germany. I could not understand how they could stumble blindfolded into the midst of this peril, the effects of which would be momentous if the openly declared aims of Marxism could be put into practice. Even as early as that time I warned people around me, just as I am warning a wider audience now, against that soothing slogan of all indolent and feckless nature: NOTHING CAN HAPPEN TO US. A similar mental contagion had already destroyed a mighty empire. Can Germany escape the operation of those laws to which all other human communities are subject?

In the years 1913 and 1914 I expressed my opinion for the first time in various circles, some of which are now members of the National Socialist Movement, that the problem of how the future of the German nation can be secured is the problem of how Marxism can be exterminated. I considered the disastrous policy of the Triple Alliance as one of the consequences resulting from the disintegrating effects of the Marxist teaching; for the alarming feature was that this teaching was invisibly corrupting the foundations of a healthy political and economic outlook.

Those who had been themselves contaminated frequently did not realise that their aims and actions sprang from this WELTANSCHAUUNG, which they otherwise openly repudiated.

Long before then the spiritual and moral decline of the German people had set in, though those who were affected by the morbid decadence were frequently unaware—as often happens—of the forces which were breaking up their very existence. Sometimes they tried to cure the disease by doctoring the symptoms, which were taken as the cause. But since nobody recognized, or wanted to recognize, the real cause of the disease this way of combating Marxism was no more effective than the application of some quack's ointment.

CHAPTER V: The World War

During the boisterous years of my youth nothing used to damp my wild spirits so much as to think that I was born at a time when the world had manifestly decided not to erect any more temples of fame except in honour of business people and State officials.

The tempest of historical achievements seemed to have permanently subsided, so much so that the future appeared to be irrevocably delivered over to what was called peaceful competition between the nations. This simply meant a system of mutual exploitation by fraudulent means, the principle of resorting to the use of force in self-defence being formally excluded. Individual countries increasingly assumed the appearance of commercial undertakings, grabbing territory and clients and concessions from each other under any and every kind of pretext. And it was all staged to an accompaniment of loud but innocuous shouting. This trend of affairs seemed destined to develop steadily and permanently. Having the support of public approbation, it seemed bound eventually to transform the world into a mammoth department store. In the vestibule of this emporium there would be rows of monumental busts which would confer immortality on those profiteers who had proved themselves the shrewdest at their trade and those administrative officials who had shown themselves the most innocuous. The salesmen could be represented by the English and the administrative functionaries by the Germans; whereas the Jews would be sacrificed to the unprofitable calling of proprietorship, for they are constantly avowing that they make no profits and are always being called upon to 'pay out'. Moreover they have the advantage of being versed in the foreign languages.

Why could I not have been born a hundred years ago? I used to ask myself. Somewhere about the time of the Wars of Liberation, when a man was still of some value even though he had no 'business'.

Thus I used to think it an ill-deserved stroke of bad luck that I had arrived too late on this terrestrial globe, and I felt chagrined at the idea that my life would have to run its course along peaceful and orderly lines. As a boy I was anything but a pacifist and all attempts to make me so turned out futile.

Then the Boer War came, like a glow of lightning on the far horizon. Day after day I used to gaze intently at the newspapers and I almost 'devoured' the telegrams and COMMUNIQUES, overjoyed to think that I could witness that heroic struggle, even though from so great a distance.

When the Russo-Japanese War came I was older and better able to judge for myself. For national reasons I then took the side of the Japanese in our discussions. I looked upon the defeat of the Russians as a blow to Austrian Slavism.

Many years had passed between that time and my arrival in Munich. I now realized that what I formerly believed to be a morbid decadence was only the lull before the storm. During my Vienna days the Balkans were already in the grip of that sultry pause which presages the violent storm. Here and there a flash of lightning could be occasionally seen; but it rapidly disappeared in sinister gloom. Then the Balkan War broke out; and therewith the first gusts of the forthcoming tornado swept across a highly-strung Europe. In the supervening calm men felt the atmosphere oppressive and foreboding, so much so that the sense of an impending catastrophe became transformed into a feeling of impatient expectance. They wished that Heaven would give free rein to the fate which could now no longer be curbed. Then the first great bolt of lightning struck the earth. The storm broke and the thunder of the heavens intermingled with the roar of the cannons in the World War.

When the news came to Munich that the Archduke Franz Ferdinand had been murdered, I had been at home all day and did not get the particulars of how it happened. At first I feared that the shots may have been fired by some German-Austrian students who had been aroused to a state of furious indignation by the persistent pro-Slav activities of the Heir to the Habsburg Throne and therefore wished to liberate the German population from this internal enemy. It was quite easy to imagine what the result of such a mistake would have been. It would have brought on a new wave of persecution, the motives of which would have been 'justified' before the whole world. But soon afterwards I heard the names of the presumed assassins and also that they were known to be Serbs. I felt somewhat dumbfounded in face of the inexorable vengeance which Destiny had wrought. The greatest friend of the Slavs had fallen a victim to the bullets of Slav patriots.

It is unjust to the Vienna government of that time to blame it now for the form and tenor of the ultimatum which was then presented. In a similar position and under similar circumstances, no other Power in the world would have acted otherwise. On her southern frontiers Austria had a relentless mortal foe who indulged in acts of provocation against the Dual Monarchy at intervals which were becoming more and more frequent.

This persistent line of conduct would not have been relaxed until the arrival of the opportune moment for the destruction of the Empire. In Austria there was good reason to fear that, at the latest, this moment would come with the death of the old Emperor. Once that had taken place, it was quite possible that the Monarchy would not be able to offer any serious resistance. For some years past the State had been so completely identified with the personality of Francis Joseph that, in the eyes of the great mass of the people, the death of this venerable personification of the Empire would be tantamount to the death of the Empire itself. Indeed it was one of the clever artifices of Slav policy to foster the impression that the Austrian State owed its very existence exclusively to the prodigies and rare talents of that monarch. This kind of flattery was particularly welcomed at the Hofburg, all the more because it had no relation whatsoever to the services actually rendered by the Emperor. No effort whatsoever was made to locate the carefully prepared sting which lay hidden in this glorifying praise. One fact which was entirely overlooked, perhaps intentionally, was that the more the Empire remained dependent on the so-called administrative talents of 'the wisest Monarch of all times', the more catastrophic would be the situation when Fate came to knock at the door and demand its tribute. Was it possible even to imagine the Austrian Empire without its venerable ruler? Would not the tragedy which befell Maria Theresa be repeated at once?

It is really unjust to the Vienna governmental circles to reproach them with having instigated a war which might have been prevented. The war was bound to come. Perhaps it might have been postponed for a year or two at the most. But it had always been the misfortune of German, as well as Austrian, diplomats that they endeavoured to put off the inevitable day of reckoning, with the result that they were finally compelled to deliver their blow at a most inopportune moment. No. Those who did not wish this war ought to have had the courage to take the consequences of the refusal upon themselves. Those consequences must necessarily have meant the sacrifice of Austria. And even then war would have come, not as a war in which all the nations would have been banded against us but in the form of a dismemberment of the Habsburg Monarchy. In that case we should have had to decide whether we should come to the assistance of the Habsburg or stand aside as spectators, with our arms folded, and thus allow Fate to run its course. Just those who are loudest in their imprecations to-day and make a great parade of wisdom in judging the causes of the war are the very same people whose collaboration was the most fatal factor in steering towards the war.

For several decades previously the German Social-Democrats had been agitating in an underhand and knavish way for war against Russia; whereas the German Centre Party, with religious ends in view, had worked to make the Austrian State the chief centre and turning-point of German policy. The consequences of this folly had now to be borne. What came was bound to come and under no circumstances could it have been avoided. The fault of the German Government lay in the fact that, merely for the sake of preserving peace at all costs, it continued to miss the occasions that were favourable for action, got entangled in an alliance for the purpose of preserving the peace of the world, and thus finally became the victim of a world coalition which opposed the German effort for the maintenance of peace and was determined to bring about the world war.

Had the Vienna Government of that time formulated its ultimatum in less drastic terms, that would not have altered the situation at all: but such a course might have aroused public indignation. For, in the eyes of the great masses, the ultimatum was too moderate and certainly not excessive or brutal. Those who would deny this to-day are either simpletons with feeble memories or else deliberate falsehood-mongers. The War of 1914 was certainly not forced on the masses; it was even desired by the whole people.

There was a desire to bring the general feeling of uncertainty to an end once and for all. And it is only in the light of this fact that we can understand how more than two million German men and youths voluntarily joined the colours, ready to shed the last drop of their blood for the cause.

For me these hours came as a deliverance from the distress that had weighed upon me during the days of my youth. I am not ashamed to acknowledge to-day that I was carried away by the enthusiasm of the moment and that I sank down upon my knees and thanked Heaven out of the fullness of my heart for the favour of having been permitted to live in such a time.

The fight for freedom had broken out on an unparalleled scale in the history of the world. From the moment that Fate took the helm in hand the conviction grew among the mass of the people that now it was not a question of deciding the destinies of Austria or Serbia but that the very existence of the German nation itself was at stake. At last, after many years of blindness, the people saw clearly into the future. Therefore, almost immediately after the gigantic struggle had begun, an excessive enthusiasm was replaced by a more earnest and more fitting undertone, because the exaltation of the popular spirit was not a mere passing frenzy. It was only too necessary that the gravity of the situation should be recognized. At that time there was, generally speaking, not the slightest presentiment or conception of how long the war might last. People dreamed of the soldiers being home by Christmas and that then they would resume their daily work in peace.

Whatever mankind desires, that it will hope for and believe in. The overwhelming majority of the people had long since grown weary of the perpetual insecurity in the general condition of public affairs. Hence it was only natural that no one believed that the Austro-Serbian conflict could be shelved. Therefore they looked forward to a radical settlement of accounts. I also belonged to the millions that desired this.

The moment the news of the Sarajevo outrage reached Munich two ideas came into my mind: First, that war was absolutely inevitable and, second, that the Habsburg State would now be forced to honour its signature to the alliance. For what I had feared most was that one day Germany herself, perhaps as a result of the Alliance, would become involved in a conflict the first direct cause of which did not affect Austria. In such a contingency, I feared that the Austrian State, for domestic political reasons, would find itself unable to decide in favour of its ally. But now this danger was removed. The old State was compelled to fight, whether it wished to do so or not.

My own attitude towards the conflict was equally simple and clear. I believed that it was not a case of Austria fighting to get satisfaction from Serbia but rather a case of Germany fighting for her own existence—the German nation for its own to-be-or-not-to-be, for its freedom and for its future. The work of Bismarck must now be carried on. Young Germany must show itself worthy of the blood shed by our fathers on so many heroic fields of battle, from Weissenburg to Sedan and Paris. And if this struggle should bring us victory our people will again rank foremost among the great nations. Only then could the German Empire assert itself as the mighty champion of peace, without the necessity of restricting the daily bread of its children for the sake of maintaining the peace.

As a boy and as a young man, I often longed for the occasion to prove that my national enthusiasm was not mere vapouring. Hurrahing sometimes seemed to me to be a kind of sinful indulgence, though I could not give any justification for that feeling; for, after all, who has the right to shout that triumphant word if he has not won the right to it there where there is no play-acting and where the hand of the Goddess of Destiny puts the truth and sincerity of nations and men through her inexorable test? Just as millions of others, I felt a proud joy in being permitted to go through this test. I had so often sung DEUTSCHLAND ÜBER ALLES and so often roared 'HEIL' that I now thought it was as a kind of retro-active grace that I was granted the right of appearing before the Court of Eternal Justice to testify to the truth of those sentiments.

One thing was clear to me from the very beginning, namely, that in the event of war, which now seemed inevitable, my books would have to be thrown aside forthwith. I also realized that my place would have to be there where the inner voice of conscience called me. I had left Austria principally for political reasons. What therefore could be more rational than that I should put into practice the logical consequences of my political opinions, now that the war had begun. I had no desire to fight for the Habsburg cause, but I was prepared to die at any time for my own kinsfolk and the Empire to which they really belonged.

On August 3rd, 1914, I presented an urgent petition to His Majesty, King Ludwig III, requesting to be allowed to serve in a Bavarian regiment. In those days the Chancellery had its hands quite full and therefore I was all the more pleased when I received the answer a day later, that my request had been granted. I opened the document with trembling hands; and no words of mine could now describe the satisfaction I felt on reading that I was instructed to report to a Bavarian regiment. Within a few days I was wearing that uniform which I was not to put oft again for nearly six years.

For me, as for every German, the most memorable period of my life now began. Face to face with that mighty struggle, all the past fell away into oblivion. With a wistful pride I look back on those days, especially because we are now approaching the tenth anniversary of that memorable happening. I recall those early weeks of war when kind fortune permitted me to take my place in that heroic struggle among the nations. As the scene unfolds itself before my mind, it seems only like yesterday. I see myself among my young comrades on our first parade drill, and so on until at last the day came on which we were to leave for the front.

In common with the others, I had one worry during those days. This was a fear that we might arrive too late for the fighting at the front. Time and again that thought disturbed me and every announcement of a victorious engagement left a bitter taste, which increased as the news of further victories arrived.

At long last the day came when we left Munich on war service. For the first time in my life I saw the Rhine, as we journeyed westwards to stand guard before that historic German river against its traditional and grasping enemy. As the first soft rays of the morning sun broke through the light mist and disclosed to us the Niederwald Statue, with one accord the whole troop train broke into the strains of DIE WACHT AM RHEIN. I then felt as if my heart could not contain its spirit.

And then followed a damp, cold night in Flanders. We marched in silence throughout the night and as the morning sun came through the mist an iron greeting suddenly burst above our heads. Shrapnel exploded in our midst and spluttered in the damp ground. But before the smoke of the explosion disappeared a wild 'Hurrah' was shouted from two hundred throats, in response to this first greeting of Death. Then began the whistling of bullets and the booming of cannons, the shouting and singing of the combatants. With eyes straining feverishly, we pressed forward, quicker and quicker, until we finally came to close-quarter fighting, there beyond the beet-fields and the meadows. Soon the strains of a song reached us from afar. Nearer and nearer, from company to company, it came. And while Death began to make havoc in our ranks we passed the song on to those beside us: DEUTSCHLAND, DEUTSCHLAND ÜBER ALLES, ÜBER ALLES IN DER WELT.

After four days in the trenches we came back. Even our step was no longer what it had been. Boys of seventeen looked now like grown men. The rank and file of the List Regiment[11] had not been properly trained in the art of warfare, but they knew how to die like old soldiers.

That was the beginning. And thus we carried on from year to year. A feeling of horror replaced the romantic fighting spirit. Enthusiasm cooled down gradually and exuberant spirits were quelled by the fear of the ever-present Death. A time came when there arose within each one of us a conflict between the urge to self-preservation and the call of duty. And I had to go through that conflict too. As Death sought its prey everywhere and unrelentingly a nameless Something rebelled within the weak body and tried to introduce itself under the name of Common Sense; but in reality it was Fear, which had taken on this cloak in order to impose itself on the individual. But the more the voice which advised prudence increased its efforts and the more clear and persuasive became its appeal, resistance became all the stronger; until finally the internal strife was over and the call of duty was triumphant. Already in the winter of 1915-16 I had come through that inner struggle. The will had asserted its incontestable mastery. Whereas in the early days I went into the fight with a cheer and a laugh, I was now habitually calm and resolute. And that frame of mind endured. Fate might now put me through the final test without my nerves or reason giving way. The young volunteer had become an old soldier.

This same transformation took place throughout the whole army. Constant fighting had aged and toughened it and hardened it, so that it stood firm and dauntless against every assault.

Only now was it possible to judge that army. After two and three years of continuous fighting, having been thrown into one battle after another, standing up stoutly against superior numbers and superior armament, suffering hunger and privation, the time had come when one could assess the value of that singular fighting force. For a thousand years to come nobody will dare to speak of heroism without recalling the German Army of the World War. And then from the dim past will emerge the immortal vision of those solid ranks of steel helmets that never flinched and never faltered. And as long as Germans live they will be proud to remember that these men were the sons of their forefathers.

I was then a soldier and did not wish to meddle in politics, all the more so because the time was inopportune. I still believe that the most modest stable-boy of those days served his country better than the best of, let us say, the 'parliamentary deputies'. My hatred for those footlers was never greater than in those days when all decent men who had anything to say said it point-blank in the enemy's face; or, failing this, kept their mouths shut and did their duty elsewhere. I despised those political fellows and if I had had my way I would have formed them into a Labour Battalion and given them the opportunity of babbling amongst themselves to their hearts' content, without offence or harm to decent people.

In those days I cared nothing for politics; but I could not help forming an opinion on certain manifestations which affected not only the whole nation but also us soldiers in particular. There were two things which caused me the greatest anxiety at that time and which I had come to regard as detrimental to our interests.

Shortly after our first series of victories a certain section of the Press already began to throw cold water, drip by drip, on the enthusiasm of the public. At first this was not obvious to many people. It was done under the mask of good intentions and a spirit of anxious care. The public was told that big celebrations of victories were somewhat out of place and were not worthy expressions of the spirit of a great nation. The fortitude and valour of German soldiers were accepted facts which did not necessarily call for outbursts of celebration. Furthermore, it was asked, what would foreign opinion have to say about these manifestations? Would not foreign opinion react more favourably to a quiet and sober form of celebration rather than to all this wild jubilation? Surely the time had come—so the Press declared—for us Germans to remember that this war was not our work and that hence there need be no feeling of shame in declaring our willingness to do our share towards effecting an understanding among the nations. For this reason it would not be wise to sully the radiant deeds of our army with unbecoming jubilation; for the rest of the world would never understand this. Furthermore, nothing is more appreciated than the modesty with which a true hero quietly and unassumingly carries on and forgets. Such was the gist of their warning.

Instead of catching these fellows by their long ears and dragging them to some ditch and looping a cord around their necks, so that the victorious enthusiasm of the nation should no longer offend the aesthetic sensibilities of these knights of the pen, a general Press campaign was now allowed to go on against what was called 'unbecoming' and 'undignified' forms of victorious celebration.

No one seemed to have the faintest idea that when public enthusiasm is once damped, nothing can enkindle it again, when the necessity arises. This enthusiasm is an intoxication and must be kept up in that form.

Without the support of this enthusiastic spirit how would it be possible to endure in a struggle which, according to human standards, made such immense demands on the spiritual stamina of the nation?

I was only too well acquainted with the psychology of the broad masses not to know that in such cases a magnaminous 'aestheticism' cannot fan the fire which is needed to keep the iron hot. In my eyes it was even a mistake not to have tried to raise the pitch of public enthusiasm still higher. Therefore I could not at all understand why the contrary policy was adopted, that is to say, the policy of damping the public spirit.

Another thing which irritated me was the manner in which Marxism was regarded and accepted. I thought that all this proved how little they knew about the Marxist plague. It was believed in all seriousness that the abolition of party distinctions during the War had made Marxism a mild and moderate thing.

But here there was no question of party. There was question of a doctrine which was being expounded for the express purpose of leading humanity to its destruction. The purport of this doctrine was not understood because nothing was said about that side of the question in our Jew-ridden universities and because our supercilious bureaucratic officials did not think it worth while to read up a subject which had not been prescribed in their university course. This mighty revolutionary trend was going on beside them; but those 'intellectuals' would not deign to give it their attention. That is why State enterprise nearly always lags behind private enterprise. Of these gentry once can truly say that their maxim is: What we don't know won't bother us. In the August of 1914 the German worker was looked upon as an adherent of Marxist socialism. That was a gross error. When those fateful hours dawned the German worker shook off the poisonous clutches of that plague; otherwise he would not have been so willing and ready to fight.

And people were stupid enough to imagine that Marxism had now become 'national', another apt illustration of the fact that those in authority had never taken the trouble to study the real tenor of the Marxist teaching. If they had done so, such foolish errors would not have been committed.

Marxism, whose final objective was and is and will continue to be the destruction of all non-Jewish national States, had to witness in those days of July 1914 how the German working classes, which it had been inveigling, were aroused by the national spirit and rapidly ranged themselves on the side of the Fatherland. Within a few days the deceptive smoke-screen of that infamous national betrayal had vanished into thin air and the Jewish bosses suddenly found themselves alone and deserted. It was as if not a vestige had been left of that folly and madness with which the masses of the German people had been inoculated for sixty years. That was indeed an evil day for the betrayers of German Labour. The moment, however, that the leaders realized the danger which threatened them they pulled the magic cap of deceit over their ears and, without being identified, played the part of mimes in the national reawakening.

The time seemed to have arrived for proceeding against the whole Jewish gang of public pests. Then it was that action should have been taken regardless of any consequent whining or protestation. At one stroke, in the August of 1914, all the empty nonsense about international solidarity was knocked out of the heads of the German working classes. A few weeks later, instead of this stupid talk sounding in their ears, they heard the noise of American-manufactured shrapnel bursting above the heads of the marching columns, as a symbol of international comradeship. Now that the German worker had rediscovered the road to nationhood, it ought to have been the duty of any Government which had the care of the people in its keeping, to take this opportunity of mercilessly rooting out everything that was opposed to the national spirit.

While the flower of the nation's manhood was dying at the front, there was time enough at home at least to exterminate this vermin. But, instead of doing so, His Majesty the Kaiser held out his hand to these hoary criminals, thus assuring them his protection and allowing them to regain their mental composure.

And so the viper could begin his work again. This time, however, more carefully than before, but still more destructively. While honest people dreamt of reconciliation these perjured criminals were making preparations for a revolution.

Naturally I was distressed at the half-measures which were adopted at that time; but I never thought it possible that the final consequences could have been so disastrous?

But what should have been done then? Throw the ringleaders into gaol, prosecute them and rid the nation of them? Uncompromising military measures should have been adopted to root out the evil. Parties should have been abolished and the Reichstag brought to its senses at the point of the bayonet, if necessary. It would have been still better if the Reichstag had been dissolved immediately. Just as the Republic to-day dissolves the parties when it wants to, so in those days there was even more justification for applying that measure, seeing that the very existence of the nation was at stake. Of course this suggestion would give rise to the question: Is it possible to eradicate ideas by force of arms? Could a WELTANSCHAUUNG be attacked by means of physical force?

At that time I turned these questions over and over again in my mind. By studying analogous cases, exemplified in history, particularly those which had arisen from religious circumstances, I came to the following fundamental conclusion:

Ideas and philosophical systems as well as movements grounded on a definite spiritual foundation, whether true or not, can never be broken by the use of force after a certain stage, except on one condition: namely, that this use of force is in the service of a new idea or WELTANSCHAUUNG which burns with a new flame.

The application of force alone, without moral support based on a spiritual concept, can never bring about the destruction of an idea or arrest the propagation of it, unless one is ready and able ruthlessly to exterminate the last upholders of that idea even to a man, and also wipe out any tradition which it may tend to leave behind. Now in the majority of cases the result of such a course has been to exclude such a State, either temporarily or for ever, from the comity of States that are of political significance; but experience has also shown that such a sanguinary method of extirpation arouses the better section of the population under the persecuting power. As a matter of fact, every persecution which has no spiritual motives to support it is morally unjust and raises opposition among the best elements of the population; so much so that these are driven more and more to champion the ideas that are unjustly persecuted. With many individuals this arises from the sheer spirit of opposition to every attempt at suppressing spiritual things by brute force.

In this way the number of convinced adherents of the persecuted doctrine increases as the persecution progresses. Hence the total destruction of a new doctrine can be accomplished only by a vast plan of extermination; but this, in the final analysis, means the loss of some of the best blood in a nation or State. And that blood is then avenged, because such an internal and total clean-up brings about the collapse of the nation's strength. And such a procedure is always condemned to futility from the very start if the attacked doctrine should happen to have spread beyond a small circle.

That is why in this case, as with all other growths, the doctrine can be exterminated in its earliest stages. As time goes on its powers of resistance increase, until at the approach of age it gives way to younger elements, but under another form and from other motives. The fact remains that nearly all attempts to exterminate a doctrine, without having some spiritual basis of attack against it, and also to wipe out all the organizations it has created, have led in many cases to the very opposite being achieved; and that for the following reasons:

When sheer force is used to combat the spread of a doctrine, then that force must be employed systematically and persistently. This means that the chances of success in the suppression of a doctrine lie only in the persistent and uniform application of the methods chosen. The moment hesitation is shown, and periods of tolerance alternate with the application of force, the doctrine against which these measures are directed will not only recover strength but every successive persecution will bring to its support new adherents who have been shocked by the oppressive methods employed. The old adherents will become more embittered and their allegiance will thereby be strengthened. Therefore when force is employed success is dependent on the consistent manner in which it is used. This persistence, however, is nothing less than the product of definite spiritual convictions. Every form of force that is not supported by a spiritual backing will be always indecisive and uncertain. Such a force lacks the stability that can be found only in a WELTANSCHAUUNG which has devoted champions. Such a force is the expression of the individual energies; therefore it is from time to time dependent on the change of persons in whose hands it is employed and also on their characters and capacities.

But there is something else to be said: Every WELTANSCHAUUNG, whether religious or political—and it is sometimes difficult to say where the one ends and the other begins—fights not so much for the negative destruction of the opposing world of ideas as for the positive realization of its own ideas. Thus its struggle lies in attack rather than in defence. It has the advantage of knowing where its objective lies, as this objective represents the realization of its own ideas. Inversely, it is difficult to say when the negative aim for the destruction of a hostile doctrine is reached and secured. For this reason alone a WELTANSCHAUUNG which is of an aggressive character is more definite in plan and more powerful and decisive in action than a WELTANSCHAUUNG which takes up a merely defensive attitude. If force be used to combat a spiritual power, that force remains a defensive measure only so long as the wielders of it are not the standard-bearers and apostles of a new spiritual doctrine.

To sum up, the following must be borne in mind: That every attempt to combat a WELTANSCHAUUNG by means of force will turn out futile in the end if the struggle fails to take the form of an offensive for the establishment of an entirely new spiritual order of' things. It is only in the struggle between two Weltan-schauungen that physical force, consistently and ruthlessly applied, will eventually turn the scales in its own favour. It was here that the fight against Marxism had hitherto failed.

This was also the reason why Bismarck's anti-socialist legislation failed and was bound to fail in the long run, despite everything. It lacked the basis of a new WELTANSCHAUUNG for whose development and extension the struggle might have been taken up. To say that the serving up of drivel about a so-called 'State-Authority' or 'Law-and-Order' was an adequate foundation for the spiritual driving force in a life-or-death struggle is only what one would expect to hear from the wiseacres in high official positions.

It was because there were no adequate spiritual motives back of this offensive that Bismarck was compelled to hand over the administration of his socialist legislative measures to the judgment and approval of those circles which were themselves the product of the Marxist teaching. Thus a very ludicrous state of affairs prevailed when the Iron Chancellor surrendered the fate of his struggle against Marxism to the goodwill of the bourgeois democracy. He left the goat to take care of the garden.

But this was only the necessary result of the failure to find a fundamentally new WELTANSCHAUUNG which would attract devoted champions to its cause and could be established on the ground from which Marxism had been driven out. And thus the result of the Bismarckian campaign was deplorable.

During the World War, or at the beginning of it, were the conditions any different? Unfortunately, they were not.

The more I then pondered over the necessity for a change in the attitude of the executive government towards Social-Democracy, as the incorporation of contemporary Marxism, the more I realized the want of a practical substitute for this doctrine. Supposing Social-Democracy were overthrown, what had one to offer the masses in its stead? Not a single movement existed which promised any success in attracting vast numbers of workers who would be now more or less without leaders, and holding these workers in its train. It is nonsensical to imagine that the international fanatic who has just severed his connection with a class party would forthwith join a bourgeois party, or, in other words, another class organization. For however unsatisfactory these various organizations may appear to be, it cannot be denied that bourgeois politicians look on the distinction between classes as a very important factor in social life, provided it does not turn out politically disadvantageous to them. If they deny this fact they show themselves not only impudent but also mendacious.

Generally speaking, one should guard against considering the broad masses more stupid than they really are. In political matters it frequently happens that feeling judges more correctly than intellect. But the opinion that this feeling on the part of the masses is sufficient proof of their stupid international attitude can be immediately and definitely refuted by the simple fact that pacifist democracy is no less fatuous, though it draws its supporters almost exclusively from bourgeois circles. As long as millions of citizens daily gulp down what the social-democratic Press tells them, it ill becomes the 'Masters' to joke at the expense of the 'Comrades'; for in the long run they all swallow the same hash, even though it be dished up with different spices. In both cases the cook is one and the same—the Jew.

One should be careful about contradicting established facts. It is an undeniable fact that the class question has nothing to do with questions concerning ideals, though that dope is administered at election time. Class arrogance among a large section of our people, as well as a prevailing tendency to look down on the manual labourer, are obvious facts and not the fancies of some day-dreamer. Nevertheless it only illustrates the mentality of our so-called intellectual circles, that they have not yet grasped the fact that circumstances which are incapable of preventing the growth of such a plague as Marxism are certainly not capable of restoring what has been lost.

The bourgeois' parties—a name coined by themselves—will never again be able to win over and hold the proletarian masses in their train. That is because two worlds stand opposed to one another here, in part naturally and in part artificially divided. These two camps have one leading thought, and that is that they must fight one another. But in such a fight the younger will come off victorious; and that is Marxism.

In 1914 a fight against Social-Democracy was indeed quite conceivable. But the lack of any practical substitute made it doubtful how long the fight could be kept up. In this respect there was a gaping void. Long before the War I was of the same opinion and that was the reason why I could not decide to join any of the parties then existing. During the course of the World War my conviction was still further confirmed by the manifest impossibility of fighting Social-Democracy in anything like a thorough way: because for that purpose there should have been a movement that was something more than a mere 'parliamentary' party, and there was none such.

I frequently discussed that want with my intimate comrades. And it was then that I first conceived the idea of taking up political work later on. As I have often assured my friends, it was just this that induced me to become active on the public hustings after the War, in addition to my professional work. And I am sure that this decision was arrived at after much earnest thought.

CHAPTER VI: War Propaganda

In watching the course of political events I was always struck by the active part which propaganda played in them. I saw that it was an instrument, which the Marxist Socialists knew how to handle in a masterly way and how to put it to practical uses. Thus I soon came to realize that the right use of propaganda was an art in itself and that this art was practically unknown to our bourgeois parties. The Christian-Socialist Party alone, especially in Lueger's time, showed a certain efficiency in the employment of this instrument and owed much of their success to it.

It was during the War, however, that we had the best chance of estimating the tremendous results which could be obtained by a propagandist system properly carried out. Here again, unfortunately, everything was left to the other side, the work done on our side being worse than insignificant. It was the total failure of the whole German system of information—a failure which was perfectly obvious to every soldier—that urged me to consider the problem of propaganda in a comprehensive way. I had ample opportunity to learn a practical lesson in this matter; for unfortunately it was only too well taught us by the enemy. The lack on our side was exploited by the enemy in such an efficient manner that one could say it showed itself as a real work of genius. In that propaganda carried on by the enemy I found admirable sources of instruction. The lesson to be learned from this had unfortunately no attraction for the geniuses on our own side. They were simply above all such things, too clever to accept any teaching. Anyhow they did not honestly wish to learn anything.

Had we any propaganda at all? Alas, I can reply only in the negative. All that was undertaken in this direction was so utterly inadequate and misconceived from the very beginning that not only did it prove useless but at times harmful. In substance it was insufficient. Psychologically it was all wrong. Anybody who had carefully investigated the German propaganda must have formed that judgment of it. Our people did not seem to be clear even about the primary question itself: Whether propaganda is a means or an end?

Propaganda is a means and must, therefore, be judged in relation to the end it is intended to serve. It must be organized in such a way as to be capable of attaining its objective. And, as it is quite clear that the importance of the objective may vary from the standpoint of general necessity, the essential internal character of the propaganda must vary accordingly. The cause for which we fought during the War was the noblest and highest that man could strive for. We were fighting for the freedom and independence of our country, for the security of our future welfare and the honour of the nation. Despite all views to the contrary, this honour does actually exist, or rather it will have to exist; for a nation without honour will sooner or later lose its freedom and independence. This is in accordance with the ruling of a higher justice, for a generation of poltroons is not entitled to freedom. He who would be a slave cannot have honour; for such honour would soon become an object of general scorn.

Germany was waging war for its very existence. The purpose of its war propaganda should have been to strengthen the fighting spirit in that struggle and help it to victory.

But when nations are fighting for their existence on this earth, when the question of 'to be or not to be' has to be answered, then all humane and aesthetic considerations must be set aside; for these ideals do not exist of themselves somewhere in the air but are the product of man's creative imagination and disappear when he disappears. Nature knows nothing of them. Moreover, they are characteristic of only a small number of nations, or rather of races, and their value depends on the measure in which they spring from the racial feeling of the latter. Humane and aesthetic ideals will disappear from the inhabited earth when those races disappear which are the creators and standard-bearers of them.

All such ideals are only of secondary importance when a nation is struggling for its existence. They must be prevented from entering into the struggle the moment they threaten to weaken the stamina of the nation that is waging war. That is always the only visible effect whereby their place in the struggle is to be judged.

In regard to the part played by humane feeling, Moltke stated that in time of war the essential thing is to get a decision as quickly as possible and that the most ruthless methods of fighting are at the same time the most humane. When people attempt to answer this reasoning by highfalutin talk about aesthetics, etc., only one answer can be given. It is that the vital questions involved in the struggle of a nation for its existence must not be subordinated to any aesthetic considerations. The yoke of slavery is and always will remain the most unpleasant experience that mankind can endure. Do the Schwabing[12] decadents look upon Germany's lot to-day as 'aesthetic'? Of course, one doesn't discuss such a question with the Jews, because they are the modern inventors of this cultural perfume. Their very existence is an incarnate denial of the beauty of God's image in His creation.

Since these ideas of what is beautiful and humane have no place in warfare, they are not to be used as standards of war propaganda.

During the War, propaganda was a means to an end. And this end was the struggle for existence of the German nation. Propaganda, therefore, should have been regarded from the standpoint of its utility for that purpose. The most cruel weapons were then the most humane, provided they helped towards a speedier decision; and only those methods were good and beautiful which helped towards securing the dignity and freedom of the nation. Such was the only possible attitude to adopt towards war propaganda in the life-or-death struggle.

If those in what are called positions of authority had realized this there would have been no uncertainty about the form and employment of war propaganda as a weapon; for it is nothing but a weapon, and indeed a most terrifying weapon in the hands of those who know how to use it. The second question of decisive importance is this: To whom should propaganda be made to appeal? To the educated intellectual classes? Or to the less intellectual?

Propaganda must always address itself to the broad masses of the people.

For the intellectual classes, or what are called the intellectual classes to-day, propaganda is not suited, but only scientific exposition. Propaganda has as little to do with science as an advertisement poster has to do with art, as far as concerns the form in which it presents its message. The art of the advertisement poster consists in the ability of the designer to attract the attention of the crowd through the form and colours he chooses. The advertisement poster announcing an exhibition of art has no other aim than to convince the public of the importance of the exhibition. The better it does that, the better is the art of the poster as such. Being meant accordingly to impress upon the public the meaning of the exposition, the poster can never take the place of the artistic objects displayed in the exposition hall. They are something entirely different. Therefore. those who wish to study the artistic display must study something that is quite different from the poster; indeed for that purpose a mere wandering through the exhibition galleries is of no use. The student of art must carefully and thoroughly study each exhibit in order slowly to form a judicious opinion about it.

The situation is the same in regard to what we understand by the word, propaganda. The purpose of propaganda is not the personal instruction of the individual, but rather to attract public attention to certain things, the importance of which can be brought home to the masses only by this means.

Here the art of propaganda consists in putting a matter so clearly and forcibly before the minds of the people as to create a general conviction regarding the reality of a certain fact, the necessity of certain things and the just character of something that is essential.

But as this art is not an end in itself and because its purpose must be exactly that of the advertisement poster, to attract the attention of the masses and not by any means to dispense individual instructions to those who already have an educated opinion on things or who wish to form such an opinion on grounds of objective study—because that is not the purpose of propaganda, it must appeal to the feelings of the public rather than to their reasoning powers.

All propaganda must be presented in a popular form and must fix its intellectual level so as not to be above the heads of the least intellectual of those to whom it is directed. Thus its purely intellectual level will have to be that of the lowest mental common denominator among the public it is desired to reach. When there is question of bringing a whole nation within the circle of its influence, as happens in the case of war propaganda, then too much attention cannot be paid to the necessity of avoiding a high level, which presupposes a relatively high degree of intelligence among the public.

The more modest the scientific tenor of this propaganda and the more it is addressed exclusively to public sentiment, the more decisive will be its success. This is the best test of the value of a propaganda, and not the approbation of a small group of intellectuals or artistic people.

The art of propaganda consists precisely in being able to awaken the imagination of the public through an appeal to their feelings, in finding the appropriate psychological form that will arrest the attention and appeal to the hearts of the national masses. That this is not understood by those among us whose wits are supposed to have been sharpened to the highest pitch is only another proof of their vanity or mental inertia.

Once we have understood how necessary it is to concentrate the persuasive forces of propaganda on the broad masses of the people, the following lessons result therefrom:

That it is a mistake to organize the direct propaganda as if it were a manifold system of scientific instruction.

The receptive powers of the masses are very restricted, and their understanding is feeble. On the other hand, they quickly forget. Such being the case, all effective propaganda must be confined to a few bare essentials and those must be expressed as far as possible in stereotyped formulas. These slogans should be persistently repeated until the very last individual has come to grasp the idea that has been put forward. If this principle be forgotten and if an attempt be made to be abstract and general, the propaganda will turn out ineffective; for the public will not be able to digest or retain what is offered to them in this way.

Therefore, the greater the scope of the message that has to be presented, the more necessary it is for the propaganda to discover that plan of action which is psychologically the most efficient. It was, for example, a fundamental mistake to ridicule the worth of the enemy as the Austrian and German comic papers made a chief point of doing in their propaganda. The very principle here is a mistaken one; for, when they came face to face with the enemy, our soldiers had quite a different impression. Therefore, the mistake had disastrous results.

Once the German soldier realised what a tough enemy he had to fight he felt that he had been deceived by the manufacturers of the information which had been given him. Therefore, instead of strengthening and stimulating his fighting spirit, this information had quite the contrary effect. Finally he lost heart.

On the other hand, British and American war propaganda was psychologically efficient. By picturing the Germans to their own people as Barbarians and Huns, they were preparing their soldiers for the horrors of war and safeguarding them against illusions. The most terrific weapons which those soldiers encountered in the field merely confirmed the information that they had already received and their belief in the truth of the assertions made by their respective governments was accordingly reinforced. Thus their rage and hatred against the infamous foe was increased. The terrible havoc caused by the German weapons of war was only another illustration of the Hunnish brutality of those barbarians; whereas on the side of the Entente no time was left the soldiers to meditate on the similar havoc which their own weapons were capable of. Thus the British soldier was never allowed to feel that the information which he received at home was untrue.

Unfortunately the opposite was the case with the Germans, who finally wound up by rejecting everything from home as pure swindle and humbug.

This result was made possible because at home they thought that the work of propaganda could be entrusted to the first ass that came along, braying of his own special talents, and they had no conception of the fact that propaganda demands the most skilled brains that can be found.

Thus the German war propaganda afforded us an incomparable example of how the work of 'enlightenment' should not be done and how such an example was the result of an entire failure to take any psychological considerations whatsoever into account.

From the enemy, however, a fund of valuable knowledge could be gained by those who kept their eyes open, whose powers of perception had not yet become sclerotic, and who during four-and-a-half years had to experience the perpetual flood of enemy propaganda.

The worst of all was that our people did not understand the very first condition which has to be fulfilled in every kind of propaganda; namely, a systematically one-sided attitude towards every problem that has to be dealt with. In this regard so many errors were committed, even from the very beginning of the war, that it was justifiable to doubt whether so much folly could be attributed solely to the stupidity of people in higher quarters.

What, for example, should we say of a poster which purported to advertise some new brand of soap by insisting on the excellent qualities of the competitive brands? We should naturally shake our heads. And it ought to be just the same in a similar kind of political advertisement.

The aim of propaganda is not to try to pass judgment on conflicting rights, giving each its due, but exclusively to emphasize the right which we are asserting. Propaganda must not investigate the truth objectively and, in so far as it is favourable to the other side, present it according to the theoretical rules of justice; yet it must present only that aspect of the truth which is favourable to its own side.

It was a fundamental mistake to discuss the question of who was responsible for the outbreak of the war and declare that the sole responsibility could not be attributed to Germany. The sole responsibility should have been laid on the shoulders of the enemy, without any discussion whatsoever.

And what was the consequence of these half-measures? The broad masses of the people are not made up of diplomats or professors of public jurisprudence nor simply of persons who are able to form reasoned judgment in given cases, but a vacillating crowd of human children who are constantly wavering between one idea and another. As soon as our own propaganda made the slightest suggestion that the enemy had a certain amount of justice on his side, then we laid down the basis on which the justice of our own cause could be questioned. The masses are not in a position to discern where the enemy's fault ends and where our own begins. In such a case they become hesitant and distrustful, especially when the enemy does not make the same mistake but heaps all the blame on his adversary. Could there be any clearer proof of this than the fact that finally our own people believed what was said by the enemy's propaganda, which was uniform and consistent in its assertions, rather than what our own propaganda said? And that, of course, was increased by the mania for objectivity which addicts our people. Everybody began to be careful about doing an injustice to the enemy, even at the cost of seriously injuring, and even ruining his own people and State.

Naturally the masses were not conscious of the fact that those in authority had failed to study the subject from this angle.

The great majority of a nation is so feminine in its character and outlook that its thought and conduct are ruled by sentiment rather than by sober reasoning. This sentiment, however, is not complex, but simple and consistent. It is not highly differentiated, but has only the negative and positive notions of love and hatred, right and wrong, truth and falsehood. Its notions are never partly this and partly that. English propaganda especially understood this in a marvellous way and put what they understood into practice. They allowed no half-measures which might have given rise to some doubt.

Proof of how brilliantly they understood that the feeling of the masses is something primitive was shown in their policy of publishing tales of horror and outrages which fitted in with the real horrors of the time, thereby cleverly and ruthlessly preparing the ground for moral solidarity at the front, even in times of great defeats. Further, the way in which they pilloried the German enemy as solely responsible for the war—which was a brutal and absolute falsehood—and the way in which they proclaimed his guilt was excellently calculated to reach the masses, realizing that these are always extremist in their feelings. And thus it was that this atrocious lie was positively believed.

The effectiveness of this kind of propaganda is well illustrated by the fact that after four-and-a-half years, not only was the enemy still carrying on his propagandist work, but it was already undermining the stamina of our people at home.

That our propaganda did not achieve similar results is not to be wondered at, because it had the germs of inefficiency lodged in its very being by reason of its ambiguity. And because of the very nature of its content one could not expect it to make the necessary impression on the masses. Only our feckless 'statesmen' could have imagined that on pacifists slops of such a kind the enthusiasm could be nourished which is necessary to enkindle that spirit which leads men to die for their country.

And so this product of ours was not only worthless but detrimental. No matter what an amount of talent employed in the organization of propaganda, it will have no result if due account is not taken of these fundamental principles. Propaganda must be limited to a few simple themes and these must be represented again and again. Here, as in innumerable other cases, perseverance is the first and most important condition of success.

Particularly in the field of propaganda, placid aesthetes and blase intellectuals should never be allowed to take the lead. The former would readily transform the impressive character of real propaganda into something suitable only for literary tea parties. As to the second class of people, one must always beware of this pest; for, in consequence of their insensibility to normal impressions, they are constantly seeking new excitements.

Such people grow sick and tired of everything. They always long for change and will always be incapable of putting themselves in the position of picturing the wants of their less callous fellow-creatures in their immediate neighbourhood, let alone trying to understand them.

The blase intellectuals are always the first to criticize propaganda, or rather its message, because this appears to them to be outmoded and trivial. They are always looking for something new, always yearning for change; and thus they become the mortal enemies of every effort that may be made to influence the masses in an effective way. The moment the organization and message of a propagandist movement begins to be orientated according to their tastes it becomes incoherent and scattered.

It is not the purpose of propaganda to create a series of alterations in sentiment with a view to pleasing these blase gentry. Its chief function is to convince the masses, whose slowness of understanding needs to be given time in order that they may absorb information; and only constant repetition will finally succeed in imprinting an idea on the memory of the crowd.

Every change that is made in the subject of a propagandist message must always emphasize the same conclusion. The leading slogan must of course be illustrated in many ways and from several angles, but in the end one must always return to the assertion of the same formula. In this way alone can propaganda be consistent and dynamic in its effects.

Only by following these general lines and sticking to them steadfastly, with uniform and concise emphasis, can final success be reached. Then one will be rewarded by the surprising and almost incredible results that such a persistent policy secures.

The success of any advertisement, whether of a business or political nature, depends on the consistency and perseverance with which it is employed.

In this respect also the propaganda organized by our enemies set us an excellent example. It confined itself to a few themes, which were meant exclusively for mass consumption, and it repeated these themes with untiring perseverance. Once these fundamental themes and the manner of placing them before the world were recognized as effective, they adhered to them without the slightest alteration for the whole duration of the War. At first all of it appeared to be idiotic in its impudent assertiveness. Later on it was looked upon as disturbing, but finally it was believed.

But in England they came to understand something further: namely, that the possibility of success in the use of this spiritual weapon consists in the mass employment of it, and that when employed in this way it brings full returns for the large expenses incurred. In England propaganda was regarded as a weapon of the first order, whereas with us it represented the last hope of a livelihood for our unemployed politicians and a snug job for shirkers of the modest hero type.

Taken all in all, its results were negative.

CHAPTER VII: The Revolution

In 1915 the enemy started his propaganda among our soldiers. From 1916 onwards it steadily became more intensive, and at the beginning of 1918 it had swollen into a storm flood. One could now judge the effects of this proselytizing movement step by step. Gradually our soldiers began to think just in the way the enemy wished them to think. On the German side there was no counter-propaganda.

At that time the army authorities, under our able and resolute Commander, were willing and ready to take up the fight in the propaganda domain also, but unfortunately they did not have the necessary means to carry that intention into effect. Moreover, the army authorities would have made a psychological mistake had they undertaken this task of mental training. To be efficacious it had come from the home front. For only thus could it be successful among men who for nearly four years now had been performing immortal deeds of heroism and undergoing all sorts of privations for the sake of that home. But what were the people at home doing? Was their failure to act merely due to unintelligence or bad faith?

In the midsummer of 1918, after the evacuation of the southern bank of the hearne, the German Press adopted a policy which was so woefully inopportune, and even criminally stupid, that I used to ask myself a question which made me more and more furious day after day: Is it really true that we have nobody who will dare to put an end to this process of spiritual sabotage which is being carried on among our heroic troops?

What happened in France during those days of 1914, when our armies invaded that country and were marching in triumph from one victory to another? What happened in Italy when their armies collapsed on the Isonzo front? What happened in France again during the spring of 1918, when German divisions took the main French positions by storm and heavy long-distance artillery bombarded Paris?

How they whipped up the flagging courage of those troops who were retreating and fanned the fires of national enthusiasm among them! How their propaganda and their marvellous aptitude in the exercise of mass-influence reawakened the fighting spirit in that broken front and hammered into the heads of the soldiers a, firm belief in final victory!

Meanwhile, what were our people doing in this sphere? Nothing, or even worse than nothing. Again and again I used to become enraged and indignant as I read the latest papers and realized the nature of the mass-murder they were committing: through their influence on the minds of the people and the soldiers. More than once I was tormented by the thought that if Providence had put the conduct of German propaganda into my hands, instead of into the hands of those incompetent and even criminal ignoramuses and weaklings, the outcome of the struggle might have been different.

During those months I felt for the first time that Fate was dealing adversely with me in keeping me on the fighting front and in a position where any chance bullet from some nigger or other might finish me, whereas I could have done the Fatherland a real service in another sphere. For I was then presumptuous enough to believe that I would have been successful in managing the propaganda business.

But I was a being without a name, one among eight millions. Hence it was better for me to keep my mouth shut and do my duty as well as I could in the position to which I had been assigned.

In the summer of 1915 the first enemy leaflets were dropped on our trenches. They all told more or less the same story, with some variations in the form of it. The story was that distress was steadily on the increase in Germany; that the War would last indefinitely; that the prospect of victory for us was becoming fainter day after day; that the people at home were yearning for peace, but that 'Militarism' and the 'Kaiser' would not permit it; that the world—which knew this very well—was not waging war against the German people but only against the man who was exclusively responsible, the Kaiser; that until this enemy of world-peace was removed there could be no end to the conflict; but that when the War was over the liberal and democratic nations would receive the Germans as colleagues in the League for World Peace. This would be done the moment 'Prussian Militarism' had been finally destroyed.

To illustrate and substantiate all these statements, the leaflets very often contained 'Letters from Home', the contents of which appeared to confirm the enemy's propagandist message.

Generally speaking, we only laughed at all these efforts. The leaflets were read, sent to base headquarters, then forgotten until a favourable wind once again blew a fresh contingent into the trenches. These were mostly dropped from aeroplanes which were used specially for that purpose.

One feature of this propaganda was very striking. It was that in sections where Bavarian troops were stationed every effort was made by the enemy propagandists to stir up feeling against the Prussians, assuring the soldiers that Prussia and Prussia alone was the guilty party who was responsible for bringing on and continuing the War, and that there was no hostility whatsoever towards the Bavarians; but that there could be no possibility of coming to their assistance so long as they continued to serve Prussian interests and helped to pull the Prussian chestnuts out of the fire. This persistent propaganda began to have a real influence on our soldiers in 1915. The feeling against Prussia grew quite noticeable among the Bavarian troops, but those in authority did nothing to counteract it. This was something more than a mere crime of omission; for sooner or later not only the Prussians were bound to have to atone severely for it but the whole German nation and consequently the Bavarians themselves also.

In this direction the enemy propaganda began to achieve undoubted success from 1916 onwards.

In a similar way letters coming directly from home had long since been exercising their effect. There was now no further necessity for the enemy to broadcast such letters in leaflet form. And also against this influence from home nothing was done except a few supremely stupid 'warnings' uttered by the executive government. The whole front was drenched in this poison which thoughtless women at home sent out, without suspecting for a moment that the enemy's chances of final victory were thus strengthened or that the sufferings of their own men at the front were thus being prolonged and rendered more severe. These stupid letters written by German women eventually cost the lives of hundreds of thousands of our men.

Thus in 1916 several distressing phenomena were already manifest. The whole front was complaining and grousing, discontented over many things and often justifiably so. While they were hungry and yet patient, and their relatives at home were in distress, in other quarters there was feasting and revelry. Yes; even on the front itself everything was not as it ought to have been in this regard.

Even in the early stages of the war the soldiers were sometimes prone to complain; but such criticism was confined to 'internal affairs'. The man who at one moment groused and grumbled ceased his murmur after a few moments and went about his duty silently, as if everything were in order. The company which had given signs of discontent a moment earlier hung on now to its bit of trench, defending it tooth and nail, as if Germany's fate depended on these few hundred yards of mud and shell-holes. The glorious old army was still at its post. A sudden change in my own fortunes soon placed me in a position where I had first-hand experience of the contrast between this old army and the home front. At the end of September 1916 my division was sent into the Battle of the Somme. For us this was the first of a series of heavy engagements, and the impression created was that of a veritable inferno, rather than war. Through weeks of incessant artillery bombardment we stood firm, at times ceding a little ground but then taking it back again, and never giving way. On October 7th, 1916, I was wounded but had the luck of being able to get back to our lines and was then ordered to be sent by ambulance train to Germany.

Two years had passed since I had left home, an almost endless period in such circumstances. I could hardly imagine what Germans looked like without uniforms. In the clearing hospital at Hermies I was startled when I suddenly heard the voice of a German woman who was acting as nursing sister and talking with one of the wounded men lying near me.

Two years! And then this voice for the first time!

The nearer our ambulance train approached the German frontier the more restless each one of us became. En route we recognised all these places through which we passed two years before as young volunteers — Brussels, Louvain, Liège — and finally we thought we recognized the first German homestead, with its familiar high gables and picturesque window-shutters. Home!

What a change! From the mud of the Somme battlefields to the spotless white beds in this wonderful building. One hesitated at first before entering them. It was only by slow stages that one could grow accustomed to this new world again. But unfortunately there were certain other aspects also in which this new world was different.

The spirit of the army at the front appeared to be out of place here. For the first time I encountered something which up to then was unknown at the front: namely, boasting of one's own cowardice. For, though we certainly heard complaining and grousing at the front, this was never in the spirit of any agitation to insubordination and certainly not an attempt to glorify one's fear. No; there at the front a coward was a coward and nothing else, And the contempt which his weakness aroused in the others was quite general, just as the real hero was admired all round. But here in hospital the spirit was quite different in some respects. Loudmouthed agitators were busy here in heaping ridicule on the good soldier and painting the weak-kneed poltroon in glorious colours. A couple of miserable human specimens were the ringleaders in this process of defamation. One of them boasted of having intentionally injured his hand in barbed-wire entanglements in order to get sent to hospital. Although his wound was only a slight one, it appeared that he had been here for a very long time and would be here interminably. Some arrangement for him seemed to be worked by some sort of swindle, just as he got sent here in the ambulance train through a swindle. This pestilential specimen actually had the audacity to parade his knavery as the manifestation of a courage which was superior to that of the brave soldier who dies a hero's death. There were many who heard this talk in silence; but there were others who expressed their assent to what the

fellow said. Personally I was disgusted at the thought that a seditious agitator of this kind should be allowed to remain in such an institution. What could be done? The hospital authorities here must have known who and what he was; and actually they did know. But still they did nothing about it. As soon as I was able to walk once again I obtained leave to visit Berlin.

Bitter want was in evidence everywhere. The metropolis, with its teeming millions, was suffering from hunger. The talk that was current in the various places of refreshment and hospices visited by the soldiers was much the same as that in our hospital. The impression given was that these agitators purposely singled out such places in order to spread their views.

But in Munich conditions were far worse. After my discharge from hospital, I was sent to a reserve battalion there. I felt as in some strange town. Anger, discontent, complaints met one's ears wherever one went. To a certain extent this was due to the infinitely maladroit manner in which the soldiers who had returned from the front were treated by the non-commissioned officers who had never seen a day's active service and who on that account were partly incapable of adopting the proper attitude towards the old soldiers. Naturally those old soldiers displayed certain characteristics which had been developed from the experiences in the trenches. The officers of the reserve units could not understand these peculiarities, whereas the officer home from active service was at least in a position to understand them for himself. As a result he received more respect from the men than officers at the home headquarters. But, apart from all this, the general spirit was deplorable. The art of shirking was looked upon as almost a proof of higher intelligence, and devotion to duty was considered a sign of weakness or bigotry. Government offices were staffed by Jews. Almost every clerk was a Jew and every Jew was a clerk. I was amazed at this multitude of combatants who belonged to the chosen people and could not help comparing it with their slender numbers in the fighting lines.

In the business world the situation was even worse. Here the Jews had actually become 'indispensable'. Like leeches, they were slowly sucking the blood from the pores of the national body. By means of newly floated War Companies an instrument had been discovered whereby all national trade was throttled so that no business could be carried on freely Special emphasis was laid on the necessity for unhampered centralization. Hence as early as 1916-17 practically all production was under the control of Jewish finance.

But against whom was the anger of the people directed? It was then that

I already saw the fateful day approaching which must finally bring the DEBACLE, unless timely preventive measures were taken.

While Jewry was busy despoiling the nation and tightening the screws of its despotism, the work of inciting the people against the Prussians increased. And just as nothing was done at the front to put a stop to the venomous propaganda, so here at home no official steps were taken against it. Nobody seemed capable of understanding that the collapse of Prussia could never bring about the rise of Bavaria. On the contrary, the collapse of the one must necessarily drag the other down with it.

This kind of behaviour affected me very deeply. In it I could see only a clever Jewish trick for diverting public attention from themselves to others. While Prussians and Bavarians were squabbling, the Jews were taking away the sustenance of both from under their very noses. While Prussians were being abused in Bavaria the Jews organized the revolution and with one stroke smashed both Prussia and Bavaria.

I could not tolerate this execrable squabbling among people of the same German stock and preferred to be at the front once again. Therefore, just after my arrival in Munich I reported myself for service again. At the beginning of March 1917 I rejoined my old regiment at the front.

Towards the end of 1917 it seemed as if we had got over the worst phases of moral depression at the front. After the Russian collapse the whole army recovered its courage and hope, and all were gradually becoming more and more convinced that the struggle would end in our favour. We could sing once again. The ravens were ceasing to croak. Faith in the future of the Fatherland was once more in the ascendant.

The Italian collapse in the autumn of 1917 had a wonderful effect; for this victory proved that it was possible to break through another front besides the Russian. This inspiring thought now became dominant in the minds of millions at the front and encouraged them to look forward with confidence to the spring of 1918. It was quite obvious that the enemy was in a state of depression. During this winter the front was somewhat quieter than usual. But that was the calm before the storm.

Just when preparations were being made to launch a final offensive which would bring this seemingly eternal struggle to an end, while endless columns of transports were bringing men and munitions to the front, and while the men were being trained for that final onslaught, then it was that the greatest act of treachery during the whole War was accomplished in Germany.

Germany must not win the War. At that moment when victory seemed ready to alight on the German standards, a conspiracy was arranged for the purpose of striking at the heart of the German spring offensive with one blow from the rear and thus making victory impossible. A general strike in the munition factories was organized.

If this conspiracy could achieve its purpose the German front would have collapsed and the wishes of the VORWÄRTS (the organ of the Social-Democratic Party) that this time victory should not take the side of the German banners, would have been fulfilled. For want of munitions the front would be broken through within a few weeks, the offensive would be effectively stopped and the Entente saved. Then International Finance would assume control over Germany and the internal objective of the Marxist national betrayal would be achieved. That objective was the destruction of the national economic system and the establishment of international capitalistic domination in its stead. And this goal has really been reached, thanks to the stupid credulity of the one side and the unspeakable treachery of the other.

The munition strike, however, did not bring the final success that had been hoped for: namely, to starve the front of ammunition. It lasted too short a time for the lack of ammunitions as such to bring disaster to the army, as was originally planned. But the moral damage was much more terrible.

In the first place. what was the army fighting for if the people at home did not wish it to be victorious? For whom then were these enormous sacrifices and privations being made and endured? Must the soldiers fight for victory while the home front goes on strike against it?

In the second place, what effect did this move have on the enemy?

In the winter of 1917-18 dark clouds hovered in the firmament of the Entente. For nearly four years onslaught after onslaught has been made against the German giant, but they failed to bring him to the ground. He had to keep them at bay with one arm that held the defensive shield because his other arm had to be free to wield the sword against his enemies, now in the East and now in the South. But at last these enemies were overcome and his rear was now free for the conflict in the West. Rivers of blood had been shed for the accomplishment of that task; but now the sword was free to combine in battle with the shield on the Western Front. And since the enemy had hitherto failed to break the German defence here, the Germans themselves had now to launch the attack. The enemy feared and trembled before the prospect of this German victory.

At Paris and London conferences followed one another in unending series. Even the enemy propaganda encountered difficulties. It was no longer so easy to demonstrate that the prospect of a German victory was hopeless.

A prudent silence reigned at the front, even among the troops of the Entente. The insolence of their masters had suddenly subsided. A disturbing truth began to dawn on them. Their opinion of the German soldier had changed. Hitherto they were able to picture him as a kind of fool whose end would be destruction; but now they found themselves face to face with the soldier who had overcome their Russian ally. The policy of restricting the offensive to the East, which had been imposed on the German military authorities by the necessities of the situation, now seemed to the Entente as a tactical stroke of genius. For three years these Germans had been battering away at the Russian front without any apparent success at first. Those fruitless efforts were almost sneered at; for it was thought that in the long run the Russian giant would triumph through sheer force of numbers. Germany would be worn out through shedding so much blood. And facts appeared to confirm this hope.

Since the September days of 1914, when for the first time interminable columns of Russian war prisoners poured into Germany after the Battle of Tannenberg, it seemed as if the stream would never end but that as soon as one army was defeated and routed another would take its place. The supply of soldiers which the gigantic Empire placed at the disposal of the Czar seemed inexhaustible; new victims were always at hand for the holocaust of war. How long could Germany hold out in this competition?

Would not the day finally have to come when, after the last victory which the Germans would achieve, there would still remain reserve armies in Russia to be mustered for the final battle? And what then? According to human standards a Russian victory over Germany might be delayed but it would have to come in the long run.

All the hopes that had been based on Russia were now lost. The Ally who had sacrificed the most blood on the altar of their mutual interests had come to the end of his resources and lay prostrate before his unrelenting foe. A feeling of terror and dismay came over the Entente soldiers who had hitherto been buoyed up by blind faith. They feared the coming spring. For, seeing that hitherto they had failed to break the Germans when the latter could concentrate only part of the fighting strength on the Western Front, how could they count on victory now that the undivided forces of that amazing land of heroes appeared to be gathered for a massed attack in the West?

The shadow of the events which had taken place in South Tyrol, the spectre of General Cadorna's defeated armies, were reflected in the gloomy faces of the Entente troops in Flanders. Faith in victory gave way to fear of defeat to come.

Then, on those cold nights, when one almost heard the tread of the German armies advancing to the great assault, and the decision was being awaited in fear and trembling, suddenly a lurid light was set aglow in Germany and sent its rays into the last shell-hole on the enemy's front.

At the very moment when the German divisions were receiving their final orders for the great offensive a general strike broke out in Germany.

At first the world was dumbfounded. Then the enemy propaganda began activities once again and pounced on this theme at the eleventh hour. All of a sudden a means had come which could be utilized to revive the sinking confidence of the Entente soldiers. The probabilities of victory could now be presented as certain, and the anxious foreboding in regard to coming events could now be transformed into a feeling of resolute assurance. The regiments that had to bear the brunt of the Greatest German onslaught in history could now be inspired with the conviction that the final decision in this war would not be won by the audacity of the German assault but rather by the powers of endurance on the side of the defence. Let the Germans now have whatever victories they liked, the revolution and not the victorious army was welcomed in the Fatherland. British, French and American newspapers began to spread this belief among their readers while a very ably managed propaganda encouraged the morale of their troops at the front.

'Germany Facing Revolution! An Allied Victory Inevitable!' That was the best medicine to set the staggering Poilu and Tommy on their feet once again. Our rifles and machine-guns could now open fire once again; but instead of effecting a panic-stricken retreat they were now met with a determined resistance that was full of confidence.

That was the result of the strike in the munitions factories. Throughout the enemy countries faith in victory was thus revived and strengthened, and that paralysing feeling of despair which had hitherto made itself felt on the Entente front was banished. Consequently the strike cost the lives of thousands of German soldiers. But the despicable instigators of that dastardly strike were candidates for the highest public positions in the Germany of the Revolution.

At first it was apparently possible to overcome the repercussion of these events on the German soldiers, but on the enemy's side they had a lasting effect. Here the resistance had lost all the character of an army fighting for a lost cause. In its place there was now a grim determination to struggle through to victory. For, according to all human rules of judgment, victory would now be assured if the Western front could hold out against the German offensive even for only a few months. The Allied parliaments recognized the possibilities of a better future and voted huge sums of money for the continuation of the propaganda which was employed for the purpose of breaking up the internal cohesion of Germany.

It was my luck that I was able to take part in the first two offensives and in the final offensive. These have left on me the most stupendous impressions of my life—

stupendous, because now for the last time the struggle lost its defensive character and assumed the character of an offensive, just as it was in 1914. A sigh of relief went up from the German trenches and dug-outs when finally, after three years of endurance in that inferno, the day for the settling of accounts had come. Once again the lusty cheering of victorious battalions was heard, as they hung the last crowns of the immortal laurel on the standards which they consecrated to Victory. Once again the strains of patriotic songs soared upwards to the heavens above the endless columns of marching troops, and for the last time the Lord smiled on his ungrateful children.

In the midsummer of 1918 a feeling of sultry oppression hung over the front. At home they were quarrelling. About what? We heard a great deal among various units at the front. The War was now a hopeless affair, and only the foolhardy could think of victory. It was not the people but the capitalists and the Monarchy who were interested in carrying on. Such were the ideas that came from home and were discussed at the front.

At first this gave rise to only very slight reaction. What did universal suffrage matter to us? Is this what we had been fighting for during four years? It was a dastardly piece of robbery thus to filch from the graves of our heroes the ideals for which they had fallen. It was not to the slogan, 'Long Live Universal Suffrage,' that our troops in Flanders once faced certain death but with the cry, 'DEUTSCHLAND ÜBER ALLES IN DER WELT'. A small but by no means an unimportant difference. And the majority of those who were shouting for this suffrage were absent when it came to fighting for it. All this political rabble were strangers to us at the front. During those days only a fraction of these parliamentarian gentry were to be seen where honest Germans foregathered.

The old soldiers who had fought at the front had little liking for those new war aims of Messrs. Ebert, Scheidemann, Barth, Liebknecht and others. We could not understand why, all of a sudden, the shirkers should abrogate all executive powers to themselves, without having any regard to the army.

From the very beginning I had my own definite personal views. I intensely loathed the whole gang of miserable party politicians who had betrayed the people. I had long ago realized that the interests of the nation played only a very small part with this disreputable crew and that what counted with them was the possibility of filling their own empty pockets. My opinion was that those people thoroughly deserved to be hanged, because they were ready to sacrifice the peace and if necessary allow Germany to be defeated just to serve their own ends. To consider their wishes would mean to sacrifice the interests of the working classes for the benefit of a gang of thieves. To meet their wishes meant that one should agree to sacrifice Germany.

Such, too, was the opinion still held by the majority of the army. But the reinforcements which came from home were fast becoming worse and worse; so much so that their arrival was a source of weakness rather than of strength to our fighting forces. The young recruits in particular were for the most part useless. Sometimes it was hard to believe that they were sons of the same nation that sent its youth into the battles that were fought round Ypres.

In August and September the symptoms of moral disintegration increased more and more rapidly, although the enemy's offensive was not at all comparable to the frightfulness of our own former defensive battles. In comparison with this offensive the battles fought on the Somme and in Flanders remained in our memories as the most terrible of all horrors.

At the end of September my division occupied, for the third time, those positions which we had once taken by storm as young volunteers. What a memory!

Here we had received our baptism of fire, in October and November 1914.

With a burning love of the homeland in their hearts and a song on their lips, our young regiment went into action as if going to a dance. The dearest blood was given freely here in the belief that it was shed to protect the freedom and independence of the Fatherland.

In July 1917 we set foot for the second time on what we regarded as sacred soil. Were not our best comrades at rest here, some of them little more than boys—the soldiers who had rushed into death for their country's sake, their eyes glowing with enthusiastic love.

The older ones among us, who had been with the regiment from the beginning, were deeply moved as we stood on this sacred spot where we had sworn 'Loyalty and Duty unto Death'. Three years ago the regiment had taken this position by storm; now it was called upon to defend it in a gruelling struggle.

With an artillery bombardment that lasted three weeks the English prepared for their great offensive in Flanders. There the spirits of the dead seemed to live again. The regiment dug itself into the mud, clung to its shell-holes and craters, neither flinching nor wavering, but growing smaller in numbers day after day. Finally the British launched their attack on July 31st, 1917.

We were relieved in the beginning of August. The regiment had dwindled down to a few companies, who staggered back, mud-crusted, more like phantoms than human beings. Besides a few hundred yards of shell-holes, death was the only reward which the English gained.

Now in the autumn of 1918 we stood for the third time on the ground we had stormed in 1914. The village of Comines, which formerly had served us as a base, was now within the fighting zone. Although little had changed in the surrounding district itself, yet the men had become different, somehow or other. They now talked politics. Like everywhere else, the poison from home was having its effect here also. The young drafts succumbed to it completely. They had come directly from home.

During the night of October 13th-14th, the British opened an attack with gas on the front south of Ypres. They used the yellow gas whose effect was unknown to us, at least from personal experience. I was destined to experience it that very night. On a hill south of Werwick, in the evening of October 13th, we were subjected for several hours to a heavy bombardment with gas bombs, which continued throughout the night with more or less intensity. About midnight a number of us were put out of action, some for ever. Towards morning I also began to feel pain. It increased with every quarter of an hour; and about seven o'clock my eyes were scorching as I staggered back and delivered the last dispatch I was destined to carry in this war. A few hours later my eyes were like glowing coals and all was darkness around me.

I was sent into hospital at Pasewalk in Pomerania, and there it was that I had to hear of the Revolution.

For a long time there had been something in the air which was indefinable and repulsive. People were saying that something was bound to happen within the next few weeks, although I could not imagine what this meant. In the first instance I thought of a strike similar to the one which had taken place in spring. Unfavourable rumours were constantly coming from the Navy, which was said to be in a state of ferment. But this seemed to be a fanciful creation of a few isolated young people. It is true that at the hospital they were all talking abut the end of the war and hoping that this was not far off, but nobody thought that the decision would come immediately. I was not able to read the newspapers.

In November the general tension increased. Then one day disaster broke in upon us suddenly and without warning. Sailors came in motor-lorries and called on us to rise in revolt. A few Jew-boys were the leaders in that combat for the 'Liberty, Beauty, and Dignity' of our National

Being. Not one of them had seen active service at the front. Through the medium of a hospital for venereal diseases these three Orientals had been sent back home. Now their red rags were being hoisted here.

During the last few days I had begun to feel somewhat better. The burning pain in the eye-sockets had become less severe. Gradually I was able to distinguish the general outlines of my immediate surroundings.

And it was permissible to hope that at least I would recover my sight sufficiently to be able to take up some profession later on. That I would ever be able to draw or design once again was naturally out of the question. Thus I was on the way to recovery when the frightful hour came.

My first thought was that this outbreak of high treason was only a local affair. I tried to enforce this belief among my comrades. My Bavarian hospital mates, in particular, were readily responsive. Their inclinations were anything but revolutionary. I could not imagine this madness breaking out in Munich; for it seemed to me that loyalty to the House of Wittelsbach was, after all, stronger than the will of a few Jews. And so I could not help believing that this was merely a revolt in the Navy and that it would be suppressed within the next few days.

With the next few days came the most astounding information of my life. The rumours grew more and more persistent. I was told that what I had considered to be a local affair was in reality a general revolution. In addition to this, from the front came the shameful news that they wished to capitulate! What! Was such a thing possible?

On November 10th the local pastor visited the hospital for the purpose of delivering a short address. And that was how we came to know the whole story.

I was in a fever of excitement as I listened to the address. The reverend old gentleman seemed to be trembling when he informed us that the House of Hohen-zollern should no longer wear the Imperial Crown, that the Fatherland had become a 'Republic', that we should pray to the Almighty not to withhold His blessing from the new order of things and not to abandon our people in the days to come. In delivering this message he could not do more than briefly express appreciation of the Royal House, its services to Pomerania, to Prussia, indeed, to the whole of the German Fatherland, and—here he began to weep. A feeling of profound dismay fell on the people in that assembly, and I do not think there was a single eye that withheld its tears. As for myself, I broke down completely when the old gentleman tried to resume his story by informing us that we must now end this long war, because the war was lost, he said, and we were at the mercy of the victor. The Fatherland would have to bear heavy burdens in the future. We were to accept the terms of the Armistice and trust to the magnanimity of our former enemies. It was impossible for me to stay and listen any longer.

Darkness surrounded me as I staggered and stumbled back to my ward and buried my aching head between the blankets and pillow. I had not cried since the day that I stood beside my mother's grave.

Whenever Fate dealt cruelly with me in my young days the spirit of determination within me grew stronger and stronger. During all those long years of war, when Death claimed many a true friend and comrade from our ranks, to me it would have appeared sinful to have uttered a word of complaint. Did they not die for Germany? And, finally, almost in the last few days of that titanic struggle, when the waves of poison gas enveloped me and began to penetrate my eyes, the thought of becoming permanently blind unnerved me; but the voice of conscience cried out immediately: Poor miserable fellow, will you start howling when there are thousands of others whose lot is a hundred times worse than yours?

And so I accepted my misfortune in silence, realizing that this was the only thing to be done and that personal suffering was nothing when compared with the misfortune of one's country.

So all had been in vain. In vain all the sacrifices and privations, in vain the hunger and thirst for endless months, in vain those hours that we stuck to our posts though the fear of death gripped our souls, and in vain the deaths of two millions who fell in discharging this duty. Think of those hundreds of thousands who set out with hearts full of faith in their fatherland, and never returned; ought not their graves to open, so that the spirits of those heroes bespattered with mud and blood should come home and take vengeance on those who had so despicably betrayed the greatest sacrifice which a human being can make for his country? Was it for this that the soldiers died in August and September 1914, for this that the volunteer regiments followed the old comrades in the autumn of the same year? Was it for this that those boys of seventeen years of age were mingled with the earth of Flanders? Was this meant to be the fruits of the sacrifice which German mothers made for their Fatherland when, with heavy hearts, they said good-bye to their sons who never returned?

Has all this been done in order to enable a gang of despicable criminals to lay hands on the Fatherland?

Was this then what the German soldier struggled for through sweltering heat and blinding snowstorm, enduring hunger and thirst and cold, fatigued from sleepless nights and endless marches? Was it for this that he lived through an inferno of artillery bombardments, lay gasping and choking during gas attacks, neither flinching nor faltering, but remaining staunch to the thought of defending the Fatherland against the enemy? Certainly these heroes also deserved the epitaph:

Traveller, when you come to Germany, tell the Homeland that we lie here, true to the Fatherland and faithful to our duty.[13]

And at Home? But—was this the only sacrifice that we had to consider?

Was the Germany of the past a country of little worth? Did she not owe a certain duty to her own history? Were we still worthy to partake in the glory of the past? How could we justify this act to future generations? What a gang of despicable and depraved criminals!

The more I tried then to glean some definite information of the terrible events that had happened the more my head became afire with rage and shame. What was all the pain I suffered in my eyes compared with this tragedy?

The following days were terrible to bear, and the nights still worse. To depend on the mercy of the enemy was a precept which only fools or criminal liars could recommend. During those nights my hatred increased—hatred for the orignators of this dastardly crime.

During the following days my own fate became clear to me. I was forced now to scoff at the thought of my personal future, which hitherto had been the cause of so much worry to me. Was it not ludicrous to think of building up anything on such a foundation? Finally, it also became clear to me that it was the inevitable that had happened, something which I had feared for a long time, though I really did not have the heart to believe it.

Emperor William II was the first German Emperor to offer the hand of friendship to the Marxist leaders, not suspecting that they were scoundrels without any sense of honour. While they held the imperial hand in theirs, the other hand was already feeling for the dagger. There is no such thing as coming to an understanding with the Jews. It must be the hard-and-fast 'Either-Or.' For my part I then decided that I would take up political work.

CHAPTER VIII:
The Beginning of My Political Activities

Towards the end of November I returned to Munich. I went to the depot of my regiment, which was now in the hands of the 'Soldiers' Councils'. As the whole administration was quite repulsive to me, I decided to leave it as soon as I possibly could. With my faithful war-comrade, Ernst-Schmidt, I came to Traunstein and remained there until the camp was broken up. In March 1919 we were back again in Munich.

The situation there could not last as it was. It tended irresistibly to a further extension of the Revolution. Eisner's death served only to hasten this development and finally led to the dictatorship of the Councils—or, to put it more correctly, to a Jewish hegemony, which turned out to be transitory but which was the original aim of those who had contrived the Revolution.

At that juncture innumerable plans took shape in my mind. I spent whole days pondering on the problem of what could be done, but unfortunately every project had to give way before the hard fact that I was quite unknown and therefore did not have even the first pre-requisite necessary for effective action. Later on I shall explain the reasons why

I could not decide to join any of the parties then in existence.

As the new Soviet Revolution began to run its course in Munich my first activities drew upon me the ill-will of the Central Council. In the early morning of April 27th, 1919, I was to have been arrested; but the three fellows who came to arrest me did not have the courage to face my rifle and withdrew just as they had arrived.

A few days after the liberation of Munich I was ordered to appear before the Inquiry Commission which had been set up in the 2nd Infantry Regiment for the purpose of watching revolutionary activities. That was my first incursion into the more or less political field.

After another few weeks I received orders to attend a course of lectures which were being given to members of the army. This course was meant to inculcate certain fundamental principles on which the soldier could base his political ideas. For me the advantage of this organization was that it gave me a chance of meeting fellow soldiers who were of the same way of thinking and with whom I could discuss the actual situation. We were all more or less firmly convinced that Germany could not be saved from imminent disaster by those who had participated in the November treachery—that is to say, the Centre and the Social-Democrats; and also that the so-called Bourgeois-National group could not make good the damage that had been done, even if they had the best intentions. They lacked a number of requisites without which such a task could never be successfully undertaken. The years that followed have justified the opinions which we held at that time.

In our small circle we discussed the project of forming a new party. The leading ideas which we then proposed were the same as those which were carried into effect afterwards, when the German Labour Party was founded. The name of the new movement which was to be founded should be such that of itself, it would appeal to the mass of the people; for all our efforts would turn out vain and useless if this condition were lacking. And that was the reason why we chose the name 'Social-Revolutionary Party', particularly because the social principles of our new organization were indeed revolutionary.

But there was also a more fundamental reason. The attention which I had given to economic problems during my earlier years was more or less confined to considerations arising directly out of the social problem. Subsequently this outlook broadened as I came to study the German policy of the Triple Alliance. This policy was very largely the result of an erroneous valuation of the economic situation, together with a confused notion as to the basis on which the future subsistence of the German people could be guaranteed. All these ideas were based on the principle that capital is exclusively the product of labour and that, just like labour, it was subject to all the factors which can hinder or promote human activity. Hence, from the national standpoint, the significance of capital depended on the greatness and freedom and power of the State, that is to say, of the nation, and that it is this dependence alone which leads capital to promote the interests of the State and the nation, from the instinct of self-preservation and for the sake of its own development.

On such principles the attitude of the State towards capital would be comparatively simple and clear. Its only object would be to make sure that capital remained subservient to the State and did not allocate to itself the right to dominate national interests. Thus it could confine its activities within the two following limits: on the one side, to assure a vital and independent system of national economy and, on the other, to safeguard the social rights of the workers.

Previously I did not recognize with adequate clearness the difference between capital which is purely the product of creative labour and the existence and nature of capital which is exclusively the result of financial speculation. Here I needed an impulse to set my mind thinking in this direction; but that impulse had hitherto been lacking. The requisite impulse now came from one of the men who delivered lectures in the course I have already mentioned. This was Gottfried Feder.

For the first time in my life I heard a discussion which dealt with the principles of stock-exchange capital and capital which was used for loan activities. After hearing the first lecture delivered by Feder, the idea immediately came into my head that I had now found a way to one of the most essential pre-requisites for the founding of a new party.

To my mind, Feder's merit consisted in the ruthless and trenchant way in which he described the double character of the capital engaged in stock-exchange and loan transaction, laying bare the fact that this capital is ever and always dependent on the payment of interest. In fundamental questions his statements were so full of common sense that those who criticized him did not deny that AU FOND his ideas were sound but they doubted whether it be possible to put these ideas into practice. To me this seemed the strongest point in Feder's teaching, though others considered it a weak point.

It is not the business of him who lays down a theoretical programme to explain the various ways in which something can be put into practice.

His task is to deal with the problem as such; and, therefore, he has to look to the end rather than the means. The important question is whether an idea is fundamentally right or not. The question of whether or not it may be difficult to carry it out in practice is quite another matter.

When a man whose task it is to lay down the principles of a programme or policy begins to busy himself with the question as to whether it is expedient and practical, instead of confining himself to the statement of the absolute truth, his work will cease to be a guiding star to those who are looking about for light and leading and will become merely a recipe for every-day iife. The man who lays down the programme of a movement must consider only the goal. It is for the political leader to point out the way in which that goal may be reached. The thought of the former will, therefore, be determined by those truths that are everlasting, whereas the activity of the latter must always be guided by taking practical account of the circumstances under which those truths have to be carried into effect.

The greatness of the one will depend on the absolute truth of his idea, considered in the abstract; whereas that of the other will depend on whether or not he correctly judges the given realities and how they may be utilized under the guidance of the truths established by the former.

The test of greatness as applied to a political leader is the success of his plans and his enterprises, which means his ability to reach the goal for which he sets out; whereas the final goal set up by the political philosopher can never be reached; for human thought may grasp truths and picture ends which it sees like clear crystal, though such ends can never be completely fulfilled because human nature is weak and imperfect. The more an idea is correct in the abstract, and, therefore, all the more powerful, the smaller is the possibility of putting it into practice, at least as far as this latter depends on human beings. The significance of a political philosopher does not depend on the practical success of the plans he lays down but rather on their absolute truth and the influence they exert on the progress of mankind. If it were otherwise, the founders of religions could not be considered as the greatest men who have ever lived, because their moral aims will never be completely or even approximately carried out in practice. Even that religion which is called the Religion of Love is really no more than a faint reflex of the will of its sublime Founder. But its significance lies in the orientation which it endeavoured to give to human civilization, and human virtue and morals.

This very wide difference between the functions of a political philosopher and a practical political leader is the reason why the qualifications necessary for both functions are scarcely ever found associated in the same person. This applies especially to the so-called successful politician of the smaller kind, whose activity is indeed hardly more than practising the art of doing the possible, as Bismarck modestly defined the art of politics in general. If such a politician resolutely avoids great ideas his success will be all the easier to attain; it will be attained more expeditely and frequently will be more tangible. By reason of this very fact, however, such success is doomed to futility and sometimes does not even survive the death of its author.

Generally speaking, the work of politicians is without significance for the following generation, because their temporary success was based on the expediency of avoiding all really great decisive problems and ideas which would be valid also for future generations.

To pursue ideals which will still be of value and significance for the future is generally not a very profitable undertaking and he who follows such a course is only very rarely understood by the mass of the people, who find beer and milk a more persuasive index of political values than far-sighted plans for the future, the realization of which can only take place later on and the advantages of which can be reaped only by posterity.

Because of a certain vanity, which is always one of the blood-relations of unintelligence, the general run of politicians will always eschew those schemes for the future which are really difficult to put into practice; and they will practise this avoidance so that they may not lose the immediate favour of the mob. The importance and the success of such politicians belong exclusively to the present and will be of no consequence for the future. But that does not worry small-minded people; they are quite content with momentary results.

The position of the constructive political philosopher is quite different. The importance of his work must always be judged from the standpoint of the future; and he is frequently described by the word WELTFREMD, or dreamer. While the ability of the politician consists in mastering the art of the possible, the founder of a political system belongs to those who are said to please the gods only because they wish for and demand the impossible. They will always have to renounce contemporary fame; but if their ideas be immortal, posterity will grant them its acknowledgment.

Within long spans of human progress it may occasionally happen that the practical politician and political philosopher are one. The more intimate this union is, the greater will be the obstacles which the activity of the politician will have to encounter. Such a man does not labour for the purpose of satisfying demands that are obvious to every philistine, but he reaches out towards ends which can be understood only by the few. His life is torn asunder by hatred and love. The protest of his contemporaries, who do not understand the man, is in conflict with the recognition of posterity, for whom he also works.

For the greater the work which a man does for the future, the less will he be appreciated by his contemporaries. His struggle will accordingly be all the more severe, and his success all the rarer. When, in the course of centuries, such a man appears who is blessed with success then, towards the end of his days, he may have a faint prevision of his future fame. But such great men are only the Marathon runners of history. The laurels of contemporary fame are only for the brow of the dying hero.

The great protagonists are those who fight for their ideas and ideals despite the fact that they receive no recognition at the hands of their contemporaries. They are the men whose memories will be enshrined in the hearts of the future generations. It seems then as if each individual felt it his duty to make retroactive atonement for the wrong which great men have suffered at the hands of their contemporaries. Their lives and their work are then studied with touching and grateful admiration. Especially in dark days of distress, such men have the power of healing broken hearts and elevating the despairing spirit of a people. To this group belong not only the genuinely great statesmen but all the great reformers as well. Beside Frederick the Great we have such men as Martin Luther and Richard Wagner.

When I heard Gottfried Feder's first lecture on 'The Abolition of the Interest-

Servitude', I understood immediately that here was a truth of transcendental importance for the future of the German people. The absolute separation of stock-exchange capital from the economic life of the nation would make it possible to oppose the process of internationalization in German business without at the same time attacking capital as such, for to do this would jeopardize the foundations of our national independence. I clearly saw what was developing in Germany and I realized then that the stiffest fight we would have to wage would not be against the enemy nations but against international capital. In Feder's speech I found an effective rallying-cry for our coming struggle.

Here, again, later events proved how correct was the impression we then had. The fools among our bourgeois politicians do not mock at us on this point any more; for even those politicians now see—if they would speak the truth—that international stock-exchange capital was not only the chief instigating factor in bringing on the War but that now when the War is over it turns the peace into a hell.

The struggle against international finance capital and loan-capital has become one of the most important points in the programme on which the German nation has based its fight for economic freedom and independence.

Regarding the objections raised by so-called practical people, the following answer must suffice: All apprehensions concerning the fearful economic consequences that would follow the abolition of the servitude that results from interest-capital are ill-timed; for, in the first place, the economic principles hitherto followed have proved quite fatal to the interests of the German people. The attitude adopted when the question of maintaining our national existence arose vividly recalls similar advice once given by experts—the Bavarian Medical College, for example—on the question of introducing railroads. The fears expressed by that august body of experts were not realized. Those who travelled in the coaches of the new 'Steam-horse' did not suffer from vertigo. Those who looked on did not become ill and the hoardings which had been erected to conceal the new invention were eventually taken down. Only those blinds which obscure the vision of the would-be 'experts', have remained. And that will be always so.

In the second place, the following must be borne in mind: Any idea may be a source of danger if it be looked upon as an end in itself, when really it is only the means to an end. For me and for all genuine National-Socialists there is only one doctrine. PEOPLE AND FATHERLAND.

What we have to fight for is the necessary security for the existence and increase of our race and people, the subsistence of its children and the maintenance of our racial stock unmixed, the freedom and independence of the Fatherland; so that our people may be enabled to fulfil the mission assigned to it by the Creator.

All ideas and ideals, all teaching and all knowledge, must serve these ends. It is from this standpoint that everything must be examined and turned to practical uses or else discarded. Thus a theory can never become a mere dead dogma since everything will have to serve the practical ends of everyday life.

Thus the judgment arrived at by Gottfried Feder determined me to make a fundamental study of a question with which I had hitherto not been very familiar.

I began to study again and thus it was that I first came to understand perfectly what was the substance and purpose of the life-work of the Jew, Karl Marx. His CAPITAL became intelligible to me now for the first time. And in the light of it I now exactly understood the fight of the Social-Democrats against national economics, a fight which was to prepare the ground for the hegemony of a real international and stock-exchange capital.

In another direction also this course of lectures had important consequences for me.

One day I put my name down as wishing to take part in the discussion. Another of the participants thought that he would break a lance for the Jews and entered into a lengthy defence of them. This aroused my opposition. An overwhelming number of those who attended the lecture course supported my views. The consequence of it all was that, a few days later, I was assigned to a regiment then stationed at Munich and given a position there as 'instruction officer'.

At that time the spirit of discipline was rather weak among those troops. It was still suffering from the after-effects of the period when the Soldiers' Councils were in control. Only gradually and carefully could a new spirit of military discipline and obedience be introduced in place of 'voluntary obedience', a term which had been used to express the ideal of military discipline under Kurt Eisner's higgledy-piggledy regime. The soldiers had to be taught to think and feel in a national and patriotic way. In these two directions lay my future line of action.

I took up my work with the greatest delight and devotion. Here I was presented with an opportunity of speaking before quite a large audience. I was now able to confirm what I had hitherto merely felt, namely, that I had a talent for public speaking. My voice had become so much better that I could be well understood, at least in all parts of the small hall where the soldiers assembled.

No task could have been more pleasing to me than this one; for now, before being demobilized, I was in a position to render useful service to an institution which had been infinitely dear to my heart: namely, the army.

I am able to state that my talks were successful. During the course of my lectures I have led back hundreds and even thousands of my fellow countrymen to their people and their fatherland. I 'nationalized' these troops and by so doing I helped to restore general discipline.

Here again I made the acquaintance of several comrades whose thought ran along the same lines as my own and who later became members of the first group out of which the new movement developed.

CHAPTER IX: The German Labour Party

One day I received an order from my superiors to investigate the nature of an association which was apparently political. It called itself 'The German Labour Party' and was soon to hold a meeting at which Gottfried Feder would speak. I was ordered to attend this meeting and report on the situation.

The spirit of curiosity in which the army authorities then regarded political parties can be very well understood. The Revolution had granted the soldiers the right to take an active part in politics and it was particularly those with the smallest experience who had availed themselves of this right. But not until the Centre and the Social-Democratic parties were reluctantly forced to recognize that the sympathies of the soldiers had turned away from the revolutionary parties towards the national movement and the national reawakening, did they feel obliged to withdraw from the army the right to vote and to forbid it all political activity.

The fact that the Centre and Marxism had adopted this policy was instructive, because if they had not thus curtailed the 'rights of the citizen'—as they described the political rights of the soldiers after the Revolution—the government which had been established in November 1918 would have been overthrown within a few years and the dishonour and disgrace of the nation would not have been further prolonged. At that time the soldiers were on the point of taking the best way to rid the nation of the vampires and valets who served the cause of the Entente in the interior of the country. But the fact that the so-called 'national' parties voted enthusiastically for the doctrinaire policy of the criminals who organized the Revolution in November (1918) helped also to render the army ineffective as an instrument of national restoration and thus showed once again where men might be led by the purely abstract notions accepted by these most gullible people.

The minds of the bourgeois middle classes had become so fossilized that they sincerely believed the army could once again become what it had previously been, namely, a rampart of German valour; while the Centre Party and the Marxists intended only to extract the poisonous tooth of nationalism, without which an army must always remain just a police force but can never be in the position of a military organization capable of fighting against the outside enemy. This truth was sufficiently proved by subsequent events.

Or did our 'national' politicians believe, after all, that the development of our army could be other than national? This belief might be possible and could be explained by the fact that during the War they were not soldiers but merely talkers. In other words, they were parliamentarians, and, as such, they did not have the slightest idea of what was passing in the hearts of those men who remembered the greatness of their own past and also remembered that they had once been the first soldiers in the world.—I decided to attend the meeting of this Party, which had hitherto been entirely unknown to me. When I arrived that evening in the guest room of the former Sternecker Brewery—which has now become a place of historical significance for us—I found approximately 20-25 persons present, most of them belonging to the lower classes.

The theme of Feder's lecture was already familiar to me; for I had heard it in the lecture course I have spoken of. Therefore, I could concentrate my attention on studying the society itself.

The impression it made upon me was neither good nor bad. I felt that here was just another one of these many new societies which were being formed at that time. In those days everybody felt called upon to found a new Party whenever he felt displeased with the course of events and had lost confidence in all the parties already existing. Thus it was that new associations sprouted up all round, to disappear just as quickly, without exercising any effect or making any noise whatsoever. Generally speaking, the founders of such associations did not have the slightest idea of what it means to bring together a number of people for the foundations of a party or a movement. Therefore these associations disappeared because of their woeful lack of anything like an adequate grasp of the necessities of the situation.

My opinion of the 'German Labour Party' was not very different after I had listened to their proceedings for about two hours. I was glad when Feder finally came to a close. I had observed enough and was just about to leave when it was announced that anybody who wished was free to open a discussion. Thereupon, I decided to remain. But the discussion seemed to proceed without anything of vital importance being mentioned, when suddenly a 'professor' commenced to speak. He opened by throwing doubt on the accuracy of what Feder had said, and then. after Feder had replied very effectively, the professor suddenly took up his position on what he called 'the basis of facts,' but before this he recommended the young party most urgently to introduce the secession of Bavaria from Prussia as one of the leading proposals in its programme. In the most self-assured way, this man kept on insisting that German-Austria would join Bavaria and that the peace would then function much better. He made other similarly extravagant statements. At this juncture I felt bound to ask for permission to speak and to tell the learned gentleman what I thought. The result was that the honourable gentleman who had last spoken slipped out of his place, like a whipped cur, without uttering a sound. While I was speaking the audience listened with an expression of surprise on their faces. When I was just about to say good-night to the assembly and to leave, a man came after me quickly and introduced himself. I did not grasp the name correctly; but he placed a little book in my hand, which was obviously a political pamphlet, and asked me very earnestly to read it.

I was quite pleased; because in this way, I could come to know about this association without having to attend its tiresome meetings. Moreover, this man, who had the appearance of a workman, made a good impression on me. Thereupon, I left the hall.

At that time I was living in one of the barracks of the 2nd Infantry Regiment. I had a little room which still bore the unmistakable traces of the Revolution. During the day I was mostly out, at the quarters of Light Infantry No. 41 or else attending meetings or lectures, held at some other branch of the army. I spent only the night at the quarters where I lodged. Since I usually woke up about five o'clock every morning

I got into the habit of amusing myself with watching little mice which played around in my small room. I used to place a few pieces of hard bread or crust on the floor and watch the funny little beasts playing around and enjoying themselves with these delicacies. I had suffered so many privations in my own life that I well knew what hunger was and could only too well picture to myself the pleasure these little creatures were experiencing.

So on the morning after the meeting I have mentioned, it happened that about five o'clock I lay fully awake in bed, watching the mice playing and vying with each other. As I was not able to go to sleep again, I suddenly remembered the pamphlet that one of the workers had given me at the meeting. It was a small pamphlet of which this worker was the author. In his little book he described how his mind had thrown off the shackles of the Marxist and trades-union phraseology, and that he had come back to the nationalist ideals. That was the reason why he had entitled his little book: "My Political Awakening". The pamphlet secured my attention the moment I began to read, and I read it with interest to the end. The process here described was similar to that which I had experienced in my own case ten years previously. Unconsciously my own experiences began to stir again in my mind. During that day my thoughts returned several times to what I had read; but I finally decided to give the matter no further attention. A week or so later, however, I received a postcard which informed me, to my astonishment, that I had been admitted into the German Labour Party. I was asked to answer this communication and to attend a meeting of the Party Committee on Wednesday next.

This manner of getting members rather amazed me, and I did not know whether to be angry or laugh at it. Hitherto I had not any idea of entering a party already in existence but wanted to found one of my own. Such an invitation as I now had received I looked upon as entirely out of the question for me.

I was about to send a written reply when my curiosity got the better of me, and I decided to attend the gathering at the date assigned, so that I might expound my principles to these gentlemen in person. Wednesday came. The tavern in which the meeting was to take place was the 'Alte Rosenbad' in the Herrnstrasse, into which apparently only an occasional guest wandered. This was not very surprising in the year 1919, when the bills of fare even at the larger restaurants were only very modest and scanty in their pretensions and thus not very attractive to clients. But I had never before heard of this restaurant.

I went through the badly-lighted guest-room, where not a single guest was to be seen, and searched for the door which led to the side room; and there I was face-to-face with the 'Congress'. Under the dim light shed by a grimy gas-lamp I could see four young people sitting around a table, one of them the author of the pamphlet. He greeted me cordially and welcomed me as a new member of the German Labour Party.

I was taken somewhat aback on being informed that actually the National President of the Party had not yet come; so I decided that I would keep back my own exposition for the time being. Finally the President appeared. He was the man who had been chairman of the meeting held in the Sternecker Brewery, when Feder spoke.

My curiosity was stimulated anew and I sat waiting for what was going to happen. Now I got at least as far as learning the names of the gentlemen who had been parties to the whole affair. The REICH National President of the Association was a certain Herr Harrer and the President for the Munich district was Anton Drexler.

The minutes of the previous meeting were read out and a vote of confidence in the secretary was passed. Then came the treasurer's report. The Society possessed a total fund of seven marks and fifty pfennigs (a sum corresponding to 7s. 6d. in English money at par), whereupon the treasurer was assured that he had the confidence of the members. This was now inserted in the minutes. Then letters of reply which had been written by the Chairman were read; first, to a letter received from Kiel, then to one from Düsseldorf and finally to one from Berlin. All three replies received the approval of all present. Then the incoming letters were read—one from Berlin, one from Düsseldorf and one from Kiel. The reception of these letters seemed to cause great satisfaction. This increasing bulk of correspondence was taken as the best and most obvious sign of the growing importance of the German Labour Party. And then? Well, there followed a long discussion of the replies which would be given to these newly-received letters.

It was all very awful. This was the worst kind of parish-pump clubbism. And was I supposed to become a member of such a club?

The question of new members was next discussed—that is to say, the question of catching myself in the trap.

I now began to ask questions. But I found that, apart from a few general principles, there was nothing—no programme, no pamphlet, nothing at all in print, no card of membership, not even a party stamp, nothing but obvious good faith and good intentions.

I no longer felt inclined to laugh; for what else was all this but a typical sign of the most complete perplexity and deepest despair in regard to all political parties, their programmes and views and activities? The feeling which had induced those few young people to join in what seemed such a ridiculous enterprise was nothing but the call of the inner voice which told them—though more intuitively than consciously—that the whole party system as it had hitherto existed was not the kind of force that could restore the German nation or repair the damages that had been done to the German people by those who hitherto controlled the internal affairs of the nation. I quickly read through the list of principles that formed the platform of the party. These principles were stated on typewritten sheets. Here again I found evidence of the spirit of longing and searching, but no sign whatever of a knowledge of the conflict that had to be fought. I myself had experienced the feelings which inspired those people. It was the longing for a movement which should be more than a party, in the hitherto accepted meaning of that word.

When I returned to my room in the barracks that evening I had formed a definite opinion on this association and I was facing the most difficult problem of my life. Should I join this party or refuse?

From the side of the intellect alone, every consideration urged me to refuse; but my feelings troubled me. The more I tried to prove to myself how senseless this club was, on the whole, the more did my feelings incline me to favour it. During the following days I was restless. I began to consider all the pros and cons. I had long ago decided to take an active part in politics. The fact that I could do so only through a new movement was quite clear to me; but I had hitherto lacked the impulse to take concrete action. I am not one of those people who will begin something to-day and just give it up the next day for the sake of something new. That was the main reason which made it so difficult for me to decide in joining something newly founded; for this must become the real fulfilment of everything I dreamt, or else it had better not be started at all. I knew that such a decision should bind me for ever and that there could be no turning back. For me there could be no idle dallying but only a cause to be championed ardently. I had already an instinctive feeling against people who took up everything, but never carried anything through to the end. I loathed these Jacks-of-all-Trades, and considered the activities of such people to be worse than if they were to remain entirely quiescent. Fate herself now seemed to supply the finger-post that pointed out the way. I should never have entered one of the big parties already in existence and shall explain my reasons for this later on. This ludicrous little formation, with its handful of members, seemed to have the unique advantage of not yet being fossilized into an 'organization' and still offered a chance for real personal activity on the part of the individual. Here it might still be possible to do some effective work; and, as the movement was still small, one could all the easier give it the required shape. Here it was still possible to determine the character of the movement, the aims to be achieved and the road to be taken, which would have been impossible in the case of the big parties already existing.

The longer I reflected on the problem, the more my opinion developed that just such a small movement would best serve as an instrument to prepare the way for the national resurgence, but that this could never be done by the political parliamentary parties which were too firmly attached to obsolete ideas or had an interest in supporting the new regime. What had to be proclaimed here was a new WELTANSCHAUUNG and not a new election cry.

It was, however, infinitely difficult to decide on putting the intention into practice. What were the qualifications which I could bring to the accomplishment of such a task?

The fact that I was poor and without resources could, in my opinion, be the easiest to bear. But the fact that I was utterly unknown raised a more difficult problem. I was only one of the millions which Chance allows to exist or cease to exist, whom even their next-door neighbours will not consent to know. Another difficulty arose from the fact that I had not gone through the regular school curriculum.

The so-called 'intellectuals' still look down with infinite superciliousness on anyone who has not been through the prescribed schools and allowed them to pump the necessary knowledge into him. The question of what a man can do is never asked but rather, what has he learned? 'Educated' people look upon any imbecile who is plastered with a number of academic certificates as superior to the ablest young fellow who lacks these precious documents. I could therefore easily imagine how this 'educated' world would receive me and I was wrong only in so far as I then believed men to be for the most part better than they proved to be in the cold light of reality. Because of their being as they are, the few exceptions stand out all the more conspicuously. I learned more and more to distinguish between those who will always be at school and those who will one day come to know something in reality.

After two days of careful brooding and reflection I became convinced that I must take the contemplated step. It was the most fateful decision of my life. No retreat was possible.

Thus I declared myself ready to accept the membership tendered me by the German Labour Party and received a provisional certificate of membership. I was numbered SEVEN.

CHAPTER X:
Why the Second Reich Collapsed

The depth of a fall is always measured by the difference between the level of the original position from which a body has fallen and that in which it is now found. The same holds good for Nations and States. The matter of greatest importance here is the height of the original level, or rather the greatest height that had been attained before the descent began.

For only the profound decline or collapse of that which was capable of reaching extraordinary heights can make a striking impression on the eye of the beholder. The collapse of the Second REICH was all the more bewildering for those who could ponder over it and feel the effect of it in their hearts, because the REICH had fallen from a height which can hardly be imagined in these days of misery and humiliation.

The Second REICH was founded in circumstances of such dazzling splendour that the whole nation had become entranced and exalted by it. Following an unparalleled series of victories, that Empire was handed over as the guerdon of immortal heroism to the children and grandchildren of the heroes. Whether they were fully conscious of it or not does not matter; anyhow, the Germans felt that this Empire had not been brought into existence by a series of able political negotiations through parliamentary channels, but that it was different from political institutions founded elsewhere by reason of the nobler circumstances that had accompanied its establishment. When its foundations were laid the accompanying music was not the chatter of parliamentary debates but the thunder and boom of war along the battle front that encircled Paris.

It was thus that an act of statesmanship was accomplished whereby the Germans, princes as well as people, established the future REICH and restored the symbol of the

Imperial Crown. Bismarck's State was not founded on treason and assassination by deserters and shirkers but by the regiments that had fought at the front. This unique birth and baptism of fire sufficed of themselves to surround the Second Empire with an aureole of historical splendour such as few of the older States could lay claim to.And what an ascension then began! A position of independence in regard to the outside world guaranteed the means of livelihood at home. The nation increased in numbers and in worldly wealth. The honour of the State and therewith the honour of the people as a whole were secured and protected by an army which was the most striking witness of the difference between this new REICH and the old German Confederation.

But the downfall of the Second Empire and the German people has been so profound that they all seem to have been struck dumbfounded and rendered incapable of feeling the significance of this downfall or reflecting on it. It seems as if people were utterly unable to picture in their minds the heights to which the Empire formerly attained, so visionary and unreal appears the greatness and splendour of those days in contrast to the misery of the present. Bearing this in mind we can understand why and how people become so dazed when they try to look back to the sublime past that they forget to look for the symptoms of the great collapse which must certainly have been present in some form or other. Naturally this applies only to those for whom Germany was more than merely a place of abode and a source of livelihood. These are the only people who have been able to feel the present conditions as really catastrophic, whereas others have considered these conditions as the fulfilment of what they had looked forward to and hitherto silently wished.

The symptoms of future collapse were definitely to be perceived in those earlier days, although very few made any attempt to draw a practical lesson from their significance. But this is now a greater necessity than it ever was before. For just as bodily ailments can be cured only when their origin has been diagnosed, so also political disease can be treated only when it has been diagnosed. It is obvious of course that the external symptoms of any disease can be more readily detected than its internal causes, for these symptoms strike the eye more easily. This is also the reason why so many people recognize only external effects and mistake them for causes. Indeed they will sometimes try to deny the existence of such causes. And that is why the majority of people among us recognize the German collapse only in the prevailing economic distress and the results that have followed therefrom. Almost everyone has to carry his share of this burden, and that is why each one looks on the economic catastrophe as the cause of the present deplorable state of affairs. The broad masses of the people see little of the cultural, political, and moral background of this collapse. Many of them completely lack both the necessary feeling and powers of understanding for it.

That the masses of the people should thus estimate the causes of Germany's downfall is quite understandable. But the fact that intelligent sections of the community regard the German collapse primarily as an economic catastrophe, and consequently think that a cure for it may be found in an economic solution, seems to me to be the reason why hitherto no improvement has been brought about. No improvement can be brought about until it be understood that economics play only a second or third role, while the main part is played by political, moral and racial factors. Only when this is understood will it be possible to understand the causes of the present evil and consequently to find the ways and means of remedying them.

Therefore the question of why Germany really collapsed is one of the most urgent significance, especially for a political movement which aims at overcoming this disaster.

In scrutinizing the past with a view to discovering the causes of the German break-up, it is necessary to be careful lest we may be unduly impressed by external results that readily strike the eye and thus ignore the less manifest causes of these results.

The most facile, and therefore the most generally accepted, way of accounting for the present misfortune is to say that it is the result of a lost war, and that this is the real cause of the present misfortune. Probably there are many who honestly believe in this absurd explanation but there are many more in whose mouths it is a deliberate and conscious falsehood. This applies to all those who are now feeding at the Government troughs. For the prophets of the Revolution again and again declared to the people that it would be immaterial to the great masses what the result of the War might be. On the contrary, they solemnly assured the public that it was High Finance which was principally interested in a victorious outcome of this gigantic struggle among the nations but that the German people and the German workers had no interest whatsoever in such an outcome. Indeed the apostles of world conciliation habitually asserted that, far from any German downfall, the opposite was bound to take place — namely, the resurgence of the German people — once 'militarism' had been crushed. Did not these self-same circles sing the praises of the Entente and did they not also lay the whole blame for the sanguinary struggle on the shoulders of Germany?

Without this explanation, would they have been able to put forward the theory that a military defeat would have no political consequences for the German people? Was not the whole Revolution dressed up in gala colours as blocking the victorious advance of the German banners and that thus the German people would be assured its liberty both at home and abroad?

Is not that so, you miserable, lying rascals?

That kind of impudence which is typical of the Jews was necessary in order to proclaim the defeat of the army as the cause of the German collapse. Indeed the Berlin VORWÄRTS, that organ and mouthpiece of sedition then wrote on this occasion that the German nation should not be permitted to bring home its banners triumphantly.

And yet they attribute our collapse to the military defeat.

Of course it would be out of the question to enter into an argument with these liars who deny at one moment what they said the moment before. I should waste no further words on them were it not for the fact that there are many thoughtless people who repeat all this in parrot fashion, without being necessarily inspired by any evil motives. But the observations I am making here are also meant for our fighting followers, seeing that nowadays one's spoken words are often forgotten and twisted in their meaning.

The assertion that the loss of the War was the cause of the German collapse can best be answered as follows: It is admittedly a fact that the loss of the War was of tragic importance for the future of our country. But that loss was not in itself a cause. It was rather the consequence of other causes. That a disastrous ending to this life-or-death conflict must have involved catastrophes in its train was clearly seen by everyone of insight who could think in a straightforward manner. But unfortunately there were also people whose powers of understanding seemed to fail them at that critical moment. And there were other people who had first questioned that truth and then altogether denied it. And there were people who, after their secret desire had been fulfilled, were suddenly faced with the subsequent facts that resulted from their own collaboration. Such people are responsible for the collapse, and not the lost war, though they now want to attribute everything to this. As a matter of fact the loss of the War was a result of their activities and not the result of bad leadership as they now would like to maintain. Our enemies were not cowards. They also know how to die. From the very first day of the War they outnumbered the German Army, and the arsenals and armament factories of the whole world were at their disposal for the replenishment of military equipment. Indeed it is universally admitted that the German victories, which had been steadily won during four years of warfare against the whole world, were due to superior leadership, apart of course from the heroism of the troops. And the organization was solely due to the German military leadership. That organization and leadership of the German Army was the most mighty thing that the world has ever seen. Any shortcomings which became evident were humanly unavoidable. The collapse of that army was not the cause of our present distress. It was itself the consequence of other faults. But this consequence in its turn ushered in a further collapse, which was more visible. That such was actually the case can be shown as follows:

Must a military defeat necessarily lead to such a complete overthrow of the State and Nation? Whenever has this been the result of an unlucky war? As a matter of fact, are nations ever ruined by a lost war and by that alone? The answer to this question can be briefly stated by referring to the fact that military defeats are the result of internal decay, cowardice, want of character, and are a retribution for such things. If such were not the causes then a military defeat would lead to a national resurgence and bring the nation to a higher pitch of effort. A military defeat is not the tombstone of national life. History affords innumerable examples to confirm the truth of that statement.

Unfortunately Germany's military overthrow was not an undeserved catastrophe, but a well-merited punishment which was in the nature of an eternal retribution. This defeat was more than deserved by us; for it represented the greatest external phenomenon of decomposition among a series of internal phenomena, which, although they were visible, were not recognized by the majority of the people, who follow the tactics of the ostrich and see only what they want to see.

Let us examine the symptoms that were evident in Germany at the time that the German people accepted this defeat. Is it not true that in several circles the misfortunes of the Fatherland were even joyfully welcomed in the most shameful manner? Who could act in such a way without thereby meriting vengeance for his attitude? Were there not people who even went further and boasted that they had gone to the extent of weakening the front and causing a collapse? Therefore it was not the enemy who brought this disgrace upon our shoulders but rather our own countrymen. If they suffered misfortune for it afterwards, was that misfortune undeserved? Was there ever a case in history where a people declared itself guilty of a war, and that even against its better conscience and its better knowledge?

No, and again no. In the manner in which the German nation reacted to its defeat we can see that the real cause of our collapse must be looked for elsewhere and not in the purely military loss of a few positions or the failure of an offensive. For if the front as such had given way and thus brought about a national disaster, then the German nation would have accepted the defeat in quite another spirit. They would have borne the subsequent misfortune with clenched teeth, or they would have been overwhelmed by sorrow. Regret and fury would have filled their hearts against an enemy into whose hands victory had been given by a chance event or the decree of Fate; and in that case the nation, following the example of the Roman Senate[14] would have faced the defeated legions on their return and expressed their thanks for the sacrifices that had been made and would have requested them not to lose faith in the Empire. Even the capitulation would have been signed under the sway of calm reason, while the heart would have beaten in the hope of the coming REVANCHE.

That is the reception that would have been given to a military defeat which had to be attributed only to the adverse decree of Fortune. There would have been neither joy-making nor dancing. Cowardice would not have been boasted of, and the defeat would not have been honoured. On returning from the Front, the troops would not have been mocked at, and the colours would not have been dragged in the dust. But above all, that disgraceful state of affairs could never have arisen which induced a British officer, Colonel Repington, to declare with scorn: Every third German is a traitor! No, in such a case this plague would never have assumed the proportions of a veritable flood which, for the past five years, has smothered every vestige of respect for the German nation in the outside world.

This shows only too clearly how false it is to say that the loss of the War was the cause of the German break-up. No. The military defeat was itself but the consequence of a whole series of morbid symptoms and their causes which had become active in the German nation before the War broke out. The War was the first catastrophal consequence, visible to all, of how traditions and national morale had been poisoned and how the instinct of self-preservation had degenerated. These were the preliminary causes which for many years had been undermining the foundations of the nation and the Empire.

But it remained for the Jews, with their unqualified capacity for falsehood, and their fighting comrades, the Marxists, to impute responsibility for the downfall precisely to the man who alone had shown a superhuman will and energy in his effort to prevent the catastrophe which he had foreseen and to save the nation from that hour of complete overthrow and shame. By placing responsibility for the loss of the world war on the shoulders of Ludendorff they took away the weapon of moral right from the only adversary dangerous enough to be likely to succeed in bringing the betrayers of the Fatherland to Justice. All this was inspired by the principle—which is quite true in itself—that in the big lie there is always a certain force of credibility; because the broad masses of a nation are always more easily corrupted in the deeper strata of their emotional nature than consciously or voluntarily; and thus in the primitive simplicity of their minds they more readily fall victims to the big lie than the small lie, since they themselves often tell small lies in little matters but would be ashamed to resort to large-scale falsehoods. It would never come into their heads to fabricate colossal untruths, and they would not believe that others could have the impudence to distort the truth so infamously. Even though the facts which prove this to be so may be brought clearly to their minds, they will still doubt and waver and will continue to think that there may be some other explanation. For the grossly impudent lie always leaves traces behind it, even after it has been nailed down, a fact which is known to all expert liars in this world and to all who conspire together in the art of lying. These people know only too well how to use falsehood for the basest purposes.

From time immemorial. however, the Jews have known better than any others how falsehood and calumny can be exploited. Is not their very existence founded on one great lie, namely, that they are a religious community, whereas in reality they are a race? And what a race! One of the greatest thinkers that mankind has produced has branded the Jews for all time with a statement which is profoundly and exactly true. He

(Schopenhauer) called the Jew "The Great Master of Lies". Those who do not realize the truth of that statement, or do not wish to believe it, will never be able to lend a hand in helping Truth to prevail.

We may regard it as a great stroke of fortune for the German nation that its period of lingering suffering was so suddenly curtailed and transformed into such a terrible catastrophe. For if things had gone on as they were the nation would have more slowly, but more surely, gone to ruin. The disease would have become chronic; whereas, in the acute form of the disaster, it at least showed itself clearly to the eyes of a considerable number of observers. It was not by accident that man conquered the black plague more easily than he conquered tuberculosis.

The first appeared in terrifying waves of death that shook the whole of mankind, the other advances insidiously; the first induces terror, the other gradual indifference. The result is, however, that men opposed the first with all the energy they were capable of, whilst they try to arrest tuberculosis by feeble means. Thus man has mastered the black plague, while tuberculosis still gets the better of him.

The same applies to diseases in nations. So long as these diseases are not of a catastrophic character, the population will slowly accustom itself to them and later succumb. It is then a stroke of luck—although a bitter one—when Fate decides to interfere in this slow process of decay and suddenly brings the victim face to face with the final stage of the disease. More often than not the result of a catastrophe is that a cure is at once undertaken and carried through with rigid determination.

But even in such a case the essential preliminary condition is always the recognition of the internal causes which have given rise to the disease in question.

The important question here is the differentiation of the root causes from the circumstances developing out of them. This becomes all the more difficult the longer the germs of disease remain in the national body and the longer they are allowed to become an integral part of that body.

It may easily happen that, as time goes on, it will become so difficult to recognize certain definite virulent poisons as such that they are accepted as belonging to the national being; or they are merely tolerated as a necessary evil, so that drastic attempts to locate those alien germs are not held to be necessary.

During the long period of peace prior to the last war certain evils were apparent here and there although, with one or two exceptions, very little effort was made to discover their origin. Here again these exceptions were first and foremost those phenomena in the economic life of the nation which were more apparent to the individual than the evil conditions existing in a good many other spheres.

There were many signs of decay which ought to have been given serious thought. As far as economics were concerned, the following may be said:—

The amazing increase of population in Germany before the war brought the question of providing daily bread into a more and more prominent position in all spheres of political and economic thought and action.

But unfortunately those responsible could not make up their minds to arrive at the only correct solution and preferred to reach their objective by cheaper methods. Repudiation of the idea of acquiring fresh territory and the substitution for it of the mad desire for the commercial conquest of the world was bound to lead eventually to unlimited and injurious industrialization.

The first and most fatal result brought about in this way was the weakening of the agricultural classes, whose decline was proportionate to the increase in the proletariat of the urban areas, until finally the equilibrium was completely upset.

The big barrier dividing rich and poor now became apparent. Luxury and poverty lived so close to each other that the consequences were bound to be deplorable. Want and frequent unemployment began to play havoc with the people and left discontent and embitterment behind them. The result of this was to divide the population into political classes. Discontent increased in spite of commercial prosperity. Matters finally reached that stage which brought about the general conviction that 'things cannot go on as they are', although no one seemed able to visualize what was really going to happen.

These were typical and visible signs of the depths which the prevailing discontent had reached. Far worse than these, however, were other consequences which became apparent as a result of the industrialization of the nation.

In proportion to the extent that commerce assumed definite control of the State, money became more and more of a God whom all had to serve and bow down to. Heavenly Gods became more and more old-fashioned and were laid away in the corners to make room for the worship of mammon. And thus began a period of utter degeneration which became specially pernicious because it set in at a time when the nation was more than ever in need of an exalted idea, for a critical hour was threatening. Germany should have been prepared to protect with the sword her efforts to win her own daily bread in a peaceful way.

Unfortunately, the predominance of money received support and sanction in the very quarter which ought to have been opposed to it. His Majesty, the Kaiser, made a mistake when he raised representatives of the new finance capital to the ranks of the nobility. Admittedly, it may be offered as an excuse that even Bismarck failed to realize the threatening danger in this respect. In practice, however, all ideal virtues became secondary considerations to those of money, for it was clear that having once taken this road, the nobility of the sword would very soon rank second to that of finance.

Financial operations succeed easier than war operations. Hence it was no longer any great attraction for a true hero or even a statesman to be brought into touch with the nearest Jew banker. Real merit was not interested in receiving cheap decorations and therefore declined them with thanks. But from the standpoint of good breeding such a development was deeply regrettable. The nobility began to lose more and more of the racial qualities that were a condition of its very existence, with the result that in many cases the term 'plebeian' would have been more appropriate.

A serious state of economic disruption was being brought about by the slow elimination of the personal control of vested interests and the gradual transference of the whole economic structure into the hands of joint stock companies.

In this way labour became degraded into an object of speculation in the hands of unscrupulous exploiters.

The de-personalization of property ownership increased on a vast scale. Financial exchange circles began to triumph and made slow but sure progress in assuming control of the whole of national life.

Before the War the internationalization of the German economic structure had already begun by the roundabout way of share issues. It is true that a section of the German industrialists made a determined attempt to avert the danger, but in the end they gave way before the united attacks of money-grabbing capitalism, which was assisted in this fight by its faithful henchmen in the Marxist movement.

The persistent war against German 'heavy industries' was the visible start of the internationalization of German economic life as envisaged by the Marxists. This, however, could only be brought to a successful conclusion by the victory which Marxism was able to gain in the Revolution. As I write these words, success is attending the general attack on the German State Railways which are now to be turned over to international capitalists. Thus 'International Social-Democracy' has once again attained one of its main objectives.

The best evidence of how far this 'commercialization' of the German nation was able to go can be plainly seen in the fact that when the War was over one of the leading captains of German industry and commerce gave it as his opinion that commerce as such was the only force which could put Germany on its feet again.

This sort of nonsense was uttered just at the time when France was restoring public education on a humanitarian basis, thus doing away with the idea that national life is dependent on commerce rather than ideal values. The statement which Stinnes broadcasted to the world at that time caused incredible confusion. It was immediately taken up and has become the leading motto of all those humbugs and babblers—the 'statesmen' whom Fate let loose on Germany after the Revolution.

One of the worst evidences of decadence in Germany before the War was the ever increasing habit of doing things by halves. This was one of the consequences of the insecurity that was felt all round. And it is to be attributed also to a certain timidity which resulted from one cause or another. And the latter malady was aggravated by the educational system. German education in pre-War times had an extraordinary number of weak features. It was simply and exclusively limited to the production of pure knowledge and paid little attention to the development of practical ability. Still less attention was given to the development of individual character, in so far as this is ever possible. And hardly any attention at all was paid to the development of a sense of responsibility, to strengthening the will and the powers of decision. The result of this method was to produce erudite people who had a passion for knowing everything. Before the War we Germans were accepted and estimated accordingly. The German was liked because good use could be made of him; but there was little esteem for him personally, on account of this weakness of character. For those who can read its significance aright, there is much instruction in the fact that among all nationalities Germans were the first to part with their national citizenship when they found themselves in a foreign country. And there is a world of meaning in the saying that was then prevalent: 'With the hat in the hand one can go through the whole country'.

This kind of social etiquette turned out disastrous when it prescribed the exclusive forms that had to be observed in the presence of His Majesty. These forms insisted that there should be no contradiction whatsoever, but that everything should be praised which His Majesty condescended to like.

It was just here that the frank expression of manly dignity, and not subservience, was most needed. Servility in the presence of monarchs may be good enough for the professional lackey and place-hunter, in fact for all those decadent beings who are more pleased to be found moving in the high circles of royalty than among honest citizens. These exceedingly 'humble' creatures however, though they grovel before their lord and bread-giver, invariably put on airs of boundless superciliousness towards other mortals, which was particularly impudent when they posed as the only people who had the right to be called 'monarchists'. This was a gross piece of impertinence such as only despicable specimens among the newly-ennobled or yet-to-be-ennobled could be capable of.

And these have always been just the people who have prepared the way for the downfall of monarchy and the monarchical principle. It could not be otherwise. For when a man is prepared to stand up for a cause, come what may, he never grovels before its representative. A man who is serious about the maintenance and welfare of an institution will not allow himself to be discouraged when the representatives of that institution show certain faults and failings. And he certainly will not run around to tell the world about it, as certain false democratic 'friends' of the monarchy have done; but he will approach His Majesty, the bearer of the Crown himself, to warn him of the seriousness of a situation and persuade the monarch to act. Furthermore, he will not take up the standpoint that it must be left to His Majesty to act as the latter thinks fit, even though the course which he would take must plainly lead to disaster. But the man I am thinking of will deem it his duty to protect the monarchy against the monarch himself, no matter what personal risk he may run in doing so. If the worth of the monarchical institution be dependent on the person of the monarch himself, then it would be the worst institution imaginable; for only in rare cases are kings found to be models of wisdom and understanding, and integrity of character, though we might like to think otherwise. But this fact is unpalatable to the professional knaves and lackeys. Yet all upright men, and they are the backbone of the nation, repudiate the nonsensical fiction that all monarchs are wise, etc. For such men history is history and truth is truth, even where monarchs are concerned. But if a nation should have the good luck to possess a great king or a great man it ought to consider itself as specially favoured above all the other nations, and these may be thankful if an adverse fortune has not allotted the worst to them.

It is clear that the worth and significance of the monarchical principle cannot rest in the person of the monarch alone, unless Heaven decrees that the crown should be set on the head of a brilliant hero like Frederick the Great, or a sagacious person like William I. This may happen once in several centuries, but hardly oftener than that. The ideal of the monarchy takes precedence of the person of the monarch, inasmuch as the meaning of the institution must lie in the institution it self. Thus the monarchy may be reckoned in the category of those whose duty it is to serve. He, too, is but a wheel in this machine and as such he is obliged to do his duty towards it. He has to adapt himself for the fulfilment of high aims. If, therefore, there were no significance attached to the idea itself and everything merely centred around the 'sacred' person, then it would never be possible to depose a ruler who has shown himself to be an imbecile.

It is essential to insist upon this truth at the present time, because recently those phenomena have appeared again and were in no small measure responsible for the collapse of the monarchy. With a certain amount of native impudence these persons once again talk about 'their King' — that is to say, the man whom they shamefully deserted a few years ago at a most critical hour. Those who refrain from participating in this chorus of lies are summarily classified as 'bad Germans'. They who make the charge are the same class of quitters who ran away in 1918 and took to wearing red badges. They thought that discretion was the better part of valour. They were indifferent about what happened to the Kaiser.

They camouflaged themselves as 'peaceful citizens' but more often than not they vanished altogether. All of a sudden these champions of royalty were nowhere to be found at that time. Circumspectly, one by one, these 'servants and counsellors' of the Crown reappeared, to resume their lip-service to royalty but only after others had borne the brunt of the anti-royalist attack and suppressed the Revolution for them. Once again they were all there. remembering wistfully the flesh-pots of Egypt and almost bursting with devotion for the royal cause. This went on until the day came when red badges were again in the ascendant. Then this whole ramshackle assembly of royal worshippers scuttled anew like mice from the cats.

If monarchs were not themselves responsible for such things one could not help sympathizing with them. But they must realize that with such champions thrones can be lost but certainly never gained.

All this devotion was a mistake and was the result of our whole system of education, which in this case brought about a particularly severe retribution. Such lamentable trumpery was kept up at the various courts that the monarchy was slowly becoming under mined. When finally it did begin to totter, everything was swept away. Naturally, grovellers and lick-spittles are never willing to die for their masters. That monarchs never realize this, and almost on principle never really take the trouble to learn it, has always been their undoing.

One visible result of wrong educational system was the fear of shouldering responsibility and the resultant weakness in dealing with obvious vital problems of existence.

The starting point of this epidemic, however, was in our parliamentary institution where the shirking of responsibility is particularly fostered. Unfortunately the disease slowly spread to all branches of everyday life but particularly affected the sphere of public affairs.

Responsibility was being shirked everywhere and this led to insufficient or half-hearted measures being taken, personal responsibility for each act being reduced to a minimum.

If we consider the attitude of various Governments towards a whole series of really pernicious phenomena in public life, we shall at once recognize the fearful significance of this policy of half-measures and the lack of courage to undertake responsibilities. I shall single out only a few from the large numbers of instances known to me.

In journalistic circles it is a pleasing custom to speak of the Press as a 'Great Power' within the State. As a matter of fact its importance is immense. One cannot easily overestimate it, for the Press continues the work of education even in adult life. Generally, readers of the Press can be classified into three groups:

First, those who believe everything they read;

Second, those who no longer believe anything;

Third, those who critically examine what they read and form their judgments accordingly.

Numerically, the first group is by far the strongest, being composed of the broad masses of the people. Intellectually, it forms the simplest portion of the nation. It cannot be classified according to occupation but only into grades of intelligence. Under this category come all those who have not been born to think for themselves or who have not learnt to do so and who, partly through incompetence and partly through ignorance, believe everything that is set before them in print. To these we must add that type of lazy individual who, although capable of thinking for himself out of sheer laziness gratefully absorbs everything that others had thought over, modestly believing this to have been thoroughly done.

The influence which the Press has on all these people is therefore enormous; for after all they constitute the broad masses of a nation. But, somehow they are not in a position or are not willing personally to sift what is being served up to them; so that their whole attitude towards daily problems is almost solely the result of extraneous influence. All this can be advantageous where public enlightenment is of a serious and truthful character, but great harm is done when scoundrels and liars take a hand at this work.

The second group is numerically smaller, being partly composed of those who were formerly in the first group and after a series of bitter disappointments are now prepared to believe nothing of what they see in print. They hate all newspapers. Either they do not read them at all or they become exceptionally annoyed at their contents, which they hold to be nothing but a congeries of lies and misstatements. These people are difficult to handle; for they will always be sceptical of the truth. Consequently, they are useless for any form of positive work.

The third group is easily the smallest, being composed of real intellectuals whom natural aptitude and education have taught to think for themselves and who in all things try to form their own judgments, while at the same time carefully sifting what they read. They will not read any newspaper without using their own intelligence to collaborate with that of the writer and naturally this does not set writers an easy task. Journalists appreciate this type of reader only with a certain amount of reservation.

Hence the trash that newspapers are capable of serving up is of little danger—much less of importance—to the members of the third group of readers. In the majority of cases these readers have learnt to regard every journalist as fundamentally a rogue who sometimes speaks the truth. Most unfortunately, the value of these readers lies in their intelligence and not in their numerical strength, an unhappy state of affairs in a period where wisdom counts for nothing and majorities for everything. Nowadays when the voting papers of the masses are the deciding factor; the decision lies in the hands of the numerically strongest group; that is to say the first group, the crowd of simpletons and the credulous.

It is an all-important interest of the State and a national duty to prevent these people from falling into the hands of false, ignorant or even evil-minded teachers. Therefore it is the duty of the State to supervise their education and prevent every form of offence in this respect. Particular attention should be paid to the Press; for its influence on these people is by far the strongest and most penetrating of all; since its effect is not transitory but continual. Its immense significance lies in the uniform and persistent repetition of its teaching. Here, if anywhere, the State should never forget that all means should converge towards the same end. It must not be led astray by the will-o'-the-wisp of so-called 'freedom of the Press', or be talked into neglecting its duty, and withholding from the nation that which is good and which does good. With ruthless determination the State must keep control of this instrument of popular education and place it at the service of the State and the Nation.

But what sort of pabulum was it that the German Press served up for the consumption of its readers in pre-War days? Was it not the worst virulent poison imaginable? Was not pacifism in its worst form inoculated into our people at a time when others were preparing slowly but surely to pounce upon Germany? Did not this self-same Press of ours in peace time already instil into the public mind a doubt as to the sovereign rights of the State itself, thereby already handicapping the State in choosing its means of defence? Was it not the German Press that under stood how to make all the nonsensical talk about 'Western democracy' palatable to our people, until an exuberant public was eventually prepared to entrust its future to the League of Nations? Was not this Press instrumental in bringing in a state of moral degradation among our people? Were not morals and public decency made to look ridiculous and classed as out-of-date and banal, until finally our people also became modernized? By means of persistent attacks, did not the Press keep on undermining the authority of the State, until one blow sufficed to bring this institution tottering to the ground? Did not the Press oppose with all its might every movement to give the State that which belongs to the State, and by means of constant criticism, injure the reputation of the army, sabotage general conscription and demand refusal of military credits, etc.—until the success of this campaign was assured?

The function of the so-called liberal Press was to dig the grave for the German people and REICH. No mention need be made of the lying Marxist Press. To them the spreading of falsehood is as much a vital necessity as the mouse is to a cat. Their sole task is to break the national backbone of the people, thus preparing the nation to become the slaves of international finance and its masters, the Jews.

And what measures did the State take to counteract this wholesale poisoning of the public mind? None, absolutely nothing at all. By this policy it was hoped to win the favour of this pest—by means of flattery, by a recognition of the 'value' of the Press, its 'importance', its 'educative mission' and similar nonsense. The Jews acknowledged all this with a knowing smile and returned thanks.

The reason for this ignominious failure on the part of the State lay not so much in its refusal to realize the danger as in the out-and-out cowardly way of meeting the situation by the adoption of faulty and ineffective measures. No one had the courage to employ any energetic and radical methods. Everyone temporised in some way or other; and instead of striking at its heart, the viper was only further irritated. The result was that not only did everything remain as it was, but the power of this institution which should have been combated grew greater from year to year.

The defence put up by the Government in those days against a mainly Jew-controlled Press that was slowly corrupting the nation, followed no definite line of action, it had no determination behind it and above all, no fixed objective whatsoever in view. This is where official understanding of the situation completely failed both in estimating the importance of the struggle, choosing the means and deciding on a definite plan. They merely tinkered with the problem. Occasionally, when bitten, they imprisoned one or another journalistic viper for a few weeks or months, but the whole poisonous brood was allowed to carry on in peace.

It must be admitted that all this was partly the result of extraordinary crafty tactics on the part of Jewry on the one hand, and obvious official stupidity or naïveté on the other hand. The Jews were too clever to allow a simultaneous attack to be made on the whole of their Press. No one section functioned as cover for the other. While the Marxist newspaper, in the most despicable manner possible, reviled everything that was sacred, furiously attacked the State and Government and incited certain classes of the community against each other, the bourgeois-democratic papers, also in Jewish hands, knew how to camouflage themselves as model examples of objectivity. They studiously avoided harsh language, knowing well that block-heads are capable of judging only by external appearances and never able to penetrate to the real depth and meaning of anything. They measure the worth of an object by its exterior and not by its content. This form of human frailty was carefully studied and understood by the Press.

For this class of blockheads the FRANKFURTER ZEITUNG would be acknowledged as the essence of respectability. It always carefully avoided calling a spade a spade. It deprecated the use of every form of physical force and persistently appealed to the nobility of fighting with 'intellectual' weapons. But this fight, curiously enough, was most popular with the least intellectual classes. That is one of the results of our defective education, which turns the youth away from the instinctive dictates of Nature, pumps into them a certain amount of knowledge without however being able to bring them to what is the supreme act of knowing. To this end diligence and goodwill are of no avail, if innate understanding fail. This final knowledge at which man must aim is the understanding of causes which are instinctively perceived.

Let me explain: Man must not fall into the error of thinking that he was ever meant to become lord and master of Nature. A lopsided education has helped to encourage that illusion. Man must realize that a fundamental law of necessity reigns throughout the whole realm of Nature and that his existence is subject to the law of eternal struggle and strife. He will then feel that there cannot be a separate law for mankind in a world in which planets and suns follow their orbits, where moons and planets trace their destined paths, where the strong are always the masters of the weak and where those subject to such laws must obey them or be destroyed. Man must also submit to the eternal principles of this supreme wisdom. He may try to understand them but he can never free himself from their sway.

It is just for intellectual DEMI-MONDE that the Jew writes those papers which he calls his 'intellectual' Press. For them the FRANKFURTER ZEITUNG and BERLINER TAGEBLATT are written, the tone being adapted to them, and it is over these people that such papers have an influence.

While studiously avoiding all forms of expression that might strike the reader as crude, the poison is injected from other vials into the hearts of the clientele. The effervescent tone and the fine phraseology lug the readers into believing that a love for knowledge and moral principle is the sole driving force that determines the policy of such papers, whereas in reality these features represent a cunning way of disarming any opposition that might be directed against the Jews and their Press.

They make such a parade of respectability that the imbecile readers are all the more ready to believe that the excesses which other papers indulge in are only of a mild nature and not such as to warrant legal action being taken against them. Indeed such action might trespass on the freedom of the Press, that expression being a euphemism under which such papers escape legal punishment for deceiving the public and poisoning the public mind. Hence the authorities are very slow indeed to take any steps against these journalistic bandits for fear of immediately alienating the sympathy of the so-called respectable Press.

A fear that is only too well founded, for the moment any attempt is made to proceed against any member of the gutter press all the others rush to its assistance at once, not indeed to support its policy but simply and solely to defend the principle of freedom of the Press and liberty of public opinion. This outcry will succeed in cowering the most stalwart; for it comes from the mouth of what is called decent journalism.

And so this poison was allowed to enter the national bloodstream and infect public life without the Government taking any effectual measures to master the course of the disease. The ridiculous half-measures that were taken were in themselves an indication of the process of disintegration that was already threatening to break up the Empire. For an institution practically surrenders its existence when it is no longer determined to defend itself with all the weapons at its command. Every half-measure is the outward expression of an internal process of decay which must lead to an external collapse sooner or later.

I believe that our present generation would easily master this danger if they were rightly led. For this generation has gone through certain experiences which must have strengthened the nerves of all those who did not become nervously broken by them. Certainly in days to come the Jews will raise a tremendous cry throughout their newspapers once a hand is laid on their favourite nest, once a move is made to put an end to this scandalous Press and once this instrument which shapes public opinion is brought under State control and no longer left in the hands of aliens and enemies of the people. I am certain that this will be easier for us than it was for our fathers. The scream of the twelve-inch shrapnel is more penetrating than the hiss from a thousand Jewish newspaper vipers.

Therefore let them go on with their hissing. A further example of the weak and hesitating way in which vital national problems were dealt with in pre-War Germany is the following: Hand in hand with the political and moral process of infecting the nation, for many years an equally virulent process of infection had been attacking the public health of the people. In large cities, particularly, syphilis steadily increased and tuberculosis kept pace with it in reaping its harvest of death almost in every part of the country.

Although in both cases the effect on the nation was alarming, it seemed as if nobody was in a position to undertake any decisive measures against these scourges.

In the case of syphilis especially the attitude of the State and public bodies was one of absolute capitulation. To combat this state of affairs something of far wider sweep should have been undertaken than was really done. The discovery of a remedy which is of a questionable nature and the excellent way in which it was placed on the market were only of little assistance in fighting such a scourge. Here again the only course to adopt is to attack the disease in its causes rather than in its symptoms. But in this case the primary cause is to be found in the manner in which love has been prostituted. Even though this did not directly bring about the fearful disease itself, the nation must still suffer serious damage thereby, for the moral havoc resulting from this prostitution would be sufficient to bring about the destruction of the nation, slowly but surely. This Judaizing of our spiritual life and mammonizing of our natural instinct for procreation will sooner or later work havoc with our whole posterity. For instead of strong, healthy children, blessed with natural feelings, we shall see miserable specimens of humanity resulting from economic calculation. For economic considerations are becoming more and more the foundations of marriage and the sole preliminary condition of it. And love looks for an outlet elsewhere.

Here, as elsewhere, one may defy Nature for a certain period of time; but sooner or later she will take her inexorable revenge. And when man realizes this truth it is often too late.

Our own nobility furnishes an example of the devastating consequences that follow from a persistent refusal to recognize the primary conditions necessary for normal wedlock. Here we are openly brought face to face with the results of those reproductive habits which on the one hand are determined by social pressure and, on the other, by financial considerations. The one leads to inherited debility and the other to adulteration of the blood-strain; for all the Jewish daughters of the department store proprietors are looked upon as eligible mates to co-operate in propagating His Lordship's stock. And the stock certainly looks it. All this leads to absolute degeneration. Nowadays our bourgeoise are making efforts to follow in the same path, They will come to the same journey's end.

These unpleasant truths are hastily and nonchalantly brushed aside, as if by so doing the real state of affairs could also be abolished. But no. It cannot be denied that the population of our great towns and cities is tending more and more to avail of prostitution in the exercise of its amorous instincts and is thus becoming more and more contaminated by the scourge of venereal disease. On the one hand, the visible effects of this mass-infection can be observed in our insane asylums and, on the other hand, alas! among the children at home. These are the doleful and tragic witnesses to the steadily increasing scourge that is poisoning our sexual life. Their sufferings are the visible results of parental vice.

There are many ways of becoming resigned to this unpleasant and terrible fact. Many people go about seeing nothing or, to be more correct, not wanting to see anything. This is by far the simplest and cheapest attitude to adopt. Others cover themselves in the sacred mantle of prudery, as ridiculous as it is false. They describe the whole condition of affairs as sinful and are profoundly indignant when brought face to face with a victim. They close their eyes in reverend abhorrence to this godless scourge and pray to the Almighty that He—if possible after their own death—may rain down fire and brimstone as on Sodom and Gomorrah and so once again make an out standing example of this shameless section of humanity. Finally, there are those who are well aware of the terrible results which this scourge will and must bring about, but they merely shrug their shoulders, fully convinced of their inability to undertake anything against this peril. Hence matters are allowed to take their own course.

Undoubtedly all this is very convenient and simple, only it must not be overlooked that this convenient way of approaching things can have fatal consequences for our national life. The excuse that other nations are also not faring any better does not alter the fact of our own deterioration, except that the feeling of sympathy for other stricken nations makes our own suffering easier to bear. But the important question that arises here is: Which nation will be the first to take the initiative in mastering this scourge, and which nations will succumb to it? This will be the final upshot of the whole situation. The present is a period of probation for racial values. The race that fails to come through the test will simply die out and its place will be taken by the healthier and stronger races, which will be able to endure greater hardships. As this problem primarily concerns posterity, it belongs to that category of which it is said with terrible justification that the sins of the fathers are visited on their offspring unto the tenth generation. This is a consequence which follows on an infringement of the laws of blood and race.

The sin against blood and race is the hereditary sin in this world and it brings disaster on every nation that commits it.

The attitude towards this one vital problem in pre-War Germany was most regrettable. What measures were undertaken to arrest the infection of our youth in the large cities? What was done to put an end to the contamination and mammonization of sexual life among us? What was done to fight the resultant spreading of syphilis throughout the whole of our national life? The reply to this question can best be illustrated by showing what should have been done.

Instead of tackling this problem in a haphazard way, the authorities should have realized that the fortunes or misfortunes of future generations depended on its solution.

But to admit this would have demanded that active measures be carried out in a ruthless manner. The primary condition would have been that the enlightened attention of the whole country should be concentrated on this terrible danger, so that every individual would realize the importance of fighting against it. It would be futile to impose obligations of a definite character—which are often difficult to bear—and expect them to become generally effective, unless the public be thoroughly instructed on the necessity of imposing and accepting such obligations. This demands a widespread and systematic method of enlightenment and all other daily problems that might distract public attention from this great central problem should be relegated to the background.

In every case where there are exigencies or tasks that seem impossible to deal with successfully public opinion must be concentrated on the one problem, under the conviction that the solution of this problem alone is a matter of life or death. Only in this way can public interest be aroused to such a pitch as will urge people to combine in a great voluntary effort and achieve important results.

This fundamental truth applies also to the individual, provided he is desirous of attaining some great end. He must always concentrate his efforts to one definitely limited stage of his progress which has to be completed before the next step be attempted. Those who do not endeavour to realize their aims step by step and who do not concentrate their energy in reaching the individual stages, will never attain the final objective. At some stage or other they will falter and fail. This systematic way of approaching an objective is an art in itself, and always calls for the expenditure of every ounce of energy in order to conquer step after step of the road.

Therefore the most essential preliminary condition necessary for an attack on such a difficult stage of the human road is that the authorities should succeed in convincing the masses that the immediate objective which is now being fought for is the only one that deserves to be considered and the only one on which everything depends. The broad masses are never able clearly to see the whole stretch of the road lying in front of them without becoming tired and thus losing faith in their ability to complete the task. To a certain extent they will keep the objective in mind, but they are only able to survey the whole road in small stages, as in the case of the traveller who knows where his journey is going to end but who masters the endless stretch far better by attacking it in degrees. Only in this way can he keep up his determination to reach the final objective.

It is in this way, with the assistance of every form of propaganda, that the problem of fighting venereal disease should be placed before the public—not as a task for the nation but as THE main task. Every possible means should be employed to bring the truth about this scourge home to the minds of the people, until the whole nation has been convinced that everything depends on the solution of this problem; that is to say, a healthy future or national decay.

Only after such preparatory measures—if necessary spread over a period of many years—will public attention and public resolution be fully aroused, and only then can serious and definite measures be undertaken without running the risk of not being fully understood or of being suddenly faced with a slackening of the public will. It must be made clear to all that a serious fight against this scourge calls for vast sacrifices and an enormous amount of work.

To wage war against syphilis means fighting against prostitution, against prejudice, against old-established customs, against current fashion, public opinion, and, last but not least, against false prudery in certain circles.

The first preliminary condition to be fulfilled before the State can claim a moral right to fight against all these things is that the young generation should be afforded facilities for contracting early marriages. Late marriages have the sanction of a custom which, from whatever angle we view it, is and will remain a disgrace to humanity.

Prostitution is a disgrace to humanity and cannot be removed simply by charitable or academic methods. Its restriction and final extermination presupposes the removal of a whole series of contributory circumstances. The first remedy must always be to establish such conditions as will make early marriages possible, especially for young men—for women are, after all, only passive subjects in this matter.

An illustration of the extent to which people have so often been led astray nowadays is afforded by the fact that not infrequently one hears mothers in so-called 'better' circles openly expressing their satisfaction at having found as a husband for their daughter a man who has already sown his wild oats, etc. As there is usually so little shortage in men of this type, the poor girl finds no difficulty in getting a mate of this description, and the children of this marriage are a visible result of such supposedly sensible unions.

When one realizes, apart from this, that every possible effort is being made to hinder the process of procreation and that Nature is being wilfully cheated of her rights, there remains really only one question:

Why is such an institution as marriage still in existence, and what are its functions? Is it really nothing better than prostitution? Does our duty to posterity no longer play any part? Or do people not realize the nature of the curse they are inflicting on themselves and their offspring by such criminally foolish neglect of one of the primary laws of Nature? This is how civilized nations degenerate and gradually perish.

Marriage is not an end in itself but must serve the greater end, which is that of increasing and maintaining the human species and the race.

This is its only meaning and purpose.

This being admitted, then it is clear that the institution of marriage must be judged by the manner in which its allotted function is fulfilled. Therefore early marriages should be the rule, because thus the young couple will still have that pristine force which is the fountain head of a healthy posterity with unimpaired powers of resistance. Of course early marriages cannot be made the rule unless a whole series of social measures are first undertaken without which early marriages cannot be even thought of. In other words, a solution of this question, which seems a small problem in itself, cannot be brought about without adopting radical measures to alter the social background. The importance of such measures ought to be studied and properly estimated, especially at a time when the so-called 'social' Republic has shown itself unable to solve the housing problem and thus has made it impossible for innumerable couples to get married. That sort of policy prepares the way for the further advance of prostitution.

Another reason why early marriages are impossible is our nonsensical method of regulating the scale of salaries, which pays far too little attention to the problem of family support. Prostitution, therefore, can only be really seriously tackled if, by means of a radical social reform, early marriage is made easier than hitherto. This is the first preliminary necessity for the solution of this problem.

Secondly, a whole series of false notions must be eradicated from our system of bringing up and educating children—things which hitherto no one seems to have worried about. In our present educational system a balance will have to be established, first and foremost, between mental instruction and physical training.

What is known as GYMNASIUM (Grammar School) to-day is a positive insult to the Greek institution. Our system of education entirely loses sight of the fact that in the long run a healthy mind can exist only in a healthy body. This statement, with few exceptions, applies particularly to the broad masses of the nation.

In the pre-War Germany there was a time when no one took the trouble to think over this truth. Training of the body was criminally neglected, the one-sided training of the mind being regarded as a sufficient guarantee for the nation's greatness. This mistake was destined to show its effects sooner than had been anticipated. It is not pure chance that the Bolshevic teaching flourishes in those regions whose degenerate population has been brought to the verge of starvation, as, for example, in the case of Central Germany, Saxony, and the Ruhr Valley. In all these districts there is a marked absence of any serious resistance, even by the so-called intellectual classes, against this Jewish contagion. And the simple reason is that the intellectual classes are themselves physically degenerate, not through privation but through education. The exclusive intellectualism of the education in vogue among our upper classes makes them unfit for life's struggle at an epoch in which physical force and not mind is the dominating factor. Thus they are neither capable of maintaining themselves nor of making their way in life. In nearly every case physical disability is the forerunner of personal cowardice.

The extravagant emphasis laid on purely intellectual education and the consequent neglect of physical training must necessarily lead to sexual thoughts in early youth. Those boys whose constitutions have been trained and hardened by sports and gymnastics are less prone to sexual indulgence than those stay-at-homes who have been fed exclusively with mental pabulum. Sound methods of education cannot, however, afford to disregard this, and we must not forget that the expectations of a healthy young man from a woman will differ from those of a weakling who has been prematurely corrupted.

Thus in every branch of our education the day's curriculum must be arranged so as to occupy a boy's free time in profitable development of his physical powers. He has no right in those years to loaf about, becoming a nuisance in public streets and in cinemas; but when his day's work is done he ought to harden his young body so that his strength may not be found wanting when the occasion arises. To prepare for this and to carry it out should be the function of our educational system and not exclusively to pump in knowledge or wisdom. Our school system must also rid itself of the notion that the training of the body is a task that should be left to the individual himself. There is no such thing as allowing freedom of choice to sin against posterity and thus against the race.

The fight against pollution of the mind must be waged simultaneously with the training of the body. To-day the whole of our public life may be compared to a hot-house for the forced growth of sexual notions and incitements. A glance at the bill-of-fare provided by our cinemas, playhouses, and theatres suffices to prove that this is not the right food, especially for our young people. Hoardings and advertisements kiosks combine to attract the public in the most vulgar manner. Anyone who has not altogether lost contact with adolescent yearnings will realize that all this must have very grave consequences. This seductive and sensuous atmosphere puts notions into the heads of our youth which, at their age, ought still to be unknown to them. Unfortunately, the results of this kind of education can best be seen in our contemporary youth who are prematurely grown up and therefore old before their time.

The law courts from time to time throw a distressing light on the spiritual life of our

14- and 15-year old children. Who, therefore, will be surprised to learn that venereal disease claims its victims at this age? And is it not a frightful shame to see the number of physically weak and intellectually spoiled young men who have been introduced to the mysteries of marriage by the whores of the big cities?

No; those who want seriously to combat prostitution must first of all assist in removing the spiritual conditions on which it thrives. They will have to clean up the moral pollution of our city 'culture' fearlessly and without regard for the outcry that will follow. If we do not drag our youth out of the morass of their present environment they will be engulfed by it. Those people who do not want to see these things are deliberately encouraging them and are guilty of spreading the effects of prostitution to the future—for the future belongs to our young generation. This process of cleansing our 'Kultur' will have to be applied in practically all spheres. The stage, art, literature, the cinema, the Press and advertisement posters, all must have the stains of pollution removed and be placed in the service of a national and cultural idea. The life of the people must be freed from the asphyxiating perfume of our modern eroticism and also from every unmanly and prudish form of insincerity. In all these things the aim and the method must be determined by thoughtful consideration for the preservation of our national well-being in body and soul. The right to personal freedom comes second in importance to the duty of maintaining the race.

Only after such measures have been put into practice can a medical campaign against this scourge begin with some hope of success. But, here again, half-measures will be valueless. Far-reaching and important decisions will have to be made. It would be doing things by halves if incurables were given the opportunity of infecting one healthy person after another. This would be that kind of humanitarianism which would allow hundreds to perish in order to save the suffering of one individual. The demand that it should be made impossible for defective people to continue to propagate defective offspring is a demand that is based on most reasonable grounds, and its proper fulfilment is the most humane task that mankind has to face. Unhappy and undeserved suffering in millions of cases will be spared, with the result that there will be a gradual improvement in national health. A determined decision to act in this manner will at the same time provide an obstacle against the further spread of venereal disease. It would then be a case, where necessary, of mercilessly isolating all incurables—perhaps a barbaric measure for those unfortunates—but a blessing for the present generation and for posterity. The temporary pain thus experienced in this century can and will spare future thousands of generations from suffering.

The fight against syphilis and its pace-maker, prostitution, is one of the gigantic tasks of mankind; gigantic, because it is not merely a case of solving a single problem but the removal of a whole series of evils which are the contributory causes of this scourge. Disease of the body in this case is merely the result of a diseased condition of the moral, social, and racial instincts.

But if for reasons of indolence or cowardice this fight is not fought to a finish we may imagine what conditions will be like 500 years hence. Little of God's image will be left in human nature, except to mock the Creator.

But what has been done in Germany to counteract this scourge? If we think calmly over the answer we shall find it distressing. It is true that in governmental circles the terrible and injurious effects of this disease were well known, but the counter-measures which were officially adopted were ineffective and a hopeless failure. They tinkered with

162

cures for the symptoms, wholly regardless of the cause of the disease.

Prostitutes were medically examined and controlled as far as possible, and when signs of infection were apparent they were sent to hospital. When outwardly cured, they were once more let loose on humanity. It is true that 'protective legislation' was introduced which made sexual intercourse a punishable offence for all those not completely cured, or those suffering from venereal disease. This legislation was correct in theory, but in practice it failed completely. In the first place, in the majority of cases women will decline to appear in court as witnesses against men who have robbed them of their health. Women would be exposed far more than men to uncharitable remarks in such cases, and one can imagine what their position would be if they had been infected by their own husbands. Should women in that case lay a charge? Or what should they do?

In the case of the man there is the additional fact that he frequently is unfortunate enough to run up against this danger when he is under the influence of alcohol. His condition makes it impossible for him to assess the qualities of his 'amorous beauty,' a fact which is well known to every diseased prostitute and makes them single out men in this ideal condition for preference. The result is that the unfortunate man is not able to recollect later on who his compassionate benefactress was, which is not surprising in cities like Berlin and Munich. Many of such cases are visitors from the provinces who, held speechless and enthralled by the magic charm of city life, become an easy prey for prostitutes. In the final analysis who is able to say whether he has been infected or not?

Are there not innumerable cases on record where an apparently cured person has a relapse and does untold harm without knowing it? Therefore in practice the results of these legislative measures are negative. The same applies to the control of prostitution, and, finally, even medical treatment and cure are nowadays unsafe and doubtful. One thing only is certain. The scourge has spread further and further in spite of all measures, and this alone suffices definitely to stamp and substantiate their inefficiency.

Everything else that was undertaken was just as inefficient as it was absurd. The spiritual prostitution of the people was neither arrested nor was anything whatsoever undertaken in this direction. Those, however, who do not regard this subject as a serious one would do well to examine the statistical data of the spread of this disease, study its growth in the last century and contemplate the possibilities of its further development. The ordinary observer, unless he were particularly stupid, would experience a cold shudder if the position were made clear to him.

The half-hearted and wavering attitude adopted in pre-War Germany towards this iniquitous condition can assuredly be taken as a visible sign of national decay. When the courage to fight for one's own health is no longer in evidence, then the right to live in this world of struggle also ceases.

One of the visible signs of decay in the old REICH was the slow setback which the general cultural level experienced. But by 'Kultur' I do not mean that which we nowadays style as civilization, which on the contrary may rather be regarded as inimical to the spiritual elevation of life.

At the turn of the last century a new element began to make its appearance in our world. It was an element which had been hitherto absolutely unknown and foreign to us. In former times there had certainly been offences against good taste; but these were mostly departures from the orthodox canons of art, and posterity could recognize a certain historical value in them. But the new products showed signs, not only of artistic aberration but of spiritual degeneration. Here, in the cultural sphere, the signs of the coming collapse first became manifest.

The Bolshevization of art is the only cultural form of life and the only spiritual manifestation of which Bolshevism is capable.

Anyone to whom this statement may appear strange need only take a glance at those lucky States which have become Bolshevized and, to his horror, he will there recognize those morbid monstrosities which have been produced by insane and degenerate people. All those artistic aberrations which are classified under the names of cubism and dadism, since the opening of the present century, are manifestations of art which have come to be officially recognized by the State itself. This phenomenon made its appearance even during the short-lived period of the Soviet Republic in Bavaria. At that time one might easily have recognized how all the official posters, propagandist pictures and newspapers, etc., showed signs not only of political but also of cultural decadence. About sixty years ago a political collapse such as we are experiencing to-day would have been just as inconceivable as the cultural decline which has been manifested in cubist and futurist pictures ever since 1900. Sixty years ago an exhibition of so-called dadistic 'experiences' would have been an absolutely preposterous idea. The organizers of such an exhibition would then have been certified for the lunatic asylum, whereas, to-day they are appointed presidents of art societies. At that time such an epidemic would never have been allowed to spread. Public opinion would not have tolerated it, and the Government would not have remained silent; for it is the duty of a Government to save its people from being stampeded into such intellectual madness. But intellectual madness would have resulted from a development that followed the acceptance of this kind of art. It would have marked one of the worst changes in human history; for it would have meant that a retrogressive process had begun to take place in the human brain, the final stages of which would be unthinkable.

If we study the course of our cultural life during the last twenty-five years we shall be astonished to note how far we have already gone in this process of retrogression. Everywhere we find the presence of those germs which give rise to protuberant growths that must sooner or later bring about the ruin of our culture. Here we find undoubted symptoms of slow corruption; and woe to the nations that are no longer able to bring that morbid process to a halt.

In almost all the various fields of German art and culture those morbid phenomena may be observed. Here everything seems to have passed the culminating point of its excellence and to have entered the curve of a hasty decline. At the beginning of the century the theatres seemed already degenerating and ceasing to be cultural factors, except the Court theatres, which opposed this prostitution of the national art.

With these exceptions, and also a few other decent institutions, the plays produced on the stage were of such a nature that the people would have benefited by not visiting them at all. A sad symptom of decline was manifested by the fact that in the case of many 'art centres' the sign was posted on the entrance doors: FOR ADULTS ONLY. Let it be borne in mind that these precautions had to be taken in regard to institutions whose main purpose should have been to promote the education of the youth and not merely to provide amusement for sophisticated adults. What would the great dramatists of other times have said of such measures and, above all, of the conditions which made these measures necessary? How exasperated Schiller would have been, and how Goethe would have turned away in disgust!

But what are Schiller, Goethe and Shakespeare when confronted with the heroes of our modern German literature? Old and frowsy and outmoded and finished. For it was typical of this epoch that not only were its own products bad but that the authors of such products and their backers reviled everything that had really been great in the past. This is a phenomenon that is very characteristic of such epochs. The more vile and miserable are the men and products of an epoch, the more they will hate and denigrate the ideal achievements of former generations. What these people would like best would be completely to destroy every vestige of the past, in order to do away with that sole standard of comparison which prevents their own daubs from being looked upon as art. Therefore the more lamentable and wretched are the products of each new era, the more it will try to obliterate all the memorials of the past. But any real innovation that is for the benefit of mankind can always face comparison with the best of what has gone before; and frequently it happens that those monuments of the past guarantee the acceptance of those modern productions. There is no fear that modern productions of real worth will look pale and worthless beside the monuments of the past. What is contributed to the general treasury of human culture often fulfils a part that is necessary in order to keep the memory of old achievements alive, because this memory alone is the standard whereby our own works are properly appreciated. Only those who have nothing of value to give to the world will oppose everything that already exists and would have it destroyed at all costs.

And this holds good not only for new phenomena in the cultural domain but also in politics. The more inferior new revolutionary movements are, the more will they try to denigrate the old forms. Here again the desire to pawn off their shoddy products as great and original achievements leads them into a blind hatred against everything which belongs to the past and which is superior to their own work. As long as the historical memory of Frederick the Great, for instance, still lives, Frederick Ebert can arouse only a problematic admiration. The relation of the hero of Sans Souci to the former republican of Bremen may be compared to that of the sun to the moon; for the moon can shine only after the direct rays of the sun have left the earth. Thus we can readily understand why it is that all the new moons in human history have hated the fixed stars. In the field of politics, if Fate should happen temporarily to place the ruling power in the hands of those nonentities they are not only eager to defile and revile the past but at the same time they will use all means to evade criticism of their own acts. The Law for the Protection of the Republic, which the new German State enacted, may be taken as one example of this truth.

One has good grounds to be suspicious in regard to any new idea, or any doctrine or philosophy, any political or economical movement, which tries to deny everything that the past has produced or to present it as inferior and worthless. Any renovation which is really beneficial to human progress will always have to begin its constructive work at the level where the last stones of the structure have been laid. It need not blush to utilize those truths which have already been established; for all human culture, as well as man himself, is only the result of one long line of development, where each generation has contributed but one stone to the building of the whole structure. The meaning and purpose of revolutions cannot be to tear down the whole building but to take away what has not been well fitted into it or is unsuitable, and to rebuild the free space thus caused, after which the main construction of the building will be carried on.

Thus alone will it be possible to talk of human progress; for otherwise the world would never be free of chaos, since each generation would feel entitled to reject the past and to destroy all the work of the past, as the necessary preliminary to any new work of its own.

The saddest feature of the condition in which our whole civilization found itself before the War was the fact that it was not only barren of any creative force to produce its own works of art and civilization but that it hated, defiled and tried to efface the memory of the superior works produced in the past. About the end of the last century people were less interested in producing new significant works of their own—particularly in the fields of dramatic art and literature—than in defaming the best works of the past and in presenting them as inferior and antiquated. As if this period of disgraceful decadence had the slightest capacity to produce anything of superior quality! The efforts made to conceal the past from the eyes of the present afforded clear evidence of the fact that these apostles of the future acted from an evil intent. These symptoms should have made it clear to all that it was not a question of new, though wrong, cultural ideas but of a process which was undermining the very foundations of civilization. It threw the artistic feeling which had hitherto been quite sane into utter confusion, thus spiritually preparing the way for political Bolshevism. If the creative spirit of the Periclean age be manifested in the Parthenon, then the Bolshevist era is manifested through its cubist grimace.

In this connection attention must be drawn once again to the want of courage displayed by one section of our people, namely, by those who, in virtue of their education and position, ought to have felt themselves obliged to take up a firm stand against this outrage on our culture. But they refrained from offering serious resistance and surrendered to what they considered the inevitable. This abdication of theirs was due, however, to sheer funk lest the apostles of Bolshevist art might raise a rumpus; for those apostles always violently attacked everyone who was not ready to recognize them as the choice spirits of artistic creation, and they tried to strangle all opposition by saying that it was the product of philistine and backwater minds. People trembled in fear lest they might be accused by these yahoos and swindlers of lacking artistic appreciation, as if it would have been a disgrace not to be able to understand and appreciate the effusions of those mental degenerates or arrant rogues. Those cultural disciples, however, had a very simple way of presenting their own effusions as works of the highest quality. They offered incomprehensible and manifestly crazy productions to their amazed contemporaries as what they called 'an inner experience'. Thus they forestalled all adverse criticism at very little cost indeed. Of course nobody ever doubted that there could have been inner experiences like that, but some doubt ought to have arisen as to whether or not there was any justification for exposing these hallucinations of psychopaths or criminals to the sane portion of human society. The works produced by a Moritz von Schwind or a Böcklin were also externalizations of an inner experience, but these were the experiences of divinely gifted artists and not of buffoons.

This situation afforded a good opportunity of studying the miserable cowardliness of our so-called intellectuals who shirked the duty of offering serious resistance to the poisoning of the sound instincts of our people. They left it to the people themselves to formulate their own attitude towards his impudent nonsense. Lest they might be considered as understanding nothing of art, they accepted every caricature of art, until they finally lost the power of judging what is really good or bad.

Taken all in all, there were superabundant symptoms to show that a diseased epoch had begun.

Still another critical symptom has to be considered. In the course of the nineteenth century our towns and cities began more and more to lose their character as centres of civilization and became more and more centres of habitation. In our great modern cities the proletariat does not show much attachment to the place where it lives. This feeling results from the fact that their dwelling-place is nothing but an accidental abode, and that feeling is also partly due to the frequent change of residence which is forced upon them by social conditions.

There is no time for the growth of any attachment to the town in which they live. But another reason lies in the cultural barrenness and superficiality of our modern cities. At the time of the German Wars of Liberation our German towns and cities were not only small in number but also very modest in size. The few that could really be called great cities were mostly the residential cities of princes; as such they had almost always a definite cultural value and also a definite cultural aspect. Those few towns which had more than fifty thousand inhabitants were, in comparison with modern cities of the same size, rich in scientific and artistic treasures. At the time when Munich had not more than sixty thousand souls it was already well on the way to become one of the first German centres of art. Nowadays almost every industrial town has a population at least as large as that, without having anything of real value to call its own. They are agglomerations of tenement houses and congested dwelling barracks, and nothing else. It would be a miracle if anybody should grow sentimentally attached to such a meaningless place. Nobody can grow attached to a place which offers only just as much or as little as any other place would offer, which has no character of its own and where obviously pains have been taken to avoid everything that might have any resemblance to an artistic appearance.

But this is not all. Even the great cities become more barren of real works of art the more they increase in population. They assume more and more a neutral atmosphere and present the same aspect, though on a larger scale, as the wretched little factory towns. Everything that our modern age has contributed to the civilization of our great cities is absolutely deficient. All our towns are living on the glory and the treasures of the past. If we take away from the Munich of to-day everything that was created under Ludwig II we should be horror-stricken to see how meagre has been the output of important artistic creations since that time. One might say much the same of Berlin and most of our other great towns.

But the following is the essential thing to be noticed: Our great modern cities have no outstanding monuments that dominate the general aspect of the city and could be pointed to as the symbols of a whole epoch. Yet almost every ancient town had a monument erected to its glory. It was not in private dwellings that the characteristic art of ancient cities was displayed but in the public monuments, which were not meant to have a transitory interest but an enduring one. And this was because they did not represent the wealth of some individual citizen but the greatness and importance of the community. It was under this inspiration that those monuments arose which bound the individual inhabitants to their own town in a manner that is often almost incomprehensible to us to-day.

What struck the eye of the individual citizen was not a number of mediocre private buildings, but imposing structures that belonged to the whole community. In contradistinction to these, private dwellings were of only very secondary importance indeed.

When we compare the size of those ancient public buildings with that of the private dwellings belonging to the same epoch then we can understand the great importance which was given to the principle that those works which reflected and affected the life of the community should take precedence of all others.

Among the broken arches and vast spaces that are covered with ruins from the ancient world the colossal riches that still arouse our wonder have not been left to us from the commercial palaces of these days but from the temples of the Gods and the public edifices that belonged to the State. The community itself was the owner of those great edifices. Even in the pomp of Rome during the decadence it was not the villas and palaces of some citizens that filled the most prominent place but rather the temples and the baths, the stadia, the circuses, the aqueducts, the basilicas, etc., which belonged to the State and therefore to the people as a whole.

In medieval Germany also the same principle held sway, although the artistic outlook was quite different. In ancient times the theme that found its expression in the Acropolis or the Pantheon was now clothed in the forms of the Gothic Cathedral. In the medieval cities these monumental structures towered gigantically above the swarm of smaller buildings with their framework walls of wood and brick. And they remain the dominant feature of these cities even to our own day, although they are becoming more and more obscured by the apartment barracks. They determine the character and appearance of the locality. Cathedrals, city-halls, corn exchanges, defence towers, are the outward expression of an idea which has its counterpart only in the ancient world.

The dimensions and quality of our public buildings to-day are in deplorable contrast to the edifices that represent private interests. If a similar fate should befall Berlin as befell Rome future generations might gaze upon the ruins of some Jewish department stores or joint-stock hotels and think that these were the characteristic expressions of the culture of our time. In Berlin itself, compare the shameful disproportion between the buildings which belong to the REICH and those which have been erected for the accommodation of trade and finance.

The credits that are voted for public buildings are in most cases inadequate and really ridiculous. They are not built as structures that were meant to last but mostly for the purpose of answering the need of the moment. No higher idea influenced those who commissioned such buildings. At the time the Berlin Schloss was built it had a quite different significance from what the new library has for our time, seeing that one battleship alone represents an expenditure of about sixty million marks, whereas less than half that sum was allotted for the building of the Reichstag, which is the most imposing structure erected for the REICH and which should have been built to last for ages. Yet, in deciding the question of internal decoration, the Upper House voted against the use of stone and ordered that the walls should be covered with stucco. For once, however, the parliamentarians made an appropriate decision on that occasion; for plaster heads would be out of place between stone walls.

The community as such is not the dominant characteristic of our contemporary cities, and therefore it is not to be wondered at if the community does not find itself architecturally represented. Thus we must eventually arrive at a veritable civic desert which will at last be reflected in the total indifference of the individual citizen towards his own country.

This is also a sign of our cultural decay and general break-up. Our era is entirely preoccupied with little things which are to no purpose, or rather it is entirely preoccupied in the service of money. Therefore it is not to be wondered at if, with the worship of such an idol, the sense of heroism should entirely disappear. But the present is only reaping what the past has sown.

All these symptoms which preceded the final collapse of the Second Empire must be attributed to the lack of a definite and uniformly accepted WELTANSCHAUUNG and the general uncertainty of outlook consequent on that lack. This uncertainty showed itself when the great questions of the time had to be considered one after another and a decisive policy adopted towards them. This lack is also accountable for the habit of doing everything by halves, beginning with the educational system, the shilly-shally, the reluctance to undertake responsibilites and, finally, the cowardly tolerance of evils that were even admitted to be destructive. Visionary humanitarianisms became the fashion. In weakly submitting to these aberrations and sparing the feelings of the individual, the future of millions of human beings was sacrificed.

An examination of the religious situation before the War shows that the general process of disruption had extended to this sphere also. A great part of the nation itself had for a long time already ceased to have any convictions of a uniform and practical character in their ideological outlook on life. In this matter the point of primary importance was by no means the number of people who renounced their church membership but rather the widespread indifference. While the two Christian denominations maintained missions in Asia and Africa, for the purpose of securing new adherents to the Faith, these same denominations were losing millions and millions of their adherents at home in Europe. These former adherents either gave up religion wholly as a directive force in their lives or they adopted their own interpretation of it. The consequences of this were specially felt in the moral life of the country. In parenthesis it may be remarked that the progress made by the missions in spreading the Christian Faith abroad was only quite modest in comparison with the spread of Mohammedanism.

It must be noted too that the attack on the dogmatic principles underlying ecclesiastical teaching increased steadily in violence. And yet this human world of ours would be inconceivable without the practical existence of a religious belief. The great masses of a nation are not composed of philosophers. For the masses of the people, especially faith is absolutely the only basis of a moral outlook on life. The various substitutes that have been offered have not shown any results that might warrant us in thinking that they might usefully replace the existing denominations. But if religious teaching and religious faith were once accepted by the broad masses as active forces in their lives, then the absolute authority of the doctrines of faith would be the foundation of all practical effort. There may be a few hundreds of thousands of superior men who can live wisely and intelligently without depending on the general standards that prevail in everyday life, but the millions of others cannot do so. Now the place which general custom fills in everyday life corresponds to that of general laws in the State and dogma in religion. The purely spiritual idea is of itself a changeable thing that may be subjected to endless interpretations. It is only through dogma that it is given a precise and concrete form without which it could not become a living faith.

Otherwise the spiritual idea would never become anything more than a mere metaphysical concept, or rather a philosophical opinion. Accordingly the attack against dogma is comparable to an attack against the general laws on which the State is founded. And so this attack would finally lead to complete political anarchy if it were successful, just as the attack on religion would lead to a worthless religious nihilism.

The political leader should not estimate the worth of a religion by taking some of its shortcomings into account, but he should ask himself whether there be any practical substitute in a view which is demonstrably better. Until such a substitute be available only fools and criminals would think of abolishing the existing religion.

Undoubtedly no small amount of blame for the present unsatisfactory religious situation must be attributed to those who have encumbered the ideal of religion with purely material accessories and have thus given rise to an utterly futile conflict between religion and science. In this conflict victory will nearly always be on the side of science, even though after a bitter struggle, while religion will suffer heavily in the eyes of those who cannot penetrate beneath the mere superficial aspects of science.

But the greatest damage of all has come from the practice of debasing religion as a means that can be exploited to serve political interests, or rather commercial interests. The impudent and loud-mouthed liars who do this make their profession of faith before the whole world in stentorian tones so that all poor mortals may hear—not that they are ready to die for it if necessary but rather that they may live all the better. They are ready to sell their faith for any political QUID PRO QUO. For ten parliamentary mandates they would ally themselves with the Marxists, who are the mortal foes of all religion. And for a seat in the Cabinet they would go the length of wedlock with the devil, if the latter had not still retained some traces of decency. If religious life in pre-war Germany had a disagreeable savour for the mouths of many people this was because Christianity had been lowered to base uses by political parties that called themselves Christian and because of the shameful way in which they tried to identify the Catholic Faith with a political party.

This substitution was fatal. It procured some worthless parliamentary mandates for the party in question, but the Church suffered damage thereby.

The consequences of that situation had to be borne by the whole nation; for the laxity that resulted in religious life set in at a juncture when everything was beginning to lose hold and vacillate and the traditional foundations of custom and of morality were threatening to fall asunder.

Yet all those cracks and clefts in the social organism might not have been dangerous if no grave burdens had been laid upon it; but they became disastrous when the internal solidarity of the nation was the most important factor in withstanding the storm of big events. In the political field also observant eyes might have noticed certain anomalies of the REICH which foretold disaster unless some alteration and correction took place in time. The lack of orientation in German policy, both domestic and foreign, was obvious to everyone who was not purposely blind. The best thing that could be said about the practice of making compromises is that it seemed outwardly to be in harmony with Bismarck's axiom that 'politics is the art of the possible'. But Bismarck was a slightly different man from the Chancellors who followed him. This difference allowed the former to apply that formula to the very essence of his policy, while in the mouths of the others it took on an utterly different significance. When he uttered that phrase Bismarck meant to say that in order to attain a definite political end all possible means should be employed or at least that all possibilities should be tried. But his successors see in that phrase only a solemn declaration that one is not necessarily bound to have political principles or any definite political aims at all. And the political leaders of the REICH at that time had no far-seeing policy. Here, again, the necessary foundation was lacking, namely, a definite WELTANSCHAUUNG, and these leaders also lacked that clear insight into the laws of political evolution which is a necessary quality in political leadership.

Many people who took a gloomy view of things at that time condemned the lack of ideas and lack of orientation which were evident in directing the policy of the REICH.

They recognized the inner weakness and futility of this policy. But such people played only a secondary role in politics. Those who had the Government of the country in their hands were quite as indifferent to principles of civil wisdom laid down by thinkers like Houston Stewart Chamberlain as our political leaders now are. These people are too stupid to think for themselves, and they have too much self-conceit to take from others the instruction which they need. Oxenstierna[15] gave expression to a truth which has lasted since time immemorial, when he said that the world is governed by only a particle of wisdom. Almost every civil servant of councillor rank might naturally be supposed to possess only an atom or so belonging to this particle. But since Germany became a Republic even this modicum is wanting. And that is why they had to promulgate the Law for the Defence of the Republic, which prohibits the holding of such views or expressing them. It was fortunate for Oxenstierna that he lived at that time and not in this wise Republic of our time.

Already before the War that institution which should have represented the strength of the Reich — the Parliament, the Reichstag — was widely recognized as its weakest feature. Cowardliness and fear of shouldering responsibilities were associated together there in a perfect fashion.

One of the silliest notions that one hears expressed to-day is that in Germany the parliamentary institution has ceased to function since the Revolution. This might easily be taken to imply that the case was different before the Revolution. But in reality the parliamentary institution never functioned except to the detriment of the country. And it functioned thus in those days when people saw nothing or did not wish to see anything. The German downfall is to be attributed in no small degree to this institution. But that the catastrophe did not take place sooner is not to be credited to the Parliament but rather to those who opposed the influence of this institution which, during peace times, was digging the grave of the German Nation and the German REICH.

From the immense mass of devastating evils that were due either directly or indirectly to the Parliament I shall select one the most intimately typical of this institution which was the most irresponsible of all time. The evil I speak of was seen in the appalling shilly-shally and weakness in conducting the internal and external affairs of the REICH. It was attributable in the first place to the action of the Reichstag and was one of the principal causes of the political collapse.

Everything subject to the influence of Parliament was done by halves, no matter from what aspect you may regard it.

The foreign policy of the REICH in the matter of alliances was an example of shilly-shally. They wished to maintain peace, but in doing so they steered straight. into war.

Their Polish policy was also carried out by half-measures. It resulted neither in a German triumph nor Polish conciliation, and it made enemies of the Russians.

They tried to solve the Alsace-Lorraine question through half-measures. Instead of crushing the head of the French hydra once and for all with the mailed fist and granting Alsace-Lorraine equal rights with the other

German States, they did neither the one nor the other. Anyhow, it was impossible for them to do otherwise, for they had among their ranks the greatest traitors to the country, such as Herr Wetterlé of the Centre Party.

But still the country might have been able to bear with all this provided the half-measure policy had not victimized that force in which, as the last resort, the existence of the Empire depended: namely, the Army.

The crime committed by the so-called German Reichstag in this regard was sufficient of itself to draw down upon it the curses of the German Nation for all time. On the most miserable of pretexts these parliamentary party henchmen filched from the hands of the nation and threw away the weapons which were needed to maintain its existence and therewith defend the liberty and independence of our people. If the graves on the plains of Flanders were to open to-day the bloodstained accusers would arise, hundreds of thousands of our best German youth who were driven into the arms of death by those conscienceless parliamentary ruffians who were either wrongly educated for their task or only half-educated. Those youths, and other millions of the killed and mutilated, were lost to the Fatherland simply and solely in order that a few hundred deceivers of the people might carry out their political manoeuvres and their exactions or even treasonably pursue their doctrinaire theories.

By means of the Marxist and democratic Press, the Jews spread the colossal falsehood about 'German Militarism' throughout the world and tried to inculpate Germany by every possible means, while at the same time the Marxist and democratic parties refused to assent to the measures that were necessary for the adequate training of our national defence forces. The appalling crime thus committed by these people ought to have been obvious to everybody who foresaw that in case of war the whole nation would have to be called to arms and that, because of the mean huckstering of these noble 'representatives of the people', as they called themselves, millions of Germans would have to face the enemy ill-equipped and insufficiently trained. But even apart from the consequences of the crude and brutal lack of conscience which these parliamentarian rascals displayed, it was quite clear that the lack of properly trained soldiers at the beginning of a war would most probably lead to the loss of such a war; and this probability was confirmed in a most terrible way during the course of the world war.

Therefore the German people lost the struggle for the freedom and independence of their country because of the half-hearted and defective policy employed during times of peace in the organization and training of the defensive strength of the nation.

The number of recruits trained for the land forces was too small; but the same half-heartedness was shown in regard to the navy and made this weapon of national self-preservation more or less ineffective.

Unfortunately, even the naval authorities themselves were contaminated with this spirit of half-heartedness. The tendency to build the ship on the stocks somewhat smaller than that just launched by the British did not show much foresight and less genius. A fleet which cannot be brought to the same numerical strength as that of the probable enemy ought to compensate for this inferiority by the superior fighting power of the individual ship. It is the weight of the fighting power that counts and not any sort of traditional quality. As a matter of fact, modern technical development is so advanced and so well proportioned among the various civilized States that it must be looked on as practically impossible for one Power to build vessels which would have a superior fighting quality to that of the vessels of equal size built by the other Powers. But it is even less feasible to build vessels of smaller displacement which will be superior in action to those of larger displacement.

As a matter of fact, the smaller proportions of the German vessels could be maintained only at the expense of speed and armament. The phrase used to justify this policy was in itself an evidence of the lack of logical thinking on the part of the naval authorities who were in charge of these matters in times of peace. They declared that the German guns were definitely superior to the British 30.5 cm. as regards striking efficiency.

But that was just why they should have adopted the policy of building 30.5 cm. guns also; for it ought to have been their object not to achieve equality but superiority in fighting strength. If that were not so then it would have been superfluous to equip the land forces with 42 cm. mortars; for the German 21 cm. mortar could be far superior to any high-angle guns which the French possessed at that time and since the fortresses could probably have been taken by means of 30.5 cm. mortars.

The army authorities unfortunately failed to do so. If they refrained from assuring superior efficiency in the artillery as in the velocity, this was because of the fundamentally false 'principle of risk' which they adopted. The naval authorities, already in times of peace, renounced the principle of attack and thus had to follow a defensive policy from the very beginning of the War. But by this attitude they renounced also the chances of final success, which can be achieved only by an offensive policy.

A vessel with slower speed and weaker armament will be crippled and battered by an adversary that is faster and stronger and can frequently shoot from a favourable distance. A large number of cruisers have been through bitter experiences in this matter. How wrong were the ideas prevalent among the naval authorities in times of peace was proved during the War. They were compelled to modify the armament of the old vessels and to equip the new ones with better armament whenever there was a chance to do so. If the German vessels in the Battle of the Skagerrak had been of equal size, the same armament and the same speed as the English, the British Fleet would have gone down under the tempest of the German 38 centimeter shells, which hit their aims more accurately and were more effective.

Japan had followed a different kind of naval policy. There, care was principally taken to create with every single new vessel a fighting force that would be superior to those of the eventual adversaries. But, because of this policy, it was afterwards possible to use the fleet for the offensive.

While the army authorities refused to adopt such fundamentally erroneous principles, the navy—which unfortunately had more representatives in Parliament—succumbed to the spirit that ruled there. The navy was not organized on a strong basis, and it was later used in an unsystematic and irresolute way. The immortal glory which the navy won, in spite of these drawbacks, must be entirely credited to the good work and the efficiency and incomparable heroism of officers and crews. If the former commanders-in-chief had been inspired with the same kind of genius all the sacrifices would not have been in vain.

It was probably the very parliamentarian skill displayed by the chief of the navy during the years of peace which later became the cause of the fatal collapse, since parliamentarian considerations had begun to play a more important role in the construction of the navy than fighting considerations. The irresolution, the weakness and the failure to adopt a logically consistent policy, which is typical of the parliamentary system, contaminated the naval authorities.

As I have already emphasized, the military authorities did not allow themselves to be led astray by such fundamentally erroneous ideas. Ludendorff, who was then a Colonel in the General Staff, led a desperate struggle against the criminal vacillations with which the Reichstag treated the most vital problems of the nation and in most cases voted against them. If the fight which this officer then waged remained unsuccessful this must be debited to the Parliament and partly also to the wretched and weak attitude of the Chancellor, Bethmann-Hollweg. Yet those who are responsible for Germany's collapse do not hesitate now to lay all the blame on the shoulders of the one man who took a firm stand against the neglectful manner in which the interests of the nation were managed. But one falsehood more or less makes no difference to these congenital tricksters.

Anybody who thinks of all the sacrifices which this nation has had to bear, as a result of the criminal neglect of those irresponsible individuals; anybody who thinks of the number of those who died or were maimed unnecessarily; anybody who thinks of the deplorable shame and dishonour which has been heaped upon us and of the illimitable distress into which our people are now plunged—anybody who realizes that in order to prepare the way to a few seats in Parliament for some unscrupulous place-hunters and arrivists will understand that such hirelings can be called by no other name than that of rascal and criminal; for otherwise those words could have no meaning. In comparison with traitors who betrayed the nation's trust every other kind of twister may be looked upon as an honourable man.

It was a peculiar feature of the situation that all the real faults of the old Germany were exposed to the public gaze only when the inner solidarity of the nation could be injured by doing so. Then, indeed, unpleasant truths were openly proclaimed in the ears of the broad masses, while many other things were at other times shamefully hushed up or their existence simply denied, especially at times when an open discussion of such problems might have led to an improvement in their regard. The higher government authorities knew little or nothing of the nature and use of propaganda in such matters. Only the Jew knew that by an able and persistent use of propaganda heaven itself can be presented to the people as if it were hell and, vice versa, the most miserable kind of life can be presented as if it were paradise. The Jew knew this and acted accordingly. But the German, or rather his Government, did not have the slightest suspicion of it. During the War the heaviest of penalties had to be paid for that ignorance.

Over against the innumerable drawbacks which I have mentioned here and which affected German life before the War there were many outstanding features on the positive side. If we take an impartial survey we must admit that most of our drawbacks were in great measure prevalent also in other countries and among the other nations, and very often in a worse form than with us; whereas among us there were many real advantages which the other did not have.

The leading phase of Germany's superiority arose from the fact that, almost alone among all the other European nations, the German nation had made the strongest effort to preserve the national character of its economic structure and for this reason was less subject than other countries to the power of international finance, though indeed there were many untoward symptoms in this regard also.

And yet this superiority was a perilous one and turned out later to be one of the chief causes of the world war.

But even if we disregard this advantage of national independence in economic matters there were certain other positive features of our social and political life which were of outstanding excellence. These features were represented by three institutions which were constant sources of regeneration. In their respective spheres they were models of perfection and were partly unrivalled.

The first of these was the statal form as such and the manner in which it had been developed for Germany in modern times. Of course we must except those monarchs who, as human beings, were subject to the failings which afflict this life and its children. If we were not so tolerant in these matters, then the case of the present generation would be hopeless; for if we take into consideration the personal capabilities and character of the representative figures in our present regime it would be difficult to imagine a more modest level of intelligence and moral character. If we measure the 'value' of the German Revolution by the personal worth and calibre of the individuals whom this revolution has presented to the German people since November 1918 then we may feel ashamed indeed in thinking of the judgment which posterity will pass on these people, when the Law for the Protection of the Republic can no longer silence public opinion. Coming generations will surely decide that the intelligence and integrity of our new German leaders were in adverse ratio to their boasting and their vices.

It must be admitted that the monarchy had become alien in spirit to many citizens and especially the broad masses. This resulted from the fact that the monarchs were not always surrounded by the highest intelligence—so to say—and certainly not always by persons of the most upright character. Unfortunately many of them preferred flatterers to honest-spoken men and hence received their 'information' from the former. This was a source of grave danger at a time when the world was passing through a period in which many of the old conditions were changing and when this change was affecting even the traditions of the Court.

The average man or woman could not have felt a wave of enthusiasm surging within the breast when, for example, at the turn of the century, a princess in uniform and on horseback had the soldiers file past her on parade. Those high circles had apparently no idea of the impression which such a parade made on the minds of ordinary people; else such unfortunate occurrences would not have taken place. The sentimental humanitarianism—not always very sincere—which was professed in those high circles was often more repulsive than attractive. When, for instance, the Princess X condescended to taste the products of a soup kitchen and found them excellent, as usual, such a gesture might have made an excellent impression in times long past, but on this occasion it had the opposite effect to what was intended. For even if we take it for granted that Her Highness did not have the slightest idea, that on the day she sampled it, the food was not quite the same as on other days, it sufficed that the people knew it. Even the best of intentions thus became an object of ridicule or a cause of exasperation.

Descriptions of the proverbial frugality practised by the monarch, his much too early rise in the morning and the drudgery he had to go through all day long until late at night, and especially the constantly expressed fears lest he might become undernourished—all this gave rise to ominous expression on the part of the people. Nobody was keen to know what and how much the monarch ate or drank. Nobody grudged him a full meal, or the necessary amount of sleep. Everybody was pleased when the monarch, as a man and a personality, brought honour on his family and his country and fulfilled his duties as a sovereign. All the legends which were circulated about him helped little and did much damage.

These and such things, however, are only mere bagatelle. What was much worse was the feeling, which spread throughout large sections of the nation, that the affairs of the individual were being taken care of from above and that he did not need to bother himself with them. As long as the Government was really good, or at least moved by goodwill, no serious objections could be raised.

But the country was destined to disaster when the old Government, which had at least striven for the best, became replaced by a new regime which was not of the same quality. Then the docile obedience and infantile credulity which formerly offered no resistance was bound to be one of the most fatal evils that can be imagined.

But against these and other defects there were certain qualities which undoubtedly had a positive effect.

First of all the monarchical form of government guarantees stability in the direction of public affairs and safeguards public offices from the speculative turmoil of ambitious politicians. Furthermore, the venerable tradition which this institution possesses arouses a feeling which gives weight to the monarchical authority. Beyond this there is the fact that the whole corps of officials, and the army in particular, are raised above the level of political party obligations. And still another positive feature was that the supreme rulership of the State was embodied in the monarch, as an individual person, who could serve as the symbol of responsibility, which a monarch has to bear more seriously than any anonymous parliamentary majority. Indeed, the proverbial honesty and integrity of the German administration must be attributed chiefly to this fact. Finally, the monarchy fulfilled a high cultural function among the German people, which made amends for many of its defects. The German residential cities have remained, even to our time, centres of that artistic spirit which now threatens to disappear and is becoming more and more materialistic. The German princes gave a great deal of excellent and practical encouragement to art and science, especially during the nineteenth century. Our present age certainly has nothing of equal worth.

During that process of disintegration which was slowly extending throughout the social order the most positive force of resistance was that offered by the army. This was the strongest source of education which the German people possessed. For that reason all the hatred of our enemies was directed against the paladin of our national self-preservation and our liberty. The strongest testimony in favour of this unique institution is the fact that it was derided, hated and fought against, but also feared, by worthless elements all round. The fact that the international profiteers who gathered at Versailles, further to exploit and plunder the nations directed their enmity specially against the old German army proved once again that it deserved to be regarded as the institution which protected the liberties of our people against the forces of the international stock-exchange. If the army had not been there to sound the alarm and stand on guard, the purposes of the Versailles representatives would have been carried out much sooner. There is only one word to express what the German people owe to this army—Everything!

It was the army that still inculcated a sense of responsibility among the people when this quality had become very rare and when the habit of shirking every kind of responsibility was steadily spreading. This habit had grown up under the evil influences of Parliament, which was itself the very model of irresponsibility. The army trained the people to personal courage at a time when the virtue of timidity threatened to become an epidemic and when the spirit of sacrificing one's personal interests for the good of the community was considered as something that amounted almost to weak-mindedness. At a time when only those were estimated as intelligent who knew how to safeguard and promote their own egotistic interests, the army was the school through which individual Germans were taught not to seek the salvation of their nation in the false ideology of international fraternization between negroes, Germans, Chinese, French and English, etc., but in the strength and unity of their own national being.

The army developed the individual's powers of resolute decision, and this at a time when a spirit of indecision and scepticism governed human conduct. At a time when the wiseacres were everywhere setting the fashion it needed courage to uphold the principle that any command is better than none. This one principle represents a robust and sound style of thought, of which not a trace would have been left in the other branches of life if the army had not furnished a constant rejuvenation of this fundamental force. A sufficient proof of this may be found in the appalling lack of decision which our present government authorities display. They cannot shake off their mental and moral lethargy and decide on some definite line of action except when they are forced to sign some new dictate for the exploitation of the German people. In that case they decline all responsibility while at the same time they sign everything which the other side places before them; and they sign with the readiness of an official stenographer. Their conduct is here explicable on the ground that in this case they are not under the necessity of coming to a decision; for the decision is dictated to them. The army imbued its members with a spirit of idealism and developed their readiness to sacrifice themselves for their country and its honour, while greed and materialism dominated in all the other branches of life. The army united a people who were split up into classes: and in this respect had only one defect, which was the One Year Military Service, a privilege granted to those who had passed through the high schools. It was a defect, because the principle of absolute equality was thereby violated; and those who had a better education were thus placed outside the cadres to which the rest of their comrades belonged. The reverse would have been better. Since our upper classes were really ignorant of what was going on in the body corporate of the nation and were becoming more and more estranged from the life of the people, the army would have accomplished a very beneficial mission if it had refused to discriminate in favour of the so-called intellectuals, especially within its own ranks. It was a mistake that this was not done; but in this world of ours can we find any institution that has not at least one defect? And in the army the good features were so absolutely predominant that the few defects it had were far below the average that generally rises from human weakness.

But the greatest credit which the army of the old Empire deserves is that, at a time when the person of the individual counted for nothing and the majority was everything, it placed individual personal values above majority values. By insisting on its faith in personality, the army opposed that typically Jewish and democratic apotheosis of the power of numbers. The army trained what at that time was most surely needed: namely, real men. In a period when men were falling a prey to effeminacy and laxity, 350,000 vigorously trained young men went from the ranks of the army each year to mingle with their fellow-men. In the course of their two years' training they had lost the softness of their young days and had developed bodies as tough as steel. The young man who had been taught obedience for two years was now fitted to command. The trained soldier could be recognized already by his walk.

This was the great school of the German nation; and it was not without reason that it drew upon its head all the bitter hatred of those who wanted the Empire to be weak and defenceless, because they were jealous of its greatness and were themselves possessed by a spirit of rapacity and greed. The rest of the world recognized a fact which many Germans did not wish to see, either because they were blind to facts or because out of malice they did not wish to see it. This fact was that the German Army was the most powerful weapon for the defence and freedom of the German nation and the best guarantee for the livelihood of its citizens.

There was a third institution of positive worth, which has to be placed beside that of the monarchy and the army. This was the civil service. German administration was better organized and better carried out than the administration of other countries. There may have been objections to the bureaucratic routine of the officials, but from this point of view the state of affairs was similar, if not worse, in the other countries.

But the other States did not have the wonderful solidarity which this organization possessed in Germany, nor were their civil servants of that same high level of scrupulous honesty. It is certainly better to be a trifle over-bureaucratic and honest and loyal than to be over-sophisticated and modern, the latter often implying an inferior type of character and also ignorance and inefficiency. For if it be insinuated to-day that the German administration of the pre-War period may have been excellent so far as bureaucratic technique goes, but that from the practical business point of view it was incompetent, I can only give the following reply: What other country in the world possessed a better-organized and administered business enterprise than the German State Railways, for instance? It was left to the Revolution to destroy this standard organization, until a time came when it was taken out of the hands of the nation and socialized, in the sense which the founders of the Republic had given to that word, namely, making it subservient to the international stock-exchange capitalists, who were the wire-pullers of the German Revolution.

The most outstanding trait in the civil service and the whole body of the civil administration was its independence of the vicissitudes of government, the political mentality of which could exercise no influence on the attitude of the German State officials. Since the Revolution this situation has been completely changed. Efficiency and capability have been replaced by the test of party-adherence; and independence of character and initiative are no longer appreciated as positive qualities in a public official. They rather tell against him.

The wonderful might and power of the old Empire was based on the monarchical form of government, the army and the civil service. On these three foundations rested that great strength which is now entirely lacking; namely, the authority of the State. For the authority of the State cannot be based on the babbling that goes on in Parliament or in the provincial diets and not upon laws made to protect the State, or upon sentences passed by the law courts to frighten those who have had the hardihood to deny the authority of the State, but only on the general confidence which the management and administration of the community establishes among the people. This confidence is in its turn, nothing else than the result of an unshakable inner conviction that the government and administration of a country is inspired by disinterested and honest goodwill and on the feeling that the spirit of the law is in complete harmony with the moral convictions of the people. In the long run, systems of government are not maintained by terrorism but on the belief of the people in the merits and sincerity of those who administer and promote the public interests.

Though it be true that in the period preceding the War certain grave evils tended to infect and corrode the inner strength of the nation, it must be remembered that the other States suffered even more than Germany from these drawbacks and yet those other States did not fail and break down when the time of crisis came. If we remember further that those defects in pre-War Germany were outweighed by great positive qualities we shall have to look elsewhere for the effective cause of the collapse. And elsewhere it lay.

The ultimate and most profound reason of the German downfall is to be found in the fact that the racial problem was ignored and that its importance in the historical development of nations was not grasped. For the events that take place in the life of nations are not due to chance but are the natural results of the effort to conserve and multiply the species and the race, even though men may not be able consciously to picture to their minds the profound motives of their conduct.

CHAPTER XI: Race and People

There are certain truths which stand out so openly on the roadsides of life, as it were, that every passer-by may see them. Yet, because of their very obviousness, the general run of people disregard such truths or at least they do not make them the object of any conscious knowledge.

People are so blind to some of the simplest facts in every-day life that they are highly surprised when somebody calls attention to what everybody ought to know. Examples of The Columbus Egg lie around us in hundreds of thousands; but observers like Columbus are rare.

Walking about in the garden of Nature, most men have the self-conceit to think that they know everything; yet almost all are blind to one of the outstanding principles that Nature employs in her work. This principle may be called the inner isolation which characterizes each and every living species on this earth.

Even a superficial glance is sufficient to show that all the innumerable forms in which the life-urge of Nature manifests itself are subject to a fundamental law—one may call it an iron law of Nature—which compels the various species to keep within the definite limits of their own life-forms when propagating and multiplying their kind. Each animal mates only with one of its own species. The titmouse cohabits only with the titmouse, the finch with the finch, the stork with the stork, the field-mouse with the field-mouse, the house-mouse with the house-mouse, the wolf with the she-wolf, etc.

Deviations from this law take place only in exceptional circumstances. This happens especially under the compulsion of captivity, or when some other obstacle makes procreative intercourse impossible between individuals of the same species. But then Nature abhors such intercourse with all her might; and her protest is most clearly demonstrated by the fact that the hybrid is either sterile or the fecundity of its descendants is limited. In most cases hybrids and their progeny are denied the ordinary powers of resistance to disease or the natural means of defence against outer attack.

Such a dispensation of Nature is quite logical. Every crossing between two breeds which are not quite equal results in a product which holds an intermediate place between the levels of the two parents. This means that the offspring will indeed be superior to the parent which stands in the biologically lower order of being, but not so high as the higher parent. For this reason it must eventually succumb in any struggle against the higher species. Such mating contradicts the will of Nature towards the selective improvements of life in general. The favourable preliminary to this improvement is not to mate individuals of higher and lower orders of being but rather to allow the complete triumph of the higher order. The stronger must dominate and not mate with the weaker, which would signify the sacrifice of its own higher nature. Only the born weakling can look upon this principle as cruel, and if he does so it is merely because he is of a feebler nature and narrower mind; for if such a law did not direct the process of evolution then the higher development of organic life would not be conceivable at all.

This urge for the maintenance of the unmixed breed, which is a phenomenon that prevails throughout the whole of the natural world, results not only in the sharply defined outward distinction between one species and another but also in the internal similarity of characteristic qualities which are peculiar to each breed or species.

The fox remains always a fox, the goose remains a goose, and the tiger will retain the character of a tiger. The only difference that can exist within the species must be in the various degrees of structural strength and active power, in the intelligence, efficiency, endurance, etc., with which the individual specimens are endowed. It would be impossible to find a fox which has a kindly and protective disposition towards geese, just as no cat exists which has a friendly disposition towards mice.

That is why the struggle between the various species does not arise from a feeling of mutual antipathy but rather from hunger and love. In both cases Nature looks on calmly and is even pleased with what happens. The struggle for the daily livelihood leaves behind in the ruck everything that is weak or diseased or wavering; while the fight of the male to possess the female gives to the strongest the right, or at least, the possibility to propagate its kind. And this struggle is a means of furthering the health and powers of resistance in the species. Thus it is one of the causes underlying the process of development towards a higher quality of being.

If the case were different the progressive process would cease, and even retrogression might set in. Since the inferior always outnumber the superior, the former would always increase more rapidly if they possessed the same capacities for survival and for the procreation of their kind; and the final consequence would be that the best in quality would be forced to recede into the background. Therefore a corrective measure in favour of the better quality must intervene. Nature supplies this by establishing rigorous conditions of life to which the weaker will have to submit and will thereby be numerically restricted; but even that portion which survives cannot indiscriminately multiply, for here a new and rigorous selection takes place, according to strength and health.

If Nature does not wish that weaker individuals should mate with the stronger, she wishes even less that a superior race should intermingle with an inferior one; because in such a case all her efforts, throughout hundreds of thousands of years, to establish an evolutionary higher stage of being, may thus be rendered futile.

History furnishes us with innumerable instances that prove this law. It shows, with a startling clarity, that whenever Aryans have mingled their blood with that of an inferior race the result has been the downfall of the people who were the standard-bearers of a higher culture. In North America, where the population is prevalently Teutonic, and where those elements intermingled with the inferior race only to a very small degree, we have a quality of mankind and a civilization which are different from those of Central and South America. In these latter countries the immigrants—who mainly belonged to the Latin races—mated with the aborigines, sometimes to a very large extent indeed. In this case we have a clear and decisive example of the effect produced by the mixture of races. But in North America the Teutonic element, which has kept its racial stock pure and did not mix it with any other racial stock, has come to dominate the American Continent and will remain master of it as long as that element does not fall a victim to the habit of adulterating its blood.

In short, the results of miscegenation are always the following:

(a) The level of the superior race becomes lowered;

(b) physical and mental degeneration sets in, thus leading slowly but steadily towards a progressive drying up of the vital sap.

The act which brings about such a development is a sin against the will of the Eternal Creator. And as a sin this act will be avenged. Man's effort to build up something that contradicts the iron logic of

Nature brings him into conflict with those principles to which he himself exclusively owes his own existence. By acting against the laws of Nature he prepares the way that leads to his ruin. Here we meet the insolent objection, which is Jewish in its inspiration and is typical of the modern pacifist. It says: "Man can control even Nature."

There are millions who repeat by rote that piece of Jewish babble and end up by imagining that somehow they themselves are the conquerors of Nature. And yet their only weapon is just a mere idea, and a very preposterous idea into the bargain; because if one accepted it, then it would be impossible even to imagine the existence of the world.

The real truth is that, not only has man failed to overcome Nature in any sphere whatsoever but that at best he has merely succeeded in getting hold of and lifting a tiny corner of the enormous veil which she has spread over her eternal mysteries and secret. He never creates anything. All he can do is to discover something. He does not master Nature but has only come to be the master of those living beings who have not gained the knowledge he has arrived at by penetrating into some of Nature's laws and mysteries. Apart from all this, an idea can never subject to its own sway those conditions which are necessary for the existence and development of mankind; for the idea itself has come only from man. Without man there would be no human idea in this world. The idea as such is therefore always dependent on the existence of man and consequently is dependent on those laws which furnish the conditions of his existence.

And not only that. Certain ideas are even confined to certain people. This holds true with regard to those ideas in particular which have not their roots in objective scientific truth but in the world of feeling. In other words, to use a phrase which is current to-day and which well and clearly expresses this truth: THEY REFLECT AN INNER EXPERIENCE. All such ideas, which have nothing to do with cold logic as such but represent mere manifestations of feeling, such as ethical and moral conceptions, etc., are inextricably bound up with man's existence. It is to the creative powers of man's imagination that such ideas owe their existence.

Now, then, a necessary condition for the maintenance of such ideas is the existence of certain races and certain types of men. For example, anyone who sincerely wishes that the pacifist idea should prevail in this world ought to do all he is capable of doing to help the Germans conquer the world; for in case the reverse should happen it may easily be that the last pacifist would disappear with the last German. I say this because, unfortunately, only our people, and no other people in the world, fell a prey to this idea. Whether you like it or not, you would have to make up your mind to forget wars if you would achieve the pacifist ideal. Nothing less than this was the plan of the American world-redeemer, Woodrow Wilson. Anyhow that was what our visionaries believed, and they thought that through his plans their ideals would be attained.

The pacifist-humanitarian idea may indeed become an excellent one when the most superior type of manhood will have succeeded in subjugating the world to such an extent that this type is then sole master of the earth.

This idea could have an injurious effect only in the measure according to which its application would become difficult and finally impossible. So, first of all, the fight and then pacifism. If the case were different it would mean that mankind has already passed the zenith of its development, and accordingly the end would not be the supremacy of some moral ideal but degeneration into barbarism and consequent chaos. People may laugh at this statement; but our planet has been moving through the spaces of ether for millions and millions of years, uninhabited by men, and at some future date may easily begin to do so again—if men should forget that wherever they have reached a superior level of existence, it was not the result of following the ideas of crazy visionaries but by acknowledging and rigorously observing the iron laws of Nature.

All that we admire in the world to-day, its science, its art, its technical developments and discoveries, are the products of the creative activities of a few peoples, and it may be true that their first beginnings must be attributed to one race. The maintenance of civilization is wholly dependent on such peoples. Should they perish, all that makes this earth beautiful will descend with them into the grave.

However great, for example, be the influence which the soil exerts on men, this influence will always vary according to the race in which it produces its effect. Dearth of soil may stimulate one race to the most strenuous efforts and highest achievement; while, for another race, the poverty of the soil may be the cause of misery and finally of undernourishment, with all its consequences. The internal characteristics of a people are always the causes which determine the nature of the effect that outer circumstances have on them. What reduces one race to starvation trains another race to harder work.

All the great civilizations of the past became decadent because the originally creative race died out, as a result of contamination of the blood.

The most profound cause of such a decline is to be found in the fact that the people ignored the principle that all culture depends on men, and not the reverse. In other words, in order to preserve a certain culture, the type of manhood that creates such a culture must be preserved. But such a preservation goes hand-in-hand with the inexorable law that it is the strongest and the best who must triumph and that they have the right to endure.

He who would live must fight. He who does not wish to fight in this world, where permanent struggle is the law of life, has not the right to exist.

Such a saying may sound hard; but, after all, that is how the matter really stands. Yet far harder is the lot of him who believes that he can overcome Nature and thus in reality insults her. Distress, misery, and disease are her rejoinders.

Whoever ignores or despises the laws of race really deprives himself of the happiness to which he believes he can attain. For he places an obstacle in the victorious path of the superior race and, by so doing, he interferes with a prerequisite condition of all human progress.

Loaded with the burden of humanitarian sentiment, he falls back to the level of those who are unable to raise themselves in the scale of being. It would be futile to attempt to discuss the question as to what race or races were the original standard-bearers of human culture and were thereby the real founders of all that we understand by the word humanity. It is much simpler to deal with this question in so far as it relates to the present time. Here the answer is simple and clear. Every manifestation of human culture, every product of art, science and technical skill, which we see before our eyes to-day, is almost exclusively the product of the Aryan creative power. This very fact fully justifies the conclusion that it was the Aryan alone who founded a superior type of humanity;

therefore he represents the architype of what we understand by the term: MAN. He is the Prometheus of mankind, from whose shining brow the divine spark of genius has at all times flashed forth, always kindling anew that fire which, in the form of knowledge, illuminated the dark night by drawing aside the veil of mystery and thus showing man how to rise and become master over all the other beings on the earth. Should he be forced to disappear, a profound darkness will descend on the earth; within a few thousand years human culture will vanish and the world will become a desert.

If we divide mankind into three categories—founders of culture, bearers of culture, and destroyers of culture—the Aryan alone can be considered as representing the first category. It was he who laid the groundwork and erected the walls of every great structure in human culture. Only the shape and colour of such structures are to be attributed to the individual characteristics of the various nations. It is the Aryan who has furnished the great building-stones and plans for the edifices of all human progress; only the way in which these plans have been executed is to be attributed to the qualities of each individual race. Within a few decades the whole of Eastern Asia, for instance, appropriated a culture and called such a culture its own, whereas the basis of that culture was the Greek mind and Teutonic skill as we know it. Only the external form—at least to a certain degree— shows the traits of an Asiatic inspiration. It is not true, as some believe, that Japan adds European technique to a culture of her own. The truth rather is that European science and technics are just decked out with the peculiar characteristics of Japanese civilization. The foundations of actual life in Japan to-day are not those of the native Japanese culture, although this characterizes the external features of the country, which features strike the eye of European observers on account of their fundamental difference from us; but the real foundations of contemporary Japanese life are the enormous scientific and technical achievements of Europe and America, that is to say, of Aryan peoples. Only by adopting these achievements as the foundations of their own progress can the various nations of the Orient take a place in contemporary world progress. The scientific and technical achievements of Europe and America provide the basis on which the struggle for daily livelihood is carried on in the Orient. They provide the necessary arms and instruments for this struggle, and only the outer forms of these instruments have become gradually adapted to Japanese ways of life.

If, from to-day onwards, the Aryan influence on Japan would cease—and if we suppose that Europe and America would collapse—then the present progress of Japan in science and technique might still last for a short duration; but within a few decades the inspiration would dry up, and native Japanese character would triumph, while the present civilization would become fossilized and fall back into the sleep from which it was aroused about seventy years ago by the impact of Aryan culture. We may therefore draw the conclusion that, just as the present Japanese development has been due to Aryan influence, so in the immemorial past an outside influence and an outside culture brought into existence the Japanese culture of that day. This opinion is very strongly supported by the fact that the ancient civilization of Japan actually became fossilizied and petrified. Such a process of senility can happen only if a people loses the racial cell which originally had been creative or if the outside influence should be withdrawn after having awakened and maintained the first cultural developments in that region. If it be shown that a people owes the fundamental elements of its culture to foreign races, assimilating and elaborating such elements, and if subsequently that culture becomes fossilized whenever the external influence ceases, then such a race may be called the depository but never the creator of a culture.

If we subject the different peoples to a strict test from this standpoint we shall find that scarcely any one of them has originally created a culture, but almost all have been merely the recipients of a culture created elsewhere.

This development may be depicted as always happening somewhat in the following way:

Aryan tribes, often almost ridiculously small in number, subjugated foreign peoples and, stimulated by the conditions of life which their new country offered them (fertility, the nature of the climate, etc.), and profiting also by the abundance of manual labour furnished them by the inferior race, they developed intellectual and organizing faculties which had hitherto been dormant in these conquering tribes. Within the course of a few thousand years, or even centuries, they gave life to cultures whose primitive traits completely corresponded to the character of the founders, though modified by adaptation to the peculiarities of the soil and the characteristics of the subjugated people. But finally the conquering race offended against the principles which they first had observed, namely, the maintenance of their racial stock unmixed, and they began to intermingle with the subjugated people. Thus they put an end to their own separate existence; for the original sin committed in Paradise has always been followed by the expulsion of the guilty parties.

After a thousand years or more the last visible traces of those former masters may then be found in a lighter tint of the skin which the Aryan blood had bequeathed to the subjugated race, and in a fossilized culture of which those Aryans had been the original creators. For just as the blood. of the conqueror, who was a conqueror not only in body but also in spirit, got submerged in the blood of the subject race, so the substance disappeared out of which the torch of human culture and progress was kindled. In so far as the blood of the former ruling race has left a light nuance of colour in the blood of its descendants, as a token and a memory, the night of cultural life is rendered less dim and dark by a mild light radiated from the products of those who were the bearers of the original fire. Their radiance shines across the barbarism to which the subjected race has reverted and might often lead the superficial observer to believe that he sees before him an image of the present race when he is really looking into a mirror wherein only the past is reflected.

It may happen that in the course of its history such a people will come into contact a second time, and even oftener, with the original founders of their culture and may not even remember that distant association. Instinctively the remnants of blood left from that old ruling race will be drawn towards this new phenomenon and what had formerly been possible only under compulsion can now be successfully achieved in a voluntary way. A new cultural wave flows in and lasts until the blood of its standard-bearers becomes once again adulterated by intermixture with the originally conquered race.

It will be the task of those who set themselves to the study of a universal history of civilization to investigate history from this point of view instead of allowing themselves to be smothered under the mass of external data, as is only too often the case with our present historical science.

This short sketch of the changes that take place among those races that are only the depositories of a culture also furnishes a picture of the development and the activity and the disappearance of those who are the true founders of culture on this earth, namely the Aryans themselves. Just as in our daily life the so-called man of genius needs a particular occasion, and sometimes indeed a special stimulus, to bring his genius to light, so too in the life of the peoples the race that has genius in it needs the occasion and stimulus to bring that genius to expression.

In the monotony and routine of everyday life even persons of significance seem just like the others and do not rise beyond the average level of their fellow-men. But as soon as such men find themselves in a special situation which disconcerts and unbalances the others, the humble person of apparently common qualities reveals traits of genius, often to the amazement of those who have hitherto known him in the small things of everyday life. That is the reason why a prophet only seldom counts for something in his own country. War offers an excellent occasion for observing this phenomenon. In times of distress, when the others despair, apparently harmless boys suddenly spring up and become heroes, full of determination, undaunted in the presence of Death and manifesting wonderful powers of calm reflection under such circumstances. If such an hour of trial did not come nobody would have thought that the soul of a hero lurked in the body of that beardless youth. A special impulse is almost always necessary to bring a man of genius into the foreground. The sledge-hammer of Fate which strikes down the one so easily suddenly finds the counter-impact of steel when it strikes at the other. And, after the common shell of everyday life is broken, the core that lay hidden in it is displayed to the eyes of an astonished world. This surrounding world then grows obstinate and will not believe that what had seemed so like itself is really of that different quality so suddenly displayed. This is a process which is repeated probably every time a man of outstanding significance appears.

Though an inventor, for example, does not establish his fame until the very day that he carries through his invention, it would be a mistake to believe that the creative genius did not become alive in him until that moment. From the very hour of his birth the spark of genius is living within the man who has been endowed with the real creative faculty. True genius is an innate quality. It can never be the result of education or training.

As I have stated already, this holds good not merely of the individual but also of the race. Those peoples who manifest creative abilities in certain periods of their history have always been fundamentally creative. It belongs to their very nature, even though this fact may escape the eyes of the superficial observer. Here also recognition from outside is only the consequence of practical achievement. Since the rest of the world is incapable of recognizing genius as such, it can only see the visible manifestations of genius in the form of inventions, discoveries, buildings, painting, etc.; but even here a long time passes before recognition is given. Just as the individual person who has been endowed with the gift of genius, or at least talent of a very high order, cannot bring that endowment to realization until he comes under the urge of special circumstances, so in the life of the nations the creative capacities and powers frequently have to wait until certain conditions stimulate them to action.

The most obvious example of this truth is furnished by that race which has been, and still is, the standard-bearer of human progress: I mean the Aryan race. As soon as Fate brings them face to face with special circumstances their powers begin to develop progressively and to be manifested in tangible form. The characteristic cultures which they create under such circumstances are almost always conditioned by the soil, the climate and the people they subjugate. The last factor—that of the character of the people—is the most decisive one. The more primitive the technical conditions under which the civilizing activity takes place, the more necessary is the existence of manual labour which can be organized and employed so as to take the place of mechanical power. Had it not been possible for them to employ members of the inferior race which they conquered, the Aryans would never have been in a position to take the first steps on the road which led them to a later type of culture; just as, without the help of certain suitable animals which they were able to tame, they would never have come to the invention of mechanical power which has subsequently enabled them to do without these beasts. The phrase, 'The Moor has accomplished his function, so let him now depart', has, unfortunately, a profound application. For thousands of years the horse has been the faithful servant of man and has helped him to lay the foundations of human progress, but now motor power has dispensed with the use of the horse.

In a few years to come the use of the horse will cease entirely; and yet without its collaboration man could scarcely have come to the stage of development which he has now created.

For the establishment of superior types of civilization the members of inferior races formed one of the most essential pre-requisites. They alone could supply the lack of mechanical means without which no progress is possible. It is certain that the first stages of human civilization were not based so much on the use of tame animals as on the employment of human beings who were members of an inferior race.

Only after subjugated races were employed as slaves was a similar fate allotted to animals, and not vice versa, as some people would have us believe. At first it was the conquered enemy who had to draw the plough and only afterwards did the ox and horse take his place. Nobody else but puling pacifists can consider this fact as a sign of human degradation.

Such people fail to recognize that this evolution had to take place in order that man might reach that degree of civilization which these apostles now exploit in an attempt to make the world pay attention to their rigmarole.

The progress of mankind may be compared to the process of ascending an infinite ladder. One does not reach the higher level without first having climbed the lower rungs. The Aryan therefore had to take that road which his sense of reality pointed out to him and not that which the modern pacifist dreams of. The path of reality is, however, difficult and hard to tread; yet it is the only one which finally leads to the goal where the others envisage mankind in their dreams. But the real truth is that those dreamers help only to lead man away from his goal rather than towards it.

It was not by mere chance that the first forms of civilization arose there where the Aryan came into contact with inferior races, subjugated them and forced them to obey his command. The members of the inferior race became the first mechanical tools in the service of a growing civilization.

Thereby the way was clearly indicated which the Aryan had to follow. As a conqueror, he subjugated inferior races and turned their physical powers into organized channels under his own leadership, forcing them to follow his will and purpose. By imposing on them a useful, though hard, manner of employing their powers he not only spared the lives of those whom he had conquered but probably made their lives easier than these had been in the former state of so-called 'freedom'. While he ruthlessly maintained his position as their master, he not only remained master but he also maintained and advanced civilization. For this depended exclusively on his inborn abilities and, therefore, on the preservation of the Aryan race as such. As soon, however, as his subject began to rise and approach the level of their conqueror, a phase of which ascension was probably the use of his language, the barriers that had distinguished master from servant broke down. The Aryan neglected to maintain his own racial stock unmixed and therewith lost the right to live in the paradise which he himself had created. He became submerged in the racial mixture and gradually lost his cultural creativeness, until he finally grew, not only mentally but also physically, more like the aborigines whom he had subjected rather than his own ancestors. For some time he could continue to live on the capital of that culture which still remained; but a condition of fossilization soon set in and he sank into oblivion.

That is how cultures and empires decline and yield their places to new formations.

The adulteration of the blood and racial deterioration conditioned thereby are the only causes that account for the decline of ancient civilizations; for it is never by war that nations are ruined, but by the loss of their powers of resistance, which are exclusively a characteristic of pure racial blood. In this world everything that is not of sound racial stock is like chaff. Every historical event in the world is nothing more nor less than a manifestation of the instinct of racial self-preservation, whether for weal or woe.

The question as to the ground reasons for the predominant importance of Aryanism can be answered by pointing out that it is not so much that the Aryans are endowed with a stronger instinct for self-preservation, but rather that this manifests itself in a way which is peculiar to themselves. Considered from the subjective standpoint, the will-to-live is of course equally strong all round and only the forms in which it is expressed are different. Among the most primitive organisms the instinct for self-preservation does not extend beyond the care of the individual ego. Egotism, as we call this passion, is so predominant that it includes even the time element; which means that the present moment is deemed the most important and that nothing is left to the future. The animal lives only for itself, searching for food only when it feels hunger and fighting only for the preservation of its own life. As long as the instinct for self-preservation manifests itself exclusively in such a way, there is no basis for the establishment of a community; not even the most primitive form of all, that is to say the family. The society formed by the male with the female, where it goes beyond the mere conditions of mating, calls for the extension of the instinct of self-preservation, since the readiness to fight for one's own ego has to be extended also to the mate. The male sometimes provides food for the female, but in most cases both parents provide food for the offspring.

Almost always they are ready to protect and defend each other; so that here we find the first, though infinitely simple, manifestation of the spirit of sacrifice. As soon as this spirit extends beyond the narrow limits of the family, we have the conditions under which larger associations and finally even States can be formed.

The lowest species of human beings give evidence of this quality only to a very small degree, so that often they do not go beyond the formation of the family society. With an increasing readiness to place their immediate personal interests in the background, the capacity for organizing more extensive communities develops.

The readiness to sacrifice one's personal work and, if necessary, even one's life for others shows its most highly developed form in the Aryan race. The greatness of the Aryan is not based on his intellectual powers, but rather on his willingness to devote all his faculties to the service of the community. Here the instinct for self-preservation has reached its noblest form; for the Aryan willingly subordinates his own ego to the common weal and when necessity calls he will even sacrifice his own life for the community.

The constructive powers of the Aryan and that peculiar ability he has for the building up of a culture are not grounded in his intellectual gifts alone. If that were so they might only be destructive and could never have the ability to organize; for the latter essentially depends on the readiness of the individual to renounce his own personal opinions and interests and to lay both at the service of the human group. By serving the common weal he receives his reward in return. For example, he does not work directly for himself but makes his productive work a part of the activity of the group to which he belongs, not only for his own benefit but for the general. The spirit underlying this attitude is expressed by the word: WORK, which to him does not at all signify a means of earning one's daily livelihood but rather a productive activity which cannot clash with the interests of the community. Whenever human activity is directed exclusively to the service of the instinct for self-preservation it is called theft or usury, robbery or burglary, etc.

This mental attitude, which forces self-interest to recede into the background in favour of the common weal, is the first prerequisite for any kind of really human civilization. It is out of this spirit alone that great human achievements have sprung for which the original doers have scarcely ever received any recompense but which turns out to be the source of abundant benefit for their descendants. It is this spirit alone which can explain why it so often happens that people can endure a harsh but honest existence which offers them no returns for their toil except a poor and modest livelihood. But such a livelihood helps to consolidate the foundations on which the community exists. Every worker and every peasant, every inventor, state official, etc., who works without ever achieving fortune or prosperity for himself, is a representative of this sublime idea, even though he may never become conscious of the profound meaning of his own activity.

Everything that may be said of that kind of work which is the fundamental condition of providing food and the basic means of human progress is true even in a higher sense of work that is done for the protection of man and his civilization. The renunciation of one's own life for the sake of the community is the crowning significance of the idea of all sacrifice. In this way only is it possible to protect what has been built up by man and to assure that this will not be destroyed by the hand of man or of nature.

In the German language we have a word which admirably expresses this underlying spirit of all work: It is Pflichterfüllung, which means the service of the common weal before the consideration of one's own interests. The fundamental spirit out of which this kind of activity springs is the contradistinction of 'Egotism' and we call it 'Idealism'.

By this we mean to signify the willingness of the individual to make sacrifices for the community and his fellow-men.

It is of the utmost importance to insist again and again that idealism is not merely a superfluous manifestation of sentiment but rather something which has been, is and always will be, a necessary precondition of human civilization; it is even out of this that the very idea of the word 'Human' arises. To this kind of mentality the Aryan owes his position in the world. And the world is indebted to the Aryan mind for having developed the concept of 'mankind'; for it is out of this spirit alone that the creative force has come which in a unique way combined robust muscular power with a first-class intellect and thus created the monuments of human civilization.

Were it not for idealism all the faculties of the intellect, even the most brilliant, would be nothing but intellect itself, a mere external phenomenon without inner value and never a creative force.

Since true idealism, however, is essentially the subordination of the interests and life of the individual to the interests and life of the community, and since the community on its part represents the pre-requisite condition of every form of organization, this idealism accords in its innermost essence with the final purpose of Nature. This feeling alone makes men voluntarily acknowledge that strength and power are entitled to take the lead and thus makes them a constituent particle in that order out of which the whole universe is shaped and formed.

Without being conscious of it, the purest idealism is always associated with the most profound knowledge. How true this is and how little genuine idealism has to do with fantastic self-dramatization will become clear the moment we ask an unspoilt child, a healthy boy for example, to give his opinion. The very same boy who listens to the rantings of an 'idealistic' pacifist without understanding them, and even rejects them, would readily sacrifice his young life for the ideal of his people.

Unconsciously his instinct will submit to the knowledge that the preservation of the species, even at the cost of the individual life, is a primal necessity and he will protest against the fantasies of pacifist ranters, who in reality are nothing better than cowardly egoists, even though camouflaged, who contradict the laws of human development. For it is a necessity of human evolution that the individual should be imbued with the spirit of sacrifice in favour of the common weal, and that he should not be influenced by the morbid notions of those knaves who pretend to know better than Nature and who have the impudence to criticize her decrees.

It is just at those junctures when the idealistic attitude threatens to disappear that we notice a weakening of this force which is a necessary constituent in the founding and maintenance of the community and is thereby a necessary condition of civilization. As soon as the spirit of egotism begins to prevail among a people then the bonds of the social order break and man, by seeking his own personal happiness, veritably tumbles out of heaven and falls into hell.

Posterity will not remember those who pursued only their own individual interests, but it will praise those heroes who renounced their own happiness.

The Jew offers the most striking contrast to the Aryan. There is probably no other people in the world who have so developed the instinct of self-preservation as the so-called 'chosen' people. The best proof of this statement is found in the simple fact that this race still exists.

Where can another people be found that in the course of the last two thousand years has undergone so few changes in mental outlook and character as the Jewish people? And yet what other people has taken such a constant part in the great revolutions? But even after having passed through the most gigantic catastrophes that have overwhelmed mankind, the Jews remain the same as ever. What an infinitely tenacious will-to-live, to preserve one's kind, is demonstrated by that fact!

The intellectual faculties of the Jew have been trained through thousands of years. To-day the Jew is looked upon as specially 'cunning'; and in a certain sense he has been so throughout the ages.

His intellectual powers, however, are not the result of an inner evolution but rather have been shaped by the object-lessons which the Jew has received from others. The human spirit cannot climb upwards without taking successive steps. For every step upwards it needs the foundation of what has been constructed before—the past—which in, the comprehensive sense here employed, can have been laid only in a general civilization. All thinking originates only to a very small degree in personal experience. The largest part is based on the accumulated experiences of the past. The general level of civilization provides the individual, who in most cases is not consciously aware of the fact, with such an abundance of preliminary knowledge that with this equipment he can more easily take further steps on the road of progress. The boy of to-day, for example, grows up among such an overwhelming mass of technical achievement which has accumulated during the last century that he takes as granted many things which a hundred years ago were still mysteries even to the greatest minds of those times. Yet these things that are not so much a matter of course are of enormous importance to those who would understand the progress we have made in these matters and would carry on that progress a step farther. If a man of genius belonging to the 'twenties of the last century were to arise from his grave to-day he would find it more difficult to understand our present age than the contemporary boy of fifteen years of age who may even have only an average intelligence. The man of genius, thus come back from the past, would need to provide himself with an extraordinary amount of preliminary information which our contemporary youth receive automatically, so to speak, during the time they are growing up among the products of our modern civilization.

Since the Jew—for reasons that I shall deal with immediately—never had a civilization of his own, he has always been furnished by others with a basis for his: intellectual work. His intellect has always developed by the use of those cultural achievements which he has found ready-to-hand around him.

The process has never been the reverse.

For, though among the Jews the instinct of self-preservation has not been weaker but has been much stronger than among other peoples, and though the impression may easily be created that the intellectual powers of the Jew are at least equal to those of other races, the Jews completely lack the most essential pre-requisite of a cultural people, namely the idealistic spirit. With the Jewish people the readiness for sacrifice does not extend beyond the simple instinct of individual preservation. In their case the feeling of racial solidarity which they apparently manifest is nothing but a very primitive gregarious instinct, similar to that which may be found among other organisms in this world. It is a remarkable fact that this herd instinct brings individuals together for mutual protection only as long as there is a common danger which makes mutual assistance expedient or inevitable. The same pack of wolves which a moment ago joined together in a common attack on their victim will dissolve into individual wolves as soon as their hunger has been satisfied. This is also sure of horses, which unite to defend themselves against any aggressor but separate the moment the danger is over.

It is much the same with the Jew. His spirit of sacrifice is only apparent. It manifests itself only so long as the existence of the individual makes this a matter of absolute necessity. But as soon as the common foe is conquered and the danger which threatened the individual Jews is overcome and the prey secured, then the apparent harmony disappears and the original conditions set in again. Jews act in concord only when a common danger threatens them or a common prey attracts them.

Where these two motives no longer exist then the most brutal egotism appears and these people who before had lived together in unity will turn into a swarm of rats that bitterly fight against each other. If the Jews were the only people in the world they would be wallowing in filth and mire and would exploit one another and try to exterminate one another in a bitter struggle, except in so far as their utter lack of the ideal of sacrifice, which shows itself in their cowardly spirit, would prevent this struggle from developing.

Therefore it would be a complete mistake to interpret the mutual help which the Jews render one another when they have to fight-or, to put it more accurately, to exploit—their fellow being, as the expression of a certain idealistic spirit of sacrifice. Here again the Jew merely follows the call of his individual egotism.

That is why the Jewish State, which ought to be a vital organization to serve the purpose of preserving or increasing the race, has absolutely no territorial boundaries. For the territorial delimitation of a State always demands a certain idealism of spirit on the part of the race which forms that State and especially a proper acceptance of the idea of work. A State which is territorially delimited cannot be established or maintained unless the general attitude towards work be a positive one. If this attitude be lacking, then the necessary basis of a civilization is also lacking.

That is why the Jewish people, despite the intellectual powers with which they are apparently endowed, have not a culture—certainly not a culture of their own. The culture which the Jew enjoys to-day is the product of the work of others and this product is debased in the hands of the Jew.

In order to form a correct judgment of the place which the Jew holds in relation to the whole problem of human civilization, we must bear in mind the essential fact that there never has been any Jewish art and consequently that nothing of this kind exists to-day. We must realize that especially in those two royal domains of art, namely architecture and music, the Jew has done no original creative work. When the Jew comes to producing something in the field of art he merely bowdler-izes something already in existence or simply steals the intellectual word, of others. The Jew essentially lacks those qualities which are characteristic of those creative races that are the founders of civilization.

To what extent the Jew appropriates the civilization built up by others—or rather corrupts it, to speak more accurately—is indicated by the fact that he cultivates chiefly the art which calls for the smallest amount of original invention, namely the dramatic art. And even here he is nothing better than a kind of juggler or, perhaps more correctly speaking, a kind of monkey imitator; for in this domain also he lacks the creative elan which is necessary for the production of all really great work. Even here, therefore, he is not a creative genius but rather a superficial imitator who, in spite of all his retouching and tricks, cannot disguise the fact that there is no inner vitality in the shape he gives his products. At this juncture the Jewish Press comes in and renders friendly assistance by shouting hosannas over the head of even the most ordinary bungler of a Jew, until the rest of the world is stampeded into thinking that the object of so much praise must really be an artist, whereas in reality he may be nothing more than a low-class mimic.

No; the Jews have not the creative abilities which are necessary to the founding of a civilization; for in them there is not, and never has been, that spirit of idealism which is an absolutely necessary element in the higher development of mankind. Therefore the Jewish intellect will never be constructive but always destructive. At best it may serve as a stimulus in rare cases but only within the meaning of the poet's lines:

'THE POWER WHICH ALWAYS WILLS THE BAD, AND ALWAYS WORKS THE GOOD' (KRAFT, DIE STETS DAS BÖSE WILL UND STETS DAS GUTE SCHAFFT). [16] It is not through his help but in spite of his help that mankind makes any progress.

Since the Jew has never had a State which was based on territorial delimitations, and therefore never a civilization of his own, the idea arose that here we were dealing with a people who had to be considered as Nomads. That is a great and mischievous mistake. The true nomad does actually possess a definite delimited territory where he lives. It is merely that he does not cultivate it, as the settled farmer does, but that he lives on the products of his herds, with which he wanders over his domain. The natural reason for this mode of existence is to be found in the fact that the soil is not fertile and that it does not give the steady produce which makes a fixed abode possible. Outside of this natural cause, however, there is a more profound cause: namely, that no mechanical civilization is at hand to make up for the natural poverty of the region in question. There are territories where the Aryan can establish fixed settlements by means of the technical skill which he has developed in the course of more than a thousand years, even though these territories would otherwise have to be abandoned, unless the Aryan were willing to wander about them in nomadic fashion; but his technical tradition and his age-long experience of the use of technical means would probably make the nomadic life unbearable for him. We ought to remember that during the first period of American colonization numerous Aryans earned their daily livelihood as trappers and hunters, etc., frequently wandering about in large groups with their women and children, their mode of existence very much resembling that of ordinary nomads. The moment, however, that they grew more numerous and were able to accumulate larger resources, they cleared the land and drove out the aborigines, at the same time establishing settlements which rapidly increased all over the country.

The Aryan himself was probably at first a nomad and became a settler in the course of ages. But yet he was never of the Jewish kind. The Jew is not a nomad; for the nomad has already a definite attitude towards the concept of 'work', and this attitude served as the basis of a later cultural development, when the necessary intellectual conditions were at hand. There is a certain amount of idealism in the general attitude of the nomad, even though it be rather primitive. His whole character may, therefore, be foreign to Aryan feeling but it will never be repulsive.

But not even the slightest trace of idealism exists in the Jewish character. The Jew has never been a nomad, but always a parasite, battening on the substance of others. If he occasionally abandoned regions where he had hitherto lived he did not do it voluntarily. He did it because from time to time he was driven out by people who were tired of having their hospitality abused by such guests. Jewish self-expansion is a parasitic phenomenon—since the Jew is always looking for new pastures for his race.

But this has nothing to do with nomadic life as such; because the Jew does not ever think of leaving a territory which he has once occupied.

He sticks where he is with such tenacity that he can hardly be driven out even by superior physical force. He expands into new territories only when certain conditions for his existence are provided therein; but even then—unlike the nomad—he will not change his former abode. He is and remains a parasite, a sponger who, like a pernicious bacillus, spreads over wider and wider areas according as some favourable area attracts him. The effect produced by his presence is also like that of the vampire; for wherever he establishes himself the people who grant him hospitality are bound to be bled to death sooner or later. Thus the Jew has at all times lived in States that have belonged to other races and within the organization of those States he had formed a State of his own, which is, however, hidden behind the mask of a 'religious community', as long as external circumstances do not make it advisable for this community to declare its true nature. As soon as the Jew feels himself sufficiently established in his position to be able to hold it without a disguise, he lifts the mask and suddenly appears in the character which so many did not formerly believe or wish to see: namely that of the Jew.

The life which the Jew lives as a parasite thriving on the substance of other nations and States has resulted in developing that specific character which Schopenhauer once described when he spoke of the Jew as 'The Great Master of Lies'. The kind of existence which he leads forces the Jew to the systematic use of falsehood, just as naturally as the inhabitants of northern climates are forced to wear warm clothes.

He can live among other nations and States only as long as he succeeds in persuading them that the Jews are not a distinct people but the representatives of a religious faith who thus constitute a 'religious community', though this be of a peculiar character.

As a matter of fact, however, this is the first of his great falsehoods. He is obliged to conceal his own particular character and mode of life that he may be allowed to continue his existence as a parasite among the nations. The greater the intelligence of the individual Jew, the better will he succeed in deceiving others. His success in this line may even go so far that the people who grant him hospitality may be led to believe that the Jew among them is a genuine Frenchman, for instance, or Englishman or German or Italian, who just happens to belong to a religious denomination which is different from that prevailing in these countries. Especially in circles concerned with the executive administration of the State, where the officials generally have only a minimum of historical sense, the Jew is able to impose his infamous deception with comparative ease. In these circles independent thinking is considered a sin against the sacred rules according to which official promotion takes place. It is therefore not surprising that even to-day in the Bavarian government offices, for example, there is not the slightest suspicion that the Jews form a distinct nation themselves and are not merely the adherents of a 'Confession', though one glance at the Press which belongs to the Jews ought to furnish sufficient evidence to the contrary even for those who possess only the smallest degree of intelligence. The JEWISH ECHO, however, is not an official gazette and therefore not authoritative in the eyes of those government potentates. Jewry has always been a nation of a definite racial character and never differentiated merely by the fact of belonging to a certain religion. At a very early date, urged on by the desire to make their way in the world, the Jews began to cast about for a means whereby they might distract such attention as might prove inconvenient for them. What could be more effective and at the same time more above suspicion than to borrow and utilize the idea of the religious community? Here also everything is copied, or rather stolen; for the Jew could not possess any religious institution which had developed out of his own consciousness, seeing that he lacks every kind of idealism; which means that belief in a life beyond this terrestrial existence is foreign to him. In the Aryan mind no religion can ever be imagined unless it embodies the conviction that life in some form or other will continue after death. As a matter of fact, the Talmud is not a book that lays down principles according to which the individual should prepare for the life to come. It only furnishes rules for a practical and convenient life in this world.

The religious teaching of the Jews is principally a collection of instructions for maintaining the Jewish blood pure and for regulating intercourse between Jews and the rest of the world: that is to say, their relation with non-Jews. But the Jewish religious teaching is not concerned with moral problems. It is rather concerned with economic problems, and very petty ones at that. In regard to the moral value of the religious teaching of the Jews there exist and always have existed quite exhaustive studies (not from the Jewish side; for whatever the Jews have written on this question has naturally always been of a tendentious character) which show up the kind of religion that the Jews have in a light that makes it look very uncanny to the Aryan mind. The Jew himself is the best example of the kind of product which this religious training evolves. His life is of this world only and his mentality is as foreign to the true spirit of Christianity as his character was foreign to the great Founder of this new creed two thousand years ago. And the Founder of Christianity made no secret indeed of His estimation of the Jewish people. When He found it necessary He drove those enemies of the human race out of the Temple of God; because then, as always, they used religion as a means of advancing their commercial interests. But at that time Christ was nailed to the Cross for his attitude towards the Jews; whereas our modern Christians enter into party politics and when elections are being held they debase themselves to beg for Jewish votes. They even enter into political intrigues with the atheistic Jewish parties against the interests of their own Christian nation.

On this first and fundamental lie, the purpose of which is to make people believe that Jewry is not a nation but a religion, other lies are subsequently based. One of those further lies, for example, is in connection with the language spoken by the Jew. For him language is not an instrument for the expression of his inner thoughts but rather a means of cloaking them. When talking French his thoughts are Jewish and when writing German rhymes he only gives expression to the character of his own race.

As long as the Jew has not succeeded in mastering other peoples he is forced to speak their language whether he likes it or not. But the moment that the world would become the slave of the Jew it would have to learn some other language (Esperanto, for example) so that by this means the Jew could dominate all the more easily.

How much the whole existence of this people is based on a permanent falsehood is proved in a unique way by 'The Protocols of the Elders of Zion', which are so violently repudiated by the Jews. With groans and moans, the FRANKFURTER ZEITUNG repeats again and again that these are forgeries. This alone is evidence in favour of their authenticity. What many Jews unconsciously wish to do is here clearly set forth. It is not necessary to ask out of what Jewish brain these revelations sprang; but what is of vital interest is that they disclose, with an almost terrifying precision, the mentality and methods of action characteristic of the Jewish people and these writings expound in all their various directions the final aims towards which the Jews are striving. The study of real happenings, however, is the best way of judging the authenticity of those documents. If the historical developments which have taken place within the last few centuries be studied in the light of this book we shall understand why the Jewish Press incessantly repudiates and denounces it. For the Jewish peril will be stamped out the moment the general public come into possession of that book and understand it.

In order to get to know the Jew properly it is necessary to study the road which he has been following among the other peoples during the last few centuries. One example will suffice to give a clear insight here.

Since his career has been the same at all epochs—just as the people at whose expense he has lived have remained the same—for the purposes of making the requisite analysis it will be best to mark his progress by stages. For the sake of simplicity we shall indicate these stages by letters of the alphabet.

The first Jews came into what was then called Germania during the period of the Roman invasion; and, as usual, they came as merchants. During the turmoil caused by the great migrations of the German tribes the Jews seem to have disappeared. We may therefore consider the period when the Germans formed the first political communities as the beginning of that process whereby Central and Northern Europe was again, and this time permanently, Judaized. A development began which has always been the same or similar wherever and whenever Jews came into contact with Aryan peoples.

(a) As soon as the first permanent settlements had been established the Jew was suddenly 'there'. He arrived as a merchant and in the beginning did not trouble to disguise his nationality. He still remained openly a Jew, partly it may be because he knew too little of the language. It may also be that people of other races refused to mix with him, so that he could not very well adopt any other appearance than that of a foreign merchant. Because of his subtlety and cunning and the lack of experience on the part of the people whose guest he became, it was not to his disadvantage openly to retain his Jewish character. This may even have been advantageous to him; for the foreigner was received kindly.

(b) Slowly but steadily he began to take part in the economic life around him; not as a producer, however, but only as a middleman. His commercial cunning, acquired through thousands of years of negotiation as an intermediary, made him superior in this field to the Aryans, who were still quite ingenuous and indeed clumsy and whose honesty was unlimited; so that after a short while commerce seemed destined to become a Jewish monopoly. The Jew began by lending out money at usurious interest, which is a permanent trade of his. It was he who first introduced the payment of interest on borrowed money. The danger which this innovation involved was not at first recognized; indeed the innovation was welcomed, because it offered momentary advantages.

(c) At this stage the Jew had become firmly settled down; that is to say, he inhabited special sections of the cities and towns and had his own quarter in the market-places. Thus he gradually came to form a State within a State. He came to look upon the commercial domain and all money transactions as a privilege belonging exclusively to himself and he exploited it ruthlessly.

(d) At this stage finance and trade had become his complete monopoly. Finally, his usurious rate of interest aroused opposition and the increasing impudence which the Jew began to manifest all round stirred up popular indignation, while his display of wealth gave rise to popular envy. The cup of his iniquity became full to the brim when he included landed property among his commercial wares and degraded the soil to the level of a market commodity. Since he himself never cultivated the soil but considered it as an object to be exploited, on which the peasant may still remain but only on condition that he submits to the most heartless exactions of his new master, public antipathy against the Jew steadily increased and finally turned into open animosity. His extortionate tyranny became so unbearable that people rebelled against his control and used physical violence against him. They began to scrutinize this foreigner somewhat more closely, and then began to discover the repulsive traits and characteristics inherent in him, until finally an abyss opened between the Jews and their hosts, across which abyss there could be no further contact.

In times of distress a wave of public anger has usually arisen against the Jew; the masses have taken the law into their own hands; they have seized Jewish property and ruined the Jew in their urge to protect themselves against what they consider to be a scourge of God. Having come to know the Jew intimately through the course of centuries, in times of distress they looked upon his presence among them as a public danger comparable only to the plague.

(e) But then the Jew began to reveal his true character. He paid court to governments, with servile flattery, used his money to ingratiate himself further and thus regularly secured for himself once again the privilege of exploiting his victim. Although public wrath flared up against this eternal profiteer and drove him out, after a few years he reappeared in those same places and carried on as before. No persecution could force him to give up his trade of exploiting other people and no amount of harrying succeeded in driving him out permanently. He always returned after a short time and it was always the old story with him.

In an effort to save at least the worst from happening, legislation was passed which debarred the Jew from obtaining possession of the land.

(f) In proportion as the powers of kings and princes increased, the Jew sidled up to them. He begged for 'charters' and 'privileges' which those gentlemen, who were generally in financial straits, gladly granted if they received adequate payment in return. However high the price he has to pay, the Jew will succeed in getting it back within a few years from operating the privilege he has acquired, even with interest and compound interest. He is a real leech who clings to the body of his unfortunate victims and cannot be removed; so that when the princes found themselves in need once again they took the blood from his swollen veins with their own hands.

This game was repeated unendingly. In the case of those who were called 'German Princes', the part they played was quite as contemptible as that played by the Jew. They were a real scourge for their people. Their compeers may be found in some of the government ministers of our time.

It was due to the German princes that the German nation could not succeed in definitely freeing itself from the Jewish peril.

Unfortunately the situation did not change at a later period. The princes finally received the reward which they had a thousand-fold deserved for all the crimes committed by them against their own people.

They had allied themselves with Satan and later on they discovered that they were in Satan's embrace.

(g) By permitting themselves to be entangled in the toils of the Jew, the princes prepared their own downfall. The position which they held among their people was slowly but steadily undermined not only by their continued failure to guard the interests of their subjects but by the positive exploitation of them. The Jew calculated exactly the time when the downfall of the princes was approaching and did his best to hasten it. He intensified their financial difficulties by hindering them in the exercise of their duty towards their people, by inveigling them through the most servile flatteries into further personal display, whereby he made himself more and more indispensable to them. His astuteness, or rather his utter unscrupulousness, in money affairs enabled him to exact new income from the princes, to squeeze the money out of them and then have it spent as quickly as possible. Every Court had its 'Court Jews', as this plague was called, who tortured the innocent victims until they were driven to despair; while at the same time this Jew provided the means which the princes squandered on their own pleasures. It is not to be wondered at that these ornaments of the human race became the recipients of official honours and even were admitted into the ranks of the hereditary nobility, thus contributing not only to expose that social institution to ridicule but also to contaminate it from the inside.

Naturally the Jew could now exploit the position to which he had attained and push himself forward even more rapidly than before. Finally he became baptized and thus entitled to all the rights and privileges which belonged to the children of the nation on which he preyed. This was a high-class stroke of business for him, and he often availed himself of it, to the great joy of the Church, which was proud of having gained a new child in the Faith, and also to the joy of Israel, which was happy at seeing the trick pulled off successfully.

(h) At this stage a transformation began to take place in the world of Jewry. Up to now they had been Jews—that is to say, they did not hitherto set any great value on pretending to be something else; and anyhow the distinctive characteristics which separated them from other races could not be easily overcome. Even as late as the time of Frederick the Great nobody looked upon the Jews as other than a 'foreign' people, and Goethe rose up in revolt against the failure legally to prohibit marriage between Christians and Jews. Goethe was certainly no reactionary and no time-server. What he said came from the voice of the blood and the voice of reason. Notwithstanding the disgraceful happenings taking place in Court circles, the people recognized instinctively that the Jew was the foreign body in their own flesh and their attitude towards him was directed by recognition of that fact.

But a change was now destined to take place. In the course of more than a thousand years the Jew had learned to master the language of his hosts so thoroughly that he considered he might now lay stress on his Jewish character and emphasize the 'Germanism' a bit more. Though it must have appeared ridiculous and absurd at first sight, he was impudent enough to call himself a 'Teuton', which in this case meant a German. In that way began one of the most infamous impositions that can be imagined. The Jew did not possess the slightest traces of the German character. He had only acquired the art of twisting the German language to his own uses, and that in a disgusting way, without having assimilated any other feature of the German character. Therefore his command of the language was the sole ground on which he could pretend to be a German. It is not however by the tie of language, but exclusively by the tie of blood that the members of a race are bound together. And the Jew himself knows this better than any other, seeing that he attaches so little importance to the preservation of his own language while at the same time he strives his utmost to maintain his blood free from intermixture with that of other races. A man may acquire and use a new language without much trouble; but it is only his old ideas that he expresses through the new language. His inner nature is not modified thereby. The best proof of this is furnished by the Jew himself. He may speak a thousand tongues and yet his Jewish nature will remain always one and the same. His distinguishing characteristics were the same when he spoke the Latin language at Ostia two thousand years ago as a merchant in grain, as they are to-day when he tries to sell adulterated flour with the aid of his German gibberish. He is always the same Jew. That so obvious a fact is not recognized by the average head-clerk in a German government department, or by an officer in the police administration, is also a self-evident and natural fact; since it would be difficult to find another class of people who are so lacking in instinct and intelligence as the civil servants employed by our modern German State authorities.

The reason why, at the stage I am dealing with, the Jew so suddenly decided to transform himself into a German is not difficult to discover.

He felt the power of the princes slowly crumbling and therefore looked about to find a new social plank on which he might stand. Furthermore, his financial domination over all the spheres of economic life had become so powerful that he felt he could no longer sustain that enormous structure or add to it unless he were admitted to the full enjoyment of the 'rights of citizenship.' He aimed at both, preservation and expansion; for the higher he could climb the more alluring became the prospect of reaching the old goal, which was promised to him in ancient times, namely world-rulership, and which he now looked forward to with feverish eyes, as he thought he saw it visibly approaching. Therefore all his efforts were now directed to becoming a fully-fledged citizen, endowed with all civil and political rights. That was the reason for his emancipation from the Ghetto.

(i) And thus the Court Jew slowly developed into the national Jew. But naturally he still remained associated with persons in higher quarters and he even attempted to push his way further into the inner circles of the ruling set. But at the same time some other representatives of his race were currying favour with the people. If we remember the crimes the Jew had committed against the masses of the people in the course of so many centuries, how repeatedly and ruthlessly he exploited them and how he sucked out even the very marrow of their substance, and when we further remember how they gradually came to hate him and finally considered him as a public scourge—then we may well understand how difficult the Jew must have found this final transformation. Yes, indeed, it must tax all their powers to be able to present themselves as 'friends of humanity' to the poor victims whom they have skinned raw.

Therefore the Jew began by making public amends for the crimes which he had committed against the people in the past. He started his metamorphosis by first appearing as the 'benefactor' of humanity. Since his new philanthropic policy had a very concrete aim in view, he could not very well apply to himself the biblical counsel, not to allow the left hand to know what the right hand is giving. He felt obliged to let as many people as possible know how deeply the sufferings of the masses grieved him and to what excesses of personal sacrifice he was ready to go in order to help them. With this manifestation of innate modesty, so typical of the Jew, he trumpeted his virtues before the world until finally the world actually began to believe him. Those who refused to share this belief were considered to be doing him an injustice. Thus after a little while he began to twist things around, so as to make it appear that it was he who had always been wronged, and vice versa. There were really some particularly foolish people who could not help pitying this poor unfortunate creature of a Jew.

Attention may be called to the fact that, in spite of his proclaimed readiness to make personal sacrifices, the Jew never becomes poor thereby. He has a happy knack of always making both ends meet.

Occasionally his benevolence might be compared to the manure which is not spread over the field merely for the purpose of getting rid of it, but rather with a view to future produce. Anyhow, after a comparatively short period of time, the world was given to know that the Jew had become a general benefactor and philanthropist. What a transformation!

What is looked upon as more or less natural when done by other people here became an object of astonishment, and even sometimes of admiration, because it was considered so unusual in a Jew. That is why he has received more credit for his acts of benevolence than ordinary mortals. And something more: The Jew became liberal all of a sudden and began to talk enthusiastically of how human progress must be encouraged.

Gradually he assumed the air of being the herald of a new age. Yet at the same time he continued to undermine the ground-work of that part of the economic system in which the people have the most practical interest. He bought up stock in the various national undertakings and thus pushed his influence into the circuit of national production, making this latter an object of buying and selling on the stock exchange, or rather what might be called the pawn in a financial game of chess, and thus ruining the basis on which personal proprietorship alone is possible. Only with the entrance of the Jew did that feeling of estrangement, between employers and employees begin which led at a later date to the political class-struggle.

Finally the Jew gained an increasing influence in all economic undertakings by means of his predominance in the stock-exchange. If not the ownership, at least he secured control of the working power of the nation.

In order to strengthen his political position, he directed his efforts towards removing the barrier of racial and civic discrimination which had hitherto hindered his advance at every turn. With characteristic tenacity he championed the cause of religious tolerance for this purpose; and in the freemason organization, which had fallen completely into his hands, he found a magnificent weapon which helped him to achieve his ends. Government circles, as well as the higher sections of the political and commercial bourgeoisie, fell a prey to his plans through his manipulation of the masonic net, though they themselves did not even suspect what was happening.

Only the people as such, or rather the masses which were just becoming conscious of their own power and were beginning to use it in the fight for their rights and liberties, had hitherto escaped the grip of the Jew. At least his influence had not yet penetrated to the deeper and wider sections of the people. This was unsatisfactory to him. The most important phase of his policy was therefore to secure control over the people. The Jew realized that in his efforts to reach the position of public despot he would need a 'peace-maker.' And he thought he could find a peace-maker if he could whip-in sufficient extensive sections of the bourgeois. But the freemasons failed to catch the glove-manufacturers and the linen-weavers in the frail meshes of their net. And so it became necessary to find a grosser and withal a more effective means. Thus another weapon beside that of freemasonry would have to be secured. This was the Press. The Jew exercised all his skill and tenacity in getting hold of it. By means of the Press he began gradually to control public life in its entirety. He began to drive it along the road which he had chosen to reach his own ends; for he was now in a position to create and direct that force which, under the name of 'public opinion' is better known to-day than it was some decades ago. Simultaneously the Jew gave himself the air of thirsting after knowledge. He lauded every phase of progress, particularly those phases which led to the ruin of others; for he judges all progress and development from the standpoint of the advantages which these bring to his own people. When it brings him no such advantages he is the deadly enemy of enlightenment and hates all culture which is real culture as such. All the knowledge which he acquires in the schools of others is exploited by him exclusively in the service of his own race.

Even more watchfully than ever before, he now stood guard over his Jewish nationality. Though bubbling over with 'enlightenment', 'progress', 'liberty', 'humanity', etc., his first care was to preserve the racial integrity of his own people. He occasionally bestowed one of his female members on an influential Christian; but the racial stock of his male descendants was always preserved unmixed fundamentally. He poisons the blood of others but preserves his own blood unadulterated.

The Jew scarcely ever marries a Christian girl, but the Christian takes a Jewess to wife. The mongrels that are a result of this latter union always declare themselves on the Jewish side. Thus a part of the higher nobility in particular became completely degenerate. The Jew was well aware of this fact and systematically used this means of disarming the intellectual leaders of the opposite race. To mask his tactics and fool his victims, he talks of the equality of all men, no matter what their race or colour may be. And the simpletons begin to believe him.

Since his whole nature still retains too foreign an odour for the broad masses of the people to allow themselves to be caught in his snare, he uses the Press to put before the public a picture of himself which is entirely untrue to life but well designed to serve his purpose. In the comic papers special efforts are made to represent the Jews as an inoffensive little race which, like all others, has its peculiarities. In spite of their manners, which may seem a bit strange, the comic papers present the Jews as fundamentally good-hearted and honourable. Attempts are generally made to make them appear insignificant rather than dangerous.

During this phase of his progress the chief goal of the Jew was the victory of democracy, or rather the supreme hegemony of the parliamentary system, which embodies his concept of democracy. This institution harmonises best with his purposes; for thus the personal element is eliminated and in its place we have the dunder-headed majority, inefficiency and, last but by no means least, knavery.

The final result must necessarily have been the overthrow of the monarchy, which had to happen sooner or later.

(j) A tremendous economic development transformed the social structure of the nation. The small artisan class slowly disappeared and the factory worker, who took its place, had scarcely any chance of establishing an independent existence of his own but sank more and more to the level of a proletariat. An essential characteristic of the factory worker is that he is scarcely ever able to provide for an independent source of livelihood which will support him in later life. In the true sense of the word, he is 'disinherited'. His old age is a misery to him and can hardly be called life at all.

In earlier times a similar situation had been created, which had imperatively demanded a solution and for which a solution was found. Side by side with the peasant and the artisan, a new class was gradually developed, namely that of officials and employees, especially those employed in the various services of the State. They also were a 'disinherited' class, in the true sense of the word. But the State found a remedy for this unhealthy situation by taking upon itself the duty of providing for the State official who could establish nothing that would be an independent means of livelihood for himself in his old age. Thus the system of pensions and retiring allowances was introduced. Private enterprises slowly followed this example in increasing numbers; so that to-day every permanent non-manual worker receives a pension in his later years, if the firm which he has served is one that has reached or gone beyond a certain size. It was only by virtue of the assurance given of State officials, that they would be cared for in their old age. that such a high degree of unselfish devotion to duty was developed, which in pre-war times was one of the distinguising characteristics of German officials.

Thus a whole class which had no personal property was saved from destitution by an intelligent system of provision, and found a place in the social structure of the national community.

The problem is now put before the State and nation, but this time in a much larger form. When the new industries sprang up and developed, millions of people left the countryside and the villages to take up employment in the big factories. The conditions under which this new class found itself forced to live were worse than miserable. The more or less mechanical transformation of the methods of work hitherto in vogue among the artisans and peasants did not fit in well with the habits or mentality of this new working-class. The way in which the peasants and artisans had formerly worked had nothing comparable to the intensive labour of the new factory worker. In the old trades time did not play a highly important role, but it became an essential element in the new industrial system. The formal taking over of the old working hours into the mammoth industrial enterprises had fatal results. The actual amount of work hitherto accomplished within a certain time was comparatively small, because the modern methods of intensive production were then unknown. Therefore, though in the older system a working day of fourteen or even fifteen hours was not unendurable, now it was beyond the possibilities of human endurance because in the new system every minute was utilized to the extreme. This absurd transference of the old working hours to the new industrial system proved fatal in two directions.

First, it ruined the health of the workers; secondly, it destroyed their faith in a superior law of justice. Finally, on the one hand a miserable wage was received and, on the other, the employer held a much more lucrative position than before. Hence a striking difference between the ways of life on the one side and on the other.

In the open country there could be no social problem, because the master and the farm-hand were doing the same kind of work and doing it together. They ate their food in common, and sometimes even out of the same dish. But in this sphere also the new system introduced an entirely different set of conditions between masters and men.

The division created between employer and employees seems not to have extended to all branches of life. How far this Judaizing process has been allowed to take effect among our people is illustrated by the fact that manual labour not only receives practically no recognition but is even considered degrading. That is not a natural German attitude. It is due to the introduction of a foreign element into our lives, and that foreign element is the Jewish spirit, one of the effects of which has been to transform the high esteem in which our handicrafts once were held into a definite feeling that all physical labour is something base and unworthy.

Thus a new social class has grown up which stands in low esteem; and the day must come when we shall have to face the question of whether the nation will be able to make this class an integral part of the social community or whether the difference of status now existing will become a permanent gulf separating this class from the others.

One thing, however, is certain: This class does not include the worst elements of the community in its ranks. Rather the contrary is the truth: it includes the most energetic parts of the nation. The sophistication which is the result of a so-called civilization has not yet exercised its disintegrating and degenerating influence on this class. The broad masses of this new lower class, constituted by the manual labourers, have not yet fallen a prey to the morbid weakness of pacifism. These are still robust and, if necessary, they can be brutal.

While our bourgeoisie middle class paid no attention at all to this momentous problem and indifferently allowed events to take their course, the Jew seized upon the manifold possibilities which the situation offered him for the future. While on the one hand he organized capitalistic methods of exploitation to their ultimate degree of efficiency, he curried favour with the victims of his policy and his power and in a short while became the leader of their struggle against himself. 'Against himself' is here only a figurative way of speaking; for this 'Great Master of Lies' knows how to appear in the guise of the innocent and throw the guilt on others. Since he had the impudence to take a personal lead among the masses, they never for a moment suspected that they were falling a prey to one of the most infamous deceits ever practised. And yet that is what it actually was.

The moment this new class had arisen out of the general economic situation and taken shape as a definite body in the social order, the Jew saw clearly where he would find the necessary pacemaker for his own progressive march. At first he had used the bourgeois class as a battering-ram against the feudal order; and now he used the worker against the bourgeois world. Just as he succeeded in obtaining civic rights by intrigues carried on under the protection of the bourgeois class, he now hoped that by joining in the struggle which the workers were waging for their own existence he would be able to obtain full control over them.

When that moment arrives, then the only objective the workers will have to fight for will be the future of the Jewish people. Without knowing it, the worker is placing himself at the service of the very power against which he believes he is fighting. Apparently he is made to fight against capital and thus he is all the more easily brought to fight for capitalist interests. Outcries are systematically raised against international capital but in reality it is against the structure of national economics that these slogans are directed. The idea is to demolish this structure and on its ruins triumphantly erect the structure of the International Stock Exchange.

In this line of action the procedure of the Jew was as follows:

He kowtowed to the worker, hypocritically pretended to feel pity for him and his lot, and even to be indignant at the misery and poverty which the worker had to endure. That is the way in which the Jew endeavoured to gain the confidence of the working class. He showed himself eager to study their various hardships, whether real or imaginary, and strove to awaken a yearning on the part of the workers to change the conditions under which they lived. The Jew artfully enkindled that innate yearning for social justice which is a typical Aryan characteristic. Once that yearning became alive it was transformed into hatred against those in more fortunate circumstances of life. The next stage was to give a precise philosophical aspect to the struggle for the elimination of social wrongs. And thus the Marxist doctrine was invented.

By presenting his doctrine as part and parcel of a just revindication of social rights, the Jew propagated the doctrine all the more effectively.

But at the same time he provoked the opposition of decent people who refused to admit these demands which, because of the form and pseudo-philosophical trimmings in which they are presented, seemed fundamentally unjust and impossible for realization. For, under the cloak of purely social concepts there are hidden aims which are of a Satanic character. These aims are even expounded in the open with the clarity of unlimited impudence. This Marxist doctrine is an individual mixture of human reason and human absurdity; but the combination is arranged in such a way that only the absurd part of it could ever be put into practice, but never the reasonable part of it. By categorically repudiating the personal worth of the individual and also the nation and its racial constituent, this doctrine destroys the fundamental basis of all civilization; for civilization essentially depends on these very factors. Such is the true essence of the Marxist WELTANSCHAUUNG, so far as the word WELTANSCHAUUNG can be applied at all to this phantom arising from a criminal brain. The destruction of the concept of personality and of race removes the chief obstacle which barred the way to domination of the social body by its inferior elements, which are the Jews.

The very absurdity of the economic and political theories of Marxism gives the doctrine its peculiar significance. Because of its pseudo-logic, intelligent people refuse to support it, while all those who are less accustomed to use their intellectual faculties, or who have only a rudimentary notion of economic principles, join the Marxist cause with flying banners. The intelligence behind the movement—for even this movement needs intelligence if it is to subsist—is supplied by the Jews themselves, naturally of course as a gratuitous service which is at the same time a sacrifice on their part.

Thus arose a movement which was composed exclusively of manual workers under the leadership of Jews. To all external appearances, this movement strives to ameliorate the conditions under which the workers live; but in reality its aim is to enslave and thereby annihilate the non-Jewish races.

The propaganda which the freemasons had carried on among the so-called intelligentsia, whereby their pacifist teaching paralysed the instinct for national self-preservation, was now extended to the broad masses of the workers and bourgeoisie by means of the Press, which was almost everywhere in Jewish hands. To those two instruments of disintegration a third and still more ruthless one was added, namely, the organization of brute physical force among the masses. As massed columns of attacks, the Marxist troops stormed those parts of the social order which had been left standing after the two former undermining operations had done their work.

The combined activity of all these forces has been marvellously managed. And it will not be surprising if it turns out that those institutions which have always appeared as the organs of the more or less traditional authority of the State should now fall before the Marxist attack. Among our higher and highest State officials, with very few exceptions, the Jew has found the cost complacent backers in his work of destruction. An attitude of sneaking servility towards 'superiors' and supercilious arrogance towards 'inferiors' are the characteristics of this class of people, as well as a grade of stupidity which is really frightening and at the same time a towering self-conceit, which has been so consistently developed to make it amusing.

But these qualities are of the greatest utility to the Jew in his dealings with our authorities. Therefore they are qualities which he appreciates most in the officials. If I were to sketch roughly the actual struggle which is now beginning I should describe it somewhat thus:

Not satisfied with the economic conquest of the world, but also demanding that it must come under his political control, the Jew subdivides the organized Marxist power into two parts, which correspond to the ultimate objectives that are to be fought for in this struggle which is carried on under the direction of the Jew. To outward appearance, these seem to be two independent movements, but in reality they constitute an indivisible unity. The two divisions are: The political movement and the trades union movement.

The trades union movement has to gather in the recruits. It offers assistance and protection to the workers in the hard struggle which they have to wage for the bare means of existence, a struggle which has been occasioned by the greediness and narrow-mindedness of many of the industrialists. Unless the workers be ready to surrender all claims to an existence which the dignity of human nature itself demands, and unless they are ready to submit their fate to the will of employers who in many cases have no sense of human responsibilities and are utterly callous to human wants, then the worker must necessarily take matters into his own hands, seeing that the organized social community—that is to say, the State—pays no attention to his needs.

The so-called national-minded bourgeoisie, blinded by its own material interests, opposes this life-or-death struggle of the workers and places the most difficult obstacles in their way. Not only does this bourgeoisie hinder all efforts to enact legislation which would shorten the inhumanly long hours of work, prohibit child-labour, grant security and protection to women and improve the hygienic conditions of the workshops and the dwellings of the working-class, but while the bourgeoisie hinders all this the shrewd Jew takes the cause of the oppressed into his own hands. He gradually becomes the leader of the trades union movements, which is an easy task for him, because he does not genuinely intend to find remedies for the social wrong: he pursues only one objective, namely, to gather and consolidate a body of followers who will act under his commands as an armed weapon in the economic war for the destruction of national economic independence. For, while a sound social policy has to move between the two poles of securing a decent level of public health and welfare on the one hand and, on the other, that of safeguarding the independence of the economic life of the nation, the Jew does not take these poles into account at all. The destruction of both is one of his main objects. He would ruin, rather than safeguard, the independence of the national economic system.

Therefore, as the leader of the trades union movement, he has no scruples about putting forward demands which not only go beyond the declared purpose of the movement but could not be carried into effect without ruining the national economic structure. On the other hand, he has no interest in seeing a healthy and sturdy population develop; he would be more content to see the people degenerate into an unthinking herd which could be reduced to total subjection. Because these are his final objectives, he can afford to put forward the most absurd claims.

He knows very well that these claims can never be realized and that therefore nothing in the actual state of affairs could be altered by them, but that the most they can do is to arouse the spirit of unrest among the masses. That is exactly the purpose which he wishes such propaganda to serve and not a real and honest improvement of the social conditions.

The Jews will therefore remain the unquestioned leaders of the trades union movement so long as a campaign is not undertaken, which must be carried out on gigantic lines, for the enlightenment of the masses; so that they will be enabled better to understand the causes of their misery. Or the same end might be achieved if the government authorities would get rid of the Jew and his work. For as long as the masses remain so ill-informed as they actually are to-day, and as long as the State remains as indifferent to their lot as it now is, the masses will follow whatever leader makes them the most extravagant promises in regard to economic matters. The Jew is a past master at this art and his activities are not hampered by moral considerations of any kind.

Naturally it takes him only a short time to defeat all his competitors in this field and drive them from the scene of action. In accordance with the general brutality and rapacity of his nature, he turns the trades union movement into an organization for the exercise of physical violence. The resistance of those whose common sense has hitherto saved them from surrendering to the Jewish dictatorship is now broken down by terrorization. The success of that kind of activity is enormous. Parallel with this, the political organization advances. It operates hand-in-hand with the trades union movement, inasmuch as the latter prepares the masses for the political organization and even forces them into it. This is also the source that provides the money which the political organization needs to keep its enormous apparatus in action.

The trades union organization is the organ of control for the political activity of its members and whips in the masses for all great political demonstrations. In the end it ceases to struggle for economic interests but places its chief weapon, the refusal to continue work which takes the form of a general strike—at the disposal of the political movement.

By means of a Press whose contents are adapted to the level of the most ignorant readers, the political and trades union organizations are provided with an instrument which prepares the lowest stratum of the nation for a campaign of ruthless destruction. It is not considered part of the purpose of this Press to inspire its readers with ideals which might help them to lift their minds above the sordid conditions of their daily lives; but, on the contrary, it panders to their lowest instincts. Among the lazy-minded and self-seeking sections of the masses this kind of speculation turns out lucrative.

It is this Press above all which carries on a fanatical campaign of calumny, strives to tear down everything that might be considered as a mainstay of national independence and to sabotage all cultural values as well as to destroy the autonomy of the national economic system. It aims its attack especially against all men of character who refuse to fall into line with the Jewish efforts to obtain control over the State or who appear dangerous to the Jews merely because of their superior intelligence. For in order to incur the enmity of the Jew it is not necessary to show any open hostility towards him. It is quite sufficient if one be considered capable of opposing the Jew some time in the future or using his abilities and character to enhance the power and position of a nation which the Jew finds hostile to himself.

The Jewish instinct, which never fails where these problems have to be dealt with, readily discerns the true mentality of those whom the Jew meets in everyday life; and those who are not of a kindred spirit with him may be sure of being listed among his enemies. Since the Jew is not the object of aggression but the aggressor himself, he considers as his enemies not only those who attack him but also those who may be capable of resisting him. The means which he employs to break people of this kind, who may show themselves decent and upright, are not the open means generally used in honourable conflict, but falsehood and calumny.

He will stop at nothing. His utterly low-down conduct is so appalling that one really cannot be surprised if in the imagination of our people the Jew is pictured as the incarnation of Satan and the symbol of evil.

The ignorance of the broad masses as regards the inner character of the Jew, and the lack of instinct and insight that our upper classes display, are some of the reasons which explain how it is that so many people fall an easy prey to the systematic campaign of falsehood which the Jew carries on.

While the upper classes, with their innate cowardliness, turn away from anyone whom the Jew thus attacks with lies and calumny, the common people are credulous of everything, whether because of their ignorance or their simple-mindedness. Government authorities wrap themselves up in a robe of silence, but more frequently they persecute the victims of Jewish attacks in order to stop the campaign in the Jewish Press. To the fatuous mind of the government official such a line of conduct appears to belong to the policy of upholding the authority of the State and preserving public order. Gradually the Marxist weapon in the hands of the Jew becomes a constant bogy to decent people. Sometimes the fear of it sticks in the brain or weighs upon them as a kind of nightmare. People begin to quail before this fearful foe and therewith become his victims.

(k) The Jewish domination in the State seems now so fully assured that not only can he now afford to call himself a Jew once again, but he even acknowledges freely and openly what his ideas are on racial and political questions. A section of the Jews avows itself quite openly as an alien people, but even here there is another falsehood. When the Zionists try to make the rest of the world believe that the new national consciousness of the Jews will be satisfied by the establishment of a Jewish State in Palestine, the Jews thereby adopt another means to dupe the simple-minded Gentile. They have not the slightest intention of building up a Jewish State in Palestine so as to live in it. What they really are aiming at is to establish a central organization for their international swindling and cheating. As a sovereign State, this cannot be controlled by any of the other States. Therefore it can serve as a refuge for swindlers who have been found out and at the same time a high-school for the training of other swindlers.

As a sign of their growing presumption and sense of security, a certain section of them openly and impudently proclaim their Jewish nationality while another section hypocritically pretend that they are German, French or English as the case may be. Their blatant behaviour in their relations with other people shows how clearly they envisage their day of triumph in the near future.

The black-haired Jewish youth lies in wait for hours on end, satanically glaring at and spying on the unsuspicious girl whom he plans to seduce, adulterating her blood and removing her from the bosom of her own people. The Jew uses every possible means to undermine the racial foundations of a subjugated people. In his systematic efforts to ruin girls and women he strives to break down the last barriers of discrimination between him and other peoples. The Jews were responsible for bringing negroes into the Rhineland, with the ultimate idea of bastardizing the white race which they hate and thus lowering its cultural and political level so that the Jew might dominate. For as long as a people remain racially pure and are conscious of the treasure of their blood, they can never be overcome by the Jew. Never in this world can the Jew become master of any people except a bastardized people.

That is why the Jew systematically endeavours to lower the racial quality of a people by permanently adulterating the blood of the individuals who make up that people.

In the field of politics he now begins to replace the idea of democracy by introducing the dictatorship of the proletariat. In the masses organized under the Marxist banners he has found a weapon which makes it possible for him to discard democracy, so as to subjugate and rule in a dictatorial fashion by the aid of brute force. He is systematically working in two ways to bring about this revolution. These ways are the economic and the political respectively.

Aided by international influences, he forms a ring of enemies around those nations which have proved themselves too sturdy for him in withstanding attacks from within. He would like to force them into war and then, if it should be necessary to his plans, he will unfurl the banners of revolt even while the troops are actually fighting at the front.

Economically he brings about the destruction of the State by a systematic method of sabotaging social enterprises until these become so costly that they are taken out of the hands of the State and then submitted to the control of Jewish finance. Politically he works to withdraw from the State its means of susbsistence, inasmuch as he undermines the foundations of national resistance and defence, destroys the confidence which the people have in their Government, reviles the past and its history and drags everything national down into the gutter. Culturally his activity consists in bowdlerizing art, literature and the theatre, holding the expressions of national sentiment up to scorn, overturning all concepts of the sublime and beautiful, the worthy and the good, finally dragging the people to the level of his own low mentality.

Of religion he makes a mockery. Morality and decency are described as antiquated prejudices and thus a systematic attack is made to undermine those last foundations on which the national being must rest if the nation is to struggle for its existence in this world.

(l) Now begins the great and final revolution. As soon as the Jew is in possession of political power he drops the last few veils which have hitherto helped to conceal his features. Out of the democratic Jew, the Jew of the People, arises the 'Jew of the Blood', the tyrant of the peoples. In the course of a few years he endeavours to exterminate all those who represent the national intelligence. And by thus depriving the peoples of their natural intellectual leaders he fits them for their fate as slaves under a lasting despotism.

Russia furnishes the most terrible example of such a slavery. In that country the Jew killed or starved thirty millions of the people, in a bout of savage fanaticism and partly by the employment of inhuman torture. And he did this so that a gang of Jewish literati and financial bandits should dominate over a great people. But the final consequence is not merely that the people lose all their freedom under the domination of the Jews, but that in the end these parasites themselves disappear. The death of the victim is followed sooner or later by that of the vampire.

If we review all the causes which contributed to bring about the downfall of the German people we shall find that the most profound and decisive cause must be attributed to the lack of insight into the racial problem and especially in the failure to recognize the Jewish danger. It would have been easy enough to endure the defeats suffered on the battlefields in August 1918. They were nothing when compared with the military victories which our nation had achieved. Our downfall was not the result of those defeats; but we were overthrown by that force which had prepared those defeats by systematically operating for several decades to destroy those political instincts and that moral stamina which alone enable a people to struggle for its existence and therewith secure the right to exist.

By neglecting the problem of preserving the racial foundations of our national life, the old Empire abrogated the sole right which entitles a people to live on this planet. Nations that make mongrels of their people, or allow their people to be turned into mongrels, sin against the Will of Eternal Providence. And thus their overthrow at the hands of a stronger opponent cannot be looked upon as a wrong but, on the contrary, as a restoration of justice. If a people refuses to guard and uphold the qualities with which it has been endowed by Nature and which have their roots in the racial blood, then such a people has no right to complain over the loss of its earthly existence.

Everything on this earth can be made into something better. Every defeat may be made the foundation of a future victory. Every lost war may be the cause of a later resurgence. Every visitation of distress can give a new impetus to human energy. And out of every oppression those forces can develop which bring about a new re-birth of the national soul — provided always that the racial blood is kept pure.

But the loss of racial purity will wreck inner happiness for ever. It degrades men for all time to come. And the physical and moral consequences can never be wiped out.

If this unique problem be studied and compared with the other problems of life we shall easily recognize how small is their importance in comparison with this. They are all limited to time; but the problem of the maintenance or loss of the purity of the racial blood will last as long as man himself lasts.

All the symptoms of decline which manifested themselves already in pre-war times can be traced back to the racial problem.

Whether one is dealing with questions of general law, or monstrous excrescences in economic life, of phenomena which point to a cultural decline or political degeneration, whether it be a question of defects in the school-system or of the evil influence which the Press exerts over the adult population—always and everywhere these phenomena are at bottom caused by a lack of consideration for the interests of the race to which one's own nation belongs, or by the failure to recognize the danger that comes from allowing a foreign race to exist within the national body.

That is why all attempts at reform, all institutions for social relief, all political striving, all economic progress and all apparent increase in the general stock of knowledge, were doomed to be unproductive of any significant results. The nation, as well as the organization which enables it to exist—namely, the State—were not developing in inner strength and stability, but, on the contrary, were visibly losing their vitality. The false brilliance of the Second Empire could not disguise the inner weakness. And every attempt to invigorate it anew failed because the main and most important problem was left out of consideration.

It would be a mistake to think that the followers of the various political parties which tried to doctor the condition of the German people, or even all their leaders, were bad in themselves or meant wrong. Their activity even at best was doomed to fail, merely because of the fact that they saw nothing but the symptoms of our general malady and they tried to doctor the symptoms while they overlooked the real cause of the disease. If one makes a methodical study of the lines along which the old Empire developed one cannot help seeing, after a careful political analysis, that a process of inner degeneration had already set in even at the time when the united Empire was formed and the German nation began to make rapid external progress. The general situation was declining, in spite of the apparent political success and in spite of the increasing economic wealth. At the elections to the Reichstag the growing number of Marxist votes indicated that the internal breakdown and the political collapse were then rapidly approaching. All the victories of the so-called bourgeois parties were fruitless, not only because they could not prevent the numerical increase in the growing mass of Marxist votes, even when the bourgeois parties triumphed at the polls, but mainly because they themselves were already infected with the germs of decay. Though quite unaware of it, the bourgeois world was infected from within with the deadly virus of Marxist ideas. The fact that they sometimes openly resisted was to be explained by the competitive strife among ambitious political leaders, rather than by attributing it to any opposition in principle between adversaries who were determined to fight one another to the bitter end. During all those years only one protagonist was fighting with steadfast perseverance.

This was the Jew. The Star of David steadily ascended as the will to national self-preservation declined.

Therefore it was not a solid national phalanx that, of itself and out of its own feeling of solidarity, rushed to the battlefields in August 1914. But it was rather the manifestation of the last flicker from the instinct of national self-preservation against the progress of the paralysis with which the pacifist and Marxist doctrine threatened our people. Even in those days when the destinies of the nation were in the balance the internal enemy was not recognized; therefore all efforts to resist the external enemy were bound to be in vain. Providence did not grant the reward to the victorious sword, but followed the eternal law of retributive justice. A profound recognition of all this was the source of those principles and tendencies which inspire our new movement. We were convinced that only by recognizing such truths could we stop the national decline in Germany and lay a granite foundation on which the State could again be built up, a State which would not be a piece of mechanism alien to our people, constituted for economic purposes and interests, but an organism created from the soul of the people themselves.

A GERMAN STATE IN A GERMAN NATION

CHAPTER XII: The First Stage in the Development of the German National Socialist Labour Party

Here at the close of the volume I shall describe the first stage in the progress of our movement and shall give a brief account of the problems we had to deal with during that period. In doing this I have no intention of expounding the ideals which we have set up as the goal of our movement; for these ideals are so momentous in their significance that an exposition of them will need a whole volume. Therefore I shall devote the second volume of this book to a detailed survey of the principles which form the programme of our movement and I shall attempt to draw a picture of what we mean by the word 'State'. When I say 'we' in this connection I mean to include all those hundreds of thousands who have fundamentally the same longing, though in the individual cases they cannot find adequate words to describe the vision that hovers before their eyes. It is a characteristic feature of all great reforms that in the beginning there is only one single protagonist to come forward on behalf of several millions of people. The final goal of a great reformation has often been the object of profound longing on the parts of hundreds of thousands for many centuries before, until finally one among them comes forward as a herald to announce the will of that multitude and become the standard-bearer of the old yearning, which he now leads to a realization in a new idea.

The fact that millions of our people yearn at heart for a radical change in our present conditions is proved by the profound discontent which exists among them. This feeling is manifested in a thousand ways. Some express it in a form of discouragement and despair. Others show it in resentment and anger and indignation. Among some the profound discontent calls forth an attitude of indifference, while it urges others to violent manifestations of wrath. Another indication of this feeling may be seen on the one hand in the attitude of those who abstain from voting at elections and, on the other, in the large numbers of those who side with the fanatical extremists of the left wing.

To these latter people our young movement had to appeal first of all. It was not meant to be an organization for contented and satisfied people, but was meant to gather in all those who were suffering from profound anxiety and could find no peace, those who were unhappy and discontented. It was not meant to float on the surface of the nation but rather to push its roots deep among the masses.

Looked at from the purely political point of view, the situation in 1918 was as follows: A nation had been torn into two parts. One part, which was by far the smaller of the two, contained the intellectual classes of the nation from which all those employed in physical labour were excluded. On the surface these intellectual classes appeared to be national-minded, but that word meant nothing else to them except a very vague and feeble concept of the duty to defend what they called the interests of the State, which in turn seemed identical with those of the dynastic regime. This class tried to defend its ideas and reach its aims by carrying on the fight with the aid of intellectual weapons, which could be used only here and there and which had only a superficial effect against the brutal measures employed by the adversaries, in the face of which the intellectual weapons were of their very nature bound to fail. With one violent blow the class which had hitherto governed was now struck down. It trembled with fear and accepted every humiliation imposed on it by the merciless victor.

Over against this class stood the broad masses of manual labourers who were organized in movements with a more or less radically Marxist tendency. These organized masses were firmly determined to break any kind of intellectual resistance by the use of brute force. They had no nationalist tendencies whatsoever and deliberately repudiated the idea of advancing the interests of the nation as such. On the contrary, they promoted the interests of the foreign oppressor. Numerically this class embraced the majority of the population and, what is more important, included all those elements of the nation without whose collaboration a national resurgence was not only a practical impossibility but was even inconceivable.

For already in 1918 one thing had to be clearly recognized; namely, that no resurgence of the German nation could take place until we had first restored our national strength to face the outside world. For this purpose arms are not the preliminary necessity, though our bourgeois 'statesmen' always blathered about it being so; what was wanted was will-power. At one time the German people had more than sufficient military armament. And yet they were not able to defend their liberty because they lacked those energies which spring from the instinct of national self-preservation and the will to hold on to one's own. The best armament is only dead and worthless material as long as the spirit is wanting which makes men willing and determined to avail themselves of such weapons. Germany was rendered defenceless not because she lacked arms, but because she lacked the will to keep her arms for the maintenance of her people.

To-day our Left-wing politicians in particular are constantly insisting that their craven-hearted and obsequious foreign policy necessarily results from the disarmament of Germany, whereas the truth is that this is the policy of traitors. To all that kind of talk the answer ought to be: No, the contrary is the truth. Your action in delivering up the arms was dictated by your anti-national and criminal policy of abandoning the interests of the nation. And now you try to make people believe that your miserable whining is fundamentally due to the fact that you have no arms. Just like everything else in your conduct, this is a lie and a falsification of the true reason.

But the politicians of the Right deserve exactly the same reproach. It was through their miserable cowardice that those ruffians of Jews who came into power in 1918 were able to rob the nation of its arms. The conservative politicians have neither right nor reason on their side when they appeal to disarmament as the cause which compelled them to adopt a policy of prudence (that is to say, cowardice). Here, again, the contrary is the truth. Disarmament is the result of their lack of spirit.

Therefore the problem of restoring Germany's power is not a question of how can we manufacture arms but rather a question of how we can produce that spirit which enables a people to bear arms. Once this spirit prevails among a people then it will find a thousand ways, each of which leads to the necessary armament. But a coward will not fire even a single shot when attacked though he may be armed with ten pistols. For him they are of less value than a blackthorn in the hands of a man of courage.

The problem of re-establishing the political power of our nation is first of all a problem of restoring the instinct of national self-preservation for if no other reason than that every preparatory step in foreign policy and every foreign judgment on the worth of a State has been proved by experience to be grounded not on the material size of the armament such a State may possess but rather on the moral capacity for resistance which such a State has or is believed to have.

The question whether or not a nation be desirable as an ally is not so much determined by the inert mass of arms which it has at hand but by the obvious presence of a sturdy will to national self-preservation and a heroic courage which will fight through to the last breath. For an alliance is not made between arms but between men.

The British nation will therefore be considered as the most valuable ally in the world as long as it can be counted upon to show that brutality and tenacity in its government, as well as in the spirit of the broad masses, which enables it to carry through to victory any struggle that it once enters upon, no matter how long such a struggle may last, or however great the sacrifice that may be necessary or whatever the means that have to be employed; and all this even though the actual military equipment at hand may be utterly inadequate when compared with that of other nations.

Once it is understood that the restoration of Germany is a question of reawakening the will to political self-preservation we shall see quite clearly that it will not be enough to win over those elements that are already national-minded but that the deliberately anti-national masses must be converted to believe in the national ideals.

A young movement that aims at re-establishing a German State with full sovereign powers will therefore have to make the task of winning over the broad masses a special objective of its plan of campaign. Our so-called 'national bourgeoisie' are so lamentably supine, generally speaking, and their national spirit appears so feckless, that we may feel sure they will offer no serious resistance against a vigorous national foreign — or domestic policy. Even though the narrow-minded German bourgeoisie should keep up a passive resistance when the hour of deliverance is at hand, as they did in Bismarck's time, we shall never have to fear any active resistance on their part, because of their recognized proverbial cowardice.

It is quite different with the masses of our population, who are imbued with ideas of internationalism. Through the primitive roughness of their natures they are disposed to accept the preaching of violence, while at the same time their Jewish leaders are more brutal and ruthless. They will crush any attempt at a German revival, just as they smashed the German Army by striking at it from the rear. Above all, these organized masses will use their numerical majority in this Parliamentarian State not only to hinder any national foreign policy, but also to prevent Germany from restoring her political power and therewith her prestige abroad. Thus she becomes excluded from the ranks of desirable allies.

For it is not we ourselves alone who are aware of the handicap that results from the existence of fifteen million Marxists, democrats, pacifists and followers of the Centre, in our midst, but foreign nations also recognize this internal burden which we have to bear and take it into their calculations when estimating the value of a possible alliance with us. Nobody would wish to form an alliance with a State where the active portion of the population is at least passively opposed to any resolute foreign policy.

The situation is made still worse by reason of the fact that the leaders of those parties which were responsible for the national betrayal are ready to oppose any and every attempt at a revival, simply because they want to retain the positions they now hold. According to the laws that govern human history it is inconceivable that the German people could resume the place they formerly held without retaliating on those who were both cause and occasion of the collapse that involved the ruin of our State. Before the judgment seat of posterity November 1918 will not be regarded as a simple rebellion but as high treason against the country.

Therefore it is not possible to think of re-establishing German sovereignty and political independence without at the same time reconstructing a united front within the nation, by a peaceful conversion of the popular will.

Looked at from the standpoint of practical ways and means, it seems absurd to think of liberating Germany from foreign bondage as long as the masses of the people are not willing to support such an ideal of freedom. After carefully considering this problem from the purely military point of view, everybody, and in particular every officer, will agree that a war cannot be waged against an outside enemy by battalions of students; but that, together with the brains of the nation, the physical strength of the nation is also necessary. Furthermore it must be remembered that the nation would be robbed of its irreplaceable assets by a national defence in which only the intellectual circles, as they are called, were engaged. The young German intellectuals who joined the volunteer regiments and fell on the battlefields of Flanders in the autumn of 1914 were bitterly missed later on. They were the dearest treasure which the nation possessed and their loss could not be made good in the course of the war. And it is not only the struggle itself which could not be waged if the working masses of the nation did not join the storm battalions, but the necessary technical preparations could not be made without a unified will and a common front within the nation itself. Our nation which has to exist disarmed, under the thousand eyes appointed by the Versailles Peace Treaty, cannot make any technical preparations for the recovery of its freedom and human independence until the whole army of spies employed within the country is cut down to those few whose inborn baseness would lead them to betray anything and everything for the proverbial thirty pieces of silver. But we can deal with such people. The millions, however, who are opposed to every kind of national revival simply because of their political opinions, constitute an insurmountable obstacle. At least the obstacle will remain insurmountable as long as the cause of their opposition, which is international Marxism, is not overcome and its teachings banished from both their hearts and heads.

From whatever point of view we may examine the possibility of recovering our independence as a State and a people, whether we consider the problem from the standpoint of technical rearmament or from that of the actual struggle itself, the necessary pre-requisite always remains the same. This pre-requisite is that the broad masses of the people must first be won over to accept the principle of our national independence. If we do not regain our external freedom every step forward in domestic reform will at best be an augmentation of our productive powers for the benefit of those nations that look upon us as a colony to be exploited.

The surplus produced by any so-called improvement would only go into the hands of our international controllers and any social betterment would at best increase the product of our labour in favour of those people. No cultural progress can be made by the German nation, because such progress is too much bound up with the political independence and dignity of a people.

Therefore, as we can find a satisfactory solution for the problem of Germany's future only by winning over the broad masses of our people for the support of the national idea, this work of education must be considered the highest and most important task to be accomplished by a movement which does not strive merely to satisfy the needs of the moment but considers itself bound to examine in the light of future results everything it decides to do or refrain from doing.

As early as 1919 we were convinced that the nationalization of the masses would have to constitute the first and paramount aim of the new movement. From the tactical standpoint, this decision laid a certain number of obligations on our shoulders.

(1) No social sacrifice could be considered too great in this effort to win over the masses for the national revival.

In the field of national economics, whatever concessions are granted to-day to the employees are negligible when compared with the benefit to be reaped by the whole nation if such concessions contribute to bring back the masses of the people once more to the bosom of their own nation. Nothing but meanness and shortsightedness, which are characteristics that unfortunately are only too prevalent among our employers, could prevent people from recognizing that in the long run no economic improvement and therefore no rise in profits are possible unless internal solidarity be restored among the bulk of the people who make up our nation.

If the German trades unions had defended the interests of the working-classes uncompromisingly during the War; if even during the War they had used the weapon of the strike to force the industrialists—who were greedy for higher dividends—to grant the demands of the workers for whom the unions acted; if at the same time they had stood up as good Germans for the defence of the nation as stoutly as for their own claims, and if they had given to their country what was their country's due—then the War would never have been lost. How ludicrously insignificant would all, and even the greatest, economic concession have been in face of the tremendous importance of such a victory.

For a movement which would restore the German worker to the German people it is therefore absolutely necessary to understand clearly that economic sacrifices must be considered light in such cases, provided of course that they do not go the length of endangering the independence and stability of the national economic system.

(2) The education of the masses along national lines can be carried out only indirectly, by improving their social conditions; for only by such a process can the economic conditions be created which enable everybody to share in the cultural life of the nation.

(3) The nationalization of the broad masses can never be achieved by half-measures—that is to say, by feebly insisting on what is called the objective side of the question—but only by a ruthless and devoted insistence on the one aim which must be achieved. This means that a people cannot be made 'national' according to the signification attached to that word by our bourgeois class to-day—that is to say, nationalism with many reservations—but national in the vehement and extreme sense. Poison can be overcome only by a counter-poison, and only the supine bourgeois mind could think that the

Kingdom of Heaven can be attained by a compromise.

The broad masses of a nation are not made up of professors and diplomats. Since these masses have only a poor acquaintance with abstract ideas, their reactions lie more in the domain of the feelings, where the roots of their positive as well as their negative attitudes are implanted. They are susceptible only to a manifestation of strength which comes definitely either from the positive or negative side, but they are never susceptible to any half-hearted attitude that wavers between one pole and the other. The emotional grounds of their attitude furnish the reason for their extraordinary stability. It is always more difficult to fight successfully against Faith than against knowledge.

Love is less subject to change than respect. Hatred is more lasting than mere aversion. And the driving force which has brought about the most tremendous revolutions on this earth has never been a body of scientific teaching which has gained power over the masses, but always a devotion which has inspired them, and often a kind of hysteria which has urged them to action.

Whoever wishes to win over the masses must know the key that will open the door to their hearts. It is not objectivity, which is a feckless attitude, but a determined will, backed up by force, when necessary.

(4) The soul of the masses can be won only if those who lead the movement for that purpose are determined not merely to carry through the positive struggle for their own aims but are also determined to destroy the enemy that opposes them.

When they see an uncompromising onslaught against an adversary the people have at all times taken this as a proof that right is on the side of the active aggressor; but if the aggressor should go only half-way and fail to push home his success by driving his opponent entirely from the scene of action, the people will look upon this as a sign that the aggressor is uncertain of the justice of his own cause and his half-way policy may even be an acknowledgment that his cause is unjust.

The masses are but a part of Nature herself. Their feeling is such that they cannot understand mutual hand-shakings between men who are declared enemies. Their wish is to see the stronger side win and the weaker wiped out or subjected unconditionally to the will of the stronger.

The nationalization of the masses can be successfully achieved only if, in the positive struggle to win the soul of the people, those who spread the international poison among them are exterminated.

(5) All the great problems of our time are problems of the moment and are only the results of certain definite causes. And among all those there is only one that has a profoundly causal significance. This is the problem of preserving the pure racial stock among the people. Human vigour or decline depends on the blood. Nations that are not aware of the importance of their racial stock, or which neglect to preserve it, are like men who would try to educate the pug-dog to do the work of the greyhound, not understanding that neither the speed of the greyhound nor the imitative faculties of the poodle are inborn qualities which cannot be drilled into the one or the other by any form of training. A people that fails to preserve the purity of its racial blood thereby destroys the unity of the soul of the nation in all its manifestations. A disintegrated national character is the inevitable consequence of a process of disintegration in the blood. And the change which takes place in the spiritual and creative faculties of a people is only an effect of the change that has modified its racial substance.

If we are to free the German people from all those failings and ways of acting which do not spring from their original character, we must first get rid of those foreign germs in the national body which are the cause of its failings and false ways.

The German nation will never revive unless the racial problem is taken into account and dealt with. The racial problem furnishes the key not only to the understanding of human history but also to the understanding of every kind of human culture.

(6) By incorporating in the national community the masses of our people who are now in the international camp we do not thereby mean to renounce the principle that the interests of the various trades and professions must be safeguarded. Divergent interests in the various branches of labour and in the trades and professions are not the same as a division between the various classes, but rather a feature inherent in the economic situation. Vocational grouping does not clash in the least with the idea of a national community, for this means national unity in regard to all those problems that affect the life of the nation as such.

To incorporate in the national community, or simply the State, a stratum of the people which has now formed a social class the standing of the higher classes must not be lowered but that of the lower classes must be raised. The class which carries through this process is never the higher class but rather the lower one which is fighting for equality of rights.

The bourgeoisie of to-day was not incorporated in the State through measures enacted by the feudal nobility but only through its own energy and a leadership that had sprung from its own ranks.

The German worker cannot be raised from his present standing and incorporated in the German folk-community by means of goody-goody meetings where people talk about the brotherhood of the people, but rather by a systematic improvement in the social and cultural life of the worker until the yawning abyss between him and the other classes can be filled in. A movement which has this for its aim must try to recruit its followers mainly from the ranks of the working class. It must include members of the intellectual classes only in so far as such members have rightly understood and accepted without reserve the ideal towards which the movement is striving. This process of transformation and reunion cannot be completed within ten or twenty years. It will take several generations, as the history of such movements has shown.

The most difficult obstacle to the reunion of our contemporary worker in the national folk-community does not consist so much in the fact that he fights for the interests of his fellow-workers, but rather in the international ideas with which he is imbued and which are of their nature at variance with the ideas of nationhood and fatherland. This hostile attitude to nation and fatherland has been inculcated by the leaders of the working class. If they were inspired by the principle of devotion to the nation in all that concerns its political and social welfare, the trades unions would make those millions of workers most valuable members of the national community, without thereby affecting their own constant struggle for their economic demands.

A movement which sincerely endeavours to bring the German worker back into his folk-community, and rescue him from the folly of internationalism, must wage a vigorous campaign against certain notions that are prevalent among the industrialists. One of these notions is that according to the concept of the folk-community, the employee is obliged to surrender all his economic rights to the employer and, further, that the workers would come into conflict with the folk-community if they should attempt to defend their own just and vital interests. Those who try to propagate such a notion are deliberate liars. The idea of a folk-community does not impose any obligations on the one side that are not imposed on the other.

A worker certainly does something which is contrary to the spirit of folk-community if he acts entirely on his own initiative and puts forward exaggerated demands without taking the common good into consideration or the maintenance of the national economic structure. But an industrialist also acts against the spirit of the folk-community if he adopts inhuman methods of exploitation and misuses the working forces of the nation to make millions unjustly for himself from the sweat of the workers. He has no right to call himself 'national' and no right to talk of a folk-community, for he is only an unscrupulous egoist who sows the seeds of social discontent and provokes a spirit of conflict which sooner or later must be injurious to the interests of the country.

The reservoir from which the young movement has to draw its members will first of all be the working masses. Those masses must be delivered from the clutches of the international mania. Their social distress must be eliminated. They must be raised above their present cultural level, which is deplorable, and transformed into a resolute and valuable factor in the folk-community, inspired by national ideas and national sentiment.

If among those intellectual circles that are nationalist in their outlook men can be found who genuinely love the people and look forward eagerly to the future of Germany, and at the same time have a sound grasp of the importance of a struggle whose aim is to win over the soul of the masses, such men are cordially welcomed in the ranks of our movement, because they can serve as a valuable intellectual force in the work that has to be done. But this movement can never aim at recruiting its membership from the unthinking herd of bourgeois voters. If it did so the movement would be burdened with a mass of people whose whole mentality would only help to paralyse the effort of our campaign to win the mass of the people. In theory it may be very fine to say that the broad masses ought to be influenced by a combined leadership of the upper and lower social strata within the framework of the one movement; but, notwithstanding all this, the fact remains that though it may be possible to exercise a psychological influence on the bourgeois classes and to arouse some enthusiasm or even awaken some understanding among them by our public demonstrations, their traditional characteristics cannot be changed. In other words, we could not eliminate from the bourgeois classes the inefficiency and supineness which are part of a tradition that has developed through centuries. The difference between the cultural levels of the two groups and between their respective attitudes towards social-economic questions is still so great that it would turn out a hindrance to the movement the moment the first enthusiasm aroused by our demonstrations calmed down.

Finally, it is not part of our programme to transform the nationalist camp itself, but rather to win over those who are anti-national in their outlook. It is from this viewpoint that the strategy of the whole movement must finally be decided.

(7) This one-sided but accordingly clear and definite attitude must be manifested in the propaganda of the movement; and, on the other hand, this is absolutely necessary to make the propaganda itself effective. If propaganda is to be of service to the movement it must be addressed to one side alone; for if it should vary the direction of its appeal it will not be understood in the one camp or may be rejected by the other, as merely insisting on obvious and uninteresting truisms; for the intellectual training of the two camps that come into question here has been very different.

Even the manner in which something is presented and the tone in which particular details are emphasized cannot have the same effect in those two strata that belong respectively to the opposite extremes of the social structure. If the propaganda should refrain from using primitive forms of expression it will not appeal to the sentiments of the masses.

If, on the other hand, it conforms to the crude sentiments of the masses in its words and gestures the intellectual circles will be averse to it because of its roughness and vulgarity. Among a hundred men who call themselves orators there are scarcely ten who are capable of speaking with effect before an audience of street-sweepers, locksmiths and navvies, etc., to-day and expound the same subject with equal effect to-morrow before an audience of university professors and students. Among a thousand public speakers there may be only one who can speak before a composite audience of locksmiths and professors in the same hall in such a way that his statements can be fully comprehended by each group while at the same time he effectively influences both and awakens enthusiasm, on the one side as well as on the other, to hearty applause.

But it must be remembered that in most cases even the most beautiful idea embodied in a sublime theory can be brought home to the public only through the medium of smaller minds. The thing that matters here is not the vision of the man of genius who created the great idea but rather the success which his apostles achieve in shaping the expression of this idea so as to bring it home to the minds of the masses. Social-Democracy and the whole Marxist movement were particularly qualified to attract the great masses of the nation, because of the uniformity of the public to which they addressed their appeal. The more limited and narrow their ideas and arguments, the easier it was for the masses to grasp and assimilate them; for those ideas and arguments were well adapted to a low level of intelligence.

These considerations led the new movement to adopt a clear and simple line of policy, which was as follows: In its message as well as in its forms of expression the propaganda must be kept on a level with the intelligence of the masses, and its value must be measured only by the actual success it achieves.

At a public meeting where the great masses are gathered together the best speaker is not he whose way of approaching a subject is most akin to the spirit of those intellectuals who may happen to be present, but the speaker who knows how to win the hearts of the masses.

An educated man who is present and who finds fault with an address because he considers it to be on an intellectual plane that is too low, though he himself has witnessed its effect on the lower intellectual groups whose adherence has to be won, only shows himself completely incapable of rightly judging the situation and therewith proves that he can be of no use in the new movement. Only intellectuals can be of use to a movement who understand its mission and its aims so well that they have learned to judge our methods of propaganda exclusively by the success obtained and never by the impression which those methods made on the intellectuals themselves. For our propaganda is not meant to serve as an entertainment for those people who already have a nationalist outlook, but its purpose is to win the adhesion of those who have hitherto been hostile to national ideas and who are nevertheless of our own blood and race.

In general, those considerations of which I have given a brief summary in the chapter on 'War Propaganda' became the guiding rules and principles which determined the kind of propaganda we were to adopt in our campaign and the manner in which we were to put it into practice. The success that has been obtained proves that our decision was right.

(8) The ends which any political reform movement sets out to attain can never be reached by trying to educate the public or influence those in power but only by getting political power into its hands. Every idea that is meant to move the world has not only the right but also the obligation of securing control of those means which will enable the idea to be carried into effect. In this world success is the only rule of judgment whereby we can decide whether such an undertaking was right or wrong. And by the word 'success' in this connection I do not mean such a success as the mere conquest of power in 1918 but the successful issue whereby the common interests of the nation have been served. A COUP D'ETAT cannot be considered successful if, as many empty-headed government lawyers in Germany now believe, the revolutionaries succeeded in getting control of the State into their hands but only if, in comparison with the state of affairs under the old regime, the lot of the nation has been improved when the aims and intentions on which the revolution was based have been put into practice. This certainly does not apply to the German Revolution, as that movement was called, which brought a gang of bandits into power in the autumn of 1918.

But if the conquest of political power be a requisite preliminary for the practical realization of the ideals that inspire a reform movement, then any movement which aims at reform must, from the very first day of its activity, be considered by its leaders as a movement of the masses and not as a literary tea club or an association of philistines who meet to play ninepins.

(9) The nature and internal organization of the new movement make it anti-parliamentarian. That is to say, it rejects in general and in its own structure all those principles according to which decisions are to be taken on the vote of the majority and according to which the leader is only the executor of the will and opinion of others. The movement lays down the principle that, in the smallest as well as in the greatest problems, one person must have absolute authority and bear all responsibility.

In our movement the practical consequences of this principle are the following:

The president of a large group is appointed by the head of the group immediately above his in authority. He is then the responsible leader of his group. All the committees are subject to his authority and not he to theirs. There is no such thing as committees that vote but only committees that work. This work is allotted by the responsible leader, who is the president of the group. The same principle applies to the higher organizations— the Bezirk (district), the KREIS (urban circuit) and the GAU (the region). In each case the president is appointed from above and is invested with full authority and executive power. Only the leader of the whole party is elected at the general meeting of the members. But he is the sole leader of the movement. All the committees are responsible to him, but he is not responsible to the committees. His decision is final, but he bears the whole responsibility of it. The members of the movement are entitled to call him to account by means of a new election, or to remove him from office if he has violated the principles of the movement or has not served its interests adequately.

He is then replaced by a more capable man. who is invested with the same authority and obliged to bear the same responsibility.

One of the highest duties of the movement is to make this principle imperative not only within its own ranks but also for the whole State.

The man who becomes leader is invested with the highest and unlimited authority, but he also has to bear the last and gravest responsibility.

The man who has not the courage to shoulder responsibility for his actions is not fitted to be a leader. Only a man of heroic mould can have the vocation for such a task.

Human progress and human cultures are not founded by the multitude. They are exclusively the work of personal genius and personal efficiency.

Because of this principle, our movement must necessarily be anti-parliamentarian, and if it takes part in the parliamentary institution it is only for the purpose of destroying this institution from within; in other words, we wish to do away with an institution which we must look upon as one of the gravest symptoms of human decline.

(10) The movement steadfastly refuses to take up any stand in regard to those problems which are either outside of its sphere of political work or seem to have no fundamental importance for us. It does not aim at bringing about a religious reformation, but rather a political reorganization of our people. It looks upon the two religious denominations as equally valuable mainstays for the existence of our people, and therefore it makes war on all those parties which would degrade this foundation, on which the religious and moral stability of our people is based, to an instrument in the service of party interests.

Finally, the movement does not aim at establishing any one form of State or trying to destroy another, but rather to make those fundamental principles prevail without which no republic and no monarchy can exist for any length of time. The movement does not consider its mission to be the establishment of a monarchy or the preservation of the Republic but rather to create a German State.

The problem concerning the outer form of this State, that is to say, its final shape, is not of fundamental importance. It is a problem which must be solved in the light of what seems practical and opportune at the moment.

Once a nation has understood and appreciated the great problems that affect its inner existence, the question of outer formalities will never lead to any internal conflict.

(11) The problem of the inner organization of the movement is not one of principle but of expediency.

The best kind of organization is not that which places a large intermediary apparatus between the leadership of the movement and the individual followers but rather that which works successfully with the smallest possible intermediary apparatus. For it is the task of such an organization to transmit a certain idea which originated in the brain of one individual to a multitude of people and to supervise the manner in which this idea is being put into practice.

Therefore, from any and every viewpoint, the organization is only a necessary evil. At best it is only a means of reaching certain ends. The worst happens when it becomes an end in itself.

Since the world produces more mechanical than intelligent beings, it will always be easier to develop the form of an organization than its substance; that is to say, the ideas which it is meant to serve.

The march of any idea which strives towards practical fulfilment, and in particular those ideas which are of a reformatory character, may be roughly sketched as follows:

A creative idea takes shape in the mind of somebody who thereupon feels himself called upon to transmit this idea to the world. He propounds his faith before others and thereby gradually wins a certain number of followers. This direct and personal way of promulgating one's ideas among one's contemporaries is the most natural and the most ideal. But as the movement develops and secures a large number of followers it gradually becomes impossible for the original founder of the doctrine on which the movement is based to carry on his propaganda personally among his innumerable followers and at the same time guide the course of the movement.

According as the community of followers increases, direct communication between the head and the individual followers becomes impossible. This intercourse must then take place through an intermediary apparatus introduced into the framework of the movement. Thus ideal conditions of inter-communication cease, and organization has to be introduced as a necessary evil. Small subsidiary groups come into existence, as in the political movement, for example, where the local groups represent the germ-cells out of which the organization develops later on.

But such sub-divisions must not be introduced into the movement until the authority of the spiritual founder and of the school he has created are accepted without reservation. Otherwise the movement would run the risk of becoming split up by divergent doctrines. In this connection too much emphasis cannot be laid on the importance of having one geographic centre as the chief seat of the movement. Only the existence of such a seat or centre, around which a magic charm such as that of Mecca or Rome is woven, can supply a movement with that permanent driving force which has its sources in the internal unity of the movement and the recognition of one head as representing this unity.

When the first germinal cells of the organization are being formed care must always be taken to insist on the importance of the place where the idea originated. The creative, moral and practical greatness of the place whence the movement went forth and from which it is governed must be exalted to a supreme symbol, and this must be honoured all the more according as the original cells of the movement become so numerous that they have to be regrouped into larger units in the structure of the organization.

When the number of individual followers became so large that direct personal contact with the head of the movement was out of the question,

then we had to form those first local groups. As those groups multiplied to an extraordinary number it was necessary to establish higher cadres into which the local groups were distributed. Examples of such cadres in the political organization are those of the region (GAU) and the district (BEZIRK).

Though it may be easy enough to maintain the original central authority over the lowest groups, it is much more difficult to do so in relation to the higher units of organization which have now developed. And yet we must succeed in doing this, for this is an indispensable condition if the unity of the movement is to be guaranteed and the idea of it carried into effect.

Finally, when those larger intermediary organizations have to be combined in new and still higher units it becomes increasingly difficult to maintain over them the absolute supremacy of the original seat of the movement and the school attached to it.

Consequently the mechanical forms of an organization must only be introduced if and in so far as the spiritual authority and the ideals of the central seat of the organization are shown to be firmly established.

In the political sphere it may often happen that this supremacy can be maintained only when the movement has taken over supreme political control of the nation.

Having taken all these considerations into account, the following principles were laid down for the inner structure of the movement:

(a) That at the beginning all activity should be concentrated in one town: namely, Munich. That a band of absolutely reliable followers should be trained and a school founded which would subsequently help to propagate the idea of the movement. That the prestige of the movement, for the sake of its subsequent extension, should first be established here through gaining as many successful and visible results as possible in this one place. To secure name and fame for the movement and its leader it was necessary, not only to give in this one town a striking example to shatter the belief that the Marxist doctrine was invincible but also to show that a counter-doctrine was possible.

(b) That local groups should not be established before the supremacy of the central authority in Munich was definitely established and acknowledged.

(c) That District, Regional, and Provincial groups should be formed only after the need for them has become evident and only after the supremacy of the central authority has been satisfactorily guaranteed.

Further, that the creation of subordinate organisms must depend on whether or not those persons can be found who are qualified to undertake the leadership of them.

Here there were only two solutions:

(a) That the movement should acquire the necessary funds to attract and train intelligent people who would be capable of becoming leaders. The personnel thus obtained could then be systematically employed according as the tactical situation and the necessity for efficiency demanded.

This solution was the easier and the more expedite. But it demanded large financial resources; for this group of leaders could work in the movement only if they could be paid a salary.

(b) Because the movement is not in a position to employ paid officials it must begin by depending on honorary helpers. Naturally this solution is slower and more difficult.

It means that the leaders of the movement have to allow vast territories to lie fallow unless in these respective districts one of the members comes forward who is capable and willing to place himself at the service of the central authority for the purpose of organizing and directing the movement in the region concerned.

It may happen that in extensive regions no such leader can be found, but that at the same time in other regions two or three or even more persons appear whose capabilities are almost on a level. The difficulty which this situation involves is very great and can be overcome only with the passing of the years.

For the establishment of any branch of the organization the decisive condition must always be that a person can be found who is capable of fulfilling the functions of a leader.

Just as the army and all its various units of organization are useless if there are no officers, so any political organization is worthless if it has not the right kind of leaders.

If an inspiring personality who has the gift of leadership cannot be found for the organization and direction of a local group it is better for the movement to refrain from establishing such a group than to run the risk of failure after the group has been founded.

The will to be a leader is not a sufficient qualification for leadership. For the leader must have the other necessary qualities.

Among these qualities will-power and energy must be considered as more serviceable than the intellect of a genius. The most valuable association of qualities is to be found in a combination of talent, determination and perseverance.

(12) The future of a movement is determined by the devotion, and even intolerance, with which its members fight for their cause. They must feel convinced that their cause alone is just, and they must carry it through to success, as against other similar organizations in the same field.

It is quite erroneous to believe that the strength of a movement must increase if it be combined with other movements of a similar kind. Any expansion resulting from such a combination will of course mean an increase in external development, which superficial observers might consider as also an increase of power; but in reality the movement thus admits outside elements which will subsequently weaken its constitutional vigour.

Though it may be said that one movement is identical in character with another, in reality no such identity exists. If it did exist then practically there would not be two movements but only one. And whatever the difference may be, even if it consist only of the measure in which the capabilities of the one set of leaders differ from those of the other, there it is. It is against the natural law of all development to couple dissimilar organisms, or the law is that the stronger must overcome the weaker and, through the struggle necessary for such a conquest, increase the constitutional vigour and effective strength of the victor.

By amalgamating political organizations that are approximately alike, certain immediate advantages may be gained, but advantages thus gained are bound in the long run to become the cause of internal weaknesses which will make their appearance later on.

A movement can become great only if the unhampered development of its internal strength be safeguarded and steadfastly augmented, until victory over all its competitors be secured.

One may safely say that the strength of a movement and its right to existence can be developed only as long as it remains true to the principle that struggle is a necessary condition of its progress and that its maximum strength will be reached only as soon as complete victory has been won.

Therefore a movement must not strive to obtain successes that will be only immediate and transitory, but it must show a spirit of uncompromising perseverance in carrying through a long struggle which will secure for it a long period of inner growth.

All those movements which owe their expansion to a so-called combination of similar organisms, which means that their external strength is due to a policy of compromise, are like plants whose growth is forced in a hothouse. They shoot up externally but they lack that inner strength which enables the natural plant to grow into a tree that will withstand the storms of centuries.

The greatness of every powerful organization which embodies a creative idea lies in the spirit of religious devotion and intolerance with which it stands out against all others, because it has an ardent faith in its own right. If an idea is right in itself and, furnished with the fighting weapons I have mentioned, wages war on this earth, then it is invincible and persecution will only add to its internal strength.

The greatness of Christianity did not arise from attempts to make compromises with those philosophical opinions of the ancient world which had some resemblance to its own doctrine, but in the unrelenting and fanatical proclamation and defence of its own teaching.

The apparent advance that a movement makes by associating itself with other movements will be easily reached and surpassed by the steady increase of strength which a doctrine and its organization acquires if it remains independent and fights its own cause alone.

(13) The movement ought to educate its adherents to the principle that struggle must not be considered a necessary evil but as something to be desired in itself. Therefore they must not be afraid of the hostility which their adversaries manifest towards them but they

must take it as a necessary condition on which their whole right to existence is based.

They must not try to avoid being hated by those who are the enemies of our people and our philosophy of life, but must welcome such hatred.

Lies and calumnies are part of the method which the enemy employs to express his chagrin.

The man who is not opposed and vilified and slandered in the Jewish Press is not a staunch German and not a true National Socialist. The best rule whereby the sincerity of his convictions, his character and strength of will, can be measured is the hostility which his name arouses among the mortal enemies of our people.

The followers of the movement, and indeed the whole nation, must be reminded again and again of the fact that, through the medium of his newspapers, the Jew is always spreading falsehood and that if he tells the truth on some occasions it is only for the purpose of masking some greater deceit, which turns the apparent truth into a deliberate falsehood. The Jew is the Great Master of Lies. Falsehood and duplicity are the weapons with which he fights.

Every calumny and falsehood published by the Jews are tokens of honour which can be worn by our comrades. He whom they decry most is nearest to our hearts and he whom they mortally hate is our best friend.

If a comrade of ours opens a Jewish newspaper in the morning and does not find himself vilified there, then he has spent yesterday to no account. For if he had achieved something he would be persecuted, slandered, derided and abused. Those who effectively combat this mortal enemy of our people, who is at the same time the enemy of all Aryan peoples and all culture, can only expect to arouse opposition on the part of this race and become the object of its slanderous attacks.

When these truths become part of the flesh and blood, as it were, of our members, then the movement will be impregnable and invincible.

(14) The movement must use all possible means to cultivate respect for the individual personality. It must never forget that all human values are based on personal values, and that every idea and achievement is the fruit of the creative power of one man. We must never forget that admiration for everything that is great is not only a tribute to one creative personality but that all those who feel such admiration become thereby united under one covenant.

Nothing can take the place of the individual, especially if the individual embodies in himself not the mechanical element but the element of cultural creativeness. No pupil can take the place of the master in completing a great picture which he has left unfinished; and just in the same way no substitute can take the place of the great poet or thinker, or the great statesman or military general. For the source of their power is in the realm of artistic creativeness. It can never be mechanically acquired, because it is an innate product of divine grace.

The greatest revolutions and the greatest achievements of this world, its greatest cultural works and the immortal creations of great statesmen, are inseparably bound up with one name which stands as a symbol for them in each respective case. The failure to pay tribute to one of those great spirits signifies a neglect of that enormous source of power which lies in the remembrance of all great men and women.

The Jew himself knows this best. He, whose great men have always been great only in their efforts to destroy mankind and its civilization, takes good care that they are worshipped as idols. But the Jew tries to degrade the honour in which nations hold their great men and women. He stigmatizes this honour as 'the cult of personality'.

As soon as a nation has so far lost its courage as to submit to this impudent defamation on the part of the Jews it renounces the most important source of its own inner strength. This inner force cannot arise from a policy of pandering to the masses but only from the worship of men of genius, whose lives have uplifted and ennobled the nation itself.

When men's hearts are breaking and their souls are plunged into the depths of despair, their great forebears turn their eyes towards them from the dim shadows of the past— those forebears who knew how to triumph over anxiety and affliction, mental servitude and physical bondage—and extend their eternal hands in a gesture of encouragement to despairing souls. Woe to the nation that is ashamed to clasp those hands.

During the initial phase of our movement our greatest handicap was the fact that none of us were known and our names meant nothing, a fact which then seemed to some of us to make the chances of final success problematical. Our most difficult task then was to make our members firmly believe that there was a tremendous future in store for the movement and to maintain this belief as a living faith; for at that time only six, seven or eight persons came to hear one of our speakers.

Consider that only six or seven poor devils who were entirely unknown came together to found a movement which should succeed in doing what the great mass-parties had failed to do: namely, to reconstruct the German REICH, even in greater power and glory than before. We should have been very pleased if we were attacked or even ridiculed. But the most depressing fact was that nobody paid any attention to us whatever. This utter lack of interest in us caused me great mental pain at that time.

When I entered the circle of those men there was not yet any question of a party or a movement. I have already described the impression which was made on me when I first came into contact with that small organization. Subsequently I had time, and also the occasion, to study the form of this so-called party which at first had made such a woeful impression.

The picture was indeed quite depressing and discouraging. There was nothing, absolutely nothing at all. There was only the name of a party. And the committee consisted of all the party members. Somehow or other it seemed just the kind of thing we were about to fight against—a miniature parliament. The voting system was employed. When the great parliament cried until they were hoarse—at least they shouted over problems of importance—here this small circle engaged in interminable discussions as to the form in which they might answer the letters which they were delighted to have received.

Needless to say, the public knew nothing of all this. In Munich nobody knew of the existence of such a party, not even by name, except our few members and their small circle of acquaintances.

Every Wednesday what was called a committee meeting was held in one of the cafés, and a debate was arranged for one evening each week. In the beginning all the members of the movement were also members of the committee, therefore the same persons always turned up at both meetings.

The first step that had to be taken was to extend the narrow limits of this small circle and get new members, but the principal necessity was to utilize all the means at our command for the purpose of making the movement known.

We chose the following methods: We decided to hold a monthly meeting to which the public would be invited. Some of the invitations were typewritten, and some were written by hand. For the first few meetings we distributed them in the streets and delivered them personally at certain houses. Each one canvassed among his own acquaintances and tried to persuade some of them to attend our meetings. The result was lamentable.

I still remember once how I personally delivered eighty of these invitations and how we waited in the evening for the crowds to come. After waiting in vain for a whole hour the chairman finally had to open the meeting. Again there were only seven people present, the old familiar seven.

We then changed our methods. We had the invitations written with a typewriter in a Munich stationer's shop and then multigraphed them. The result was that a few more people attended our next meeting. The number increased gradually from eleven to thirteen to seventeen, to twenty-three and finally to thirty-four. We collected some money within our own circle, each poor devil giving a small contribution, and in that way we raised sufficient funds to be able to advertise one of our meetings in the MUNICH OBSERVER, which was still an independent paper.

This time we had an astonishing success. We had chosen the Munich HOFBRÄU HAUS KELLER (which must not be confounded with the Munich HOFBRÄU HAUS FESTSAAL) as our meeting-place. It was a small hall and would accommodate scarcely more than 130 people. To me, however, the hall seemed enormous, and we were all trembling lest this tremendous edifice would remain partly empty on the night of the meeting.

At seven o'clock 111 persons were present, and the meeting was opened. A Munich professor delivered the principal address, and I spoke after him.

That was my first appearance in the role of public orator. The whole thing seemed a very daring adventure to Herr Harrer, who was then chairman of the party. He was a very decent fellow; but he had an A PRIORI conviction that, although I might have quite a number of good qualities, I certainly did not have a talent for public speaking. Even later he could not be persuaded to change his opinion. But he was mistaken. Twenty minutes had been allotted to me for my speech on this occasion, which might be looked upon as our first public meeting.

I talked for thirty minutes, and what I always had felt deep down in my heart, without being able to put it to the test, was here proved to be true: I could make a good speech. At the end of the thirty minutes it was quite clear that all the people in the little hall had been profoundly impressed. The enthusiasm aroused among them found its first expression in the fact that my appeal to those present brought us donations which amounted to three hundred marks. That was a great relief for us. Our finances were at that time so meagre that we could not afford to have our party prospectus printed, or even leaflets. Now we possessed at least the nucleus of a fund from which we could pay the most urgent and necessary expenses.

But the success of this first larger meeting was also important from another point of view. I had already begun to introduce some young and fresh members into the committee. During the long period of my military service I had come to know a large number of good comrades whom I was now able to persuade to join our party. All of them were energetic and disciplined young men who, through their years of military service, had been imbued with the principle that nothing is impossible and that where there's a will there's a way.

The need for this fresh blood supply became evident to me after a few weeks of collaboration with the new members. Herr Harrer, who was then chairman of the party, was a journalist by profession, and as such he was a man of general knowledge. But as leader of the party he had one very serious handicap: he could not speak to the crowd. Though he did his work conscientiously, it lacked the necessary driving force, probably for the reason that he had no oratorical gifts whatsoever. Herr Drexler, at that time chairman of the Munich local group, was a simple working man. He, too, was not of any great importance as a speaker.

Moreover, he was not a soldier. He had never done military service, even during the War. So that this man who was feeble and diffident by nature had missed the only school which knows how to transform diffident and weakly natures into real men. Therefore neither of those two men were of the stuff that would have enabled them to stir up an ardent and indomitable faith in the ultimate triumph of the movement and to brush aside, with obstinate force and if necessary with brutal ruthlessness, all obstacles that stood in the path of the new idea. Such a task could be carried out only by men who had been trained, body and soul, in those military virtues which make a man, so to speak, agile as a greyhound, tough as leather, and hard as Krupp steel.

At that time I was still a soldier. Physically and mentally I had the polish of six years of service, so that in the beginning this circle must have looked on me as quite a stranger. In common with my army comrades, I had forgotten such phrases as: "That will not go", or "That is not possible", or "We ought not to take such a risk; it is too dangerous".

The whole undertaking was of its very nature dangerous. At that time there were many parts of Germany where it would have been absolutely impossible openly to invite people to a national meeting that dared to make a direct appeal to the masses. Those who attended such meetings were usually dispersed and driven away with broken heads. It certainly did not call for any great qualities to be able to do things in that way. The largest so-called bourgeois mass meetings were accustomed to dissolve, and those in attendance would run away like rabbits when frightened by a dog as soon as a dozen communists appeared on the scene.

The Reds used to pay little attention to those bourgeois organizations where only babblers talked. They recognized the inner triviality of such associations much better than the members themselves and therefore felt that they need not be afraid of them. On the contrary, however, they were all the more determined to use every possible means of annihilating once and for all any movement that appeared to them to be a danger to their own interests. The most effective means which they always employed in such cases were terror and brute force.

The Marxist leaders, whose business consisted in deceiving and misleading the public, naturally hated most of all a movement whose declared aim was to win over those masses which hitherto had been exclusively at the service of international Marxism in the Jewish and Stock Exchange parties. The title alone, 'German Labour party', irritated them. It could easily be foreseen that at the first opportune moment we should have to face the opposition of the Marxist despots, who were still intoxicated with their triumph in 1918.

People in the small circles of our own movement at that time showed a certain amount of anxiety at the prospect of such a conflict. They wanted to refrain as much as possible from coming out into the open, because they feared that they might be attacked and beaten. In their minds they saw our first public meetings broken up and feared that the movement might thus be ruined for ever. I found it difficult to defend my own position, which was that the conflict should not be evaded but that it should be faced openly and that we should be armed with those weapons which are the only protection against brute force. Terror cannot be overcome by the weapons of the mind but only by counter-terror. The success of our first public meeting strengthened my own position. The members felt encouraged to arrange for a second meeting, even on a larger scale.

Some time in October 1919 the second larger meeting took place in the EBERLBRÄU KELLER. The theme of our speeches was 'Brest-Litowsk and Versailles'. There were four speakers. I talked for almost an hour, and the success was even more striking than at our first meeting. The number of people who attended had grown to more than 130. An attempt to disturb the proceedings was immediately frustrated by my comrades. The would-be disturbers were thrown down the stairs, bearing imprints of violence on their heads.

A fortnight later another meeting took place in the same hall. The number in attendance had now increased to more than 170, which meant that the room was fairly well filled. I spoke again, and once more the success obtained was greater than at the previous meeting.

Then I proposed that a larger hall should be found. After looking around for some time we discovered one at the other end of the town, in the 'Deutschen REICH' in the Dachauer Strasse. The first meeting at this new rendezvous had a smaller attendance than the previous meeting. There were just less than 140 present. The members of the committee began to be discouraged, and those who had always been sceptical were now convinced that this falling-off in the attendance was due to the fact that we were holding the meetings at too short intervals. There were lively discussions, in which I upheld my own opinion that a city with 700,000 inhabitants ought to be able not only to stand one meeting every fortnight but ten meetings every week. I held that we should not be discouraged by one comparative setback, that the tactics we had chosen were correct, and that sooner or later success would be ours if we only continued with determined perseverance to push forward on our road. This whole winter of 1919-20 was one continual struggle to strengthen confidence in our ability to carry the movement through to success and to intensify this confidence until it became a burning faith that could move mountains.

Our next meeting in the small hall proved the truth of my contention.

Our audience had increased to more than 200. The publicity effect and the financial success were splendid. I immediately urged that a further meeting should be held. It took place in less than a fortnight, and there were more than 270 people present. Two weeks later we invited our followers and their friends, for the seventh time, to attend our meeting. The same hall was scarcely large enough for the number that came. They amounted to more than four hundred.

During this phase the young movement developed its inner form. Sometimes we had more or less hefty discussions within our small circle. From various sides—it was then just the same as it is to-day—objections were made against the idea of calling the young movement a party. I have always considered such criticism as a demonstration of practical incapability and narrow-mindedness on the part of the critic. Those objections have always been raised by men who could not differentiate between external appearances and inner strength, but tried to judge the movement by the high-sounding character of the name attached to it. To this end they ransacked the vocabulary of our ancestors, with unfortunate results.

At that time it was very difficult to make the people understand that every movement is a party as long as it has not brought its ideals to final triumph and thus achieved its purpose. It is a party even if it give itself a thousand different names.

Any person who tries to carry into practice an original idea whose realization would be for the benefit of his fellow men will first have to look for disciples who are ready to fight for the ends he has in view. And if these ends did not go beyond the destruction of the party system and therewith put a stop to the process of disintegration, then all those who come forward as protagonists and apostles of such an ideal are a party in themselves as long as their final goal is reached. It is only hair-splitting and playing with words when these antiquated theorists, whose practical success is in reverse ratio to their wisdom, presume to think they can change the character of a movement which is at the same time a party, by merely changing its name.

On the contrary, it is entirely out of harmony with the spirit of the nation to keep harping on that far-off and forgotten nomenclature which belongs to the ancient Germanic times and does not awaken any distinct association in our age. This habit of borrowing words from the dead past tends to mislead the people into thinking that the external trappings of its vocabulary are the important feature of a movement. It is really a mischievous habit; but it is quite prevalent nowadays.

At that time, and subsequently, I had to warn followers repeatedly against these wandering scholars who were peddling Germanic folk-lore and who never accomplished anything positive or practical, except to cultivate their own superabundant self-conceit. The new movement must guard itself against an influx of people whose only recommendation is their own statement that they have been fighting for these very same ideals during the last thirty or forty years.

Now if somebody has fought for forty years to carry into effect what he calls an idea, and if these alleged efforts not only show no positive results but have not even been able to hinder the success of the opposing party, then the story of those forty years of futile effort furnishes sufficient proof for the incompetence of such a protagonist. People of that kind are specially dangerous because they do not want to participate in the movement as ordinary members. They talk rather of the leading positions which would be the only fitting posts for them, in view of their past work and also so that they might be enabled to carry on that work further. But woe to a young movement if the conduct of it should fall into the hands of such people. A business man who has been in charge of a great firm for forty years and who has completely ruined it through his mismanagement is not the kind of person one would recommend for the founding of a new firm. And it is just the same with a new national movement. Nobody of common sense would appoint to a leading post in such a movement some Teutonic Methuselah who had been ineffectively preaching some idea for a period of forty years, until himself and his idea had entered the stage of senile decay.

Furthermore, only a very small percentage of such people join a new movement with the intention of serving its end unselfishly and helping in the spread of its principles. In most cases they come because they think that, under the aegis of the new movement, it will be possible for them to promulgate their old ideas to the misfortune of their new listeners. Anyhow, nobody ever seems able to describe what exactly these ideas are.

It is typical of such persons that they rant about ancient Teutonic heroes of the dim and distant ages, stone axes, battle spears and shields, whereas in reality they themselves are the woefullest poltroons imaginable. For those very same people who brandish Teutonic tin swords that have been fashioned carefully according to ancient models and wear padded bear-skins, with the horns of oxen mounted over their bearded faces, proclaim that all contemporary conflicts must be decided by the weapons of the mind alone. And thus they skedaddle when the first communist cudgel appears. Posterity will have little occasion to write a new epic on these heroic gladiators.

I have seen too much of that kind of people not to feel a profound contempt for their miserable play-acting. To the masses of the nation they are just an object of ridicule; but the Jew finds it to his own interest to treat these folk-lore comedians with respect and to prefer them to real men who are fighting to establish a German State. And yet these comedians are extremely proud of themselves. Notwithstanding their complete fecklessness, which is an established fact, they pretend to know everything better than other people; so much so that they make themselves a veritable nuisance to all sincere and honest patriots, to whom not only the heroism of the past is worthy of honour but who also feel bound to leave examples of their own work for the inspiration of the coming generation.

Among those people there were some whose conduct can be explained by their innate stupidity and incompetence; but there are others who have a definite ulterior purpose in view. Often it is difficult to distinguish between the two classes. The impression which I often get, especially of those so-called religious reformers whose creed is grounded on ancient Germanic customs, is that they are the missionaries and protégés of those forces which do not wish to see a national revival taking place in Germany. All their activities tend to turn the attention of the people away from the necessity of fighting together in a common cause against the common enemy, namely the Jew. Moreover, that kind of preaching induces the people to use up their energies, not in fighting for the common cause, but in absurd and ruinous religious controversies within their own ranks. There are definite grounds that make it absolutely necessary for the movement to be dominated by a strong central force which is embodied in the authoritative leadership. In this way alone is it possible to counteract the activity of such fatal elements. And that is just the reason why these folk-lore Ahasueruses are vigorously hostile to any movement whose members are firmly united under one leader and one discipline. Those people of whom I have spoken hate such a movement because it is capable of putting a stop to their mischief.

It was not without good reason that when we laid down a clearly defined programme for the new movement we excluded the word VÖLKISCH from it.

The concept underlying the term VÖLKISCH cannot serve as the basis of a movement, because it is too indefinite and general in its application.

Therefore, if somebody called himself VÖLKISCH such a designation could not be taken as the hall-mark of some definite, party affiliation.

Because this concept is so indefinite from the practical viewpoint, it gives rise to various interpretations and thus people can appeal to it all the more easily as a sort of personal recommendation. Whenever such a vague concept, which is subject to so many interpretations, is admitted into a political movement it tends to break up the disciplined solidarity of the fighting forces. No such solidarity can be maintained if each individual member be allowed to define for himself what he believes and what he is willing to do.

One feels it a disgrace when one notices the kind of people who float about nowadays with the VÖLKISCH symbol stuck in their buttonholes, and at the same time to notice how many people have various ideas of their own as to the significance of that symbol. A well-known professor in Bavaria, a famous combatant who fights only with the weapons of the mind and who boasts of having marched against Berlin—by shouldering the weapons of the mind, of course—believes that the word VÖLKISCH is synonymous with 'monarchical'. But this learned authority has hitherto neglected to explain how our German monarchs of the past can be identified with what we generally mean by the word VÖLKISCH to-day. I am afraid he will find himself at a loss if he is asked to give a precise answer. For it would be very difficult indeed to imagine anything less VÖLKISCH than most of those German monarchical States were. Had they been otherwise they would not have disappeared; or if they were VÖLKISCH, then the fact of their downfall may be taken as evidence that the VÖLKISCH outlook on the world (WELTANSCHAUUNG) is a false outlook.

Everybody interprets this concept in his own way. But such multifarious opinions cannot be adopted as the basis of a militant political movement. I need not call attention to the absolute lack of worldly wisdom, and especially the failure to understand the soul of the nation, which is displayed by these Messianic Precursors of the Twentieth Century. Sufficient attention has been called to those people by the ridicule which the left-wing parties have bestowed on them. They allow them to babble on and sneer at them.

I do not set much value on the friendship of people who do not succeed in getting disliked by their enemies. Therefore, we considered the friendship of such people as not only worthless but even dangerous to our young movement. That was the principal reason why we first called ourselves a PARTY. We hoped that by giving ourselves such a name we might scare away a whole host of VÖLKISCH dreamers. And that was the reason also why we named our Party, THE NATIONAL SOCIALIST GERMAN LABOUR PARTY.

The first term, Party, kept away all those dreamers who live in the past and all the lovers of bombastic nomenclature, as well as those who went around beating the big drum for the VÖLKISCH idea. The full name of the Party kept away all those heroes whose weapon is the sword of the spirit and all those whining poltroons who take refuge behind their so-called 'intelligence' as if it were a kind of shield.

It was only to be expected that this latter class would launch a massed attack against us after our movement had started; but, of course, it was only a pen-and-ink attack, for the goose-quill is the only weapon which these VÖLKISCH lancers wield. We had declared one of our principles thus: "We shall meet violence with violence in our own defence".

Naturally that principle disturbed the equanimity of the knights of the pen. They reproached us bitterly not only for what they called our crude worship of the cudgel but also because, according to them, we had no intellectual forces on our side. These charlatans did not think for a moment that a Demosthenes could be reduced to silence at a mass-meeting by fifty idiots who had come there to shout him down and use their fists against his supporters. The innate cowardice of the pen-and-ink charlatan prevents him from exposing himself to such a danger, for he always works in safe retirement and never dares to make a noise or come forward in public.

Even to-day I must warn the members of our young movement in the strongest possible terms to guard against the danger of falling into the snare of those who call themselves 'silent workers'. These 'silent workers' are not only a whitelivered lot but are also, and always will be, ignorant do-nothings. A man who is aware of certain happenings and knows that a certain danger threatens, and at the same time sees a certain remedy which can be employed against it, is in duty bound not to work in silence but to come into the open and publicly fight for the destruction of the evil and the acceptance of his own remedy. If he does not do so, then he is neglecting his duty and shows that he is weak in character and that he fails to act either because of his timidity, or indolence or incompetence. Most of these 'silent workers' generally pretend to know God knows what. Not one of them is capable of any real achievement, but they keep on trying to fool the world with their antics. Though quite indolent, they try to create the impression that their 'silent work' keeps them very busy. To put it briefly, they are sheer swindlers, political jobbers who feel chagrined by the honest work which others are doing. When you find one of these VÖLKISCH moths buzzing over the value of his 'silent work' you may be sure that you are dealing with a fellow who does no productive work at all but steals from others the fruits of their honest labour.

In addition to all this one ought to note the arrogance and conceited impudence with which these obscurantist idlers try to tear to pieces the work of other people, criticizing it with an air of superiority, and thus playing into the hands of the mortal enemy of our people. Even the simplest follower who has the courage to stand on the table in some beer-hall where his enemies are gathered, and manfully and openly defend his position against them, achieves a thousand times more than these slinking hypocrites. He at least will convert one or two people to believe in the movement. One can examine his work and test its effectiveness by its actual results. But those knavish swindlers—who praise their own 'silent work' and shelter themselves under the cloak of anonymity, are just worthless drones, in the truest sense of the term, and are utterly useless for the purpose of our national reconstruction. In the beginning of 1920 I put forward the idea of holding our first mass meeting. On this proposal there were differences of opinion amongst us. Some leading members of our party thought that the time was not ripe for such a meeting and that the result might be detrimental. The Press of the Left had begun to take notice of us and we were lucky enough in being able gradually to arouse their wrath. We had begun to appear at other meetings and to ask questions or contradict the speakers, with the natural result that we were shouted down forthwith. But still we thereby gained some of our ends. People began to know of our existence and the better they understood us, the stronger became their aversion and their enmity. Therefore we might expect that a large contingent of our friends from the Red Camp would attend our first mass meeting.

I fully realized that our meeting would probably be broken up. But we had to face the fight; if not now, then some months later. Since the first day of our foundation we were resolved to secure the future of the movement by fighting our way forward in a spirit of blind faith and ruthless determination. I was well acquainted with the mentality of all those who belonged to the Red Camp, and I knew quite well that if we opposed them tooth and nail not only would we make an impression on them but that we even might win new followers for ourselves. Therefore I felt that we must decide on a policy of active opposition.

Herr Harrer was then chairman of our party. He did not see eye to eye with me as to the opportune time for our first mass meeting. Accordingly he felt himself obliged to resign from the leadership of the movement, as an upright and honest man. Herr Anton Drexler took his place. I kept the work of organizing the propaganda in my own hands and I listened to no compromise in carrying it out.

We decided on February 24th 1920 as the date for the first great popular meeting to be held under the aegis of this movement which was hitherto unknown.

I made all the preparatory arrangements personally. They did not take very long. The whole apparatus of our organization was set in motion for the purpose of being able to secure a rapid decision as to our policy. Within twenty-four hours we had to decide on the attitude we should take in regard to the questions of the day which would be put forward at the mass meeting. The notices which advertised the meeting had to bring these points before the public. In this direction we were forced to depend on the use of posters and leaflets, the contents of which and the manner in which they were displayed were decided upon in accordance with the principles which I have already laid down in dealing with propaganda in general. They were produced in a form which would appeal to the crowd. They concentrated on a few points which were repeated again and again. The text was concise and definite, an absolutely dogmatic form of expression being used. We distributed these posters and leaflets with a dogged energy and then we patiently waited for the effect they would produce.

For our principal colour we chose red, as it has an exciting effect on the eye and was therefore calculated to arouse the attention of our opponents and irritate them. Thus they would have to take notice of us—whether they liked it or not—and would not forget us.

One result of our tactics was to show up clearly the close political fraternization that existed also here in Bavaria between the Marxists and the Centre Party. The political party that held power in Bavaria, which was the Bavarian People's Party (affiliated with the Centre Party) did its best to counteract the effect which our placards were having on the 'Red' masses. Thus they made a definite step to fetter our activities. If the police could find no other grounds for prohibiting our placards, then they might claim that we were disturbing the traffic in the streets. And thus the so-called German National People's Party calmed the anxieties of their 'Red' allies by completely prohibiting those placards which proclaimed a message that was bringing back to the bosom of their own people hundreds of thousands of workers who had been misled by international agitators and incensed against their own nation.

These placards bear witness to the bitterness of the struggle in which the young movement was then engaged. Future generations will find in these placards a documentary proof of our determination and the justice of our own cause. And these placards will also prove how the so-called national officials took arbitrary action to strangle a movement that did not please them, because it was nationalizing the broad masses of the people and winning them back to their own racial stock.

These placards will also help to refute the theory that there was then a national government in Bavaria and they will afford documentary confirmation of the fact that if Bavaria remained nationally-minded during the years 1919, 1920, 1921, 1922 and 1923, this was not due to a national government but it was because the national spirit gradually gained a deeper hold on the people and the Government was forced to follow public feeling. The Government authorities themselves did everything in their power to hamper this process of recovery and make it impossible. But in this connection two officials must be mentioned as outstanding exceptions.

Ernst Pöhner was Chief of Police at the time. He had a loyal counsellor in Dr. Frick, who was his chief executive official. These were the only men among the higher officials who had the courage to place the interests of their country before their own interests in holding on to their jobs. Of those in responsible positions Ernst Pöhner was the only one who did not pay court to the mob but felt that his duty was towards the nation as such and was ready to risk and sacrifice everything, even his personal livelihood, to help in the restoration of the German people, whom he dearly loved. For that reason he was a bitter thorn in the side of the venal group of Government officials. It was not the interests of the nation or the necessity of a national revival that inspired or directed their conduct. They simply truckled to the wishes of the Government, so as to secure their daily bread for themselves, but they had no thought whatsoever for the national welfare that had been entrusted to their care.

Above all, Pöhner was one of those people who, in contradistinction to the majority of our so-called defenders of the authority of the State, did not fear to incur the enmity of the traitors to the country and the nation but rather courted it as a mark of honour and honesty. For such men the hatred of the Jews and Marxists and the lies and calumnies they spread, were their only source of happiness in the midst of the national misery. Pöhner was a man of granite loyalty. He was like one of the ascetic characters of the classical era and was at the same time that kind of straightforward German for whom the saying 'Better dead than a slave' is not an empty phrase but a veritable heart's cry.

In my opinion he and his collaborator, Dr. Frick, are the only men holding positions then in Bavaria who have the right to be considered as having taken active part in the creation of a national Bavaria. Before holding our first great mass meeting it was necessary not only to have our propaganda material ready but also to have the main items of our programme printed.

In the second volume of this book I shall give a detailed account of the guiding principles which we then followed in drawing up our programme. Here I will only say that the programme was arranged not merely to set forth the form and content of the young movement but also with an eye to making it understood among the broad masses. The so-called intellectual circles made jokes and sneered at it and then tried to criticize it. But the effect of our programme proved that the ideas which we then held were right.

During those years I saw dozens of new movements arise and disappear without leaving a trace behind. Only one movement has survived. It is the National Socialist German Labour Party. To-day I am more convinced than ever before that, though they may combat us and try to paralyse our movement, and though pettifogging party ministers may forbid us the right of free speech, they cannot prevent the triumph of our ideas. When the present system of statal administration and even the names of the political parties that represent it will be forgotten, the programmatic basis of the National Socialist movement will supply the groundwork on which the future State will be built.

The meetings which we held before January 1920 had enabled us to collect the financial means that were necessary to have our first pamphlets and posters and programmes printed.

I shall bring the first part of this book to a close by referring to our first great mass meeting, because that meeting marked the occasion on which our framework as a small party had to be broken up and we started to become the most powerful factor of this epoch in the influence we exercised on public opinion. At that time my chief anxiety was that we might not fill the hall and that we might have to face empty benches. I myself was firmly convinced that if only the people would come this day would turn out a great success for the young movement. That was my feeling as I waited impatiently for the hour to come.

It had been announced that the meeting would begin at 7.30. A quarter-of-an-hour before the opening time I walked through the chief hall of the Hofbräuhaus on the PLATZ in Munich and my heart was nearly bursting with joy. The great hall—for at that time it seemed very big to me—was filled to overflowing. Nearly 2,000 people were present. And, above all, those people had come whom we had always wished to reach.

More than half the audience consisted of persons who seemed to be communists or independents. Our first great demonstration was destined, in their view, to come to an abrupt end.

But things happened otherwise. When the first speaker had finished I got up to speak. After a few minutes I was met with a hailstorm of interruptions and violent encounters broke out in the body of the hall.

A handful of my loyal war comrades and some other followers grappled with the disturbers and restored order in a little while. I was able to continue my speech. After half an hour the applause began to drown the interruptions and the hootings. Then interruptions gradually ceased and applause took their place. When I finally came to explain the twenty-five points and laid them, point after point, before the masses gathered there and asked them to pass their own judgment on each point, one point after another was accepted with increasing enthusiasm. When the last point was reached I had before me a hall full of people united by a new conviction, a new faith and a new will.

Nearly four hours had passed when the hall began to clear. As the masses streamed towards the exits, crammed shoulder to shoulder, shoving and pushing, I knew that a movement was now set afoot among the German people which would never pass into oblivion.

A fire was enkindled from whose glowing heat the sword would be fashioned which would restore freedom to the German Siegfried and bring back life to the German nation. Beside the revival which I then foresaw, I also felt that the Goddess of Vengeance was now getting ready to redress the treason of the 9th of November, 1918. The hall was emptied. The movement was on the march.

VOLUME II: THE NATIONAL SOCIALIST MOVEMENT

CHAPTER I: Weltanschauung and Party

On February 24th, 1920, the first great mass meeting under the auspices of the new movement took place. In the Banquet Hall of the Hofbräuhaus in Munich the twenty-five theses which constituted the programme of our new party were expounded to an audience of nearly two thousand people and each thesis was enthusiastically received.

Thus we brought to the knowledge of the public those first principles and lines of action along which the new struggle was to be conducted for the abolition of a confused mass of obsolete ideas and opinions which had obscure and often pernicious tendencies. A new force was to make its appearance among the timid and feckless bourgeoisie. This force was destined to impede the triumphant advance of the Marxists and bring the Chariot of Fate to a standstill just as it seemed about to reach its goal.

It was evident that this new movement could gain the public significance and support which are necessary pre-requisites in such a gigantic struggle only if it succeeded from the very outset in awakening a sacrosanct conviction in the hearts of its followers, that here it was not a case of introducing a new electoral slogan into the political field but that an entirely new WELTANSCHAUUNG, which was of a radical significance, had to be promoted.

One must try to recall the miserable jumble of opinions that used to be arrayed side by side to form the usual Party Programme, as it was called, and one must remember how these opinions used to be brushed up or dressed in a new form from time to time. If we would properly understand these programmatic monstrosities we must carefully investigate the motives which inspired the average bourgeois 'programme committee'.

Those people are always influenced by one and the same preoccupation when they introduce something new into their programme or modify something already contained in it. That preoccupation is directed towards the results of the next election. The moment these artists in parliamentary government have the first glimmering of a suspicion that their darling public may be ready to kick up its heels and escape from the harness of the old party wagon they begin to paint the shafts with new colours. On such occasions the party astrologists and horoscope readers, the so-called 'experienced men' and 'experts', come forward. For the most part they are old parliamentary hands whose political schooling has furnished them with ample experience. They can remember former occasions when the masses showed signs of losing patience and they now diagnose the menace of a similar situation arising. Resorting to their old prescription, they form a 'committee'. They go around among the darling public and listen to what is being said. They dip their noses into the newspapers and gradually begin to scent what it is that their darlings, the broad masses, are wishing for, what they reject and what they are hoping for. The groups that belong to each trade or business, and even office employees, are carefully studied and their innermost desires are investigated. The 'malicious slogans' of the opposition from which danger is threatened are now suddenly looked upon as worthy of reconsideration, and it often happens that these slogans, to the great astonishment of those who originally coined and circulated them, now appear to be quite harmless and indeed are to be found among the dogmas of the old parties.

So the committees meet to revise the old programme and draw up a new one.

For these people change their convictions just as the soldier changes his shirt in war — when the old one is bug-eaten. In the new programme everyone gets everything he wants. The farmer is assured that the interests of agriculture will be safeguarded. The industrialist is assured of protection for his products. The consumer is assured that his interests will be protected in the market prices. Teachers are given higher salaries and civil servants will have better pensions. Widows and orphans will receive generous assistance from the State. Trade will be promoted. The tariff will be lowered and even the taxes, though they cannot be entirely abolished, will be almost abolished. It sometimes happens that one section of the public is forgotten or that one of the demands mooted among the public has not reached the ears of the party. This is also hurriedly patched on to the whole, should there be any space available for it: until finally it is felt that there are good grounds for hoping that the whole normal host of philistines, including their wives, will have their anxieties laid to rest and will beam with satisfaction once again. And so, internally armed with faith in the goodness of God and the impenetrable stupidity of the electorate, the struggle for what is called 'the reconstruction of the REICH' can now begin.

When the election day is over and the parliamentarians have held their last public meeting for the next five years, when they can leave their job of getting the populace to toe the line and can now devote themselves to higher and more pleasing tasks — then the programme committee is dissolved and the struggle for the progressive reorganization of public affairs becomes once again a business of earning one's daily bread, which for the parliamentarians means merely the attendance that is required in order to be able to draw their daily remunerations. Morning after morning the honourable deputy wends his way to the House, and though he may not enter the Chamber itself he gets at least as far as the front hall, where he will find the register on which the names of the deputies in attendance have to be inscribed. As a part of his onerous service to his constituents he enters his name, and in return receives a small indemnity as a well-earned reward for his unceasing and exhausting labours.

When four years have passed, or in the meantime if there should be some critical weeks during which the parliamentary corporations have to face the danger of being dissolved, these honourable gentlemen become suddenly seized by an irresistible desire to act. Just as the grub-worm cannot help growing into a cock-chafer, these parliamentarian worms leave the great House of Puppets and flutter on new wings out among the beloved public. They address the electors once again, give an account of the enormous labours they have accomplished and emphasize the malicious obstinacy of their opponents. They do not always meet with grateful applause; for occasionally the unintelligent masses throw rude and unfriendly remarks in their faces. When this spirit of public ingratitude reaches a certain pitch there is only one way of saving the situation. The prestige of the party must be burnished up again. The programme has to be amended. The committee is called into existence once again. And the swindle begins anew. Once we understand the impenetrable stupidity of our public we cannot be surprised that such tactics turn out successful. Led by the Press and blinded once again by the alluring appearance of the new programme, the bourgeois as well as the proletarian herds of voters faithfully return to the common stall and re-elect their old deceivers. The 'people's man' and labour candidate now change back again into the parliamentarian grub and become fat and rotund as they batten on the leaves that grow on the tree of public life—to be retransformed into the glittering butterfly after another four years have passed.

Scarcely anything else can be so depressing as to watch this process in sober reality and to be the eyewitness of this repeatedly recurring fraud. On a spiritual training ground of that kind it is not possible for the bourgeois forces to develop the strength which is necessary to carry on the fight against the organized might of Marxism. Indeed they have never seriously thought of doing so. Though these parliamentary quacks who represent the white race are generally recognized as persons of quite inferior mental capacity, they are shrewd enough to know that they could not seriously entertain the hope of being able to use the weapon of Western Democracy to fight a doctrine for the advance of which Western Democracy, with all its accessories, is employed as a means to an end. Democracy is exploited by the Marxists for the purpose of paralysing their opponents and gaining for themselves a free hand to put their own methods into action. When certain groups of Marxists use all their ingenuity for the time being to make it be believed that they are inseparably attached to the principles of democracy, it may be well to recall the fact that when critical occasions arose these same gentlemen snapped their fingers at the principle of decision by majority vote, as that principle is understood by Western Democracy. Such was the case in those days when the bourgeois parliamentarians, in their monumental shortsightedness, believed that the security of the REICH was guaranteed because it had an overwhelming numerical majority in its favour, and the Marxists did not hesitate suddenly to grasp supreme power in their own hands, backed by a mob of loafers, deserters, political place-hunters and Jewish dilettanti. That was a blow in the face for that democracy in which so many parliamentarians believed. Only those credulous parliamentary wizards who represented bourgeois democracy could have believed that the brutal determination of those whose interest it is to spread the Marxist world-pest, of which they are the carriers, could for a moment, now or in the future, be held in check by the magical formulas of Western Parliamentarianism. Marxism will march shoulder to shoulder with democracy until it succeeds indirectly in securing for its own criminal purposes even the support of those whose minds are nationally orientated and whom Marxism strives to exterminate. But if the Marxists should one day come to believe that there was a danger that from this witch's cauldron of our parliamentary democracy a majority vote might be concocted, which by reason of its numerical majority would be empowered to enact legislation and might use that power seriously to combat Marxism, then the whole parliamentarian hocus-pocus would be at an end. Instead of appealing to the democratic conscience, the standard bearers of the Red International would immediately send forth a furious rallying-cry among the proletarian masses and the ensuing fight would not take place in the sedate atmosphere of Parliament but in the factories and the streets. Then democracy would be annihilated forthwith. And what the intellectual prowess of the apostles who represented the people in Parliament had failed to accomplish would now be successfully carried out by the crow-bar and the sledge-hammer of the exasperated proletarian masses—just as in the autumn of 1918. At a blow they would awaken the bourgeois world to see the madness of thinking that the Jewish drive towards world-conquest can be effectually opposed by means of Western Democracy.

As I have said, only a very credulous soul could think of binding himself to observe the rules of the game when he has to face a player for whom those rules are nothing but a mere bluff or a means of serving his own interests, which means he will discard them when they prove no longer useful for his purpose.

All the parties that profess so-called bourgeois principles look upon political life as in reality a struggle for seats in Parliament. The moment their principles and convictions are of no further use in that struggle they are thrown overboard, as if they were sand ballast. And the programmes are constructed in such a way that they can be dealt with in like manner. But such practice has a correspondingly weakening effect on the strength of those parties. They lack the great magnetic force which alone attracts the broad masses; for these masses always respond to the compelling force which emanates from absolute faith in the ideas put forward, combined with an indomitable zest to fight for and defend them.

At a time in which the one side, armed with all the fighting power that springs from a systematic conception of life—even though it be criminal in a thousand ways—makes an attack against the established order the other side will be able to resist when it draws its strength from a new faith, which in our case is a political faith. This faith must supersede the weak and cowardly command to defend. In its stead we must raise the battle-cry of a courageous and ruthless attack. Our present movement is accused, especially by the so-called national bourgeois cabinet ministers—the Bavarian representatives of the Centre, for example—of heading towards a revolution. We have one answer to give to those political pigmies. We say to them: We are trying to make up for that which you, in your criminal stupidity, have failed to carry out. By your parliamentarian jobbing you have helped to drag the nation into ruin. But we, by our aggressive policy, are setting up a new WELTANSCHAUUNG which we shall defend with indomitable devotion. Thus we are building the steps on which our nation once again may ascend to the temple of freedom.

And so during the first stages of founding our movement we had to take special care that our militant group which fought for the establishment of a new and exalted political faith should not degenerate into a society for the promotion of parliamentarian interests.

The first preventive measure was to lay down a programme which of itself would tend towards developing a certain moral greatness that would scare away all the petty and weakling spirits who make up the bulk of our present party politicians.

Those fatal defects which finally led to Germany's downfall afford the clearest proof of how right we were in considering it absolutely necessary to set up programmatic aims which were sharply and distinctly defined.

Because we recognized the defects above mentioned, we realized that a new conception of the State had to be formed, which in itself became a part of our new conception of life in general.

In the first volume of this book I have already dealt with the term VÖLKISCH, and I said then that this term has not a sufficiently precise meaning to furnish the kernel around which a closely consolidated militant community could be formed. All kinds of people, with all kinds of divergent opinions, are parading about at the present moment under the device VÖLKISCH on their banners. Before I come to deal with the purposes and aims of the National Socialist Labour Party I want to establish a clear understanding of what is meant by the concept VÖLKISCH and herewith explain its relation to our party movement. The word VÖLKISCH does not express any clearly specified idea. It may be interpreted in several ways and in practical application it is just as general as the word 'religious', for instance. It is difficult to attach any precise meaning to this latter word, either as a theoretical concept or as a guiding principle in practical life. The word 'religious' acquires a precise meaning only when it is associated with a distinct and definite form through which the concept is put into practice. To say that a person is 'deeply religious' may be very fine phraseology; but, generally speaking, it tells us little or nothing. There may be some few people who are content with such a vague description and there may even be some to whom the word conveys a more or less definite picture of the inner quality of a person thus described. But, since the masses of the people are not composed of philosophers or saints, such a vague religious idea will mean for them nothing else than to justify each individual in thinking and acting according to his own bent. It will not lead to that practical faith into which the inner religious yearning is transformed only when it leaves the sphere of general metaphysical ideas and is moulded to a definite dogmatic belief. Such a belief is certainly not an end in itself, but the means to an end. Yet it is a means without which the end could never be reached at all. This end, however, is not merely something ideal; for at the bottom it is eminently practical. We must always bear in mind the fact that, generally speaking, the highest ideals are always the outcome of some profound vital need, just as the most sublime beauty owes its nobility of shape, in the last analysis, to the fact that the most beautiful form is the form that is best suited to the purpose it is meant to serve.

By helping to lift the human being above the level of mere animal existence, Faith really contributes to consolidate and safeguard its own existence. Taking humanity as it exists to-day and taking into consideration the fact that the religious beliefs which it generally holds and which have been consolidated through our education, so that they serve as moral standards in practical life, if we should now abolish religious teaching and not replace it by anything of equal value the result would be that the foundations of human existence would be seriously shaken. We may safely say that man does not live merely to serve higher ideals, but that these ideals, in their turn, furnish the necessary conditions of his existence as a human being. And thus the circle is closed.

Of course, the word 'religious' implies some ideas and beliefs that are fundamental. Among these we may reckon the belief in the immortality of the soul, its future existence in eternity, the belief in the existence of a Higher Being, and so on. But all these ideas, no matter how firmly the individual believes in them, may be critically analysed by any person and accepted or rejected accordingly, until the emotional concept or yearning has been transformed into an active service that is governed by a clearly defined doctrinal faith. Such a faith furnishes the practical outlet for religious feeling to express itself and thus opens the way through which it can be put into practice.

Without a clearly defined belief, the religious feeling would not only be worthless for the purposes of human existence but even might contribute towards a general disorganization, on account of its vague and multifarious tendencies.

What I have said about the word 'religious' can also be applied to the term VÖLKISCH. This word also implies certain fundamental ideas. Though these ideas are very important indeed, they assume such vague and indefinite forms that they cannot be estimated as having a greater value than mere opinions, until they become constituent elements in the structure of a political party. For in order to give practical force to the ideals that grow out of a WELTANSCHAUUNG and to answer the demands which are a logical consequence of such ideals, mere sentiment and inner longing are of no practical assistance, just as freedom cannot be won by a universal yearning for it. No. Only when the idealistic longing for independence is organized in such a way that it can fight for its ideal with military force, only then can the urgent wish of a people be transformed into a potent reality.

Any WELTANSCHAUUNG, though a thousandfold right and supremely beneficial to humanity, will be of no practical service for the maintenance of a people as long as its principles have not yet become the rallying point of a militant movement. And, on its own side, this movement will remain a mere party until is has brought its ideals to victory and transformed its party doctrines into the new foundations of a State which gives the national community its final shape.

If an abstract conception of a general nature is to serve as the basis of a future development, then the first prerequisite is to form a clear understanding of the nature and character and scope of this conception. For only on such a basis can a movement he founded which will be able to draw the necessary fighting strength from the internal cohesion of its principles and convictions. From general ideas a political programme must be constructed and a general WELTANSCHAUUNG must receive the stamp of a definite political faith. Since this faith must be directed towards ends that have to be attained in the world of practical reality, not only must it serve the general ideal as such but it must also take into consideration the means that have to be employed for the triumph of the ideal. Here the practical wisdom of the statesman must come to the assistance of the abstract idea, which is correct in itself. In that way an eternal ideal, which has everlasting significance as a guiding star to mankind, must be adapted to the exigencies of human frailty so that its practical effect may not be frustrated at the very outset through those shortcomings which are general to mankind. The exponent of truth must here go hand in hand with him who has a practical knowledge of the soul of the people, so that from the realm of eternal verities and ideals what is suited to the capacities of human nature may be selected and given practical form. To take abstract and general principles, derived from a WELTANSCHAUUNG which is based on a solid foundation of truth, and transform them into a militant community whose members have the same political faith—a community which is precisely defined, rigidly organized, of one mind and one will—such a transformation is the most important task of all; for the possibility of successfully carrying out the idea is dependent on the successful fulfilment of that task. Out of the army of millions who feel the truth of these ideas, and even may understand them to some extent, one man must arise. This man must have the gift of being able to expound general ideas in a clear and definite form, and, from the world of vague ideas shimmering before the minds of the masses, he must formulate principles that will be as clear-cut and firm as granite. He must fight for these principles as the only true ones, until a solid rock of common faith and common will emerges above the troubled waves of vagrant ideas. The general justification of such action is to be sought in the necessity for it and the individual will be justified by his success.

If we try to penetrate to the inner meaning of the word VÖLKISCH we arrive at the following conclusions:

The current political conception of the world is that the State, though it possesses a creative force which can build up civilizations, has nothing in common with the concept of race as the foundation of the State. The State is considered rather as something which has resulted from economic necessity, or, at best, the natural outcome of the play of political forces and impulses. Such a conception of the foundations of the State, together with all its logical consequences, not only ignores the primordial racial forces that underlie the State, but it also leads to a policy in which the importance of the individual is minimized. If it be denied that races differ from one another in their powers of cultural creativeness, then this same erroneous notion must necessarily influence our estimation of the value of the individual. The assumption that all races are alike leads to the assumption that nations and individuals are equal to one another. And international Marxism is nothing but the application—effected by the Jew, Karl Marx—of a general conception of life to a definite profession of political faith; but in reality that general concept had existed long before the time of Karl Marx. If it had not already existed as a widely diffused infection the amazing political progress of the Marxist teaching would never have been possible. In reality what distinguished Karl Marx from the millions who were affected in the same way was that, in a world already in a state of gradual decomposition, he used his keen powers of prognosis to detect the essential poisons, so as to extract them and concentrate them, with the art of a necromancer, in a solution which would bring about the rapid destruction of the independent nations on the globe. But all this was done in the service of his race.

Thus the Marxist doctrine is the concentrated extract of the mentality which underlies the general concept of life to-day. For this reason alone it is out of the question and even ridiculous to think that what is called our bourgeois world can put up any effective fight against Marxism. For this bourgeois world is permeated with all those same poisons and its conception of life in general differs from Marxism only in degree and in the character of the persons who hold it. The bourgeois world is Marxist but believes in the possibility of a certain group of people—that is to say, the bourgeoisie—being able to dominate the world, while Marxism itself systematically aims at delivering the world into the hands of the Jews.

Over against all this, the VÖLKISCH concept of the world recognizes that the primordial racial elements are of the greatest significance for mankind. In principle, the State is looked upon only as a means to an end and this end is the conservation of the racial characteristics of mankind. Therefore on the VÖLKISCH principle we cannot admit that one race is equal to another. By recognizing that they are different, the VÖLKISCH concept separates mankind into races of superior and inferior quality. On the basis of this recognition it feels bound in conformity with the eternal Will that dominates the universe, to postulate the victory of the better and stronger and the subordination of the inferior and weaker. And so it pays homage to the truth that the principle underlying all Nature's operations is the aristocratic principle and it believes that this law holds good even down to the last individual organism. It selects individual values from the mass and thus operates as an organizing principle, whereas Marxism acts as a disintegrating solvent. The VÖLKISCH belief holds that humanity must have its ideals, because ideals are a necessary condition of human existence itself. But, on the other hand, it denies that an ethical ideal has the right to prevail if it endangers the existence of a race that is the standard-bearer of a higher ethical ideal. For in a world which would be composed of mongrels and negroids all ideals of human beauty and nobility and all hopes of an idealized future for our humanity would be lost forever.

On this planet of ours human culture and civilization are indissolubly bound up with the presence of the Aryan. If he should be exterminated or subjugated, then the dark shroud of a new barbarian era would enfold the earth.

To undermine the existence of human culture by exterminating its founders and custodians would be an execrable crime in the eyes of those who believe that the folk-idea lies at the basis of human existence. Whoever would dare to raise a profane hand against that highest image of God among His creatures would sin against the bountiful Creator of this marvel and would collaborate in the expulsion from Paradise.

Hence the folk concept of the world is in profound accord with Nature's will; because it restores the free play of the forces which will lead the race through stages of sustained reciprocal education towards a higher type, until finally the best portion of mankind will possess the earth and will be free to work in every domain all over the world and even reach spheres that lie outside the earth.

We all feel that in the distant future many may be faced with problems which can be solved only by a superior race of human beings, a race destined to become master of all the other peoples and which will have at its disposal the means and resources of the whole world.

It is evident that such a general sketch of the ideas implied in the folk concept of the world may easily be interpreted in a thousand different ways. As a matter of fact there is scarcely one of our recent political movements that does not refer at some point to this conception of the world. But the fact that this conception of the world still maintains its independent existence in face of all the others proves that their ways of looking at life are quite difierent from this. Thus the Marxist conception, directed by a central organization endowed with supreme authority, is opposed by a motley crew of opinions which is not very impressive in face of the solid phalanx presented by the enemy. Victory cannot be achieved with such weak weapons. Only when the international idea, politically organized by Marxism, is confronted by the folk idea, equally well organized in a systematic way and equally well led—only then will the fighting energy in the one camp be able to meet that of the other on an equal footing; and victory will be found on the side of eternal truth.

But a general conception of life can never be given an organic embodiment until it is precisely and definitely formulated. The function which dogma fulfils in religious belief is parallel to the function which party principles fulfil for a political party which is in the process of being built up. Therefore, for the conception of life that is based on the folk idea it is necessary that an instrument be forged which can be used in fighting for this ideal, similar to the Marxist party organization which clears the way for internationalism.

And this is the aim which the German National Socialist Labour Movement pursues.

The folk conception must therefore be definitely formulated so that it may be organically incorporated in the party. That is a necessary prerequisite for the success of this idea. And that it is so is very clearly proved even by the indirect acknowledgment of those who oppose such an amalgamation of the folk idea with party principles. The very people who never tire of insisting again and again that the conception of life based on the folk idea can never be the exclusive property of a single group, because it lies dormant or 'lives' in myriads of hearts, only confirm by their own statements the simple fact that the general presence of such ideas in the hearts of millions of men has not proved sufficient to impede the victory of the opposing ideas, which are championed by a political party organized on the principle of class conflict. If that were not so, the German people ought already to have gained a gigantic victory instead of finding themselves on the brink of the abyss. The international ideology achieved success because it was organized in a militant political party which was always ready to take the offensive. If hitherto the ideas opposed to the international concept have had to give way before the latter the reason is that they lacked a united front to fight for their cause. A doctrine which forms a definite outlook on life cannot struggle and triumph by allowing the right of free interpretation of its general teaching, but only by defining that teaching in certain articles of faith that have to be accepted and incorporating it in a political organization.

Therefore I considered it my special duty to extract from the extensive but vague contents of a general WELTANSCHAUUNG the ideas which were essential and give them a more or less dogmatic form. Because of their precise and clear meaning, these ideas are suited to the purpose of uniting in a common front all those who are ready to accept them as principles. In other words: The German National Socialist Labour Party extracts the essential principles from the general conception of the world which is based on the folk idea. On these principles it establishes a political doctrine which takes into account the practical realities of the day, the nature of the times, the available human material and all its deficiencies. Through this political doctrine it is possible to bring great masses of the people into an organization which is constructed as rigidly as it could be. Such an organization is the main preliminary that is necessary for the final triumph of this ideal.

CHAPTER II: The State

Already in 1920-1921 certain circles belonging to the effete bourgeois class accused our movement again and again of taking up a negative attitude towards the modern State. For that reason the motley gang of camp followers attached to the various political parties, representing a heterogeneous conglomeration of political views, assumed the right of utilizing all available means to suppress the protagonists of this young movement which was preaching a new political gospel. Our opponents deliberately ignored the fact that the bourgeois class itself stood for no uniform opinion as to what the State really meant and that the bourgeoisie did not and could not give any coherent definition of this institution. Those whose duty it is to explain what is meant when we speak of the State, hold chairs in State universities, often in the department of constitutional law, and consider it their highest duty to find explanations and justifications for the more or less fortunate existence of that particular form of State which provides them with their daily bread. The more absurd such a form of State is the more obscure and artificial and incomprehensible are the definitions which are advanced to explain the purpose of its existence. What, for instance, could a royal and imperial university professor write about the meaning and purpose of a State in a country whose statal form represented the greatest monstrosity of the twentieth century? That would be a difficult undertaking indeed, in view of the fact that the contemporary professor of constitutional law is obliged not so much to serve the cause of truth but rather to serve a certain definite purpose. And this purpose is to defend at all costs the existence of that monstrous human mechanism which we now call the State. Nobody can be surprised if concrete facts are evaded as far as possible when the problem of the State is under discussion and if professors adopt the tactics of concealing themselves in morass of abstract values and duties and purposes which are described as 'ethical' and 'moral'.

Generally speaking, these various theorists may be classed in three groups:

1. Those who hold that the State is a more or less voluntary association of men who have agreed to set up and obey a ruling authority.

This is numerically the largest group. In its ranks are to be found those who worship our present principle of legalized authority. In their eyes the will of the people has no part whatever in the whole affair. For them the fact that the State exists is sufficient reason to consider it sacred and inviolable. To accept this aberration of the human brain one would have to have a sort of canine adoration for what is called the authority of the State. In the minds of these people the means is substituted for the end, by a sort of sleight-of-hand movement. The State no longer exists for the purpose of serving men but men exist for the purpose of adoring the authority of the State, which is vested in its functionaries, even down to the smallest official. So as to prevent this placid and ecstatic adoration from changing into something that might become in any way disturbing, the authority of the State is limited simply to the task of preserving order and tranquillity. Therewith it is no longer either a means or an end. The State must see that public peace and order are preserved and, in their turn, order and peace must make the existence of the State possible. All life must move between these two poles. In Bavaria this view is upheld by the artful politicians of the Bavarian Centre, which is called the 'Bavarian Populist Party'. In Austria the Black-and-Yellow legitimists adopt a similar attitude. In the REICH, unfortunately, the so-called conservative elements follow the same line of thought.

2. The second group is somewhat smaller in numbers. It includes those who would make the existence of the State dependent on some conditions at least. They insist that not only should there be a uniform system of government but also, if possible, that only one language should be used, though solely for technical reasons of administration. In this view the authority of the State is no longer the sole and exclusive end for which the State exists. It must also promote the good of its subjects. Ideas of 'freedom', mostly based on a misunderstanding of the meaning of that word, enter into the concept of the State as it exists in the minds of this group. The form of government is no longer considered inviolable simply because it exists. It must submit to the test of practical efficiency. Its venerable age no longer protects it from being criticized in the light of modern exigencies. Moreover, in this view the first duty laid upon the State is to guarantee the economic well-being of the individual citizens. Hence it is judged from the practical standpoint and according to general principles based on the idea of economic returns. The chief representatives of this theory of the State are to be found among the average German bourgeoisie, especially our liberal democrats.

3. The third group is numerically the smallest. In the State they discover a means for the realization of tendencies that arise from a policy of power, on the part of a people who are ethnically homogeneous and speak the same language. But those who hold this view are not clear about what they mean by 'tendencies arising from a policy of power'. A common language is postulated not only because they hope that thereby the State would be furnished with a solid basis for the extension of its power outside its own frontiers, but also because they think—though falling into a fundamental error by doing so—that such a common language would enable them to carry out a process of nationalization in a definite direction.

During the last century it was lamentable for those who had to witness it, to notice how in these circles I have just mentioned the word 'Germanization' was frivolously played with, though the practice was often well intended. I well remember how in the days of my youth this very term used to give rise to notions which were false to an incredible degree. Even in Pan-German circles one heard the opinion expressed that the Austrian Germans might very well succeed in Germanizing the Austrian Slavs, if only the Government would be ready to co-operate. Those people did not understand that a policy of Germanization can be carried out only as regards human beings. What they mostly meant by Germanization was a process of forcing other people to speak the German language. But it is almost inconceivable how such a mistake could be made as to think that a Nigger or a Chinaman will become a German because he has learned the German language and is willing to speak German for the future, and even to cast his vote for a German political party. Our bourgeois nationalists could never clearly see that such a process of Germanization is in reality de-Germanization; for even if all the outstanding and visible differences between the various peoples could be bridged over and finally wiped out by the use of a common language, that would produce a process of bastardization which in this case would not signify Germanization but the annihilation of the German element. In the course of history it has happened only too often that a conquering race succeeded by external force in compelling the people whom they subjected to speak the tongue of the conqueror and that after a thousand years their language was spoken by another people and that thus the conqueror finally turned out to be the conquered.

What makes a people or, to be more correct, a race, is not language but blood. Therefore it would be justifiable to speak of Germanization only if that process could change the blood of the people who would be subjected to it, which is obviously impossible. A change would be possible only by a mixture of blood, but in this case the quality of the superior race would be debased. The final result of such a mixture would be that precisely those qualities would be destroyed which had enabled the conquering race to achieve victory over an inferior people. It is especially the cultural creativeness which disappears when a superior race intermixes with an inferior one, even though the resultant mongrel race should excel a thousandfold in speaking the language of the race that once had been superior. For a certain time there will be a conflict between the different mentalities, and it may be that a nation which is in a state of progressive degeneration will at the last moment rally its cultural creative power and once again produce striking examples of that power. But these results are due only to the activity of elements that have remained over from the superior race or hybrids of the first crossing in whom the superior blood has remained dominant and seeks to assert itself. But this will never happen with the final descendants of such hybrids. These are always in a state of cultural retrogression.

We must consider it as fortunate that a Germanization of Austria according to the plan of Joseph II did not succeed. Probably the result would have been that the Austrian State would have been able to survive, but at the same time participation in the use of a common language would have debased the racial quality of the German element. In the course of centuries a certain herd instinct might have been developed but the herd itself would have deteriorated in quality. A national State might have arisen, but a people who had been culturally creative would have disappeared.

For the German nation it was better that this process of intermixture did not take place, although it was not renounced for any high-minded reasons but simply through the short-sighted pettiness of the Habsburgs. If it had taken place the German people could not now be looked upon as a cultural factor.

Not only in Austria, however, but also in the REICH, these so-called national circles were, and still are, under the influence of similar erroneous ideas. Unfortunately, a policy towards Poland, whereby the East was to be Germanized, was demanded by many and was based on the same false reasoning. Here again it was believed that the Polish people could be Germanized by being compelled to use the German language. The result would have been fatal. A people of foreign race would have had to use the German language to express modes of thought that were foreign to the German, thus compromising by its own inferiority the dignity and nobility of our nation.

It is revolting to think how much damage is indirectly done to German prestige to-day through the fact that the German patois of the Jews when they enter the United States enables them to be classed as Germans, because many Americans are quite ignorant of German conditions. Among us, nobody would think of taking these unhygienic immigrants from the East for members of the German race and nation merely because they mostly speak German.

What has been beneficially Germanized in the course of history was the land which our ancestors conquered with the sword and colonized with German tillers of the soil. To the extent that they introduced foreign blood into our national body in this colonization, they have helped to disintegrate our racial character, a process which has resulted in our German hyper-individualism, though this latter characteristic is even now frequently praised.

In this third group also there are people who, to a certain degree, consider the State as an end in itself. Hence they consider its preservation as one of the highest aims of human existence. Our analysis may be summed up as follows:

All these opinions have this common feature and failing: that they are not grounded in a recognition of the profound truth that the capacity for creating cultural values is essentially based on the racial element and that, in accordance with this fact, the paramount purpose of the State is to preserve and improve the race; for this is an indispensable condition of all progress in human civilization.

Thus the Jew, Karl Marx, was able to draw the final conclusions from these false concepts and ideas on the nature and purpose of the State. By eliminating from the concept of the State all thought of the obligation which the State bears towards the race, without finding any other formula that might be universally accepted, the bourgeois teaching prepared the way for that doctrine which rejects the State as such.

That is why the bourgeois struggle against Marxist internationalism is absolutely doomed to fail in this field. The bourgeois classes have already sacrificed the basic principles which alone could furnish a solid footing for their ideas. Their crafty opponent has perceived the defects in their structure and advances to the assault on it with those weapons which they themselves have placed in his hands though not meaning to do so.

Therefore any new movement which is based on the racial concept of the world will first of all have to put forward a clear and logical doctrine of the nature and purpose of the State. The fundamental principle is that the State is not an end in itself but the means to an end. It is the preliminary condition under which alone a higher form of human civilization can be developed, but it is not the source of such a development. This is to be sought exclusively in the actual existence of a race which is endowed with the gift of cultural creativeness. There may be hundreds of excellent States on this earth, and yet if the Aryan, who is the creator and custodian of civilization, should disappear, all culture that is on an adequate level with the spiritual needs of the superior nations to-day would also disappear. We may go still further and say that the fact that States have been created by human beings does not in the least exclude the possiblity that the human race may become extinct, because the superior intellectual faculties and powers of adaptation would be lost when the racial bearer of these faculties and powers disappeared.

If, for instance, the surface of the globe should be shaken to-day by some seismic convulsion and if a new Himalaya would emerge from the waves of the sea, this one catastrophe alone might annihilate human civilization. No State could exist any longer. All order would be shattered. And all vestiges of cultural products which had been evolved through thousands of years would disappear. Nothing would be left but one tremendous field of death and destruction submerged in floods of water and mud. If, however, just a few people would survive this terrible havoc, and if these people belonged to a definite race that had the innate powers to build up a civilization, when the commotion had passed, the earth would again bear witness to the creative power of the human spirit, even though a span of a thousand years might intervene. Only with the extermination of the last race that possesses the gift of cultural creativeness, and indeed only if all the individuals of that race had disappeared, would the earth definitely be turned into a desert. On the other hand, modern history furnishes examples to show that statal institutions which owe their beginnings to members of a race which lacks creative genius are not made of stuff that will endure. Just as many varieties of prehistoric animals had to give way to others and leave no trace behind them, so man will also have to give way, if he loses that definite faculty which enables him to find the weapons that are necessary for him to maintain his own existence.

It is not the State as such that brings about a certain definite advance in cultural progress. The State can only protect the race that is the cause of such progress. The State as such may well exist without undergoing any change for hundreds of years, though the cultural faculties and the general life of the people, which is shaped by these faculties, may have suffered profound changes by reason of the fact that the State did not prevent a process of racial mixture from taking place. The present State, for instance, may continue to exist in a mere mechanical form, but the poison of miscegenation permeating the national body brings about a cultural decadence which manifests itself already in various symptoms that are of a detrimental character.

Thus the indispensable prerequisite for the existence of a superior quality of human beings is not the State but the race, which is alone capable of producing that higher human quality.

This capacity is always there, though it will lie dormant unless external circumstances awaken it to action. Nations, or rather races, which are endowed with the faculty of cultural creativeness possess this faculty in a latent form during periods when the external circumstances are unfavourable for the time being and therefore do not allow the faculty to express itself effectively. It is therefore outrageously unjust to speak of the pre-Christian Germans as barbarians who had no civilization. They never have been such. But the severity of the climate that prevailed in the northern regions which they inhabited imposed conditions of life which hampered a free development of their creative faculties. If they had come to the fairer climate of the South, with no previous culture whatsoever, and if they acquired the necessary human material—that is to say, men of an inferior race—to serve them as working implements, the cultural faculty dormant in them would have splendidly blossomed forth, as happened in the case of the Greeks, for example. But this primordial creative faculty in cultural things was not solely due to their northern climate. For the Laplanders or the Eskimos would not have become creators of a culture if they were transplanted to the South. No, this wonderful creative faculty is a special gift bestowed on the Aryan, whether it lies dormant in him or becomes active, according as the adverse conditions of nature prevent the active expression of that faculty or favourable circumstances permit it.

From these facts the following conclusions may be drawn:

The State is only a means to an end. Its end and its purpose is to preserve and promote a community of human beings who are physically as well as spiritually kindred. Above all, it must preserve the existence of the race, thereby providing the indispensable condition for the free development of all the forces dormant in this race. A great part of these faculties will always have to be employed in the first place to maintain the physical existence of the race, and only a small portion will be free to work in the field of intellectual progress. But, as a matter of fact, the one is always the necessary counterpart of the other.

Those States which do not serve this purpose have no justification for their existence. They are monstrosities. The fact that they do exist is no more of a justification than the successful raids carried out by a band of pirates can be considered a justification of piracy.

We National Socialists, who are fighting for a new WELTANSCHAUUNG, must never take our stand on the famous 'basis of facts', and especially not on mistaken facts. If we did so, we should cease to be the protagonists of a new and great idea and would become slaves in the service of the fallacy which is dominant to-day. We must make a clear-cut distinction between the vessel and its contents. The State is only the vessel and the race is what it contains. The vessel can have a meaning only if it preserves and safeguards the contents. Otherwise it is worthless.

Hence the supreme purpose of the ethnical State is to guard and preserve those racial elements which, through their work in the cultural field, create that beauty and dignity which are characteristic of a higher mankind. As Aryans, we can consider the State only as the living organism of a people, an organism which does not merely maintain the existence of a people, but functions in such a way as to lead its people to a position of supreme liberty by the progressive development of the intellectual and cultural faculties.

What they want to impose upon us as a State to-day is in most cases nothing but a monstrosity, the product of a profound human aberration which brings untold suffering in its train.

We National Socialists know that in holding these views we take up a revolutionary stand in the world of to-day and that we are branded as revolutionaries. But our views and our conduct will not be determined by the approbation or disapprobation of our contemporaries, but only by our duty to follow a truth which we have acknowledged. In doing this we have reason to believe that posterity will have a clearer insight, and will not only understand the work we are doing to-day, but will also ratify it as the right work and will exalt it accordingly.

On these principles we National Socialists base our standards of value in appraising a State. This value will be relative when viewed from the particular standpoint of the individual nation, but it will be absolute when considered from the standpoint of humanity as a whole. In other words, this means:

That the excellence of a State can never be judged by the level of its culture or the degree of importance which the outside world attaches to its power, but that its excellence must be judged by the degree to which its institutions serve the racial stock which belongs to it.

A State may be considered as a model example if it adequately serves not only the vital needs of the racial stock it represents but if it actually assures by its own existence the preservation of this same racial stock, no matter what general cultural significance this statal institution may have in the eyes of the rest of the world. For it is not the task of the State to create human capabilities, but only to assure free scope for the exercise of capabilities that already exist. On the other hand, a State may be called bad if, in spite of the existence of a high cultural level, it dooms to destruction the bearers of that culture by breaking up their racial uniformity. For the practical effect of such a policy would be to destroy those conditions that are indispensable for the ulterior existence of that culture, which the State did not create but which is the fruit of the creative power inherent in the racial stock whose existence is assured by being united in the living organism of the State. Once again let me emphasize the fact that the State itself is not the substance but the form. Therefore, the cultural level is not the standard by which we can judge the value of the State in which that people lives. It is evident that a people which is endowed with high creative powers in the cultural sphere is of more worth than a tribe of negroes. And yet the statal organization of the former, if judged from the standpoint of efficiency, may be worse than that of the negroes. Not even the best of States and statal institutions can evolve faculties from a people which they lack and which they never possessed, but a bad State may gradually destroy the faculties which once existed. This it can do by allowing or favouring the suppression of those who are the bearers of a racial culture.

Therefore, the worth of a State can be determined only by asking how far it actually succeeds in promoting the well-being of a definite race and not by the role which it plays in the world at large. Its relative worth can be estimated readily and accurately; but it is difficult to judge its absolute worth, because the latter is conditioned not only by the State but also by the quality and cultural level of the people that belong to the individual State in question.

Therefore, when we speak of the high mission of the State we must not forget that the high mission belongs to the people and that the business of the State is to use its organizing powers for the purpose of furnishing the necessary conditions which allow this people freely to unfold its creative faculties. And if we ask what kind of statal institution we Germans need, we must first have a clear notion as to the people which that State must embrace and what purpose it must serve.

Unfortunately the German national being is not based on a uniform racial type. The process of welding the original elements together has not gone so far as to warrant us in saying that a new race has emerged. On the contrary, the poison which has invaded the national body, especially since the Thirty Years' War, has destroyed the uniform constitution not only of our blood but also of our national soul. The open frontiers of our native country, the association with non-German foreign elements in the territories that lie all along those frontiers, and especially the strong influx of foreign blood into the interior of the REICH itself, has prevented any complete assimilation of those various elements, because the influx has continued steadily. Out of this melting-pot no new race arose. The heterogeneous elements continue to exist side by side. And the result is that, especially in times of crisis, when the herd usually flocks together, the Germans disperse in all directions. The fundamental racial elements are not only different in different districts, but there are also various elements in the single districts. Beside the Nordic type we find the East-European type, beside the Eastern there is the Dinaric, the Western type intermingling with both, and hybrids among them all. That is a grave drawback for us. Through it the Germans lack that strong herd instinct which arises from unity of blood and saves nations from ruin in dangerous and critical times; because on such occasions small differences disappear, so that a united herd faces the enemy. What we understand by the word hyper-individualism arises from the fact that our primordial racial elements have existed side by side without ever consolidating. During times of peace such a situation may offer some advantages, but, taken all in all, it has prevented us from gaining a mastery in the world. If in its historical development the German people had possessed the unity of herd instinct by which other peoples have so much benefited, then the German REICH would probably be mistress of the globe to-day. World history would have taken another course and in this case no man can tell if what many blinded pacifists hope to attain by petitioning, whining and crying, may not have been reached in this way: namely, a peace which would not be based upon the waving of olive branches and tearful misery-mongering of pacifist old women, but a peace that would be guaranteed by the triumphant sword of a people endowed with the power to master the world and administer it in the service of a higher civilization.

The fact that our people did not have a national being based on a unity of blood has been the source of untold misery for us. To many petty German potentates it gave residential capital cities, but the German people as a whole was deprived of its right to rulership.

Even to-day our nation still suffers from this lack of inner unity; but what has been the cause of our past and present misfortunes may turn out a blessing for us in the future. Though on the one hand it may be a drawback that our racial elements were not welded together, so that no homogeneous national body could develop, on the other hand, it was fortunate that, since at least a part of our best blood was thus kept pure, its racial quality was not debased.

A complete assimilation of all our racial elements would certainly have brought about a homogeneous national organism; but, as has been proved in the case of every racial mixture, it would have been less capable of creating a civilization than by keeping intact its best original elements. A benefit which results from the fact that there was no all-round assimilation is to be seen in that even now we have large groups of German Nordic people within our national organization, and that their blood has not been mixed with the blood of other races. We must look upon this as our most valuable treasure for the sake of the future. During that dark period of absolute ignorance in regard to all racial laws, when each individual was considered to be on a par with every other, there could be no clear appreciation of the difference between the various fundamental racial characteristics. We know to-day that a complete assimilation of all the various elements which constitute the national being might have resulted in giving us a larger share of external power: but, on the other hand, the highest of human aims would not have been attained, because the only kind of people which fate has obviously chosen to bring about this perfection would have been lost in such a general mixture of races which would constitute such a racial amalgamation.

But what has been prevented by a friendly Destiny, without any assistance on our part, must now be reconsidered and utilized in the light of our new knowledge.

He who talks of the German people as having a mission to fulfil on this earth must know that this cannot be fulfilled except by the building up of a State whose highest purpose is to preserve and promote those nobler elements of our race and of the whole of mankind which have remained unimpaired.

Thus for the first time a high inner purpose is accredited to the State. In face of the ridiculous phrase that the State should do no more than act as the guardian of public order and tranquillity, so that everybody can peacefully dupe everybody else, it is given a very high mission indeed to preserve and encourage the highest type of humanity which a beneficent Creator has bestowed on this earth. Out of a dead mechanism which claims to be an end in itself a living organism shall arise which has to serve one purpose exclusively: and that, indeed, a purpose which belongs to a higher order of ideas.

As a State the German REICH shall include all Germans. Its task is not only to gather in and foster the most valuable sections of our people but to lead them slowly and surely to a dominant position in the world.

Thus a period of stagnation is superseded by a period of effort. And here, as in every other sphere, the proverb holds good that to rest is to rust; and furthermore the proverb that victory will always be won by him who attacks. The higher the final goal which we strive to reach, and the less it be understood at the time by the broad masses, the more magnificent will be its success. That is what the lesson of history teaches. And the achievement will be all the more significant if the end is conceived in the right way and the fight carried through with unswerving persistence. Many of the officials who direct the affairs of State nowadays may find it easier to work for the maintenance of the present order than to fight for a new one. They will find it more comfortable to look upon the State as a mechanism, whose purpose is its own preservation, and to say that 'their lives belong to the State,' as if anything that grew from the inner life of the nation can logically serve anything but the national being, and as if man could be made for anything else than for his fellow beings. Naturally, it is easier, as I have said, to consider the authority of the State as nothing but the formal mechanism of an organization, rather than as the sovereign incarnation of a people's instinct for self-preservation on this earth. For these weak minds the State and the authority of the State is nothing but an aim in itself, while for us it is an effective weapon in the service of the great and eternal struggle for existence, a weapon which everyone must adopt, not because it is a mere formal mechanism, but because it is the main expression of our common will to exist.

Therefore, in the fight for our new idea, which conforms completely to the primal meaning of life, we shall find only a small number of comrades in a social order which has become decrepit not only physically but mentally also. From these strata of our population only a few exceptional people will join our ranks, only those few old people whose hearts have remained young and whose courage is still vigorous, but not those who consider it their duty to maintain the state of affairs that exists.

Against us we have the innumerable army of all those who are lazy-minded and indifferent rather than evil, and those whose self-interest leads them to uphold the present state of affairs. On the apparent hopelessness of our great struggle is based the magnitude of our task and the possibilities of success. A battle-cry which from the very start will scare off all the petty spirits, or at least discourage them, will become the signal for a rally of all those temperaments that are of the real fighting metal. And it must be clearly recognized that if a highly energetic and active body of men emerge from a nation and unite in the fight for one goal, thereby ultimately rising above the inert masses of the people, this small percentage will become masters of the whole. World history is made by minorities if these numerical minorities represent in themselves the will and energy and initiative of the people as a whole.

What seems an obstacle to many persons is really a preliminary condition of our victory. Just because our task is so great and because so many difficulties have to be overcome, the highest probability is that only the best kind of protagonists will join our ranks. This selection is the guarantee of our success. Nature generally takes certain measures to correct the effect which racial mixture produces in life. She is not much in favour of the mongrel. The later products of cross-breeding have to suffer bitterly, especially the third, fourth and fifth generations. Not only are they deprived of the higher qualities that belonged to the parents who participated in the first mixture, but they also lack definite will-power and vigorous vital energies owing to the lack of harmony in the quality of their blood. At all critical moments in which a person of pure racial blood makes correct decisions, that is to say, decisions that are coherent and uniform, the person of mixed blood will become confused and take measures that are incoherent. Hence we see that a person of mixed blood is not only relatively inferior to a person of pure blood, but is also doomed to become extinct more rapidly. In innumerable cases wherein the pure race holds its ground the mongrel breaks down. Therein we witness the corrective provision which Nature adopts. She restricts the possibilities of procreation, thus impeding the fertility of cross-breeds and bringing them to extinction.

For instance, if an individual member of a race should mingle his blood with the member of a superior race the first result would be a lowering of the racial level, and furthermore the descendants of this cross-breeding would be weaker than those of the people around them who had maintained their blood unadulterated. Where no new blood from the superior race enters the racial stream of the mongrels, and where those mongrels continue to cross-breed among themselves, the latter will either die out because they have insufficient powers of resistance, which is Nature's wise provision, or in the course of many thousands of years they will form a new mongrel race in which the original elements will become so wholly mixed through this millennial crossing that traces of the original elements will be no longer recognizable. And thus a new people would be developed which possessed a certain resistance capacity of the herd type, but its intellectual value and its cultural significance would be essentially inferior to those which the first cross-breeds possessed. But even in this last case the mongrel product would succumb in the mutual struggle for existence with a higher racial group that had maintained its blood unmixed. The herd solidarity which this mongrel race had developed through thousands of years will not be equal to the struggle. And this is because it would lack elasticity and constructive capacity to prevail over a race of homogeneous blood that was mentally and culturally superior.

Therewith we may lay down the following principle as valid: every racial mixture leads, of necessity, sooner or later to the downfall of the mongrel product, provided the higher racial strata of this cross-breed has not retained within itself some sort of racial homogeneity. The danger to the mongrels ceases only when this higher stratum, which has maintained certain standards of homogeneous breeding, ceases to be true to its pedigree and intermingles with the mongrels.

This principle is the source of a slow but constant regeneration whereby all the poison which has invaded the racial body is gradually eliminated so long as there still remains a fundamental stock of pure racial elements which resists further crossbreeding.

Such a process may set in automatically among those people where a strong racial instinct has remained. Among such people we may count those elements which, for some particular cause such as coercion, have been thrown out of the normal way of reproduction along strict racial lines. As soon as this compulsion ceases, that part of the race which has remained intact will tend to marry with its own kind and thus impede further intermingling. Then the mongrels recede quite naturally into the background unless their numbers had increased so much as to be able to withstand all serious resistance from those elements which had preserved the purity of their race.

When men have lost their natural instincts and ignore the obligations imposed on them by Nature, then there is no hope that Nature will correct the loss that has been caused, until recognition of the lost instincts has been restored. Then the task of bringing back what has been lost will have to be accomplished. But there is serious danger that those who have become blind once in this respect will continue more and more to break down racial barriers and finally lose the last remnants of what is best in them. What then remains is nothing but a uniform mish-mash, which seems to be the dream of our fine Utopians. But that mish-mash would soon banish all ideals from the world. Certainly a great herd could thus be formed. One can breed a herd of animals; but from a mixture of this kind men such as have created and founded civilizations would not be produced. The mission of humanity might then be considered at an end.

Those who do not wish that the earth should fall into such a condition must realize that it is the task of the German State in particular to see to it that the process of bastardization is brought to a stop.

Our contemporary generation of weaklings will naturally decry such a policy and whine and complain about it as an encroachment on the most sacred of human rights. But there is only one right that is sacrosanct and this right is at the same time a most sacred duty. This right and obligation are: that the purity of the racial blood should be guarded, so that the best types of human beings may be preserved and that thus we should render possible a more noble development of humanity itself.

A folk-State should in the first place raise matrimony from the level of being a constant scandal to the race. The State should consecrate it as an institution which is called upon to produce creatures made in the likeness of the Lord and not create monsters that are a mixture of man and ape. The protest which is put forward in the name of humanity does not fit the mouth of a generation that makes it possible for the most depraved degenerates to propagate themselves, thereby imposing unspeakable suffering on their own products and their contemporaries, while on the other hand contraceptives are permitted and sold in every drug store and even by street hawkers, so that babies should not be born even among the healthiest of our people. In this present State of ours, whose function it is to be the guardian of peace and good order, our national bourgeoisie look upon it as a crime to make procreation impossible for syphilitics and those who suffer from tuberculosis or other hereditary diseases, also cripples and imbeciles. But the practical prevention of procreation among millions of our very best people is not considered as an evil, nor does it offend against the noble morality of this social class but rather encourages their short-sightedness and mental lethargy. For otherwise they would at least stir their brains to find an answer to the question of how to create conditions for the feeding and maintaining of those future beings who will be the healthy representatives of our nation and must also provide the conditions on which the generation that is to follow them will have to support itself and live.

How devoid of ideals and how ignoble is the whole contemporary system! The fact that the churches join in committing this sin against the image of God, even though they continue to emphasize the dignity of that image, is quite in keeping with their present activities. They talk about the Spirit, but they allow man, as the embodiment of the Spirit, to degenerate to the proletarian level. Then they look on with amazement when they realize how small is the influence of the Christian Faith in their own country and how depraved and ungodly is this riff-raff which is physically degenerate and therefore morally degenerate also. To balance this state of affairs they try to convert the Hottentots and the Zulus and the Kaffirs and to bestow on them the blessings of the Church. While our European people, God be praised and thanked, are left to become the victims of moral depravity, the pious missionary goes out to Central Africa and establishes missionary stations for negroes. Finally, sound and healthy—though primitive and backward—people will be transformed, under the name of our 'higher civilization', into a motley of lazy and brutalized mongrels.

It would better accord with noble human aspirations if our two Christian denominations would cease to bother the negroes with their preaching, which the negroes do not want and do not understand. It would be better if they left this work alone, and if, in its stead, they tried to teach people in Europe, kindly and seriously, that it is much more pleasing to God if a couple that is not of healthy stock were to show loving kindness to some poor orphan and become a father and mother to him, rather than give life to a sickly child that will be a cause of suffering and unhappiness to all.

In this field the People's State will have to repair the damage that arises from the fact that the problem is at present neglected by all the various parties concerned. It will be the task of the People's State to make the race the centre of the life of the community. It must make sure that the purity of the racial strain will be preserved. It must proclaim the truth that the child is the most valuable possession a people can have. It must see to it that only those who are healthy shall beget children; that there is only one infamy, namely, for parents that are ill or show hereditary defects to bring children into the world and that in such cases it is a high honour to refrain from doing so. But, on the other hand, it must be considered as reprehensible conduct to refrain from giving healthy children to the nation. In this matter the State must assert itself as the trustee of a millennial future, in face of which the egotistic desires of the individual count for nothing and will have to give way before the ruling of the State. In order to fulfil this duty in a practical manner the State will have to avail itself of modern medical discoveries. It must proclaim as unfit for procreation all those who are inflicted with some visible hereditary disease or are the carriers of it; and practical measures must be adopted to have such people rendered sterile. On the other hand, provision must be made for the normally fertile woman so that she will not be restricted in child-bearing through the financial and economic system operating in a political regime that looks upon the blessing of having children as a curse to their parents. The State will have to abolish the cowardly and even criminal indifference with which the problem of social amenities for large families is treated, and it will have to be the supreme protector of this greatest blessing that a people can boast of. Its attention and care must be directed towards the child rather than the adult.

Those who are physically and mentally unhealthy and unfit must not perpetuate their own suffering in the bodies of their children. From the educational point of view there is here a huge task for the People's State to accomplish. But in a future era this work will appear greater and more significant than the victorious wars of our present bourgeois epoch. Through educational means the State must teach individuals that illness is not a disgrace but an unfortunate accident which has to be pitied, yet that it is a crime and a disgrace to make this affliction all the worse by passing on disease and defects to innocent creatures out of mere egotism.

And the State must also teach the people that it is an expression of a really noble nature and that it is a humanitarian act worthy of admiration if a person who innocently suffers from hereditary disease refrains from having a child of his own but gives his love and affection to some unknown child who, through its health, promises to become a robust member of a healthy community. In accomplishing such an educational task the State integrates its function by this activity in the moral sphere. It must act on this principle without paying any attention to the question of whether its conduct will be understood or misconstrued, blamed or praised.

If for a period of only 600 years those individuals would be sterilized who are physically degenerate or mentally diseased, humanity would not only be delivered from an immense misfortune but also restored to a state of general health such as we at present can hardly imagine. If the fecundity of the healthy portion of the nation should be made a practical matter in a conscientious and methodical way, we should have at least the beginnings of a race from which all those germs would be eliminated which are to-day the cause of our moral and physical decadence. If a people and a State take this course to develop that nucleus of the nation which is most valuable from the racial standpoint and thus increase its fecundity, the people as a whole will subsequently enjoy that most precious of gifts which consists in a racial quality fashioned on truly noble lines.

To achieve this the State should first of all not leave the colonization of newly acquired territory to a haphazard policy but should have it carried out under the guidance of definite principles. Specially competent committees ought to issue certificates to individuals entitling them to engage in colonization work, and these certificates should guarantee the racial purity of the individuals in question. In this way frontier colonies could gradually be founded whose inhabitants would be of the purest racial stock, and hence would possess the best qualities of the race. Such colonies would be a valuable asset to the whole nation. Their development would be a source of joy and confidence and pride to each citizen of the nation, because they would contain the pure germ which would ultimately bring about a great development of the nation and indeed of mankind itself.

The WELTANSCHAUUNG which bases the State on the racial idea must finally succeed in bringing about a nobler era, in which men will no longer pay exclusive attention to breeding and rearing pedigree dogs and horses and cats, but will endeavour to improve the breed of the human race itself. That will be an era of silence and renunciation for one class of people, while the others will give their gifts and make their sacrifices joyfully.

That such a mentality may be possible cannot be denied in a world where hundreds and thousands accept the principle of celibacy from their own choice, without being obliged or pledged to do so by anything except an ecclesiastical precept. Why should it not be possible to induce people to make this sacrifice if, instead of such a precept, they were simply told that they ought to put an end to this truly original sin of racial corruption which is steadily being passed on from one generation to another. And, further, they ought to be brought to realize that it is their bounden duty to give to the Almighty Creator beings such as He himself made to His own image.

Naturally, our wretched army of contemporary philistines will not understand these things. They will ridicule them or shrug their round shoulders and groan out their everlasting excuses: "Of course it is a fine thing, but the pity is that it cannot be carried out." And we reply: "With you indeed it cannot be done, for your world is incapable of such an idea. You know only one anxiety and that is for your own personal existence. You have one God, and that is your money. We do not turn to you, however, for help, but to the great army of those who are too poor to consider their personal existence as the highest good on earth. They do not place their trust in money but in other gods, into whose hands they confide their lives. Above all we turn to the vast army of our German youth. They are coming to maturity in a great epoch, and they will fight against the evils which were due to the laziness and indifference of their fathers." Either the German youth will one day create a new State founded on the racial idea or they will be the last witnesses of the complete breakdown and death of the bourgeois world.

For if a generation suffers from defects which it recognizes and even admits and is nevertheless quite pleased with itself, as the bourgeois world is to-day, resorting to the cheap excuse that nothing can be done to remedy the situation, then such a generation is doomed to disaster. A marked characteristic of our bourgeois world is that they no longer can deny the evil conditions that exist. They have to admit that there is much which is foul and wrong; but they are not able to make up their minds to fight against that evil, which would mean putting forth the energy to mobilize the forces of 60 or 70 million people and thus oppose this menace. They do just the opposite. When such an effort is made elsewhere they only indulge in silly comment and try from a safe distance to show that such an enterprise is theoretically impossible and doomed to failure. No arguments are too stupid to be employed in the service of their own pettifogging opinions and their knavish moral attitude. If, for instance, a whole continent wages war against alcoholic intoxication, so as to free a whole people from this devastating vice, our bourgeois European does not know better than to look sideways stupidly, shake the head in doubt and ridicule the movement with a superior sneer—a state of mind which is effective in a society that is so ridiculous. But when all these stupidities miss their aim and in that part of the world this sublime and intangible attitude is treated effectively and success attends the movement, then such success is called into question or its importance minimized. Even moral principles are used in this slanderous campaign against a movement which aims at suppressing a great source of immorality.

No. We must not permit ourselves to be deceived by any illusions on this point. Our contemporary bourgeois world has become useless for any such noble human task because it has lost all high quality and is evil, not so much—as I think—because evil is wished but rather because these people are too indolent to rise up against it. That is why those political societies which call themselves 'bourgeois parties' are nothing but associations to promote the interests of certain professional groups and classes. Their highest aim is to defend their own egoistic interests as best they can. It is obvious that such a guild, consisting of bourgeois politicians, may be considered fit for anything rather than a struggle, especially when the adversaries are not cautious shopkeepers but the proletarian masses, goaded on to extremities and determined not to hesitate before deeds of violence.

If we consider it the first duty of the State to serve and promote the general welfare of the people, by preserving and encouraging the development of the best racial elements, the logical consequence is that this task cannot be limited to measures concerning the birth of the infant members of the race and nation but that the State will also have to adopt educational means for making each citizen a worthy factor in the further propagation of the racial stock.

Just as, in general, the racial quality is the preliminary condition for the mental efficiency of any given human material, the training of the individual will first of all have to be directed towards the development of sound bodily health. For the general rule is that a strong and healthy mind is found only in a strong and healthy body. The fact that men of genius are sometimes not robust in health and stature, or even of a sickly constitution, is no proof against the principle I have enunciated. These cases are only exceptions which, as everywhere else, prove the rule. But when the bulk of a nation is composed of physical degenerates it is rare for a great spirit to arise from such a miserable motley. And in any case his activities would never meet with great success. A degenerate mob will either be incapable of understanding him at all or their will-power is so feeble that they cannot follow the soaring of such an eagle.

The State that is grounded on the racial principle and is alive to the significance of this truth will first of all have to base its educational work not on the mere imparting of knowledge but rather on physical training and development of healthy bodies. The cultivation of the intellectual facilities comes only in the second place. And here again it is character which has to be developed first of all, strength of will and decision. And the educational system ought to foster the spirit of readiness to accept responsibilities gladly. Formal instruction in the sciences must be considered last in importance. Accordingly the State which is grounded on the racial idea must start with the principle that a person whose formal education in the sciences is relatively small but who is physically sound and robust, of a steadfast and honest character, ready and able to make decisions and endowed with strength of will, is a more useful member of the national community than a weakling who is scholarly and refined. A nation composed of learned men who are physical weaklings, hesitant about decisions of the will, and timid pacifists, is not capable of assuring even its own existence on this earth. In the bitter struggle which decides the destiny of man it is very rare that an individual has succumbed because he lacked learning. Those who fail are they who try to ignore these consequences and are too faint-hearted about putting them into effect. There must be a certain balance between mind and body. An ill-kept body is not made a more beautiful sight by the indwelling of a radiant spirit. We should not be acting justly if we were to bestow the highest intellectual training on those who are physically deformed and crippled, who lack decision and are weak-willed and cowardly. What has made the Greek ideal of beauty immortal is the wonderful union of a splendid physical beauty with nobility of mind and spirit.

Moltke's saying, that in the long run fortune favours only the efficient, is certainly valid for the relationship between body and spirit. A mind which is sound will generally maintain its dwelling in a body that is sound.

Accordingly, in the People's State physical training is not a matter for the individual alone. Nor is it a duty which first devolves on the parents and only secondly or thirdly a public interest; but it is necessary for the preservation of the people, who are represented and protected by the State. As regards purely formal education the State even now interferes with the individual's right of self-determination and insists upon the right of the community by submitting the child to an obligatory system of training, without paying attention to the approval or disapproval of the parents. In a similar way and to a higher degree the new People's State will one day make its authority prevail over the ignorance and incomprehension of individuals in problems appertaining to the safety of the nation. It must organize its educational work in such a way that the bodies of the young will be systematically trained from infancy onwards, so as to be tempered and hardened for the demands to be made on them in later years. Above all, the State must see to it that a generation of stay-at-homes is not developed.

The work of education and hygiene has to begin with the young mother. The painstaking efforts carried on for several decades have succeeded in abolishing septic infection at childbirth and reducing puerperal fever to a relatively small number of cases. And so it ought to be possible by means of instructing sisters and mothers in an opportune way, to institute a system of training the child from early infancy onwards so that this may serve as an excellent basis for future development.

The People's State ought to allow much more time for physical training in the school. It is nonsense to burden young brains with a load of material of which, as experience shows, they retain only a small part, and mostly not the essentials, but only the secondary and useless portion; because the young mind is incapable of sifting the right kind of learning out of all the stuff that is pumped into it. To-day, even in the curriculum of the high schools, only two short hours in the week are reserved for gymnastics; and worse still, it is left to the pupils to decide whether or not they want to take part. This shows a grave disproportion between this branch of education and purely intellectual instruction. Not a single day should be allowed to pass in which the young pupil does not have one hour of physical training in the morning and one in the evening; and every kind of sport and gymnastics should be included. There is one kind of sport which should be specially encouraged, although many people who call themselves VÖLKISCH consider it brutal and vulgar, and that is boxing. It is incredible how many false notions prevail among the 'cultivated' classes. The fact that the young man learns how to fence and then spends his time in duels is considered quite natural and respectable. But boxing—that is brutal. Why? There is no other sport which equals this in developing the militant spirit, none that demands such a power of rapid decision or which gives the body the flexibility of good steel. It is no more vulgar when two young people settle their differences with their fists than with sharp-pointed pieces of steel. One who is attacked and defends himself with his fists surely does not act less manly than one who runs off and yells for the assistance of a policeman. But, above all, a healthy youth has to learn to endure hard knocks. This principle may appear savage to our contemporary champions who fight only with the weapons of the intellect. But it is not the purpose of the People's State to educate a colony of aesthetic pacifists and physical degenerates. This State does not consider that the human ideal is to be found in the honourable philistine or the maidenly spinster, but in a dareful personification of manly force and in women capable of bringing men into the world.

Generally speaking, the function of sport is not only to make the individual strong, alert and daring, but also to harden the body and train it to endure an adverse environment.

If our superior class had not received such a distinguished education, and if, on the contrary, they had learned boxing, it would never have been possible for bullies and deserters and other such CANAILLE to carry through a German revolution. For the success of this revolution was not due to the courageous, energetic and audacious activities of its authors but to the lamentable cowardice and irresolution of those who ruled the German State at that time and were responsible for it. But our educated leaders had received only an 'intellectual' training and thus found themselves defenceless when their adversaries used iron bars instead of intellectual weapons. All this could happen only because our superior scholastic system did not train men to be real men but merely to be civil servants, engineers, technicians, chemists, litterateurs, jurists and, finally, professors; so that intellectualism should not die out.

Our leadership in the purely intellectual sphere has always been brilliant, but as regards will-power in practical affairs our leadership has been beneath criticism.

Of course education cannot make a courageous man out of one who is temperamentally a coward. But a man who naturally possesses a certain degree of courage will not be able to develop that quality if his defective education has made him inferior to others from the very start as regards physical strength and prowess. The army offers the best example of the fact that the knowledge of one's physical ability develops a man's courage and militant spirit. Outstanding heroes are not the rule in the army, but the average represents men of high courage. The excellent schooling which the German soldiers received before the War imbued the members of the whole gigantic organism with a degree of confidence in their own superiority such as even our opponents never thought possible. All the immortal examples of dauntless courage and daring which the German armies gave during the late summer and autumn of 1914, as they advanced from triumph to triumph, were the result of that education which had been pursued systematically. During those long years of peace before the last War men who were almost physical weaklings were made capable of incredible deeds, and thus a self-confidence was developed which did not fail even in the most terrible battles.

It is our German people, which broke down and were delivered over to be kicked by the rest of the world, that had need of the power that comes by suggestion from self-confidence. But this confidence in one's self must be instilled into our children from their very early years. The whole system of education and training must be directed towards fostering in the child the conviction that he is unquestionably a match for any- and everybody. The individual has to regain his own physical strength and prowess in order to believe in the invincibility of the nation to which he belongs. What has formerly led the German armies to victory was the sum total of the confidence which each individual had in himself, and which all of them had in those who held the positions of command. What will restore the national strength of the German people is the conviction that they will be able to reconquer their liberty. But this conviction can only be the final product of an equal feeling in the millions of individuals. And here again we must have no illusions.

The collapse of our people was overwhelming, and the efforts to put an end to so much misery must also be overwhelming. It would be a bitter and grave error to believe that our people could be made strong again simply by means of our present bourgeois training in good order and obedience. That will not suffice if we are to break up the present order of things, which now sanctions the acknowledgment of our defeat and cast the broken chains of our slavery in the face of our opponents. Only by a superabundance of national energy and a passionate thirst for liberty can we recover what has been lost.

Also the manner of clothing the young should be such as harmonizes with this purpose. It is really lamentable to see how our young people have fallen victims to a fashion mania which perverts the meaning of the old adage that clothes make the man.

Especially in regard to young people clothes should take their place in the service of education. The boy who walks about in summer-time wearing long baggy trousers and clad up to the neck is hampered even by his clothes in feeling any inclination towards strenuous physical exercise. Ambition and, to speak quite frankly, even vanity must be appealed to. I do not mean such vanity as leads people to want to wear fine clothes, which not everybody can afford, but rather the vanity which inclines a person towards developing a fine bodily physique. And this is something which everybody can help to do.

This will come in useful also for later years. The young girl must become acquainted with her sweetheart. If the beauty of the body were not completely forced into the background to-day through our stupid manner of dressing, it would not be possible for thousands of our girls to be led astray by Jewish mongrels, with their repulsive crooked waddle. It is also in the interests of the nation that those who have a beautiful physique should be brought into the foreground, so that they might encourage the development of a beautiful bodily form among the people in general.

Military training is excluded among us to-day, and therewith the only institution which in peace-times at least partly made up for the lack of physical training in our education. Therefore what I have suggested is all the more necessary in our time. The success of our old military training not only showed itself in the education of the individual but also in the influence which it exercised over the mutual relationship between the sexes. The young girl preferred the soldier to one who was not a soldier. The People's State must not confine its control of physical training to the official school period, but it must demand that, after leaving school and while the adolescent body is still developing, the boy continues this training. For on such proper physical development success in after-life largely depends. It is stupid to think that the right of the State to supervise the education of its young citizens suddenly comes to an end the moment they leave school and recommences only with military service. This right is a duty, and as such it must continue uninterruptedly. The present State, which does not interest itself in developing healthy men, has criminally neglected this duty. It leaves our contemporary youth to be corrupted on the streets and in the brothels, instead of keeping hold of the reins and continuing the physical training of these youths up to the time when they are grown into healthy young men and women.

For the present it is a matter of indifference what form the State chooses for carrying on this training. The essential matter is that it should be developed and that the most suitable ways of doing so should be investigated. The People's State will have to consider the physical training of the youth after the school period just as much a public duty as their intellectual training; and this training will have to be carried out through public institutions. Its general lines can be a preparation for subsequent service in the army. And then it will no longer be the task of the army to teach the young recruit the most elementary drill regulations. In fact the army will no longer have to deal with recruits in the present sense of the word, but it will rather have to transform into a soldier the youth whose bodily prowess has been already fully trained.

In the People's State the army will no longer be obliged to teach boys how to walk and stand erect, but it will be the final and supreme school of patriotic education. In the army the young recruit will learn the art of bearing arms, but at the same time he will be equipped for his other duties in later life. And the supreme aim of military education must always be to achieve that which was attributed to the old army as its highest merit: namely, that through his military schooling the boy must be transformed into a man, that he must not only learn to obey but also acquire the fundamentals that will enable him one day to command. He must learn to remain silent not only when he is rightly rebuked but also when he is wrongly rebuked.

Furthermore, on the self-consciousness of his own strength and on the basis of that ESPRIT DE CORPS which inspires him and his comrades, he must become convinced that he belongs to a people who are invincible.

After he has completed his military training two certificates shall be handed to the soldier. The one will be his diploma as a citizen of the State, a juridical document which will enable him to take part in public affairs. The second will be an attestation of his physical health, which guarantees his fitness for marriage.

The People's State will have to direct the education of girls just as that of boys and according to the same fundamental principles. Here again special importance must be given to physical training, and only after that must the importance of spiritual and mental training be taken into account. In the education of the girl the final goal always to be kept in mind is that she is one day to be a mother.

It is only in the second place that the People's State must busy itself with the training of character, using all the means adapted to that purpose.

Of course the essential traits of the individual character are already there fundamentally before any education takes place. A person who is fundamentally egoistic will always remain fundamentally egoistic, and the idealist will always remain fundamentally an idealist. Besides those, however, who already possess a definite stamp of character there are millions of people with characters that are indefinite and vague. The born delinquent will always remain a delinquent, but numerous people who show only a certain tendency to commit criminal acts may become useful members of the community if rightly trained; whereas, on the other hand, weak and unstable characters may easily become evil elements if the system of education has been bad.

During the War it was often lamented that our people could be so little reticent. This failing made it very difficult to keep even highly important secrets from the knowledge of the enemy. But let us ask this question: What did the German educational system do in pre-War times to teach the Germans to be discreet? Did it not very often happen in schooldays that the little tell-tale was preferred to his companions who kept their mouths shut? Is it not true that then, as well as now, complaining about others was considered praiseworthy 'candour', while silent discretion was taken as obstinacy? Has any attempt ever been made to teach that discretion is a precious and manly virtue? No, for such matters are trifles in the eyes of our educators. But these trifles cost our State innumerable millions in legal expenses; for 90 per cent of all the processes for defamation and such like charges arise only from a lack of discretion. Remarks that are made without any sense of responsibility are thoughtlessly repeated from mouth to mouth; and our economic welfare is continually damaged because important methods of production are thus disclosed. Secret preparations for our national defence are rendered illusory because our people have never learned the duty of silence. They repeat everything they happen to hear. In times of war such talkative habits may even cause the loss of battles and therefore may contribute essentially to the unsuccessful outcome of a campaign. Here, as in other matters, we may rest assured that adults cannot do what they have not learnt to do in youth. A teacher must not try to discover the wild tricks of the boys by encouraging the evil practice of tale-bearing. Young people form a sort of State among themselves and face adults with a certain solidarity. That is quite natural. The ties which unite the ten-year boys to one another are stronger and more natural than their relationship to adults. A boy who tells on his comrades commits an act of treason and shows a bent of character which is, to speak bluntly, similar to that of a man who commits high treason.

Such a boy must not be classed as 'good', 'reliable', and so on, but rather as one with undesirable traits of character. It may be rather convenient for the teacher to make use of such unworthy tendencies in order to help his own work, but by such an attitude the germ of a moral habit is sown in young hearts and may one day show fatal consequences. It has happened more often than once that a young informer developed into a big scoundrel.

This is only one example among many. The deliberate training of fine and noble traits of character in our schools to-day is almost negative. In the future much more emphasis will have to be laid on this side of our educational work. Loyalty, self-sacrifice and discretion are virtues which a great nation must possess. And the teaching and development of these in the school is a more important matter than many others things now included in the curriculum. To make the children give up habits of complaining and whining and howling when they are hurt, etc., also belongs to this part of their training. If the educational system fails to teach the child at an early age to endure pain and injury without complaining we cannot be surprised if at a later age, when the boy has grown to be the man and is, for example, in the trenches, the postal service is used for nothing else than to send home letters of weeping and complaint. If our youths, during their years in the primary schools, had had their minds crammed with a little less knowledge, and if instead they had been better taught how to be masters of themselves, it would have served us well during the years 1914-1918.

In its educational system the People's State will have to attach the highest importance to the development of character, hand-in-hand with physical training. Many more defects which our national organism shows at present could be at least ameliorated, if not completely eliminated, by education of the right kind.

Extreme importance should be attached to the training of will-power and the habit of making firm decisions, also the habit of being always ready to accept responsibilities.

In the training of our old army the principle was in vogue that any order is always better than no order. Applied to our youth this principle ought to take the form that any answer is better than no answer. The fear of replying, because one fears to be wrong, ought to be considered more humiliating than giving the wrong reply. On this simple and primitive basis our youth should be trained to have the courage to act.

It has been often lamented that in November and December 1918 all the authorities lost their heads and that, from the monarch down to the last divisional commander, nobody had sufficient mettle to make a decision on his own responsibility. That terrible fact constitutes a grave rebuke to our educational system; because what was then revealed on a colossal scale at that moment of catastrophe was only what happens on a smaller scale everywhere among us. It is the lack of will-power, and not the lack of arms, which renders us incapable of offering any serious resistance to-day. This defect is found everywhere among our people and prevents decisive action wherever risks have to be taken, as if any great action can be taken without also taking the risk. Quite unsuspectingly, a German General found a formula for this lamentable lack of the will-to-act when he said: "I act only when I can count on a 51 per cent probability of success." In that '51 per cent probability' we find the very root of the German collapse. The man who demands from Fate a guarantee of his success deliberately denies the significance of an heroic act. For this significance consists in the very fact that, in the definite knowledge that the situation in question is fraught with mortal danger, an action is undertaken which may lead to success. A patient suffering from cancer and who knows that his death is certain if he does not undergo an operation, needs no 51 per cent probability of a cure before facing the operation. And if the operation promises only half of one per cent probability of success a man of courage will risk it and would not whine if it turned out unsuccessful.

All in all, the cowardly lack of will-power and the incapacity for making decisions are chiefly results of the erroneous education given us in our youth. The disastrous effects of this are now widespread among us. The crowning examples of that tragic chain of consequences are shown in the lack of civil courage which our leading statesmen display.

The cowardice which leads nowadays to the shirking of every kind of responsibility springs from the same roots. Here again it is the fault of the education given our young people. This drawback permeates all sections of public life and finds its immortal consummation in the institutions of government that function under the parliamentary regime.

Already in the school, unfortunately, more value is placed on 'confession and full repentance' and 'contrite renouncement', on the part of little sinners, than on a simple and frank avowal. But this latter seems to-day, in the eyes of many an educator, to savour of a spirit of utter incorrigibility and depravation. And, though it may seem incredible, many a boy is told that the gallows tree is waiting for him because he has shown certain traits which might be of inestimable value in the nation as a whole.

Just as the People's State must one day give its attention to training the will-power and capacity for decision among the youth, so too it must inculcate in the hearts of the young generation from early childhood onwards a readiness to accept responsibilities, and the courage of open and frank avowal. If it recognizes the full significance of this necessity, finally—after a century of educative work—it will succeed in building up a nation which will no longer be subject to those defeats that have contributed so disastrously to bring about our present overthrow.

The formal imparting of knowledge, which constitutes the chief work of our educational system to-day, will be taken over by the People's State with only few modifications. These modifications must be made in three branches.

First of all, the brains of the young people must not generally be burdened with subjects of which ninety-five per cent are useless to them and are therefore forgotten again. The curriculum of the primary and secondary schools presents an odd mixture at the present time. In many branches of study the subject matter to be learned has become so enormous that only a very small fraction of it can be remembered later on, and indeed only a very small fraction of this whole mass of knowledge can be used. On the other hand, what is learned is insufficient for anybody who wishes to specialize in any certain branch for the purpose of earning his daily bread. Take, for example, the average civil servant who has passed through the GYMNASIUM or High School, and ask him at the age of thirty or forty how much he has retained of the knowledge that was crammed into him with so much pains.

How much is retained from all that was stuffed into his brain? He will certainly answer: "Well, if a mass of stuff was then taught, it was not for the sole purpose of supplying the student with a great stock of knowledge from which he could draw in later years, but it served to develop the understanding, the memory, and above all it helped to strengthen the thinking powers of the brain." That is partly true. And yet it is somewhat dangerous to submerge a young brain in a flood of impressions which it can hardly master and the single elements of which it cannot discern or appreciate at their just value. It is mostly the essential part of this knowledge, and not the accidental, that is forgotten and sacrificed. Thus the principal purpose of this copious instruction is frustrated, for that purpose cannot be to make the brain capable of learning by simply offering it an enormous and varied amount of subjects for acquisition, but rather to furnish the individual with that stock of knowledge which he will need in later life and which he can use for the good of the community. This aim, however, is rendered illusory if, because of the superabundance of subjects that have been crammed into his head in childhood, a person is able to remember nothing, or at least not the essential portion, of all this in later life. There is no reason why millions of people should learn two or three languages during the school years, when only a very small fraction will have the opportunity to use these languages in later life and when most of them will therefore forget those languages completely. To take an instance: Out of 100,000 students who learn French there are probably not 2,000 who will be in a position to make use of this accomplishment in later life, while 98,000 will never have a chance to utilize in practice what they have learned in youth. They have spent thousands of hours on a subject which will afterwards be without any value or importance to them. The argument that these matters form part of the general process of educating the mind is invalid. It would be sound if all these people were able to use this learning in after life. But, as the situation stands, 98,000 are tortured to no purpose and waste their valuable time, only for the sake of the 2,000 to whom the language will be of any use.

In the case of that language which I have chosen as an example it cannot be said that the learning of it educates the student in logical thinking or sharpens his mental acumen, as the learning of Latin, for instance, might be said to do. It would therefore be much better to teach young students only the general outline, or, better, the inner structure of such a language: that is to say, to allow them to discern the characteristic features of the language, or perhaps to make them acquainted with the rudiments of its grammar, its pronunciation, its syntax, style, etc. That would be sufficient for average students, because it would provide a clearer view of the whole and could be more easily remembered. And it would be more practical than the present-day attempt to cram into their heads a detailed knowledge of the whole language, which they can never master and which they will readily forget. If this method were adopted, then we should avoid the danger that, out of the superabundance of matter taught, only some fragments will remain in the memory; for the youth would then have to learn what is worth while, and the selection between the useful and the useless would thus have been made beforehand.

As regards the majority of students the knowledge and understanding of the rudiments of a language would be quite sufficient for the rest of their lives. And those who really do need this language subsequently would thus have a foundation on which to start, should they choose to make a more thorough study of it.

By adopting such a curriculum the necessary amount of time would be gained for physical exercises as well as for a more intense training in the various educational fields that have already been mentioned.

A reform of particular importance is that which ought to take place in the present methods of teaching history. Scarcely any other people are made to study as much of history as the Germans, and scarcely any other people make such a bad use of their historical knowledge. If politics means history in the making, then our way of teaching history stands condemned by the way we have conducted our politics. But there would be no point in bewailing the lamentable results of our political conduct unless one is now determined to give our people a better political education. In 99 out of 100 cases the results of our present teaching of history are deplorable. Usually only a few dates, years of birth and names, remain in the memory, while a knowledge of the main and clearly defined lines of historical development is completely lacking. The essential features which are of real significance are not taught. It is left to the more or less bright intelligence of the individual to discover the inner motivating urge amid the mass of dates and chronological succession of events.

You may object as strongly as you like to this unpleasant statement. But read with attention the speeches which our parliamentarians make during one session alone on political problems and on questions of foreign policy in particular. Remember that those gentlemen are, or claim to be, the elite of the German nation and that at least a great number of them have sat on the benches of our secondary schools and that many of them have passed through our universities. Then you will realize how defective the historical education of these people has been. If these gentlemen had never studied history at all but had possessed a sound instinct for public affairs, things would have gone better, and the nation would have benefited greatly thereby.

The subject matter of our historical teaching must be curtailed. The chief value of that teaching is to make the principal lines of historical development understood. The more our historical teaching is limited to this task, the more we may hope that it will turn out subsequently to be of advantage to the individual and, through the individual, to the community as a whole. For history must not be studied merely with a view to knowing what happened in the past but as a guide for the future, and to teach us what policy would be the best to follow for the preservation of our own people. That is the real end; and the teaching of history is only a means to attain this end. But here again the means has superseded the end in our contemporary education. The goal is completely forgotten. Do not reply that a profound study of history demands a detailed knowledge of all these dates because otherwise we could not fix the great lines of development. That task belongs to the professional historians. But the average man is not a professor of history. For him history has only one mission and that is to provide him with such an amount of historical knowledge as is necessary in order to enable him to form an independent opinion on the political affairs of his own country. The man who wants to become a professor of history can devote himself to all the details later on. Naturally he will have to occupy himself even with the smallest details. Of course our present teaching of history is not adequate to all this. Its scope is too vast for the average student and too limited for the student who wishes to be an historical expert.

Finally, it is the business of the People's State to arrange for the writing of a world history in which the race problem will occupy a dominant position.

To sum up: The People's State must reconstruct our system of general instruction in such a way that it will embrace only what is essential. Beyond this it will have to make provision for a more advanced teaching in the various subjects for those who want to specialize in them. It will suffice for the average individual to be acquainted with the fundamentals of the various subjects to serve as the basis of what may be called an all-round education. He ought to study exhaustively and in detail only that subject in which he intends to work during the rest of his life. A general instruction in all subjects should be obligatory, and specialization should be left to the choice of the individual.

In this way the scholastic programme would be shortened, and thus several school hours would be gained which could be utilized for physical training and character training, in will-power, the capacity for making practical judgments, decisions, etc.

The little account taken by our school training to-day, especially in the secondary schools, of the callings that have to be followed in after life is demonstrated by the fact that men who are destined for the same calling in life are educated in three different kinds of schools. What is of decisive importance is general education only and not the special teaching. When special knowledge is needed it cannot be given in the curriculum of our secondary schools as they stand to-day.

Therefore the People's State will one day have to abolish such half-measures.

The second modification in the curriculum which the People's State will have to make is the following:

It is a characteristic of our materialistic epoch that our scientific education shows a growing emphasis on what is real and practical: such subjects, for instance, as applied mathematics, physics, chemistry, etc. Of course they are necessary in an age that is dominated by industrial technology and chemistry, and where everyday life shows at least the external manifestations of these. But it is a perilous thing to base the general culture of a nation on the knowledge of these subjects. On the contrary, that general culture ought always to be directed towards ideals. It ought to be founded on the humanist disciplines and should aim at giving only the ground work of further specialized instruction in the various practical sciences. Otherwise we should sacrifice those forces that are more important for the preservation of the nation than any technical knowledge. In the historical department the study of ancient history should not be omitted. Roman history, along general lines, is and will remain the best teacher, not only for our own time but also for the future. And the ideal of Hellenic culture should be preserved for us in all its marvellous beauty. The differences between the various peoples should not prevent us from recognizing the community of race which unites them on a higher plane. The conflict of our times is one that is being waged around great objectives. A civilization is fighting for its existence. It is a civilization that is the product of thousands of years of historical development, and the Greek as well as the German forms part of it.

A clear-cut division must be made between general culture and the special branches. To-day the latter threaten more and more to devote themselves exclusively to the service of Mammon. To counterbalance this tendency, general culture should be preserved, at least in its ideal forms. The principle should be repeatedly emphasized, that industrial and technical progress, trade and commerce, can flourish only so long as a folk community exists whose general system of thought is inspired by ideals, since that is the preliminary condition for a flourishing development of the enterprises I have spoken of. That condition is not created by a spirit of materialist egotism but by a spirit of self-denial and the joy of giving one's self in the service of others.

The system of education which prevails to-day sees its principal object in pumping into young people that knowledge which will help them to make their way in life. This principle is expressed in the following terms: "The young man must one day become a useful member of human society." By that phrase they mean the ability to gain an honest daily livelihood. The superficial training in the duties of good citizenship, which he acquires merely as an accidental thing, has very weak foundations. For in itself the State represents only a form, and therefore it is difficult to train people to look upon this form as the ideal which they will have to serve and towards which they must feel responsible. A form can be too easily broken. But, as we have seen, the idea which people have of the State to-day does not represent anything clearly defined. Therefore, there is nothing but the usual stereotyped 'patriotic' training. In the old Germany the greatest emphasis was placed on the divine right of the small and even the smallest potentates. The way in which this divine right was formulated and presented was never very clever and often very stupid. Because of the large numbers of those small potentates, it was impossible to give adequate biographical accounts of the really great personalities that shed their lustre on the history of the German people. The result was that the broad masses received a very inadequate knowledge of German history. Here, too, the great lines of development were missing.

It is evident that in such a way no real national enthusiasm could be aroused. Our educational system proved incapable of selecting from the general mass of our historical personages the names of a few personalities which the German people could be proud to look upon as their own. Thus the whole nation might have been united by the ties of a common knowledge of this common heritage. The really important figures in German history were not presented to the present generation. The attention of the whole nation was not concentrated on them for the purpose of awakening a common national spirit. From the various subjects that were taught, those who had charge of our training seemed incapable of selecting what redounded most to the national honour and lifting that above the common objective level, in order to inflame the national pride in the light of such brilliant examples. At that time such a course would have been looked upon as rank chauvinism, which did not then have a very pleasant savour. Pettifogging dynastic patriotism was more acceptable and more easily tolerated than the glowing fire of a supreme national pride. The former could be always pressed into service, whereas the latter might one day become a dominating force. Monarchist patriotism terminated in Associations of Veterans, whereas passionate national patriotism might have opened a road which would be difficult to determine. This national passion is like a highly tempered thoroughbred who is discriminate about the sort of rider he will tolerate in the saddle. No wonder that most people preferred to shirk such a danger. Nobody seemed to think it possible that one day a war might come which would put the mettle of this kind of patriotism to the test, in artillery bombardment and waves of attacks with poison gas. But when it did come our lack of this patriotic passion was avenged in a terrible way. None were very enthusiastic about dying for their imperial and royal sovereigns; while on the other hand the 'Nation' was not recognized by the greater number of the soldiers.

Since the revolution broke out in Germany and the monarchist patriotism was therefore extinguished, the purpose of teaching history was nothing more than to add to the stock of objective knowledge. The present State has no use for patriotic enthusiasm; but it will never obtain what it really desires. For if dynastic patriotism failed to produce a supreme power of resistance at a time when the principle of nationalism dominated, it will be still less possible to arouse republican enthusiasm. There can be no doubt that the German people would not have stood on the field of battle for four and a half years to fight under the battle slogan 'For the Republic,' and least of all those who created this grand institution.

In reality this Republic has been allowed to exist undisturbed only by grace of its readiness and its promise to all and sundry, to pay tribute and reparations to the stranger and to put its signature to any kind of territorial renunciation. The rest of the world finds it sympathetic, just as a weakling is always more pleasing to those who want to bend him to their own uses than is a man who is made of harder metal. But the fact that the enemy likes this form of government is the worst kind of condemnation. They love the

German Republic and tolerate its existence because no better instrument could be found which would help them to keep our people in slavery. It is to this fact alone that this magnanimous institution owes its survival. And that is why it can renounce any REAL system of national education and can feel satisfied when the heroes of the REICH banner shout their hurrahs, but in reality these same heroes would scamper away like rabbits if called upon to defend that banner with their blood.

The People's State will have to fight for its existence. It will not gain or secure this existence by signing documents like that of the Dawes Plan. But for its existence and defence it will need precisely those things which our present system believes can be repudiated. The more worthy its form and its inner national being, the greater will be the envy and opposition of its adversaries. The best defence will not be in the arms it possesses but in its citizens. Bastions of fortresses will not save it, but the living wall of its men and women, filled with an ardent love for their country and a passionate spirit of national patriotism.

Therefore the third point which will have to be considered in relation to our educational system is the following:

The People's State must realize that the sciences may also be made a means of promoting a spirit of pride in the nation. Not only the history of the world but the history of civilization as a whole must be taught in the light of this principle. An inventor must appear great not only as an inventor but also, and even more so, as a member of the nation. The admiration aroused by the contemplation of a great achievement must be transformed into a feeling of pride and satisfaction that a man of one's own race has been chosen to accomplish it. But out of the abundance of great names in German history the greatest will have to be selected and presented to our young generation in such a way as to become solid pillars of strength to support the national spirit.

The subject matter ought to be systematically organized from the standpoint of this principle. And the teaching should be so orientated that the boy or girl, after leaving school, will not be a semi-pacifist, a democrat or of something else of that kind, but a whole-hearted German. So that this national feeling be sincere from the very beginning, and not a mere pretence, the following fundamental and inflexible principle should be impressed on the young brain while it is yet malleable: The man who loves his nation can prove the sincerity of this sentiment only by being ready to make sacrifices for the nation's welfare. There is no such thing as a national sentiment which is directed towards personal interests. And there is no such thing as a nationalism that embraces only certain classes. Hurrahing proves nothing and does not confer the right to call oneself national if behind that shout there is no sincere preoccupation for the conservation of the nation's well-being. One can be proud of one's people only if there is no class left of which one need to be ashamed. When one half of a nation is sunk in misery and worn out by hard distress, or even depraved or degenerate, that nation presents such an unattractive picture that nobody can feel proud to belong to it. It is only when a nation is sound in all its members, physically and morally, that the joy of belonging to it can properly be intensified to the supreme feeling which we call national pride. But this pride, in its highest form, can be felt only by those who know the greatness of their nation.

The spirit of nationalism and a feeling for social justice must be fused into one sentiment in the hearts of the youth. Then a day will come when a nation of citizens will arise which will be welded together through a common love and a common pride that shall be invincible and indestructible for ever.

The dread of chauvinism, which is a symptom of our time, is a sign of its impotence. Since our epoch not only lacks everything in the nature of exuberant energy but even finds such a manifestation disagreeable, fate will never elect it for the accomplishment of any great deeds. For the greatest changes that have taken place on this earth would have been inconceivable if they had not been inspired by ardent and even hysterical passions, but only by the bourgeois virtues of peacefulness and order.

One thing is certain: our world is facing a great revolution. The only question is whether the outcome will be propitious for the Aryan portion of mankind or whether the everlasting Jew will profit by it.

By educating the young generation along the right lines, the People's State will have to see to it that a generation of mankind is formed which will be adequate to this supreme combat that will decide the destinies of the world.

That nation will conquer which will be the first to take this road. The whole organization of education and training which the People's State is to build up must take as its crowning task the work of instilling into the hearts and brains of the youth entrusted to it the racial instinct and understanding of the racial idea. No boy or girl must leave school without having attained a clear insight into the meaning of racial purity and the importance of maintaining the racial blood unadulterated. Thus the first indispensable condition for the preservation of our race will have been established and thus the future cultural progress of our people will be assured.

For in the last analysis all physical and mental training would be in vain unless it served an entity which is ready and determined to carry on its own existence and maintain its own characteristic qualities.

If it were otherwise, something would result which we Germans have cause to regret already, without perhaps having hitherto recognized the extent of the tragic calamity. We should be doomed to remain also in the future only manure for civilization. And that not in the banal sense of the contemporary bourgeois mind, which sees in a lost fellow member of our people only a lost citizen, but in a sense which we should have painfully to recognize: namely, that our racial blood would be destined to disappear. By continually mixing with other races we might lift them from their former lower level of civilization to a higher grade; but we ourselves should descend for ever from the heights we had reached.

Finally, from the racial standpoint this training also must find its culmination in the military service. The term of military service is to be a final stage of the normal training which the average German receives.

While the People's State attaches the greatest importance to physical and mental training, it has also to consider, and no less importantly, the task of selecting men for the service of the State itself. This important matter is passed over lightly at the present time. Generally the children of parents who are for the time being in higher situations are in their turn considered worthy of a higher education. Here talent plays a subordinate part. But talent can be estimated only relatively. Though in general culture he may be inferior to the city child, a peasant boy may be more talented than the son of a family that has occupied high positions through many generations. But the superior culture of the city child has in itself nothing to do with a greater or lesser degree of talent; for this culture has its roots in the more copious mass of impressions which arise from the more varied education and the surroundings among which this child lives. If the intelligent son of peasant parents were educated from childhood in similar surroundings his intellectual accomplishments would be quite otherwise. In our day there is only one sphere where the family in which a person has been born means less than his innate gifts. That is the sphere of art. Here, where a person cannot just 'learn,' but must have innate gifts that later on may undergo a more or less happy development (in the sense of a wise development of what is already there), money and parental property are of no account. This is a good proof that genius is not necessarily connected with the higher social strata or with wealth. Not rarely the greatest artists come from poor families. And many a boy from the country village has eventually become a celebrated master.

It does not say much for the mental acumen of our time that advantage is not taken of this truth for the sake of our whole intellectual life. The opinion is advanced that this principle, though undoubtedly valid in the field of art, has not the same validity in regard to what are called the applied sciences. It is true that a man can be trained to a certain amount of mechanical dexterity, just as a poodle can be taught incredible tricks by a clever master. But such training does not bring the animal to use his intelligence in order to carry out those tricks. And the same holds good in regard to man. It is possible to teach men, irrespective of talent or no talent, to go through certain scientific exercises, but in such cases the results are quite as inanimate and mechanical as in the case of the animal. It would even be possible to force a person of mediocre intelligence, by means of a severe course of intellectual drilling, to acquire more than the average amount of knowledge; but that knowledge would remain sterile. The result would be a man who might be a walking dictionary of knowledge but who will fail miserably on every critical occasion in life and at every juncture where vital decisions have to be taken. Such people need to be drilled specially for every new and even most insignificant task and will never be capable of contributing in the least to the general progress of mankind. Knowledge that is merely drilled into people can at best qualify them to fill government positions under our present regime.

It goes without saying that, among the sum total of individuals who make up a nation, gifted people are always to be found in every sphere of life. It is also quite natural that the value of knowledge will be all the greater the more vitally the dead mass of learning is animated by the innate talent of the individual who possesses it. Creative work in this field can be done only through the marriage of knowledge and talent.

One example will suffice to show how much our contemporary world is at fault in this matter. From time to time our illustrated papers publish, for the edification of the German philistine, the news that in some quarter or other of the globe, and for the first time in that locality, a Negro has become a lawyer, a teacher, a pastor, even a grand opera tenor or something else of that kind. While the bourgeois blockhead stares with amazed admiration at the notice that tells him how marvellous are the achievements of our modern educational technique, the more cunning Jew sees in this fact a new proof to be utilized for the theory with which he wants to infect the public, namely that all men are equal. It does not dawn on the murky bourgeois mind that the fact which is published for him is a sin against reason itself, that it is an act of criminal insanity to train a being who is only an anthropoid by birth until the pretence can be made that he has been turned into a lawyer; while, on the other hand, millions who belong to the most civilized races have to remain in positions which are unworthy of their cultural level. The bourgeois mind does not realize that it is a sin against the will of the eternal Creator to allow hundreds of thousands of highly gifted people to remain floundering in the swamp of proletarian misery while Hottentots and Zulus are drilled to fill positions in the intellectual professions. For here we have the product only of a drilling technique, just as in the case of the performing dog. If the same amount of care and effort were applied among intelligent races each individual would become a thousand times more capable in such matters.

This state of affairs would become intolerable if a day should arrive when it no longer refers to exceptional cases. But the situation is already intolerable where talent and natural gifts are not taken as decisive factors in qualifying for the right to a higher education. It is indeed intolerable to think that year after year hundreds of thousands of young people without a single vestige of talent are deemed worthy of a higher education, while other hundreds of thousands who possess high natural gifts have to go without any sort of higher schooling at all. The practical loss thus caused to the nation is incalculable. If the number of important discoveries which have been made in America has grown considerably in recent years one of the reasons is that the number of gifted persons belonging to the lowest social classes who were given a higher education in that country is proportionately much larger than in Europe.

A stock of knowledge packed into the brain will not suffice for the making of discoveries. What counts here is only that knowledge which is illuminated by natural talent. But with us at the present time no value is placed on such gifts. Only good school reports count.

Here is another educative work that is waiting for the People's State to do. It will not be its task to assure a dominant influence to a certain social class already existing, but it will be its duty to attract the most competent brains in the total mass of the nation and promote them to place and honour. It is not merely the duty of the State to give to the average child a certain definite education in the primary school, but it is also its duty to open the road to talent in the proper direction. And above all, it must open the doors of the higher schools under the State to talent of every sort, no matter in what social class it may appear. This is an imperative necessity; for thus alone will it be possible to develop a talented body of public leaders from the class which represents learning that in itself is only a dead mass.

There is still another reason why the State should provide for this situation. Our intellectual class, particularly in Germany, is so shut up in itself and fossilized that it lacks living contact with the classes beneath it. Two evil consequences result from this: First, the intellectual class neither understands nor sympathizes with the broad masses. It has been so long cut off from all connection with them that it cannot now have the necessary psychological ties that would enable it to understand them. It has become estranged from the people. Secondly, the intellectual class lacks the necessary will-power; for this faculty is always weaker in cultivated circles, which live in seclusion, than among the primitive masses of the people. God knows we Germans have never been lacking in abundant scientific culture, but we have always had a considerable lack of will-power and the capacity for making decisions. For example, the more 'intellectual' our statesmen have been the more lacking they have been, for the most part, in practical achievement. Our political preparation and our technical equipment for the world war were defective, certainly not because the brains governing the nation were too little educated, but because the men who directed our public affairs were over-educated, filled to over-flowing with knowledge and intelligence, yet without any sound instinct and simply without energy, or any spirit of daring. It was our nation's tragedy to have to fight for its existence under a Chancellor who was a dillydallying philosopher. If instead of a Bethmann von Hollweg we had had a rough man of the people as our leader the heroic blood of the common grenadier would not have been shed in vain. The exaggeratedly intellectual material out of which our leaders were made proved to be the best ally of the scoundrels who carried out the November revolution. These intellectuals safeguarded the national wealth in a miserly fashion, instead of launching it forth and risking it, and thus they set the conditions on which the others won success.

Here the Catholic Church presents an instructive example. Clerical celibacy forces the Church to recruit its priests not from their own ranks but progressively from the masses of the people. Yet there are not many who recognize the significance of celibacy in this relation. But therein lies the cause of the inexhaustible vigour which characterizes that ancient institution. For by thus unceasingly recruiting the ecclesiastical dignitaries from the lower classes of the people, the Church is enabled not only to maintain the contact of instinctive understanding with the masses of the population but also to assure itself of always being able to draw upon that fund of energy which is present in this form only among the popular masses. Hence the surprising youthfulness of that gigantic organism, its mental flexibility and its iron will-power.

It will be the task of the Peoples' State so to organize and administer its educational system that the existing intellectual class will be constantly furnished with a supply of fresh blood from beneath. From the bulk of the nation the State must sift out with careful scrutiny those persons who are endowed with natural talents and see that they are employed in the service of the community. For neither the State itself nor the various departments of State exist to furnish revenues for members of a special class, but to fulfil the tasks allotted to them. This will be possible, however, only if the State trains individuals specially for these offices. Such individuals must have the necessary fundamental capabilities and will-power. The principle does not hold true only in regard to the civil service but also in regard to all those who are to take part in the intellectual and moral leadership of the people, no matter in what sphere they may be employed. The greatness of a people is partly dependent on the condition that it must succeed in training the best brains for those branches of the public service for which they show a special natural aptitude and in placing them in the offices where they can do their best work for the good of the community. If two nations of equal strength and quality engage in a mutual conflict that nation will come out victorious which has entrusted its intellectual and moral leadership to its best talents and that nation will go under whose government represents only a common food trough for privileged groups or classes and where the inner talents of its individual members are not availed of.

Of course such a reform seems impossible in the world as it is to-day. The objection will at once be raised, that it is too much to expect from the favourite son of a highly-placed civil servant, for instance, that he shall work with his hands simply because somebody else whose parents belong to the working-class seems more capable for a job in the civil service. That argument may be valid as long as manual work is looked upon in the same way as it is looked upon to-day. Hence the Peoples' State will have to take up an attitude towards the appreciation of manual labour which will be fundamentally different from that which now exists. If necessary, it will have to organize a persistent system of teaching which will aim at abolishing the present-day stupid habit of looking down on physical labour as an occupation to be ashamed of.

The individual will have to be valued, not by the class of work he does but by the way in which he does it and by its usefulness to the community. This statement may sound

272

monstrous in an epoch when the most brainless columnist on a newspaper staff is more esteemed than the most expert mechanic, merely because the former pushes a pen. But, as I have said, this false valuation does not correspond to the nature of things. It has been artificially introduced, and there was a time when it did not exist at all. The present unnatural state of affairs is one of those general morbid phenomena that have arisen from our materialistic epoch. Fundamentally every kind of work has a double value; the one material, the other ideal. The material value depends on the practical importance of the work to the life of the community. The greater the number of the population who benefit from the work, directly or indirectly, the higher will be its material value. This evaluation is expressed in the material recompense which the individual receives for his labour. In contradistinction to this purely material value there is the ideal value. Here the work performed is not judged by its material importance but by the degree to which it answers a necessity. Certainly the material utility of an invention may be greater than that of the service rendered by an everyday workman; but it is also certain that the community needs each of those small daily services just as much as the greater services. From the material point of view a distinction can be made in the evaluation of different kinds of work according to their utility to the community, and this distinction is expressed by the differentiation in the scale of recompense; but on the ideal or abstract plans all workmen become equal the moment each strives to do his best in his own field, no matter what that field may be. It is on this that a man's value must be estimated, and not on the amount of recompense received.

In a reasonably directed State care must be taken that each individual is given the kind of work which corresponds to his capabilities. In other words, people will be trained for the positions indicated by their natural endowments; but these endowments or faculties are innate and cannot be acquired by any amount of training, being a gift from Nature and not merited by men. Therefore, the way in which men are generally esteemed by their fellow-citizens must not be according to the kind of work they do, because that has been more or less assigned to the individual. Seeing that the kind of work in which the individual is employed is to be accounted to his inborn gifts and the resultant training which he has received from the community, he will have to be judged by the way in which he performs this work entrusted to him by the community. For the work which the individual performs is not the purpose of his existence, but only a means. His real purpose in life is to better himself and raise himself to a higher level as a human being; but this he can only do in and through the community whose cultural life he shares. And this community must always exist on the foundations on which the State is based. He ought to contribute to the conservation of those foundations. Nature determines the form of this contribution. It is the duty of the individual to return to the community, zealously and honestly, what the community has given him. He who does this deserves the highest respect and esteem. Material remuneration may be given to him whose work has a corresponding utility for the community; but the ideal recompense must lie in the esteem to which everybody has a claim who serves his people with whatever powers Nature has bestowed upon him and which have been developed by the training he has received from the national community. Then it will no longer be dishonourable to be an honest craftsman; but it will be a cause of disgrace to be an inefficient State official, wasting God's day and filching daily bread from an honest public. Then it will be looked upon as quite natural that positions should not be given to persons who of their very nature are incapable of filling them.

Furthermore, this personal efficiency will be the sole criterion of the right to take part on an equal juridical footing in general civil affairs.

The present epoch is working out its own ruin. It introduces universal suffrage, chatters about equal rights but can find no foundation for this equality. It considers the material wage as the expression of a man's value and thus destroys the basis of the noblest kind of equality that can exist. For equality cannot and does not depend on the work a man does, but only on the manner in which each one does the particular work allotted to him. Thus alone will mere natural chance be set aside in determining the work of a man and thus only does the individual become the artificer of his own social worth.

At the present time, when whole groups of people estimate each other's value only by the size of the salaries which they respectively receive, there will be no understanding of all this. But that is no reason why we should cease to champion those ideas. Quite the opposite: in an epoch which is inwardly diseased and decaying anyone who would heal it must have the courage first to lay bare the real roots of the disease. And the National Socialist Movement must take that duty on its shoulders. It will have to lift its voice above the heads of the small bourgeoisie and rally together and co-ordinate all those popular forces which are ready to become the protagonists of a new WELTANSCHAUUNG.

Of course the objection will be made that in general it is difficult to differentiate between the material and ideal values of work and that the lower prestige which is attached to physical labour is due to the fact that smaller wages are paid for that kind of work. It will be said that the lower wage is in its turn the reason why the manual worker has less chance to participate in the culture of the nation; so that the ideal side of human culture is less open to him because it has nothing to do with his daily activities. It may be added that the reluctance to do physical work is justified by the fact that, on account of the small income, the cultural level of manual labourers must naturally be low, and that this in turn is a justification for the lower estimation in which manual labour is generally held.

There is quite a good deal of truth in all this. But that is the very reason why we ought to see that in the future there should not be such a wide difference in the scale of remuneration. Don't say that under such conditions poorer work would be done. It would be the saddest symptom of decadence if finer intellectual work could be obtained only through the stimulus of higher payment. If that point of view had ruled the world up to now humanity would never have acquired its greatest scientific and cultural heritage. For all the greatest inventions, the greatest discoveries, the most profoundly revolutionary scientific work, and the most magnificent monuments of human culture, were never given to the world under the impulse or compulsion of money. Quite the contrary: not rarely was their origin associated with a renunciation of the worldly pleasures that wealth can purchase.

It may be that money has become the one power that governs life to-day. Yet a time will come when men will again bow to higher gods. Much that we have to-day owes its existence to the desire for money and property; but there is very little among all this which would leave the world poorer by its lack.

It is also one of the aims before our movement to hold out the prospect of a time when the individual will be given what he needs for the purposes of his life and it will be a time in which, on the other hand, the principle will be upheld that man does not live for material enjoyment alone. This principle will find expression in a wiser scale of wages and salaries which will enable everyone, including the humblest workman who fulfils his duties conscientiously, to live an honourable and decent life both as a man and as a citizen. Let it not be said that this is merely a visionary ideal, that this world would never tolerate it in practice and that of itself it is impossible to attain.

Even we are not so simple as to believe that there will ever be an age in which there will be no drawbacks. But that does not release us from the obligation to fight for the removal of the defects which we have recognized, to overcome the shortcomings and to strive towards the ideal. In any case the hard reality of the facts to be faced will always place only too many limits to our aspirations. But that is precisely why man must strive again and again to serve the ultimate aim and no failures must induce him to renounce his intentions, just as we cannot spurn the sway of justice because mistakes creep into the administration of the law, and just as we cannot despise medical science because, in spite of it, there will always be diseases.

Man should take care not to have too low an estimate of the power of an ideal. If there are some who may feel disheartened over the present conditions, and if they happen to have served as soldiers, I would remind them of the time when their heroism was the most convincing example of the power inherent in ideal motives. It was not preoccupation about their daily bread that led men to sacrifice their lives, but the love of their country, the faith which they had in its greatness, and an all round feeling for the honour of the nation. Only after the German people had become estranged from these ideals, to follow the material promises offered by the Revolution, only after they threw away their arms to take up the rucksack, only then—instead of entering an earthly paradise—did they sink into the purgatory of universal contempt and at the same time universal want.

That is why we must face the calculators of the materialist Republic with faith in an idealist REICH.

CHAPTER III:
Citizens and Subjects of the State

The institution that is now erroneously called the State generally classifies people only into two groups: citizens and aliens. Citizens are all those who possess full civic rights, either by reason of their birth or by an act of naturalization. Aliens are those who enjoy the same rights in some other State. Between these two categories there are certain beings who resemble a sort of meteoric phenomena. They are people who have no citizenship in any State and consequently no civic rights anywhere.

In most cases nowadays a person acquires civic rights by being born within the frontiers of a State. The race or nationality to which he may belong plays no role whatsoever. The child of a Negro who once lived in one of the German protectorates and now takes up his residence in Germany automatically becomes a 'German Citizen' in the eyes of the world. In the same way the child of any Jew, Pole, African or Asian may automatically become a German Citizen.

Besides naturalization that is acquired through the fact of having been born within the confines of a State there exists another kind of naturalization which can be acquired later. This process is subject to various preliminary requirements. For example one condition is that, if possible, the applicant must not be a burglar or a common street thug. It is required of him that his political attitude is not such as to give cause for uneasiness; in other words he must be a harmless simpleton in politics. It is required that he shall not be a burden to the State of which he wishes to become a citizen. In this realistic epoch of ours this last condition naturally only means that he must not be a financial burden. If the affairs of the candidate are such that it appears likely he will turn out to be a good taxpayer, that is a very important consideration and will help him to obtain civic rights all the more rapidly.

The question of race plays no part at all.

The whole process of acquiring civic rights is not very different from that of being admitted to membership of an automobile club, for instance. A person files his application. It is examined. It is sanctioned. And one day the man receives a card which informs him that he has become a citizen. The information is given in an amusing way. An applicant who has hitherto been a Zulu or Kaffir is told: "By these presents you are now become a German Citizen."

The President of the State can perform this piece of magic. What God Himself could not do is achieved by some Theophrastus Paracelsus[17] of a civil servant through a mere twirl of the hand. Nothing but a stroke of the pen, and a Mongolian slave is forthwith turned into a real German. Not only is no question asked regarding the race to which the new citizen belongs; even the matter of his physical health is not inquired into. His flesh may be corrupted with syphilis; but he will still be welcome in the State as it exists to-day so long as he may not become a financial burden or a political danger.

In this way, year after year, those organisms which we call States take up poisonous matter which they can hardly ever overcome.

Another point of distinction between a citizen and an alien is that the former is admitted to all public offices, that he may possibly have to do military service and that in return he is permitted to take a passive or active part at public elections. Those are his chief privileges. For in regard to personal rights and personal liberty the alien enjoys the same amount of protection as the citizen, and frequently even more. Anyhow that is how it happens in our present German Republic.

I realize fully that nobody likes to hear these things. But it would be difficult to find anything more illogical or more insane than our contemporary laws in regard to State citizenship.

At present there exists one State which manifests at least some modest attempts that show a better appreciation of how things ought to be done in this matter. It is not, however, in our model German Republic but in the U.S.A. that efforts are made to conform at least partly to the counsels of commonsense. By refusing immigrants to enter there if they are in a bad state of health, and by excluding certain races from the right to become naturalized as citizens, they have begun to introduce principles similar to those on which we wish to ground the People's State.

The People's State will classify its population in three groups: Citizens, subjects of the State, and aliens.

The principle is that birth within the confines of the State gives only the status of a subject. It does not carry with it the right to fill any position under the State or to participate in political life, such as taking an active or passive part in elections. Another principle is that the race and nationality of every subject of the State will have to be proved. A subject is at any time free to cease being a subject and to become a citizen of that country to which he belongs in virtue of his nationality. The only difference between an alien and a subject of the State is that the former is a citizen of another country.

The young boy or girl who is of German nationality and is a subject of the German State is bound to complete the period of school education which is obligatory for every German. Thereby he submits to the system of training which will make him conscious of his race and a member of the folk-community. Then he has to fulfil all those requirements laid down by the State in regard to physical training after he has left school; and finally he enters the army. The training in the army is of a general kind. It must be given to each individual German and will render him competent to fulfil the physical and mental requirements of military service. The rights of citizenship shall be conferred on every young man whose health and character have been certified as good, after having completed his period of military service. This act of inauguration in citizenship shall be a solemn ceremony. And the diploma conferring the rights of citizenship will be preserved by the young man as the most precious testimonial of his whole life. It entitles him to exercise all the rights of a citizen and to enjoy all the privileges attached thereto. For the State must draw a sharp line of distinction between those who, as members of the nation, are the foundation and the support of its existence and greatness, and those who are domiciled in the State simply as earners of their livelihood there.

On the occasion of conferring a diploma of citizenship the new citizen must take a solemn oath of loyalty to the national community and the State. This diploma must be a bond which unites together all the various classes and sections of the nation. It shall be a greater honour to be a citizen of this REICH, even as a street-sweeper, than to be the King of a foreign State.

The citizen has privileges which are not accorded to the alien. He is the master in the REICH. But this high honour has also its obligations. Those who show themselves without personal honour or character, or common criminals, or traitors to the fatherland, can at any time be deprived of the rights of citizenship. Therewith they become merely subjects of the State.

The German girl is a subject of the State but will become a citizen when she marries. At the same time those women who earn their livelihood independently have the right to acquire citizenship if they are German subjects.

CHAPTER IV: Personality and the Ideal of the People's State

I f the principal duty of the National Socialist People's State be to educate and promote the existence of those who are the material out of which the State is formed, it will not be sufficient to promote those racial elements as such, educate them and finally train them for practical life, but the State must also adapt its own organization to meet the demands of this task.

It would be absurd to appraise a man's worth by the race to which he belongs and at the same time to make war against the Marxist principle, that all men are equal, without being determined to pursue our own principle to its ultimate consequences. If we admit the significance of blood, that is to say, if we recognize the race as the fundamental element on which all life is based, we shall have to apply to the individual the logical consequences of this principle. In general I must estimate the worth of nations differently, on the basis of the different races from which they spring, and I must also differentiate in estimating the worth of the individual within his own race. The principle, that one people is not the same as another, applies also to the individual members of a national community. No one brain, for instance, is equal to another; because the constituent elements belonging to the same blood vary in a thousand subtle details, though they are fundamentally of the same quality.

The first consequence of this fact is comparatively simple. It demands that those elements within the folk-community which show the best racial qualities ought to be encouraged more than the others and especially they should be encouraged to increase and multiply.

This task is comparatively simple because it can be recognized and carried out almost mechanically. It is much more difficult to select from among a whole multitude of people all those who actually possess the highest intellectual and spiritual characteristics and assign them to that sphere of influence which not only corresponds to their outstanding talents but in which their activities will above all things be of benefit to the nation. This selection according to capacity and efficiency cannot be effected in a mechanical way. It is a work which can be accomplished only through the permanent struggle of everyday life itself.

A WELTANSCHAUUNG which repudiates the democratic principle of the rule of the masses and aims at giving this world to the best people—that is, to the highest quality of mankind—must also apply that same aristocratic postulate to the individuals within the folk-community. It must take care that the positions of leadership and highest influence are given to the best men. Hence it is not based on the idea of the majority, but on that of personality.

Anyone who believes that the People's National Socialist State should distinguish itself from the other States only mechanically, as it were, through the better construction of its economic life—thanks to a better equilibrium between poverty and riches, or to the extension to broader masses of the power to determine the economic process, or to a fairer wage, or to the elimination of vast differences in the scale of salaries—anyone who thinks this understands only the superficial features of our movement and has not the least idea of what we mean when we speak of our WELTANSCHAUUNG. All these features just mentioned could not in the least guarantee us a lasting existence and certainly would be no warranty of greatness. A nation that could content itself with external reforms would not have the slightest chance of success in the general struggle for life among the nations of the world. A movement that would confine its mission to such adjustments, which are certainly right and equitable, would effect no far-reaching or profound reform in the existing order. The whole effect of such measures would be limited to externals. They would not furnish the nation with that moral armament which alone will enable it effectively to overcome the weaknesses from which we are suffering to-day.

In order to elucidate this point of view it may be worth while to glance once again at the real origins and causes of the cultural evolution of mankind.

The first step which visibly brought mankind away from the animal world was that which led to the first invention. The invention itself owes its origin to the ruses and stratagems which man employed to assist him in the struggle with other creatures for his existence and often to provide him with the only means he could adopt to achieve success in the struggle. Those first very crude inventions cannot be attributed to the individual; for the subsequent observer, that is to say the modern observer, recognizes them only as collective phenomena. Certain tricks and skilful tactics which can be observed in use among the animals strike the eye of the observer as established facts which may be seen everywhere; and man is no longer in a position to discover or explain their primary cause and so he contents himself with calling such phenomena 'instinctive.'

In our case this term has no meaning. Because everyone who believes in the higher evolution of living organisms must admit that every manifestation of the vital urge and struggle to live must have had a definite beginning in time and that one subject alone must have manifested it for the first time. It was then repeated again and again; and the practice of it spread over a widening area, until finally it passed into the subconscience of every member of the species, where it manifested itself as 'instinct.'

This is more easily understood and more easy to believe in the case of man. His first skilled tactics in the struggle with the rest of the animals undoubtedly originated in his management of creatures which possessed special capabilities.

There can be no doubt that personality was then the sole factor in all decisions and achievements, which were afterwards taken over by the whole of humanity as a matter of course. An exact exemplification of this may be found in those fundamental military principles which have now become the basis of all strategy in war. Originally they sprang from the brain of a single individual and in the course of many years, maybe even thousands of years, they were accepted all round as a matter of course and this gained universal validity.

Man completed his first discovery by making a second. Among other things he learned how to master other living beings and make them serve him in his struggle for existence. And thus began the real inventive activity of mankind, as it is now visible before our eyes. Those material inventions, beginning with the use of stones as weapons, which led to the domestication of animals, the production of fire by artificial means, down to the marvellous inventions of our own days, show clearly that an individual was the originator in each case. The nearer we come to our own time and the more important and revolutionary the inventions become, the more clearly do we recognize the truth of that statement. All the material inventions which we see around us have been produced by the creative powers and capabilities of individuals. And all these inventions help man to raise himself higher and higher above the animal world and to separate himself from that world in an absolutely definite way. Hence they serve to elevate the human species and continually to promote its progress. And what the most primitive artifice once did for man in his struggle for existence, as he went hunting through the primeval forest, that same sort of assistance is rendered him to-day in the form of marvellous scientific inventions which help him in the present day struggle for life and to forge weapons for future struggles. In their final consequences all human thought and invention help man in his life-struggle on this planet, even though the so-called practical utility of an invention, a discovery or a profound scientific theory, may not be evident at first sight. Everything contributes to raise man higher and higher above the level of all the other creatures that surround him, thereby strengthening and consolidating his position; so that he develops more and more in every direction as the ruling being on this earth.

Hence all inventions are the result of the creative faculty of the individual. And all such individuals, whether they have willed it or not, are the benefactors of mankind, both great and small. Through their work millions and indeed billions of human beings have been provided with means and resources which facilitate their struggle for existence.

Thus at the origin of the material civilization which flourishes to-day we always see individual persons. They supplement one another and one of them bases his work on that of the other. The same is true in regard to the practical application of those inventions and discoveries. For all the various methods of production are in their turn inventions also and consequently dependent on the creative faculty of the individual. Even the purely theoretical work, which cannot be measured by a definite rule and is preliminary to all subsequent technical discoveries, is exclusively the product of the individual brain. The broad masses do not invent, nor does the majority organize or think; but always and in every case the individual man, the person.

Accordingly a human community is well organized only when it facilitates to the highest possible degree individual creative forces and utilizes their work for the benefit of the community. The most valuable factor of an invention, whether it be in the world of material realities or in the world of abstract ideas, is the personality of the inventor himself. The first and supreme duty of an organized folk community is to place the inventor in a position where he can be of the greatest benefit to all. Indeed the very purpose of the organization is to put this principle into practice. Only by so doing can it ward off the curse of mechanization and remain a living thing. In itself it must personify the effort to place men of brains above the multitude and to make the latter obey the former.

Therefore not only does the organization possess no right to prevent men of brains from rising above the multitude but, on the contrary, it must use its organizing powers to enable and promote that ascension as far as it possibly can. It must start out from the principle that the blessings of mankind never came from the masses but from the creative brains of individuals, who are therefore the real benefactors of humanity. It is in the interest of all to assure men of creative brains a decisive influence and facilitate their work. This common interest is surely not served by allowing the multitude to rule, for they are not capable of thinking nor are they efficient and in no case whatsoever can they be said to be gifted. Only those should rule who have the natural temperament and gifts of leadership.

Such men of brains are selected mainly, as I have already said, through the hard struggle for existence itself. In this struggle there are many who break down and collapse and thereby show that they are not called by Destiny to fill the highest positions; and only very few are left who can be classed among the elect. In the realm of thought and of artistic creation, and even in the economic field, this same process of selection takes place, although—especially in the economic field—its operation is heavily handicapped. This same principle of selection rules in the administration of the State and in that department of power which personifies the organized military defence of the nation. The idea of personality rules everywhere, the authority of the individual over his subordinates and the responsibility of the individual towards the persons who are placed over him. It is only in political life that this very natural principle has been completely excluded. Though all human civilization has resulted exclusively from the creative activity of the individual, the principle that it is the mass which counts—through the decision of the majority—makes its appearance only in the administration of the national community especially in the higher grades; and from there downwards the poison gradually filters into all branches of national life, thus causing a veritable decomposition. The destructive workings of Judaism in different parts of the national body can be ascribed fundamentally to the persistent Jewish efforts at undermining the importance of personality among the nations that are their hosts and, in place of personality, substituting the domination of the masses. The constructive principle of Aryan humanity is thus displaced by the destructive principle of the Jews, They become the 'ferment of decomposition' among nations and races and, in a broad sense, the wreckers of human civilization.

Marxism represents the most striking phase of the Jewish endeavour to eliminate the dominant significance of personality in every sphere of human life and replace it by the numerical power of the masses. In politics the parliamentary form of government is the expression of this effort. We can observe the fatal effects of it everywhere, from the smallest parish council upwards to the highest governing circles of the nation. In the field of economics we see the trade union movement, which does not serve the real interests of the employees but the destructive aims of international Jewry. Just to the same degree in which the principle of personality is excluded from the economic life of the nation, and the influence and activities of the masses substituted in its stead, national economy, which should be for the service and benefit of the community as a whole, will gradually deteriorate in its creative capacity. The shop committees which, instead of caring for the interests of the employees, strive to influence the process of production, serve the same destructive purpose. They damage the general productive system and consequently injure the individual engaged in industry. For in the long run it is impossible to satisfy popular demands merely by high-sounding theoretical phrases. These can be satisfied only by supplying goods to meet the individual needs of daily life and by so doing create the conviction that, through the productive collaboration of its members, the folk community serves the interests of the individual.

Even if, on the basis of its mass-theory, Marxism should prove itself capable of taking over and developing the present economic system, that would not signify anything. The question as to whether the Marxist doctrine be right or wrong cannot be decided by any test which would show that it can administer for the future what already exists to-day, but only by asking whether it has the creative power to build up according to its own principles a civilization which would be a counterpart of what already exists. Even if Marxism were a thousandfold capable of taking over the economic life as we now have it and maintaining it in operation under Marxist direction, such an achievement would prove nothing; because, on the basis of its own principles, Marxism would never be able to create something which could supplant what exists to-day.

And Marxism itself has furnished the proof that it cannot do this. Not only has it been unable anywhere to create a cultural or economic system of its own; but it was not even able to develop, according to its own principles, the civilization and economic system it found ready at hand. It has had to make compromises, by way of a return to the principle of personality, just as it cannot dispense with that principle in its own organization.

The racial WELTANSCHAUUNG is fundamentally distinguished from the Marxist by reason of the fact that the former recognizes the significance of race and therefore also personal worth and has made these the pillars of its structure. These are the most important factors of its WELTANSCHAUUNG.

If the National Socialist Movement should fail to understand the fundamental importance of this essential principle, if it should merely varnish the external appearance of the present State and adopt the majority principle, it would really do nothing more than compete with Marxism on its own ground. For that reason it would not have the right to call itself a WELTANSCHAUUNG. If the social programme of the movement consisted in eliminating personality and putting the multitude in its place, then National Socialism would be corrupted with the poison of Marxism, just as our national-bourgeois parties are.

The People's State must assure the welfare of its citizens by recognizing the importance of personal values under all circumstances and by preparing the way for the maximum of productive efficiency in all the various branches of economic life, thus securing to the individual the highest possible share in the general output.

Hence the People's State must mercilessly expurgate from all the leading circles in the government of the country the parliamentarian principle, according to which decisive power through the majority vote is invested in the multitude. Personal responsibility must be substituted in its stead.

From this the following conclusion results:

The best constitution and the best form of government is that which makes it quite natural for the best brains to reach a position of dominant importance and influence in the community. Just as in the field of economics men of outstanding ability cannot be designated from above but must come forward in virtue of their own efforts, and just as there is an unceasing educative process that leads from the smallest shop to the largest undertaking, and just as life itself is the school in which those lessons are taught, so in the political field it is not possible to 'discover' political talent all in a moment. Genius of an extraordinary stamp is not to be judged by normal standards whereby we judge other men.

In its organization the State must be established on the principle of personality, starting from the smallest cell and ascending up to the supreme government of the country.

There are no decisions made by the majority vote, but only by responsible persons. And the word 'council' is once more restored to its original meaning. Every man in a position of responsibility will have councillors at his side, but the decision is made by that individual person alone.

The principle which made the former Prussian Army an admirable instrument of the German nation will have to become the basis of our statal constitution, that is to say, full authority over his subordinates must be invested in each leader and he must be responsible to those above him.

Even then we shall not be able to do without those corporations which at present we call parliaments. But they will be real councils, in the sense that they will have to give advice. The responsibility can and must be borne by one individual, who alone will be vested with authority and the right to command.

Parliaments as such are necessary because they alone furnish the opportunity for leaders to rise gradually who will be entrusted subsequently with positions of special responsibility.

The following is an outline of the picture which the organization will present:

From the municipal administration up to the government of the REICH, the People's State will not have any body of representatives which makes its decisions through the majority vote. It will have only advisory bodies to assist the chosen leader for the time being and he will distribute among them the various duties they are to perform. In certain fields they may, if necessary, have to assume full responsibility, such as the leader or president of each corporation possesses on a larger scale.

In principle the People's State must forbid the custom of taking advice on certain political problems—economics, for instance—from persons who are entirely incompetent because they lack special training and practical experience in such matters. Consequently the State must divide its representative bodies into a political chamber and a corporative chamber that represents the respective trades and professions.

To assure an effective co-operation between those two bodies, a selected body will be placed over them. This will be a special senate.

No vote will be taken in the chambers or senate. They are to be organizations for work and not voting machines. The individual members will have consultive votes but no right of decision will be attached thereto. The right of decision belongs exclusively to the president, who must be entirely responsible for the matter under discussion.

This principle of combining absolute authority with absolute responsibility will gradually cause a selected group of leaders to emerge; which is not even thinkable in our present epoch of irresponsible parliamentarianism.

The political construction of the nation will thereby be brought into harmony with those laws to which the nation already owes its greatness in the economic and cultural spheres.

Regarding the possibility of putting these principles into practice, I should like to call attention to the fact that the principle of parliamentarian democracy, whereby decisions are enacted through the majority vote, has not always ruled the world. On the contrary, we find it prevalent only during short periods of history, and those have always been periods of decline in nations and States.

One must not believe, however, that such a radical change could be effected by measures of a purely theoretical character, operating from above downwards; for the change I have been describing could not be limited to transforming the constitution of a State but would have to include the various fields of legislation and civic existence as a whole. Such a revolution can be brought about only by means of a movement which is itself organized under the inspiration of these principles and thus bears the germ of the future State in its own organism.

Therefore it is well for the National Socialist Movement to make itself completely familiar with those principles to-day and actually to put them into practice within its own organization, so that not only will it be in a position to serve as a guide for the future State but will have its own organization such that it can subsequently be placed at the disposal of the State itself.

CHAPTER V:
Weltanschauung and Organization

The People's State, which I have tried to sketch in general outline, will not become a reality in virtue of the simple fact that we know the indispensable conditions of its existence. It does not suffice to know what aspect such a State would present. The problem of its foundation is far more important. The parties which exist at present and which draw their profits from the State as it now is cannot be expected to bring about a radical change in the regime or to change their attitude on their own initiative. This is rendered all the more impossible because the forces which now have the direction of affairs in their hands are Jews here and Jews there and Jews everywhere. The trend of development which we are now experiencing would, if allowed to go on unhampered, lead to the realization of the Pan-Jewish prophecy that the Jews will one day devour the other nations and become lords of the earth.

In contrast to the millions of 'bourgeois' and 'proletarian' Germans, who are stumbling to their ruin, mostly through timidity, indolence and stupidity, the Jew pursues his way persistently and keeps his eye always fixed on his future goal. Any party that is led by him can fight for no other interests than his, and his interests certainly have nothing in common with those of the Aryan nations.

If we would transform our ideal picture of the People's State into a reality we shall have to keep independent of the forces that now control public life and seek for new forces that will be ready and capable of taking up the fight for such an ideal. For a fight it will have to be, since the first objective will not be to build up the idea of the People's State but rather to wipe out the Jewish State which is now in existence. As so often happens in the course of history, the main difficulty is not to establish a new order of things but to clear the ground for its establishment. Prejudices and egotistic interests join together in forming a common front against the new idea and in trying by every means to prevent its triumph, because it is disagreeable to them or threatens their existence.

That is why the protagonist of the new idea is unfortunately, in spite of his {254}desire for constructive work, compelled to wage a destructive battle first, in order to abolish the existing state of affairs.

A doctrine whose principles are radically new and of essential importance must adopt the sharp probe of criticism as its weapon, though this may show itself disagreeable to the individual followers.

It is evidence of a very superficial insight into historical developments if the so-called folkists emphasize again and again that they will adopt the use of negative criticism under no circumstances but will engage only in constructive work. That is nothing but puerile chatter and is typical of the whole lot of folkists. It is another proof that the history of our own times has made no impression on these minds. Marxism too has had its aims to pursue and it also recognizes constructive work, though by this it understands only the establishment of despotic rule in the hands of international Jewish finance. Nevertheless for seventy years its principal work still remains in the field of criticism. And what disruptive and destructive criticism it has been! Criticism repeated again and again, until the corrosive acid ate into the old State so thoroughly that it finally crumbled to pieces. Only then did the so-called 'constructive' critical work of Marxism begin. And that was natural, right and logical. An existing order of things is not abolished by merely proclaiming and insisting on a new one. It must not be hoped that those who are the partisans of the existing order and have their interests bound up with it will be converted and won over to the new movement simply by being shown that something new is necessary. On the contrary, what may easily happen is that two different situations will exist side by side and that a WELTANSCHAUUNG is transformed into a party, above which level it will not be able to raise itself afterwards. For a WELTANSCHAUUNG is intolerant and cannot permit another to exist side by side with it. It imperiously demands its own recognition as unique and exclusive and a complete transformation in accordance with its views throughout all the branches of public life. It can never allow the previous state of affairs to continue in existence by its side.

And the same holds true of religions.

Christianity was not content with erecting an altar of its own. It had first to destroy the pagan altars. It was only in virtue of this passionate intolerance that an apodictic faith could grow up. And intolerance is an indispensable condition for the growth of such a faith.

It may be objected here that in these phenomena which we find throughout the history of the world we have to recognize mostly a specifically Jewish mode of thought and that such fanaticism and intolerance are typical symptoms of Jewish mentality. That may be a thousandfold true; and it is a fact deeply to be regretted. The appearance of intolerance and fanaticism in the history of mankind may be deeply regrettable, and it may be looked upon as foreign to human nature, but the fact does not change conditions as they exist to-day. The men who wish to liberate our German nation from the conditions in which it now exists cannot cudgel their brains with thinking how excellent it would be if this or that had never arisen. They must strive to find ways and means of abolishing what actually exists. A philosophy of life which is inspired by an infernal spirit of intolerance can only be set aside by a doctrine that is advanced in an equally ardent spirit and fought for with as determined a will and which is itself a new idea, pure and absolutely true.

Each one of us to-day may regret the fact that the advent of Christianity was the first occasion on which spiritual terror was introduced into the much freer ancient world, but the fact cannot be denied that ever since then the world is pervaded and dominated by this kind of coercion and that violence is broken only by violence and terror by terror. Only then can a new regime be created by means of constructive work. Political parties are prone to enter compromises; but a WELTANSCHAUUNG never does this. A political party is inclined to adjust its teachings with a view to meeting those of its opponents, but a WELTANSCHAUUNG proclaims its own infallibility.

In the beginning, political parties have also and nearly always the intention of {255}securing an exclusive and despotic domination for themselves. They always show a slight tendency to become WELTANSCHHAUUNGen. But the limited nature of their programme is in itself enough to rob them of that heroic spirit which a WELTANSCHAUUNG demands. The spirit of conciliation which animates their will attracts those petty and chicken-hearted people who are not fit to be protagonists in any crusade. That is the reason why they mostly become struck in their miserable pettiness very early on the march. They give up fighting for their ideology and, by way of what they call 'positive collaboration,' they try as quickly as possible to wedge themselves into some tiny place at the trough of the existent regime and to stick there as long as possible. Their whole effort ends at that. And if they should get shouldered away from the common manger by a competition of more brutal manners then their only idea is to force themselves in again, by force or chicanery, among the herd of all the others who have similar appetites, in order to get back into the front row, and finally—even at the expense of their most sacred convictions—participate anew in that beloved spot where they find their fodder. They are the jackals of politics.

But a general WELTANSCHAUUNG will never share its place with something else. Therefore it can never agree to collaborate in any order of things that it condemns. On the contrary it feels obliged to employ every means in fighting against the old order and the whole world of ideas belonging to that order and prepare the way for its destruction.

These purely destructive tactics, the danger of which is so readily perceived by the enemy that he forms a united front against them for his common defence, and also the constructive tactics, which must be aggressive in order to carry the new world of ideas to success—both these phases of the struggle call for a body of resolute fighters. Any new philosophy of life will bring its ideas to victory only if the most courageous and active elements of its epoch and its people are enrolled under its standards and grouped firmly together in a powerful fighting organization. To achieve this purpose it is absolutely necessary to select from the general system of doctrine a certain number of ideas which will appeal to such individuals and which, once they are expressed in a precise and clear-cut form, will serve as articles of faith for a new association of men. While the programme of the ordinary political party is nothing but the recipe for cooking up favourable results out of the next general elections, the programme of a WELTANSCHAUUNG represents a declaration of war against an existing order of things, against present conditions, in short, against the established WELTANSCHAUUNG.

It is not necessary, however, that every individual fighter for such a new doctrine need have a full grasp of the ultimate ideas and plans of those who are the leaders of the movement. It is only necessary that each should have a clear notion of the fundamental ideas and that he should thoroughly assimilate a few of the most fundamental principles, so that he will be convinced of the necessity of carrying the movement and its doctrines to success. The individual soldier is not initiated in the knowledge of high strategical plans. But he is trained to submit to a rigid discipline, to be passionately convinced of the justice and inner worth of his cause and that he must devote himself to it without reserve. So, too, the individual follower of a movement must be made acquainted with its far-reaching purpose, how it is inspired by a powerful will and has a great future before it.

Supposing that each soldier in an army were a general, and had the training and capacity for generalship, that army would not be an efficient fighting instrument. Similarly a political movement would not be very efficient in fighting for a WELTANSCHAUUNG if it were made up exclusively of intellectuals. No, we need the simple soldier also. Without him no discipline can be established.

By its very nature, an organization can exist only if leaders of high intellectual ability are served by a large mass of men who are emotionally devoted to the cause. To maintain discipline in a company of two hundred men who are equally intelligent and capable would turn out more difficult in the long run than in a company of one hundred and ninety less gifted men and ten who have had a higher education.

{256}The Social-Democrats have profited very much by recognizing this truth. They took the broad masses of our people who had just completed military service and learned to submit to discipline, and they subjected this mass of men to the discipline of the Social-Democratic organization, which was no less rigid than the discipline through which the young men had passed in their military training. The Social-Democratic organization consisted of an army divided into officers and men. The German worker who had passed through his military service became the private soldier in that army, and the Jewish intellectual was the officer. The German trade union functionaries may be compared to the non-commissioned officers. The fact, which was always looked upon with indifference by our middle-classes, that only the so-called uneducated classes joined Marxism was the very ground on which this party achieved its success. For while the bourgeois parties, because they mostly consisted of intellectuals, were only a feckless band of undisciplined individuals, out of much less intelligent human material the Marxist leaders formed an army of party combatants who obey their Jewish masters just as blindly as they formerly obeyed their German officers. The German middle-classes, who never; bothered their heads about psychological problems because they felt themselves superior to such matters, did not think it necessary to reflect on the profound significance of this fact and the secret danger involved in it. Indeed they believed. that a political movement which draws its followers exclusively from intellectual circles must, for that very reason, be of greater importance and have better grounds. for its chances of success, and even a greater probability of taking over the government of the country than a party made up of the ignorant masses. They completely failed to realize the fact that the strength of a political party never consists in the intelligence and independent spirit of the rank-and-file of its members but rather in the spirit of willing obedience with which they follow their intellectual leaders. What is of decisive importance is the leadership itself. When two bodies of troops are arrayed in mutual combat victory will not fall to that side in which every soldier has an expert knowledge of the rules of strategy, but rather to that side which has the best leaders and at the same time the best disciplined, most blindly obedient and best drilled troops.

That is a fundamental piece of knowledge which we must always bear in mind when we examine the possibility of transforming a WELTANSCHAUUNG into a practical reality.

If we agree that in order to carry a WELTANSCHAUUNG into practical effect it must be incorporated in a fighting movement, then the logical consequence is that the programme of such a movement must take account of the human material at its disposal. Just as the ultimate aims and fundamental principles must be absolutely definite and unmistakable, so the propagandist programme must be well drawn up and must be inspired by a keen sense of its psychological appeals to the minds of those without whose help the noblest ideas will be doomed to remain in the eternal, realm of ideas.

If the idea of the People's State, which is at present an obscure wish, is one day to attain a clear and definite success, from its vague and vast mass of thought it will have to put forward certain definite principles which of their very nature and content are calculated to attract a broad mass of adherents; in other words, such a group of people as can guarantee that these principles will be fought for. That group of people are the German workers.

That is why the programme of the new movement was condensed into a few fundamental postulates, twenty-five in all. They are meant first of all to give the ordinary man a rough sketch of what the movement is aiming at. They are, so to say, a profession of faith which on the one hand is meant to win adherents to the movement and, on the other, they are meant to unite such adherents together in a covenant to which all have subscribed.

In these matters we must never lose sight of the following: What we call the programme of the movement is absolutely right as far as its ultimate aims are concerned, but as regards the manner in which that programme is formulated, certain psychological considerations had to be taken into account. Hence, in the course of time, the opinion may well arise that certain principles should be expressed differently and might be better formulated. But any attempt at a different formulation has a fatal effect in most cases. For something that ought to be fixed and unshakable thereby becomes the subject of discussion. As soon as one point alone is removed from the sphere of dogmatic certainty, the discussion will not simply result in a new and better formulation which will have greater consistency but may easily lead to endless debates and general confusion. In such cases the question must always be carefully considered as to whether a new and more adequate formulation is to be preferred, though it may cause a controversy within the movement, or whether it may not be better to retain the old formula which, though probably not the best, represents an organism enclosed in itself, solid and internally homogeneous. All experience shows that the second of these alternatives is preferable. For since in these changes one is dealing only with external forms such corrections will always appear desirable and possible. But in the last analysis the generality of people think superficially and therefore the great danger is that in what is merely an external formulation of the programme people will see an essential aim of the movement. In that way the will and the combative force at the service of the ideas are weakened and the energies that ought to be directed towards the outer world are dissipated in programmatic discussions within the ranks of the movement.

For a doctrine that is actually right in its main features it is less dangerous to retain a formulation which may no longer be quite adequate instead of trying to improve it and thereby allowing a fundamental principle of the movement, which had hitherto been considered as solid as granite, to become the subject of a general discussion which may have unfortunate consequences. This is particularly to be avoided as long as a movement is still fighting for victory. For would it be possible to inspire people with blind faith in the truth of a doctrine if doubt and uncertainty are encouraged by continual alterations in its external formulation?

The essentials of a teaching must never be looked for in its external formulas, but always in its inner meaning. And this meaning is unchangeable. And in its interest one can only wish that a movement should exclude everything that tends towards disintegration and uncertainty in order to preserve the unified force that is necessary for its triumph.

Here again the Catholic Church has a lesson to teach us. Though sometimes, and often quite unnecessarily, its dogmatic system is in conflict with the exact sciences and with scientific discoveries, it is not disposed to sacrifice a syllable of its teachings. It has rightly recognized that its powers of resistance would be weakened by introducing greater or less doctrinal adaptations to meet the temporary conclusions of science, which in reality are always vacillating. And thus it holds fast to its fixed and established dogmas which alone can give to the whole system the character of a faith. And that is the reason why it stands firmer to-day than ever before. We may prophesy that, as a fixed pole amid fleeting phenomena, it will continue to attract increasing numbers of people who will be blindly attached to it the more rapid the rhythm of changing phenomena around it.

Therefore whoever really and seriously desires that the idea of the People's State should triumph must realize that this triumph can be assured only through a militant movement and that this movement must ground its strength only on the granite firmness of an impregnable and firmly coherent programme. In regard to its formulas it must never make concessions to the spirit of the time but must maintain the form that has once and for all been decided upon as the right one; in any case until victory has crowned its efforts. Before this goal has been reached any attempt to open a discussion on the opportuneness of this or that point in the programme might tend to disintegrate the solidity and fighting strength of the movement, according to the measures in which its followers might take part in such an internal dispute. Some 'improvements' introduced to-day might be subjected to a critical examination to-morrow, in order to substitute it with something better {258}the day after. Once the barrier has been taken down the road is opened and we know only the beginning, but we do not know to what shoreless sea it may lead.

This important principle had to be acknowledged in practice by the members of the National Socialist Movement at its very beginning. In its programme of twenty-five points the National Socialist German Labour Party has been furnished with a basis that must remain unshakable. The members of the movement, both present and future, must never feel themselves called upon to undertake a critical revision of these leading postulates, but rather feel themselves obliged to put them into practice as they stand. Otherwise the next generation would, in its turn and with equal right, expend its energy in such purely formal work within the party, instead of winning new adherents to the movement and thus adding to its power. For the majority of our followers the essence of the movement will consist not so much in the letter of our theses but in the meaning that we attribute to them.

The new movement owes its name to these considerations, and later on its programme was drawn up in conformity with them. They are the basis of our propaganda. In order to carry the idea of the People's State to victory, a popular party had to be founded, a party that did not consist of intellectual leaders only but also of manual labourers. Any attempt to carry these theories into effect without the aid of a militant organization would be doomed to failure to-day, as it has failed in the past and must fail in the future. That is why the movement is not only justified but it is also obliged to consider itself as the champion and representative of these ideas. Just as the fundamental principles of the National Socialist Movement are based on the folk idea, folk ideas are National Socialist. If National Socialism would triumph it will have to hold firm to this fact unreservedly, and here again it has not only the right but also the duty to emphasize most rigidly that any attempt to represent the folk idea outside of the National Socialist German Labour Party is futile and in most cases fraudulent.

If the reproach should be launched against our movement that it has 'monopolized' the folk idea, there is only one answer to give.

Not only have we monopolized the folk idea but, to all practical intents and purposes, we have created it.

For what hitherto existed under this name was not in the least capable of influencing the destiny of our people, since all those ideas lacked a political and coherent formulation. In most cases they are nothing but isolated and incoherent notions which are more or less right. Quite frequently these were in open contradiction to one another and in no case was there any internal cohesion among them. And even if this internal cohesion existed it would have been much too weak to form the basis of any movement.

Only the National Socialist Movement proved capable of fulfilling this task. All kinds of associations and groups, big as well as little, now claim the title VÖLKISCH. This is one result of the work which National Socialism has done. Without this work, not one of all these parties would have thought of adopting the word VÖLKISCH at all. That expression would have meant nothing to them and especially their directors would never have had anything to do with such an idea. Not until the work of the German National Socialist Labour Party had given this idea a pregnant meaning did it appear in the mouths of all kinds of people. Our party above all, by the success of its propaganda, has shown the force of the folk idea; so much so that the others, in an effort to gain proselytes, find themselves forced to copy our example, at least in words.

Just as heretofore they exploited everything to serve their petty electoral purposes, to-day they use the word VÖLKISCH only as an external and hollow-sounding phrase for the purpose of counteracting the force of the impression which the National Socialist Party makes on the members of those other parties. Only the desire to maintain their existence and the fear that our movement may prevail, because it is based on a WELTANSCHAUUNG that is of universal importance, and because they feel that the exclusive character of our movement betokens danger for them—only for these reasons do they use words which they repudiated eight {259}years ago, derided seven years ago, branded as stupid six years ago, combated five years ago, hated four years ago, and finally, two years ago, annexed and incorporated them in their present political vocabulary, employing them as war slogans in their struggle.

And so it is necessary even now not to cease calling attention to the fact that not one of those parties has the slightest idea of what the German nation needs. The most striking proof of this is represented by the superficial way in which they use the word VÖLKISCH.

Not less dangerous are those who run about as semi-folkists formulating fantastic schemes which are mostly based on nothing else than a fixed idea which in itself might be right but which, because it is an isolated notion, is of no use whatsoever for the formation of a great homogeneous fighting association and could by no means serve as the basis of its organization. Those people who concoct a programme which consists partly of their own ideas and partly of ideas taken from others, about which they have read somewhere, are often more dangerous than the outspoken enemies of the VÖLKISCH idea. At best they are sterile theorists but more frequently they are mischievous agitators of the public mind. They believe that they can mask their intellectual vanity, the futility of their efforts, and their lack of stability, by sporting flowing beards and indulging in ancient German gestures.

In face of all those futile attempts, it is therefore worth while to recall the time when the new National Socialist Movement began its fight.

CHAPTER VI:
The First Period of our Struggle

T
he echoes of our first great meeting, in the banquet hall of the Hofbräuhaus on
February 24th, 1920, had not yet died away when we began preparations for our
next meeting. Up to that time we had to consider carefully the venture of holding a small
meeting every month or at most every fortnight in a city like Munich; but now it was
decided that we should hold a mass meeting every week. I need not say that we anxiously
asked ourselves on each occasion again and again: Will the people come and will they
listen? Personally I was firmly convinced that if once they came they would remain and
listen.

During that period the hall of the Hofbrau Haus in Munich acquired for us, National
Socialists, a sort of mystic significance. Every week there was a meeting, almost always
in that hall, and each time the hall was better filled than on the former occasion, and our
public more attentive.

Starting with the theme, 'Responsibility for the War,' which nobody at that time cared
about, and passing on to the discussion of the peace treaties, we dealt with almost
everything that served to stimulate the minds of our audience and make them interested
in our ideas. We drew attention to the peace treaties. What the new movement prophesied
again and again before those great masses of people has been fulfilled almost in every
detail. To-day it is easy to talk and write about these things. But in those days a public
mass meeting which was attended not by the small bourgeoisie but by proletarians who
had been aroused by agitators, to criticize the Peace Treaty of Versailles meant an attack
on the Republic and an evidence of reaction, if not of monarchist tendencies. The moment
one uttered the first criticism of the Versailles Treaty one could expect an immediate
reply, which became almost stereotyped: 'And Brest-Litowsk?' 'Brest-Litowsk!' And
then the crowd would murmur and the murmur would gradually swell into a roar, until
the speaker would have to give up his attempt to persuade them. It would be like knocking
one's head against a wall, so desperate were these people. They would not listen nor
understand that Versailles was a scandal and a disgrace and that the dictate signified an
act of highway robbery against our people. The disruptive work done by the Marxists
and the poisonous propaganda of the external enemy had robbed these people of their
reason. And one had no right to complain. For the guilt on this side was enormous. What
had the German bourgeoisie done to call a halt to this terrible campaign of disintegration,
to oppose it and open a way to a recognition of the truth by giving a better and more
thorough explanation of the situation than that of the Marxists? Nothing, nothing. At that
time I never saw those who are now the great apostles of the people. Perhaps they spoke
to select groups, at tea parties of their own little coteries; but there where they should
have been, where the wolves were at work, they never risked their appearance, unless it
gave them the opportunity of yelling in concert with the wolves.

As for myself, I then saw clearly that for the small group which first composed our
movement the question of war guilt had to be cleared up, and cleared up in the light of
historical truth. A preliminary condition for the future success of our movement was that
it should bring knowledge of the meaning of the peace treaties to the minds of the popular
masses. In the opinion of the masses, the peace treaties then signified a democratic

success. Therefore, it was necessary to take the opposite side and dig ourselves into the minds of the people as the enemies of the peace treaties; so that later on, when the naked truth of this despicable swindle would be disclosed in all its hideousness, the people would recall the position which we then took and would give us their confidence.

Already at that time I took up my stand on those important fundamental questions where public opinion had gone wrong as a whole. I opposed these wrong notions without regard either for popularity or for hatred, and I was ready to face the fight. The National Socialist German Labour Party ought not to be the beadle but rather the master of public opinion. It must not serve the masses but rather dominate them.

In the case of every movement, especially during its struggling stages, there is naturally a temptation to conform to the tactics of an opponent and use the same battle-cries, when his tactics have succeeded in leading the people to crazy conclusions or to adopt mistaken attitudes towards the questions at issue. This temptation is particularly strong when motives can be found, though they are entirely illusory, that seem to point towards the same ends which the young movement is aiming at. Human poltroonery will then all the more readily adopt those arguments which give it a semblance of justification, 'from its own point of view,' in participating in the criminal policy which the adversary is following.

On several occasions I have experienced such cases, in which the greatest energy had to be employed to prevent the ship of our movement from being drawn into a general current which had been started artificially, and indeed from sailing with it. The last occasion was when our German Press, the Hecuba of the existence of the German nation, succeeded in bringing the question of South Tyrol into a position of importance which was seriously damaging to the interests of the German people. Without considering what interests they were serving, several so-called 'national' men, parties and leagues, joined in the general cry, simply for fear of public opinion which had been excited by the Jews, and foolishly contributed to help in the struggle against a system which we Germans ought, particularly in those days, to consider as the one ray of light in this distracted world. While the international World-Jew is slowly but surely strangling us, our so-called patriots vociferate against a man and his system which have had the courage to liberate themselves from the shackles of Jewish Freemasonry at least in one quarter of the globe and to set the forces of national resistance against the international world-poison. But weak characters were tempted to set their sails according to the direction of the wind and capitulate before the shout of public opinion. For it was veritably a capitulation. They are so much in the habit of lying and so morally base that men may not admit this even to themselves, but the truth remains that only cowardice and fear of the public feeling aroused by the Jews induced certain people to join in the hue and cry. All the other reasons put forward were only miserable excuses of paltry culprits who were conscious of their own crime.

There it was necessary to grasp the rudder with an iron hand and turn the movement about, so as to save it from a course that would have led it on the rocks. Certainly to attempt such a change of course was not a popular manoeuvre at that time, because all the leading forces of public opinion had been active and a great flame of public feeling illuminated only one direction. Such a decision almost always brings disfavour on those who dare to take it. In the course of history not a few men have been stoned for an act for which posterity has afterwards thanked them on its knees.

But a movement must count on posterity and not on the plaudits of the movement. It may well be that at such moments certain individuals have to endure hours of anguish; but they should not forget that the moment of liberation will come and that a movement which purposes to reshape the world must serve the future and not the passing hour.

On this point it may be asserted that the greatest and most enduring successes in history are mostly those which were least understood at the beginning, because they were in strong contrast to public opinion and the views and wishes of the time.

We had experience of this when we made our own first public appearance. In all truth it can be said that we did not court public favour but made an onslaught on the follies of our people. In those days the following happened almost always: I presented myself before an assembly of men who believed the opposite of what I wished to say and who wanted the opposite of what I believed in. Then I had to spend a couple of hours in persuading two or three thousand people to give up the opinions they had first held, in destroying the foundations of their views with one blow after another and finally in leading them over to take their stand on the grounds of our own convictions and our WELTANSCHAUUNG.

I learned something that was important at that time, namely, to snatch from the hands of the enemy the weapons which he was using in his reply. I soon noticed that our adversaries, especially in the persons of those who led the discussion against us, were furnished with a definite repertoire of arguments out of which they took points against our claims which were being constantly repeated. The uniform character of this mode of procedure pointed to a systematic and unified training. And so we were able to recognize the incredible way in which the enemy's propagandists had been disciplined, and I am proud to-day that I discovered a means not only of making this propaganda ineffective but of beating the artificers of it at their own work. Two years later I was master of that art.

In every speech which I made it was important to get a clear idea beforehand of the probable form and matter of the counter-arguments we had to expect in the discussion, so that in the course of my own speech these could be dealt with and refuted. To this end it was necessary to mention all the possible objections and show their inconsistency; it was all the easier to win over an honest listener by expunging from his memory the arguments which had been impressed upon it, so that we anticipated our replies. What he had learned was refuted without having been mentioned by him and that made him all the more attentive to what I had to say.

That was the reason why, after my first lecture on the 'Peace Treaty of Versailles,' which I delivered to the troops while I was still a political instructor in my regiment, I made an alteration in the title and subject and henceforth spoke on 'The Treaties of Brest-Litowsk and Versailles.' For after the discussion which followed my first lecture I quickly ascertained that in reality people knew nothing about the Treaty of Brest-Litowsk and that able party propaganda had succeeded in presenting that Treaty as one of the most scandalous acts of violence in the history of the world.

As a result of the persistency with which this falsehood was repeated again and again before the masses of the people, millions of Germans saw in the Treaty of Versailles a just castigation for the crime we had committed at Brest-Litowsk. Thus they considered all opposition to Versailles as unjust and in many cases there was an honest moral dislike to such a proceeding. And this was also the reason why the shameless and monstrous word 'Reparations' came into common use in Germany. This hypocritical falsehood appeared to millions of our exasperated fellow countrymen as the fulfilment of a higher justice. It is a terrible thought, but the fact was so. The best proof of this was the propaganda which I initiated against Versailles by explaining the Treaty of Brest-Litowsk. I compared the two treaties with one another, point by point, and showed how in truth the one treaty was immensely humane, in contradistinction to the inhuman barbarity of the other. The effect was very striking. Then I spoke on this theme before an assembly of two thousand persons, during which I often saw three thousand six hundred hostile eyes fixed on me. And three hours later I had in front of me a swaying mass of righteous indignation and fury. A great lie had been uprooted from the hearts and brains of a crowd composed of thousands of individuals and a truth had been implanted in its place.

The two lectures—that 'On the Causes of the World War' and 'On the Peace Treaties of Brest-Litowsk and Versailles' respectively—I then considered as the most important of all. Therefore I repeated them dozens of times, always giving them a new intonation; until at least on those points a definitely clear and unanimous opinion reigned among those from whom our movement recruited its first members.

Furthermore, these gatherings brought me the advantage that I slowly became a platform orator at mass meetings, and gave me practice in the pathos and gesture required in large halls that held thousands of people.

Outside of the small circles which I have mentioned, at that time I found no party engaged in explaining things to the people in this way. Not one of these parties was then active which talk to-day as if it was they who had brought about the change in public opinion. If a political leader, calling himself a nationalist, pronounced a discourse somewhere or other on this theme it was only before circles which for the most part were already of his own conviction and among whom the most that was done was to confirm them in their opinions. But that was not what was needed then. What was needed was to win over through propaganda and explanation those whose opinions and mental attitudes held them bound to the enemy's camp.

The one-page circular was also adopted by us to help in this propaganda. While still a soldier I had written a circular in which I contrasted the Treaty of Brest-Litowsk with that of Versailles. That circular was printed and distributed in large numbers. Later on I used it for the party, and also with good success. Our first meetings were distinguished by the fact that there were tables covered with leaflets, papers, and pamphlets of every kind. But we relied principally on the spoken word. And, in fact, this is the only means capable of producing really great revolutions, which can be explained on general psychological grounds.

In the first volume I have already stated that all the formidable events which have changed the aspect of the world were carried through, not by the written but by the spoken word. On that point there was a long discussion in a certain section of the Press during the course of which our shrewd bourgeois people strongly opposed my thesis. But the reason for this attitude confounded the sceptics. The bourgeois intellectuals protested against my attitude simply because they themselves did not have the force or ability to influence the masses through the spoken word; for they always relied exclusively on the help of writers and did not enter the arena themselves as orators for the purpose of arousing the people. The development of events necessarily led to that condition of affairs which is characteristic of the bourgeoisie to-day, namely, the loss of the psychological instinct to act upon and influence the masses.

An orator receives continuous guidance from the people before whom he speaks. This helps him to correct the direction of his speech; for he can always gauge, by the faces of his hearers, how far they follow and understand him, and whether his words are producing the desired effect. But the writer does not know his reader at all. Therefore, from the outset he does not address himself to a definite human group of persons which he has before his eyes but must write in a general way. Hence, up to a certain extent he must fail in psychological finesse and flexibility. Therefore, in general it may be said that a brilliant orator writes better than a brilliant writer can speak, unless the latter has continual practice in public speaking. One must also remember that of itself the multitude is mentally inert, that it remains attached to its old habits and that it is not naturally prone to read something which does not conform with its own pre-established beliefs when such writing does not contain what the multitude hopes to find there. Therefore, some piece of writing which has a particular tendency is for the most part read only by those who are in sympathy with it. Only a leaflet or a placard, on account of its brevity, can hope to arouse a momentary interest in those whose opinions differ from it. The picture, in all its forms, including the film, has better prospects. Here there is less need of elaborating the appeal to the intelligence. It is sufficient if one be careful to have quite short texts, because many people are more ready to accept a pictorial presentation than to read a long written description. In a much shorter time, at one stroke I might say, people will understand a pictorial presentation of something which it would take them a long and laborious effort of reading to understand.

The most important consideration, however, is that one never knows into what hands a piece of written material comes and yet the form in which its subject is presented must remain the same. In general the effect is greater when the form of treatment corresponds to the mental level of the reader and suits his nature. Therefore, a book which is meant for the broad masses of the people must try from the very start to gain its effects through a style and level of ideas which would be quite different from a book intended to be read by the higher intellectual classes.

Only through his capacity for adaptability does the force of the written word approach that of oral speech. The orator may deal with the same subject as a book deals with; but if he has the genius of a great and popular orator he will scarcely ever repeat the same argument or the same material in the same form on two consecutive occasions. He will always follow the lead of the great mass in such a way that from the living emotion of his hearers the apt word which he needs will be suggested to him and in its turn this will go straight to the hearts of his hearers. Should he make even a slight mistake he has the living correction before him. As I have already said, he can read the play of expression on the faces of his hearers, first to see if they understand what he says, secondly to see if they take in the whole of his argument, and, thirdly, in how far they are convinced of the justice of what has been placed before them. Should he observe, first, that his hearers do not understand him he will make his explanation so elementary and clear that they will be able to grasp it, even to the last individual. Secondly, if he feels that they are not capable of following him he will make one idea follow another carefully and slowly until the most slow-witted hearer no longer lags behind. Thirdly, as soon as he has the feeling that they do not seem convinced that he is right in the way he has put things to them he will repeat his argument over and over again, always giving fresh illustrations, and he himself will state their unspoken objection. He will repeat these objections, dissecting them and refuting them, until the last group of the opposition show him by their behaviour and play of expression that they have capitulated before his exposition of the case.

Not infrequently it is a case of overcoming ingrained prejudices which are mostly unconscious and are supported by sentiment rather than reason. It is a thousand times more difficult to overcome this barrier of instinctive aversion, emotional hatred and preventive dissent than to correct opinions which are founded on defective or erroneous knowledge. False ideas and ignorance may be set aside by means of instruction, but emotional resistance never can. Nothing but an appeal to these hidden forces will be effective here. And that appeal can be made by scarcely any writer. Only the orator can hope to make it. A very striking proof of this is found in the fact that, though we had a bourgeois Press which in many cases was well written and produced and had a circulation of millions among the people, it could not prevent the broad masses from becoming the implacable enemies of the bourgeois class. The deluge of papers and books published by the intellectual circles year after year passed over the millions of the lower social strata like water over glazed leather. This proves that one of two things must be true: either that the matter offered in the bourgeois Press was worthless or that it is impossible to reach the hearts of the broad masses by means of the written word alone. Of course, the latter would be specially true where the written material shows such little psychological insight as has hitherto been the case.

It is useless to object here, as certain big Berlin papers of German-National tendencies have attempted to do, that this statement is refuted by the fact that the Marxists have exercised their greatest influence through their writings, and especially through their principal book, published by Karl Marx. Seldom has a more superficial argument been based on a false assumption. What gave Marxism its amazing influence over the broad masses was not that formal printed work which sets forth the Jewish system of ideas, but the tremendous oral propaganda carried on for years among the masses. Out of one hundred thousand German workers scarcely one hundred know of Marx's book. It has been studied much more in intellectual circles and especially by the Jews than by the genuine followers of the movement who come from the lower classes. That work was not written for the masses, but exclusively for the intellectual leaders of the Jewish machine for conquering the world. The engine was heated with quite different stuff: namely, the journalistic Press. What differentiates the bourgeois Press from the Marxist Press is that the latter is written by agitators, whereas the bourgeois Press would like to carry on agitation by means of professional writers. The Social-Democrat sub-editor, who almost always came directly from the meeting to the editorial offices of his paper, felt his job on his finger-tips. But the bourgeois writer who left his desk to appear before the masses already felt ill when he smelled the very odour of the crowd and found that what he had written was useless to him.

What won over millions of workpeople to the Marxist cause was not the EX CATHEDRA style of the Marxist writers but the formidable propagandist work done by tens of thousands of indefatigable agitators, commencing with the leading fiery agitator down to the smallest official in the syndicate, the trusted delegate and the platform orator. Furthermore, there were the hundreds of thousands of meetings where these orators, standing on tables in smoky taverns, hammered their ideas into the heads of the masses, thus acquiring an admirable psychological knowledge of the human material they had to deal with. And in this way they were enabled to select the best weapons for their assault on the citadel of public opinion. In addition to all this there were the gigantic mass-demonstrations with processions in which a hundred thousand men took part. All this was calculated to impress on the petty-hearted individual the proud conviction that, though a small worm, he was at the same time a cell of the great dragon before whose devastating breath the hated bourgeois world would one day be consumed in fire and flame, and the dictatorship of the proletariat would celebrate its conclusive victory.

This kind of propaganda influenced men in such a way as to give them a taste for reading the Social Democratic Press and prepare their minds for its teaching. That Press, in its turn, was a vehicle of the spoken word rather than of the written word. Whereas in the bourgeois camp professors and learned writers, theorists and authors of all kinds, made attempts at talking, in the Marxist camp real speakers often made attempts at writing. And it was precisely the Jew who was most prominent here. In general and because of his shrewd dialectical skill and his knack of twisting the truth to suit his own purposes, he was an effective writer but in reality his MÉTIER was that of a revolutionary orator rather than a writer.

For this reason the journalistic bourgeois world, setting aside the fact that here also the Jew held the whip hand and that therefore this press did not really interest itself in the instructtion of the broad masses, was not able to exercise even the least influence over the opinions held by the great masses of our people.

It is difficult to remove emotional prejudices, psychological bias, feelings, etc., and to put others in their place. Success depends here on imponderable conditions and influences. Only the orator who is gifted with the most sensitive insight can estimate all this. Even the time of day at which the speech is delivered has a decisive influence on its results. The same speech, made by the same orator and on the same theme, will have very different results according as it is delivered at ten o'clock in the forenoon, at three in the afternoon, or in the evening. When I first engaged in public speaking I arranged for meetings to take place in the forenoon and I remember particularly a demonstration that we held in the Munich Kindl Keller 'Against the Oppression of German Districts.' That was the biggest hall then in Munich and the audacity of our undertaking was great. In order to make the hour of the meeting attractive for all the members of our movement and the other people who might come, I fixed it for ten o'clock on a Sunday morning. The result was depressing. But it was very instructive. The hall was filled. The impression was profound, but the general feeling was cold as ice. Nobody got warmed up, and I myself, as the speaker of the occasion, felt profoundly unhappy at the thought that I could not establish the slightest contact with my audience. I do not think I spoke worse than before, but the effect seemed absolutely negative. I left the hall very discontented, but also feeling that I had gained a new experience. Later on I tried the same kind of experiment, but always with the same results.

That was nothing to be wondered at. If one goes to a theatre to see a matinée performance and then attends an evening performance of the same play one is astounded at the difference in the impressions created. A sensitive person recognizes for himself the fact that these two states of mind caused by the matinee and the evening performance respectively are quite different in themselves. The same is true of cinema productions. This latter point is important; for one may say of the theatre that perhaps in the afternoon the actor does not make the same effort as in the evening. But surely it cannot be said that the cinema is different in the afternoon from what it is at nine o'clock in the evening. No, here the time exercises a distinct influence, just as a room exercises a distinct influence on a person. There are rooms which leave one cold, for reasons which are difficult to explain. There are rooms which refuse steadfastly to allow any favourable atmosphere to be created in them. Moreover, certain memories and traditions which are present as pictures in the human mind may have a determining influence on the impression produced. Thus, a representation of Parsifal at Bayreuth will have an effect quite different from that which the same opera produces in any other part of the world. The mysterious charm of the House on the 'Festival Heights' in the old city of The Margrave cannot be equalled or substituted anywhere else.

In all these cases one deals with the problem of influencing the freedom of the human will. And that is true especially of meetings where there are men whose wills are opposed to the speaker and who must be brought around to a new way of thinking. In the morning and during the day it seems that the power of the human will rebels with its strongest energy against any attempt to impose upon it the will or opinion of another. On the other hand, in the evening it easily succumbs to the domination of a stronger will. Because really in such assemblies there is a contest between two opposite forces. The superior oratorical art of a man who has the compelling character of an apostle will succeed better in bringing around to a new way of thinking those who have naturally been subjected to a weakening of their forces of resistance rather than in converting those who are in full possession of their volitional and intellectual energies.

The mysterious artificial dimness of the Catholic churches also serves this purpose, the burning candles, the incense, the thurible, etc.

In this struggle between the orator and the opponent whom he must convert to his cause this marvellous sensibility towards the psychological influences of propaganda can hardly ever be availed of by an author. Generally speaking, the effect of the writer's work helps rather to conserve, reinforce and deepen the foundations of a mentality already existing. All really great historical revolutions were not produced by the written word. At most, they were accompanied by it.

It is out of the question to think that the French Revolution could have been carried into effect by philosophizing theories if they had not found an army of agitators led by demagogues of the grand style. These demagogues inflamed popular passion that had been already aroused, until that volcanic eruption finally broke out and convulsed the whole of Europe. And the same happened in the case of the gigantic Bolshevik revolution which recently took place in Russia. It was not due to the writers on Lenin's side but to the oratorical activities of those who preached the doctrine of hatred and that of the innumerable small and great orators who took part in the agitation.

The masses of illiterate Russians were not fired to Communist revolutionary enthusiasm by reading the theories of Karl Marx but by the promises of paradise made to the people by thousands of agitators in the service of an idea.

It was always so, and it will always be so.

It is just typical of our pig-headed intellectuals, who live apart from the practical world, to think that a writer must of necessity be superior to an orator in intelligence. This point of view was once exquisitely illustrated by a critique, published in a certain National paper which I have already mentioned, where it was stated that one is often disillusioned by reading the speech of an acknowledged great orator in print. That reminded me of another article which came into my hands during the War. It dealt with the speeches of Lloyd George, who was then Minister of Munitions, and examined them in a painstaking way under the microscope of criticism. The writer made the brilliant statement that these speeches showed inferior intelligence and learning and that, moreover, they were banal and commonplace productions. I myself procured some of these speeches, published in pamphlet form, and had to laugh at the fact that a normal German quill-driver did not in the least understand these psychological masterpieces in the art of influencing the masses.

298

This man criticized these speeches exclusively according to the impression they made on his own blasé mind, whereas the great British Demagogue had produced an immense effect on his audience through them, and in the widest sense on the whole of the British populace. Looked at from this point of view, that Englishman's speeches were most wonderful achievements, precisely because they showed an astounding knowledge of the soul of the broad masses of the people. For that reason their effect was really penetrating. Compare with them the futile stammerings of a Bethmann-Hollweg. On the surface his speeches were undoubtedly more intellectual, but they just proved this man's inability to speak to the people, which he really could not do. Nevertheless, to the average stupid brain of the German writer, who is, of course, endowed with a lot of scientific learning, it came quite natural to judge the speeches of the English Minister—which were made for the purpose of influencing the masses—by the impression which they made on his own mind, fossilized in its abstract learning. And it was more natural for him to compare them in the light of that impression with the brilliant but futile talk of the German statesman, which of course appealed to the writer's mind much more favourably. That the genius of Lloyd George was not only equal but a thousandfold superior to that of a Bethmann-Hollweg is proved by the fact that he found for his speeches that form and expression which opened the hearts of his people to him and made these people carry out his will absolutely. The primitive quality itself of those speeches, the originality of his expressions, his choice of clear and simple illustration, are examples which prove the superior political capacity of this Englishman. For one must never judge the speech of a statesman to his people by the impression which it leaves on the mind of a university professor but by the effect it produces on the people. And this is the sole criterion of the orator's genius.

The astonishing development of our movement, which was created from nothing a few years ago and is to-day singled out for persecution by all the internal and external enemies of our nation, must be attributed to the constant recognition and practical application of those principles.

Written matter also played an important part in our movement; but at the stage of which I am writing it served to give an equal and uniform education to the directors of the movement, in the upper as well as in the lower grades, rather than to convert the masses of our adversaries. It was only in very rare cases that a convinced and devoted Social Democrat or Communist was induced to acquire an understanding of our WELTANSCHAUUNG or to study a criticism of his own by procuring and reading one of our pamphlets or even one of our books. Even a newspaper is rarely read if it does not bear the stamp of a party affiliation. Moreover, the reading of newspapers helps little; because the general picture given by a single number of a newspaper is so confused and produces such a fragmentary impression that it really does not influence the occasional reader. And where a man has to count his pennies it cannot be assumed that, exclusively for the purpose of being objectively informed, he will become a regular reader or subscriber to a paper which opposes his views. Only one who has already joined a movement will regularly read the party organ of that movement, and especially for the purpose of keeping himself informed of what is happening in the movement.

It is quite different with the 'spoken' leaflet. Especially if it be distributed gratis it will be taken up by one person or another, all the more willingly if its display title refers to a question about which everybody is talking at the moment. Perhaps the reader, after having read through such a leaflet more or less thoughtfully, will have new viewpoints and mental attitudes and may give his attention to a new movement. But with these, even in the best of cases, only a small impulse will be given, but no definite conviction will be created; because the leaflet can do nothing more than draw attention to something and can become effective only by bringing the reader subsequently into a situation where he is more fundamentally informed and instructed. Such instruction must always be given at the mass assembly.

Mass assemblies are also necessary for the reason that, in attending them, the individual who felt himself formerly only on the point of joining the new movement, now begins to feel isolated and in fear of being left alone as he acquires for the first time the picture of a great community which has a strengthening and encouraging effect on most people. Brigaded in a company or battalion, surrounded by his companions, he will march with a lighter heart to the attack than if he had to march alone. In the crowd he feels himself in some way thus sheltered, though in reality there are a thousand arguments against such a feeling.

Mass demonstrations on the grand scale not only reinforce the will of the individual but they draw him still closer to the movement and help to create an ESPRIT DE CORPS. The man who appears first as the representative of a new doctrine in his place of business or in his factory is bound to feel himself embarrassed and has need of that reinforcement which comes from the consciousness that he is a member of a great community. And only a mass demonstration can impress upon him the greatness of this community. If, on leaving the shop or mammoth factory, in which he feels very small indeed, he should enter a vast assembly for the first time and see around him thousands and thousands of men who hold the same opinions; if, while still seeking his way, he is gripped by the force of mass-suggestion which comes from the excitement and enthusiasm of three or four thousand other men in whose midst he finds himself; if the manifest success and the concensus of thousands confirm the truth and justice of the new teaching and for the first time raise doubt in his mind as to the truth of the opinions held by himself up to now—then he submits himself to the fascination of what we call mass-suggestion. The will, the yearning and indeed the strength of thousands of people are in each individual. A man who enters such a meeting in doubt and hesitation leaves it inwardly fortified; he has become a member of a community.

The National Socialist Movement should never forget this, and it should never allow itself to be influenced by these bourgeois duffers who think they know everything but who have foolishly gambled away a great State, together with their own existence and the supremacy of their own class. They are overflowing with ability; they can do everything, and they know everything. But there is one thing they have not known how to do, and that is how to save the German people from falling into the arms of Marxism. In that they have shown themselves most pitiably and miserably impotent. So that the present opinion they have of themselves is only equal to their conceit. Their pride and stupidity are fruits of the same tree.

If these people try to disparage the importance of the spoken word to-day, they do it only because they realize—God be praised and thanked—how futile all their own speechifying has been.

CHAPTER VII:
The Conflict with the Red Forces

In 1919-20 and also in 1921 I attended some of the bourgeois meetings. Invariably I had the same feeling towards these as towards the compulsory dose of castor oil in my boyhood days. It just had to be taken because it was good for one: but it certainly tasted unpleasant. If it were possible to tie ropes round the German people and forcibly drag them to these bourgeois meetings, keeping them there behind barred doors and allowing nobody to escape until the meeting closed, then this procedure might prove successful in the course of a few hundred years. For my own part, I must frankly admit that, under such circumstances, I could not find life worth living; and indeed I should no longer wish to be a German. But, thank God, all this is impossible. And so it is not surprising that the sane and unspoilt masses shun these 'bourgeois mass meetings' as the devil shuns holy water.

I came to know the prophets of the bourgeois WELTANSCHAUUNG, and I was not surprised at what I learned, as I knew that they attached little importance to the spoken word. At that time I attended meetings of the Democrats, the German Nationalists, the German People's Party and the Bavarian People's Party (the Centre Party of Bavaria). What struck me at once was the homogeneous uniformity of the audiences. Nearly always they were made up exclusively of party members. The whole affair was more like a yawning card party than an assembly of people who had just passed through a great revolution. The speakers did all they could to maintain this tranquil atmosphere. They declaimed, or rather read out, their speeches in the style of an intellectual newspaper article or a learned treatise, avoiding all striking expressions. Here and there a feeble professorial joke would be introduced, whereupon the people sitting at the speaker's table felt themselves obliged to laugh — not loudly but encouragingly and with well-bred reserve.

And there were always those people at the speaker's table. I once attended a meeting in the Wagner Hall in Munich. It was a demonstration to celebrate the anniversary of the Battle of Leipzig.[18] The speech was delivered or rather read out by a venerable old professor from one or other of the universities. The committee sat on the platform: one monocle on the right, another monocle on the left, and in the centre a gentleman with no monocle. All three of them were punctiliously attired in morning coats, and I had the impression of being present before a judge's bench just as the death sentence was about to be pronounced or at a christening or some more solemn religious ceremony. The so-called speech, which in printed form may have read quite well, had a disastrous effect. After three quarters of an hour the audience fell into a sort of hypnotic trance, which was interrupted only when some man or woman left the hall, or by the clatter which the waitresses made, or by the increasing yawns of slumbering individuals. I had posted myself behind three workmen who were present either out of curiosity or because they were sent there by their parties. From time to time they glanced at one another with an ill-concealed grin, nudged one another with the elbow, and then silently left the hall. One could see that they had no intention whatsoever of interrupting the proceedings, nor indeed was it necessary to interrupt them. At long last the celebration showed signs of drawing to a close. After the professor, whose voice had meanwhile become more and more inaudible, finally ended his speech, the gentleman without the monocle delivered a rousing peroration to the assembled 'German sisters and brothers.' On behalf of the audience and himself he expressed gratitude for the magnificent lecture which they had just heard from Professor X and emphasized how deeply the Professor's words had moved them all. If a general discussion on the lecture were to take place it would be tantamount to profanity, and he thought he was voicing the opinion of all present in suggesting that such a discussion should not be held. Therefore, he would ask the assembly to rise from their seats and join in singing the patriotic song, WIR SIND EIN EINIG VOLK VON BRÜDERN. The proceedings finally closed with the anthem, DEUTSCHLAND ÜBER ALLES.

And then they all sang. It appeared to me that when the second verse was reached the voices were fewer and that only when the refrain came on they swelled loudly. When we reached the third verse my belief was confirmed that a good many of those present were not very familiar with the text.

But what has all this to do with the matter when such a song is sung wholeheartedly and fervidly by an assembly of German nationals?

After this the meeting broke up and everyone hurried to get outside, one to his glass of beer, one to a cafe, and others simply into the fresh air.

Out into the fresh air! That was also my feeling. And was this the way to honour an heroic struggle in which hundreds of thousands of Prussians and Germans had fought? To the devil with it all!

That sort of thing might find favour with the Government, it being merely a 'peaceful' meeting. The Minister responsible for law and order need not fear that enthusiasm might suddenly get the better of public decorum and induce these people to pour out of the room and, instead of dispersing to beer halls and cafes, march in rows of four through the town singing DEUTSCHLAND hoch in Ehren and causing some unpleasantness to a police force in need of rest.

No. That type of citizen is of no use to anyone.

On the other hand the National Socialist meetings were by no means 'peaceable' affairs. Two distinct WELTANSCHHAUUNGen raged in bitter opposition to one another, and these meetings did not close with the mechanical rendering of a dull patriotic song but rather with a passionate outbreak of popular national feeling.

It was imperative from the start to introduce rigid discipline into our meetings and establish the authority of the chairman absolutely. Our purpose was not to pour out a mixture of soft-soap bourgeois talk; what we had to say was meant to arouse the opponents at our meetings! How often did they not turn up in masses with a few individual agitators among them and, judging by the expression on all their faces, ready to finish us off there and then.

Yes, how often did they not turn up in huge numbers, those supporters of the Red Flag, all previously instructed to smash up everything once and for all and put an end to these meetings. More often than not everything hung on a mere thread, and only the chairman's ruthless determination and the rough handling by our ushers baffled our adversaries' intentions. And indeed they had every reason for being irritated.

The fact that we had chosen red as the colour for our posters sufficed to attract them to our meetings. The ordinary bourgeoisie were very shocked to see that, we had also chosen the symbolic red of Bolshevism and they regarded this as something ambiguously significant. The suspicion was whispered in German Nationalist circles that we also were merely another variety of Marxism, perhaps even Marxists suitably disguised, or better still, Socialists. The actual difference between Socialism and Marxism still remains a mystery to these people up to this day. The charge of Marxism was conclusively proved when it was discovered that at our meetings we deliberately substituted the words 'Fellow-countrymen and Women' for 'Ladies and Gentlemen' and addressed each other as 'Party Comrade'. We used to roar with laughter at these silly faint-hearted bourgeoisie and their efforts to puzzle out our origin, our intentions and our aims.

We chose red for our posters after particular and careful deliberation, our intention being to irritate the Left, so as to arouse their attention and tempt them to come to our meetings—if only in order to break them up—so that in this way we got a chance of talking to the people.

In those years' it was indeed a delightful experience to follow the constantly changing tactics of our perplexed and helpless adversaries. First of all they appealed to their followers to ignore us and keep away from our meetings. Generally speaking this appeal was heeded. But, as time went on, more and more of their followers gradually found their way to us and accepted our teaching. Then the leaders became nervous and uneasy. They clung to their belief that such a development should not be ignored for ever, and that terror must be applied in order to put an end to it.

Appeals were then made to the 'class-conscious proletariat' to attend our meetings in masses and strike with the clenched hand of the proletarian at the representatives of a 'monarchist and reactionary agitation'.

Our meetings suddenly became packed with work-people fully three-quarters of an hour before the proceedings were scheduled to begin. These gatherings resembled a powder cask ready to explode at any moment; and the fuse was conveniently at hand. But matters always turned out differently. People came as enemies and left, not perhaps prepared to join us, yet in a reflective mood and disposed critically to examine the correctness of their own doctrine. Gradually as time went on my three-hour lectures resulted in supporters and opponents becoming united in one single enthusiastic group of people. Every signal for the breaking-up of the meeting failed. The result was that the opposition leaders became frightened and once again looked for help to those quarters that had formerly discountenanced these tactics and, with some show of right, had been of the opinion that on principle the workers should be forbidden to attend our meetings.

Then they did not come any more, or only in small numbers. But after a short time the whole game started all over again. The instructions to keep away from us were ignored; the comrades came in steadily increasing numbers, until finally the advocates of the radical tactics won the day. We were to be broken up.

Yet when, after two, three and even eight meetings, it was realized that to break up these gatherings was easier said than done and that every meeting resulted in a decisive weakening of the red fighting forces, then suddenly the other password was introduced: 'Proletarians, comrades and comradesses, avoid meetings of the National Socialist agitators'.

The same eternally alternating tactics were also to be observed in the Red Press. Soon they tried to silence us but discovered the uselessness of such an attempt. After that they swung round to the opposite tactics. Daily 'reference' was made to us solely for the purpose of absolutely ridiculing us in the eyes of the working-classes. After a time these gentlemen must have felt that no harm was being done to us, but that, on the contrary, we were reaping an advantage in that people were asking themselves why so much space was being devoted to a subject which was supposed to be so ludicrous. People became curious. Suddenly there was a change of tactics and for a time we were treated as veritable criminals against mankind. One article followed the other, in which our criminal intentions were explained and new proofs brought forward to support what was said. Scandalous tales, all of them fabricated from start to finish, were published in order to help to poison the public mind. But in a short time even these attacks also proved futile; and in fact they assisted materially because they attracted public attention to us.

In those days I took up the standpoint that it was immaterial whether they laughed at us or reviled us, whether they depicted us as fools or criminals; the important point was that they took notice of us and that in the eyes of the working-classes we came to be regarded as the only force capable of putting up a fight. I said to myself that the followers of the Jewish Press would come to know all about us and our real aims.

One reason why they never got so far as breaking up our meetings was undoubtedly the incredible cowardice displayed by the leaders of the opposition. On every critical occasion they left the dirty work to the smaller fry whilst they waited outside the halls for the results of the break up.

We were exceptionally well informed in regard to our opponents' intentions, not only because we allowed several of our party colleagues to remain members of the Red organizations for reasons of expediency, but also because the Red wire-pullers, fortunately for us, were afflicted with a degree of talkativeness that is still unfortunately very prevalent among Germans. They could not keep their own counsel, and more often than not they started cackling before the proverbial egg was laid. Hence, time and again our precautions were such that Red agitators had no inkling of how near they were to being thrown out of the meetings.

This state of affairs compelled us to take the work of safeguarding our meetings into our own hands. No reliance could be placed on official protection. On the contrary; experience showed that such protection always favoured only the disturbers. The only real outcome of police intervention would be that the meeting would be dissolved, that is to say, closed. And that is precisely what our opponents granted.

Generally speaking, this led the police to adopt a procedure which, to say the least, was a most infamous sample of official malpractice. The moment they received information of a threat that the one or other meeting was to be broken up, instead of arresting the would-be disturbers, they promptly advised the innocent parties that the meeting was forbidden. This step the police proclaimed as a 'precautionary measure in the interests of law and order'.

The political work and activities of decent people could therefore always be hindered by desperate ruffians who had the means at their disposal. In the name of peace and order State authority bowed down to these ruffians and demanded that others should not provoke them. When National Socialism desired to hold meetings in certain parts and the labour unions declared that their members would resist, then it was not these blackmailers that were arrested and gaoled. No. Our meetings were forbidden by the police. Yes, this organ of the law had the unspeakable impudence to advise us in writing to this effect in innumerable instances. To avoid such eventualities, it was necessary to see to it that every attempt to disturb a meeting was nipped in the bud. Another feature to be taken into account in this respect is that all meetings which rely on police protection must necessarily bring discredit to their promoters in the eyes of the general public. Meetings that are only possible with the protective assistance of a strong force of police convert nobody; because in order to win over the lower strata of the people there must be a visible show of strength on one's own side. In the same way that a man of courage will win a woman's affection more easily than a coward, so a heroic movement will be more successful in winning over the hearts of a people than a weak movement which relies on police support for its very existence.

It is for this latter reason in particular that our young movement was to be charged with the responsibility of assuring its own existence, defending itself; and conducting its own work of smashing the Red opposition.

The work of organizing the protective measures for our meetings was based on the following:

(1) An energetic and psychologically judicious way of conducting the meeting.

(2) An organized squad of troops to maintain order.

In those days we and no one else were masters of the situation at our meetings and on no occasion did we fail to emphasize this. Our opponents fully realized that any provocation would be the occasion of throwing them out of the hall at once, whatever the odds against us. At meetings, particularly outside Munich, we had in those days from five to eight hundred opponents against fifteen to sixteen National Socialists; yet we brooked no interference, for we were ready to be killed rather than capitulate. More than once a handful of party colleagues offered a heroic resistance to a raging and violent mob of Reds. Those fifteen or twenty men would certainly have been overwhelmed in the end had not the opponents known that three or four times as many of themselves would first get their skulls cracked. Arid that risk they were not willing to run. We had done our best to study Marxist and bourgeois methods of conducting meetings, and we had certainly learnt something.

The Marxists had always exercised a most rigid discipline so that the question of breaking up their meetings could never have originated in bourgeois quarters. This gave the Reds all the more reason for acting on this plan. In time they not only became past-masters in this art but in certain large districts of the REICH they went so far as to declare that non-Marxist meetings were nothing less than a cause of' provocation against the proletariat. This was particularly the case when the wire-pullers suspected that a meeting might call attention to their own transgressions and thus expose their own treachery and chicanery. Therefore the moment such a meeting was announced to be held a howl of rage went up from the Red Press. These detractors of the law nearly always turned first to the authorities and requested in imperative and threatening language that this 'provocation of the proletariat' be stopped forthwith in the 'interests of law and order'. Their language was chosen according to the importance of the official blockhead they were dealing with and thus success was assured. If by chance the official happened to be a true German—and not a mere figurehead—and he declined the impudent request, then the time-honoured appeal to stop 'provocation of the proletariat' was issued together with instructions to attend such and such a meeting on a certain date in full strength for the purpose of 'putting a stop to the disgraceful machinations of the bourgeoisie by means of the proletarian fist'.

The pitiful and frightened manner in which these bourgeois meetings are conducted must be seen in order to be believed. Very frequently these threats were sufficient to call off such a meeting at once. The feeling of fear was so marked that the meeting, instead of commencing at eight o'clock, very seldom was opened before a quarter to nine or nine o'clock. The Chairman thereupon did his best, by showering compliments on the 'gentleman of the opposition' to prove how he and all others present were pleased (a palpable lie) to welcome a visit from men who as yet were not in sympathy with them for the reason that only by mutual discussion (immediately agreed to) could they be brought closer together in mutual understanding. Apart from this the Chairman also assured them that the meeting had no intention whatsoever of interfering with the professed convictions of anybody. Indeed no. Everyone had the right to form and hold his own political views, but others should be allowed to do likewise. He therefore requested that the speaker be allowed to deliver his speech without interruption — the speech in any case not being a long affair. People abroad, he continued, would thus not come to regard this meeting as another shameful example of the bitter fraternal strife that is raging in Germany. And so on and so forth

The brothers of the Left had little if any appreciation for that sort of talk; the speaker had hardly commenced when he was shouted down. One gathered the impression at times that these speakers were graceful for being peremptorily cut short in their martyr-like discourse. These bourgeois toreadors left the arena in the midst of a vast uproar, that is to say, provided that they were not thrown down the stairs with cracked skulls, which was very often the case.

Therefore, our methods of organization at National Socialist meetings were something quite strange to the Marxists. They came to our meetings in the belief that the little game which they had so often played could as a matter of course be also repeated on us. "To-day we shall finish them off." How often did they bawl this out to each other on entering the meeting hall, only to be thrown out with lightning speed before they had time to repeat it.

In the first place our method of conducting a meeting was entirely different. We did not beg and pray to be allowed to speak, and we did not straightway give everybody the right to hold endless discussions. We curtly gave everyone to understand that we were masters of the meeting and that we would do as it pleased us and that everyone who dared to interrupt would be unceremoniously thrown out. We stated clearly our refusal to accept responsibility for anyone treated in this manner. If time permitted and if it suited us, a discussion would be allowed to take place. Our party colleague would now make his speech.... That kind of talk was sufficient in itself to astonish the Marxists.

Secondly, we had at our disposal a well-trained and organized body of men for maintaining order at our meetings. On the other hand the bourgeois parties protected their meetings with a body of men better classified as ushers who by virtue of their age thought they were entitled to-authority and respect. But as Marxism has little or no respect for these things, the question of suitable self-protection at these bourgeois meetings was, so to speak, in practice non-existent.

When our political meetings first started I made it a special point to organize a suitable defensive squad — a squad composed chiefly of young men. Some of them were comrades who had seen active service with me; others were young party members who, right from the start, had been trained and brought up to realize that only terror is capable of smashing terror — that only courageous and determined people had made a success of things in this world and that, finally, we were fighting for an idea so lofty that it was worth the last drop of our blood. These young men had been brought up to realize that where force replaced common sense in the solution of a problem, the best means of defence was attack and that the reputation of our hall-guard squads should stamp us as a political fighting force and not as a debating society.

And it was extraordinary how eagerly these boys of the War generation responded to this order. They had indeed good reason for being bitterly disappointed and indignant at the miserable milksop methods employed by the bourgeoise.

Thus it became clear to everyone that the Revolution had only been possible thanks to the dastardly methods of a bourgeois government. At that time there was certainly no lack of man-power to suppress the revolution, but unfortunately there was an entire lack of directive brain power. How often did the eyes of my young men light up with enthusiasm when I explained to them the vital functions connected with their task and assured them time and again that all earthly wisdom is useless unless it be supported by a measure of strength, that the gentle goddess of Peace can only walk in company with the god of War, and that every great act of peace must be protected and assisted by force. In this way the idea of military service came to them in a far more realistic form — not in the fossilized sense of the souls of decrepit officials serving the dead authority of a dead State, but in the living realization of the duty of each man to sacrifice his life at all times so that his country might live.

How those young men did their job!

Like a swarm of hornets they tackled disturbers at our meetings, regardless of superiority of numbers, however great, indifferent to wounds and bloodshed, inspired with the great idea of blazing a trail for the sacred mission of our movement.

As early as the summer of 1920 the organization of squads of men as hall guards for maintaining order at our meetings was gradually assuming definite shape. By the spring of 1921 this body of men were sectioned off into squads of one hundred, which in turn were sub-divided into smaller groups.

The urgency for this was apparent, as meanwhile the number of our meetings had steadily increased. We still frequently met in the Munich Hofbräuhaus but more frequently in the large meeting halls throughout the city itself. In the autumn and winter of 1920-1921 our meetings in the Bürgerbräu and Munich Kindlbräu had assumed vast proportions and it was always the same picture that presented itself; namely, meetings of the NSDAP (The German National Socialist Labour Party) were always crowded out so that the police were compelled to close and bar the doors long before proceedings commenced.

The organization of defence guards for keeping order at our meetings cleared up a very difficult question. Up till then the movement had possessed no party badge and no party flag. The lack of these tokens was not only a disadvantage at that time but would prove intolerable in the future. The disadvantages were chiefly that members of the party possessed no outward broken of membership which linked them together, and it was absolutely unthinkable that for the future they should remain without some token which would be a symbol of the movement and could be set against that of the International.

More than once in my youth the psychological importance of such a symbol had become clearly evident to me and from a sentimental point of view also it was advisable. In Berlin, after the War, I was present at a mass-demonstration of Marxists in front of the Royal Palace and in the Lustgarten. A sea of red flags, red armlets and red flowers was in itself sufficient to give that huge assembly of about 120,000 persons an outward appearance of strength. I was now able to feel and understand how easily the man in the street succumbs to the hypnotic magic of such a grandiose piece of theatrical presentation.

The bourgeoisie, which as a party neither possesses or stands for any WELTANSCHAUUNG, had therefore not a single banner. Their party was composed of 'patriots' who went about in the colours of the REICH. If these colours were the symbol of a definite WELTANSCHAUUNG then one could understand the rulers of the State regarding this flag as expressive of their own WELTANSCHAUUNG, seeing that through their efforts the official REICH flag was expressive of their own WELTANSCHAUUNG.

But in reality the position was otherwise.

The REICH was morticed together without the aid of the German bourgeoisie and the flag itself was born of the War and therefore merely a State flag possessing no importance in the sense of any particular ideological mission.

Only in one part of the German-speaking territory—in German-Austria—was there anything like a bourgeois party flag in evidence. Here a section of the national bourgeoisie selected the 1848 colours (black, red and gold) as their party flag and therewith created a symbol which, though of no importance from a weltanschauliche viewpoint, had, nevertheless, a revolutionary character from a national point of view. The most bitter opponents of this flag at that time, and this should not be forgotten to-day, were the Social Democrats and the Christian Socialists or clericals. They, in particular, were the ones who degraded and besmirched these colours in the same way as in 1918 they dragged black, white and red into the gutter. Of course, the black, red and gold of the German parties in the old Austria were the colours of the year 1848: that is to say, of a period likely to be regarded as somewhat visionary, but it was a period that had honest German souls as its representatives, although the Jews were lurking unseen as wire-pullers in the background. It was high treason and the shameful enslavement of the German territory that first of all made these colours so attractive to the Marxists of the Centre Party; so much so that to-day they revere them as their most cherished possession and use them as their own banners for the protection of the flag they once foully besmirched.

It is a fact, therefore, that, up till 1920, in opposition to the Marxists there was no flag that would have stood for a consolidated resistance to them. For even if the better political elements of the German bourgeoisie were loath to accept the suddenly discovered black, red and gold colours as their symbol after the year 1918, they nevertheless were incapable of counteracting this with a future programme of their own that would correspond to the new trend of affairs. At the most, they had a reconstruction of the old REICH in mind.

And it is to this way of thinking that the black, white and red colours of the old REICH are indebted for their resurrection as the flag of our so-called national bourgeois parties.

It was obvious that the symbol of a régime which had been overthrown by the Marxists under inglorious circumstances was not now worthy to serve as a banner under which the same Marxism was to be crushed in its turn. However much any decent German may love and revere those old colours, glorious when placed side by side in their youthful freshness, when he had fought under them and seen the sacrifice of so many lives, that flag had little value for the struggle of the future.

In our Movement I have always adopted the standpoint that it was a really lucky thing for the German nation that it had lost its old flag[19]. This standpoint of mine was in strong contrast to that of the bourgeois politicians. It may be immaterial to us what the Republic does under its flag. But let us be deeply grateful to fate for having so graciously spared the most glorious war flag for all time from becoming an ignominious rag. The REICH of to-day, which sells itself and its people, must never be allowed to adopt the honourable and heroic black, white and red colours.

As long as the November outrage endures, that outrage may continue to bear its own external sign and not steal that of an honourable past. Our bourgeois politicians should awaken their consciences to the fact that whoever desires this State to have the black, white and red colours is pilfering from the past. The old flag was suitable only for the old REICH and, thank Heaven, the Republic chose the colours best suited to itself.

This was also the reason why we National Socialists recognized that hoisting the old colours would be no symbol of our special aims; for we had no wish to resurrect from the dead the old REICH which had been ruined through its own blunders, but to build up a new State.

The Movement which is fighting Marxism to-day along these lines must display on its banner the symbol of the new State.

The question of the new flag, that is to say the form and appearance it must take, kept us very busy in those days. Suggestions poured in from all quarters, which although well meant were more or less impossible in practice. The new flag had not only to become a symbol expressing our own struggle but on the other hand it was necessary that it should prove effective as a large poster. All those who busy themselves with the tastes of the public will recognize and appreciate the great importance of these apparently petty matters. In hundreds of thousands of cases a really striking emblem may be the first cause of awakening interest in a movement.

For this reason we declined all suggestions from various quarters for identifying our movement by means of a white flag with the old State or rather with those decrepit parties whose sole political objective is the restoration of past conditions. And, apart from this, white is not a colour capable of attracting and focusing public attention. It is a colour suitable only for young women's associations and not for a movement that stands for reform in a revolutionary period.

Black was also suggested—certainly well-suited to the times, but embodying no significance to empress the will behind our movement. And, finally, black is incapable of attracting attention.

White and blue was discarded, despite its admirable aesthetic appeal—as being the colours of an individual German Federal State—a State that, unfortunately, through its political attitude of particularist narrow-mindedness did not enjoy a good reputation. And, generally speaking, with these colours it would have been difficult to attract attention to our movement. The same applies to black and white.

Black, red and gold did not enter the question at all.

And this also applies to black, white and red for reasons already stated. At least, not in the form hitherto in use. But the effectiveness of these three colours is far superior to all the others and they are certainly the most strikingly harmonious combination to be found.

I myself was always for keeping the old colours, not only because I, as a soldier, regarded them as my most sacred possession, but because in their aesthetic effect, they conformed more than anything else to my personal taste. Accordingly I had to discard all the innumerable suggestions and designs which had been proposed for the new movement, among which were many that had incorporated the swastika into the old colours. I, as leader, was unwilling to make public my own design, as it was possible that someone else could come forward with a design just as good, if not better, than my own. As a matter of fact, a dental surgeon from Starnberg submitted a good design very similar to mine, with only one mistake, in that his swastika with curved corners was set upon a white background.

After innumerable trials I decided upon a final form—a flag of red material with a white disc bearing in its centre a black swastika. After many trials I obtained the correct proportions between the dimensions of the flag and of the white central disc, as well as that of the swastika. And this is how it has remained ever since.

At the same time we immediately ordered the corresponding armlets for our squad of men who kept order at meetings, armlets of red material, a central white disc with the black swastika upon it. Herr Füss, a Munich goldsmith, supplied the first practical and permanent design.

The new flag appeared in public in the midsummer of 1920. It suited our movement admirably, both being new and young. Not a soul had seen this flag before; its effect at that time was something akin to that of a blazing torch. We ourselves experienced almost a boyish delight when one of the ladies of the party who had been entrusted with the making of the flag finally handed it over to us. And a few months later those of us in Munich were in possession of six of these flags. The steadily increasing strength of our hall guards was a main factor in popularizing the symbol.

And indeed a symbol it proved to be.

Not only because it incorporated those revered colours expressive of our homage to the glorious past and which once brought so much honour to the German nation, but this symbol was also an eloquent expression of the will behind the movement. We National Socialists regarded our flag as being the embodiment of our party programme. The red expressed the social thought underlying the movement. White the national thought. And the swastika signified the mission allotted to us—the struggle for the victory of Aryan mankind and at the same time the triumph of the ideal of creative work which is in itself and always will be anti-Semitic.

Two years later, when our squad of hall guards had long since grown into storm detachments, it seemed necessary to give this defensive organization of a young WELTANSCHAUUNG a particular symbol of victory, namely a Standard. I also designed this and entrusted the execution of it to an old party comrade, Herr Gahr, who was a goldsmith. Ever since that time this Standard has been the distinctive token of the National Socialist struggle.

The increasing interest taken in our meetings, particularly during 1920, compelled us at times to hold two meetings a week. Crowds gathered round our posters; the large meeting halls in the town were always filled and tens of thousands of people, who had been led astray by the teachings of Marxism, found their way to us and assisted in the work of fighting for the liberation of the REICH. The public in Munich had got to know us. We were being spoken about. The words 'National Socialist' had become common property to many and signified for them a definite party programme. Our circle of supporters and even of members was constantly increasing, so that in the winter of 1920-21 we were able to appear as a strong party in Munich.

At that time there was no party in Munich with the exception of the Marxist parties—certainly no nationalist party—which was able to hold such mass demonstrations as ours. The Munich Kindl Hall, which held 5,000 people, was more than once overcrowded and up till then there was only one other hall, the Krone Circus Hall, into which we had not ventured.

At the end of January 1921 there was again great cause for anxiety in Germany. The Paris Agreement, by which Germany pledged herself to pay the crazy sum of a hundred milliards of gold marks, was to be confirmed by the London Ultimatum.

Thereupon an old-established Munich working committee, representative of so-called VÖLKISCH groups, deemed it advisable to call for a public meeting of protest. I became nervous and restless when I saw that a lot of time was being wasted and nothing undertaken. At first a meeting was suggested in the KÖNIG PLATZ; on second thoughts this was turned down, as someone feared the proceedings might be wrecked by Red elements. Another suggestion was a demonstration in front of the Feldherrn Hall, but this also came to nothing. Finally a combined meeting in the Munich Kindl Hall was suggested. Meanwhile, day after day had gone by; the big parties had entirely ignored the terrible event, and the working committee could not decide on a definite date for holding the demonstration.

On Tuesday, February 1st, I put forward an urgent demand for a final decision. I was put off until Wednesday. On that day I demanded to be told clearly if and when the meeting was to take place. The reply was again uncertain and evasive, it being stated that it was 'intended' to arrange a demonstration that day week.

At that I lost all patience and decided to conduct a demonstration of protest on my own. At noon on Wednesday I dictated in ten minutes the text of the poster and at the same time hired the Krone Circus Hall for the next day, February 3rd.

In those days this was a tremendous venture. Not only because of the uncertainty of filling that vast hall, but also because of the risk of the meeting being wrecked.

Numerically our squad of hall guards was not strong enough for this vast hall. I was also uncertain about what to do in case the meeting was broken up—a huge circus building being a different proposition from an ordinary meeting hall. But events showed that my fears were misplaced, the opposite being the case. In that vast building a squad of wreckers could be tackled and subdued more easily than in a cramped hall.

One thing was certain: A failure would throw us back for a long time to come. If one meeting was wrecked our prestige would be seriously injured and our opponents would be encouraged to repeat their success. That would lead to sabotage of our work in connection with further meetings and months of difficult struggle would be necessary to overcome this.

We had only one day in which to post our bills, Thursday. Unfortunately it rained on the morning of that day and there was reason to fear that many people would prefer to remain at home rather than hurry to a meeting through rain and snow, especially when there was likely to be violence and bloodshed.

And indeed on that Thursday morning I was suddenly struck with fear that the hall might never be filled to capacity, which would have made me ridiculous in the eyes of the working committee. I therefore immediately dictated various leaflets, had them printed and distributed in the afternoon. Of course they contained an invitation to attend the meeting.

Two lorries which I hired were draped as much as possible in red, each had our new flag hoisted on it and was then filled with fifteen or twenty members of our party. Orders were given the members to canvas the streets thoroughly, distribute leaflets and conduct propaganda for the mass meeting to be held that evening. It was the first time that lorries had driven through the streets bearing flags and not manned by Marxists. The public stared open-mouthed at these red-draped cars, and in the outlying districts clenched fists were angrily raised at this new evidence of 'provocation of the proletariat'. Were not the Marxists the only ones entitled to hold meetings and drive about in motor lorries?

At seven o'clock in the evening only a few had gathered in the circus hall. I was being kept informed by telephone every ten minutes and was becoming uneasy. Usually at seven or a quarter past our meeting halls were already half filled; sometimes even packed. But I soon found out the reason why I was uneasy. I had entirely forgotten to take into account the huge dimensions of this new meeting place. A thousand people in the Hofbräuhaus was quite an impressive sight, but the same number in the Circus building was swallowed up in its dimensions and was hardly noticeable. Shortly afterwards I received more hopeful reports and at a quarter to eight I was informed that the hall was three-quarters filled, with huge crowds still lined up at the pay boxes. I then left for the meeting.

I arrived at the Circus building at two minutes past eight. There was still a crowd of people outside, partly inquisitive people and many opponents who preferred to wait outside for developments.

When I entered the great hall I felt the same joy I had felt a year previously at the first meeting in the Munich Hofbräu Banquet Hall; but it was not until I had forced my way through the solid wall of people and reached the platform that I perceived the full measure of our success. The hall was before me, like a huge shell, packed with thousands and thousands of people. Even the arena was densely crowded. More than 5,600 tickets had been sold and, allowing for the unemployed, poor students and our own detachments of men for keeping order, a crowd of about 6,500 must have been present.

My theme was 'Future or Downfall' and I was filled with joy at the conviction that the future was represented by the crowds that I was addressing.

I began, and spoke for about two and a half hours. I had the feeling after the first half-hour that the meeting was going to be a big success. Contact had been at once established with all those thousands of individuals. After the first hour the speech was already being received by spontaneous outbreaks of applause, but after the second hour this died down to a solemn stillness which I was to experience so often later on in this same hall, and which will for ever be remembered by all those present. Nothing broke this impressive silence and only when the last word had been spoken did the meeting give vent to its feelings by singing the national anthem.

I watched the scene during the next twenty minutes, as the vast hall slowly emptied itself, and only then did I leave the platform, a happy man, and made my way home.

Photographs were taken of this first meeting in the Krone Circus Hall in Munich. They are more eloquent than words to demonstrate the success of this demonstration. The bourgeois papers reproduced photographs and reported the meeting as having been merely 'nationalist' in character; in their usual modest fashion they omitted all mention of its promoters.

Thus for the first time we had developed far beyond the dimensions of an ordinary party. We could no longer be ignored. And to dispel all doubt that the meeting was merely an isolated success, I immediately arranged for another at the Circus Hall in the following week, and again we had the same success. Once more the vast hall was overflowing with people; so much so that I decided to hold a third meeting during the following week, which also proved a similar success.

After these initial successes early in 1921 I increased our activity in Munich still further. I not only held meetings once a week, but during some weeks even two were regularly held and very often during midsummer and autumn this increased to three. We met regularly at the Circus Hall and it gave us great satisfaction to see that every meeting brought us the same measure of success.

The result was shown in an ever-increasing number of supporters and members into our party.

Naturally, such success did not allow our opponents to sleep soundly. At first their tactics fluctuated between the use of terror and silence in our regard. Then they recognized that neither terror nor silence could hinder the progress of our movement. So they had recourse to a supreme act of terror which was intended to put a definite end to our activities in the holding of meetings.

As a pretext for action along this line they availed themselves of a very mysterious attack on one of the Landtag deputies, named Erhard Auer. It was declared that someone had fired several shots at this man one evening. This meant that he was not shot but that an attempt had been made to shoot him. A fabulous presence of mind and heroic courage on the part of Social Democratic leaders not only prevented the sacrilegious intention from taking effect but also put the crazy would-be assassins to flight, like the cowards that they were. They were so quick and fled so far that subsequently the police could not find even the slightest traces of them. This mysterious episode was used by the organ of the Social Democratic Party to arouse public feeling against the movement, and while doing this it delivered its old rigmarole about the tactics that were to be employed the next time. Their purpose was to see to it that our movement should not grow but should be immediately hewn down root and branch by the hefty arm of the proletariat.

A few days later the real attack came. It was decided finally to interrupt one of our meetings which was billed to take place in the Munich Hofbräuhaus, and at which I myself was to speak.

On November 4th, 1921, in the evening between six and seven o'clock I received the first precise news that the meeting would positively be broken up and that to carry out this action our adversaries had decided to send to the meeting great masses of workmen employed in certain 'Red' factories.

It was due to an unfortunate accident that we did not receive this news sooner. On that day we had given up our old business office in the Sternecker Gasse in Munich and moved into other quarters; or rather we had given up the old offices and our new quarters were not yet in functioning order. The telephone arrangements had been cut off by the former tenants and had not yet been reinstalled. Hence it happened that several attempts made that day to inform us by telephone of the break-up which had been planned for the evening did not reach us.

Consequently our order troops were not present in strong force at that meeting. There was only one squad present, which did not consist of the usual one hundred men, but only of about forty-six. And our telephone connections were not yet sufficiently organized to be able to give the alarm in the course of an hour or so, so that a sufficiently powerful number of order troops to deal with the situation could be called. It must also be added that on several previous occasions we had been forewarned, but nothing special happened. The old proverb, 'Revolutions which were announced have scarcely ever come off', had hitherto been proved true in our regard.

Possibly for this reason also sufficiently strong precautions had not been taken on that day to cope with the brutal determination of our opponents to break up our meeting.

Finally, we did not believe that the Hofbräuhaus in Munich was suitable for the interruptive tactics of our adversaries. We had feared such a thing far more in the bigger halls, especially that of the Krone Circus. But on this point we learned a very serviceable lesson that evening. Later, we studied this whole question according to a scientific system and arrived at results, both interesting and incredible, and which subsequently were an essential factor in the direction of our organization and in the tactics of our Storm Troops.

When I arrived in the entrance halt of the Hofbräuhaus at 7.45 that evening I realized that there could be no doubt as to what the 'Reds' intended. The hall was filled, and for that reason the police had barred the entrances. Our adversaries, who had arrived very early, were in the hall, and our followers were for the most part outside. The small bodyguard awaited me at the entrance. I had the doors leading to the principal hall closed and then asked the bodyguard of forty-five or forty-six men to come forward. I made it clear to the boys that perhaps on that evening for the first time they would have to show their unbending and unbreakable loyalty to the movement and that not one of us should leave the hall unless carried out dead. I added that I would remain in the hall and that I did not believe that one of them would abandon me, and that if I saw any one of them act the coward I myself would personally tear off his armlet and his badge. I demanded of them that they should come forward if the slightest attempt to sabotage the meeting were made and that they must remember that the best defence is always attack.

I was greeted with a triple 'HEIL' which sounded more hoarse and violent than usual.

Then I advanced through the hall and could take in the situation with my own eyes. Our opponents sat closely huddled together and tried to pierce me through with their looks. Innumerable faces glowing with hatred and rage were fixed on me, while others with sneering grimaces shouted at me together. Now they would 'Finish with us. We must look out for our entrails. To-day they would smash in our faces once and for all.' And there were other expressions of an equally elegant character. They knew that they were there in superior numbers and they acted accordingly.

Yet we were able to open the meeting; and I began to speak. In the Hall of the Hofbräuhaus I stood always at the side, away from the entry and on top of a beer table. Therefore I was always right in the midst of the audience. Perhaps this circumstance was responsible for creating a certain feeling and a sense of agreement which I never found elsewhere.

Before me, and especially towards my left, there were only opponents, seated or standing. They were mostly robust youths and men from the Maffei Factory, from Kustermann's, and from the factories on the Isar, etc. Along the right-hand wall of the hall they were thickly massed quite close to my table. They now began to order litre mugs of beer, one after the other, and to throw the empty mugs under the table. In this way whole batteries were collected. I should have been surprised had this meeting ended peacefully.

In spite of all the interruptions, I was able to speak for about an hour and a half and I felt as if I were master of the situation. Even the ringleaders of the disturbers appeared to be convinced of this; for they steadily became more uneasy, often left the hall, returned and spoke to their men in an obviously nervous way.

A small psychological error which I committed in replying to an interruption, and the mistake of which I myself was conscious the moment the words had left my mouth, gave the sign for the outbreak.

There were a few furious outbursts and all in a moment a man jumped on a seat and shouted "Liberty". At that signal the champions of liberty began their work.

In a few moments the hall was filled with a yelling and shrieking mob. Numerous beer-mugs flew like howitzers above their heads. Amid this uproar one heard the crash of chair legs, the crashing of mugs, groans and yells and screams.

It was a mad spectacle. I stood where I was and could observe my boys doing their duty, every one of them.

There I had the chance of seeing what a bourgeois meeting could be.

The dance had hardly begun when my Storm Troops, as they were called from that day onwards, launched their attack. Like wolves they threw themselves on the enemy again and again in parties of eight or ten and began steadily to thrash them out of the hall. After five minutes I could see hardly one of them that was not streaming with blood. Then I realized what kind of men many of them were, above all my brave Maurice Hess, who is my private secretary to-day, and many others who, even though seriously wounded, attacked again and again as long as they could stand on their feet. Twenty minutes long the pandemonium continued. Then the opponents, who had numbered seven or eight hundred, had been driven from the hall or hurled out headlong by my men, who had not numbered fifty. Only in the left corner a big crowd still stood out against our men and put up a bitter fight. Then two pistol shots rang out from the entrance to the hall in the direction of the platform and now a wild din of shooting broke out from all sides. One's heart almost rejoiced at this spectacle which recalled memories of the War.

At that moment it was not possible to identify the person who had fired the shots. But at any rate I could see that my boys renewed the attack with increased fury until finally the last disturbers were overcome and flung out of the hall.

About twenty-five minutes had passed since it all began. The hall looked as if a bomb had exploded there. Many of my comrades had to be bandaged and others taken away. But we remained masters of the situation. Hermann Essen, who was chairman of the meeting, announced: "The meeting will continue. The speaker shall proceed." So I went on with my speech.

When we ourselves declared the meeting at an end an excited police officer rushed in, waved his hands and declared: "The meeting is dissolved."

Without wishing to do so I had to laugh at this example of the law's delay. It was the authentic constabulary officiosiousness. The smaller they are the greater they must always appear.

That evening we learned a real lesson. And our adversaries never forgot the lesson they had received.

Up to the autumn of 1923 the Münchener post did not again mention the clenched fists of the Proletariat.

CHAPTER VIII:
The Strong is Strongest When Alone

In the preceding chapter I mentioned the existence of a co-operative union between the German patriotic associations. Here I shall deal briefly with this question. In speaking of a co-operative union we generally mean a group of associations which, for the purpose of facilitating their work, establish mutual relations for collaborating with one another along certain lines, appointing a common directorate with varying powers and thenceforth carrying out a common line of action. The average citizen is pleased and reassured when he hears that these associations, by establishing a co-operative union among one another, have at long last discovered a common platform on which they can stand united and have eliminated all grounds of mutual difference. Therewith a general conviction arises, to the effect that such a union is an immense gain in strength and that small groups which were weak as long as they stood alone have now suddenly become strong. Yet this conviction is for the most part a mistaken one.

It will be interesting and, in my opinion, important for the better understanding of this question if we try to get a clear notion of how it comes about that these associations, unions, etc., are established, when all of them declare that they have the same ends in view. In itself it would be logical to expect that one aim should be fought for by a single association and it would be more reasonable if there were not a number of associations fighting for the same aim. In the beginning there was undoubtedly only one association which had this one fixed aim in view. One man proclaimed a truth somewhere and, calling for the solution of a definite question, fixed his aim and founded a movement for the purpose of carrying his views into effect.

That is how an association or a party is founded, the scope of whose programme is either the abolition of existing evils or the positive establishment of a certain order of things in the future.

Once such a movement has come into existence it may lay practical claim to certain priority rights. The natural course of things would now be that all those who wish to fight for the same objective as this movement is striving for should identify themselves with it and thus increase its strength, so that the common purpose in view may be all the better served. Especially men of superior intelligence must feel, one and all, that by joining the movement they are establishing precisely those conditions which are necessary for practical success in the common struggle. Accordingly it is reasonable and, in a certain sense, honest—which honesty, as I shall show later, is an element of very great importance—that only one movement should be founded for the purpose of attaining the one aim.

The fact that this does not happen must be attributed to two causes. The first may almost be described as tragic. The second is a matter for pity, because it has its foundation in the weaknesses of human nature. But, on going to the bottom of things, I see in both causes only facts which give still another ground for strengthening our will, our energy and intensity of purpose; so that finally, through the higher development of the human faculties, the solution of the problem in question may be rendered possible.

The tragic reason why it so often happens that the pursuit of one definite task is not left to one association alone is as follows: Generally speaking, every action carried out on the grand style in this world is the expression of a desire that has already existed for a long time in millions of human hearts, a longing which may have been nourished in silence. Yes, it may happen that throughout centuries men may have been yearning for the solution of a definite problem, because they have been suffering under an unendurable order of affairs, without seeing on the far horizon the coming fulfilment of the universal longing. Nations which are no longer capable of finding an heroic deliverance from such a sorrowful fate may be looked upon as effete. But, on the other hand, nothing gives better proof of the vital forces of a people and the consequent guarantee of its right to exist than that one day, through a happy decree of Destiny, a man arises who is capable of liberating his people from some great oppression, or of wiping out some bitter distress, or of calming the national soul which had been tormented through its sense of insecurity, and thus fulfilling what had long been the universal yearning of the people.

An essential characteristic of what are called the great questions of the time is that thousands undertake the task of solving them and that many feel themselves called to this task: yea, even that Destiny itself has proposed many for the choice, so that through the free play of forces the stronger and bolder shall finally be victorious and to him shall be entrusted the task of solving the problem.

Thus it may happen that for centuries many are discontented with the form in which their religious life expresses itself and yearn for a renovation of it; and so it may happen that through this impulse of the soul some dozens of men may arise who believe that, by virtue of their understanding and their knowledge, they are called to solve the religious difficulties of the time and accordingly present themselves as the prophets of a new teaching or at least as declared adversaries of the standing beliefs.

Here also it is certain that the natural law will take its course, inasmuch as the strongest will be destined to fulfil the great mission. But usually the others are slow to acknowledge that only one man is called. On the contrary, they all believe that they have an equal right to engage in the solution of the diffculties in question and that they are equally called to that task. Their contemporary world is generally quite unable to decide which of all these possesses the highest gifts and accordingly merits the support of all.

So in the course of centuries, or indeed often within the same epoch, different men establish different movements to struggle towards the same end. At least the end is declared by the founders of the movements to be the same, or may be looked upon as such by the masses of the people. The populace nourishes vague desires and has only general opinions, without having any precise notion of their own ideals and desires or of the question whether and how it is impossible for these ideals and desires to be fulfilled.

The tragedy lies in the fact that many men struggle to reach the same objective by different roads, each one genuinely believing in his own mission and holding himself in duty bound to follow his own road without any regard for the others.

These movements, parties, religious groups, etc., originate entirely independently of one another out of the general urge of the time, and all with a view to working towards the same goal. It may seem a tragic thing, at least at first sight, that this should be so, because people are too often inclined to think that forces which are dispersed in different directions would attain their ends far more quickly and more surely if they were united in one common effort. But that is not so. For Nature herself decides according to the rules of her inexorable logic. She leaves these diverse groups to compete with one another and dispute the palm of victory and thus she chooses the clearest, shortest and surest way along which she leads the movement to its final goal.

How could one decide from outside which is the best way, if the forces at hand were not allowed free play, if the final decision were to rest with the doctrinaire judgment of men who are so infatuated with their own superior knowledge that their minds are not open to accept the indisputable proof presented by manifest success, which in the last analysis always gives the final confirmation of the justice of a course of action.

Hence, though diverse groups march along different routes towards the same objective, as soon as they come to know that analogous efforts are being made around them, they will have to study all the more carefully whether they have chosen the best way and whether a shorter way may not be found and how their efforts can best be employed to reach the objective more quickly.

Through this rivalry each individual protagonist develops his faculties to a still higher pitch of perfection and the human race has frequently owed its progress to the lessons learned from the misfortunes of former attempts which have come to grief. Therefore we may conclude that we come to know the better ways of reaching final results through a state of things which at first sight appeared tragic; namely, the initial dispersion of individual efforts, wherein each group was unconsciously responsible for such dispersion.

In studying the lessons of history with a view to finding a way for the solution of the German problem, the prevailing opinion at one time was that there were two possible paths along which that problem might be solved and that these two paths should have united from the very beginning. The chief representatives and champions of these two paths were Austria and Prussia respectively, Habsburg and Hohenzollern. All the rest, according to this prevalent opinion, ought to have entrusted their united forces to the one or the other party. But at that time the path of the most prominent representative, the Habsburg, would have been taken, though the Austrian policy would never have led to the foundation of a united German REICH.

Finally, a strong and united German REICH arose out of that which many millions of Germans deplored in their hearts as the last and most terrible manifestation of our fratricidal strife. The truth is that the German Imperial Crown was retrieved on the battle field of Königgrätz and not in the fights that were waged before Paris, as was commonly asserted afterwards.

Thus the foundation of the German REICH was not the consequence of any common will working along common lines, but it was much more the outcome of a deliberate struggle for hegemony, though the protagonists were often hardly conscious of this. And from this struggle Prussia finally came out victorious. Anybody who is not so blinded by partisan politics as to deny this truth will have to agree that the so-called wisdom of men would never have come to the same wise decision as the wisdom of Life itself, that is to say, the free play of forces, finally brought to realization. For in the German lands of two hundred years before who would seriously have believed that Hohenzollern Prussia, and not Habsburg, would become the germ cell, the founder and the tutor of the new REICH? And, on the other hand, who would deny to-day that Destiny thus acted wiser than human wisdom. Who could now imagine a German REICH based on the foundations of an effete and degenerate dynasty?

No. The general evolution of things, even though it took a century of struggle, placed the best in the position that it had merited.

And that will always be so. Therefore it is not to be regretted if different men set out to attain the same objective. In this way the strongest and swiftest becomes recognized and turns out to be the victor.

Now there is a second cause for the fact that often in the lives of nations several movements which show the same characteristics strive along different ways to reach what appears to be the same goal. This second cause is not at all tragic, but just something that rightly calls forth pity. It arises from a sad mixture of envy, jealousy, ambition, and the itch for taking what belongs to others. Unfortunately these failings are often found united in single specimens of the human species.

The moment a man arises who profoundly understands the distress of his people and, having diagnosed the evil with perfect accuracy, takes measures to cure it; the moment he fixes his aim and chooses the means to reach it—then paltry and pettifogging people become all attention and eagerly follow the doings of this man who has thus come before the public gaze. Just like sparrows who are apparently indifferent, but in reality are firmly intent on the movements of the fortunate companion with the morsel of bread so that they may snatch it from him if he should momentarily relax his hold on it, so it is also with the human species. All that is needed is that one man should strike out on a new road and then a crowd of poltroons will prick up their ears and begin to sniff for whatever little booty may possibly lie at the end of that road. The moment they think they have discovered where the booty is to be gathered they hurry to find another way which may prove to be quicker in reaching that goal.

As soon as a new movement is founded and has formulated a definite programme, people of that kind come forward and proclaim that they are fighting for the same cause. This does not imply that they are ready honestly to join the ranks of such a movement and thus recognize its right of priority. It implies rather that they intend to steal the programme and found a new party on it. In doing this they are shameless enough to assure the unthinking public that for a long time they had intended to take the same line of action as the other has now taken, and frequently they succeed in thus placing themselves in a favourable light, instead of arousing the general disapprobation which they justly deserve. For it is a piece of gross impudence to take what has already been inscribed on another's flag and display it on one's own, to steal the programme of another, and then to form a separate group as if all had been created by the new founder of this group. The impudence of such conduct is particularly demonstrated when the individuals who first caused dispersion and disruption by their new foundation are those who—as experience has shown—are most emphatic in proclaiming the necessity of union and unity the moment they find they cannot catch up with their adversary's advance.

It is to that kind of conduct that the so-called 'patriotic disintegration' is to be attributed.

Certainly in the years 1918—1919 the founding of a multitude of new groups, parties, etc., calling themselves 'Patriotic,' was a natural phenomenon of the time, for which the founders were not at all responsible. By 1920 the National Socialist German Labour Party had slowly crystallized from all these parties and had become supreme. There could be no better proof of the sterling honesty of certain individual founders than the fact that many of them decided, in a really admirable manner, to sacrifice their manifestly less successful movements to the stronger movement, by joining it unconditionally and dissolving their own.

This is specially true in regard to Julius Streicher, who was at that time the protagonist of the German Socialist party in Nürnberg. The National Socialist German Labour Party had been founded with similar aims in view, but quite independently of the other. I have already said that Streicher, then a teacher in Nürnberg, was the chief protagonist of the German Socialist Party. He had a sacred conviction of the mission and future of his own movement. As soon, however, as the superior strength and stronger growth of the National Socialist Party became clear and unquestionable to his mind, he gave up his work in the German Socialist Party and called upon his followers to fall into line with the National Socialist German Labour Party, which had come out victorious from the mutual contest, and carry on the fight within its ranks for the common cause. The decision was personally a difficult one for him, but it showed a profound sense of honesty.

When that first period of the movement was over there remained no further dispersion of forces: for their honest intentions had led the men of that time to the same honourable, straightforward and just conclusion. What we now call the 'patriotic disintegration' owes its existence exclusively to the second of the two causes which I have mentioned. Ambitious men who at first had no ideas of their own, and still less any concept of aims to be pursued, felt themselves 'called' exactly at that moment in which the success of the National Socialist German Labour Party became unquestionable.

Suddenly programmes appeared which were mere transcripts of ours. Ideas were proclaimed which had been taken from us. Aims were set up on behalf of which we had been fighting for several years, and ways were mapped out which the National Socialists had for a long time trodden. All kinds of means were resorted to for the purpose of trying to convince the public that, although the National Socialist German Labour Party had now been for a long time in existence, it was found necessary to establish these new parties. But all these phrases were just as insincere as the motives behind them were ignoble.

In reality all this was grounded only on one dominant motive. That motive was the personal ambition of the founders, who wished to play a part in which their own pigmy talents could contribute nothing original except the gross effrontery which they displayed in appropriating the ideas of others, a mode of conduct which in ordinary life is looked upon as thieving.

At that time there was not an idea or concept launched by other people which these political kleptomaniacs did not seize upon at once for the purpose of applying to their own base uses. Those who did all this were the same people who subsequently, with tears in their eyes, profoundly deplored the 'patriotic disintegration' and spoke unceasingly about the 'necessity of unity'. In doing this they nurtured the secret hope that they might be able to cry down the others, who would tire of hearing these loud-mouthed accusations and would end up by abandoning all claim to the ideas that had been stolen from them and would abandon to the thieves not only the task of carrying these ideas into effect but also the task of carrying on the movements of which they themselves were the original founders.

When that did not succeed, and the new enterprises, thanks to the paltry mentality of their promoters, did not show the favourable results which had been promised beforehand, then they became more modest in their pretences and were happy if they could land themselves in one of the so-called 'co-operative unions'.

At that period everything which could not stand on its own feet joined one of those co-operative unions, believing that eight lame people hanging on to one another could force a gladiator to surrender to them.

But if among all these cripples there was one who was sound of limb he had to use all his strength to sustain the others and thus he himself was practically paralysed.

We ought to look upon the question of joining these working coalitions as a tactical problem, but, in coming to a decision, we must never forget the following fundamental principle:

Through the formation of a working coalition associations which are weak in themselves can never be made strong, whereas it can and does happen not infrequently that a strong association loses its strength by joining in a coalition with weaker ones. It is a mistake to believe that a factor of strength will result from the coalition of weak groups; because experience shows that under all forms and all conditions the majority represents the duffers and poltroons. Hence a multiplicity of associations, under a directorate of many heads, elected by these same associations, is abandoned to the control of poltroons and weaklings. Through such a coalition the free play of forces is paralysed, the struggle for the selection of the best is abolished and therewith the necessary and final victory of the healthier and stronger is impeded. Coalitions of that kind are inimical to the process of natural development, because for the most part they hinder rather than advance the solution of the problem which is being fought for.

It may happen that, from considerations of a purely tactical kind, the supreme command of a movement whose goal is set in the future will enter into a coalition with such associations for the treatment of special questions and may also stand on a common platform with them, but this can be only for a short and limited period. Such a coalition must not be permanent, if the movement does not wish to renounce its liberating mission. Because if it should become indissolubly tied up in such a combination it would lose the capacity and the right to allow its own forces to work freely in following out a natural development, so as to overcome rivals and attain its own objective triumphantly.

It must never be forgotten that nothing really great in this world has ever been achieved through coalitions, but that such achievements have always been due to the triumph of the individual. Successes achieved through coalitions, owing to the very nature of their source, carry the germs of future disintegration in them from the very start; so much so that they have already forfeited what has been achieved. The great revolutions which have taken place in human thought and have veritably transformed the aspect of the world would have been inconceivable and impossible to carry out except through titanic struggles waged between individual natures, but never as the enterprises of coalitions.

And, above all things, the People's State will never be created by the desire for compromise inherent in a patriotic coalition, but only by the iron will of a single movement which has successfully come through in the struggle with all the others.

CHAPTER IX: Fundamental Ideas Regarding the Nature and Organization of the Storm Troops

The strength of the old state rested on three pillars: the monarchical form of government, the civil service, and the army. The Revolution of 1918 abolished the form of government, dissolved the army and abandoned the civil service to the corruption of party politics. Thus the essential supports of what is called the Authority of the State were shattered. This authority nearly always depends on three elements, which are the essential foundations of all authority.

Popular support is the first element which is necessary for the creation of authority. But an authority resting on that foundation alone is still quite frail, uncertain and vacillating. Hence everyone who finds himself vested with an authority that is based only on popular support must take measures to improve and consolidate the foundations of that authority by the creation of force. Accordingly we must look upon power, that is to say, the capacity to use force, as the second foundation on which all authority is based. This foundation is more stable and secure, but not always stronger, than the first. If popular support and power are united together and can endure for a certain time, then an authority may arise which is based on a still stronger foundation, namely, the authority of tradition. And, finally, if popular support, power, and tradition are united together, then the authority based on them may be looked upon as invincible.

In Germany the Revolution abolished this last foundation. There was no longer even a traditional authority. With the collapse of the old REICH, the suppression of the monarchical form of government, the destruction of all the old insignia of greatness and the imperial symbols, tradition was shattered at a blow. The result was that the authority of the State was shaken to its foundations.

The second pillar of statal authority, namely POWER, also ceased to exist. In order to carry through the Revolution it was necessary to dissolve that body which had hitherto incorporated the organized force and power of the State, namely, the Army. Indeed, some detached fragments of the Army itself had to be employed as fighting elements in the Revolution. The Armies at the front were not subjected in the same measure to this process of disruption; but as they gradually left farther behind them the fields of glory on which they had fought heroically for four-and-half years, they were attacked by the solvent acid that had permeated the Fatherland; and when they arrived at the demobilizing centres they fell into that state of confusion which was styled voluntary obedience in the time of the Soldiers' Councils.

Of course it was out of the question to think of founding any kind of authority on this crowd of mutineering soldiers, who looked upon military service as a work of eight hours per day. Therefore the second element, that which guarantees the stability of authority, was also abolished and the Revolution had only the original element, popular support, on which to build up its authority. But this basis was extraordinarily insecure. By means of a few violent thrusts the Revolution had shattered the old statal edifice to its deepest foundations, but only because the normal equilibrium within the social structure of the nation had already been destroyed by the war.

Every national body is made up of three main classes. At one extreme we have the best of the people, taking the word 'best' here to indicate those who are highly endowed with the civic virtues and are noted for their courage and their readiness to sacrifice their private interests. At the other extreme are the worst dregs of humanity, in whom vice and egotistic interests prevail. Between these two extremes stands the third class, which is made up of the broad middle stratum, who do not represent radiant heroism or vulgar vice.

The stages of a nation's rise are accomplished exclusively under the leadership of the best extreme.

Times of normal and symmetrical development, or of stable conditions, owe their existence and outwardly visible characteristics to the preponderating influence of the middle stratum. In this stage the two extreme classes are balanced against one another; in other words, they are relatively cancelled out.

Times of national collapse are determined by the preponderating influence of the worst elements.

It must be noted here, however, that the broad masses, which constitute what I have called the middle section, come forward and make their influence felt only when the two extreme sections are engaged in mutual strife. In case one of the extreme sections comes out victorious the middle section will readily submit to its domination. If the best dominate, the broad masses will follow it. Should the worst extreme turn out triumphant, then the middle section will at least offer no opposition to it; for the masses that constitute the middle class never fight their own battles.

The outpouring of blood for four-and-a-half years during the war destroyed the inner equilibrium between these three sections in so far as it can be said—though admitting the sacrifices made by the middle section—that the class which consisted of the best human elements almost completely disappeared through the loss of so much of its blood in the war, because it was impossible to replace the truly enormous quantity of heroic German blood which had been shed during those four-and-a-half years. In hundreds of thousands of cases it was always a matter of 'VOLUNTEERS to the front', VOLUNTEERS for patrol and duty, VOLUNTEER dispatch carriers, VOLUNTEERS for establishing and working telephonic communications, VOLUNTEERS for bridge-building, VOLUNTEERS for the submarines, VOLUNTEERS for the air service, VOLUNTEERS for the storm battalions, and so on, and so on. During four-and-a-half years, and on thousands of occasions, there was always the call for volunteers and again for volunteers. And the result was always the same. Beardless young fellows or fully developed men, all filled with an ardent love for their country, urged on by their own courageous spirit or by a lofty sense of their duty—it was always such men who answered the call for volunteers. Tens of thousands, indeed hundreds of thousands, of such men came forward, so that that kind of human material steadily grew scarcer and scarcer. What did not actually fall was maimed in the fight or gradually had to join the ranks of the crippled because of the wounds they were constantly receiving, and thus they had to carry on interminably owing to the steady decrease in the supply of such men. In 1914 whole armies were composed of volunteers who, owing to a criminal lack of conscience on the part of our feckless parliamentarians, had not received any proper training in times of peace, and so were thrown as defenceless cannon-fodder to the enemy. The four hundred thousand who thus fell or were permanently maimed on the battlefields of Flanders could not be replaced any more. Their loss was something far more than merely numerical. With their death the scales, which were already too lightly weighed at that end of the social structure which represented our best human quality, now moved upwards rapidly, becoming heavier on the other end with those vulgar elements of infamy and cowardice—in short, there was an increase in the elements that constituted the worst extreme of our population.

And there was something more: While for four-and-a-half years our best human material was being thinned to an exceptional degree on the battlefields, our worst people wonderfully succeeded in saving themselves. For each hero who made the supreme sacrifice and ascended the steps of Valhalla, there was a shirker who cunningly dodged death on the plea of being engaged in business that was more or less useful at home.

And so the picture which presented itself at the end of the war was this: The great middle stratum of the nation had fulfilled its duty and paid its toll of blood. One extreme of the population, which was constituted of the best elements, had given a typical example of its heroism and had sacrificed itself almost to a man. The other extreme, which was constituted of the worst elements of the population, had preserved itself almost intact, through taking advantage of absurd laws and also because the authorities failed to enforce certain articles of the military code.

This carefully preserved scum of our nation then made the Revolution. And the reason why it could do so was that the extreme section composed of the best elements was no longer there to oppose it. It no longer existed.

Hence the German Revolution, from the very beginning, depended on only one section of the population. This act of Cain was not committed by the German people as such, but by an obscure CANAILLE of deserters, hooligans, etc.

The man at the front gladly welcomed the end of the strife in which so much blood had been shed. He was happy to be able to return home and see his wife and children once again. But he had no moral connection with the Revolution. He did not like it, nor did he like those who had provoked and organized it. During the four-and-a-half years of that bitter struggle at the front he had come to forget the party hyenas at home and all their wrangling had become foreign to him.

The Revolution was really popular only with a small section of the German people: namely, that class and their accomplices who had selected the rucksack as the hall-mark of all honourable citizens in this new State. They did not like the Revolution for its own sake, though many people still erroneously believe the contrary, but for the consequences which followed in its train.

But it was very difficult to establish any abiding authority on the popular support given to these Marxist freebooters. And yet the young Republic stood in need of authority at any cost, unless it was ready to agree to be overthrown after a short period of chaos by an elementary force assembled from those last elements that still remained among the best extreme of the population.

The danger which those who were responsible for the Revolution feared most at that time was that, in the turmoil of the confusion which they themselves had created, the ground would suddenly be taken from under their feet, that they might be suddenly seized and transported to another terrain by an iron grip, such as has often appeared at these junctures in the history of nations. The Republic must be consolidated at all costs.

Hence it was forced almost immediately after its foundation to erect another pillar beside that wavering pillar of popularity. They found that power must be organized once again in order to procure a firmer foundation for their authority.

When those who had been the matadors of the Revolution in December 1918, and January and February 1919, felt the ground trembling beneath their feet they looked around them for men who would be ready to reinforce them with military support; for their feeble position was dependent only on whatever popular favour they enjoyed. The 'anti-militarist' Republic had need of soldiers. But the first and only pillar on which the authority of the State rested, namely, its popularity, was grounded only on a conglomeration of rowdies and thieves, burglars, deserters, shirkers, etc. Therefore in that section of the nation which we have called the evil extreme it was useless to look for men who would be willing to sacrifice their lives on behalf of a new ideal. The section which had nourished the revolutionary idea and carried out the Revolution was neither able nor willing to call on the soldiers to protect it. For that section had no wish whatsoever to organize a republican State, but to disorganize what already existed and thus satisfy its own instincts all the better. Their password was not the organization and construction of the German Republic, but rather the plundering of it.

Hence the cry for help sent out by the public representatives, who were beset by a thousand anxieties, did not find any response among this class of people, but rather provoked a feeling of bitterness and repudiation. For they looked upon this step as the beginning of a breach of faith and trust, and in the building up of an authority which was no longer based on popular support but also on force they saw the beginning of a hostile move against what the Revolution meant essentially for those elements. They feared that measures might be taken against the right to robbery and absolute domination on the part of a horde of thieves and plunderers—in short, the worst rabble—who had broken out of the convict prisons and left their chains behind.

The representatives of the people might cry out as much as they liked, but they could get no help from that rabble. The cries for help were met with the counter-cry 'traitors' by those very people on whose support the popularity of the regime was founded.

Then for the first time large numbers of young Germans were found who were ready to button on the military uniform once again in the service of 'Peace and Order', as they believed, shouldering the carbine and rifle and donning the steel helmet to defend the wreckers of the Fatherland. Volunteer corps were assembled and, although hating the Revolution, they began to defend it. The practical effect of their action was to render the Revolution firm and stable. In doing this they acted in perfect good faith.

The real organizer of the Revolution and the actual wire-puller behind it, the international Jew, had sized up the situation correctly. The German people were not yet ripe to be drawn into the blood swamp of Bolshevism, as the Russian people had been drawn. And that was because there was a closer racial union between the intellectual classes in Germany and the manual workers, and also because broad social strata were permeated with cultured people, such as was the case also in the other States of Western Europe; but this state of affairs was completely lacking in Russia. In that country the intellectual classes were mostly not of Russian nationality, or at least they did not have the racial characteristics of the Slav. The thin upper layer of intellectuals which then existed in Russia might be abolished at any time, because there was no intermediate stratum connecting it organically with the great mass of the people. There the mental and moral level of the great mass of the people was frightfully low.

In Russia the moment the agitators were successful in inciting broad masses of the people, who could not read or write, against the upper layer of intellectuals who were not in contact with the masses or permanently linked with them in any way — at that moment the destiny of Russia was decided, the success of the Revolution was assured. Thereupon the analphabetic Russian became the slave of his Jewish dictators who, on their side, were shrewd enough to name their dictatorship 'The Dictatorship of the People'.

In the case of Germany an additional factor must be taken into account. Here the Revolution could be carried into effect only if the Army could first be gradually dismembered. But the real author of the Revolution and of the process of disintegration in the Army was not the soldier who had fought at the front but the CANAILLE which more or less shunned the light and which were either quartered in the home garrisons or were officiating as 'indispensables' somewhere in the business world at home. This army was reinforced by ten thousand deserters who, without running any particular risk, could turn their backs on the Front. At all times the real poltroon fears nothing so much as death. But at the Front he had death before his eyes every day in a thousand different shapes. There has always been one possible way, and one only, of making weak or wavering men, or even downright poltroons, face their duty steadfastly. This means that the deserter must be given to understand that his desertion will bring upon him just the very thing he is flying from. At the Front a man may die, but the deserter MUST die. Only this draconian threat against every attempt to desert the flag can have a terrifying effect, not merely on the individual but also on the mass. Therein lay the meaning and purpose of the military penal code.

It was a fine belief to think that the great struggle for the life of a nation could be carried through if it were based solely on voluntary fidelity arising from and sustained by the knowledge that such a struggle was necessary. The voluntary fulfilment of one's duty is a motive that determines the actions of only the best men, but not of the average type of men. Hence special laws are necessary; just as, for instance, the law against stealing, which was not made for men who are honest on principle but for the weak and unstable elements. Such laws are meant to hinder the evil-doer through their deterrent effect and thus prevent a state of affairs from arising in which the honest man is considered the more stupid, and which would end in the belief that it is better to have a share in the robbery than to stand by with empty hands or allow oneself to be robbed.

It was a mistake to believe that in a struggle which, according to all human foresight, might last for several years it would be possible to dispense with those expedients which the experience of hundreds and even of thousands of years had proved to be effective in making weak and unstable men face and fulfil their duty in difficult times and at moments of great nervous stress.

For the voluntary war hero it is, of course, not necessary to have the death penalty in the military code, but it is necessary for the cowardly egoists who value their own lives more than the existence of the community in the hour of national need. Such weak and characterless people can be held back from surrendering to their cowardice only by the application of the heaviest penalties. When men have to struggle with death every day and remain for weeks in trenches of mire, often very badly supplied with food, the man who is unsure of himself and begins to waver cannot be made to stick to his post by threats of imprisonment or even penal servitude. Only by a ruthless enforcement of the death penalty can this be effected. For experience shows that at such a time the recruit considers prison a thousand times more preferable than the battlefield. In prison at least his precious life is not in danger. The practical abolition of the death penalty during the war was a mistake for which we had to pay dearly. Such omission really meant that the military penal code was no longer recognized as valid. An army of deserters poured into the stations at the rear or returned home, especially in 1918, and there began to form that huge criminal organization with which we were suddenly faced, after November 7th, 1918, and which perpetrated the Revolution.

The Front had nothing to do with all this. Naturally, the soldiers at the Front were yearning for peace. But it was precisely that fact which represented a special danger for the Revolution. For when the German soldiers began to draw near home, after the Armistice, the revolutionaries were in trepidation and asked the same question again and again: What will the troops from the Front do? Will the field-greys stand for it?

During those weeks the Revolution was forced to give itself at least an external appearance of moderation, if it were not to run the risk of being wrecked in a moment by a few German divisions. For at that time, even if the commander of one division alone had made up his mind to rally the soldiers of his division, who had always remained faithful to him, in an onslaught to tear down the red flag and put the 'councils' up against the wall, or, if there was any resistance, to break it with trench-mortars and hand grenades, that division would have grown into an army of sixty divisions in less than four weeks. The Jew wire-pullers were terrified by this prospect more than by anything else; and to forestall this particular danger they found it necessary to give the Revolution a certain aspect of moderation. They dared not allow it to degenerate into Bolshevism, so they had to face the existing conditions by putting up the hypocritical picture of 'order and tranquillity'. Hence many important concessions, the appeal to the old civil service and to the heads of the old Army. They would be needed at least for a certain time, and only when they had served the purpose of Turks' Heads could the deserved kick-out be administered with impunity. Then the Republic would be taken entirely out of the hands of the old servants of the State and delivered into the claws of the revolutionaries.

They thought that this was the only plan which would succeed in duping the old generals and civil servants and disarm any eventual opposition beforehand through the apparently harmless and mild character of the new regime.

Practical experience has shown to what extent the plan succeeded.

The Revolution, however, was not made by the peaceful and orderly elements of the nation but rather by rioters, thieves and robbers. And the way in which the Revolution was developing did not accord with the intentions of these latter elements; still, on tactical grounds, it was not possible to explain to them the reasons for the course things were taking and make that course acceptable.

As Social Democracy gradually gained power it lost more and more the character of a crude revolutionary party. Of course in their inner hearts the Social Democrats wanted a revolution; and their leaders had no other end in view. Certainly not. But what finally resulted was only a revolutionary programme; but not a body of men who would be able to carry it out. A revolution cannot be carried through by a party of ten million members. If such a movement were attempted the leaders would find that it was not an extreme section of the population on which they had to depend butrather the broad masses of the middle stratum; hence the inert masses.

Recognizing all this, already during the war, the Jews caused the famous split in the Social Democratic Party. While the Social Democratic Party, conforming to the inertia of its mass following, clung like a leaden weight on the neck of the national defence, the actively radical elements were extracted from it and formed into new aggressive columns for purposes of attack. The Independent Socialist Party and the Spartacist League were the storm battalions of revolutionary Marxism. The objective assigned to them was to create a FAIT ACCOMPLI, on the grounds of which the masses of the Social Democratic Party could take their stand, having been prepared for this event long beforehand. The feckless bourgeoisie had been estimated at its just value by the Marxists and treated EN CANAILLE. Nobody bothered about it, knowing well that in their canine servility the representatives of an old and worn-out generation would not be able to offer any serious resistance.

When the Revolution had succeeded and its artificers believed that the main pillars of the old State had been broken down, the Army returning from the Front began to appear in the light of a sinister sphinx and thus made it necessary to slow down the national course of the Revolution. The main body of the Social Democratic horde occupied the conquered positions, and the Independent Socialist and Spartacist storm battalions were side-tracked.

But that did not happen without a struggle.

The activist assault formations that had started the Revolution were dissatisfied and felt that they had been betrayed. They now wanted to continue the fight on their own account. But their illimitable racketeering became odious even to the wire-pullers of the Revolution. For the Revolution itself had scarcely been accomplished when two camps appeared. In the one camp were the elements of peace and order; in the other were those of blood and terror. Was it not perfectly natural that our bourgeoisie should rush with flying colours to the camp of peace and order? For once in their lives their piteous political organizations found it possible to act, inasmuch as the ground had been prepared for them on which they were glad to get a new footing; and thus to a certain extent they found themselves in coalition with that power which they hated but feared. The German political bourgeoisie achieved the high honour of being able to associate itself with the accursed Marxist leaders for the purpose of combating Bolshevism.

Thus the following state of affairs took shape as early as December 1918 and January 1919:

A minority constituted of the worst elements had made the Revolution. And behind this minority all the Marxist parties immediately fell into step. The Revolution itself had an outward appearance of moderation, which aroused against it the enmity of the fanatical extremists. These began to launch hand-grenades and fire machine-guns, occupying public buildings, thus threatening to destroy the moderate appearance of the Revolution. To prevent this terror from developing further a truce was concluded between the representatives of the new regime and the adherents of the old order, so as to be able to wage a common fight against the extremists. The result was that the enemies of the Republic ceased to oppose the Republic as such and helped to subjugate those who were also enemies of the Republic, though for quite different reasons. But a further result was that all danger of the adherents of the old State putting up a fight against the new was now definitely averted.

This fact must always be clearly kept in mind. Only by remembering it can we understand how it was possible that a nation in which nine-tenths of the people had not joined in a revolution, where seven-tenths repudiated it and six-tenths detested it—how this nation allowed the Revolution to be imposed upon it by the remaining one-tenth of the population.

Gradually the barricade heroes in the Spartacist camp petered out, and so did the nationalist patriots and idealists on the other side. As these two groups steadily dwindled, the masses of the middle stratum, as always happens, triumphed. The Bourgeoisie and the Marxists met together on the grounds of accomplished facts, and the Republic began to be consolidated. At first, however, that did not prevent the bourgeois parties from propounding their monarchist ideas for some time further, especially at the elections, whereby they endeavoured to conjure up the spirits of the dead past to encourage their own feeble-hearted followers. It was not an honest proceeding. In their hearts they had broken with the monarchy long ago; but the foulness of the new regime had begun to extend its corruptive action and make itself felt in the camp of the bourgeois parties. The common bourgeois politician now felt better in the slime of republican corruption than in the severe decency of the defunct State, which still lived in his memory.

As I have already pointed out, after the destruction of the old Army the revolutionary leaders were forced to strengthen statal authority by creating a new factor of power. In the conditions that existed they could do this only by winning over to their side the adherents of a WELTANSCHAUUNG which was a direct contradiction of their own. From those elements alone it was possible slowly to create a new army which, limited numerically by the peace treaties, had to be subsequently transformed in spirit so as to become an instrument of the new regime.

Setting aside the defects of the old State, which really became the cause of the Revolution, if we ask how it was possible to carry the Revolution to a successful issue as a political act, we arrive at the following conclusions:

1. It was due to a process of dry rot in our conceptions of duty and obedience.

2. It was due also to the passive timidity of the Parties who were supposed to uphold the State.

To this the following must be added: The dry rot which attacked our concepts of duty and obedience was fundamentally due to our wholly non-national and purely State education. From this came the habit of confusing means and ends. Consciousness of duty, fulfilment of duty, and obedience, are not ends in themselves no more than the State is an end in itself; but they all ought to be employed as means to facilitate and assure the existence of a community of people who are kindred both physically and spiritually. At a moment when a nation is manifestly collapsing and when all outward signs show that it is on the point of becoming the victim of ruthless oppression, thanks to the conduct of a few miscreants, to obey these people and fulfil one's duty towards them is merely doctrinaire formalism, and indeed pure folly; whereas, on the other hand, the refusal of obedience and fulfilment of duty in such a case might save the nation from collapse. According to our current bourgeois idea of the State, if a divisional general received from above the order not to shoot he fulfilled his duty and therefore acted rightly in not shooting, because to the bourgeois mind blind formal obedience is a more valuable thing than the life of a nation. But according to the National Socialist concept it is not obedience to weak superiors that should prevail at such moments, in such an hour the duty of assuming personal responsibility towards the whole nation makes its appearance.

The Revolution succeeded because that concept had ceased to be a vital force with our people, or rather with our governments, and died down to something that was merely formal and doctrinaire.

As regards the second point, it may be said that the more profound cause of the fecklessness of the bourgeois parties must be attributed to the fact that the most active and upright section of our people had lost their lives in the war. Apart from that, the bourgeois parties, which may be considered as the only political formations that stood by the old State, were convinced that they ought to defend their principles only by intellectual ways and means, since the use of physical force was permitted only to the State. That outlook was a sign of the weakness and decadence which had been gradually developing. And it was also senseless at a period when there was a political adversary who had long ago abandoned that standpoint and, instead of this, had openly declared that he meant to attain his political ends by force whenever that became possible. When Marxism emerged in the world of bourgeois democracy, as a consequence of that democracy itself, the appeal sent out by the bourgeois democracy to fight Marxism with intellectual weapons was a piece of folly for which a terrible expiation had to be made later on. For Marxism always professed the doctrine that the use of arms was a matter which had to be judged from the standpoint of expediency and that success justified the use of arms.

This idea was proved correct during the days from November 7 to 10, 1918. The Marxists did not then bother themselves in the least about parliament or democracy, but they gave the death blow to both by turning loose their horde of criminals to shoot and raise hell.

When the Revolution was over the bourgeois parties changed the title of their firm and suddenly reappeared, the heroic leaders emerging from dark cellars or more lightsome storehouses where they had sought refuge. But, just as happens in the case of all representatives of antiquated institutions, they had not forgotten their errors or learned anything new. Their political programme was grounded in the past, even though they themselves had become reconciled to the new regime. Their aim was to secure a share in the new establishment, and so they continued the use of words as their sole weapon.

Therefore after the Revolution the bourgeois parties also capitulated to the street in a miserable fashion.

When the law for the Protection of the Republic was introduced the majority was not at first in favour of it. But, confronted with two hundred thousand Marxists demonstrating in the streets, the bourgeois 'statesmen' were so terror-stricken that they voted for the Law against their wills, for the edifying reason that otherwise they feared they might get their heads smashed by the enraged masses on leaving the Reichstag.

And so the new State developed along its own course, as if there had been no national opposition at all.

The only organizations which at that time had the strength and courage to face Marxism and its enraged masses were first of all the volunteer corps[20], and subsequently the organizations for self-defence, the civic guards and finally the associations formed by the demobilized soldiers of the old Army.

But the existence of these bodies did not appreciably change the course of German history; and that for the following causes:

As the so-called national parties were without influence, because they had no force which could effectively demonstrate in the street, the Leagues of Defence could not exercise any influence because they had no political idea and especially because they had no definite political aim in view.

The success which Marxism once attained was due to perfect co-operation between political purposes and ruthless force. What deprived nationalist Germany of all practical hopes of shaping German development was the lack of a determined co-operation between brute force and political aims wisely chosen.

Whatever may have been the aspirations of the 'national' parties, they had no force whatsoever to fight for these aspirations, least of all in the streets.

The Defence Leagues had force at their disposal. They were masters of the street and of the State, but they lacked political ideas and aims on behalf of which their forces might have been or could have been employed in the interests of the German nation. The cunning Jew was able in both cases, by his astute powers of persuasion, in reinforcing an already existing tendency to make this unfortunate state of affairs permanent and at the same time to drive the roots of it still deeper.

The Jew succeeded brilliantly in using his Press for the purpose of spreading abroad the idea that the defence associations were of a 'non-political' character just as in politics he was always astute enough to praise the purely intellectual character of the struggle and demand that it must always be kept on that plane

Millions of German imbeciles then repeated this folly without having the slightest suspicion that by so doing they were, for all practical purposes, disarming themselves and delivering themselves defenceless into the hands of the Jew.

But there is a natural explanation of this also. The lack of a great idea which would re-shape things anew has always meant a limitation in fighting power. The conviction of the right to employ even the most brutal weapons is always associated with an ardent faith in the necessity for a new and revolutionary transformation of the world.

A movement which does not fight for such high aims and ideals will never have recourse to extreme means.

The appearance of a new and great idea was the secret of success in the French Revolution. The Russian Revolution owes its triumph to an idea. And it was only the idea that enabled Fascism triumphantly to subject a whole nation to a process of complete renovation.

Bourgeois parties are not capable of such an achievement. And it was not the bourgeois parties alone that fixed their aim in a restoration of the past. The defence associations also did so, in so far as they concerned themselves with political aims at all. The spirit of the old war legions and Kyffauser tendencies lived in them and therewith helped politically to blunt the sharpest weapons which the German nation then possessed and allow them to rust in the hands of republican serfs. The fact that these associations were inspired by the best of intentions in so doing, and certainly acted in good faith, does not alter in the slightest degree the foolishness of the course they adopted.

In the consolidated REICHSWEHR Marxism gradually acquired the support of force, which it needed for its authority. As a logical consequence it proceeded to abolish those defence associations which it considered dangerous, declaring that they were now no longer necessary. Some rash leaders who defied the Marxist orders were summoned to court and sent to prison. But they all got what they had deserved.

The founding of the National Socialist German Labour Party incited a movement which was the first to fix its aim, not in a mechanical restoration of the past—as the bourgeois parties did—but in the substitution of an organic People's State for the present absurd statal mechanism.

From the first day of its foundation the new movement took its stand on the principle that its ideas had to be propagated by intellectual means but that, wherever necessary, muscular force must be employed to support this propaganda. In accordance with their conviction of the paramount importance of the new doctrine, the leaders of the new movement naturally believe that no sacrifice can be considered too great when it is a question of carrying through the purpose of the movement.

I have emphasized that in certain circumstances a movement which is meant to win over the hearts of the people must be ready to defend itself with its own forces against terrorist attempts on the part of its adversaries. It has invariably happened in the history of the world that formal State authority has failed to break a reign of terror which was inspired by a WELTANSCHAUUNG. It can only be conquered by a new and different WELTANSCHAUUNG whose representatives are quite as audacious and determined. The acknowledgment of this fact has always been very unpleasant for the bureaucrats who are the protectors of the State, but the fact remains nevertheless. The rulers of the State can guarantee tranquillity and order only in case the State embodies a WELTANSCHAUUNG which is shared in by the people as a whole; so that elements of disturbance can be treated as isolated criminals, instead of being considered as the champions of an idea which is diametrically opposed to official opinions. If such should be the case the State may employ the most violent measures for centuries long against the terror that threatens it; but in the end all these measures will prove futile, and the State will have to succumb.

The German State is intensely overrun by Marxism. In a struggle that went on for seventy years the State was not able to prevent the triumph of the Marxist idea. Even though the sentences to penal servitude and imprisonment amounted in all to thousands of years, and even though the most sanguinary methods of repression were in innumerable instances threatened against the champions of the Marxist WELTANSCHAUUNG, in the end the State was forced to capitulate almost completely. The ordinary bourgeois political leaders will deny all this, but their protests are futile.

Seeing that the State capitulated unconditionally to Marxism on November 9th, 1918, it will not suddenly rise up tomorrow as the conqueror of Marxism. On the contrary. Bourgeois simpletons sitting on office stools in the various ministries babble about the necessity of not governing against the wishes of the workers, and by the word 'workers' they mean the Marxists. By identifying the German worker with Marxism not only are they guilty of a vile falsification of the truth, but they thus try to hide their own collapse before the Marxist idea and the Marxist organization.

In view of the complete subordination of the present State to Marxism, the National Socialist Movement feels all the more bound not only to prepare the way for the triumph of its idea by appealing to the reason and understanding of the public but also to take upon itself the responsibility of organizing its own defence against the terror of the International, which is intoxicated with its own victory.

I have already described how practical experience in our young movement led us slowly to organize a system of defence for our meetings. This gradually assumed the character of a military body specially trained for the maintenance of order, and tended to develop into a service which would have its properly organized cadres.

This new formation might resemble the defence associations externally, but in reality there were no grounds of comparison between the one and the other.

As I have already said, the German defence organizations did not have any definite political ideas of their own. They really were only associations for mutual protection, and they were trained and organized accordingly, so that they were an illegal complement or auxiliary to the legal forces of the State. Their character as free corps arose only from the way in which they were constructed and the situation in which the State found itself at that time. But they certainly could not claim to be free corps on the grounds that they were associations formed freely and privately for the purpose of fighting for their own freely formed political convictions. Such they were not, despite the fact that some of their leaders and some associations as such were definitely opposed to the Republic. For before we can speak of political convictions in the higher sense we must be something more than merely convinced that the existing regime is defective. Political convictions in the higher sense mean that one has the picture of a new regime clearly before one's mind, feels that the establishment of this regime is an absolute necessity and sets himself to carry out that purpose as the highest task to which his life can be devoted.

The troops for the preservation of order, which were then formed under the National Socialist Movement, were fundamentally different from all the other defence associations by reason of the fact that our formations were not meant in any way to defend the state of things created by the Revolution, but rather that they were meant exclusively to support our struggle for the creation of a new Germany.

In the beginning this body was merely a guard to maintain order at our meetings. Its first task was limited to making it possible for us to hold our meetings, which otherwise would have been completely prevented by our opponents. These men were at that time trained merely for purposes of attack, but they were not taught to adore the big stick exclusively, as was then pretended in stupid German patriotic circles. They used the cudgel because they knew that it can be made impossible for high ideals to be put forward if the man who endeavours to propagate them can be struck down with the cudgel. As a matter of fact, it has happened in history not infrequently that some of the greatest minds have perished under the blows of the most insignificant helots. Our bodyguards did not look upon violence as an end in itself, but they protected the expositors of ideal aims and purposes against hostile coercion by violence. They also understood that there was no obligation to undertake the defence of a State which did not guarantee the defence of the nation, but that, on the contrary, they had to defend the nation against those who were threatening to destroy nation and State.

After the fight which took place at the meeting in the Munich Hofbräuhaus, where the small number of our guards who were present won everlasting fame for themselves by the heroic manner in which they stormed the adversaries; these guards were called THE STORM DETACHMENT. As the name itself indicates, they represent only a DETACHMENT of the Movement. They are one constituent element of it, just as is the Press, the propaganda, educational institutes, and other sections of the Party.

We learned how necessary was the formation of such a body, not only from our experience on the occasion of that memorable meeting but also when we sought gradually to carry the Movement beyond Munich and extend it to the other parts of Germany. Once we had begun to appear as a danger to Marxism the Marxists lost no opportunity of trying to crush beforehand all preparations for the holding of National Socialist meetings. When they did not succeed in this they tried to break up the meeting itself. It goes without saying that all the Marxist organizations, no matter of what grade or view, blindly supported the policy and activities of their representations in every case. But what is to be said of the bourgeois parties who, when they were reduced to silence by these same Marxists and in many places did not dare to send their speakers to appear before the public, yet showed themselves pleased, in a stupid and incomprehensible manner, every time we received any kind of set-back in our fight against Marxism. The bourgeois parties were happy to think that those whom they themselves could not stand up against, but had to knuckle down to, could not be broken by us. What must be said of those State officials, chiefs of police, and even cabinet ministers, who showed a scandalous lack of principle in presenting themselves externally to the public as 'national' and yet shamelessly acted as the henchmen of the Marxists in the disputes which we, National Socialists, had with the latter. What can be said of persons who debased themselves so far, for the sake of a little abject praise in the Jewish Press, that they persecuted those men to whose heroic courage and intervention, regardless of risk, they were partly indebted for not having been torn to pieces by the Red mob a few years previously and strung up to the lamp-posts?

One day these lamentable phenomena fired the late but unforgotten Prefect Pöhner— a man whose unbending straightforwardness forced him to hate all twisters and to hate them as only a man with an honest heart can hate—to say: "In all my life I wished to be first a German and then an official, and I never wanted to mix up with these creatures who, as if they were kept officials, prostituted themselves before anybody who could play lord and master for the time being."

It was a specially sad thing that gradually tens of thousands of honest and loyal servants of the State did not only come under the power of such people but were also slowly contaminated by their unprincipled morals. Moreover, these kind of men pursued honest officials with a furious hatred, degrading them and driving them from their positions, and yet passed themselves off as 'national' by the aid of their lying hypocrisy.

From officials of that kind we could expect no support, and only in very rare instances was it given. Only by building up its own defence could our movement become secure and attract that amount of public attention and general respect which is given to those who can defend themselves when attacked.

As an underlying principle in the internal development of the Storm Detachment, we came to the decision that not only should it be perfectly trained in bodily efficiency but that the men should be so instructed as to make them indomitably convinced champions of the National Socialist ideas and, finally, that they should be schooled to observe the strictest discipline. This body was to have nothing to do with the defence organizations of the bourgeois type and especially not with any secret organization.

My reasons at that time for guarding strictly against letting the Storm Detachment of the German National Socialist Labour Party appear as a defence association were as follows:

On purely practical grounds it is impossible to build up a national defence organization by means of private associations, unless the State makes an enormous contribution to it. Whoever thinks otherwise overestimates his own powers. Now it is entirely out of the question to form organizations of any military value for a definite purpose on the principle of so-called 'voluntary discipline'. Here the chief support for enforcing orders, namely, the power of inflicting punishment, is lacking. In the autumn, or rather in the spring, of 1919 it was still possible to raise 'volunteer corps', not only because most of the men who came forward at that time had been through the school of the old Army, but also because the kind of duty imposed there constrained the individual to absolute obedience at least for a definite period of time.

That spirit is entirely lacking in the volunteer defence organizations of to-day. The more the defence association grows, the weaker its discipline becomes and so much the less can one demand from the individual members. Thus the whole organization will more and more assume the character of the old non-political associations of war comrades and veterans.

It is impossible to carry through a voluntary training in military service for larger masses unless one is assured absolute power of command. There will always be few men who will voluntarily and spontaneously submit to that kind of obedience which is considered natural and necessary in the Army.

Moreover, a proper system of military training cannot be developed where there are such ridiculously scanty means as those at the disposal of the defence associations. The principal task of such an institution must be to impart the best and most reliable kind of instruction. Eight years have passed since the end of the War, and during that time none of our German youth, at an age when formerly they would have had to do military service, have received any systematic training at all. The aim of a defence association cannot be to enlist here and now all those who have already received a military training; for in that case it could be reckoned with mathematical accuracy when the last member would leave the association. Even the younger soldier from 1918 will no longer be fit for front-line service twenty years later, and we are approaching that state of things with a rapidity that gives cause for anxiety. Thus the defence associations must assume more and more the aspect of the old ex-service men's societies. But that cannot be the meaning and purpose of an institution which calls itself, not an association of ex-service men but a DEFENCE association, indicating by this title that it considers its task to be, not only to preserve the tradition of the old soldiers and hold them together but also to propagate the idea of national defence and be able to carry this idea into practical effect, which means the creation of a body of men who are fit and trained for military defence.

But this implies that those elements will receive a military training which up to now have received none. This is something that in practice is impossible for the defence associations. Real soldiers cannot be made by a training of one or two hours per week.

In view of the enormously increasing demands which modern warfare imposes on each individual soldier to-day, a military service of two years is barely sufficient to transform a raw recruit into a trained soldier. At the Front during the War we all saw the fearful consequences which our young recruits had to suffer from their lack of a thorough military training. Volunteer formations which had been drilled for fifteen or twenty weeks under an iron discipline and shown unlimited self-denial proved nevertheless to be no better than cannon fodder at the Front. Only when distributed among the ranks of the old and experienced soldiers could the young recruits, who had been trained for four or six months, become useful members of a regiment. Guided by the 'old men', they adapted themselves gradually to their task.

In the light of all this, how hopeless must the attempt be to create a body of fighting troops by a so-called training of one or two hours in the week, without any definite power of command and without any considerable means. In that way perhaps one could refresh military training in old soldiers, but raw recruits cannot thus be transformed into expert soldiers.

How such a proceeding produces utterly worthless results may also be demonstrated by the fact that at the same time as these so-called volunteer defence associations, with great effort and outcry and under difficulties and lack of necessities, try to educate and train a few thousand men of goodwill (the others need not be taken into account) for purposes of national defence, the State teaches our young men democratic and pacifist ideas and thus deprives millions and millions of their national instincts, poisons their logical sense of patriotism and gradually turns them into a herd of sheep who will patiently follow any arbitrary command. Thus they render ridiculous all those attempts made by the defence associations to inculcate their ideas in the minds of the German youth.

Almost more important is the following consideration, which has always made me take up a stand against all attempts at a so-called military training on the basis of the volunteer associations.

Assuming that, in spite of all the difficulties just mentioned, a defence association were successful in training a certain number of Germans every year to be efficient soldiers, not only as regards their mental outlook but also as regards bodily efficiency and the expert handling of arms, the result must necessarily be null and void in a State whose whole tendency makes it not only look upon such a defensive formation as undesirable but even positively hate it, because such an association would completely contradict the intimate aims of the political leaders, who are the corrupters of this State.

But anyhow, such a result would be worthless under governments which have demonstrated by their own acts that they do not lay the slightest importance on the military power of the nation and are not disposed to permit an appeal to that power only in case that it were necessary for the protection of their own malignant existence.

And that is the state of affairs to-day. It is not ridiculous to think of training some ten thousand men in the use of arms, and carry on that training surreptitiously, when a few years previously the State, having shamefully sacrificed eight-and-a-half million highly trained soldiers, not merely did not require their services any more, but, as a mark of gratitude for their sacrifices, held them up to public contumely. Shall we train soldiers for a regime which besmirched and spat upon our most glorious soldiers, tore the medals and badges from their breasts, trampled on their flags and derided their achievements? Has the present regime taken one step towards restoring the honour of the old army and bringing those who destroyed and outraged it to answer for their deeds? Not in the least. On the contrary, the people I have just referred to may be seen enthroned in the highest positions under the State to-day. And yet it was said at Leipzig: "Right goes with might." Since, however, in our Republic to-day might is in the hands of the very men who arranged for the Revolution, and since that Revolution represents a most despicable act of high treason against the nation — yea, the vilest act in German history — there can surely be no grounds for saying that might of this character should be enhanced by the formation of a new young army. It is against all sound reason.

The importance which this State attached, after the Revolution of 1918, to the reinforcement of its position from the military point of view is clearly and unmistakably demonstrated by its attitude towards the large self-defence organizations which existed in that period. They were not unwelcome as long as they were of use for the personal protection of the miserable creatures cast up by the Revolution.

But the danger to these creatures seemed to disappear as the debasement of our people gradually increased. As the existence of the defence associations no longer implied a reinforcement of the national policy they became superfluous. Hence every effort was made to disarm them and suppress them wherever that was possible.

History records only a few examples of gratitude on the part of princes. But there is not one patriot among the new bourgeoisie who can count on the gratitude of revolutionary incendiaries and assassins, persons who have enriched themselves from the public spoil and betrayed the nation. In examining the problem as to the wisdom of forming these defence associations I have never ceased to ask: 'For whom shall I train these young men? For what purpose will they be employed when they will have to be called out?' The answer to these questions lays down at the same time the best rule for us to follow.

If the present State should one day have to call upon trained troops of this kind it would never be for the purpose of defending the interests of the nation VIS-À-VIS those of the stranger but rather to protect the oppressors of the nation inside the country against the danger of a general outbreak of wrath on the part of a nation which has been deceived and betrayed and whose interests have been bartered away.

For this reason it was decided that the Storm Detachment of the German National Socialist Labour Party ought not to be in the nature of a military organization. It had to be an instrument of protection and education for the National Socialist Movement and its duties should be in quite a different sphere from that of the military defence association.

And, of course, the Storm Detachment should not be in the nature of a secret organization. Secret organizations are established only for purposes that are against the law. Therewith the purpose of such an organization is limited by its very nature. Considering the loquacious propensities of the German people, it is not possible to build up any vast organization, keeping it secret at the same time and cloaking its purpose. Every attempt of that kind is destined to turn out absolutely futile. It is not merely that our police officials to-day have at their disposal a staff of eaves-droppers and other such rabble who are ready to play traitor, like Judas, for thirty pieces of silver and will betray whatever secrets they can discover and will invent what they would like to reveal. In order to forestall such eventualities, it is never possible to bind one's own followers to the silence that is necessary. Only small groups can become really secret societies, and that only after long years of filtration. But the very smallness of such groups would deprive them of all value for the National Socialist Movement. What we needed then and need now is not one or two hundred dare-devil conspirators but a hundred thousand devoted champions of our WELTANSCHAUUNG. The work must not be done through secret conventicles but through formidable mass demonstrations in public. Dagger and pistol and poison-vial cannot clear the way for the progress of the movement. That can be done only by winning over the man in the street. We must overthrow Marxism, so that for the future National Socialism will be master of the street, just as it will one day become master of the State.

There is another danger connected with secret societies. It lies in the fact that their members often completely misunderstand the greatness of the task in hand and are apt to believe that a favourable destiny can be assured for the nation all at once by means of a single murder. Such a belief may find historical justification by appealing to cases where a nation had been suffering under the tyranny of some oppressor who at the same time was a man of genius and whose extraordinary personality guaranteed the internal solidity of his position and enabled him to maintain his fearful oppression. In such cases a man may suddenly arise from the ranks of the people who is ready to sacrifice himself and plunge the deadly steel into the heart of the hated individual. In order to look upon such a deed as abhorrent one must have the republican mentality of that petty CANAILLE who are conscious of their own crime. But the greatest champion[21] of liberty that the German people have ever had has glorified such a deed in WILLIAM TELL.

During 1919 and 1920 there was danger that the members of secret organizations, under the influence of great historical examples and overcome by the immensity of the nation's misfortunes, might attempt to wreak vengeance on the destroyers of their country, under the belief that this would end the miseries of the people. All such attempts were sheer folly, for the reason that the Marxist triumph was not due to the superior genius of one remarkable person but rather to immeasurable incompetence and cowardly shirking on the part of the bourgeoisie. The hardest criticism that can be uttered against our bourgeoisie is simply to state the fact that it submitted to the Revolution, even though the Revolution did not produce one single man of eminent worth. One can always understand how it was possible to capitulate before a Robespierre, a Danton, or a Marat; but it was utterly scandalous to go down on all fours before the withered Scheidemann, the obese Herr Erzberger, Frederick Ebert, and the innumerable other political pigmies of the Revolution. There was not a single man of parts in whom one could see the revolutionary man of genius. Therein lay the country's misfortune; for they were only revolutionary bugs, Spartacists wholesale and retail. To suppress one of them would be an act of no consequence. The only result would be that another pair of bloodsuckers, equally fat and thirsty, would be ready to take his place.

During those years we had to take up a determined stand against an idea which owed its origin and foundation to historical episodes that were really great, but to which our own despicable epoch did not bear the slightest similarity.

The same reply may be given when there is question of putting somebody 'on the spot' who has acted as a traitor to his country. It would be ridiculous and illogical to shoot a poor wretch[22] who had betrayed the position of a howitzer to the enemy while the highest positions of the government are occupied by a rabble who bartered away a whole empire, who have on their consciences the deaths of two million men who were sacrificed in vain, fellows who were responsible for the millions maimed in the war and who make a thriving business out of the republican regime without allowing their souls to be disturbed in any way. It would be absurd to do away with small traitors in a State whose government has absolved the great traitors from all punishment. For it might easily happen that one day an honest idealist, who, out of love for his country, had removed from circulation some miserable informer that had given information about secret stores of arms might now be called to answer for his act before the chief traitors of the country. And there is still an important question: Shall some small traitorous creature be suppressed by another small traitor, or by an idealist? In the former case the result would be doubtful and the deed would almost surely be revealed later on. In the second case a petty rascal is put out of the way and the life of an idealist who may be irreplaceable is in jeopardy.

For myself, I believe that small thieves should not be hanged while big thieves are allowed to go free. One day a national tribunal will have to judge and sentence some tens of thousands of organizers who were responsible for the criminal November betrayal and all the consequences that followed on it. Such an example will teach the necessary lesson, once and for ever, to those paltry traitors who revealed to the enemy the places where arms were hidden.

On the grounds of these considerations I steadfastly forbade all participation in secret societies, and I took care that the Storm Detachment should not assume such a character. During those years I kept the National Socialist Movement away from those experiments which were being undertaken by young Germans who for the most part were inspired with a sublime idealism but who became the victims of their own deeds, because they could not ameliorate the lot of their fatherland to the slightest degree.

If then the Storm Detachment must not be either a military defence organization or a secret society, the following conclusions must result:

1. Its training must not be organized from the military standpoint but from the standpoint of what is most practical for party purposes. Seeing that its members must undergo a good physical training, the place of chief importance must not be given to military drill but rather to the practice of sports. I have always considered boxing and ju-jitsu more important than some kind of bad, because mediocre, training in rifle-shooting. If the German nation were presented with a body of young men who had been perfectly trained in athletic sports, who were imbued with an ardent love for their country and a readiness to take the initiative in a fight, then the national State could make an army out of that body within less than two years if it were necessary, provided the cadres already existed. In the actual state of affairs only the REICHSWEHR could furnish the cadres and not a defence organization that was neither one thing nor the other. Bodily efficiency would develop in the individual a conviction of his superiority and would give him that confidence which is always based only on the consciousness of one's own powers. They must also develop that athletic agility which can be employed as a defensive weapon in the service of the Movement.

2. In order to safeguard the Storm Detachment against any tendency towards secrecy, not only must the uniform be such that it can immediately be recognized by everybody, but the large number of its effectives show the direction in which the Movement is going and which must be known to the whole public. The members of the Storm Detachment must not hold secret gatherings but must march in the open and thus, by their actions, put an end to all legends about a secret organization. In order to keep them away from all temptations towards finding an outlet for their activities in small conspiracies, from the very beginning we had to inculcate in their minds the great idea of the Movement

and educate them so thoroughly to the task of defending this idea that their horizon became enlarged and that the individual no longer considered it his mission to remove from circulation some rascal or other, whether big or small, but to devote himself entirely to the task of bringing about the establishment of a new National Socialist People's State. In this way the struggle against the present State was placed on a higher plane than that of petty revenge and small conspiracies. It was elevated to the level of a spiritual struggle on behalf of a WELTANSCHAUUNG, for the destruction of Marxism in all its shapes and forms.

3. The form of organization adopted for the Storm Detachment, as well as its uniform and equipment, had to follow different models from those of the old Army. They had to be specially suited to the requirements of the task that was assigned to the Storm Detachment.

These were the ideas I followed in 1920 and 1921. I endeavoured to instil them gradually into the members of the young organization. And the result was that by the midsummer of 1922 we had a goodly number of formations which consisted of a hundred men each. By the late autumn of that year these formations received their distinctive uniforms. There were three events which turned out to be of supreme importance for the subsequent development of the Storm Detachment.

1. The great mass demonstration against the Law for the Protection of the Republic. This demonstration was held in the late summer of 1922 on the KÖNIGS-PLATZ in Munich, by all the patriotic societies. The National Socialist Movement also participated in it. The march-past of our party, in serried ranks, was led by six Munich companies of a hundred men each, followed by the political sections of the Party. Two bands marched with us and about fifteen flags were carried. When the National Socialists arrived at the great square it was already half full, but no flag was flying. Our entry aroused unbounded enthusiasm. I myself had the honour of being one of the speakers who addressed that mass of about sixty thousand people.

The demonstration was an overwhelming success; especially because it was proved for the first time that nationalist Munich could march on the streets, in spite of all threats from the Reds. Members of the organization for the defence of the Red Republic endeavoured to hinder the marching columns by their terrorist activities, but they were scattered by the companies of the Storm Detachment within a few minutes and sent off with bleeding skulls. The National Socialist Movement had then shown for the first time that in future it was determined to exercise the right to march on the streets and thus take this monopoly away from the international traitors and enemies of the country.

The result of that day was an incontestable proof that our ideas for the creation of the Storm Detachment were right, both from the psychological viewpoint and as to the manner in which this body was organized.

On the basis of this success the enlistment progressed so rapidly that within a few weeks the number of Munich companies of a hundred men each became doubled.

2. The expedition to Coburg in October 1922.

Certain People's Societies had decided to hold a German Day at Coburg. I was invited to take part, with the intimation that they wished me to bring a following along. This invitation, which I received at eleven o'clock in the morning, arrived just in time. Within an hour the arrangements for our participation in the German Congress were ready. I picked eight hundred men of the Storm Detachment to accompany me. These were divided into about fourteen companies and had to be brought by special train from

Munich to Coburg, which had just voted by plebiscite to be annexed to Bavaria. Corresponding orders were given to other groups of the National Socialist Storm Detachment which had meanwhile been formed in various other localities.

This was the first time that such a special train ran in Germany. At all the places where the new members of the Storm Detachment joined us our train caused a sensation. Many of the people had never seen our flag. And it made a very great impression.

As we arrived at the station in Coburg we were received by a deputation of the organizing committee of the German Day. They announced that it had been 'arranged' at the orders of local trades unions—that is to say, the Independent and Communist Parties—that we should not enter the town with our flags unfurled and our band playing (we had a band consisting of forty-two musicians with us) and that we should not march with closed ranks.

I immediately rejected these unmilitary conditions and did not fail to declare before the gentlemen who had arranged this 'day' how astonished I was at the idea of their negotiating with such people and coming to an agreement with them. Then I announced that the Storm Troops would immediately march into the town in company formation, with our flags flying and the band playing.

And that is what happened.

As we came out into the station yard we were met by a growling and yelling mob of several thousand, that shouted at us: 'Assassins', 'Bandits', 'Robbers', 'Criminals'. These were the choice names which these exemplary founders of the German Republic showered on us. The young Storm Detachment gave a model example of order. The companies fell into formation on the square in front of the station and at first took no notice of the insults hurled at them by the mob. The police were anxious. They did not pilot us to the quarters assigned to us on the outskirts of Coburg, a city quite unknown to us, but to the Hofbräuhaus Keller in the centre of the town. Right and left of our march the tumult raised by the accompanying mob steadily increased. Scarcely had the last company entered the courtyard of the Hofbräuhaus when the huge mass made a rush to get in after them, shouting madly. In order to prevent this, the police closed the gates. Seeing the position was untenable I called the Storm Detachment to attention and then asked the police to open the gates immediately. After a good deal of hesitation, they consented.

We now marched back along the same route as we had come, in the direction of our quarters, and there we had to make a stand against the crowd. As their cries and yells all along the route had failed to disturb the equanimity of our companies, the champions of true Socialism, Equality, and Fraternity now took to throwing stones. That brought our patience to an end. For ten minutes long, blows fell right and left, like a devastating shower of hail. Fifteen minutes later there were no more Reds to be seen in the street.

The collisions which took place when the night came on were more serious. Patrols of the Storm Detachment had discovered National Socialists who had been attacked singly and were in an atrocious state. Thereupon we made short work of the opponents. By the following morning the Red terror, under which Coburg had been suffering for years, was definitely smashed.

Adopting the typically Marxist and Jewish method of spreading falsehoods, leaflets were distributed by hand on the streets, bearing the caption: "Comrades and Comradesses of the International Proletariat." These leaflets were meant to arouse the wrath of the populace. Twisting the facts completely around, they declared that our 'bands of assasins' had commenced 'a war of extermination against the peaceful workers of Coburg'. At half-past one that day there was to be a 'great popular demonstration', at which it was hoped that the workers of the whole district would turn up. I was determined finally to crush this Red terror and so I summoned the Storm Detachment to meet at midday. Their number had now increased to 1,500. I decided to march with these men to the Coburg Festival and to cross the big square where the Red demonstration was to take place. I wanted to see if they would attempt to assault us again. When we entered the square we found that instead of the ten thousand that had been advertised, there were only a few hundred people present. As we approached they remained silent for the most part, and some ran away. Only at certain points along the route some bodies of Reds, who had arrived from outside the city and had not yet come to know us, attempted to start a row. But a few fisticuffs put them to flight. And now one could see how the population, which had for such a long time been so wretchedly intimidated, slowly woke up and recovered their courage. They welcomed us openly, and in the evening, on our return march, spontaneous shouts of jubilation broke out at several points along the route.

At the station the railway employees informed us all of a sudden that our train would not move. Thereupon I had some of the ringleaders told that if this were the case I would have all the Red Party heroes arrested that fell into our hands, that we would drive the train ourselves, but that we would take away with us, in the locomotive and tender and in some of the carriages, a few dozen members of this brotherhood of international solidarity. I did not omit to let those gentry know that if we had to conduct the train the journey would undoubtedly be a very risky adventure and that we might all break our necks. It would be a consolation, however, to know that we should not go to Eternity alone, but in equality and fraternity with the Red gentry.

Thereupon the train departed punctually and we arrived next morning in Munich safe and sound.

Thus at Coburg, for the first time since 1914, the equality of all citizens before the law was re-established. For even if some coxcomb of a higher official should assert to-day that the State protects the lives of its citizens, at least in those days it was not so. For at that time the citizens had to defend themselves against the representatives of the present State.

At first it was not possible fully to estimate the importance of the consequences which resulted from that day. The victorious Storm Troops had their confidence in themselves considerably reinforced and also their faith in the sagacity of their leaders. Our contemporaries began to pay us special attention and for the first time many recognized the National Socialist Movement as an organization that in all probability was destined to bring the Marxist folly to a deserving end.

Only the democrats lamented the fact that we had not the complaisance to allow our skulls to be cracked and that we had dared, in a democratic Republic, to hit back with fists and sticks at a brutal assault, rather than with pacifist chants.

Generally speaking, the bourgeois Press was partly distressed and partly vulgar, as always. Only a few decent newspapers expressed their satisfaction that at least in one locality the Marxist street bullies had been effectively dealt with.

And in Coburg itself at least a part of the Marxist workers who must be looked upon as misled, learned from the blows of National Socialist fists that these workers were also fighting for ideals, because experience teaches that the human being fights only for something in which he believes and which he loves.

The Storm Detachment itself benefited most from the Coburg events. It grew so quickly in numbers that at the Party Congress in January 1923 six thousand men participated in the ceremony of consecrating the flags and the first companies were fully clad in their new uniform.

Our experience in Coburg proved how essential it is to introduce one distinctive uniform for the Storm Detachment, not only for the purpose of strengthening the ESPRIT DE CORPS but also to avoid confusion and the danger of not recognizing the opponent in a squabble. Up to that time they had merely worn the armlet, but now the tunic and the well-known cap were added.

But the Coburg experience had also another important result. We now determined to break the Red Terror in all those localities where for many years it had prevented men of other views from holding their meetings. We were determined to restore the right of free assembly. From that time onwards we brought our battalions together in such places and little by little the red citadels of Bavaria, one after another, fell before the National Socialist propaganda. The Storm Troops became more and more adept at their job. They increasingly lost all semblance of an aimless and lifeless defence movement and came out into the light as an active militant organization, fighting for the establishment of a new German State.

This logical development continued until March 1923. Then an event occurred which made me divert the Movement from the course hitherto followed and introduce some changes in its outer formation.

In the first months of 1923 the French occupied the Ruhr district. The consequence of this was of great importance in the development of the Storm Detachment.

It is not yet possible, nor would it be in the interest of the nation, to write or speak openly and freely on the subject. I shall speak of it only as far as the matter has been dealt with in public discussions and thus brought to the knowledge of everybody.

The occupation of the Ruhr district, which did not come as a surprise to us, gave grounds for hoping that Germany would at last abandon its cowardly policy of submission and therewith give the defensive associations a definite task to fulfil. The Storm Detachment also, which now numbered several thousand of robust and vigorous young men, should not be excluded from this national service. During the spring and summer of 1923 it was transformed into a fighting military organization. It is to this reorganization that we must in great part attribute the later developments that took place during 1923, in so far as it affected our Movement.

Elsewhere I shall deal in broad outline with the development of events in 1923. Here I wish only to state that the transformation of the Storm Detachment at that time must have been detrimental to the interests of the Movement if the conditions that had motivated the change were not to be carried into effect, namely, the adoption of a policy of active resistance against France.

The events which took place at the close of 1923, terrible as they may appear at first sight, were almost a necessity if looked at from a higher standpoint; because, in view of the attitude taken by the Government of the German REICH, conversion of the Storm Troops into a military force would be meaningless and thus a transformation which would also be harmful to the Movement was ended at one stroke. At the same time it was made possible for us to reconstruct at the point where we had been diverted from the proper course.

In the year 1925 the German National Socialist Labour Party was re-founded and had to organize and train its Storm Detachment once again according to the principles I have laid down. It must return to the original idea and once more it must consider its most essential task to function as the instrument of defence and reinforcement in the spiritual struggle to establish the ideals of the Movement.

The Storm Detachment must not be allowed to sink to the level of something in the nature of a defence organization or a secret society. Steps must be taken rather to make it a vanguard of 100,000 men in the struggle for the National Socialist ideal which is based on the profound principle of a People's State.

CHAPTER X: The Mask of Federalism

In the winter of 1919, and still more in the spring and summer of 1920, the young Party felt bound to take up a definite stand on a question which already had become quite serious during the War. In the first volume of this book I have briefly recorded certain facts which I had personally witnessed and which foreboded the break-up of Germany. In describing these facts I made reference to the special nature of the propaganda which was directed by the English as well as the French towards reopening the breach that had existed between North and South in Germany. In the spring of 1915 there appeared the first of a series of leaflets which was systematically followed up and the aim of which was to arouse feeling against Prussia as being solely responsible for the war. Up to 1916 this system had been developed and perfected in a cunning and shameless manner. Appealing to the basest of human instincts, this propaganda endeavoured to arouse the wrath of the South Germans against the North Germans and after a short time it bore fruit. Persons who were then in high positions under the Government and in the Army, especially those attached to headquarters in the Bavarian Army, merited the just reproof of having blindly neglected their duty and failed to take the necessary steps to counter such propaganda. But nothing was done. On the contrary, in some quarters it did not appear to be quite unwelcome and probably they were short-sighted enough to think that such propaganda might help along the development of unification in Germany but even that it might automatically bring about consolidation of the federative forces. Scarcely ever in history was such a wicked neglect more wickedly avenged. The weakening of Prussia, which they believed would result from this propaganda, affected the whole of Germany. It resulted in hastening the collapse which not only wrecked Germany as a whole but even more particularly the federal states.

In that town where the artificially created hatred against Prussia raged most violently the revolt against the reigning House was the beginning of the Revolution.

It would be a mistake to think that the enemy propaganda was exclusively responsible for creating an anti-Prussian feeling and that there were no reasons which might excuse the people for having listened to this propaganda. The incredible fashion in which the national economic interests were organized during the War, the absolutely crazy system of centralization which made the whole REICH its ward and exploited the REICH, furnished the principal grounds for the growth of that anti-Prussian feeling. The average citizen looked upon the companies for the placing of war contracts, all of which had their headquarters in Berlin, as identical with Berlin and Berlin itself as identical with Prussia. The average citizen did not know that the organization of these robber companies, which were called War Companies, was not in the hands of Berlin or Prussia and not even in German hands at all. People recognized only the gross irregularities and the continual encroachments of that hated institution in the Metropolis of the REICH and directed their anger towards Berlin and Prussia, all the more because in certain quarters (the Bavarian Government) nothing was done to correct this attitude, but it was even welcomed with silent rubbing of hands.

The Jew was far too shrewd not to understand that the infamous campaign which he had organized, under the cloak of War Companies, for plundering the German nation would and must eventually arouse opposition. As long as that opposition did not spring directly at his own throat he had no reason to be afraid. Hence he decided that the best way of forestalling an outbreak on the part of the enraged and desperate masses would be to inflame their wrath and at the same time give it another outlet.

Let Bavaria quarrel as much as it liked with Prussia and Prussia with Bavaria. The more, the merrier. This bitter strife between the two states assured peace to the Jew. Thus public attention was completely diverted from the international maggot in the body of the nation; indeed, he seemed to have been forgotten. Then when there came a danger that level-headed people, of whom there are many to be found also in Bavaria, would advise a little more reserve and a more judicious evaluation of things, thus calming the rage against Prussia, all the Jew had to do in Berlin was to stage a new provocation and await results. Every time that was done all those who had profiteered out of the conflict between North and South filled their lungs and again fanned the flame of indignation until it became a blaze.

It was a shrewd and expert manoeuvre on the part of the Jew, to set the different branches of the German people quarrelling with one another, so that their attention would be turned away from himself and he could plunder them all the more completely.

Then came the Revolution.

Until the year 1918, or rather until the November of that year, the average German citizen, particularly the less educated lower middle-class and the workers, did not rightly understand what was happening and did not realize what must be the inevitable consequences, especially for Bavaria, of this internecine strife between the branches of the German people; but at least those sections which called themselves 'National' ought to have clearly perceived these consequences on the day that the Revolution broke out. For the moment the COUP D'ÉTAT had succeeded, the leader and organizer of the Revolution in Bavaria put himself forward as the defender of 'Bavarian' interests. The international Jew, Kurt Eisner, began to play off Bavaria against Prussia. This Oriental was just about the last person in the world that could be pointed to as the logical defender of Bavarian interests. In his trade as newspaper reporter he had wandered from place to place all over Germany and to him it was a matter of sheer indifference whether Bavaria or any other particular part of God's whole world continued to exist.

In deliberately giving the revolutionary rising in Bavaria the character of an offensive against Prussia, Kurt Eisner was not acting in the slightest degree from the standpoint of Bavarian interests, but merely as the commissioned representative of Jewry. He exploited existing instincts and antipathies in Bavaria as a means which would help to make the dismemberment of Germany all the more easy. When once dismembered, the REICH would fall an easy prey to Bolshevism.

The tactics employed by him were continued for a time after his death. The Marxists, who had always derided and exploited the individual German states and their princes, now suddenly appealed, as an 'Independent Party' to those sentiments and instincts which had their strongest roots in the families of the reigning princes and the individual states.

The fight waged by the Bavarian Soviet Republic against the military contingents that were sent to free Bavaria from its grasp was represented by the Marxist propagandists as first of all the 'Struggle of the Bavarian Worker' against 'Prussian Militarism.' This explains why it was that the suppression of the Soviet Republic in Munich did not have the same effect there as in the other German districts. Instead of recalling the masses to a sense of reason, it led to increased bitterness and anger against Prussia.

The art of the Bolshevik agitators, in representing the suppression of the Bavarian Soviet Republic as a victory of 'Prussian Militarism' over the 'Anti-militarists' and 'Anti-Prussian' people of Bavaria, bore rich fruit. Whereas on the occasion of the elections to the Bavarian Legislative Diet, Kurt Eisner did not have ten thousand followers in Munich and the Communist party less than three thousand, after the fall of the Bavarian Republic the votes given to the two parties together amounted to nearly one hundred thousand.

It was then that I personally began to combat that crazy incitement of some branches of the German people against other branches.

I believe that never in my life did I undertake a more unpopular task than I did when I took my stand against the anti-Prussian incitement. During the Soviet regime in Munich great public meetings were held at which hatred against the rest of Germany, but particularly against Prussia, was roused up to such a pitch that a North German would have risked his life in attending one of those meetings. These meetings often ended in wild shouts: "Away from Prussia", "Down with the Prussians", "War against Prussia", and so on. This feeling was openly expressed in the Reichstag by a particularly brilliant defender of Bavarian sovereign rights when he said: "Rather die as a Bavarian than rot as a Prussian".

One should have attended some of the meetings held at that time in order to understand what it meant for one when, for the first time and surrounded by only a handful of friends, I raised my voice against this folly at a meeting held in the Munich Löwenbräu Keller. Some of my War comrades stood by me then. And it is easy to imagine how we felt when that raging crowd, which had lost all control of its reason, roared at us and threatened to kill us. During the time that we were fighting for the country the same crowd were for the most part safely ensconced in the rear positions or were peacefully circulating at home as deserters and shirkers. It is true that that scene turned out to be of advantage to me. My small band of comrades felt for the first time absolutely united with me and readily swore to stick by me through life and death.

These conflicts, which were constantly repeated in 1919, seemed to become more violent soon after the beginning of 1920. There were meetings—I remember especially one in the Wagner Hall in the Sonnenstrasse in Munich—during the course of which my group, now grown much larger, had to defend themselves against assaults of the most violent character. It happened more than once that dozens of my followers were mishandled, thrown to the floor and stamped upon by the attackers and were finally thrown out of the hall more dead than alive.

The struggle which I had undertaken, first by myself alone and afterwards with the support of my war comrades, was now continued by the young movement, I might say almost as a sacred mission.

I am proud of being able to say to-day that we—depending almost exclusively on our followers in Bavaria—were responsible for putting an end, slowly but surely, to the coalition of folly and treason. I say folly and treason because, although convinced that the masses who joined in it meant well but were stupid, I cannot attribute such simplicity as an extenuating circumstance in the case of the organizers and their abetters. I then looked upon them, and still look upon them to-day, as traitors in the payment of France. In one case, that of Dorten, history has already pronounced its judgment.

The situation became specially dangerous at that time by reason of the fact that they were very astute in their ability to cloak their real tendencies, by insisting primarily on their federative intentions and claiming that those were the sole motives of the agitation. Of course it is quite obvious that the agitation against Prussia had nothing to do with federalism. Surely 'Federal Activities' is not the phrase with which to describe an effort to dissolve and dismember another federal state. For an honest federalist, for whom the formula used by Bismarck to define his idea of the REICH is not a counterfeit phrase, could not in the same breath express the desire to cut off portions of the Prussian State, which was created or at least completed by Bismarck. Nor could he publicly support such a separatist attempt.

What an outcry would be raised in Munich if some prussian conservative party declared itself in favour of detaching Franconia from Bavaria or took public action in demanding and promoting such a separatist policy. Nevertheless, one can only have sympathy for all those real and honest federalists who did not see through this infamous swindle, for they were its principal victims. By distorting the federalist idea in such a way its own champions prepared its grave. One cannot make propaganda for a federalist configuration of the REICH by debasing and abusing and besmirching the essential element of such a political structure, namely Prussia, and thus making such a Confederation impossible, if it ever had been possible. It is all the more incredible by reason of the fact that the fight carried on by those so-called federalists was directed against that section of the Prussian people which was the last that could be looked upon as connected with the November democracy. For the abuse and attacks of these so-called federalists were not levelled against the fathers of the Weimar Constitution—the majority of whom were South Germans or Jews—but against those who represented the old conservative Prussia, which was the antipodes of the Weimar Constitution. The fact that the directors of this campaign were careful not to touch the Jews is not to be wondered at and perhaps gives the key to the whole riddle.

Before the Revolution the Jew was successful in distracting attention from himself and his War Companies by inciting the masses, and especially the Bavarians, against Prussia. Similarly he felt obliged, after the Revolution, to find some way of camouflaging his new plunder campaign which was nine or ten times greater. And again he succeeded, in this case by provoking the so-called 'national' elements against one another: the conservative Bavarians against the Prussians, who were just as conservative. He acted again with extreme cunning, inasmuch as he who held the reins of Prussia's destiny in his hands provoked such crude and tactless aggressions that again and again they set the blood boiling in those who were being continually duped. Never against the Jew, however, but always the German against his own brother. The Bavarian did not see the Berlin of four million industrious and efficient working people, but only the lazy and decadent Berlin which is to be found in the worst quarters of the West End. And his antipathy was not directed against this West End of Berlin but against the 'Prussian' city.

In many cases it tempted one to despair.

The ability which the Jew has displayed in turning public attention away from himself and giving it another direction may be studied also in what is happening to-day.

In 1918 there was nothing like an organized anti-Semitic feeling. I still remember the difficulties we encountered the moment we mentioned the Jew. We were either confronted with dumb-struck faces or else a lively and hefty antagonism. The efforts we made at the time to point out the real enemy to the public seemed to be doomed to failure. But then things began to change for the better, though only very slowly. The 'League for Defence and Offence' was defectively organized but at least it had the great merit of opening up the Jewish question once again. In the winter of 1918-1919 a kind of anti-semitism began slowly to take root. Later on the National Socialist Movement presented the Jewish problem in a new light. Taking the question beyond the restricted circles of the upper classes and small bourgeoisie we succeeded in transforming it into the driving motive of a great popular movement. But the moment we were successful in placing this problem before the German people in the light of an idea that would unite them in one struggle the Jew reacted. He resorted to his old tactics. With amazing alacrity he hurled the torch of discord into the patriotic movement and opened a rift there. In bringing forward the ultramontane question and in the mutual quarrels that it gave rise to between Catholicism and Protestantism lay the sole possibility, as conditions then were, of occupying public attention with other problems and thus ward off the attack which had been concentrated against Jewry. The men who dragged our people into this controversy can never make amends for the crime they then committed against the nation. Anyhow, the Jew has attained the ends he desired. Catholics and Protestants are fighting with one another to their hearts' content, while the enemy of Aryan humanity and all Christendom is laughing up his sleeve.

Once it was possible to occupy the attention of the public for several years with the struggle between federalism and unification, wearing out their energies in this mutual friction while the Jew trafficked in the freedom of the nation and sold our country to the masters of international high finance. So in our day he has succeeded again, this time by raising ructions between the two German religious denominations while the foundations on which both rest are being eaten away and destroyed through the poison injected by the international and cosmopolitan Jew.

Look at the ravages from which our people are suffering daily as a result of being contaminated with Jewish blood. Bear in mind the fact that this poisonous contamination can be eliminated from the national body only after centuries, or perhaps never. Think further of how the process of racial decomposition is debasing and in some cases even destroying the fundamental Aryan qualities of our German people, so that our cultural creativeness as a nation is gradually becoming impotent and we are running the danger, at least in our great cities, of falling to the level where Southern Italy is to-day. This pestilential adulteration of the blood, of which hundreds of thousands of our people take no account, is being systematically practised by the Jew to-day. Systematically these negroid parasites in our national body corrupt our innocent fair-haired girls and thus destroy something which can no longer be replaced in this world.

The two Christian denominations look on with indifference at the profanation and destruction of a noble and unique creature who was given to the world as a gift of God's grace. For the future of the world, however, it does not matter which of the two triumphs

347

over the other, the Catholic or the Protestant. But it does matter whether Aryan humanity survives or perishes. And yet the two Christian denominations are not contending against the destroyer of Aryan humanity but are trying to destroy one another. Everybody who has the right kind of feeling for his country is solemnly bound, each within his own denomination, to see to it that he is not constantly talking about the Will of God merely from the lips but that in actual fact he fulfils the Will of God and does not allow God's handiwork to be debased. For it was by the Will of God that men were made of a certain bodily shape, were given their natures and their faculties. Whoever destroys His work wages war against God's Creation and God's Will. Therefore everyone should endeavour, each in his own denomination of course, and should consider it as his first and most solemn duty to hinder any and everyone whose conduct tends, either by word or deed, to go outside his own religious body and pick a quarrel with those of another denomination. For, in view of the religious schism that exists in Germany, to attack the essential characteristics of one denomination must necessarily lead to a war of extermination between the two Christian denominations. Here there can be no comparison between our position and that of France, or Spain or Italy. In those three countries one may, for instance, make propaganda for the side that is fighting against ultramontanism without thereby incurring the danger of a national rift among the French, or Spanish or Italian people. In Germany, however, that cannot be so, for here the Protestants would also take part in such propaganda. And thus the defence which elsewhere only Catholics organize against clerical aggression in political matters would assume with us the character of a Protestant attack against Catholicism. What may be tolerated by the faithful in one denomination even when it seems unjust to them, will at once be indignantly rejected and opposed on A PRIORI grounds if it should come from the militant leaders of another denomination. This is so true that even men who would be ready and willing to fight for the removal of manifest grievances within their own religious denomination will drop their own fight and turn their activities against the outsider the moment the abolition of such grievances is counselled or demanded by one who is not of the same faith. They consider it unjustified and inadmissible and incorrect for outsiders to meddle in matters which do not affect them at all. Such attempts are not excused even when they are inspired by a feeling for the supreme interests of the national community; because even in our day religious feelings still have deeper roots than all feeling for political and national expediency. That cannot be changed by setting one denomination against another in bitter conflict. It can be changed only if, through a spirit of mutual tolerance, the nation can be assured of a future the greatness of which will gradually operate as a conciliating factor in the sphere of religion also. I have no hesitation in saying that in those men who seek to-day to embroil the patriotic movement in religious quarrels I see worse enemies of my country than the international communists are. For the National Socialist Movement has set itself to the task of converting those communists. But anyone who goes outside the ranks of his own Movement and tends to turn it away from the fulfilment of its mission is acting in a manner that deserves the severest condemnation. He is acting as a champion of Jewish interests, whether consciously or unconsciously does not matter. For it is in the interests of the Jews to-day that the energies of the patriotic movement should be squandered in a religious conflict, because it is beginning to be dangerous for the Jews. I have purposely used the phrase about SQUANDERING the energies of the Movement, because nobody but some person who is entirely ignorant of history could imagine that this movement can solve a question which the greatest statesmen have tried for centuries to solve, and tried in vain.

Anyhow the facts speak for themselves. The men who suddenly discovered, in 1924, that the highest mission of the patriotic movement was to fight ultramontanism, have not succeeded in smashing ultramontanism, but they succeeded in splitting the patriotic movement. I have to guard against the possibility of some immature brain arising in the patriotic movement which thinks that it can do what even a Bismarck failed to do. It will be always one of the first duties of those who are directing the National Socialist Movement to oppose unconditionally any attempt to place the National Socialist Movement at the service of such a conflict. And anybody who conducts a propaganda with that end in view must be expelled forthwith from its ranks.

As a matter of fact we succeeded until the autumn of 1923 in keeping our movement away from such controversies. The most devoted Protestant could stand side by side with the most devoted Catholic in our ranks without having his conscience disturbed in the slightest as far as concerned his religious convictions. The bitter struggle which both waged in common against the wrecker of Aryan humanity taught them natural respect and esteem. And it was just in those years that our movement had to engage in a bitter strife with the Centre Party not for religious ends but for national, racial, political and economic ends. The success we then achieved showed that we were right, but it does not speak to-day in favour of those who thought they knew better.

In recent years things have gone so far that patriotic circles, in god-forsaken blindness of their religious strife, could not recognize the folly of their conduct even from the fact that atheist Marxist newspapers advocated the cause of one religious denomination or the other, according as it suited Marxist interests, so as to create confusion through slogans and declarations which were often immeasurably stupid, now molesting the one party and again the other, and thus poking the fire to keep the blaze at its highest.

But in the case of a people like the Germans, whose history has so often shown them capable of fighting for phantoms to the point of complete exhaustion, every war-cry is a mortal danger. By these slogans our people have often been drawn away from the real problems of their existence. While we were exhausting our energies in religious wars the others were acquiring their share of the world. And while the patriotic movement is debating with itself whether the ultramontane danger be greater than the Jewish, or vice versa, the Jew is destroying the racial basis of our existence and thereby annihilating our people. As far as regards that kind of 'patriotic' warrior, on behalf of the National Socialist Movement and therefore of the German people I pray with all my heart: "Lord, preserve us from such friends, and then we can easily deal with our enemies."

The controversy over federation and unification, so cunningly propagandized by the Jews in 1919-1920 and onwards, forced National Socialism, which repudiated the quarrel, to take up a definite stand in relation to the essential problem concerned in it. Ought Germany to be a confederacy or a military State? What is the practical significance of these terms? To me it seems that the second question is more important than the first, because it is fundamental to the understanding of the whole problem and also because the answer to it may help to clear up confusion and therewith have a conciliating effect.

What is a Confederacy?

By a Confederacy we mean a union of sovereign states which of their own free will and in virtue of their sovereignty come together and create a collective unit, ceding to that unit as much of their own sovereign rights as will render the existence of the union possible and will guarantee it.

But the theoretical formula is not wholly put into practice by any confederacy that exists to-day. And least of all by the American Union, where it is impossible to speak of original sovereignty in regard to the majority of the states. Many of them were not included in the federal complex until long after it had been established. The states that make up the American Union are mostly in the nature of territories, more or less, formed for technical administrative purposes, their boundaries having in many cases been fixed in the mapping office. Originally these states did not and could not possess sovereign rights of their own. Because it was the Union that created most of the so-called states. Therefore the sovereign rights, often very comprehensive, which were left, or rather granted, to the various territories correspond not only to the whole character of the Confederation but also to its vast space, which is equivalent to the size of a Continent. Consequently, in speaking of the United States of America one must not consider them as sovereign states but as enjoying rights or, better perhaps, autarchic powers, granted to them and guaranteed by the Constitution.

Nor does our definition adequately express the condition of affairs in Germany. It is true that in Germany the individual states existed as states before the REICH and that the REICH was formed from them. The REICH, however, was not formed by the voluntary and equal co-operation of the individual states, but rather because the state of Prussia gradually acquired a position of hegemony over the others. The difference in the territorial area alone between the German states prevents any comparison with the American Union. The great difference in territorial area between the very small German states that then existed and the larger, or even still more the largest, demonstrates the inequality of their achievements and shows that they could not take an equal part in founding and shaping the federal Empire. In the case of most of these individual states it cannot be maintained that they ever enjoyed real sovereignty; and the term 'State Sovereignty' was really nothing more than an administrative formula which had no inner meaning. As a matter of fact, not only developments in the past but also in our own time wiped out several of these so-called 'Sovereign States' and thus proved in the most definite way how frail these 'sovereign' state formations were.

I cannot deal here with the historical question of how these individual states came to be established, but I must call attention to the fact that hardly in any case did their frontiers coincide with ethical frontiers of the inhabitants. They were purely political phenomena which for the most part emerged during the sad epoch when the German Empire was in a state of exhaustion and was dismembered. They represented both cause and effect in the process of exhaustion and partition of our fatherland.

The Constitution of the old REICH took all this into account, at least up to a certain degree, in so far as the individual states were not accorded equal representation in the Reichstag, but a representation proportionate to their respective areas, their actual importance and the role which they played in the formation of the REICH.

The sovereign rights which the individual states renounced in order to form the REICH were voluntarily ceded only to a very small degree. For the most part they had no practical existence or they were simply taken by Prussia under the pressure of her preponderant power. The principle followed by Bismarck was not to give the REICH what he could take from the individual states but to demand from the individual states only what was absolutely necessary for the REICH. A moderate and wise policy. On the one side Bismarck showed the greatest regard for customs and traditions; on the other side his policy secured for the new REICH from its foundation onwards a great measure of love and willing co-operation. But it would be a fundamental error to attribute Bismarck's decision to any conviction on his part that the REICH was thus acquiring all the rights of sovereignty which would suffice for all time. That was far from Bismarck's idea. On the contrary, he wished to leave over for the future what it would be difficult to carry through at the moment and might not have been readily agreed to by the individual states. He trusted to the levelling effect of time and to the pressure exercised by the process of evolution, the steady action of which appeared more effective than an attempt to break the resistance which the individual states offered at the moment. By this policy he showed his great ability in the art of statesmanship. And, as a matter of fact, the sovereignty of the REICH has continually increased at the cost of the sovereignty of the individual states. The passing of time has achieved what Bismarck hoped it would.

The German collapse and the abolition of the monarchical form of government necessarily hastened this development. The German federal states, which had not been grounded on ethnical foundations but arose rather out of political conditions, were bound to lose their importance the moment the monarchical form of government and the dynasties connected with it were abolished, for it was to the spirit inherent in these that the individual states owned their political origin and development. Thus deprived of their internal RAISON D'ÊTRE, they renounced all right to survival and were induced by purely practical reasons to fuse with their neighbours or else they joined the more powerful states out of their own free will. That proved in a striking manner how extraordinarily frail was the actual sovereignty these small phantom states enjoyed, and it proved too how lightly they were estimated by their own citizens.

Though the abolition of the monarchical regime and its representatives had dealt a hard blow to the federal character of the REICH, still more destructive, from the federal point of view, was the acceptance of the obligations that resulted from the 'peace' treaty.

It was only natural and logical that the federal states should lose all sovereign control over the finances the moment the REICH, in consequence of a lost war, was subjected to financial obligations which could never be guaranteed through separate treaties with the individual states. The subsequent steps which led the REICH to take over the posts and railways were an enforced advance in the process of enslaving our people, a process which the peace treaties gradually developed. The REICH was forced to secure possession of resources which had to be constantly increased in order to satisfy the demands made by further extortions.

The form in which the powers of the REICH were thus extended to embrace the federal states was often ridiculously stupid, but in itself the procedure was logical and natural. The blame for it must be laid at the door of these men and those parties that failed in the hour of need to concentrate all their energies in an effort to bring the war to a victorious issue. The guilt lies on those parties which, especially in Bavaria, catered for their own egotistic interests during the war and refused to the REICH what the REICH had to requisition to a tenfold greater measure when the war was lost. The retribution of History! Rarely has the vengeance of Heaven followed so closely on the crime as it did in this case. Those same parties which, a few years previously, placed the interests of their own states — especially in Bavaria — before those of the REICH had now to look on passively while the pressure of events forced the REICH, in its own interests, to abolish the existence of the individual states. They were the victims of their own defaults.

It was an unparalleled example of hypocrisy to raise the cry of lamentation over the loss which the federal states suffered in being deprived of their sovereign rights. This cry was raised before the electorate, for it is only to the electorate that our contemporary parties address themselves. But these parties, without exception, outbid one another in accepting a policy of fulfilment which, by the sheer force of circumstances and in its ultimate consequences, could not but lead to a profound alteration in the internal structure of the REICH. Bismarck's REICH was free and unhampered by any obligations towards the outside world.

Bismarck's REICH never had to shoulder such heavy and entirely unproductive obligations as those to which Germany was subjected under the Dawes Plan. Also in domestic affairs Bismarck's REICH was able to limit its powers to a few matters that were absolutely necessary for its existence. Therefore it could dispense with the necessity of a financial control over these states and could live from their contributions. On the other side the relatively small financial tribute which the federal states had to pay to the REICH induced them to welcome its existence. But it is untrue and unjust to state now, as certain propagandists do, that the federal states are displeased with the REICH merely because of their financial subjection to it. No, that is not how the matter really stands. The lack of sympathy for the political idea embodied in the REICH is not due to the loss of sovereign rights on the part of the individual states. It is much more the result of the deplorable fashion in which the present régime cares for the interests of the German people. Despite all the celebrations in honour of the national flag and the Constitution, every section of the German people feels that the present REICH is not in accordance with its heart's desire. And the Law for the Protection of the Republic may prevent outrages against republican institutions, but it will not gain the love of one single German. In its constant anxiety to protect itself against its own citizens by means of laws and sentences of imprisonment, the Republic has aroused sharp and humiliating criticism of all republican institutions as such.

For another reason also it is untrue to say, as certain parties affirm to-day, that the REICH has ceased to be popular on account of its overbearing conduct in regard to certain sovereign rights which the individual states had heretofore enjoyed. Supposing the REICH had not extended its authority over the individual states, there is no reason to believe that it would find more favour among those states if the general obligations remained so heavy as they now are. On the contrary, if the individual states had to pay their respective shares of the highly increased tribute which the REICH has to meet to-day in order to fulfil the provisions of the Versailles Dictate, the hostility towards the REICH would be infinitely greater. For then not only would it prove difficult to collect the respective contributions due to the REICH from the federal states, but coercive methods would have to be employed in making the collections. The Republic stands on the footing of the peace treaties and has neither the courage nor the intention to break them. That being so, it must observe the obligations which the peace treaties have imposed on it. The responsibility for this situation is to be attributed solely to those parties who preach unceasingly to the patient electoral masses on the necessity of maintaining the autonomy of the federal states, while at the same time they champion and demand of the REICH a policy which must necessarily lead to the suppression of even the very last of those so-called 'sovereign' rights.

I say NECESSARILY because the present REICH has no other possible means of bearing the burden of charges which an insane domestic and foreign policy has laid on it. Here still another wedge is placed on the former, to drive it in still deeper. Every new debt which the REICH contracts, through the criminal way in which the interests of

Germany are represented VIS-À-VIS foreign countries, necessitates a new and stronger blow which drives the under wedges still deeper, That blow demands another step in the progressive abolition of the sovereign rights of the individual states, so as not to allow the germs of opposition to rise up into activity or even to exist.

The chief characteristic difference between the policy of the present REICH and that of former times lies in this: The old REICH gave freedom to its people at home and showed itself strong towards the outside world, whereas the Republic shows itself weak towards the stranger and oppresses its own citizens at home. In both cases one attitude determines the other. A vigorous national State does not need to make many laws for the interior, because of the affection and attachment of its citizens. The international servile State can live only by coercing its citizens to render it the services it demands. And it is a piece of impudent falsehood for the present regime to speak of 'Free citizens'. Only the old Germany could speak in that manner. The present Republic is a colony of slaves at the service of the stranger. At best it has subjects, but not citizens. Hence it does not possess a national flag but only a trade mark, introduced and protected by official decree and legislative measures. This symbol, which is the Gessler's cap of German Democracy, will always remain alien to the spirit of our people. On its side, the Republic having no sense of tradition or respect for past greatness, dragged the symbol of the past in the mud, but it will be surprised one day to discover how superficial is the devotion of its citizens to its own symbol. The Republic has given to itself the character of an intermezzo in German history. And so this State is bound constantly to restrict more and more the sovereign rights of the individual states, not only for general reasons of a financial character but also on principle. For by enforcing a policy of financial blackmail, to squeeze the last ounce of substance out of its people, it is forced also to take their last rights away from them, lest the general discontent may one day flame up into open rebellion.

We, National Socialists, would reverse this formula and would adopt the following axiom: A strong national REICH which recognizes and protects to the largest possible measure the rights of its citizens both within and outside its frontiers can allow freedom to reign at home without trembling for the safety of the State. On the other hand, a strong national Government can intervene to a considerable degree in the liberties of the individual subject as well as in the liberties of the constituent states without thereby weakening the ideal of the REICH; and it can do this while recognizing its responsibility for the ideal of the REICH, because in these particular acts and measures the individual citizen recognizes a means of promoting the prestige of the nation as a whole.

Of course, every State in the world has to face the question of unification in its internal organization. And Germany is no exception in this matter. Nowadays it is absurd to speak of 'statal sovereignty' for the constituent states of the REICH, because that has already become impossible on account of the ridiculously small size of so many of these states. In the sphere of commerce as well as that of administration the importance of the individual states has been steadily decreasing. Modern means of communication and mechanical progress have been increasingly restricting distance and space. What was once a State is to-day only a province and the territory covered by a modern State had once the importance of a continent. The purely technical difficulty of administering a State like Germany is not greater than that of governing a province like Brandenburg a hundred years ago. And to-day it is easier to cover the distance from Munich to Berlin than it was to cover the distance from Munich to Starnberg a hundred years ago. In view of the modern means of transport, the whole territory of the REICH to-day is smaller than that of certain German federal states at the time of the Napoleonic wars. To close one's eyes to the consequences of these facts means to live in the past. There always were, there are and always will be, men who do this. They may retard but they cannot stop the revolutions of history.

We, National Socialists, must not allow the consequences of that truth to pass by us unnoticed. In these matters also we must not permit ourselves to be misled by the phrases of our so-called national bourgeois parties. I say 'phrases', because these same parodies do not seriously believe that it is possible for them to carry out their proposals, and because they themselves are the chief culprits and also the accomplices responsible for the present state of affairs. Especially in Bavaria, the demands for a halt in the process of centralization can be no more than a party move behind which there is no serious idea. If these parties ever had to pass from the realm of phrase-making into that of practical deeds they would present a sorry spectacle. Every so-called 'Robbery of Sovereign Rights' from Bavaria by the REICH has met with no practical resistance, except for some fatuous barking by way of protest. Indeed, when anyone seriously opposed the madness that was shown in carrying out this system of centralization he was told by those same parties that he understood nothing of the nature and needs of the State to-day. They slandered him and pronounced him anathema and persecuted him until he was either shut up in prison or illegally deprived of the right of public speech. In the light of these facts our followers should become all the more convinced of the profound hypocrisy which characterizes these so-called federalist circles. To a certain extent they use the federalist doctrine just as they use the name of religion, merely as a means of promoting their own base party interests.

A certain unification, especially in the field of transport, appears logical. But we, National Socialists, feel it our duty to oppose with all our might such a development in the modern State, especially when the measures proposed are solely for the purpose of screening a disastrous foreign policy and making it possible. And just because the present REICH has threatened to take over the railways, the posts, the finances, etc., not from the high standpoint of a national policy, but in order to have in its hands the means and pledges for an unlimited policy of fulfilment—for that reason we, National Socialists, must take every step that seems suitable to obstruct and, if possible, definitely to prevent such a policy. We must fight against the present system of amalgamating institutions that are vitally important for the existence of our people, because this system is being adopted solely to facilitate the payment of milliards and the transference of pledges to the stranger, under the post-War provisions which our politicians have accepted.

For these reasons also the National Socialist Movement has to take up a stand against such tendencies.

Moreover, we must oppose such centralization because in domestic affairs it helps to reinforce a system of government which in all its manifestations has brought the greatest misfortunes on the German nation. The present Jewish-Democratic REICH, which has become a veritable curse for the German people, is seeking to negative the force of the criticism offered by all the federal states which have not yet become imbued with the spirit of the age, and is trying to carry out this policy by crushing them to the point of annihilation. In face of this we National Socialists must try to ground the opposition of the individual states on such a basis that it will be able to operate with a good promise of success. We must do this by transforming the struggle against centralization into something that will be an expression of the higher interests of the German nation as such. Therefore, while the Bavarian Populist Party, acting from its own narrow and particularist standpoint, fights to maintain the 'special rights' of the Bavarian State, we ought to stand on quite a different ground in fighting for the same rights. Our grounds ought to be those of the higher national interests in opposition to the November Democracy.

A still further reason for opposing a centralizing process of that kind arises from the certain conviction that in great part this so-called nationalization does not make for unification at all and still less for simplification. In many cases it is adopted simply as a means of removing from the sovereign control of the individual states certain institutions which they wish to place in the hands of the revolutionary parties. In German History favouritism has never been of so base a character as in the democratic republic. A great portion of this centralization to-day is the work of parties which once promised that they would open the way for the promotion of talent, meaning thereby that they would fill those posts and offices entirely with their own partisans. Since the foundation of the Republic the Jews especially have been obtaining positions in the economic institutions taken over by the REICH and also positions in the national administration, so that the one and the other have become preserves of Jewry.

For tactical reasons, this last consideration obliges us to watch with the greatest attention every further attempt at centralization and fight it at each step. But in doing this our standpoint must always be that of a lofty national policy and never a pettifogging particularism.

This last observation is necessary, lest an opinion might arise among our own followers that we do not accredit to the REICH the right of incorporating in itself a sovereignty which is superior to that of the constituent states. As regards this right we cannot and must not entertain the slightest doubt. Because for us the State is nothing but a form. Its substance, or content, is the essential thing. And that is the nation, the people. It is clear therefore that every other interest must be subordinated to the supreme interests of the nation. In particular we cannot accredit to any other state a sovereign power and sovereign rights within the confines of the nation and the REICH, which represents the nation. The absurdity which some federal states commit by maintaining 'representations' abroad and corresponding foreign 'representations' among themselves—that must cease and will cease. Until this happens we cannot be surprised if certain foreign countries are dubious about the political unity of the REICH and act accordingly. The absurdity of these 'representations' is all the greater because they do harm and do not bring the slightest advantage. If the interests of a German abroad cannot be protected by the ambassador of the REICH, much less can they be protected by the minister from some small federal state which appears ridiculous in the framework of the present world order. The real truth is that these small federal states are envisaged as points of attack for attempts at secession, which prospect is always pleasing to a certain foreign State. We, National Socialists, must not allow some noble caste which has become effete with age to occupy an ambassadorial post abroad, with the idea that by engrafting one of its withered branches in new soil the green leaves may sprout again. Already in the time of the old REICH our diplomatic representatives abroad were such a sorry lot that a further trial of that experience would be out of the question.

It is certain that in the future the importance of the individual states will be transferred to the sphere of our cultural policy. The monarch who did most to make Bavaria an important centre was not an obstinate particularist with anti-German tendencies, but

Ludwig I who was as much devoted to the ideal of German greatness as he was to that of art. His first consideration was to use the powers of the state to develop the cultural position of Bavaria and not its political power. And in doing this he produced better and more durable results than if he had followed any other line of conduct. Up to this time Munich was a provincial residence town of only small importance, but he transformed it into the metropolis of German art and by doing so he made it an intellectual centre which even to-day holds Franconia to Bavaria, though the Franconians are of quite a different temperament. If Munich had remained as it had been earlier, what has happened in Saxony would have been repeated in Bavaria, with the difference that Leipzig and Bavarian Nürnberg would have become, not Bavarian but Franconian cities. It was not the cry of "Down with Prussia" that made Munich great. What made this a city of importance was the King who wished to present it to the German nation as an artistic jewel that would have to be seen and appreciated, and so it has turned out in fact. Therein lies a lesson for the future. The importance of the individual states in the future will no longer lie in their political or statal power. I look to them rather as important ethnical and cultural centres. But even in this respect time will do its levelling work. Modern travelling facilities shuffle people among one another in such a way that tribal boundaries will fade out and even the cultural picture will gradually become more of a uniform pattern.

The army must definitely be kept clear of the influence of the individual states. The coming National Socialist State must not fall back into the error of the past by imposing on the army a task which is not within its sphere and never should have been assigned to it. The German army does not exist for the purpose of being a school in which tribal particularisms are to be cultivated and preserved, but rather as a school for teaching all the Germans to understand and adapt their habits to one another. Whatever tends to have a separating influence in the life of the nation ought to be made a unifying influence in the army. The army must raise the German boy above the narrow horizon of his own little native province and set him within the broad picture of the nation. The youth must learn to know, not the confines of his own region but those of the fatherland, because it is the latter that he will have to defend one day. It is therefore absurd to have the German youth do his military training in his own native region. During that period he ought to learn to know Germany. This is all the more important to-day, since young Germans no longer travel on their own account as they once used to do and thus enlarge their horizon. In view of this, is it not absurd to leave the young Bavarian recruit at Munich, the recruit from Baden at Baden itself and the Württemberger at Stuttgart and so on? And would it not be more reasonable to show the Rhine and the North Sea to the Bavarian, the Alps to the native of Hamburg and the mountains of Central Germany to the boy from East Prussia? The character proper to each region ought to be maintained in the troops but not in the training garrisons. We may disapprove of every attempt at unification but not that of unifying the army. On the contrary, even though we should wish to welcome no other kind of unification, this must be greeted with joy. In view of the size of the present army of the REICH, it would be absurd to maintain the federal divisions among the troops. Moreover, in the unification of the German army which has actually been effected we see a fact which we must not renounce but restore in the future national army.

Finally a new and triumphant idea should burst every chain which tends to paralyse its efforts to push forward. National Socialism must claim the right to impose its principles on the whole German nation, without regard to what were hitherto the confines

356

of federal states. And we must educate the German nation in our ideas and principles. As the Churches do not feel themselves bound or limited by political confines, so the National Socialist Idea cannot feel itself limited to the territories of the individual federal states that belong to our Fatherland.

The National Socialist doctrine is not handmaid to the political interests of the single federal states. One day it must become teacher to the whole German nation. It must determine the life of the whole people and shape that life anew. For this reason we must imperatively demand the right to overstep boundaries that have been traced by a political development which we repudiate.

The more completely our ideas triumph, the more liberty can we concede in particular affairs to our citizens at home.

CHAPTER XI:
Propaganda and Organization

The year 1921 was specially important for me from many points of view. When I entered the German Labour Party I at once took charge of the propaganda, believing this branch to be far the most important for the time being. Just then it was not a matter of pressing necessity to cudgel one's brains over problems of organization. The first necessity was to spread our ideas among as many people as possible. Propaganda should go well ahead of organization and gather together the human material for the latter to work up. I have never been in favour of hasty and pedantic methods of organization, because in most cases the result is merely a piece of dead mechanism and only rarely a living organization. Organization is a thing that derives its existence from organic life, organic evolution. When the same set of ideas have found a lodgement in the minds of a certain number of people they tend of themselves to form a certain degree of order among those people and out of this inner formation something that is very valuable arises. Of course here, as everywhere else, one must take account of those human weaknesses which make men hesitate, especially at the beginning, to submit to the control of a superior mind. If an organization is imposed from above downwards in a mechanical fashion, there is always the danger that some individual may push himself forward who is not known for what he is and who, out of jealousy, will try to hinder abler persons from taking a leading place in the movement. The damage that results from that kind of thing may have fatal consequences, especially in a new movement.

For this reason it is advisable first to propagate and publicly expound the ideas on which the movement is founded. This work of propaganda should continue for a certain time and should be directed from one centre. When the ideas have gradually won over a number of people this human material should be carefully sifted for the purpose of selecting those who have ability in leadership and putting that ability to the test. It will often be found that apparently insignificant persons will nevertheless turn out to be born leaders.

Of course, it is quite a mistake to suppose that those who show a very intelligent grasp of the theory underlying a movement are for that reason qualified to fill responsible positions on the directorate. The contrary is very frequently the case.

Great masters of theory are only very rarely great organizers also. And this is because the greatness of the theorist and founder of a system consists in being able to discover and lay down those laws that are right in the abstract, whereas the organizer must first of all be a man of psychological insight. He must take men as they are, and for that reason he must know them, not having too high or too low an estimate of human nature. He must take account of their weaknesses, their baseness and all the other various characteristics, so as to form something out of them which will be a living organism, endowed with strong powers of resistance, fitted to be the carrier of an idea and strong enough to ensure the triumph of that idea.

But it is still more rare to find a great theorist who is at the same time a great leader. For the latter must be more of an agitator, a truth that will not be readily accepted by many of those who deal with problems only from the scientific standpoint. And yet what I say is only natural. For an agitator who shows himself capable of expounding ideas to the great masses must always be a psychologist, even though he may be only a demagogue. Therefore he will always be a much more capable leader than the contemplative theorist who meditates on his ideas, far from the human throng and the world. For to be a leader means to be able to move the masses. The gift of formulating ideas has nothing whatsoever to do with the capacity for leadership. It would be entirely futile to discuss the question as to which is the more important: the faculty of conceiving ideals and human aims or that of being able to have them put into practice. Here, as so often happens in life, the one would be entirely meaningless without the other. The noblest conceptions of the human understanding remain without purpose or value if the leader cannot move the masses towards them. And, conversely, what would it avail to have all the genius and elan of a leader if the intellectual theorist does not fix the aims for which mankind must struggle. But when the abilities of theorist and organizer and leader are united in the one person, then we have the rarest phenomenon on this earth. And it is that union which produces the great man.

As I have already said, during my first period in the Party I devoted myself to the work of propaganda. I had to succeed in gradually gathering together a small nucleus of men who would accept the new teaching and be inspired by it. And in this way we should provide the human material which subsequently would form the constituent elements of the organization. Thus the goal of the propagandist is nearly always fixed far beyond that of the organizer.

If a movement proposes to overthrow a certain order of things and construct a new one in its place, then the following principles must be clearly understood and must dominate in the ranks of its leadership: Every movement which has gained its human material must first divide this material into two groups: namely, followers and members.

It is the task of the propagandist to recruit the followers and it is the task of the organizer to select the members.

The follower of a movement is he who understands and accepts its aims; the member is he who fights for them.

The follower is one whom the propaganda has converted to the doctrine of the movement. The member is he who will be charged by the organization to collaborate in winning over new followers from which in turn new members can be formed.

To be a follower needs only the passive recognition of the idea. To be a member means to represent that idea and fight for it. From ten followers one can have scarcely more than two members. To be a follower simply implies that a man has accepted the teaching of the movement; whereas to be a member means that a man has the courage to participate actively in diffusing that teaching in which he has come to believe.

Because of its passive character, the simple effort of believing in a political doctrine is enough for the majority, for the majority of mankind is mentally lazy and timid. To be a member one must be intellectually active, and therefore this applies only to the minority.

Such being the case, the propagandist must seek untiringly to acquire new followers for the movement, whereas the organizer must diligently look out for the best elements among such followers, so that these elements may be transformed into members. The propagandist need not trouble too much about the personal worth of the individual proselytes he has won for the movement. He need not inquire into their abilities, their intelligence or character. From these proselytes, however, the organizer will have to select those individuals who are most capable of actively helping to bring the movement to victory.

The propagandist aims at inducing the whole people to accept his teaching. The organizer includes in his body of membership only those who, on psychological grounds, will not be an impediment to the further diffusion of the doctrines of the movement.

The propagandist inculcates his doctrine among the masses, with the idea of preparing them for the time when this doctrine will triumph, through the body of combatant members which he has formed from those followers who have given proof of the necessary ability and will-power to carry the struggle to victory.

The final triumph of a doctrine will be made all the more easy if the propagandist has effectively converted large bodies of men to the belief in that doctrine and if the organization that actively conducts the fight be exclusive, vigorous and solid.

When the propaganda work has converted a whole people to believe in a doctrine, the organization can turn the results of this into practical effect through the work of a mere handful of men. Propaganda and organization, therefore follower and member, then stand towards one another in a definite mutual relationship. The better the propaganda has worked, the smaller will the organization be. The greater the number of followers, so much the smaller can be the number of members. And conversely. If the propaganda be bad, the organization must be large. And if there be only a small number of followers, the membership must be all the larger—if the movement really counts on being successful.

The first duty of the propagandist is to win over people who can subsequently be taken into the organization. And the first duty of the organization is to select and train men who will be capable of carrying on the propaganda. The second duty of the organization is to disrupt the existing order of things and thus make room for the penetration of the new teaching which it represents, while the duty of the organizer must be to fight for the purpose of securing power, so that the doctrine may finally triumph.

A revolutionary conception of the world and human existence will always achieve decisive success when the new WELTANSCHAUUNG has been taught to a whole people, or subsequently forced upon them if necessary, and when, on the other hand, the central organization, the movement itself, is in the hands of only those few men who are absolutely indispensable to form the nerve-centres of the coming State.

Put in another way, this means that in every great revolutionary movement that is of world importance the idea of this movement must always be spread abroad through the operation of propaganda. The propagandist must never tire in his efforts to make the new ideas clearly understood, inculcating them among others, or at least he must place himself in the position of those others and endeavour to upset their confidence in the convictions they have hitherto held. In order that such propaganda should have backbone to it, it must be based on an organization. The organization chooses its members from among those followers whom the propaganda has won. That organization will become all the more vigorous if the work of propaganda be pushed forward intensively. And the propaganda will work all the better when the organization back of it is vigorous and strong in itself.

Hence the supreme task of the organizer is to see to it that any discord or differences which may arise among the members of the movement will not lead to a split and thereby cramp the work within the movement. Moreover, it is the duty of the organization to see that the fighting spirit of the movement does not flag or die out but that it is constantly reinvigorated and restrengthened. It is not necessary the number of members should increase indefinitely. Quite the contrary would be better. In view of the fact that only a fraction of humanity has energy and courage, a movement which increases its own organization indefinitely must of necessity one day become plethoric and inactive. Organizations, that is to say, groups of members, which increase their size beyond certain dimensions gradually lose their fighting force and are no longer in form to back up the propagation of a doctrine with aggressive elan and determination.

Now the greater and more revolutionary a doctrine is, so much the more active will be the spirit inspiring its body of members, because the subversive energy of such a doctrine will frighten way the chicken-hearted and small-minded bourgeoisie. In their hearts they may believe in the doctrine but they are afraid to acknowledge their belief openly. By reason of this very fact, however, an organization inspired by a veritable revolutionary idea will attract into the body of its membership only the most active of those believers who have been won for it by its propaganda. It is in this activity on the part of the membership body, guaranteed by the process of natural selection, that we are to seek the prerequisite conditions for the continuation of an active and spirited propaganda and also the victorious struggle for the success of the idea on which the movement is based.

The greatest danger that can threaten a movement is an abnormal increase in the number of its members, owing to its too rapid success. So long as a movement has to carry on a hard and bitter fight, people of weak and fundamentally egotistic temperament will steer very clear of it; but these will try to be accepted as members the moment the party achieves a manifest success in the course of its development.

It is on these grounds that we are to explain why so many movements which were at first successful slowed down before reaching the fulfilment of their purpose and, from an inner weakness which could not otherwise be explained, gave up the struggle and finally disappeared from the field. As a result of the early successes achieved, so many undesirable, unworthy and especially timid individuals became members of the movement that they finally secured the majority and stifled the fighting spirit of the others. These inferior elements then turned the movement to the service of their personal interests and, debasing it to the level of their own miserable heroism, no longer struggled for the triumph of the original idea. The fire of the first fervour died out, the fighting spirit flagged and, as the bourgeois world is accustomed to say very justly in such cases, the party mixed water with its wine.

For this reason it is necessary that a movement should, from the sheer instinct of self-preservation, close its lists to new membership the moment it becomes successful. And any further increase in its organization should be allowed to take place only with the most careful foresight and after a painstaking sifting of those who apply for membership. Only thus will it be possible to keep the kernel of the movement intact and fresh and sound. Care must be taken that the conduct of the movement is maintained exclusively in the hands of this original nucleus. This means that the nucleus must direct the propaganda which aims at securing general recognition for the movement. And the movement itself, when it has secured power in its hands, must carry out all those acts and measures which are necessary in order that its ideas should be finally established in practice.

With those elements that originally made the movement, the organization should occupy all the important positions that have been conquered and from those elements the whole directorate should be formed. This should continue until the maxims and doctrines of the party have become the foundation and policy of the new State. Only then will it be permissible gradually to give the reins into the hands of the Constitution of that State which the spirit of the movement has created. But this usually happens through a process of mutual rivalry, for here it is less a question of human intelligence than of the play and effect of the forces whose development may indeed be foreseen from the start but not perpetually controlled.

All great movements, whether of a political or religious nature, owe their imposing success to the recognition and adoption of those principles. And no durable success is conceivable if these laws are not observed.

As director of propaganda for the party, I took care not merely to prepare the ground for the greatness of the movement in its subsequent stages, but I also adopted the most radical measures against allowing into the organization any other than the best material. For the more radical and exciting my propaganda was, the more did it frighten weak and wavering characters away, thus preventing them from entering the first nucleus of our organization. Perhaps they remained followers, but they did not raise their voices. On the contrary, they maintained a discreet silence on the fact. Many thousands of persons then assured me that they were in full agreement with us but they could not on any account become members of our party. They said that the movement was so radical that to take part in it as members would expose them to grave censures and grave dangers, so that they would rather continue to be looked upon as honest and peaceful citizens and remain aside, for the time being at least, though devoted to our cause with all their hearts.

And that was all to the good. If all these men who in their hearts did not approve of revolutionary ideas came into our movement as members at that time, we should be looked upon as a pious confraternity to-day and not as a young movement inspired with the spirit of combat.

The lively and combative form which I gave to all our propaganda fortified and guaranteed the radical tendency of our movement, and the result was that, with a few exceptions, only men of radical views were disposed to become members.

It was due to the effect of our propaganda that within a short period of time hundreds of thousands of citizens became convinced in their hearts that we were right and wished us victory, although personally they were too timid to make sacrifices for our cause or even participate in it.

Up to the middle of 1921 this simple activity of gathering in followers was sufficient and was of value to the movement. But in the summer of that year certain events happened which made it seem opportune for us to bring our organization into line with the manifest successes which the propaganda had achieved.

An attempt made by a group of patriotic visionaries, supported by the chairman of the party at that time, to take over the direction of the party led to the break up of this little intrigue and, by a unanimous vote at a general meeting, entrusted the entire direction of the party to my own hands. At the same time a new statute was passed which invested sole responsibility in the chairman of the movement, abolished the system of resolutions in committee and in its stead introduced the principle of division of labour which since that time has worked excellently.

From August 1st, 1921, onwards I undertook this internal reorganization of the party and was supported by a number of excellent men. I shall mention them and their work individually later on.

In my endeavour to turn the results gained by the propaganda to the advantage of the organization and thus stabilize them, I had to abolish completely a number of old customs and introduce regulations which none of the other parties possessed or had adopted.

In the years 1920-21 the movement was controlled by a committee elected by the members at a general meeting. The committee was composed of a first and second treasurer, a first and second secretary, and a first and second chairman at the head of it. In addition to these there was a representative of the members, the director of propaganda, and various assessors.

Comically enough, the committee embodied the very principle against which the movement itself wanted to fight with all its energy, namely, the principle of parliamentarianism. Here was a principle which personified everything that was being opposed by the movement, from the smallest local groups to the district and regional groups, the state groups and finally the national directorate itself. It was a system under which we all suffered and are still suffering.

It was imperative to change this state of affairs forthwith, if this bad foundation in the internal organization was not to keep the movement insecure and render the fulfilment of its high mission impossible.

The sessions of the committee, which were ruled by a protocol, and in which decisions were made according to the vote of the majority, presented the picture of a miniature parliament. Here also there was no such thing as personal responsibility. And here reigned the same absurdities and illogical state of affairs as flourish in our great representative bodies of the State. Names were presented to this committee for election as secretaries, treasurers, representatives of the members of the organization, propaganda agents and God knows what else. And then they all acted in common on every particular question and decided it by vote. Accordingly, the director of propaganda voted on a question that concerned the man who had to do with the finances and the latter in his turn voted on a question that concerned only the organization as such, the organizer voting on a subject that had to do with the secretarial department, and so on.

Why select a special man for propaganda if treasurers and scribes and commissaries, etc., had to deliver judgment on questions concerning it? To a person of commonsense that sort of thing seemed as incomprehensible as it would be if in a great manufacturing concern the board of directors were to decide on technical questions of production or if, inversely, the engineers were to decide on questions of administration.

I refused to countenance that kind of folly and after a short time I ceased to appear at the meetings of the committee. I did nothing else except attend to my own department of propaganda and I did not permit any of the others to poke their heads into my activities.

Conversely, I did not interfere in the affairs of others.

When the new statute was approved and I was appointed as president, I had the necessary authority in my hands and also the corresponding right to make short shrift of all that nonsense. In the place of decisions by the majority vote of the committee, the principle of absolute responsibility was introduced.

The chairman is responsible for the whole control of the movement. He apportions the work among the members of the committee subordinate to him and for special work he selects other individuals. Each of these gentlemen must bear sole responsibility for the task assigned to him. He is subordinate only to the chairman, whose duty is to supervise the general collaboration, selecting the personnel and giving general directions for the co-ordination of the common work.

This principle of absolute responsibility is being adopted little by little throughout the movement. In the small local groups and perhaps also in the regional and district groups it will take yet a long time before the principle can be thoroughly imposed, because timid and hesitant characters are naturally opposed to it. For them the idea of bearing absolute responsibility for an act opens up an unpleasant prospect. They would like to hide behind the shoulders of the majority in the so-called committee, having their acts covered by decisions passed in that way. But it seems to me a matter of absolute necessity to take a decisive stand against that view, to make no concessions whatsoever to this fear of responsibility, even though it takes some time before we can put fully into effect this concept of duty and ability in leadership, which will finally bring forward leaders who have the requisite abilities to occupy the chief posts.

In any case, a movement which must fight against the absurdity of parliamentary institutions must be immune from this sort of thing. Only thus will it have the requisite strength to carry on the struggle.

At a time when the majority dominates everywhere else a movement which is based on the principle of one leader who has to bear personal responsibility for the direction of the official acts of the movement itself will one day overthrow the present situation and triumph over the existing regime. That is a mathematical certainty.

This idea made it necessary to reorganize our movement internally. The logical development of this reorganization brought about a clear-cut distinction between the economic section of the movement and the general political direction. The principle of personal responsibility was extended to all the administrative branches of the party and it brought about a healthy renovation, by liberating them from political influences and allowing them to operate solely on economic principles.

In the autumn of 1921, when the party was founded, there were only six members. The party did not have any headquarters, nor officials, nor formularies, nor a stamp, nor printed material of any sort. The committee first held its sittings in a restaurant on the Herrengasse and then in a café at Gasteig. This state of affairs could not last. So I at once took action in the matter. I went around to several restaurants and hotels in Munich, with the idea of renting a room in one of them for the use of the Party. In the old Sterneckerbräu im Tal, there was a small room with arched roof, which in earlier times was used as a sort of festive tavern where the Bavarian Counsellors of the Holy Roman Empire foregathered. It was dark and dismal and accordingly well suited to its ancient uses, though less suited to the new purpose it was now destined to serve. The little street on which its one window looked out was so narrow that even on the brightest summer day the room remained dim and sombre. Here we took up our first fixed abode. The rent came to fifty marks per month, which was then an enormous sum for us. But our exigencies had to be very modest. We dared not complain even when they removed the wooden wainscoting a few days after we had taken possession. This panelling had been specially put up for the Imperial Counsellors. The place began to look more like a grotto than an office.

Still it marked an important step forward. Slowly we had electric light installed and later on a telephone. A table and some borrowed chairs were brought, an open paper-stand and later on a cupboard. Two sideboards, which belonged to the landlord, served to store our leaflets, placards, etc.

As time went on it turned out impossible to direct the course of the movement merely by holding a committee meeting once a week. The current business administration of the movement could not be regularly attended to except we had a salaried official.

But that was then very difficult for us. The movement had still so few members that it was hard to find among them a suitable person for the job who would be content with very little for himself and at the same time would be ready to meet the manifold demands which the movement would make on his time and energy.

After long searching we discovered a soldier who consented to become our first administrator. His name was Schüssler, an old war comrade of mine. At first he came to our new office every day between six and eight o'clock in the evening. Later on he came from five to eight and subsequently for the whole afternoon. Finally it became a full-time job and he worked in the office from morning until late at night. He was an industrious, upright and thoroughly honest man, faithful and devoted to the movement. He brought with him a small Adler typewriter of his own. It was the first machine to be used in the service of the party. Subsequently the party bought it by paying for it in installments. We needed a small safe in order to keep our papers and register of membership from danger of being stolen—not to guard our funds, which did not then exist. On the contrary, our financial position was so miserable that I often had to dip my hand into my own personal savings.

After eighteen months our business quarters had become too small, so we moved to a new place in the Cornelius Strasse. Again our office was in a restaurant, but instead of one room we now had three smaller rooms and one large room with great windows. At that time this appeared a wonderful thing to us. We remained there until the end of November 1923.

In December 1920, we acquired the VÖLKISCHER BEOBACHTER. This newspaper which, as its name implies, championed the claims of the people, was now to become the organ of the German National Socialist Labour Party. At first it appeared twice weekly; but at the beginning of 1928 it became a daily paper, and at the end of August in the same year it began to appear in the large format which is now well known.

As a complete novice in journalism I then learned many a lesson for which I had to pay dearly.

In contradistinction to the enormous number of papers in Jewish hands, there was at that time only one important newspaper that defended the cause of the people. This was a matter for grave consideration. As I have often learned by experience, the reason for that state of things must be attributed to the incompetent way in which the business side of the so-called popular newspapers was managed. These were conducted too much according to the rule that opinion should prevail over action that produces results. Quite a wrong standpoint, for opinion is of itself something internal and finds its best expression in productive activity. The man who does valuable work for his people expresses thereby his excellent sentiments, whereas another who merely talks about his opinions and does nothing that is of real value or use to the people is a person who perverts all right thinking. And that attitude of his is also pernicious for the community.

The VÖLKISCHE BEOBACHTER was a so-called 'popular' organ, as its name indicated. It had all the good qualities, but still more the errors and weaknesses, inherent in all popular institutions. Though its contents were excellent, its management as a business concern was simply impossible. Here also the underlying idea was that popular newspapers ought to be subsidized by popular contributions, without recognizing that it had to make its way in competition with the others and that it was dishonest to expect the subscriptions of good patriots to make up for the mistaken management of the undertaking.

I took care to alter those conditions promptly, for I recognized the danger lurking in them. Luck was on my side here, inasmuch as it brought me the man who since that time has rendered innumerable services to the movement, not only as business manager of the newspaper but also as business manager of the party. In 1914, in the War, I made the acquaintance of Max Amann, who was then my superior and is to-day general business Director of the Party. During four years in the War I had occasion to observe almost continually the unusual ability, the diligence and the rigorous conscientiousness of my future collaborator.

In the summer of 1921 I applied to my old regimental comrade, whom I met one day by chance, and asked him to become business manager of the movement. At that time the movement was passing through a grave crisis and I had reason to be dissatisfied with several of our officials, with one of whom I had had a very bitter experience. Amann then held a good situation in which there were also good prospects for him.

After long hesitation he agreed to my request, but only on condition that he must not be at the mercy of incompetent committees. He must be responsible to one master, and only one.

It is to the inestimable credit of this first business manager of the party, whose commercial knowledge is extensive and profound, that he brought order and probity into the various offices of the party. Since that time these have remained exemplary and cannot be equalled or excelled in this by any other branches of the movement. But, as often happens in life, great ability provokes envy and disfavour. That had also to be expected in this case and borne patiently.

Since 1922 rigorous regulations have been in force, not only for the commercial construction of the movement but also in the organization of it as such. There exists now a central filing system, where the names and particulars of all the members are enrolled. The financing of the party has been placed on sound lines. The current expenditure must be covered by the current receipts and special receipts can be used only for special expenditures. Thus, notwithstanding the difficulties of the time the movement remained practically without any debts, except for a few small current accounts. Indeed, there was a permanent increase in the funds. Things are managed as in a private business. The employed personnel hold their jobs in virtue of their practical efficiency and could not in any manner take cover behind their professed loyalty to the party. A good National Socialist proves his soundness by the readiness, diligence and capability with which he discharges whatever duties are assigned to him in whatever situation he holds within the national community. The man who does not fulfil his duty in the job he holds cannot boast of a loyalty against which he himself really sins.

Adamant against all kinds of outer influence, the new business director of the party firmly maintained the standpoint that there were no sinecure posts in the party administration for followers and members of the movement whose pleasure is not work. A movement which fights so energetically against the corruption introduced into our civil service by the various political parties must be immune from that vice in its own administrative department. It happened that some men were taken on the staff of the paper who had formerly been adherents of the Bavarian People's Party, but their work showed that they were excellently qualified for the job. The result of this experiment was generally excellent. It was owing to this honest and frank recognition of individual efficiency that the movement won the hearts of its employees more swiftly and more profoundly than had ever been the case before. Subsequently they became good National Socialists and remained so. Not in word only, but they proved it by the steady and honest and conscientious work which they performed in the service of the new movement. Naturally a well qualified party member was preferred to another who had equal qualifications but did not belong to the party. The rigid determination with which our new business chief applied these principles and gradually put them into force, despite all misunderstandings, turned out to be of great advantage to the movement. To this we owe the fact that it was possible for us — during the difficult period of the inflation, when thousands of businesses failed and thousands of newspapers had to cease publication — not only to keep the commercial department of the movement going and meet all its obligations but also to make steady progress with the VÖLKISCHE BEOBACHTER. At that time it came to be ranked among the great newspapers.

The year 1921 was of further importance for me by reason of the fact that in my position as chairman of the party I slowly but steadily succeeded in putting a stop to the criticisms and the intrusions of some members of the committee in regard to the detailed activities of the party administration. This was important, because we could not get a capable man to take on a job if nincompoops were constantly allowed to butt in, pretending that they knew everything much better; whereas in reality they had left only general chaos behind them. Then these wise-acres retired, for the most part quite modestly, to seek another field for their activities where they could supervise and tell how things ought to be done. Some men seemed to have a mania for sniffing behind everything and were, so to say, always in a permanent state of pregnancy with magnificent plans and ideas and projects and methods. Naturally their noble aim and ideal were always the formation of a committee which could pretend to be an organ of control in order to be able to sniff as experts into the regular work done by others. But it is offensive and contrary to the spirit of National Socialism when incompetent people constantly interfere in the work of capable persons. But these makers of committees do not take that very much into account. In those years I felt it my duty to safeguard against such annoyance all those who were entrusted with regular and responsible work, so that there should be no spying over the shoulder and they would be guaranteed a free hand in their day's work.

The best means of making committees innocuous, which either did nothing or cooked up impracticable decisions, was to give them some real work to do. It was then amusing to see how the members would silently fade away and were soon nowhere to be found. It made me think of that great institution of the same kind, the Reichstag. How quickly they would evanesce if they were put to some real work instead of talking, especially if each member were made personally responsible for the work assigned to him.

I always demanded that, just as in private life so also in the movement, one should not tire of seeking until the best and honestest and manifestly the most competent person could be found for the position of leader or administrator in each section of the movement. Once installed in his position he was given absolute authority and full freedom of action towards his subordinates and full responsibility towards his superiors. Nobody was placed in a position of authority towards his subordinates unless he himself was competent in the work entrusted to them. In the course of two years I brought my views more and more into practice; so that to-day, at least as far as the higher direction of the movement is concerned, they are accepted as a matter of course.

The manifest success of this attitude was shown on November 9th, 1923. Four years previously, when I entered the movement, it did not have even a rubber stamp. On November 9th, 1923, the party was dissolved and its property confiscated. The total sum realized by all the objects of value and the paper amounted to more than 170,000 gold marks.

CHAPTER XII:
The Problem of the Trade Unions

Owing to the rapid growth of the movement, in 1922 we felt compelled to take a definite stand on a question which has not been fully solved even yet. In our efforts to discover the quickest and easiest way for the movement to reach the heart of the broad masses we were always confronted with the objection that the worker could never completely belong to us while his interests in the purely vocational and economic sphere were cared for by a political organization conducted by men whose principles were quite different from ours.

That was quite a serious objection. The general belief was that a workman engaged in some trade or other could not exist if he did not belong to a trade union. Not only were his professional interests thus protected but a guarantee of permanent employment was simply inconceivable without membership in a trade union. The majority of the workers were in the trades unions. Generally speaking, the unions had successfully conducted the battle for the establishment of a definite scale of wages and had concluded agreements which guaranteed the worker a steady income. Undoubtedly the workers in the various trades benefited by the results of that campaign and, for honest men especially, conflicts of conscience must have arisen if they took the wages which had been assured through the struggle fought by the trades unions and if at the same time the men themselves withdrew from the fight.

It was difficult to discuss this problem with the average bourgeois employer. He had no understanding (or did not wish to have any) for either the material or moral side of the question. Finally he declared that his own economic interests were in principle opposed to every kind of organization which joined together the workmen that were dependent on him. Hence it was for the most part impossible to bring these bourgeois employers to take an impartial view of the situation. Here, therefore, as in so many other cases, it was necessary to appeal to disinterested outsiders who would not be subject to the temptation of fixing their attention on the trees and failing to see the forest. With a little good will on their part, they could much more easily understand a state of affairs which is of the highest importance for our present and future existence.

In the first volume of this book I have already expressed my views on the nature and purpose and necessity of trade unions. There I took up the standpoint that unless measures are undertaken by the State (usually futile in such cases) or a new ideal is introduced in our education, which would change the attitude of the employer towards the worker, no other course would be open to the latter except to defend his own interests himself by appealing to his equal rights as a contracting party within the economic sphere of the nation's existence. I stated further that this would conform to the interests of the national community if thereby social injustices could be redressed which otherwise would cause serious damage to the whole social structure. I stated, moreover, that the worker would always find it necessary to undertake this protective action as long as there were men among the employers who had no sense of their social obligations nor even of the most elementary human rights. And I concluded by saying that if such self-defence be considered necessary its form ought to be that of an association made up of the workers themselves on the basis of trades unions.

This was my general idea and it remained the same in 1922. But a clear and precise formula was still to be discovered. We could not be satisfied with merely understanding the problem. It was necessary to come to some conclusions that could be put into practice. The following questions had to be answered:

(1) Are trade unions necessary?

(2) Should the German National Socialist Labour Party itself operate on a trade unionist basis or have its members take part in trade unionist activities in some form or other?

(3) What form should a National Socialist Trades Union take? What are the tasks confronting us and the ends we must try to attain?

(4) How can we establish trade unions for such tasks and aims?

I think that I have already answered the first question adequately. In the present state of affairs I am convinced that we cannot possibly dispense with the trades unions. On the contrary, they are among the most important institutions in the economic life of the nation. Not only are they important in the sphere of social policy but also, and even more so, in the national political sphere. For when the great masses of a nation see their vital needs satisfied through a just trade unionist movement the stamina of the whole nation in its struggle for existence will be enormously reinforced thereby.

Before everything else, the trades unions are necessary as building stones for the future economic parliament, which will be made up of chambers representing the various professions and occupations.

The second question is also easy to answer. If the trade unionist movement is important, then it is clear that National Socialism ought to take a definite stand on that question, not only theoretically but also in practice. But how? That is more difficult to see clearly.

The National Socialist Movement, which aims at establishing the National Socialist People's State, must always bear steadfastly in mind the principle that every future institution under that State must be rooted in the movement itself. It is a great mistake to believe that by acquiring possession of supreme political power we can bring about a definite reorganization, suddenly starting from nothing, without the help of a certain reserve stock of men who have been trained beforehand, especially in the spirit of the movement. Here also the principle holds good that the spirit is always more important than the external form which it animates; since this form can be created mechanically and quickly. For instance, the leadership principle may be imposed on an organized political community in a dictatorial way. But this principle can become a living reality only by passing through the stages that are necessary for its own evolution. These stages lead from the smallest cell of the State organism upwards. As its bearers and representatives, the leadership principle must have a body of men who have passed through a process of selection lasting over several years, who have been tempered by the hard realities of life and thus rendered capable of carrying the principle into practical effect.

It is out of the question to think that a scheme for the Constitution of a State can be pulled out of a portfolio at a moment's notice and 'introduced' by imperative orders from above. One may try that kind of thing but the result will always be something that has not sufficient vitality to endure. It will be like a stillborn infant. The idea of it calls to mind the origin of the Weimar Constitution and the attempt to impose on the German people a new Constitution and a new flag, neither of which had any inner relation to the vicissitudes of our people's history during the last half century.

The National Socialist State must guard against all such experiments. It must grow out of an organization which has already existed for a long time. This organization must possess National Socialist life in itself, so that finally it may be able to establish a National Socialist State that will be a living reality.

As I have already said, the germ cells of this State must lie in the administrative chambers which will represent the various occupations and professions, therefore first of all in the trades unions. If this subsequent vocational representation and the Central Economic Parliament are to be National Socialist institutions, these important germ cells must be vehicles of the National Socialist concept of life. The institutions of the movement are to be brought over into the State; for the State cannot call into existence all of a sudden and as if by magic those institutions which are necessary to its existence, unless it wishes to have institutions that are bound to remain completely lifeless.

Looking at the matter from the highest standpoint, the National Socialist Movement will have to recognize the necessity of adopting its own trade-unionist policy.

It must do this for a further reason, namely because a real National Socialist education for the employer as well as for the employee, in the spirit of a mutual co-operation within the common framework of the national community, cannot be secured by theoretical instruction, appeals and exhortations, but through the struggles of daily life. In this spirit and through this spirit the movement must educate the several large economic groups and bring them closer to one another under a wider outlook. Without this preparatory work it would be sheer illusion to hope that a real national community can be brought into existence. The great ideal represented by its philosophy of life and for which the movement fights can alone form a general style of thought steadily and slowly. And this style will show that the new state of things rests on foundations that are internally sound and not merely an external façade.

Hence the movement must adopt a positive attitude towards the trade-unionist idea. But it must go further than this. For the enormous number of members and followers of the trade-unionist movement it must provide a practical education which will meet the exigencies of the coming National Socialist State.

The answer to the third question follows from what has been already said.

The National Socialist Trades Union is not an instrument for class warfare, but a representative organ of the various occupations and callings. The National Socialist State recognizes no 'classes'. But, under the political aspect, it recognizes only citizens with absolutely equal rights and equal obligations corresponding thereto. And, side by side with these, it recognizes subjects of the State who have no political rights whatsoever.

According to the National Socialist concept, it is not the task of the trades union to band together certain men within the national community and thus gradually transform these men into a class, so as to use them in a conflict against other groups similarly organized within the national community. We certainly cannot assign this task to the trades union as such. This was the task assigned to it the moment it became a fighting weapon in the hands of the Marxists. The trades union is not naturally an instrument of class warfare; but the Marxists transformed it into an instrument for use in their own class struggle. They created the economic weapon which the international Jew uses for the purpose of destroying the economic foundations of free and independent national States, for ruining their national industry and trade and thereby enslaving free nations to serve Jewish world-finance, which transcends all State boundaries.

In contradistinction to this, the National Socialist Trades Union must organize definite groups and those who participate in the economic life of the nation and thus enhance the security of the national economic system itself, reinforcing it by the elimination of all those anomalies which ultimately exercise a destructive influence on the social body of the nation, damaging the vital forces of the national community, prejudicing the welfare of the State and, by no means as a last consequence, bringing evil and destruction on economic life itself.

Therefore in the hands of the National Socialist Trades Union the strike is not an instrument for disturbing and dislocating the national production, but for increasing it and making it run smoothly, by fighting against all those annoyances which by reason of their unsocial character hinder efficiency in business and thereby hamper the existence of the whole nation. For individual efficiency stands always in casual relation to the general social and juridical position of the individual in the economic process. Individual efficiency is also the sole root of the conviction that the economic prosperity of the nation must necessarily redound to the benefit of the individual citizen.

The National Socialist employee will have to recognize the fact that the economic prosperity of the nation brings with it his own material happiness.

The National Socialist employer must recognize that the happiness and contentment of his employees are necessary pre-requisites for the existence and development of his own economic prosperity. National Socialist workers and employers are both together the delegates and mandatories of the whole national community. The large measure of personal freedom which is accorded to them for their activities must be explained by the fact that experience has shown that the productive powers of the individual are more enhanced by being accorded a generous measure of freedom than by coercion from above. Moreover, by according this freedom we give free play to the natural process of selection which brings forward the ablest and most capable and most industrious. For the National Socialist Trades Union, therefore, the strike is a means that may, and indeed must, be resorted to as long as there is not a National Socialist State yet. But when that State is established it will, as a matter of course, abolish the mass struggle between the two great groups made up of employers and employees respectively, a struggle which has always resulted in lessening the national production and injuring the national community. In place of this struggle, the National Socialist State will take over the task of caring for and defending the rights of all parties concerned. It will be the duty of the Economic Chamber itself to keep the national economic system in smooth working order and to remove whatever defects or errors it may suffer from. Questions that are now fought over through a quarrel that involves millions of people will then be settled in the Representative Chambers of Trades and Professions and in the Central Economic Parliament. Thus employers and employees will no longer find themselves drawn into a mutual conflict over wages and hours of work, always to the detriment of their mutual interests. But they will solve these problems together on a higher plane, where the welfare of the national community and of the State will be as a shining ideal to throw light on all their negotiations.

Here again, as everywhere else, the inflexible principle must be observed, that the interests of the country must come before party interests.

The task of the National Socialist Trades Union will be to educate and prepare its members to conform to these ideals. That task may be stated as follows: All must work together for the maintenance and security of our people and the People's State, each one according to the abilities and powers with which Nature has endowed him and which have been developed and trained by the national community.

Our fourth question was: How shall we establish trades unions for such tasks and aims? That is far more difficult to answer.

Generally speaking, it is easier to establish something in new territory than in old territory which already has its established institutions. In a district where there is no existing business of a special character one can easily establish a new business of this character. But it is more difficult if the same kind of enterprise already exists and it is most difficult of all when the conditions are such that only one enterprise of this kind can prosper. For here the promoters of the new enterprise find themselves confronted not only with the problem of introducing their own business but also that of how to bring about the destruction of the other business already existing in the district, so that the new enterprise may be able to exist.

It would be senseless to have a National Socialist Trades Union side by side with other trades unions. For this Trades Union must be thoroughly imbued with a feeling for the ideological nature of its task and of the resulting obligation not to tolerate other similar or hostile institutions. It must also insist that itself alone is necessary, to the exclusion of all the rest. It can come to no arrangement and no compromise with kindred tendencies but must assert its own absolute and exclusive right.

There were two ways which might lead to such a development:

(1) We could establish our Trades Union and then gradually take up the fight against the Marxist International Trades Union.

(2) Or we could enter the Marxist Trades Union and inculcate a new spirit in it, with the idea of transforming it into an instrument in the service of the new ideal.

The first way was not advisable, by reason of the fact that our financial situation was still the cause of much worry to us at that time and our resources were quite slender. The effects of the inflation were steadily spreading and made the particular situation still more difficult for us, because in those years one could scarcely speak of any material help which the trades unions could extend to their members. From this point of view, there was no reason why the individual worker should pay his dues to the union. Even the Marxist unions then existing were already on the point of collapse until, as the result of Herr Cuno's enlightened Ruhr policy, millions were suddenly poured into their coffers. This so-called 'national' Chancellor of the REICH should go down in history as the Redeemer of the Marxist trades unions.

We could not count on similar financial facilities. And nobody could be induced to enter a new Trades Union which, on account of its financial weakness, could not offer him the slightest material benefit. On the other hand, I felt bound absolutely to guard against the creation of such an organization which would only be a shelter for shirkers of the more or less intellectual type.

At that time the question of personnel played the most important role. I did not have a single man whom I might call upon to carry out this important task. Whoever could have succeeded at that time in overthrowing the Marxist unions to make way for the triumph of the National Socialist corporative idea, which would then take the place of the ruinous class warfare—such a person would be fit to rank with the very greatest men our nation has produced and his bust should be installed in the Valhalla at Regensburg for the admiration of posterity.

But I knew of no person who could qualify for such a pedestal.

In this connection we must not be led astray by the fact that the international trades unions are conducted by men of only mediocre significance, for when those unions were founded there was nothing else of a similar kind already in existence. To-day the National Socialist Movement must fight against a monster organization which has existed for a long time, rests on gigantic foundations and is carefully constructed even in the smallest details. An assailant must always exercise more intelligence than the defender, if he is to overthrow the latter. The Marxist trade-unionist citadel may be governed to-day by mediocre leaders, but it cannot be taken by assault except through the dauntless energy and genius of a superior leader on the other side. If such a leader cannot be found it is futile to struggle with Fate and even more foolish to try to overthrow the existing state of things without being able to construct a better in its place.

Here one must apply the maxim that in life it is often better to allow something to go by the board rather than try to half do it or do it badly, owing to a lack of suitable means.

To this we must add another consideration, which is not at all of a demagogic character. At that time I had, and I still have to-day, a firmly rooted conviction that when one is engaged in a great ideological struggle in the political field it would be a grave mistake to mix up economic questions with this struggle in its earlier stages. This applies particularly to our German people. For if such were to happen in their case the economic struggle would immediately distract the energy necessary for the political fight. Once the people are brought to believe that they can buy a little house with their savings they will devote themselves to the task of increasing their savings and no spare time will be left to them for the political struggle against those who, in one way or another, will one day secure possession of the pennies that have been saved. Instead of participating in the political conflict on behalf of the opinions and convictions which they have been brought to accept they will now go further with their 'settlement' idea and in the end they will find themselves for the most part sitting on the ground amidst all the stools.

To-day the National Socialist Movement is at the beginning of its struggle. In great part it must first of all shape and develop its ideals. It must employ every ounce of its energy in the struggle to have its great ideal accepted, and the success of this effort is not conceivable unless the combined energies of the movement be entirely at the service of this struggle.

To-day we have a classical example of how the active strength of a people becomes paralysed when that people is too much taken up with purely economic problems.

The Revolution which took place in November 1918 was not made by the trades unions, but it was carried out in spite of them. And the people of Germany did not wage any political fight for the future of their country because they thought that the future could be sufficiently secured by constructive work in the economic field.

We must learn a lesson from this experience, because in our case the same thing must happen under the same circumstances. The more the combined strength of our movement is concentrated in the political struggle, the more confidently may we count on being successful along our whole front. But if we busy ourselves prematurely with trade unionist problems, settlement problems, etc., it will be to the disadvantage of our own cause, taken as a whole. For, though these problems may be important, they cannot be solved in an adequate manner until we have political power in our hand and are able to use it in the service of this idea. Until that day comes these problems can have only a paralysing effect on the movement. And if it takes them up too soon they will only be a hindrance in the effort to attain its own ideological aims. It may then easily happen that trade unionist considerations will control the political direction of the movement, instead of the ideological aims of the movement directing the way that the trades unions are to take.

The movement and the nation can derive advantage from a National Socialist trade unionist organization only if the latter be so thoroughly inspired by National Socialist ideas that it runs no danger of falling into step behind the Marxist movement. For a National Socialist Trades Union which would consider itself only as a competitor against the Marxist unions would be worse than none. It must declare war against the Marxist Trades Union, not only as an organization but, above all, as an idea. It must declare itself hostile to the idea of class and class warfare and, in place of this, it must declare itself as the defender of the various occupational and professional interests of the German people.

Considered from all these points of view it was not then advisable, nor is it yet advisable, to think of founding our own Trades Union. That seemed clear to me, at least until somebody appeared who was obviously called by fate to solve this particular problem.

Therefore there remained only two possible ways. Either to recommend our own party members to leave the trades unions in which they were enrolled or to remain in them for the moment, with the idea of causing as much destruction in them as possible.

In general, I recommended the latter alternative.

Especially in the year 1922-23 we could easily do that. For, during the period of inflation, the financial advantages which might be reaped from a trades union organization would be negligible, because we could expect to enroll only a few members owing to the undeveloped condition of our movement. The damage which might result from such a policy was all the greater because its bitterest critics and opponents were to be found among the followers of the National Socialist Party.

I had already entirely discountenanced all experiments which were destined from the very beginning to be unsuccessful. I would have considered it criminal to run the risk of depriving a worker of his scant earnings in order to help an organization which, according to my inner conviction, could not promise real advantages to its members.

Should a new political party fade out of existence one day nobody would be injured thereby and some would have profited, but none would have a right to complain. For what each individual contributes to a political movement is given with the idea that it may ultimately come to nothing. But the man who pays his dues to a trade union has the right to expect some guarantee in return. If this is not done, then the directors of such a trade union are swindlers or at least careless people who ought to be brought to a sense of their responsibilities.

We took all these viewpoints into consideration before making our decision in 1922. Others thought otherwise and founded trades unions. They upbraided us for being short-sighted and failing to see into the future. But it did not take long for these organizations to disappear and the result was what would have happened in our own case. But the difference was that we should have deceived neither ourselves nor those who believed in us.

CHAPTER XIII:
The German Post-War Policy of Alliances

The erratic manner in which the foreign affairs of the REICH were conducted was due to a lack of sound guiding principles for the formation of practical and useful alliances. Not only was this state of affairs continued after the Revolution, but it became even worse.

For the confused state of our political ideas in general before the War may be looked upon as the chief cause of our defective statesmanship; but in the post-War period this cause must be attributed to a lack of honest intentions. It was natural that those parties who had fully achieved their destructive purpose by means of the Revolution should feel that it would not serve their interests if a policy of alliances were adopted which must ultimately result in the restoration of a free German State. A development in this direction would not be in conformity with the purposes of the November crime. It would have interrupted and indeed put an end to the internationalization of German national economy and German Labour. But what was feared most of all was that a successful effort to make the REICH independent of foreign countries might have an influence in domestic politics which one day would turn out disastrous for those who now hold supreme power in the government of the REICH. One cannot imagine the revival of a nation unless that revival be preceded by a process of nationalization. Conversely, every important success in the field of foreign politics must call forth a favourable reaction at home. Experience proves that every struggle for liberty increases the national sentiment and national self-consciousness and therewith gives rise to a keener sensibility towards anti-national elements and tendencies. A state of things, and persons also, that may be tolerated and even pass unnoticed in times of peace will not only become the object of aversion when national enthusiasm is aroused but will even provoke positive opposition, which frequently turns out disastrous for them. In this connection we may recall the spy-scare that became prevalent when the war broke out, when human passion suddenly manifested itself to such a heightened degree as to lead to the most brutal persecutions, often without any justifiable grounds, although everybody knew that the danger resulting from spies is greater during the long periods of peace; but, for obvious reasons, they do not then attract a similar amount of public attention. For this reason the subtle instinct of the State parasites who came to the surface of the national body through the November happenings makes them feel at once that a policy of alliances which would restore the freedom of our people and awaken national sentiment might possibly ruin their own criminal existence.

Thus we may explain the fact that since 1918 the men who have held the reins of government adopted an entirely negative attitude towards foreign affairs and that the business of the State has been almost constantly conducted in a systematic way against the interests of the German nation. For that which at first sight seemed a matter of chance proved, on closer examination, to be a logical advance along the road which was first publicly entered upon by the November Revolution of 1918.

Undoubtedly a distinction ought to be made between (1) the responsible administrators of our affairs of State, or rather those who ought to be responsible; (2) the average run of our parliamentary politicasters, and (3) the masses of our people, whose sheepish docility corresponds to their want of intelligence.

The first know what they want. The second fall into line with them, either because they have been already schooled in what is afoot or because they have not the courage to take an uncompromising stand against a course which they know and feel to be detrimental. The third just submit to it because they are too stupid to understand.

While the German National Socialist Labour Party was only a small and practically unknown society, problems of foreign policy could have only a secondary importance in the eyes of many of its members. This was the case especially because our movement has always proclaimed the principle, and must proclaim it, that the freedom of the country in its foreign relations is not a gift that will be bestowed upon us by Heaven or by any earthly Powers, but can only be the fruit of a development of our inner forces. We must first root out the causes which led to our collapse and we must eliminate all those who are profiting by that collapse. Then we shall be in a position to take up the fight for the restoration of our freedom in the management of our foreign relations.

It will be easily understood therefore why we did not attach so much importance to foreign affairs during the early stages of our young movement, but preferred to concentrate on the problem of internal reform.

But when the small and insignificant society expanded and finally grew too large for its first framework, the young organization assumed the importance of a great association and we then felt it incumbent on us to take a definite stand on problems regarding the development of a foreign policy. It was necessary to lay down the main lines of action which would not only be in accord with the fundamental ideas of our WELTANSCHAUUNG but would actually be an expansion of it in the practical world of foreign affairs.

Just because our people have had no political education in matters concerning our relations abroad, it was necessary to teach the leaders in the various sections of our movement, and also the masses of the people, the chief principles which ought to guide the development of our foreign relations. That was one of the first tasks to be accomplished in order to prepare the ground for the practical carrying out of a foreign policy which would win back the independence of the nation in managing its external affairs and thus restore the real sovereignty of the REICH.

The fundamental and guiding principles which we must always bear in mind when studying this question is that foreign policy is only a means to an end and that the sole end to be pursued is the welfare of our own people. Every problem in foreign politics must be considered from this point of view, and this point of view alone. Shall such and such a solution prove advantageous to our people now or in the future, or will it injure their interests? That is the question.

This is the sole preoccupation that must occupy our minds in dealing with a question. Party politics, religious considerations, humanitarian ideals—all such and all other preoccupations must absolutely give way to this.

Before the War the purpose to which German foreign policy should have been devoted was to assure the supply of material necessities for the maintenance of our people and their children. And the way should have been prepared which would lead to this goal. Alliances should have been established which would have proved beneficial to us from this point of view and would have brought us the necessary auxiliary support. The task to be accomplished is the same to-day, but with this difference: In pre-War times it was a question of caring for the maintenance of the German people, backed up by the power which a strong and independent State then possessed, but our task to-day is to make our nation powerful once again by re-establishing a strong and independent State. The re-establishment of such a State is the prerequisite and necessary condition which must be fulfilled in order that we may be able subsequently to put into practice a foreign policy which will serve to guarantee the existence of our people in the future, fulfilling their needs and furnishing them with those necessities of life which they lack. In other words, the aim which Germany ought to pursue to-day in her foreign policy is to prepare the way for the recovery of her liberty to-morrow. In this connection there is a fundamental principle which we must keep steadily before our minds. It is this: The possibility of winning back the independence of a nation is not absolutely bound up with the question of territorial reintegration but it will suffice if a small remnant, no matter how small, of this nation and State will exist, provided it possesses the necessary independence to become not only the vehicle of' the common spirit of the whole people but also to prepare the way for the military fight to reconquer the nation's liberty.

When a people who amount to a hundred million souls tolerate the yoke of common slavery in order to prevent the territory belonging to their State from being broken up and divided, that is worse than if such a State and such a people were dismembered while one fragment still retained its complete independence. Of course, the natural proviso here is that this fragment must be inspired with a consciousness of the solemn duty that devolves upon it, not only to proclaim persistently the inviolable unity of its spiritual and cultural life with that of its detached members but also to prepare the means that are necessary for the military conflict which will finally liberate and re-unite the fragments that are suffering under oppression.

One must also bear in mind the fact that the restoration of lost districts which were formerly parts of the State, both ethnically and politically, must in the first instance be a question of winning back political power and independence for the motherland itself, and that in such cases the special interests of the lost districts must be uncompromisingly regarded as a matter of secondary importance in the face of the one main task, which is to win back the freedom of the central territory. For the detached and oppressed fragments of a nation or an imperial province cannot achieve their liberation through the expression of yearnings and protests on the part of the oppressed and abandoned, but only when the portion which has more or less retained its sovereign independence can resort to the use of force for the purpose of reconquering those territories that once belonged to the common fatherland.

Therefore, in order to reconquer lost territories the first condition to be fulfilled is to work energetically for the increased welfare and reinforcement of the strength of that portion of the State which has remained over after the partition. Thus the unquenchable yearning which slumbers in the hearts of the people must be awakened and restrengthened by bringing new forces to its aid, so that when the hour comes all will be devoted to the one purpose of liberating and uniting the whole people. Therefore, the interests of the separated territories must be subordinated to the one purpose. That one purpose must aim at obtaining for the central remaining portion such a measure of power and might that will enable it to enforce its will on the hostile will of the victor and thus redress the wrong. For flaming protests will not restore the oppressed territories to the bosom of a common REICH. That can be done only through the might of the sword.

The forging of this sword is a work that has to be done through the domestic policy which must be adopted by a national government. To see that the work of forging these arms is assured, and to recruit the men who will bear them, that is the task of the foreign policy.

In the first volume of this book I discussed the inadequacy of our policy of alliances before the War. There were four possible ways to secure the necessary foodstuffs for the maintenance of our people. Of these ways the fourth, which was the most unfavourable, was chosen. Instead of a sound policy of territorial expansion in Europe, our rulers embarked on a policy of colonial and trade expansion. That policy was all the more mistaken inasmuch as they presumed that in this way the danger of an armed conflict would be averted. The result of the attempt to sit on many stools at the same time might have been foreseen. It let us fall to the ground in the midst of them all. And the World War was only the last reckoning presented to the REICH to pay for the failure of its foreign policy.

The right way that should have been taken in those days was the third way I indicated: namely, to increase the strength of the REICH as a Continental Power by the acquisition of new territory in Europe. And at the same time a further expansion, through the subsequent acquisition of colonial territory, might thus be brought within the range of practical politics. Of course, this policy could not have been carried through except in alliance with England, or by devoting such abnormal efforts to the increase of military force and armament that, for forty or fifty years, all cultural undertakings would have to be completely relegated to the background. This responsibility might very well have been undertaken. The cultural importance of a nation is almost always dependent on its political freedom and independence. Political freedom is a prerequisite condition for the existence, or rather the creation, of great cultural undertakings. Accordingly no sacrifice can be too great when there is question of securing the political freedom of a nation. What might have to be deducted from the budget expenses for cultural purposes, in order to meet abnormal demands for increasing the military power of the State, can be generously paid back later on. Indeed, it may be said that after a State has concentrated all its resources in one effort for the purpose of securing its political independence a certain period of ease and renewed equilibrium sets in. And it often happens that the cultural spirit of the nation, which had been heretofore cramped and confined, now suddenly blooms forth. Thus Greece experienced the great Periclean era after the miseries it had suffered during the Persian Wars. And the Roman Republic turned its energies to the cultivation of a higher civilization when it was freed from the stress and worry of the

Punic Wars.

Of course, it could not be expected that a parliamentary majority of feckless and stupid people would be capable of deciding on such a resolute policy for the absolute subordination of all other national interests to the one sole task of preparing for a future conflict of arms which would result in establishing the security of the State. The father of Frederick the Great sacrificed everything in order to be ready for that conflict; but the fathers of our absurd parliamentarian democracy, with the Jewish hall-mark, could not do it.

That is why, in pre-War times, the military preparation necessary to enable us to conquer new territory in Europe was only very mediocre, so that it was difficult to obtain the support of really helpful allies.

Those who directed our foreign affairs would not entertain even the idea of systematically preparing for war. They rejected every plan for the acquisition of territory in Europe. And by preferring a policy of colonial and trade expansion, they sacrificed the alliance with England, which was then possible. At the same time they neglected to seek the support of Russia, which would have been a logical proceeding. Finally they stumbled into the World War, abandoned by all except the ill-starred Habsburgs.

The characteristic of our present foreign policy is that it follows no discernible or even intelligible lines of action. Whereas before the War a mistake was made in taking the fourth way that I have mentioned, and this was pursued only in a halfhearted manner, since the Revolution not even the sharpest eye can detect any way that is being followed. Even more than before the War, there is absolutely no such thing as a systematic plan, except the systematic attempts that are made to destroy the last possibility of a national revival.

If we make an impartial examination of the situation existing in Europe to-day as far as concerns the relation of the various Powers to one another, we shall arrive at the following results:

For the past three hundred years the history of our Continent has been definitely determined by England's efforts to keep the European States opposed to one another in an equilibrium of forces, thus assuring the necessary protection of her own rear while she pursued the great aims of British world-policy.

The traditional tendency of British diplomacy ever since the reign of Queen Elizabeth has been to employ systematically every possible means to prevent any one Power from attaining a preponderant position over the other European Powers and, if necessary, to break that preponderance by means of armed intervention. The only parallel to this has been the tradition of the Prussian Army. England has made use of various forces to carry out its purpose, choosing them according to the actual situation or the task to be faced; but the will and determination to use them has always been the same. The more difficult England's position became in the course of history the more the British Imperial Government considered it necessary to maintain a condition of political paralysis among the various European States, as a result of their mutual rivalries. When the North American colonies obtained their political independence it became still more necessary for England to use every effort to establish and maintain the defence of her flank in Europe. In accordance with this policy she reduced Spain and the Netherlands to the position of inferior naval Powers. Having accomplished this, England concentrated all her forces against the increasing strength of France, until she brought about the downfall of Napoleon Bonaparte and therewith destroyed the military hegemony of France, which was the most dangerous rival that England had to fear.

The change of attitude in British statesmanship towards Germany took place only very slowly, not only because the German nation did not represent an obvious danger for England as long as it lacked national unification, but also because public opinion in England, which had been directed to other quarters by a system of propaganda that had been carried out for a long time, could be turned to a new direction only by slow degrees. In order to reach the proposed ends the calmly reflecting statesman had to bow to popular sentiment, which is the most powerful motive-force and is at the same time the most lasting in its energy. When the statesman has attained one of his ends, he must immediately turn his thoughts to others; but only by degrees and the slow work of propaganda can the sentiment of the masses be shaped into an instrument for the attainment of the new aims which their leaders have decided on.

As early as 1870-71 England had decided on the new stand it would take. On certain occasions minor oscillations in that policy were caused by the growing influence of America in the commercial markets of the world and also by the increasing political power of Russia; but, unfortunately, Germany did not take advantage of these and, therefore, the original tendency of British diplomacy was only reinforced.

England looked upon Germany as a Power which was of world importance commercially and politically and which, partly because of its enormous industrial development, assumed such threatening proportions that the two countries already contended against one another in the same sphere and with equal energy. The so-called peaceful conquest of the world by commercial enterprise, which, in the eyes of those who governed our public affairs at that time, represented the highest peak of human wisdom, was just the thing that led English statesmen to adopt a policy of resistance. That this resistance assumed the form of an organized aggression on a vast scale was in full conformity with a type of statesmanship which did not aim at the maintenance of a dubious world peace but aimed at the consolidation of British world-hegemony. In carrying out this policy, England allied herself with those countries which had a definite military importance. And that was in keeping with her traditional caution in estimating the power of her adversary and also in recognizing her own temporary weakness. That line of conduct cannot be called unscrupulous; because such a comprehensive organization for war purposes must not be judged from the heroic point of view but from that of expediency. The object of a diplomatic policy must not be to see that a nation goes down heroically but rather that it survives in a practical way. Hence every road that leads to this goal is opportune and the failure to take it must be looked upon as a criminal neglect of duty.

When the German Revolution took place England's fears of a German world hegemony came to a satisfactory end.

From that time it was not an English interest to see Germany totally cancelled from the geographic map of Europe. On the contrary, the astounding collapse which took place in November 1918 found British diplomacy confronted with a situation which at first appeared untenable.

For four-and-a-half years the British Empire had fought to break the presumed preponderance of a Continental Power. A sudden collapse now happened which removed this Power from the foreground of European affairs. That collapse disclosed itself finally in the lack of even the primordial instinct of self-preservation, so that European equilibrium was destroyed within forty-eight hours. Germany was annihilated and France became the first political Power on the Continent of Europe.

The tremendous propaganda which was carried on during this war for the purpose of encouraging the British public to stick it out to the end aroused all the primitive instincts and passions of the populace and was bound eventually to hang as a leaden weight on the decisions of British statesmen. With the colonial, economical and commercial destruction of Germany, England's war aims were attained. Whatever went beyond those aims was an obstacle to the furtherance of British interests. Only the enemies of England could profit by the disappearance of Germany as a Great Continental Power in Europe. In November 1918, however, and up to the summer of 1919, it was not possible for England to change its diplomatic attitude; because during the long war it had appealed, more than it had ever done before, to the feelings of the populace. In view of the feeling prevalent among its own people, England could not change its foreign policy; and another reason which made that impossible was the military strength to which other European Powers had now attained. France had taken the direction of peace negotiations into her own hands and could impose her law upon the others. During those months of negotiations and bargaining the only Power that could have altered the course which things were taking was Germany herself; but Germany was torn asunder by a civil war, and her so-called statesmen had declared themselves ready to accept any and every dictate imposed on them.

Now, in the comity of nations, when one nation loses its instinct for self-preservation and ceases to be an active member it sinks to the level of an enslaved nation and its territory will have to suffer the fate of a colony.

To prevent the power of France from becoming too great, the only form which English negotiations could take was that of participating in France's lust for aggrandizement.

As a matter of fact, England did not attain the ends for which she went to war. Not only did it turn out impossible to prevent a Continental Power from obtaining a preponderance over the ratio of strength in the Continental State system of Europe, but a large measure of preponderance had been obtained and firmly established.

In 1914 Germany, considered as a military State, was wedged in between two countries, one of which had equal military forces at its disposal and the other had greater military resources. Then there was England's overwhelming supremacy at sea. France and Russia alone hindered and opposed the excessive aggrandizement of Germany. The unfavourable geographical situation of the REICH, from the military point of view, might be looked upon as another coefficient of security against an exaggerated increase of German power. From the naval point of view, the configuration of the coast-line was unfavourable in case of a conflict with England. And though the maritime frontier was short and cramped, the land frontier was widely extended and open.

France's position is different to-day. It is the first military Power without a serious rival on the Continent. It is almost entirely protected by its southern frontier against Spain and Italy. Against Germany it is safeguarded by the prostrate condition of our country. A long stretch of its coast-line faces the vital nervous system of the British Empire. Not only could French aeroplanes and long-range batteries attack the vital centres of the British system, but submarines can threaten the great British commercial routes. A submarine campaign based on France's long Atlantic coast and on the European and North African coasts of the Mediterranean would have disastrous consequences for England.

Thus the political results of the war to prevent the development of German power was the creation of a French hegemony on the Continent. The military result was the consolidation of France as the first Continental Power and the recognition of American equality on the sea. The economic result was the cession of great spheres of British interests to her former allies and associates.

The Balkanization of Europe, up to a certain degree, was desirable and indeed necessary in the light of the traditional policy of Great Britain, just as France desired the Balkanization of Germany. What England has always desired, and will continue to desire, is to prevent any one Continental Power in Europe from attaining a position of world importance. Therefore England wishes to maintain a definite equilibrium of forces among the European States—for this equilibrium seems a necessary condition of England's world-hegemony.

What France has always desired, and will continue to desire, is to prevent Germany from becoming a homogeneous Power. Therefore France wants to maintain a system of small German States whose forces would balance one another and over which there should be no central government. Then, by acquiring possession of the left bank of the Rhine, she would have fulfilled the pre-requisite conditions for the establishment and security of her hegemony in Europe.

The final aims of French diplomacy must be in perpetual opposition to the final tendencies of British statesmanship.

Taking these considerations as a starting-point, anyone who investigates the possibilities that exist for Germany to find allies must come to the conclusion that there remains no other way of forming an alliance except to approach England. The consequences of England's war policy were and are disastrous for Germany. However, we cannot close our eyes to the fact that, as things stand to-day, the necessary interests of England no longer demand the destruction of Germany. On the contrary, British diplomacy must tend more and more, from year to year, towards curbing France's unbridled lust after hegemony. Now, a policy of alliances cannot be pursued by bearing past grievances in mind, but it can be rendered fruitful by taking account of past experiences. Experience should have taught us that alliances formed for negative purposes suffer from intrinsic weakness. The destinies of nations can be welded together only under the prospect of a common success, of common gain and conquest, in short, a common extension of power for both contracting parties.

The ignorance of our people on questions of foreign politics is clearly demonstrated by the reports in the daily Press which talk about "friendship towards Germany" on the part of one or the other foreign statesman, whereby this professed friendship is taken as a special guarantee that such persons will champion a policy that will be advantageous to our people. That kind of talk is absurd to an incredible degree. It means speculating on the unparalleled simplicity of the average German philistine when he comes to talking politics. There is not any British, American, or Italian statesman who could ever be described as 'pro-German'. Every Englishman must naturally be British first of all. The same is true of every American. And no Italian statesman would be prepared to adopt a policy that was not pro-Italian. Therefore, anyone who expects to form alliances with foreign nations on the basis of a pro-German feeling among the statesmen of other countries is either an ass or a deceiver. The necessary condition for linking together the destinies of nations is never mutual esteem or mutual sympathy, but rather the prospect of advantages accruing to the contracting parties. It is true that a British statesman will always follow a pro-British and not a pro-German policy; but it is also true that certain definite interests involved in this pro-British policy may coincide on various grounds with German interests. Naturally that can be so only to a certain degree and the situation may one day be completely reversed. But the art of statesmanship is shown when at certain periods there is question of reaching a certain end and when allies are found who must take the same road in order to defend their own interests.

The practical application of these principles at the present time must depend on the answer given to the following questions: What States are not vitally interested in the fact that, by the complete abolition of a German Central Europe, the economic and military power of France has reached a position of absolute hegemony? Which are the States that, in consideration of the conditions which are essential to their own existence and in view of the tradition that has hitherto been followed in conducting their foreign policy, envisage such a development as a menace to their own future?

Finally, we must be quite clear on the following point: France is and will remain the implacable enemy of Germany. It does not matter what Governments have ruled or will rule in France, whether Bourbon or Jacobin, Napoleonic or Bourgeois-Democratic, Clerical Republican or Red Bolshevik, their foreign policy will always be directed towards acquiring possession of the Rhine frontier and consolidating France's position on this river by disuniting and dismembering Germany.

England did not want Germany to be a world Power. France desired that there should be no Power called Germany. Therefore there was a very essential difference. To-day we are not fighting for our position as a World-Power but only for the existence of our country, for national unity and the daily bread of our children. Taking this point of view into consideration, only two States remain to us as possible allies in Europe—England and Italy.

England is not pleased to see a France on whose military power there is no check in Europe, so that one day she might undertake the support of a policy which in some way or other might come into conflict with British interests. Nor can England be pleased to see France in possession of such enormous coal and iron mines in Western Europe as would make it possible for her one day to play a role in world-commerce which might threaten danger to British interests. Moreover, England can never be pleased to see a France whose political position on the Continent, owing to the dismemberment of the rest of Europe, seems so absolutely assured that she is not only able to resume a French world-policy on great lines but would even find herself compelled to do so. The bombs which were once dropped by the Zeppelins might be multiplied by the thousand every night. The military predominance of France is a weight that presses heavily on the hearts of the World Empire over which Great Britain rules.

Nor can Italy desire, nor will she desire, any further strengthening of France's power in Europe. The future of Italy will be conditioned by the development of events in the Mediterranean and by the political situation in the area surrounding that sea. The reason that led Italy into the War was not a desire to contribute towards the aggrandizement of France but rather to deal her hated Adriatic rival a mortal blow. Any further increase of France's power on the Continent would hamper the development of Italy's future, and Italy does not deceive herself by thinking that racial kindred between the nations will in any way eliminate rivalries.

Serious and impartial consideration proves that it is these two States, Great Britain and Italy, whose natural interests not only do not contrast with the conditions essential to the existence of the German nation but are identical with them, to a certain extent.

But when we consider the possibilities of alliances we must be careful not to lose sight of three factors. The first factor concerns ourselves; the other two concern the two States I have mentioned.

Is it at all possible to conclude an alliance with Germany as it is to-day? Can a Power which would enter into an alliance for the purpose of securing assistance in an effort to carry out its own OFFENSIVE aims—can such a Power form an alliance with a State whose rulers have for years long presented a spectacle of deplorable incompetence and pacifist cowardice and where the majority of the people, blinded by democratic and Marxist teachings, betray the interests of their own people and country in a manner that cries to Heaven for vengeance? As things stand to-day, can any Power hope to establish useful relations and hope to fight together for the furtherance of their common interests with this State which manifestly has neither the will nor the courage to move a finger even in the defence of its bare existence? Take the case of a Power for which an alliance must be much more than a pact to guarantee a state of slow decomposition, such as happened with the old and disastrous Triple Alliance. Can such a Power associate itself for life or death with a State whose most characteristic signs of activity consist of a rampant servility in external relations and a scandalous repression of the national spirit at home? Can such a Power be associated with a State in which there is nothing of greatness, because its whole policy does not deserve it? Or can alliances be made with Governments which are in the hands of men who are despised by their own fellow-citizens and consequently are not respected abroad?

No. A self-respecting Power which expects something more from alliances than commissions for greedy Parliamentarians will not and cannot enter into an alliance with our present-day Germany. Our present inability to form alliances furnishes the principle and most solid basis for the combined action of the enemies who are robbing us. Because Germany does not defend itself in any other way except by the flamboyant protests of our parliamentarian elect, there is no reason why the rest of the world should take up the fight in our defence. And God does not follow the principle of granting freedom to a nation of cowards, despite all the implications of our 'patriotic' associations. Therefore, for those States which have not a direct interest in our annihilation no other course remains open except to participate in France's campaign of plunder, at least to make it impossible for the strength of France to be exclusively aggrandized thereby.

In the second place, we must not forget that among the nations which were formerly our enemies mass-propaganda has turned the opinions and feelings of large sections of the population in a fixed direction. When for years long a foreign nation has been presented to the public as a horde of 'Huns', 'Robbers', 'Vandals', etc., they cannot suddenly be presented as something different, and the enemy of yesterday cannot be recommended as the ally of tomorrow.

But the third factor deserves greater attention, since it is of essential importance for establishing future alliances in Europe. From the political point of view it is not in the interests of Great Britain that Germany should be ruined even still more, but such a proceeding would be very much in the interests of the international money-markets manipulated by the Jew. The cleavage between the official, or rather traditional, British statesmanship and the controlling influence of the Jew on the money-markets is nowhere so clearly manifested as in the various attitudes taken towards problems of British foreign policy. Contrary to the interests and welfare of the British State, Jewish finance demands not only the absolute economic destruction of Germany but its complete political enslavement. The internationalization of our German economic system, that is to say, the transference of our productive forces to the control of Jewish international finance, can be completely carried out only in a State that has been politically Bolshevized. But the Marxist fighting forces, commanded by international and Jewish stock-exchange capital, cannot finally smash the national resistance in Germany without friendly help from outside. For this purpose French armies would first have to invade and overcome the territory of the German REICH until a state of international chaos would set in, and then the country would have to succumb to Bolshevik storm troops in the service of Jewish international finance.

Hence it is that at the present time the Jew is the great agitator for the complete destruction of Germany. Whenever we read of attacks against Germany taking place in any part of the world the Jew is always the instigator. In peace-time, as well as during the War, the Jewish-Marxist stock-exchange Press systematically stirred up hatred against Germany, until one State after another abandoned its neutrality and placed itself at the service of the world coalition, even against the real interests of its own people.

The Jewish way of reasoning thus becomes quite clear. The Bolshevization of Germany, that is to say, the extermination of the patriotic and national German intellectuals, thus making it possible to force German Labour to bear the yoke of international Jewish finance—that is only the overture to the movement for expanding Jewish power on a wider scale and finally subjugating the world to its rule. As has so often happened in history, Germany is the chief pivot of this formidable struggle. If our people and our State should fall victims to these oppressors of the nations, lusting after blood and money, the whole earth would become the prey of that hydra. Should Germany be freed from its grip, a great menace for the nations of the world would thereby be eliminated.

It is certain that Jewry uses all its subterranean activities not only for the purpose of keeping alive old national enmities against Germany but even to spread them farther and render them more acute wherever possible. It is no less certain that these activities are only very partially in keeping with the true interests of the nations among whose people the poison is spread. As a general principle, Jewry carries on its campaign in the various countries by the use of arguments that are best calculated to appeal to the mentality of the respective nations and are most likely to produce the desired results; for Jewry knows what the public feeling is in each country. Our national stock has been so much adulterated by the mixture of alien elements that, in its fight for power, Jewry can make use of the more or less 'cosmopolitan' circles which exist among us, inspired by the pacifist and international ideologies. In France they exploit the well-known and accurately estimated chauvinistic spirit. In England they exploit the commercial and world-political outlook. In short, they always work upon the essential characteristics that belong to the mentality of each nation. When they have in this way achieved a decisive influence in the political and economic spheres they can drop the limitations which their former tactics necessitated, now disclosing their real intentions and the ends for which they are fighting. Their work of destruction now goes ahead more quickly, reducing one State after another to a mass of ruins on which they will erect the everlasting and sovereign Jewish Empire.

In England, and in Italy, the contrast between the better kind of solid statesmanship and the policy of the Jewish stock-exchange often becomes strikingly evident.

Only in France there exists to-day more than ever before a profound accord between the views of the stock-exchange, controlled by the Jews, and the chauvinistic policy pursued by French statesmen. This identity of views constitutes an immense, danger for Germany. And it is just for this reason that France is and will remain by far the most dangerous enemy. The French people, who are becoming more and more obsessed by negroid ideas, represent a threatening menace to the existence of the white race in Europe, because they are bound up with the Jewish campaign for world-domination. For the contamination caused by the influx of negroid blood on the Rhine, in the very heart of Europe, is in accord with the sadist and perverse lust for vengeance on the part of the hereditary enemy of our people, just as it suits the purpose of the cool calculating Jew who would use this means of introducing a process of bastardization in the very centre of the European Continent and, by infecting the white race with the blood of an inferior stock, would destroy the foundations of its independent existence.

France's activities in Europe to-day, spurred on by the French lust for vengeance and systematically directed by the Jew, are a criminal attack against the life of the white race and will one day arouse against the French people a spirit of vengeance among a generation which will have recognized the original sin of mankind in this racial pollution.

As far as concerns Germany, the danger which France represents involves the duty of relegating all sentiment to a subordinate place and extending the hand to those who are threatened with the same menace and who are not willing to suffer or tolerate France's lust for hegemony.

For a long time yet to come there will be only two Powers in Europe with which it may be possible for Germany to conclude an alliance. These Powers are Great Britain and Italy.

If we take the trouble to cast a glance backwards on the way in which German foreign policy has been conducted since the Revolution we must, in view of the constant and incomprehensible acts of submission on the part. of our governments, either lose heart or become fired with rage and take up the cudgels against such a regime. Their way of acting cannot be attributed to a want of understanding, because what seemed to every thinking man to be inconceivable was accomplished by the leaders of the November parties with their Cyclopean intellects. They bowed to France and begged her favour. Yes, during all these recent years, with the touching simplicity of incorrigible visionaries, they went on their knees to France again and again. They perpetuaily wagged their tails before the GRANDE NATION. And in each trick-o'-the-loop which the French hangmen performed with his rope they recognized a visible change of feeling. Our real political wire-pullers never shared in this absurd credulity. The idea of establishing a friendship with France was for them only a means of thwarting every attempt on Germany's part to adopt a practical policy of alliances. They had no illusions about French aims or those of the men behind the scenes in France. What induced them to take up such an attitude and to act as if they honestly believed that the fate of Germany could possibly be changed in this way was the cool calculation that if this did not happen our people might take the reins into their own hands and choose another road.

Of course it is difficult for us to propose England as our possible ally in the future. Our Jewish Press has always been adept in concentrating hatred against England particularly. And many of our good German simpletons perch on these branches which the Jews have limed to capture them. They babble about a restoration of German sea power and protest against the robbery of our colonies. Thus they furnish material which the contriving Jew transmits to his clansmen in England, so that it can be used there for purposes of practical propaganda. For our simple-minded bourgeoisie who indulge in politics can take in only little by little the idea that to-day we have not to fight for 'sea-power' and such things. Even before the War it was absurd to direct the national energies of Germany towards this end without first having secured our position in Europe. Such a hope to-day reaches that peak of absurdity which may be called criminal in the domain of politics.

Often one becomes really desperate on seeing how the Jewish wire-pullers succeeded in concentrating the attention of the people on things which are only of secondary importance to-day, They incited the people to demonstrations and protests while at the same time France was tearing our nation asunder bit by bit and systematically removing the very foundations of our national independence.

In this connection I have to think of the Wooden Horse in the riding of which the Jew showed extraordinary skill during these years. I mean South Tyrol.

Yes, South Tyrol. The reason why I take up this question here is just because I want to call to account that shameful CANAILLE who relied on the ignorance and short memories of large sections of our people and stimulated a national indignation which is as foreign to the real character of our parliamentary impostors as the idea of respect for private property is to a magpie.

I should like to state here that I was one of those who, at the time when the fate of South Tyrol was being decided—that is to say, from August 1914 to November 1918—took my place where that country also could have been effectively defended, namely, in the Army. I did my share in the fighting during those years, not merely to save South Tyrol from being lost but also to save every other German province for the Fatherland.

The parliamentary sharpers did not take part in that combat. The whole CANAILLE played party politics. On the other hand, we carried on the fight in the belief that a victorious issue of the War would enable the German nation to keep South Tyrol also; but the loud-mouthed traitor carried on a seditious agitation against such a victorious issue, until the fighting Siegfried succumbed to the dagger plunged in his back. It was only natural that the inflammatory and hypocritical speeches of the elegantly dressed parliamentarians on the Vienna RATHAUS PLATZ or in front of the FELDHERRNHALLE in Munich could not save South Tyrol for Germany. That could be done only by the fighting battalions at the Front. Those who broke up that fighting front betrayed South Tyrol, as well as the other districts of Germany.

Anyone who thinks that the South Tyrol question can be solved to-day by protests and manifestations and processions organized by various associations is either a humbug or merely a German philistine.

In this regard it must be quite clearly understood that we cannot get back the territories we have lost if we depend on solemn imprecations before the throne of the Almighty God or on pious hopes in a League of Nations, but only by the force of arms.

Therefore the only remaining question is: Who is ready to take up arms for the restoration of the lost territories?

As far as concerns myself personally, I can state with a good conscience that I would have courage enough to take part in a campaign for the reconquest of South Tyrol, at the head of parliamentarian storm battalions consisting of parliamentarian gasconaders and all the party leaders, also the various Councillors of State. Only the Devil knows whether I might have the luck of seeing a few shells suddenly burst over this 'burning' demonstration of protest. I think that if a fox were to break into a poultry yard his presence would not provoke such a helter-skelter and rush to cover as we should witness in the band of 'protesters'.

The vilest part of it all is that these talkers themselves do not believe that anything can be achieved in this way. Each one of them knows very well how harmless and ineffective their whole pretence is. They do it only because it is easier now to babble about the restoration of South Tyrol than to fight for its preservation in days gone by.

Each one plays the part that he is best capable of playing in life. In those days we offered our blood. To-day these people are engaged in whetting their tusks.

It is particularly interesting to note to-day how legitimist circles in Vienna preen themselves on their work for the restoration of South Tyrol. Seven years ago their august and illustrious Dynasty helped, by an act of perjury and treason, to make it possible for the victorious world-coalition to take away South Tyrol. At that time these circles supported the perfidious policy adopted by their Dynasty and did not trouble themselves in the least about the fate of South Tyrol or any other province. Naturally it is easier to-day to take up the fight for this territory, since the present struggle is waged with 'the weapons of the mind'. Anyhow, it is easier to join in a 'meeting of protestation' and talk yourself hoarse in giving vent to the noble indignation that fills your breast, or stain your finger with the writing of a newspaper article, than to blow up a bridge, for instance, during the occupation of the Ruhr.

The reason why certain circles have made the question of South Tyrol the pivot of German-Italian relations during the past few years is quite evident. Jews and Habsburg legitimists are greatly interested in preventing Germany from pursuing a policy of alliance which might lead one day to the resurgence of a free German fatherland. It is not out of love for South Tyrol that they play this role to-day—for their policy would turn out detrimental rather than helpful to the interests of that province—but through fear of an agreement being established between Germany and Italy.

A tendency towards lying and calumny lies in the nature of these people, and that explains how they can calmly and brazenly attempt to twist things in such a way as to make it appear that we have 'betrayed' South Tyrol.

There is one clear answer that must be given to these gentlemen. It is this: Tyrol has been betrayed, in the first place, by every German who was sound in limb and body and did not offer himself for service at the Front during 1914-1918 to do his duty towards his country.

In the second place, Tyrol was betrayed by every man who, during those years did not help to reinforce the national spirit and the national powers of resistance, so as to enable the country to carry through the War and keep up the fight to the very end.

In the third place, South Tyrol was betrayed by everyone who took part in the November Revolution, either directly by his act or indirectly by a cowardly toleration of it, and thus broke the sole weapon that could have saved South Tyrol.

In the fourth place, South Tyrol was betrayed by those parties and their adherents who put their signatures to the disgraceful treaties of Versailles and St. Germain.

And so the matter stands, my brave gentlemen, who make your protests only with words.

To-day I am guided by a calm and cool recognition of the fact that the lost territories cannot be won back by the whetted tongues of parliamentary spouters but only by the whetted sword; in other words, through a fight where blood will have to be shed.

Now, I have no hesitations in saying that to-day, once the die has been cast, it is not only impossible to win back South Tyrol through a war but I should definitely take my stand against such a movement, because I am convinced that it would not be possible to arouse the national enthusiasm of the German people and maintain it in such a way as would be necessary in order to carry through such a war to a successful issue. On the contrary, I believe that if we have to shed German blood once again it would be criminal to do so for the sake of liberating 200,000 Germans, when more than seven million neighbouring Germans are suffering under foreign domination and a vital artery of the German nation has become a playground for hordes of African niggers.

If the German nation is to put an end to a state of things which threatens to wipe it off the map of Europe it must not fall into the errors of the pre-War period and make the whole world its enemy. But it must ascertain who is its most dangerous enemy so that it can concentrate all its forces in a struggle to beat him. And if, in order to carry through this struggle to victory, sacrifices should be made in other quarters, future generations will not condemn us for that. They will take account of the miseries and anxieties which led us to make such a bitter decision, and in the light of that consideration they will more clearly recognize the brilliancy of our success.

Again I must say here that we must always be guided by the fundamental principle that, as a preliminary to winning back lost provinces, the political independence and strength of the motherland must first be restored.

The first task which has to be accomplished is to make that independence possible and to secure it by a wise policy of alliances, which presupposes an energetic management of our public affairs.

But it is just on this point that we, National Socialists, have to guard against being dragged into the tow of our ranting bourgeois patriots who take their cue from the Jew. It would be a disaster if, instead of preparing for the coming struggle, our Movement also were to busy itself with mere protests by word of mouth.

It was the fantastic idea of a Nibelungen alliance with the decomposed body of the Habsburg State that brought about Germany's ruin. Fantastic sentimentality in dealing with the possibilities of foreign policy to-day would be the best means of preventing our revival for innumerable years to come.

Here I must briefly answer the objections which may be raised in regard to the three questions I have put.

1. Is it possible at all to form an alliance with the present Germany, whose weakness is so visible to all eyes?

2. Can the ex-enemy nations change their attitude towards Germany?

3. In other nations is not the influence of Jewry stronger than the recognition of their own interests, and does not this influence thwart all their good intentions and render all their plans futile?

I think that I have already dealt adequately with one of the two aspects of the first point. Of course nobody will enter into an alliance with the present Germany. No Power in the world would link its fortunes with a State whose government does not afford grounds for the slightest confidence. As regards the attempt which has been made by many of our compatriots to explain the conduct of the Government by referring to the woeful state of public feeling and thus excuse such conduct, I must strongly object to that way of looking at things.

The lack of character which our people have shown during the last six years is deeply distressing. The indifference with which they have treated the most urgent necessities of our nation might veritably lead one to despair. Their cowardice is such that it often cries to heaven for vengeance. But one must never forget that we are dealing with a people who gave to the world, a few years previously, an admirable example of the highest human qualities. From the first days of August 1914 to the end of the tremendous struggle between the nations, no people in the world gave a better proof of manly courage, tenacity and patient endurance, than this people gave who are so cast down and dispirited to-day. Nobody will dare to assert that the lack of character among our people to-day is typical of them. What we have to endure to-day, among us and around us, is due only to the influence of the sad and distressing effects that followed the high treason committed on November 9th, 1918. More than ever before the word of the poet is true: that evil can only give rise to evil. But even in this epoch those qualities among our people which are fundamentally sound are not entirely lost. They slumber in the depths of the national conscience, and sometimes in the clouded firmament we see certain qualities like shining lights which Germany will one day remember as the first symptoms of a revival. We often see young Germans assembling and forming determined resolutions, as they did in 1914, freely and willingly to offer themselves as a sacrifice on the altar of their beloved Fatherland. Millions of men have resumed work, whole-heartedly and zealously, as if no revolution had ever affected them. The smith is at his anvil once again. And the farmer drives his plough. The scientist is in his laboratory. And everybody is once again attending to his duty with the same zeal and devotion as formerly.

The oppression which we suffer from at the hands of our enemies is no longer taken, as it formerly was, as a matter for laughter; but it is resented with bitterness and anger. There can be no doubt that a great change of attitude has taken place.

This evolution has not yet taken the shape of a conscious intention and movement to restore the political power and independence of our nation; but the blame for this must be attributed to those utterly incompetent people who have no natural endowments to qualify them for statesmanship and yet have been governing our nation since 1918 and leading it to ruin.

Yes. If anybody accuses our people to-day he ought to be asked: What is being done to help them? What are we to say of the poor support which the people give to any measures introduced by the Government? Is it not true that such a thing as a Government hardly exists at all? And must we consider the poor support which it receives as a sign of a lack of vitality in the nation itself; or is it not rather a proof of the complete failure of the methods employed in the management of this valuable trust? What have our Governments done to re-awaken in the nation a proud spirit of self-assertion, up-standing manliness, and a spirit of righteous defiance towards its enemies?

In 1919, when the Peace Treaty was imposed on the German nation, there were grounds for hoping that this instrument of unrestricted oppression would help to reinforce the outcry for the freedom of Germany. Peace treaties which make demands that fall like a whip-lash on the people turn out not infrequently to be the signal of a future revival.

To what purpose could the Treaty of Versailles have been exploited?

In the hands of a willing Government, how could this instrument of unlimited blackmail and shameful humiliation have been applied for the purpose of arousing national sentiment to its highest pitch? How could a well-directed system of propaganda have utilized the sadist cruelty of that treaty so as to change the indifference of the people to a feeling of indignation and transform that indignation into a spirit of dauntless resistance?

Each point of that Treaty could have been engraved on the minds and hearts of the German people and burned into them until sixty million men and women would find their souls aflame with a feeling of rage and shame; and a torrent of fire would burst forth as from a furnace, and one common will would be forged from it, like a sword of steel. Then the people would join in the common cry: "To arms again!"

Yes. A treaty of that kind can be used for such a purpose. Its unbounded oppression and its impudent demands were an excellent propaganda weapon to arouse the sluggish spirit of the nation and restore its vitality.

Then, from the child's story-book to the last newspaper in the country, and every theatre and cinema, every pillar where placards are posted and every free space on the hoardings should be utilized in the service of this one great mission, until the faint-hearted cry, "Lord, deliver us," which our patriotic associations send up to Heaven to-day would be transformed into an ardent prayer: "Almighty God, bless our arms when the hour comes. Be just, as Thou hast always been just. Judge now if we deserve our freedom. Lord, bless our struggle."

All opportunities were neglected and nothing was done.

Who will be surprised now if our people are not such as they should be or might be? The rest of the world looks upon us only as its valet, or as a kindly dog that will lick its master's hand after he has been whipped.

Of course the possibilities of forming alliances with other nations are hampered by the indifference of our own people, but much more by our Governments. They have been and are so corrupt that now, after eight years of indescribable oppression, there exists only a faint desire for liberty.

In order that our nation may undertake a policy of alliances, it must restore its prestige among other nations, and it must have an authoritative Government that is not a drudge in the service of foreign States and the taskmaster of its own people, but rather the herald of the national will.

If our people had a government which would look upon this as its mission, six years would not have passed before a courageous foreign policy on the part of the REICH would find a corresponding support among the people, whose desire for freedom would be encouraged and intensified thereby.

The third objection referred to the difficulty of changing the ex-enemy nations into friendly allies. That objection may be answered as follows:

The general anti-German psychosis which has developed in other countries through the war propaganda must of necessity continue to exist as long as there is not a renaissance of the national conscience among the German people, so that the German REICH may once again become a State which is able to play its part on the chess-board of European politics and with whom the others feel that they can play. Only when the Government and the people feel absolutely certain of being able to undertake a policy of alliances can one Power or another, whose interests coincide with ours, think of instituting a system of propaganda for the purpose of changing public opinion among its own people. Naturally it will take several years of persevering and ably directed work to reach such a result. Just because a long period is needed in order to change the public opinion of a country, it is necessary to reflect calmly before such an enterprise be undertaken. This means that one must not enter upon this kind of work unless one is absolutely convinced that it is worth the trouble and that it will bring results which will be valuable in the future. One must not try to change the opinions and feelings of a people by basing one's actions on the vain cajolery of a more or less brilliant Foreign Minister, but only if there be a tangible guarantee that the new orientation will be really useful. Otherwise public opinion in the country dealt with may be just thrown into a state of complete confusion. The most reliable guarantee that can be given for the possibility of subsequently entering into an alliance with a certain State cannot be found in the loquacious suavity of some individual member of the Government, but in the manifest stability of a definite and practical policy on the part of the Government as a whole, and in the support which is given to that policy by the public opinion of the country. The faith of the public in this policy will be strengthened all the more if the Government organize one active propaganda to explain its efforts and secure public support for them, and if public opinion favourably responds to the Government's policy.

Therefore a nation in such a position as ours will be looked upon as a possible ally if public opinion supports the Government's policy and if both are united in the same enthusiastic determination to carry through the fight for national freedom. That condition of affairs must be firmly established before any attempt can be made to change public opinion in other countries which, for the sake of defending their most elementary interests, are disposed to take the road shoulder-to-shoulder with a companion who seems able to play his part in defending those interests. In other words, this means that they will be ready to establish an alliance.

For this purpose, however, one thing is necessary. Seeing that the task of bringing about a radical change in the public opinion of a country calls for hard work, and many do not at first understand what it means, it would be both foolish and criminal to commit mistakes which could be used as weapons in the hands of those who are opposed to such a change.

One must recognize the fact that it takes a long time for a people to understand completely the inner purposes which a Government has in view, because it is not possible to explain the ultimate aims of the preparations that are being made to carry through a certain policy. In such cases the Government has to count on the blind faith of the masses or the intuitive instinct of the ruling caste that is more developed intellectually. But since many people lack this insight, this political acumen and faculty for seeing into the trend of affairs, and since political considerations forbid a public explanation of why such and such a course is being followed, a certain number of leaders in intellectual circles will always oppose new tendencies which, because they are not easily grasped, can be pointed to as mere experiments. And that attitude arouses opposition among conservative circles regarding the measures in question.

For this reason a strict duty devolves upon everybody not to allow any weapon to fall into the hands of those who would interfere with the work of bringing about a mutual understanding with other nations. This is specially so in our case, where we have to deal with the pretentions and fantastic talk of our patriotic associations and our small bourgeoisie who talk politics in the cafes. That the cry for a new war fleet, the restoration of our colonies, etc., has no chance of ever being carried out in practice will not be denied by anyone who thinks over the matter calmly and seriously. These harmless and sometimes half-crazy spouters in the war of protests are serving the interests of our mortal enemy, while the manner in which their vapourings are exploited for political purposes in England cannot be considered as advantageous to Germany.

They squander their energies in futile demonstrations against the whole world. These demonstrations are harmful to our interests and those who indulge in them forget the fundamental principle which is a preliminary condition of all success. What thou doest, do it thoroughly. Because we keep on howling against five or ten States we fail to concentrate all the forces of our national will and our physical strength for a blow at the heart of our bitterest enemy. And in this way we sacrifice the possibility of securing an alliance which would reinforce our strength for that decisive conflict.

Here, too, there is a mission for National Socialism to fulfil. It must teach our people not to fix their attention on the little things but rather on the great things, not to exhaust their energies on secondary objects, and not to forget that the object we shall have to fight for one day is the bare existence of our people and that the sole enemy we shall have to strike at is that Power which is robbing us of this existence.

It may be that we shall have many a heavy burden to bear. But this is by no means an excuse for refusing to listen to reason and raise nonsensical outcries against the rest of the world, instead of concentrating all our forces against the most deadly enemy.

Moreover, the German people will have no moral right to complain of the manner in which the rest of the world acts towards them, as long as they themselves have not called to account those criminals who sold and betrayed their own country. We cannot hope to be taken very seriously if we indulge in long-range abuse and protests against England and Italy and then allow those scoundrels to circulate undisturbed in our own country who were in the pay of the enemy war propaganda, took the weapons out of our hands, broke the backbone of our resistance and bartered away the REICH for thirty pieces of silver.

The enemy did only what was expected. And we ought to learn from the stand he took and the way he acted.

Anyone who cannot rise to the level of this outlook must reflect that otherwise there would remain nothing else than to renounce the idea of adopting any policy of alliances for the future. For if we cannot form an alliance with England because she has robbed us of our colonies, or with Italy because she has taken possession of South Tyrol, or with Poland or Czechoslovakia, then there remains no other possibility of an alliance in Europe except with France which, inter alia, has robbed us of Alsace and Lorraine.

There can scarcely be any doubt as to whether this last alternative would be advantageous to the interests of the German people. But if it be defended by somebody one is always doubtful whether that person be merely a simpleton or an astute rogue.

As far as concerns the leaders in these activities, I think the latter hypothesis is true.

A change in public feeling among those nations which have hitherto been enemies and whose true interests will correspond in the future with ours could be effected, as far as human calculation goes, if the internal strength of our State and our manifest determination to secure our own existence made it clear that we should be valuable allies. Moreover, it is necessary that our incompetent way of doing things and our criminal conduct in some matters should not furnish grounds which may be utilized for purposes of propaganda by those who would oppose our projects of establishing an alliance with one or other of our former enemies.

The answer to the third question is still more difficult: Is it conceivable that they who represent the true interests of those nations which may possibly form an alliance with us could put their views into practice against the will of the Jew, who is the mortal enemy of national and independent popular States?

For instance, could the motive-forces of Great Britain's traditional statesmanship smash the disastrous influence of the Jew, or could they not?

This question, as I have already said, is very difficult to answer. The answer depends on so many factors that it is impossible to form a conclusive judgment. Anyhow, one thing is certain: The power of the Government in a given State and at a definite period may be so firmly established in the public estimation and so absolutely at the service of the country's interests that the forces of international Jewry could not possibly organize a real and effective obstruction against measures considered to be politically necessary.

The fight which Fascist Italy waged against Jewry's three principal weapons, the profound reasons for which may not have been consciously understood (though I do not believe this myself) furnishes the best proof that the poison fangs of that Power which transcends all State boundaries are being drawn, even though in an indirect way. The prohibition of Freemasonry and secret societies, the suppression of the supernational Press and the definite abolition of Marxism, together with the steadily increasing consolidation of the Fascist concept of the State—all this will enable the Italian Government, in the course of some years, to advance more and more the interests of the Italian people without paying any attention to the hissing of the Jewish world-hydra.

The English situation is not so favourable. In that country which has 'the freest democracy' the Jew dictates his will, almost unrestrained but indirectly, through his influence on public opinion. And yet there is a perpetual struggle in England between those who are entrusted with the defence of State interests and the protagonists of Jewish world-dictatorship.

After the War it became clear for the first time how sharp this contrast is, when British statesmanship took one stand on the Japanese problem and the Press took a different stand.

Just after the War had ceased the old mutual antipathy between America and Japan began to reappear. Naturally the great European Powers could not remain indifferent to this new war menace. In England, despite the ties of kinship, there was a certain amount of jealousy and anxiety over the growing importance of the United States in all spheres of international economics and politics. What was formerly a colonial territory, the daughter of a great mother, seemed about to become the new mistress of the world. It is quite understandable that to-day England should re-examine her old alliances and that British statesmanship should look anxiously to the danger of a coming moment when the cry would no longer be: "Britain rules the waves", but rather: "The Seas belong to the United States".

The gigantic North American State, with the enormous resources of its virgin soil, is much more invulnerable than the encircled German REICH. Should a day come when the die which will finally decide the destinies of the nations will have to be cast in that country, England would be doomed if she stood alone. Therefore she eagerly reaches out her hand to a member of the yellow race and enters an alliance which, from the racial point of view is perhaps unpardonable; but from the political viewpoint it represents the sole possibility of reinforcing Britain's world position in face of the strenuous developments taking place on the American continent.

Despite the fact that they fought side by side on the European battlefields, the British Government did not decide to conclude an alliance with the Asiatic partner, yet the whole Jewish Press opposed the idea of a Japanese alliance.

How can we explain the fact that up to 1918 the Jewish Press championed the policy of the British Government against the German REICH and then suddenly began to take its own way and showed itself disloyal to the Government?

It was not in the interests of Great Britain to have Germany annihilated, but primarily a Jewish interest. And to-day the destruction of Japan would serve British political interests less than it would serve the far-reaching intentions of those who are leading the movement that hopes to establish a Jewish world-empire. While England is using all her endeavours to maintain her position in the world, the Jew is organizing his aggressive plans for the conquest of it.

He already sees the present European States as pliant instruments in his hands, whether indirectly through the power of so-called Western Democracy or in the form of a direct domination through Russian Bolshevism. But it is not only the old world that he holds in his snare; for a like fate threatens the new world. Jews control the financial forces of America on the stock exchange. Year after year the Jew increases his hold on Labour in a nation of 120 million souls. But a very small section still remains quite independent and is thus the cause of chagrin to the Jew.

The Jews show consummate skill in manipulating public opinion and using it as an instrument in fighting for their own future.

The great leaders of Jewry are confident that the day is near at hand when the command given in the Old Testament will be carried out and the Jews will devour the other nations of the earth.

Among this great mass of denationalized countries which have become Jewish colonies one independent State could bring about the ruin of the whole structure at the last moment. The reason for doing this would be that Bolshevism as a world-system cannot continue to exist unless it encompasses the whole earth. Should one State preserve its national strength and its national greatness the empire of the Jewish satrapy, like every other tyranny, would have to succumb to the force of the national idea.

As a result of his millennial experience in accommodating himself to surrounding circumstances, the Jew knows very well that he can undermine the existence of European nations by a process of racial bastardization, but that he could hardly do the same to a national Asiatic State like Japan. To-day he can ape the ways of the German and the Englishman, the American and the Frenchman, but he has no means of approach to the yellow Asiatic. Therefore he seeks to destroy the Japanese national State by using other national States as his instruments, so that he may rid himself of a dangerous opponent before he takes over supreme control of the last national State and transforms that control into a tyranny for the oppression of the defenceless.

He does not want to see a national Japanese State in existence when he founds his millennial empire of the future, and therefore he wants to destroy it before establishing his own dictatorship.

And so he is busy to-day in stirring up antipathy towards Japan among the other nations, as he stirred it up against Germany. Thus it may happen that while British statesmanship is still endeavouring to ground its policy in the alliance with Japan, the Jewish Press in Great Britain may be at the same time leading a hostile movement against that ally and preparing for a war of destruction by pretending that it is for the triumph of democracy and at the same time raising the war-cry: Down with Japanese militarism and imperialism.

Thus in England to-day the Jew opposes the policy of the State. And for this reason the struggle against the Jewish world-danger will one day begin also in that country.

And here again the National Socialist Movement has a tremendous task before it.

It must open the eyes of our people in regard to foreign nations and it must continually remind them of the real enemy who menaces the world to-day. In place of preaching hatred against Aryans from whom we may be separated on almost every other ground but with whom the bond of kindred blood and the main features of a common civilization unite us, we must devote ourselves to arousing general indignation against the maleficent enemy of humanity and the real author of all our sufferings.

The National Socialist Movement must see to it that at least in our own country the mortal enemy is recognized and that the fight against him may be a beacon light pointing to a new and better period for other nations as well as showing the way of salvation for Aryan humanity in the struggle for its existence.

Finally, may reason be our guide and will-power our strength. And may the sacred duty of directing our conduct as I have pointed out give us perseverance and tenacity; and may our faith be our supreme protection.

CHAPTER XIV:
Germany's Policy In Eastern Europe

There are two considerations which induce me to make a special analysis of Germany's position in regard to Russia. These are:

(1) This may prove to be the most decisive point in determining Germany's foreign policy.

(2) The problem which has to be solved in this connection is also a touchstone to test the political capacity of the young National Socialist Movement for clear thinking and acting along the right lines.

I must confess that the second consideration has often been a source of great anxiety to me. The members of our movement are not recruited from circles which are habitually indifferent to public affairs, but mostly from among men who hold more or less extreme views. Such being the case, it is only natural that their understanding of foreign politics should suffer from the prejudice and inadequate knowledge of those circles to which they were formerly attached by political and ideological ties. And this is true not merely of the men who come to us from the Left. On the contrary, however subversive may have been the kind of teaching they formerly received in regard to these problems, in very many cases this was at least partly counterbalanced by the residue of sound and natural instincts which remained. In such cases it is only necessary to substitute a better teaching in place of the earlier influences, in order to transform the instinct of self-preservation and other sound instincts into valuable assets.

On the other hand, it is much more difficult to impress definite political ideas on the minds of men whose earlier political education was not less nonsensical and illogical than that given to the partisans of the Left. These men have sacrificed the last residue of their natural instincts to the worship of some abstract and entirely objective theory. It is particularly difficult to induce these representatives of our so-called intellectual circles to take a realistic and logical view of their own interests and the interests of their nation in its relations with foreign countries. Their minds are overladen with a huge burden of prejudices and absurd ideas and they have lost or renounced every instinct of self-preservation. With those men also the National Socialist Movement has to fight a hard battle. And the struggle is all the harder because, though very often they are utterly incompetent, they are so self-conceited that, without the slightest justification, they look down with disdain on ordinary commonsense people. These arrogant snobs who pretend to know better than other people, are wholly incapable of calmly and coolly analysing a problem and weighing its pros and cons, which are the necessary preliminaries of any decision or action in the field of foreign politics.

It is just this circle which is beginning to-day to divert our foreign policy into most disastrous directions and turn it away from the task of promoting the real interests of the nation. Seeing that they do this in order to serve their own fantastic ideologies, I feel myself obliged to take the greatest pains in laying before my own colleagues a clear exposition of the most important problem in our foreign policy, namely, our position in relation to Russia. I shall deal with it, as thoroughly as may be necessary to make it generally understood and as far as the limits of this book permit. Let me begin by laying down the following postulate:

When we speak of foreign politics we understand that domain of government which has set before it the task of managing the affairs of a nation in its relations with the rest of the world. Now the guiding principles which must be followed in managing these affairs must be based on the definite facts that are at hand. Moreover, as National Socialists, we must lay down the following axiom regarding the manner in which the foreign policy of a People's State should be conducted:

The foreign policy of a People's State must first of all bear in mind the duty of securing the existence of the race which is incorporated in this State. And this must be done by establishing a healthy and natural proportion between the number and growth of the population on the one hand and the extent and resources of the territory they inhabit, on the other. That balance must be such that it accords with the vital necessities of the people.

What I call a HEALTHY proportion is that in which the support of a people is guaranteed by the resources of its own soil and sub-soil. Any situation which falls short of this condition is none the less unhealthy even though it may endure for centuries or even a thousand years. Sooner or later, this lack of proportion must of necessity lead to the decline or even annihilation of the people concerned.

Only a sufficiently large space on this earth can assure the independent existence of a people.

The extent of the territorial expansion that may be necessary for the settlement of the national population must not be estimated by present exigencies nor even by the magnitude of its agricultural productivity in relation to the number of the population. In the first volume of this book, under the heading "Germany's Policy of Alliances before the War," I have already explained that the geometrical dimensions of a State are of importance not only as the source of the nation's foodstuffs and raw materials, but also from the political and military standpoints. Once a people is assured of being able to maintain itself from the resources of the national territory, it must think of how this national territory can be defended. National security depends on the political strength of a State, and this strength, in its turn, depends on the military possibilities inherent in the geographical situation.

Thus the German nation could assure its own future only by being a World Power. For nearly two thousand years the defence of our national interests was a matter of world history, as can be seen from our more or less successful activities in the field of foreign politics. We ourselves have been witnesses to this, seeing that the gigantic struggle that went on from 1914 to 1918 was only the struggle of the German people for their existence on this earth, and it was carried out in such a way that it has become known in history as the World War.

When Germany entered this struggle it was presumed that she was a World Power. I say PRESUMED, because in reality she was no such thing. In 1914, if there had been a different proportion between the German population and its territorial area, Germany would have been really a World Power and, if we leave other factors out of count, the War would have ended in our favour.

It is not my task nor my intention here to discuss what would have happened if certain conditions had been fulfilled. But I feel it absolutely incumbent on me to show the present conditions in their bare and unadorned reality, insisting on the weakness inherent in them, so that at least in the ranks of the National Socialist Movement they should receive the necessary recognition.

Germany is not at all a World Power to-day. Even though our present military weakness could be overcome, we still would have no claim to be called a World Power. What importance on earth has a State in which the proportion between the size of the population and the territorial area is so miserable as in the present German REICH? At an epoch in which the world is being gradually portioned out among States many of whom almost embrace whole continents one cannot speak of a World Power in the case of a State whose political motherland is confined to a territorial area of barely five-hundred-thousand square kilometres.

Looked at purely from the territorial point of view, the area comprised in the German REICH is insignificant in comparison with the other States that are called World Powers. England must not be cited here as an example to contradict this statement; for the English motherland is in reality the great metropolis of the British World Empire, which owns almost a fourth of the earth's surface. Next to this we must consider the American Union as one of the foremost among the colossal States, also Russia and China. These are enormous spaces, some of which are more than ten times greater in territorial extent than the present German REICH. France must also be ranked among these colossal States. Not only because she is adding to the strength of her army in a constantly increasing measure by recruiting coloured troops from the population of her gigantic empire, but also because France is racially becoming more and more negroid, so much so that now one can actually speak of the creation of an African State on European soil. The contemporary colonial policy of France cannot be compared with that of Germany in the past. If France develops along the lines it has taken in our day, and should that development continue for the next three hundred years, all traces of French blood will finally be submerged in the formation of a Euro-African Mulatto State. This would represent a formidable and compact colonial territory stretching from the Rhine to the Congo, inhabited by an inferior race which had developed through a slow and steady process of bastardization.

That process distinguishes French colonial policy from the policy followed by the old Germany.

The former German colonial policy was carried out by half-measures, as was almost everything they did at that time. They did not gain an expanse of territory for the settlement of German nationals nor did they attempt to reinforce the power of the REICH through the enlistment of black troops, which would have been a criminal undertaking.

The Askari in German East Africa represented a small and hesitant step along this road; but in reality they served only for the defence of the colony itself. The idea of importing black troops to a European theatre of war—apart entirely from the practical impossibility of this in the World War—was never entertained as a proposal to be carried out under favourable circumstances; whereas, on the contrary, the French always looked on such an idea as fundamental in their colonial activities.

Thus we find in the world to-day not only a number of States that are much greater than the German in the mere numerical size of their populations, but also possess a greater support for their political power. The proportion between the territorial dimensions of the German REICH and the numerical size of its population was never so unfavourable in comparison with the other world States as at the beginning of our history two thousand years ago and again to-day. At the former juncture we were a young people and we stormed a world which was made up of great States that were already in a decadent condition, of which the last giant was Rome, to whose overthrow we contributed. To-day we find ourselves in a world of great and powerful States, among which the importance of our own REICH is constantly declining more and more.

We must always face this bitter truth with clear and calm minds. We must study the area and population of the German REICH in relation to the other States and compare them down through the centuries. Then we shall find that, as I have said, Germany is not a World Power whether its military strength be great or not.

There is no proportion between our position and that of the other States throughout the world. And this lack of proportion is to be attributed to the fact that our foreign policy never had a definite aim to attain, and also to the fact that we lost every sound impulse and instinct for self-preservation.

If the historians who are to write our national history at some future date are to give the National Socialist Movement the credit of having devoted itself to a sacred duty in the service of our people, this movement will have to recognize the real truth of our situation in regard to the rest of the world. However painful this recognition may be, the movement must draw courage from it and a sense of practical realities in fighting against the aimlessness and incompetence which has hitherto been shown by our people in the conduct of their foreign policy. Without respect for 'tradition,' and without any preconceived notions, the movement must find the courage to organize our national forces and set them on the path which will lead them away from that territorial restriction which is the bane of our national life to-day, and win new territory for them. Thus the movement will save the German people from the danger of perishing or of being slaves in the service of any other people.

Our movement must seek to abolish the present disastrous proportion between our population and the area of our national territory, considering national territory as the source of our maintenance or as a basis of political power. And it ought to strive to abolish the contrast between past history and the hopelessly powerless situation in which we are to-day. In striving for this it must bear in mind the fact that we are members of the highest species of humanity on this earth, that we have a correspondingly high duty, and that we shall fulfil this duty only if we inspire the German people with the racial idea, so that they will occupy themselves not merely with the breeding of good dogs and horses and cats, but also care for the purity of their own blood.

When I say that the foreign policy hitherto followed by Germany has been without aim and ineffectual, the proof of my statement will be found in the actual failures of this policy. Were our people intellectually backward, or if they lacked courage, the final results of their efforts could not have been worse than what we see to-day. What happened during the last decades before the War does not permit of any illusions on this point; because we must not measure the strength of a State taken by itself, but in comparison with other States. Now, this comparison shows that the other States increased their strength in such a measure that not only did it balance that of Germany but turned out in the end to be greater; so that, contrary to appearances, when compared with the other States Germany declined more and more in power until there was a large margin in her disfavour. Yes, even in the size of our population we remained far behind, and kept on losing ground. Though it is true that the courage of our people was not surpassed by that of any other in the world and that they poured out more blood than any other nation in defence of their existence, their failure was due only to the erroneous way in which that courage was turned to practical purposes.

In this connection, if we examine the chain of political vicissitudes through which our people have passed during more than a thousand years, recalling the innumerable struggles and wars and scrutinizing it all in the light of the results that are before our eyes to-day, we must confess that from the ocean of blood only three phenomena have emerged which we must consider as lasting fruits of political happenings definitely determined by our foreign policy.

(1) The colonization of the Eastern Mark, which was mostly the work of the Bajuvari.

(2) The conquest and settlement of the territory east of the Elbe.

(3) The organization of the Brandenburg-Prussian State, which was the work of the Hohenzollerns and which became the model for the crystallization of a new REICH.

An instructive lesson for the future.

These first two great successes of our foreign policy turned out to be the most enduring. Without them our people would play no role in the world to-day. These achievements were the first and unfortunately the only successful attempts to establish a harmony between our increasing population and the territory from which it drew its livelihood. And we must look upon it as of really fatal import that our German historians have never correctly appreciated these formidable facts which were so full of importance for the following generations. In contradistinction to this, they wrote panegyrics on many other things, fantastic heroism, innumerable adventures and wars, without understanding that these latter had no significance whatsoever for the main line of our national development.

The third great success achieved by our political activity was the establishment of the Prussian State and the development of a particular State concept which grew out of this. To the same source we are to attribute the organization of the instinct of national self-preservation and self-defence in the German Army, an achievement which suited the modern world. The transformation of the idea of self-defence on the part of the individual into the duty of national defence is derived from the Prussian State and the new statal concept which it introduced. It would be impossible to over-estimate the importance of this historical process. Disrupted by excessive individualism, the German nation became disciplined under the organization of the Prussian Army and in this way recovered at least some of the capacity to form a national community, which in the case of other people had originally arisen through the constructive urge of the herd instinct. Consequently the abolition of compulsory national military service—which may have no meaning for dozens of other nations—had fatal consequences for us. Ten generations of Germans left without the corrective and educative effect of military training and delivered over to the evil effects of those dissensions and divisions the roots of which lie in their blood and display their force also in a disunity of world-outlook—these ten generations would be sufficient to allow our people to lose the last relics of an independent existence on this earth.

The German spirit could then make its contribution to civilization only through individuals living under the rule of foreign nations and the origin of those individuals would remain unknown. They would remain as the fertilizing manure of civilization, until the last residue of Nordic-Aryan blood would become corrupted or drained out.

It is a remarkable fact that the real political successes achieved by our people during their millennial struggles are better appreciated and understood among our adversaries than among ourselves. Even still to-day we grow enthusiastic about a heroism which robbed our people of millions of their best racial stock and turned out completely fruitless in the end.

The distinction between the real political successes which our people achieved in the course of their long history and the futile ends for which the blood of the nation has been shed is of supreme importance for the determination of our policy now and in the future.

We, National Socialists, must never allow ourselves to re-echo the hurrah patriotism of our contemporary bourgeois circles. It would be a fatal danger for us to look on the immediate developments before the War as constituting a precedent which we should be obliged to take into account, even though only to the very smallest degree, in choosing our own way. We can recognize no obligation devolving on us which may have its historical roots in any part of the nineteenth century. In contradistinction to the policy of those who represented that period, we must take our stand on the principles already mentioned in regard to foreign policy: namely, the necessity of bringing our territorial area into just proportion with the number of our population. From the past we can learn only one lesson. And this is that the aim which is to be pursued in our political conduct must be twofold: namely (1) the acquisition of territory as the objective of our foreign policy and (2) the establishment of a new and uniform foundation as the objective of our political activities at home, in accordance with our doctrine of nationhood.

I shall briefly deal with the question of how far our territorial aims are justified according to ethical and moral principles. This is all the more necessary here because, in our so-called nationalist circles, there are all kinds of plausible phrase-mongers who try to persuade the German people that the great aim of their foreign policy ought to be to right the wrongs of 1918, while at the same time they consider it incumbent on them to assure the whole world of the brotherly spirit and sympathy of the German people towards all other nations.

In regard to this point I should like to make the following statement: To demand that the 1914 frontiers should be restored is a glaring political absurdity that is fraught with such consequences as to make the claim itself appear criminal. The confines of the REICH as they existed in 1914 were thoroughly illogical; because they were not really complete, in the sense of including all the members of the German nation. Nor were they reasonable, in view of the geographical exigencies of military defence. They were not the consequence of a political plan which had been well considered and carried out. But they were temporary frontiers established in virtue of a political struggle that had not been brought to a finish; and indeed they were partly the chance result of circumstances. One would have just as good a right, and in many cases a better right, to choose some other outstanding year than 1914 in the course of our history and demand that the objective of our foreign policy should be the re-establishment of the conditions then existing. The demands I have mentioned are quite characteristic of our bourgeois compatriots, who in such matters take no political thought of the future, They live only in the past and indeed only in the immediate past; for their retrospect does not go back beyond their own times. The law of inertia binds them to the present order of things, leading them to oppose every attempt to change this. Their opposition, however, never passes over into any kind of active defence. It is only mere passive obstinacy. Therefore, we must regard it as quite natural that the political horizon of such people should not reach beyond 1914. In proclaiming that the aim of their political activities is to have the frontiers of that time restored, they only help to close up the rifts that are already becoming apparent in the league which our enemies have formed against us. Only on these grounds can we explain the fact that eight years after a world conflagration in which a number of Allied belligerents had aspirations and aims that were partly in conflict with one another, the coalition of the victors still remains more or less solid.

Each of those States in its turn profited by the German collapse. In the fear which they all felt before the proof of strength that we had given, the Great Powers maintained a mutual silence about their individual feelings of envy and enmity towards one another. They felt that the best guarantee against a resurgence of our strength in the future would be to break up and dismember our REICH as thoroughly as possible. A bad conscience and fear of the strength of our people made up the durable cement which has held the members of that league together, even up to the present moment.

And our conduct does not tend to change this state of affairs. Inasmuch as our bourgeoisie sets up the restoration of the 1914 frontiers as the aim of Germany's political programme, each member of the enemy coalition who otherwise might be inclined to withdraw from the combination sticks to it, out of fear lest he might be attacked by us if he isolated himself and in that case would not have the support of his allies. Each individual State feels itself aimed at and threatened by this programme. And the programme is absurd, for the following two reasons:

(1) Because there are no available means of extricating it from the twilight atmosphere of political soirees and transforming it into reality.

(2) Even if it could be really carried into effect the result would be so miserable that, surely to God, it would not be worth while to risk the blood of our people once again for such a purpose.

For there can be scarcely any doubt whatsoever that only through bloodshed could we achieve the restoration of the 1914 frontiers. One must have the simple mind of a child to believe that the revision of the Versailles Treaty can be obtained by indirect means and by beseeching the clemency of the victors; without taking into account the fact that for this we should need somebody who had the character of a Talleyrand, and there is no Talleyrand among us. Fifty percent of our politicians consists of artful dodgers who have no character and are quite hostile to the sympathies of our people, while the other fifty per cent is made up of well-meaning, harmless, and complaisant incompetents. Times have changed since the Congress of Vienna. It is no longer princes or their courtesans who contend and bargain about State frontiers, but the inexorable cosmopolitan Jew who is fighting for his own dominion over the nations. The sword is the only means whereby a nation can thrust that clutch from its throat. Only when national sentiment is organized and concentrated into an effective force can it defy that international menace which tends towards an enslavement of the nations. But this road is and will always be marked with bloodshed.

If we are once convinced that the future of Germany calls for the sacrifice, in one way or another, of all that we have and are, then we must set aside considerations of political prudence and devote ourselves wholly to the struggle for a future that will be worthy of our country.

For the future of the German nation the 1914 frontiers are of no significance. They did not serve to protect us in the past, nor do they offer any guarantee for our defence in the future. With these frontiers the German people cannot maintain themselves as a compact unit, nor can they be assured of their maintenance. From the military viewpoint these frontiers are not advantageous or even such as not to cause anxiety. And while we are bound to such frontiers it will not be possible for us to improve our present position in relation to the other World Powers, or rather in relation to the real World Powers. We shall not lessen the discrepancy between our territory and that of Great Britain, nor shall we reach the magnitude of the United States of America. Not only that, but we cannot substantially lessen the importance of France in international politics.

One thing alone is certain: The attempt to restore the frontiers of 1914, even if it turned out successful, would demand so much bloodshed on the part of our people that no future sacrifice would be possible to carry out effectively such measures as would be necessary to assure the future existence of the nation. On the contrary, under the intoxication of such a superficial success further aims would be renounced, all the more so because the so-called 'national honour' would seem to be revindicated and new ports would be opened, at least for a certain time, to our commercial development.

Against all this we, National Socialists, must stick firmly to the aim that we have set for our foreign policy; namely, that the German people must be assured the territorial area which is necessary for it to exist on this earth. And only for such action as is undertaken to secure those ends can it be lawful in the eyes of God and our German posterity to allow the blood of our people to be shed once again. Before God, because we are sent into this world with the commission to struggle for our daily bread, as creatures to whom nothing is donated and who must be able to win and hold their position as lords of the earth only through their own intelligence and courage. And this justification must be established also before our German posterity, on the grounds that for each one who has shed his blood the life of a thousand others will be guaranteed to posterity. The territory on which one day our German peasants will be able to bring forth and nourish their sturdy sons will justify the blood of the sons of the peasants that has to be shed to-day. And the statesmen who will have decreed this sacrifice may be persecuted by their contemporaries, but posterity will absolve them from all guilt for having demanded this offering from their people.

Here I must protest as sharply as possible against those nationalist scribes who pretend that such territorial extension would be a "violation of the sacred rights of man" and accordingly pour out their literary effusions against it. One never knows what are the hidden forces behind the activities of such persons. But it is certain that the confusion which they provoke suits the game our enemies are playing against our nation and is in accordance with their wishes. By taking such an attitude these scribes contribute criminally to weaken from the inside and to destroy the will of our people to promote their own vital interests by the only effective means that can be used for that purpose. For no nation on earth possesses a square yard of ground and soil by decree of a higher Will and in virtue of a higher Right. The German frontiers are the outcome of chance, and are only temporary frontiers that have been established as the result of political struggles which took place at various times. The same is also true of the frontiers which demarcate the territories on which other nations live. And just as only an imbecile could look on the physical geography of the globe as fixed and unchangeable—for in reality it represents a definite stage in a given evolutionary epoch which is due to the formidable forces of Nature and may be altered to-morrow by more powerful forces of destruction and change—so, too, in the lives of the nations the confines which are necessary for their sustenance are subject to change. State frontiers are established by human beings and may be changed by human beings.

The fact that a nation has acquired an enormous territorial area is no reason why it should hold that territory perpetually. At most, the possession of such territory is a proof of the strength of the conqueror and the weakness of those who submit to him. And in this strength alone lives the right of possession. If the German people are imprisoned within an impossible territorial area and for that reason are face to face with a miserable future, this is not by the command of Destiny, and the refusal to accept such a situation is by no means a violation of Destiny's laws. For just as no Higher Power has promised more territory to other nations than to the German, so it cannot be blamed for an unjust distribution of the soil. The soil on which we now live was not a gift bestowed by Heaven on our forefathers. But they had to conquer it by risking their lives. So also in the future our people will not obtain territory, and therewith the means of existence, as a favour from any other people, but will have to win it by the power of a triumphant sword.

To-day we are all convinced of the necessity of regulating our situation in regard to France; but our success here will be ineffective in its broad results if the general aims of our foreign policy will have to stop at that. It can have significance for us only if it serves to cover our flank in the struggle for that extension of territory which is necessary for the existence of our people in Europe. For colonial acquisitions will not solve that question. It can be solved only by the winning of such territory for the settlement of our people as will extend the area of the motherland and thereby will not only keep the new settlers in the closest communion with the land of their origin, but will guarantee to this territorial ensemble the advantages which arise from the fact that in their expansion over greater territory the people remain united as a political unit.

The National Movement must not be the advocate for other nations, but the protagonist for its own nation. Otherwise it would be something superfluous and, above all, it would have no right to clamour against the action of the past; for then it would be repeating the action of the past. The old German policy suffered from the mistake of having been determined by dynastic considerations. The new German policy must not follow the sentimentality of cosmopolitan patriotism. Above all, we must not form a police guard for the famous 'poor small nations'; but we must be the soldiers of the German nation.

We National Socialists have to go still further. The right to territory may become a duty when a great nation seems destined to go under unless its territory be extended. And that is particularly true when the nation in question is not some little group of negro people but the Germanic mother of all the life which has given cultural shape to the modern world. Germany will either become a World Power or will not continue to exist at all. But in order to become a World Power it needs that territorial magnitude which gives it the necessary importance to-day and assures the existence of its citizens.

Therefore we National Socialists have purposely drawn a line through the line of conduct followed by pre-War Germany in foreign policy. We put an end to the perpetual

Germanic march towards the South and West of Europe and turn our eyes towards the lands of the East. We finally put a stop to the colonial and trade policy of pre-War times and pass over to the territorial policy of the future.

But when we speak of new territory in Europe to-day we must principally think of Russia and the border States subject to her.

Destiny itself seems to wish to point out the way for us here. In delivering Russia over to Bolshevism, Fate robbed the Russian people of that intellectual class which had once created the Russian State and were the guarantee of its existence. For the Russian State was not organized by the constructive political talent of the Slav element in Russia, but was much more a marvellous exemplification of the capacity for State-building possessed by the Germanic element in a race of inferior worth. Thus were many powerful Empires created all over the earth. More often than once inferior races with Germanic organizers and rulers as their leaders became formidable States and continued to exist as long as the racial nucleus remained which had originally created each respective State. For centuries Russia owed the source of its livelihood as a State to the Germanic nucleus of its governing class. But this nucleus is now almost wholly broken up and abolished. The Jew has taken its place. Just as it is impossible for the Russian to shake off the Jewish yoke by exerting his own powers, so, too, it is impossible for the Jew to keep this formidable State in existence for any long period of time. He himself is by no means an organizing element, but rather a ferment of decomposition. This colossal Empire in the East is ripe for dissolution. And the end of the Jewish domination in Russia will also be the end of Russia as a State. We are chosen by Destiny to be the witnesses of a catastrophe which will afford the strongest confirmation of the nationalist theory of race.

But it is our task, and it is the mission of the National Socialist Movement, to develop in our people that political mentality which will enable them to realize that the aim which they must set to themselves for the fulfilment of their future must not be some wildly enthusiastic adventure in the footsteps of Alexander the Great but industrious labour with the German plough, for which the German sword will provide the soil.

That the Jew should declare himself bitterly hostile to such a policy is only quite natural. For the Jews know better than any others what the adoption of this line of conduct must mean for their own future. That fact alone ought to teach all genuine nationalists that this new orientation is the right and just one. But, unfortunately, the opposite is the case. Not only among the members of the German-National Party but also in purely nationalist circles violent opposition is raised against this Eastern policy. And in connection with that opposition, as in all such cases, the authority of great names is appealed to. The spirit of Bismarck is evoked in defence of a policy which is as stupid as it is impossible, and is in the highest degree detrimental to the interests of the German people. They say that Bismarck laid great importance on the value of good relations with Russia. To a certain extent, that is true. But they quite forget to add that he laid equal stress on the importance of good relations with Italy, for example. Indeed, the same Herr von Bismarck once concluded an alliance with Italy so that he might more easily settle accounts with Austria. Why is not this policy now advocated? They will reply that the Italy of to-day is not the Italy of that time. Good. But then, honourable sirs, permit me to remind you that the Russia of to-day is no longer the Russia of that time. Bismarck never laid down a policy which would be permanently binding under all circumstances and should be adhered to on principle. He was too much the master of the moment to burden himself with that kind of obligation. Therefore, the question ought not to be what

Bismarck then did, but rather what he would do to-day. And that question is very easy to answer. His political sagacity would never allow him to ally himself with a State that is doomed to disappear.

Moreover, Bismarck looked upon the colonial and trade policy of his time with mixed feelings, because what he most desired was to assure the best possibilities of consolidating and internally strengthening the state system which he himself had created. That was the sole ground on which he then welcomed the Russian defence in his rear, so as to give him a free hand for his activities in the West. But what was advantageous then to Germany would now be detrimental.

As early as 1920-21, when the young movement began slowly to appear on the political horizon and movements for the liberation of the German nation were formed here and there, the Party was approached from various quarters in an attempt to bring it into definite connection with the liberationist movements in other countries. This was in line with the plans of the 'League of Oppressed Nations', which had been advertised in many quarters and was composed principally of representatives of some of the Balkan States and also of Egypt and India. These always impressed me as charlatans who gave themselves big airs but had no real background at all. Not a few Germans, however, especially in the nationalist camp, allowed themselves to be taken in by these pompous Orientals, and in the person of some wandering Indian or Egyptian student they believed at once that they were face to face with a 'representative' of India or Egypt. They did not realize that in most cases they were dealing with persons who had no backing whatsoever, who were not authorized by anybody to conclude any sort of agreement whatsoever; so that the practical result of every negotiation with such individuals was negative and the time spent in such dealings had to be reckoned as utterly lost. I was always on my guard against these attempts. Not only that I had something better to do than to waste weeks in such sterile 'discussions', but also because I believed that even if one were dealing with genuine representatives that whole affair would be bound to turn out futile, if not positively harmful.

In peace-time it was already lamentable enough that the policy of alliances, because it had no active and aggressive aims in view, ended in a defensive association with antiquated States that had been pensioned off by the history of the world. The alliance with Austria, as well as that with Turkey, was not much to be joyful about. While the great military and industrial States of the earth had come together in a league for purposes of active aggression, a few old and effete States were collected, and with this antique bric-à-brac an attempt was made to face an active world coalition. Germany had to pay dearly for that mistaken foreign policy and yet not dearly enough to prevent our incorrigible visionaries from falling back into the same error again. For the attempt to make possible the disarmament of the all-powerful victorious States through a 'League of Oppressed Nations' is not only ridiculous but disastrous. It is disastrous because in that way the German people are again being diverted from real possibilities, which they abandon for the sake of fruitless hopes and illusions. In reality the German of to-day is like a drowning man that clutches at any straw which may float beside him. And one finds people doing this who are otherwise highly educated. Wherever some will-o'-the-wisp of a fantastic hope appears these people set off immediately to chase it. Let this be a League of Oppressed Nations, a League of Nations, or some other fantastic invention, thousands of ingenuous souls will always be found to believe in it.

I remember well the childish and incomprehensible hopes which arose suddenly in nationalist circles in the years 1920-21 to the effect that England was just nearing its downfall in India. A few Asiatic mountebanks, who put themselves forward as "the champions of Indian Freedom", then began to peregrinate throughout Europe and succeeded in inspiring otherwise quite reasonable people with the fixed notion that the British World Empire, which had its pivot in India, was just about to collapse there. They never realized that their own wish was the father of all these ideas. Nor did they stop to think how absurd their wishes were. For inasmuch as they expected the end of the British Empire and of England's power to follow the collapse of its dominion over India, they themselves admitted that India was of the most outstanding importance for England.

Now in all likelihood the deep mysteries of this most important problem must have been known not only to the German-National prophets but also to those who had the direction of British history in their hands. It is right down puerile to suppose that in England itself the importance of India for the British Empire was not adequately appreciated. And it is a proof of having learned nothing from the world war and of thoroughly misunderstanding or knowing nothing about Anglo-Saxon determination, when they imagine that England could lose India without first having put forth the last ounce of her strength in the struggle to hold it. Moreover, it shows how complete is the ignorance prevailing in Germany as to the manner in which the spirit of England permeates and administers her Empire. England will never lose India unless she admits racial disruption in the machinery of her administration (which at present is entirely out of the question in India) or unless she is overcome by the sword of some powerful enemy. But Indian risings will never bring this about. We Germans have had sufficient experience to know how hard it is to coerce England. And, apart from all this, I as a German would far rather see India under British domination than under that of any other nation.

The hopes of an epic rising in Egypt were just as chimerical. The 'Holy War' may bring the pleasing illusion to our German nincompoops that others are now ready to shed their blood for them. Indeed, this cowardly speculation is almost always the father of such hopes. But in reality the illusion would soon be brought to an end under the fusillade from a few companies of British machine-guns and a hail of British bombs.

A coalition of cripples cannot attack a powerful State which is determined, if necessary, to shed the last drop of its blood to maintain its existence. To me, as a nationalist who appreciates the worth of the racial basis of humanity, I must recognize the racial inferiority of the so-called 'Oppressed Nations', and that is enough to prevent me from linking the destiny of my people with the destiny of those inferior races.

To-day we must take up the same sort of attitude also towards Russia. The Russia of to-day, deprived of its Germanic ruling class, is not a possible ally in the struggle for German liberty, setting aside entirely the inner designs of its new rulers. From the purely military viewpoint a Russo-German coalition waging war against Western Europe, and probably against the whole world on that account, would be catastrophic for us. The struggle would have to be fought out, not on Russian but on German territory, without Germany being able to receive from Russia the slightest effective support. The means of power at the disposal of the present German REICH are so miserable and so inadequate to the waging of a foreign war that it would be impossible to defend our frontiers against Western Europe, England included. And the industrial area of Germany would have to be abandoned undefended to the concentrated attack of our adversaries. It must be added that between Germany and Russia there is the Polish State, completely in the hands of the French. In case Germany and Russia together should wage war against Western

Europe, Russia would have to overthrow Poland before the first Russian soldier could arrive on the German front. But it is not so much a question of soldiers as of technical equipment. In this regard we should have our situation in the world war repeated, but in a more terrible manner. At that time German industry had to be drained to help our glorious allies, and from the technical side Germany had to carry on the war almost alone. In this new hypothetical war Russia, as a technical factor, would count for nothing. We should have practically nothing to oppose to the general motorization of the world, which in the next war will make its appearance in an overwhelming and decisive form. In this important field Germany has not only shamefully lagged behind, but with the little it has it would have to reinforce Russia, which at the present moment does not possess a single factory capable of producing a motor gun-wagon. Under such conditions the presupposed coming struggle would assume the character of sheer slaughter. The German youth would have to shed more of its blood than it did even in the world war; for, as always, the honour of fighting will fall on us alone, and the result would be an inevitable catastrophe. But even admitting that a miracle were produced and that this war did not end in the total annihilation of Germany, the final result would be that the German nation would be bled white, and, surrounded by great military States, its real situation would be in no way ameliorated.

It is useless to object here that in case of an alliance with Russia we should not think of an immediate war or that, anyhow, we should have means of making thorough preparations for war. No. An alliance which is not for the purpose of waging war has no meaning and no value. Even though at the moment when an alliance is concluded the prospect of war is a distant one, still the idea of the situation developing towards war is the profound reason for entering into an alliance. It is out of the question to think that the other Powers would be deceived as to the purpose of such an alliance. A Russo-German coalition would remain either a matter of so much paper—and in this case it would have no meaning for us—or the letter of the treaty would be put into practice visibly, and in that case the rest of the world would be warned. It would be childish to think that in such circumstances England and France would wait for ten years to give the Russo-German alliance time to complete its technical preparations. No. The storm would break over Germany immediately.

Therefore the fact of forming an alliance with Russia would be the signal for a new war. And the result of that would be the end of Germany.

To these considerations the following must be added:

(1) Those who are in power in Russia to-day have no idea of forming an honourable alliance or of remaining true to it, if they did.

It must never be forgotten that the present rulers of Russia are blood-stained criminals, that here we have the dregs of humanity which, favoured by the circumstances of a tragic moment, overran a great State, degraded and extirpated millions of educated people out of sheer blood-lust, and that now for nearly ten years they have ruled with such a savage tyranny as was never known before. It must not be forgotten that these rulers belong to a people in whom the most bestial cruelty is allied with a capacity for artful mendacity and believes itself to-day more than ever called to impose its sanguinary despotism on the rest of the world. It must not be forgotten that the international Jew, who is to-day the absolute master of Russia, does not look upon Germany as an ally but as a State condemned to the same doom as Russia. One does not form an alliance with a partner whose only aim is the destruction of his fellow-partner. Above all, one does not enter into alliances with people for whom no treaty is sacred; because they do not move about this earth as men of honour and sincerity but as the representatives of lies and deception, thievery and plunder and robbery. The man who thinks that he can bind himself by treaty with parasites is like the tree that believes it can form a profitable bargain with the ivy that surrounds it.

(2) The menace to which Russia once succumbed is hanging steadily over Germany. Only a bourgeois simpleton could imagine that Bolshevism can be tamed. In his superficial way of thinking he does not suspect that here we are dealing with a phenomenon that is due to an urge of the blood: namely, the aspiration of the Jewish people to become the despots of the world. That aspiration is quite as natural as the impulse of the Anglo-Saxon to sit in the seats of rulership all over the earth. And as the Anglo-Saxon chooses his own way of reaching those ends and fights for them with his characteristic weapons, so also does the Jew. The Jew wriggles his way in among the body of the nations and bores them hollow from inside. The weapons with which he works are lies and calumny, poisonous infection and disintegration, until he has ruined his hated adversary. In Russian Bolshevism we ought to recognize the kind of attempt which is being made by the Jew in the twentieth century to secure dominion over the world. In other epochs he worked towards the same goal but with different, though at bottom similar, means. The kind of effort which the Jew puts forth springs from the deepest roots in the nature of his being. A people does not of itself renounce the impulse to increase its stock and power. Only external circumstances or senile impotence can force them to renounce this urge. In the same way the Jew will never spontaneously give up his march towards the goal of world dictatorship or repress his external urge. He can be thrown back on his road only by forces that are exterior to him, for his instinct towards world domination will die out only with himself. The impotence of nations and their extinction through senility can come only when their blood has remained no longer pure. And the Jewish people preserve the purity of their blood better than any other nation on earth. Therefore the Jew follows his destined road until he is opposed by a force superior to him. And then a desperate struggle takes place to send back to Lucifer him who would assault the heavens.

To-day Germany is the next battlefield for Russian Bolshevism. All the force of a fresh missionary idea is needed to raise up our nation once more, to rescue it from the coils of the international serpent and stop the process of corruption which is taking place in the internal constitution of our blood; so that the forces of our nation, once liberated, may be employed to preserve our nationality and prevent the repetition of the recent catastrophe from taking place even in the most distant future. If this be the goal we set to ourselves it would be folly to ally ourselves with a country whose master is the mortal enemy of our future. How can we release our people from this poisonous grip if we accept the same grip ourselves? How can we teach the German worker that Bolshevism is an infamous crime against humanity if we ally ourselves with this infernal abortion and recognize its existence as legitimate. With what right shall we condemn the members of the broad masses whose sympathies lie with a certain WELTANSCHAUUNG if the rulers of our State choose the representatives of that WELTANSCHAUUNG as their allies? The struggle against the Jewish Bolshevization of the world demands that we should declare our position towards Soviet Russia. We cannot cast out the Devil through Beelzebub. If nationalist circles to-day grow enthusiastic about the idea of an alliance with Bolshevism, then let them look around only in Germany and recognize from what quarter they are being supported. Do these nationalists believe that a policy which is recommended and acclaimed by the Marxist international Press can be beneficial for the German people? Since when has the Jew acted as shield-bearer for the militant nationalist?

One special reproach which could be made against the old German REICH with regard to its policy of alliances was that it spoiled its relations towards all others by continually swinging now this way and now that way and by its weakness in trying to preserve world peace at all costs. But one reproach which cannot be made against it is that it did not continue to maintain good relations with Russia.

I admit frankly that before the War I thought it would have been better if Germany had abandoned her senseless colonial policy and her naval policy and had joined England in an alliance against Russia, therewith renouncing her weak world policy for a determined European policy, with the idea of acquiring new territory on the Continent. I do not forget the constant insolent threats which Pan-Slavist Russia made against Germany. I do not forget the continual trial mobilizations, the sole object of which was to irritate Germany. I cannot forget the tone of public opinion in Russia which in pre-War days excelled itself in hate-inspired outbursts against our nation and REICH. Nor can I forget the big Russian Press which was always more favourable to France than to us.

But, in spite of everything, there was still a second way possible before the War. We might have won the support of Russia and turned against England. Circumstances are entirely different to-day. If, before the War, throwing all sentiment to the winds, we could have marched by the side of Russia, that is no longer possible for us to-day. Since then the hand of the world-clock has moved forward. The hour has struck and struck loudly, when the destiny of our people must be decided one way or another.

The present consolidation of the great States of the world is the last warning signal for us to look to ourselves and bring our people back from their land of visions to the land of hard truth and point the way into the future, on which alone the old REICH can march triumphantly once again.

If, in view of this great and most important task placed before it, the National Socialist Movement sets aside all illusions and takes reason as its sole effective guide the catastrophe of 1918 may turn out to be an infinite blessing for the future of our nation. From the lesson of that collapse it may formulate an entirely new orientation for the conduct of its foreign policy. Internally reinforced through its new WELTANSCHAUUNG, the German nation may reach a final stabilization of its policy towards the outside world. It may end by gaining what England has, what even Russia had, and what France again and again utilized as the ultimate grounds on which she was able to base correct decisions for her own interests: namely, A Political Testament. Political Testament of the German Nation ought to lay down the following rules, which will be always valid for its conduct towards the outside world:

Never permit two Continental Powers to arise in Europe. Should any attempt be made to organize a second military Power on the German frontier by the creation of a State which may become a Military Power, with the prospect of an aggression against Germany in view, such an event confers on Germany not only the right but the duty to prevent by every means, including military means, the creation of such a State and to crush it if created. See to it that the strength of our nation does not rest on colonial foundations but on those of our own native territory in Europe. Never consider the REICH secure unless, for centuries to come, it is in a position to give every descendant of our race a piece of ground and soil that he can call his own. Never forget that the most sacred of all rights in this world is man's right to the earth which he wishes to cultivate for himself and that the holiest of all sacrifices is that of the blood poured out for it.

I should not like to close this chapter without referring once again to the one sole possibility of alliances that exists for us in Europe at the present moment. In speaking of the German alliance problem in the present chapter I mentioned England and Italy as the only countries with which it would be worth while for us to strive to form a close alliance and that this alliance would be advantageous. I should like here to underline again the military importance of such an alliance.

The military consequences of forming this alliance would be the direct opposite of the consequences of an alliance with Russia. Most important of all is the fact that a RAPPROCHEMENT with England and Italy would in no way involve a danger of war. The only Power that could oppose such an arrangement would be France; and France would not be in a position to make war. But the alliance should allow to Germany the possibility of making those preparations in all tranquillity which, within the framework of such a coalition, might in one way or another be requisite in view of a regulation of accounts with France. For the full significance of such an alliance lies in the fact that on its conclusion Germany would no longer be subject to the threat of a sudden invasion. The coalition against her would disappear automatically; that is to say, the Entente which brought such disaster to us. Thus France, the mortal enemy of our people, would be isolated. And even though at first this success would have only a moral effect, it would be sufficient to give Germany such liberty of action as we cannot now imagine. For the new Anglo-German-Italian alliance would hold the political initiative and no longer France.

A further success would be that at one stroke Germany would be delivered from her unfavourable strategical situation. On the one side her flank would be strongly protected; and, on the other, the assurance of being able to import her foodstuffs and raw materials would be a beneficial result of this new alignment of States. But almost of greater importance would be the fact that this new League would include States that possess technical qualities which mutually supplement each other. For the first time Germany would have allies who would not be as vampires on her economic body but would contribute their part to complete our technical equipment. And we must not forget a final fact: namely, that in this case we should not have allies resembling Turkey and Russia to-day. The greatest World Power on this earth and a young national State would supply far other elements for a struggle in Europe than the putrescent carcasses of the States with which Germany was allied in the last war.

As I have already said, great difficulties would naturally be made to hinder the conclusion of such an alliance. But was not the formation of the Entente somewhat more difficult? Where King Edward VII succeeded partly against interests that were of their nature opposed to his work we must and will succeed, if the recognition of the necessity of such a development so inspires us that we shall be able to act with skill and conquer our own feelings in carrying the policy through. This will be possible when, incited to action by the miseries of our situation, we shall adopt a definite purpose and follow it out systematically instead of the defective foreign policy of the last decades, which never had a fixed purpose in view.

The future goal of our foreign policy ought not to involve an orientation to the East or the West, but it ought to be an Eastern policy which will have in view the acquisition of such territory as is necessary for our German people. To carry out this policy we need that force which the mortal enemy of our nation, France, now deprives us of by holding us in her grip and pitilessly robbing us of our strength. Therefore we must stop at no sacrifice in our effort to destroy the French striving towards hegemony over Europe. As our natural ally to-day we have every Power on the Continent that feels France's lust for hegemony in Europe unbearable. No attempt to approach those Powers ought to appear too difficult for us, and no sacrifice should be considered too heavy, if the final outcome would be to make it possible for us to overthrow our bitterest enemy. The minor wounds will be cured by the beneficent influence of time, once the ground wounds have been cauterized and closed.

Naturally the internal enemies of our people will howl with rage. But this will not succeed in forcing us as National Socialists to cease our preaching in favour of that which our most profound conviction tells us to be necessary. We must oppose the current of public opinion which will be driven mad by Jewish cunning in exploiting our German thoughtlessness. The waves of this public opinion often rage and roar against us; but the man who swims with the current attracts less attention than he who buffets it. To-day we are but a rock in the river. In a few years Fate may raise us up as a dam against which the general current will be broken, only to flow forward in a new bed. Therefore it is necessary that in the eyes of the rest of the world our movement should be recognized as representing a definite and determined political programme. We ought to bear on our visors the distinguishing sign of that task which Heaven expects us to fulfil.

When we ourselves are fully aware of the ineluctable necessity which determines our external policy this knowledge will fill us with the grit which we need in order to stand up with equanimity under the bombardment launched against us by the enemy Press and to hold firm when some insinuating voice whispers that we ought to give ground here and there in order not to have all against us and that we might sometimes howl with the wolves.

CHAPTER XV: The Right to Self-Defence

After we had laid down our arms, in November 1918, a policy was adopted which in all human probability was bound to lead gradually to our complete subjugation. Analogous examples from history show that those nations which lay down their arms without being absolutely forced to do so subsequently prefer to submit to the greatest humiliations and exactions rather than try to change their fate by resorting to arms again.

That is intelligible on purely human grounds. A shrewd conqueror will always enforce his exactions on the conquered only by stages, as far as that is possible. Then he may expect that a people who have lost all strength of character—which is always the case with every nation that voluntarily submits to the threats of an opponent—will not find in any of these acts of oppression, if one be enforced apart from the other, sufficient grounds for taking up arms again. The more numerous the extortions thus passively accepted so much the less will resistance appear justified in the eyes of other people, if the vanquished nation should end by revolting against the last act of oppression in a long series. And that is specially so if the nation has already patiently and silently accepted impositions which were much more exacting.

The fall of Carthage is a terrible example of the slow agony of a people which ended in destruction and which was the fault of the people themselves.

In his THREE ARTICLES OF FAITH Clausewitz expressed this idea admirably and gave it a definite form when he said: "The stigma of shame incurred by a cowardly submission can never be effaced. The drop of poison which thus enters the blood of a nation will be transmitted to posterity. It will undermine and paralyse the strength of later generations." But, on the contrary, he added: "Even the loss of its liberty after a sanguinary and honourable struggle assures the resurgence of the nation and is the vital nucleus from which one day a new tree can draw firm roots."

Naturally a nation which has lost all sense of honour and all strength of character will not feel the force of such a doctrine. But any nation that takes it to heart will never fall very low. Only those who forget it or do not wish to acknowledge it will collapse. Hence those responsible for a cowardly submission cannot be expected suddenly to take thought with themselves, for the purpose of changing their former conduct and directing it in the way pointed out by human reason and experience. On the contrary, they will repudiate such a doctrine, until the people either become permanently habituated to the yoke of slavery or the better elements of the nation push their way into the foreground and forcibly take power away from the hands of an infamous and corrupt regime. In the first case those who hold power will be pleased with the state of affairs, because the conquerors often entrust them with the task of supervising the slaves. And these utterly characterless beings then exercise that power to the detriment of their own people, more cruelly than the most cruel-hearted stranger that might be nominated by the enemy himself.

The events which happened subsequent to 1918 in Germany prove how the hope of securing the clemency of the victor by making a voluntary submission had the most disastrous influence on the political views and conduct of the broad masses. I say the broad masses explicitly, because I cannot persuade myself that the things which were done or left undone by the leaders of the people are to be attributed to a similar disastrous illusion. Seeing that the direction of our historical destiny after the war was now openly controlled by the Jews, it is impossible to admit that a defective knowledge of the state of affairs was the sole cause of our misfortunes. On the contrary, the conclusion that must be drawn from the facts is that our people were intentionally driven to ruin. If we examine it from this point of view we shall find that the direction of the nation's foreign policy was not so foolish as it appeared; for on scrutinizing the matter closely we see clearly that this conduct was a procedure which had been calmly calculated, shrewdly defined and logically carried out in the service of the Jewish idea and the Jewish endeavour to secure the mastery of the world.

From 1806 to 1813 Prussia was in a state of collapse. But that period sufficed to renew the vital energies of the nation and inspire it once more with a resolute determination to fight. An equal period of time has passed over our heads from 1918 until to-day, and no advantage has been derived from it. On the contrary, the vital strength of our State has been steadily sapped.

Seven years after November 1918 the Locarno Treaty was signed.

Thus the development which took place was what I have indicated above. Once the shameful Armistice had been signed our people were unable to pluck up sufficient courage and energy to call a halt suddenly to the conduct of our adversary as the oppressive measures were being constantly renewed. The enemy was too shrewd to put forward all his demands at once. He confined his duress always to those exactions which, in his opinion and that of our German Government, could be submitted to for the moment: so that in this way they did not risk causing an explosion of public feeling. But according as the single impositions were increasingly subscribed to and tolerated it appeared less justifiable to do now in the case of one sole imposition or act of duress what had not been previously done in the case of so many others, namely, to oppose it. That is the 'drop of poison' of which Clausewitz speaks. Once this lack of character is manifested the resultant condition becomes steadily aggravated and weighs like an evil inheritance on all future decisions. It may become as a leaden weight around the nation's neck, which cannot be shaken off but which forces it to drag out its existence in slavery.

Thus, in Germany, edicts for disarmament and oppression and economic plunder followed one after the other, making us politically helpless. The result of all this was to create that mood which made so many look upon the Dawes Plan as a blessing and the Locarno Treaty as a success. From a higher point of view we may speak of one sole blessing in the midst of so much misery. This blessing is that, though men may be fooled, Heaven can't be bribed. For Heaven withheld its blessing. Since that time Misery and Anxiety have been the constant companions of our people, and Distress is the one Ally that has remained loyal to us. In this case also Destiny has made no exceptions. It has given us our deserts. Since we did not know how to value honour any more, it has taught us to value the liberty to seek for bread. Now that the nation has learned to cry for bread, it may one day learn to pray for freedom.

The collapse of our nation in the years following 1918 was bitter and manifest. And yet that was the time chosen to persecute us in the most malicious way our enemies could devise, so that what happened afterwards could have been foretold by anybody then. The government to which our people submitted was as hopelessly incompetent as it was conceited, and this was especially shown in repudiating those who gave any warning that disturbed or displeased. Then we saw—and to-day also—the greatest parliamentary nincompoops, really common saddlers and glove-makers—not merely by trade, for that would signify very little—suddenly raised to the rank of statesmen and sermonizing to humble mortals from that pedestal. It did not matter, and it still does not matter, that such a 'statesman', after having displayed his talents for six months or so as a mere windbag, is shown up for what he is and becomes the object of public raillery and sarcasm. It does not matter that he has given the most evident proof of complete incompetency. No. That does not matter at all. On the contrary, the less real service the parliamentary statesmen of this Republic render the country, the more savagely they persecute all who expect that parliamentary deputies should show some positive results of their activities. And they persecute everybody who dares to point to the failure of these activities and predict similar failures for the future. If one finally succeeds in nailing down one of these parliamentarians to hard facts, so that this political artist can no longer deny the real failure of his whole action and its results, then he will find thousands of grounds for excuse, but will in no way admit that he himself is the chief cause of the evil.

In the winter of 1922-23, at the latest, it ought to have been generally recognized that, even after the conclusion of peace, France was still endeavouring with iron consistency to attain those ends which had been originally envisaged as the final purpose of the War.

For nobody could think of believing that for four and a half years France continued to pour out the not abundant supply of her national blood in the most decisive struggle throughout all her history in order subsequently to obtain compensation through reparations for the damages sustained. Even Alsace and Lorraine, taken by themselves, would not account for the energy with which the French conducted the War, if Alsace-Lorraine were not already considered as a part of the really vast programme which French foreign policy had envisaged for the future. The aim of that programme was: Disintegration of Germany into a collection of small states. It was for this that Chauvinist France waged war; and in doing so she was in reality selling her people to be the serfs of the international Jew.

French war aims would have been obtained through the World War if, as was originally hoped in Paris, the struggle had been carried out on German soil. Let us imagine the bloody battles of the World War not as having taken place on the Somme, in Flanders, in Artois, in front of Warsaw, Nizhni-Novogorod, Kowno, and Riga but in Germany, in the Ruhr or on the Maine, on the Elbe, in front of Hanover, Leipzig, Nürnberg, etc. If such happened, then we must admit that the destruction of Germany might have been accomplished. It is very much open to question if our young federal State could have borne the hard struggle for four and a half years, as it was borne by a France that had been centralized for centuries, with the whole national imagination focused on Paris. If this titanic conflict between the nations developed outside the frontiers of our fatherland, not only is all the merit due to the immortal service rendered by our old army but it was also very fortunate for the future of Germany. I am fully convinced that if things had taken a different course there would no longer be a German REICH to-day but only 'German States'. And that is the only reason why the blood which was shed by our friends and brothers in the War was at least not shed in vain.

The course which events took was otherwise. In November 1918 Germany did indeed collapse with lightning suddenness. But when the catastrophe took place at home the armies under the Commander-in-Chief were still deep in the enemy's country. At that time France's first preoccupation was not the dismemberment of Germany but the problem of how to get the German armies out of France and Belgium as quickly as possible. And so, in order to put an end to the War, the first thing that had to be done by the Paris Government was to disarm the German armies and push them back into Germany if possible. Until this was done the French could not devote their attention to carrying out their own particular and original war aims. As far as concerned England, the War was really won when Germany was destroyed as a colonial and commercial Power and was reduced to the rank of a second-class State. It was not in England's interest to wipe out the German State altogether. In fact, on many grounds it was desirable for her to have a future rival against France in Europe. Therefore French policy was forced to carry on by peaceful means the work for which the War had opened the way; and Clemenceau's statement, that for him Peace was merely a continuation of the War, thus acquired an enhanced significance.

Persistently and on every opportunity that arose, the effort to dislocate the framework of the REICH was to have been carried on. By perpetually sending new notes that demanded disarmament, on the one hand, and by the imposition of economic levies which, on the other hand, could be carried out as the process of disarmament progressed, it was hoped in Paris that the framework of the REICH would gradually fall to pieces. The more the Germans lost their sense of national honour the more could economic pressure and continued economic distress be effective as factors of political destruction. Such a policy of political oppression and economic exploitation, carried out for ten or twenty years, must in the long run steadily ruin the most compact national body and, under certain circumstances, dismember it. Then the French war aims would have been definitely attained.

By the winter of 1922-23 the intentions of the French must already have been known for a long time back. There remained only two possible ways of confronting the situation. If the German national body showed itself sufficiently tough-skinned, it might gradually blunt the will of the French or it might do—once and for all—what was bound to become inevitable one day: that is to say, under the provocation of some particularly brutal act of oppression it could put the helm of the German ship of state to roundabout and ram the enemy. That would naturally involve a life-and-death-struggle. And the prospect of coming through the struggle alive depended on whether France could be so far isolated that in this second battle Germany would not have to fight against the whole world but in defence of Germany against a France that was persistently disturbing the peace of the world.

I insist on this point, and I am profoundly convinced of it, namely, that this second alternative will one day be chosen and will have to be chosen and carried out in one way or another. I shall never believe that France will of herself alter her intentions towards us, because, in the last analysis, they are only the expression of the French instinct for self-preservation. Were I a Frenchman and were the greatness of France so dear to me as that of Germany actually is, in the final reckoning I could not and would not act otherwise than a Clemenceau. The French nation, which is slowly dying out, not so much through depopulation as through the progressive disappearance of the best elements of the race, can continue to play an important role in the world only if Germany be destroyed. French policy may make a thousand detours on the march towards its fixed goal, but the destruction of Germany is the end which it always has in view as the fulfilment of the most profound yearning and ultimate intentions of the French. Now it is a mistake to believe that if the will on one side should remain only PASSIVE and intent on its own self-preservation it can hold out permanently against another will which is not less forceful but is ACTIVE. As long as the eternal conflict between France and Germany is waged only in the form of a German defence against the French attack, that conflict can never be decided; and from century to century Germany will lose one position after another. If we study the changes that have taken place, from the twelfth century up to our day, in the frontiers within which the German language is spoken, we can hardly hope for a successful issue to result from the acceptance and development of a line of conduct which has hitherto been so detrimental for us.

Only when the Germans have taken all this fully into account will they cease from allowing the national will-to-life to wear itself out in merely passive defence, but they will rally together for a last decisive contest with France. And in this contest the essential objective of the German nation will be fought for. Only then will it be possible to put an end to the eternal Franco-German conflict which has hitherto proved so sterile. Of course it is here presumed that Germany sees in the suppression of France nothing more than a means which will make it possible for our people finally to expand in another quarter. To-day there are eighty million Germans in Europe. And our foreign policy will be recognized as rightly conducted only when, after barely a hundred years, there will be 250 million Germans living on this Continent, not packed together as the coolies in the factories of another Continent but as tillers of the soil and workers whose labour will be a mutual assurance for their existence.

In December 1922 the situation between Germany and France assumed a particularly threatening aspect. France had new and vast oppressive measures in view and needed sanctions for her conduct. Political pressure had to precede the economic plunder, and the French believed that only by making a violent attack against the central nervous system of German life would they be able to make our 'recalcitrant' people bow to their galling yoke. By the occupation of the Ruhr District, it was hoped in France that not only would the moral backbone of Germany be broken finally but that we should be reduced to such a grave economic condition that we should be forced, for weal or woe, to subscribe to the heaviest possible obligations.

It was a question of bending and breaking Germany. At first Germany bent and subsequently broke in pieces completely.

Through the occupation of the Ruhr, Fate once more reached out its hand to the German people and bade them arise. For what at first appeared as a heavy stroke of misfortune was found, on closer examination, to contain extremely encouraging possibilities of bringing Germany's sufferings to an end.

As regards foreign politics, the action of France in occupying the Ruhr really estranged England for the first time in quite a profound way. Indeed it estranged not merely British diplomatic circles, which had concluded the French alliance and had upheld it from motives of calm and objective calculation, but it also estranged large sections of the English nation. The English business world in particular scarcely concealed the displeasure it felt at this incredible forward step in strengthening the power of France on the Continent. From the military standpoint alone France now assumed a position in Europe such as Germany herself had not held previously. Moreover, France thus obtained control over economic resources which practically gave her a monopoly that consolidated her political and commercial strength against all competition. The most important iron and coal mines of Europe were now united in the hand of one nation which, in contrast to Germany, had hitherto defended her vital interests in an active and resolute fashion and whose military efficiency in the Great War was still fresh in the memories of the whole world. The French occupation of the Ruhr coal field deprived England of all the successes she had gained in the War. And the victors were now Marshal Foch and the France he represented, no longer the calm and painstaking British statesmen.

In Italy also the attitude towards France, which had not been very favourable since the end of the War, now became positively hostile. The great historic moment had come when the Allies of yesterday might become the enemies of to-morrow. If things happened otherwise and if the Allies did not suddenly come into conflict with one another, as in the Second Balkan War, that was due to the fact that Germany had no Enver Pasha but merely a Cuno as Chancellor of the REICH.

Nevertheless, the French invasion of the Ruhr opened up great possibilities for the future not only in Germany's foreign politics but also in her internal politics. A considerable section of our people who, thanks to the persistent influence of a mendacious Press, had looked upon France as the champion of progress and liberty, were suddenly cured of this illusion. In 1914 the dream of international solidarity suddenly vanished from the brain of our German working class. They were brought back into the world of everlasting struggle, where one creature feeds on the other and where the death of the weaker implies the life of the stronger. The same thing happened in the spring of

1923.

When the French put their threats into effect and penetrated, at first hesitatingly and cautiously, into the coal-basin of Lower Germany the hour of destiny had struck for Germany. It was a great and decisive moment. If at that moment our people had changed not only their frame of mind but also their conduct the German Ruhr District could have been made for France what Moscow turned out to be for Napoleon. Indeed, there were only two possibilities: either to leave this move also to take its course and do nothing or to turn to the German people in that region of sweltering forges and flaming furnaces. An effort might have been made to set their wills afire with determination to put an end to this persistent disgrace and to face a momentary terror rather than submit to a terror that was endless.

Cuno, who was then Chancellor of the REICH, can claim the immortal merit of having discovered a third way; and our German bourgeois political parties merit the still more glorious honour of having admired him and collaborated with him.

Here I shall deal with the second way as briefly as possible.

By occupying the Ruhr France committed a glaring violation of the Versailles Treaty. Her action brought her into conflict with several of the guarantor Powers, especially with England and Italy. She could no longer hope that those States would back her up in her egotistic act of brigandage. She could count only on her own forces to reap anything like a positive result from that adventure, for such it was at the start. For a German National Government there was only one possible way left open. And this was the way which honour prescribed. Certainly at the beginning we could not have opposed France with an active armed resistance. But it should have been clearly recognized that any negotiations which did not have the argument of force to back them up would turn out futile and ridiculous. If it were not possible to organize an active resistance, then it was absurd to take up the standpoint: "We shall not enter into any negotiations." But it was still more absurd finally to enter into negotiations without having organized the necessary force as a support.

Not that it was possible for us by military means to prevent the occupation of the Ruhr. Only a madman could have recommended such a decision. But under the impression produced by the action which France had taken, and during the time that it was being carried out, measures could have been, and should have been, undertaken without any regard to the Versailles Treaty, which France herself had violated, to provide those military resources which would serve as a collateral argument to back up the negotiations later on. For it was quite clear from the beginning that the fate of this district occupied by the French would one day be decided at some conference table or other. But it also must have been quite to everybody that even the best negotiators could have little success as long as the ground on which they themselves stood and the chair on which they sat were not under the armed protection of their own people. A weak pigmy cannot contend against athletes, and a negotiator without any armed defence at his back must always bow in obeisance when a Brennus throws the sword into the scales on the enemy's side, unless an equally strong sword can be thrown into the scales at the other end and thus maintain the balance. It was really distressing to have to observe the comedy of negotiations which, ever since 1918, regularly preceded each arbitrary dictate that the enemy imposed upon us. We offered a sorry spectacle to the eyes of the whole world when we were invited, for the sake of derision, to attend conference tables simply to be presented with decisions and programmes which had already been drawn up and passed a long time before, and which we were permitted to discuss, but from the beginning had to be considered as unalterable. It is true that in scarcely a single instance were our negotiators men of more than mediocre abilities. For the most part they justified only too well the insolent observation made by Lloyd George when he sarcastically remarked, in the presence of a former Chancellor of the REICH, Herr Simon, that the Germans were not able to choose men of intelligence as their leaders and representatives. But in face of the resolute determination and the power which the enemy held in his hands, on the one side, and the lamentable impotence of Germany on the other, even a body of geniuses could have obtained only very little for Germany.

In the spring of 1923, however, anyone who might have thought of seizing the opportunity of the French invasion of the Ruhr to reconstruct the military power of Germany would first have had to restore to the nation its moral weapons, to reinforce its will-power, and to extirpate those who had destroyed this most valuable element of national strength.

Just as in 1918 we had to pay with our blood for the failure to crush the Marxist serpent underfoot once and for all in 1914 and 1915, now we have to suffer retribution for the fact that in the spring of 1923 we did not seize the opportunity then offered us for finally wiping out the handiwork done by the Marxists who betrayed their country and were responsible for the murder of our people.

Any idea of opposing French aggression with an efficacious resistance was only pure folly as long as the fight had not been taken up against those forces which, five years previously, had broken the German resistance on the battlefields by the influences which they exercised at home. Only bourgeois minds could have arrived at the incredible belief that Marxism had probably become quite a different thing now and that the CANAILLE of ringleaders in 1918, who callously used the bodies of our two million dead as stepping-stones on which they climbed into the various Government positions, would now, in the year 1923, suddenly show themselves ready to pay their tribute to the national conscience. It was veritably a piece of incredible folly to expect that those traitors would suddenly appear as the champions of German freedom. They had no intention of doing it. Just as a hyena will not leave its carrion, a Marxist will not give up indulging in the betrayal of his country. It is out of the question to put forward the stupid retort here, that so many of the workers gave their blood for Germany. German workers, yes, but no longer international Marxists. If the German working class, in 1914, consisted of real Marxists the War would have ended within three weeks. Germany would have collapsed before the first soldier had put a foot beyond the frontiers. No. The fact that the German people carried on the War proved that the Marxist folly had not yet been able to penetrate deeply. But as the War was prolonged German soldiers and workers gradually fell back into the hands of the Marxist leaders, and the number of those who thus relapsed became lost to their country. At the beginning of the War, or even during the War, if twelve or fifteen thousand of these Jews who were corrupting the nation had been forced to submit to poison-gas, just as hundreds of thousands of our best German workers from every social stratum and from every trade and calling had to face it in the field, then the millions of sacrifices made at the front would not have been in vain. On the contrary: If twelve thousand of these malefactors had been eliminated in proper time probably the lives of a million decent men, who would be of value to Germany in the future, might have been saved. But it was in accordance with bourgeois 'statesmanship' to hand over, without the twitch of an eyelid, millions of human beings to be slaughtered on the battlefields, while they looked upon ten or twelve thousand public traitors, profiteers, usurers and swindlers, as the dearest and most sacred national treasure and proclaimed their persons to be inviolable. Indeed it would be hard to say what is the most outstanding feature of these bourgeois circles: mental debility, moral weakness and cowardice, or a mere down-at-heel mentality. It is a class that is certainly doomed to go under but, unhappily, it drags down the whole nation with it into the abyss.

The situation in 1923 was quite similar to that of 1918. No matter what form of resistance was decided upon, the first prerequisite for taking action was the elimination of the Marxist poison from the body of the nation. And I was convinced that the first task then of a really National Government was to seek and find those forces that were determined to wage a war of destruction against Marxism and to give these forces a free hand. It was their duty not to bow down before the fetish of 'order and tranquillity' at a moment when the enemy from outside was dealing the Fatherland a death-blow and when high treason was lurking behind every street corner at home. No. A really National Government ought then to have welcomed disorder and unrest if this turmoil would afford an opportunity of finally settling with the Marxists, who are the mortal enemies of our people. If this precaution were neglected, then it was sheer folly to think of resisting, no matter what form that resistance might take.

Of course, such a settlement of accounts with the Marxists as would be of real historical importance could not be effected along lines laid down by some secret council or according to some plan concocted by the shrivelled mind of some cabinet minister. It would have to be in accordance with the eternal laws of life on this Earth which are and will remain those of a ceaseless struggle for existence. It must always be remembered that in many instances a hardy and healthy nation has emerged from the ordeal of the most bloody civil wars, while from peace conditions which had been artificially maintained there often resulted a state of national putrescence that reeked to the skies. The fate of a nation cannot be changed in kid gloves. And so in the year 1923 brutal action should have been taken to stamp out the vipers that battened on the body of the nation. If this were done, then the first prerequisite for an active opposition would have been fulfilled.

At that time I often talked myself hoarse in trying to make it clear, at least to the so-called national circles, what was then at stake and that by repeating the errors committed in 1914 and the following years we must necessarily come to the same kind of catastrophe as in 1918. I frequently implored of them to let Fate have a free hand and to make it possible for our Movement to settle with the Marxists. But I preached to deaf ears. They all thought they knew better, including the Chief of the Defence Force, until finally they found themselves forced to subscribe to the vilest capitulation that history records.

I then became profoundly convinced that the German bourgeoisie had come to the end of its mission and was not capable of fulfilling any further function. And then also I recognized the fact that all the bourgeois parties had been fighting Marxism merely from the spirit of competition without sincerely wishing to destroy it. For a long time they had been accustomed to assist in the destruction of their country, and their one great care was to secure good seats at the funeral banquet. It was for this alone that they kept on 'fighting'.

At that time—I admit it openly—I conceived a profound admiration for the great man beyond the Alps, whose ardent love for his people inspired him not to bargain with Italy's internal enemies but to use all possible ways and means in an effort to wipe them out.

What places Mussolini in the ranks of the world's great men is his decision not to share Italy with the Marxists but to redeem his country from Marxism by destroying internationalism.

What miserable pigmies our sham statesmen in Germany appear by comparison with him. And how nauseating it is to witness the conceit and effrontery of these nonentities in criticizing a man who is a thousand times greater than them. And how painful it is to think that this takes place in a country which could point to a Bismarck as its leader as recently as fifty years ago.

The attitude adopted by the bourgeoisie in 1923 and the way in which they dealt kindly with Marxism decided from the outset the fate of any attempt at active resistance in the Ruhr. With that deadly enemy in our own ranks it was sheer folly to think of fighting France. The most that could then be done was to stage a sham fight in order to satisfy the German national element to some extent, to tranquillize the 'boiling state of the public mind', or dope it, which was what was really intended. Had they really believed in what they did, they ought to have recognized that the strength of a nation lies, first of all, not in its arms but in its will, and that before conquering the external enemy the enemy at home would have to be eliminated. If not, then disaster must result if victory be not achieved on the very first day of the fight. The shadow of one defeat is sufficient to break up the resistance of a nation that has not been liberated from its internal enemies, and give the adversary a decisive victory.

In the spring of 1923 all this might have been predicted. It is useless to ask whether it was then possible to count on a military success against France. For if the result of the German action in regard to the French invasion of the Ruhr had been only the destruction of Marxism at home, success would have been on our side. Once liberated from the deadly enemies of her present and future existence, Germany would possess forces which no power in the world could strangle again. On the day when Marxism is broken in Germany the chains that bind Germany will be smashed for ever. For never in our history have we been conquered by the strength of our outside enemies but only through our own failings and the enemy in our own camp.

Since it was not able to decide on such heroic action at that time, the Government could have chosen the first way: namely, to allow things to take their course and do nothing at all.

But at that great moment Heaven made Germany a present of a great man. This was Herr Cuno. He was neither a statesman nor a politician by profession, still less a politician by birth. But he belonged to that type of politician who is merely used for liGYMNASIUMating some definite question. Apart from that, he had business experience. It was a curse for Germany that, in the practice of politics, this business man looked upon politics also as a business undertaking and regulated his conduct accordingly.

"France occupies the Ruhr. What is there in the Ruhr? Coal. And so France occupies the Ruhr for the sake of its coal?" What could come more naturally to the mind of Herr Cuno than the idea of a strike, which would prevent the French from obtaining any coal? And therefore, in the opinion of Herr Cuno, one day or other they would certainly have to get out of the Ruhr again if the occupation did not prove to be a paying business. Such were approximately the lines along which that OUTSTANDING NATIONAL STATESMAN reasoned. At Stuttgart and other places he spoke to 'his people' and this people became lost in admiration for him. Of course they needed the Marxists for the strike, because the workers would have to be the first to go on strike. Now, in the brain of a bourgeois statesman such as Cuno, a Marxist and a worker are one and the same thing. Therefore it was necessary to bring the worker into line with all the other Germans in a united front. One should have seen how the countenances of these party politicians beamed with the light of their moth-eaten bourgeois culture when the great genius spoke the word of revelation to them. Here was a nationalist and also a man of genius. At last they had discovered what they had so long sought. For now the abyss between Marxism and themselves could be bridged over. And thus it became possible for the pseudo-nationalist to ape the German manner and adopt nationalist phraseology in reaching out the ingenuous hand of friendship to the internationalist traitors of their country. The traitor readily grasped that hand, because, just as Herr Cuno had need of the Marxist chiefs for his 'united front', the Marxist chiefs needed Herr Cuno's money. So that both parties mutually benefited by the transaction. Cuno obtained his united front, constituted of nationalist charlatans and international swindlers. And now, with the help of the money paid to them by the State, these people were able to pursue their glorious mission, which was to destroy the national economic system. It was an immortal thought, that of saving a nation by means of a general strike in which the strikers were paid by the State. It was a command that could be enthusiastically obeyed by the most indifferent of loafers.

Everybody knows that prayers will not make a nation free. But that it is possible to liberate a nation by giving up work has yet to be proved by historical experience. Instead of promoting a paid general strike at that time, and making this the basis of his 'united front', if Herr Cuno had demanded two hours more work from every German, then the swindle of the 'united front' would have been disposed of within three days. Nations do not obtain their freedom by refusing to work but by making sacrifices.

Anyhow, the so-called passive resistance could not last long. Nobody but a man entirely ignorant of war could imagine that an army of occupation might be frightened and driven out by such ridiculous means. And yet this could have been the only purpose of an action for which the country had to pay out milliards and which contributed seriously to devaluate the national currency.

Of course the French were able to make themselves almost at home in the Ruhr basin the moment they saw that such ridiculous measures were being adopted against them. They had received the prescription directly from ourselves of the best way to bring a recalcitrant civil population to a sense of reason if its conduct implied a serious danger for the officials which the army of occupation had placed in authority. Nine years previously we wiped out with lightning rapidity bands of Belgian FRANCS-TIREURS and made the civil population clearly understand the seriousness of the situation, when the activities of these bands threatened grave danger for the German army. In like manner if the passive resistance of the Ruhr became really dangerous for the French, the armies of occupation would have needed no more than eight days to bring the whole piece of childish nonsense to a gruesome end. For we must always go back to the original question in all this business: What were we to do if the passive resistance came to the point where it really got on the nerves of our opponents and they proceeded to suppress it with force and bloodshed? Would we still continue to resist? If so, then, for weal or woe, we would have to submit to a severe and bloody persecution. And in that case we should be faced with the same situation as would have faced us in the case of an active resistance. In other words, we should have to fight. Therefore the so-called passive resistance would be logical only if supported by the determination to come out and wage an open fight in case of necessity or adopt a kind of guerilla warfare. Generally speaking, one undertakes such a struggle when there is a possibility of success. The moment a besieged fortress is taken by assault there is no practical alternative left to the defenders except to surrender, if instead of probable death they are assured that their lives will be spared. Let the garrison of a citadel which has been completely encircled by the enemy once lose all hope of being delivered by their friends, then the strength of the defence collapses totally.

That is why passive resistance in the Ruhr, when one considers the final consequences which it might and must necessarily have if it were to turn out really successful, had no practical meaning unless an active front had been organized to support it. Then one might have demanded immense efforts from our people. If each of these Westphalians in the Ruhr could have been assured that the home country had mobilized an army of eighty or a hundred divisions to support them, the French would have found themselves treading on thorns. Surely a greater number of courageous men could be found to sacrifice themselves for a successful enterprise than for an enterprise that was manifestly futile.

This was the classic occasion that induced us National Socialists to take up a resolute stand against the so-called national word of command. And that is what we did. During those months I was attacked by people whose patriotism was a mixture of stupidity and humbug and who took part in the general hue and cry because of the pleasant sensation they felt at being suddenly enabled to show themselves as nationalists, without running any danger thereby. In my estimation, this despicable 'united front' was one of the most ridiculous things that could be imagined. And events proved that I was right.

As soon as the Trades Unions had nearly filled their treasuries with Cuno's contributions, and the moment had come when it would be necessary to transform the passive resistance from a mere inert defence into active aggression, the Red hyenas suddenly broke out of the national sheepfold and returned to be what they always had been. Without sounding any drums or trumpets, Herr Cuno returned to his ships. Germany was richer by one experience and poorer by the loss of one great hope.

Up to midsummer of that year several officers, who certainly were not the least brave and honourable of their kind, had not really believed that the course of things could take a turn that was so humiliating. They had all hoped that—if not openly, then at least secretly—the necessary measures would be taken to make this insolent French invasion a turning-point in German history. In our ranks also there were many who counted at least on the intervention of the REICHSWEHR. That conviction was so ardent that it decisively influenced the conduct and especially the training of innumerable young men.

But when the disgraceful collapse set in and the most humiliating kind of capitulation was made, indignation against such a betrayal of our unhappy country broke out into a blaze. Millions of German money had been spent in vain and thousands of young Germans had been sacrificed, who were foolish enough to trust in the promises made by the rulers of the REICH. Millions of people now became clearly convinced that Germany could be saved only if the whole prevailing system were destroyed root and branch.

There never had been a more propitious moment for such a solution. On the one side an act of high treason had been committed against the country, openly and shamelessly. On the other side a nation found itself delivered over to die slowly of hunger. Since the State itself had trodden down all the precepts of faith and loyalty, made a mockery of the rights of its citizens, rendered the sacrifices of millions of its most loyal sons fruitless and robbed other millions of their last penny, such a State could no longer expect anything but hatred from its subjects. This hatred against those who had ruined the people and the country was bound to find an outlet in one form or another. In this connection I shall quote here the concluding sentence of a speech which I delivered at the great court trial that took place in the spring of 1924.

"The judges of this State may tranquilly condemn us for our conduct at that time, but History, the goddess of a higher truth and a better legal code, will smile as she tears up this verdict and will acquit us all of the crime for which this verdict demands punishment."

But History will then also summon before its own tribunal those who, invested with power to-day, have trampled on law and justice, condemning our people to misery and ruin, and who, in the hour of their country's misfortune, took more account of their own ego than of the life of the community.

Here I shall not relate the course of events which led to November 8th, 1923, and closed with that date. I shall not do so because I cannot see that this would serve any beneficial purpose in the future and also because no good could come of opening old sores that have been just only closed. Moreover, it would be out of place to talk about the guilt of men who perhaps in the depths of their hearts have as much love for their people as I myself, and who merely did not follow the same road as I took or failed to recognize it as the right one to take.

In the face of the great misfortune which has befallen our fatherland and affects all us, I must abstain from offending and perhaps disuniting those men who must at some future date form one great united front which will be made up of true and loyal Germans and which will have to withstand the common front presented by the enemy of our people. For I know that a time will come when those who then treated us as enemies will venerate the men who trod the bitter way of death for the sake of their people.

I have dedicated the first volume of this book to our eighteen fallen heroes. Here at the end of this second volume let me again bring those men to the memory of the adherents and champions of our ideals, as heroes who, in the full consciousness of what they were doing, sacrificed their lives for us all. We must never fail to recall those names in order to encourage the weak and wavering among us when duty calls, that duty which they fulfilled with absolute faith, even to its extreme consequences. Together with those, and as one of the best of all, I should like to mention the name of a man who devoted his life to reawakening his and our people, through his writing and his ideas and finally through positive action. I mean: Dietrich Eckart.

Epilogue

On November 9th, 1923, four and a half years after its foundation, the German National Socialist Labour Party was dissolved and forbidden throughout the whole of the REICH. To-day, in November 1926, it is again established throughout the REICH, enjoying full liberty, stronger and internally more compact than ever before.

All persecutions of the Movement and the individuals at its head, all the imputations and calumnies, have not been able to prevail against it. Thanks to the justice of its ideas, the integrity of its intentions and the spirit of self-denial that animates its members, it has overcome all oppression and increased its strength through the ordeal. If, in our contemporary world of parliamentary corruption, our Movement remains always conscious of the profound nature of its struggle and feels that it personifies the values of individual personality and race, and orders its action accordingly—then it may count with mathematical certainty on achieving victory some day in the future. And Germany must necessarily win the position which belongs to it on this Earth if it is led and organized according to these principles.

A State which, in an epoch of racial adulteration, devotes itself to the duty of preserving the best elements of its racial stock must one day become ruler of the Earth.

The adherents of our Movements must always remember this, whenever they may have misgivings lest the greatness of the sacrifices demanded of them may not be justified by the possibilities of success.

THE END

Endnotes

1. In order to understand the reference here, and similar references in later portions of MEIN KAMPF, the following must be borne in mind:
From 1792 to 1814 the French Revolutionary Armies overran Germany. In 1800 Bavaria shared in the Austrian defeat at Hohenlinden and the French occupied Munich. In 1805 the Bavarian Elector was made King of Bavaria by Napoleon and stipulated to back up Napoleon in all his wars with a force of 30,000 men. Thus Bavaria became the absolute vassal of the French. This was 'TheTime of Germany's Deepest Humiliation', which is referred to again and again by Hitler.
In 1806 a pamphlet entitled 'Germany's Deepest Humiliation' was published in South Germany. Among those who helped to circulate the pamphlet was the Nürnberg bookseller, Johannes Philipp Palm. He was denounced to the French by a Bavarian police agent. At his trial he refused to disclose the name of the author. By Napoleon's orders, he was shot at Braunau-on-the-Innon August 26th, 1806. A monument erected to him on the site of the execution was one of the first public objects that made an impression on Hitler asa little boy.
Leo Schlageter's case was in many respects parallel to that of Johannes Palm. Schlageter was a German theological student who volunteered for service in 1914. He became an artillery officer and won the Iron Cross of both classes. When the French occupied the Ruhr in 1923 Schlageter helped to organize the passive resistance on the German side. He and his companions blew up a railway bridge for the purpose of making the transport of coal to France more difficult.
Those who took part in the affair were denounced to the French by a German informer. Schlageter took the whole responsibility on his own shoulders and was condemned to death, his companions being sentenced to various terms of imprisonment and penal servitude by the French Court. Schlageter refused to disclose the identity of those who issued the order to blow up the railway bridge and he would not plead for mercy before a French Court. He was shot by a French firing-squad on May 26th, 1923. Severing was at that time German Minister of the Interior. It is said that representations were made, to him on Schlageter's behalf and that he refused to interfere.
Schlageter has become the chief martyr of the German resistance to the French occupation of the Ruhr and also one of the great heroes of the National Socialist Movement. He had joined the Movement at a very early stage, his card of membership bearing the number 61.

2. Non-classical secondary school. The Lyceum and GYMNASIUM were classical or semi-classical secondary schools.

3. See Translator's Introduction

4. When Francis II had laid down his title as Emperor of the Holy Roman Empire of the German Nation, which he did at the command of Napoleon, the Crown and Mace, as the Imperial Insignia, were kept in Vienna. After the German Empire was refounded, in 1871, under William I, there were many demands to have the Insignia transferred to Berlin. But these went unheeded. Hitler had them brought to Germany after the Austrian Anschluss and displayed at Nuremberg during the Party Congress in September 1938.

5. The Phaecians were a legendary people, mentioned in Homer's Odyssey. They were supposed to live on some unknown island in the Eastern Mediterranean, sometimes suggested to be Corcyra, the modern Corfu. They loved good living more than work, and so the name Phaecian has come to be a synonym for parasite.

6. SPOTTGEBURT VON DRECK UND FEUER. This is the epithet that Faust hurls at Mephistopheles as the latter intrudes on the conversation between Faust and Martha in the garden: Mephistopheles: Thou, full of sensual, super-sensual desire, A girl by the nose is leading thee.
Faust: Abortion, thou of filth and fire.

7. Herodotus (Book VII, 213-218) tells the story of how a Greek traitor, Ephialtes, helped the Persian invaders at the Battle of Thermopylae (480 B.C.) When the Persian King, Xerxes, had begun to despair of being able to break through the Greek defence, Ephialtes came to him and, on being promised a definite payment, told the King of a pathway over the shoulder of the mountain to the Greek end of the Pass.
The bargain being clinched, Ephialtes led a detachment of the Persian troops under General Hydarnes over the mountain pathway. Thus taken in the rear, the Greek defenders, under Leonidas, King of Sparta, had to fight in two opposite directions within the narrow pass. Terrible slaughter ensued and Leonidas fell in the thick of the fighting.
The bravery of Leonidas and the treason of Ephialtes impressed Hitler, as it does almost every schoolboy. The incident is referred to again in MEIN KAMPF (Chap. VIII, Vol. I), where Hitler compares the German troops that fell in France and Flanders to the Greeks at Thermopylae, the treachery of Ephialtes being suggested as the prototype of the defeatist policy of the German politicians towards the end of the Great War.

8. German Austria was the East Mark on the South and East Prussia was the East Mark on the North.

9. Carlyle explains the epithet thus: "First then, let no one from the title GEHOERNTE (Horned, Behorned),

fancy that our brave Siegfried, who was the loveliest as well as the bravest of men, was actually cornuted, and had horns on his brow, though like Michael Angelo's Moses; or even that his skin, to which the epithet BEHORNED refers, was hard like a crocodile's, and not softer than the softest shamey, for the truth is, his Hornedness means only an Invulnerability, like that of Achilles..."

10. Lines quoted from the Song of the Curassiers in Schiller's WALLENSTEIN.

11. The Second Infantry Bavarian Regiment, in which Hitler served as a volunteer.

12. Schwabing is the artistic quarter in Munich where artists have their studios and litterateurs, especially of the Bohemian class, foregather.

13. Here again we have the defenders of Thermopylae recalled as the prototype of German valour in the Great War. Hitler's quotation is a German variant of the couplet inscribed on the monument erected at Thermopylae to the memory of Leonidas and his Spartan soldiers who fell defending the Pass. As given by Herodotus, who claims that he saw the inscription himself, the original text may be literally translated thus:
Go, tell the Spartans, thou who passeth by, That here, obedient to their laws, we lie.

14. Probably the author has two separate incidents in mind. The first happened in 390 B.C., when, as the victorious Gauls descended on Rome, the Senators ordered their ivory chairs to be placed in the Forum before the Temples of the Gods. There, clad in their robes of state, they awaited the invader, hoping to save the city by sacrificing themselves.
This noble gesture failed for the time being; but it had an inspiring influence on subsequent generations. The second incident, which has more historical authenticity, occurred after the Roman defeat at Cannae in 216 B.C. On that occasion Varro, the Roman commander, who, though in great part responsible for the disaster, made an effort to carry on the struggle, was, on his return to Rome, met by the citizens of all ranks and publicly thanked because he had not despaired of the Republic. The consequence was that the Republic refused to make peace with the victorious Carthagenians.

15. Swedish Chancellor who took over the reins of Government after the death of Gustavus Adolphus

16. When Mephistopheles first appears to Faust, in the latter's study, Faust inquires: "What is thy name?" To which Mephistopheles replies: "A part of the Power which always wills the Bad and always works the Good." And when Faust asks him what is meant by this riddle and why he should call himself 'a part,' the gist of Mephistopheles' reply is that he is the Spirit of Negation and exists through opposition to the positive Truth and Order and Beauty which proceed from the never-ending creative energy of the Deity. In the Prologue to Faust the Lord declares that man's active nature would grow sluggish in working the good and that therefore he has to be aroused by the Spirit of Opposition. This Spirit wills the Bad, but of itself it can do nothing positive, and by its opposition always works the opposite of what it wills.

17. The last and most famous of the medieval alchemists. He was born at Basle about the year 1490 and died at Salzburg in 1541. He taught that all metals could be transmuted through the action of one primary element common to them all. This element he called ALCAHEST. If it could be found it would prove to be at once the philosopher's stone, the universal medicine and their resistible solvent. There are many aspects of his teaching which are now looked upon as by no means so fantastic as they were considered in his own time.

18. The Battle of Leipzig (1813), where the Germans inflicted an overwhelming defeat on Napoleon, was the decisive event which put an end to the French occupation of Germany.
The occupation had lasted about twenty years. After the Great War, and the partial occupation of Germany once again by French forces, the Germans used to celebrate the anniversary of the Battle of Leipzig as a symbol of their yearning.

19. The flag of the German Empire, founded in 1871, was Black-White-Red. This was discarded in 1918 and Black-Red-Gold was chosen as the flag of the German Republic founded at Weimar in 1919. The flag designed by Hitler—red with a white disc in the centre, bearing the black swastika—is now the national flag.

20. After the DEBACLE of 1918 several semi-military associations were formed by demobilized officers who had fought at the Front. These were semi-clandestine associations and were known as FREIKORPS (Volunteer corps). Their principal purpose was to act as rallying centres for the old nationalist elements.

21. Schiller, who wrote the famous drama of WILLIAM TELL.

22. The reference here is to those who gave information to the Allied Commissions about hidden stores of arms in Germany. Before 1918 Germany was a federal Empire, composed of twenty-five federal states.

ABOUT CODA BOOKS www.codahistory.com

Most Coda books are edited and endorsed by Emmy Award winning film maker and military historian Bob Carruthers, producer of Discovery Channel's Line of Fire and Weapons of War and BBC's Both Sides of the Line. Long experience and strong editorial control gives the military history enthusiast the ability to buy with confidence. The series advisor is David McWhinnie, producer of the acclaimed Battlefield series for Discovery Channel. David and Bob have co-produced books and films with a wide variety of the UK's leading historians including Professor John Erickson and Dr David Chandler. Where possible the books draw on rare primary sources to give the military enthusiast new insights into a fascinating subject.

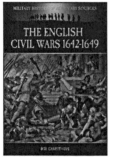

The English Civil Wars

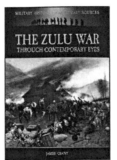

The Zulu Wars

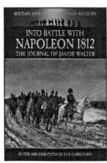

Into Battle with Napoleon 1812

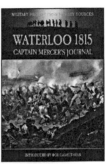

Waterloo 1815

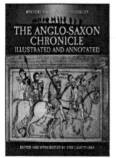

The Anglo-Saxon Chronicle

The Battle of the Bulge

The Normandy Campaign 1944

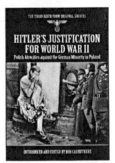

Hitler's Justification for WWII

Hitler's Mein Kampf -
The Roots of Evil

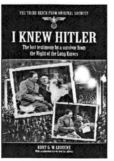

I Knew Hitler

Mein Kampf - The 1939
Illustrated Edition

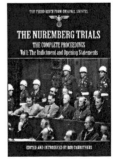

The Nuremberg Trials Volume 1

Tiger I in Combat

Tiger I Crew Manual

Panzers at War 1939-1942

Panzers at War 1943-1945

Wolf Pack - the U boats

Poland 1939

Luftwaffe Combat Reports

Eastern Front Night Combat

Eastern Front Encirclement

Panzer Combat Reports

The Panther V in Combat

The Red Army in Combat

Barbarossa - Hitler Turns East

The Russian Front

The Wehrmacht in Russia

Servants of Evil